ANDEAN COCAINE

ANDEAN

THE MAKING OF A

THE UNIVERSITY OF
NORTH CAROLINA PRESS
Chapel Hill

COCAINE

GLOBAL DRUG *Paul Gootenberg*

Designed by Rebecca Evans
Set in Cycles and Chevalier
by Rebecca Evans

The paper in this book meets the guidelines for
permanence and durability of the Committee on
Production Guidelines for Book Longevity of the
Council on Library Resources.

The University of North Carolina Press has been
a member of the Green Press Initiative since 2003.

Library of Congress Cataloging-in-Publication Data
Gootenberg, Paul, 1954–
Andean cocaine: the making of a global drug / Paul Gootenberg.
p.   cm.
Includes bibliographical references and index.
ISBN 978-0-8078-3229-5 (cloth: alk. paper)
ISBN 978-0-8078-5905-6 (pbk.: alk. paper)
1. Cocaine Industry—History—Peru.
2. Drug traffic—Peru.
I. Title.
HV5840.P4G66 2008
338.4'761532379—dc22   2008032901
cloth   12 11 10 09 08   5 4 3 2 1
paper   12 11 10 09 08   5 4 3 2 1

CONTENTS

Acknowledgments ix

Chronology: Cocaine, 1850–2000 xv

Introduction: Cocaine as Andean History 1

I

COCAINE RISING

CHAPTER 1 Imagining Coca, Discovering Cocaine, 1850–1890 15

CHAPTER 2 Making a National Commodity:
Peruvian Crude Cocaine, 1885–1910 55

II

COCAINE FALLING

CHAPTER 3 Cocaine Enchained: Global Commodity
Circuits, 1890s–1930s 105

CHAPTER 4 Withering Cocaine: Peruvian Responses, 1910–1945 143

CHAPTER 5 Anticocaine: From Reluctance to
Global Prohibitions, 1910–1950 189

III

ILLICIT COCAINE

CHAPTER 6 Birth of the *Narcos*: Pan-American
Illicit Networks, 1945–1965 245

CHAPTER 7 The Drug Boom (1965–1975) and Beyond 291

APPENDIX

Quantifying Cocaine 325

TABLE A.1 Sample Peruvian Exchange Rates, 1875–1965 328

TABLE A.2 Coca and Cocaine Exports from Peru, 1888–1910 329

TABLE A.3 Reported Cocaine Factories by Region, Peru, 1885–1920s 331

TABLE A.4 Active Cocaine Factories in Peru, 1920–1950 334

TABLE A.5 Cocaine Smuggling: Reported Seizures, 1935–1970s 336

Notes 337

Bibliographic Essay: A Guide to the Historiography of Cocaine 377

Bibliography 385

Index 413

ILLUSTRATIONS, TABLES, FIGURES, AND MAPS

ILLUSTRATIONS

French perspective on the coca leaf, nineteenth century 25

Informe of commission to evaluate Bignon's cocaine method, 1885 40

Merck factory at Darmstadt, late nineteenth century 59

Trade journal ad, 1890s 61

Ad for Lima-made cocaine, Meyer and Hafemann Pharmacy, 1885 67

Scene from the Austrian Amazonian colony of Pozuzo, ca. 1900 79

Crude cocaine factory, Monzón, ca. 1900 92

Dr. Augusto Durand, caudillo of cocaine 97

Layout of equipment in Peruvian cocaine workshop, ca. 1910 151

A Huánuco cocaine maker, 1920s 160

Paz Soldán's national cocaine *estanco* scheme, 1929 170

Eduardo Balarezo, pioneer Peruvian cocaine trafficker, 1949 255

Blanca Ibáñez de Sánchez, Bolivian drug trafficker, ca. 1960 281

Pan-American cocaine routes, mid-1960s 288

Pasta básica de cocaína commodity chain, mid-1960s 298

Illicit crude cocaine diagram, Drug Enforcement
Administration, 1970s 300

TABLES

3.1 Merck Cocaine Production and Imports of
Coca and Cocaine, 1879–1918 110

3.2 Bolivian Coca Production and Exports, 1900–1942 117

3.3 U.S. Coca Imports and Cocaine, 1882–1931 120

3.4 Japanese Cocaine Imports, Cocaine Production, and
Colonial Coca, 1910–1939 130

3.5 Peruvian Exports of Coca and Crude Cocaine, 1877–1933 133

4.1 Peruvian Cocaine and Coca Exports, 1910–1950 158

5.1 U.S. Coca: Medicinal and Special Imports, 1925–1959 203

FIGURES

3.1 The Rise and Fall of Java Coca Leaf, 1904–1940 127

3.2 Peruvian Coca Regions and Coca Uses, ca. 1940 136

4.1 The Decline of Peruvian Coca and Cocaine, 1904–1933 146

5.1 League of Nations World Cocaine Accounts, Mid-1930s 213

MAPS

2.1 The Huánuco-Huallaga Cocaine Region, 1930s 87

3.1 Andean Coca Regions, Early Twentieth Century 134

ACKNOWLEDGMENTS

In writing an academic history of cocaine, I have suffered a lot of gentle teasing over the years from friends and colleagues. Cocaine is admittedly interesting stuff, and not just to the millions of people whose lives the drug has touched for better or for worse since the 1970s. But what began for me as a kind of follow-up "commodity study"—my previous monographs dealt with nineteenth-century Peruvian guano—soon became an addictive line of research. Not only is little known about cocaine in history, even compared to other popularly used mind-altering drugs, but drug studies as a field affords boundless possibilities for intellectual trespassing. Over the past decade, I've been able to dig into developments all across the globe, given the crucial worldly connections of drugs like cocaine, and I have wandered through fields I barely thought twice about before: ethnobotany, the sociology of the illicit, the history of medicine, diplomatic history, psycho-pharmacology, the anthropology of goods, and cultural studies. I also gathered some memorable stories from my journeys chasing down new archives about cocaine. Once I found genuine (albeit century-old) test samples of cocaine in a British depository that will remain unnamed; later, I was trapped in the dungeon of the head of the Sociedad de Croatas, whom I was hoping to interview about his drug-making ancestors. There were dawn train rides to the friendly Merck corporate archive in New Jersey and flights over the Andes in rickety Russian transports and the equally scary *narco*-style business jets of AeroContinente for research in the forgotten upland town of Huánuco, Peru. Perhaps the weirdest moment of all was frantically copying documents amid the pin-and-map cubicles at the heart of the global drug war in the DEA's Virginia headquarters. "What a long, strange trip" this research has been, to take a lyric from one of cocaine's chief enthusiasts of the 1970s.

During the halcyon days of the American cocaine culture of the late 1970s and early 1980s, I was an enslaved graduate student, so, truth be told, I had neither the time, the cash, nor the inclination to indulge in that long party. I'm not sure that detachment necessarily makes my study of the drug more "objective." For I'll also admit to being a child of the sixties, peace signs and all, and if I harbor any hidden bias about cocaine, it is a negative one. Cocaine represented the glitzy new drug culture that drowned out, to the beat of disco, the mellower chords of my youth. That said, over the past years of research I've found the history of cocaine to be far more compelling and complex than a "bad" drug story. If any moralistic thread runs through this book, it's that what matters is our larger and longer *relationship* to this drug (including the self-destructive "drug war" our government still wages against the Andes and domestic minorities over cocaine) rather than the drug's inherent good or bad qualities or whether we like the drug or not. We as a society must work on maturing our relationship to this product of a faraway land.

There are actually quite a few books about cocaine on the market or gathering dust: journalistic surveys, trade books, and readers, some of which offer tidbits of cocaine history background. Not all are useless to scholars, although none actually builds from genuine and new archival work. This book, readers should know, is definitely not another popular drug book, even if it brims with intriguing and pertinent stories. My purpose here is the scholarly one of presenting new data and narratives from the critical perspectives of university professors such as myself who work at the borders of academic history and the social sciences. This book, I hope, is an antidote to these received and mainly superficial accounts of cocaine. At the end, for curious or specialized readers, I include a bibliographic essay about the slim but serious new field of cocaine history.

I have many people to thank, or blame, for feeding my interest in drugs. In Peru, Patricia Wieland, Pierina Traverso, Julio Cotler, Miguel Léon, Richard Kernaghan, and especially Enrique Mayer and Marcos Cueto all helped in various ways. Academics Francisco and Jorge Durand and Ricardo Soberón talked to me about their families' long-ago involvements with cocaine. Staff at the Biblioteca Nacional del Perú, Archivo General de la Nación, San Marcos Medical School, and Archivo Provincial de Huánuco were professional and gracious. The late Felix Denegri Luna allowed me to use his vast personal library (now at La Universidad Católica), as did Maestro Manuel Nieves his rare collection of Huánuco regional periodicals. A handful of *huanuqueño* old-timers also shared their personal cocaine stories. Some Peruvianists—Paulo Drinot, Shane Hunt, Nils Jacobsen, Carmen McEvoy, Alfonso Quiroz, Nuria Sala i Vila—have likely forgotten the clues they lent me. Elsewhere around the world, Joseph Spillane and Michael Kenney (in the United States), Marcel de Kort (Holland), Laurent Laniel (France), Tilmann Holzer (Germany), Luis Astorga (Mexico), Daniel Palma and Marcos Fernández Labbé (Chile), Jyri Soininen (Finland), Mary Roldán (Colombia), Silvia Rivera (Bolivia), and my Bolivianist colleague at Stony Brook, Brooke Larson, provided international insight. Fellow contributors to my volume *Cocaine: Global Histories* (Routledge, 1999) helped round out the global terrain for my own research—most are noted above, but this group also includes Dr. Steven Karch, Marek Kohn, and H. Richard Friman. In this country, there are many colleagues to thank from drug studies and among my fellow Latin American historians. Writer JoAnn Kawell first piqued my interest in cocaine's unresearched past, and I hope she will still find something of value here. Among my interlocutors were Isaac Campos, Pablo Piccato, Sinclair Thompson, Hernán Pruden, Martín Monsalve, Natalia Sobrevilla, Amy Chazkel, Debbie Poole, and Eric Hershberg (the last three as neighbors), Steve Topik (who never doubted the validity of this commodity), Itty Abraham and Willem van Schendel (the SSRC illicit flows group), and Ethan Nadelmann, my reminder that bright guys need not stay on the sidelines.

A number of fellowships and institutions generously allowed me to pursue this project: a John Simon Guggenheim Fellowship and St Antony's College, Oxford (1993–94), the Lindesmith Center / Open Society Institute (1995–96), the Social Science Research Council (1995), the Russell Sage Foundation (1996–97), the Woodrow Wilson Center for International Scholars (1999–2000), and the American Council of Learned Societies (2006–7). In the two residential centers, I thank Eric Wanner, Joe Tulchin, and Cindy Arnson for their hospitality, and for the research assistance of Cecilia Russo-Walsh, Lisa Kahraman, Stephanie Smith, and Peter Newman. Archivists and librarians at many institutions pitched in, notably Fred Romansky at the U.S. National Archives (who helped declassify what proved to be eye-opening DEA historical papers about this subject) and helpful staff at the National Library of Medicine, the Pan-American Union, the Library of Congress, the DEA Library and Information Center, and the Food and Drug Administration; in London, the Wellcome Institute, Public Record Office, Kew Gardens Archive, and Guildhouse Library; elsewhere, at the Penn State University Library (Anslinger papers), New York Public Library, New York Academy of Medicine, United Nations Library and

UN Archives, Merck Archives, and university libraries at Columbia, NYU, Yale, and Oxford. Portions of and arguments from this book have also been through a long mill of academic seminars and workshops, of which I would like to mention (chronologically, as I recall) colleagues at the Russell Sage Foundation, Harvard, Fordham, Yale, the Lindesmith Center, Stanford, the University of Florida, Columbia, Stony Brook, the University of Texas, the New York City Workshop on Latin American History, El Instituto de Investigaciones Sociales (UNAM), the University of British Columbia, Simon Fraser University, Wellesley, the New School, Amherst, the College of New Jersey, the Drug Policy Reform Biennial Conference (the Meadowlands), the International Economic History Association (Buenos Aires), the European Social Science History Conference (Amsterdam), the Sawyer Seminar at the University of Toronto, and the "narco-historia" panel at LASA-Montreal. I am ever grateful for all that feedback.

Aspects of this research have appeared in the *Hispanic American Historical Review*, the *Journal of Latin American Studies*, *Comparative Studies in Society and History*, *The Americas*, and in volumes published by Routledge, Indiana University Press, and Duke University Press. James Goldwasser, a friend, read and critiqued the entire draft manuscript in fall 2006 and thus guided a much-needed editorial revision. At Stony Brook, Domenica Tafuro and Greg Jackson assisted in preparing tables and graphics, while Magally Alegre Henderson hunted for maps in Peru. My entire experience publishing this book with the University of North Carolina Press has been a pleasure and an eye-opener about the professionalism and ideals of a great academic press. Elaine Maisner, my editor, was from start to finish amazingly smart and supportive about the book. The two external readers, William O. Walker III and Marcos Cueto, were the best people imaginable for this study. Project editor Paula Wald, as well as Vicky Wells in rights, helped push the final manuscript swiftly through its last throes, and the copyeditor, Ruth Homrighaus, among other feats caught every kind of inconsistency imaginable. Jen Burton prepared the book's index.

Most of this book was written in my research-crammed basement *cueva* (home office) in the beautiful environs of Cobble Hill, Brooklyn, surrounded by my expanding family, the warm sound of vinyl records, and a far-too-enticing neighborhood outside. At times, if I can confess this now, I felt overwhelmed by and lost in the complexity of my archival treasure trove on Andean cocaine and the enormity of the book's canvas. I felt — to paraphrase Aerosmith guitarist Steven Tyler's fuzzy memory of the 1980s — that I had "all of Peru up my nose." Despite this addiction to cocaine history, I was able to hold on to a job at Stony Brook University, where I also survived a 2000–2005 stint as director of Latin American and Caribbean Studies (with the help of LACS assistant Domenica Tafuro) and had the company of many fine colleagues and grad students. At times, it was a struggle to write on, as my wife, Laura (who put up with this book for way too long), and I brought our beautiful children, Dany and Léa, into the world. They have opened up a new and inspiring universe for us. Cocaine could wait.

CHRONOLOGY

Cocaine, 1850–2000

PRE-1880S

1550–1800: Coca tolerated as indigenous vice; no spread from colonial region

1800s: Slow awakening of scientific curiosity in leaf

1855–60: Cocaine alkaloid derived in Germany from Peruvian leaf

1860–80s: Coca's European flowering — age of Vin Mariani

1884–1905: CONSTRUCTING A COMMERCIAL COMMODITY, COCAINE

Era when United States and Peru actively promote herbal-cure coca and modern medical cocaine

United States largest and most avid market (e.g., Coca-Cola), but rival in German manufacturers

Peru rapidly develops coca exports and dynamic legal crude cocaine industry

Cocaine lauded as a model of modernizing and "Peruvian" industry

1905–1940: THE DECLINE OF COCAINE

Medical and legal prestige of cocaine sinks fast in United States; the cocaine "fiend" emerges

United States fully outlaws by 1920 and mostly eliminates within borders as abusable drug

United States launches international drive to ban drug, but League of Nations and producers lag

New colonialist coca-cocaine circuits erupt in Dutch Java and then Japanese Formosa

Peru retains depressed legal industry, centered in Huánuco, at head of Huallaga Valley

Peruvians defend legal national cocaine but turn against "backward" native coca use

1940–1970: ERECTION OF GLOBAL PROHIBITIONS / BIRTH OF THE ILLICIT

United States / UN emerge as uncontested leaders of world antidrug forces, including now cocaine

Germany, Javan, and Japanese industries and plantations destroyed in war and occupation

1947–50: Isolated Peru, led by pro-U.S. military junta, finally criminalizes cocaine

1948–61: UN adopts goal of eradication at source, that is, the Andean coca bush

1950–70: Underground circuits begin, disperse, intensify from Bolivia to Cuba and Chile

1960s: Huallaga and Bolivia's Chapare become development poles in government, U.S.-aided agricultural projects

1970–75: Cocaine demand returns to United States in Nixon era as pricey, glamorous "soft" drug

1970S–2000: THE ERA OF ILLICIT COCAINE AND HEMISPHERIC DRUG WARS

U.S. demand and Huallaga-led supply dramatically on rise

Peruvian state falls into deep two-decade political/social crises; abandonment of Huallaga peasantry and "development"

Colombians after 1973 Chile coup capture, concentrate, and expand illicit trades to north

1980s: U.S. anticocaine measures intensify, with little effectiveness

Price continues to slide, rise of retail "crack" (1984–); 1986–87, height of U.S. cocaine scare

Peru, Bolivia allow production; trade shifts through Cali and northern Mexico

1990s: Fujimori's Peru (and Bolivia) reassert control over coca zones; illicit crop declines

Coca and cocaine concentrate in southeast Colombia; U.S. Plan Colombia resolves to confront there

U.S. consumption steady, though crack use falls; spread to Brazil, Russia, Africa, and beyond

ANDEAN COCAINE

INTRODUCTION

Cocaine as Andean History

LINKS IN A CHAIN

Pharmacist Alfredo Bignon was burning the midnight oil in the backroom laboratory of his Droguería y Botica Francesa, just around the corner from Lima's main Plaza de Armas. Once more, he went over in his head his hard-won new formula for making cocaine. Tomorrow, the thirteenth of March 1885, he would present his findings at the Academia Libre de Medicina de Lima, where a distinguished panel of Peruvian doctors and chemists would judge his innovation in a ten-page official *informe*. Bignon felt satisfied. Using simple precipitation methods and local ingredients — fresh-grown Andean coca leaf, kerosene, soda ash — he was able to produce a chemically active "crude" cocaine in "an easy and economic preparation in the same place as coca cultivation": at home in Peru. This would surely bring him scientific glory, if not riches — a dream he shared with the young Sigmund Freud, who was working on his own "cocaine papers" in far-off Vienna at precisely the same time.[1] It would help his adopted country meet the skyrocketing world demand for cocaine exports, satisfying the commercial interest recently unleashed by news of the drug's miraculous power as a local anesthetic. It was precisely what respected European drug firms like Merck of Darmstadt wanted. For Bignon, this was just the first of a dozen original experiments with the new drug he would report in prestigious Lima, Parisian, and New York medical journals over the next few years. Turning the humble Indian coca leaf into modern cocaine was to be, Bignon imagined, one of Peru's heroic national endeavors.

Exactly seventy-four years later, on the streets of New York City, another enterprising Peruvian named Eduardo Balarezo was making cocaine history, though this time of a less respectable kind. The *New York Daily Mirror* headline of 20 August 1949 blared, "Smash Biggest Dope Ring Here: Seize Leader in City; Peru Jails 80." It was the world's first international cocaine bust. Balarezo, a former sailor from Lambayeque, was arrested as the presumed head of a cocaine-running ring operating up and down the Pacific coast. Authorities described him as a bowlegged *zambo* (a Peruvian mixed-race category) and a rumored associate of mobster "Lucky" Luciano. In the process of Balarezo's arrest, police and officials of Harry J. Anslinger's Federal Bureau of Narcotics (FBN), assisted by the head of Peru's national police, Captain Alfonso Mier y Terán, raided nine houses, seizing thirteen kilos of powder with an estimated street value of $154,000. Balarezo, a naturalized U.S. citizen, saw his good life in New York evaporate. Within months, Joseph Martin, the high-profile cold war prosecutor of the Alger Hiss case, had overseen Balarezo's trial and conviction.[2] The ring led all the way to the coca fields of the Upper Amazon near Huánuco, Peru, through the turbulent right-wing military politics of Lima via small-time sailor smugglers on the Grace Line to the Puerto Rican bars of Harlem. *Time* dubbed this brief blast of illicit coke "Peru's White Goddess." Anslinger, touting the theme of his infamous reefer madness campaign of the decade before, assured the American public that with Balarezo and company behind bars, a dangerous new drug epidemic had been nipped in the bud: "Suppression of this traffic has averted a serious crime wave." He was only partly right. It was not until the 1970s that Andean cocaine—on a scale never imagined by either Alfredo Bignon or Eduardo Balarezo—became both a global temptation and a global menace.

This book, a new history of the now-notorious Andean commodity, unravels the hidden processes and transformations linking these distant events. It traces the emergence of cocaine, using fresh historical sources and new historical methods, through three long arcs and global processes: first, its birth as a successful heroic medical commodity of the late nineteenth century (1850–1910); second, the drug's depression and inward retreat of the early twentieth century (1910–45); and third, its reemergence, phoenixlike, as a dynamic transnational *illicit* good after World War II (1945–75). These stages, I argue, are hidden developments that came and went well before cocaine's fate passed into the hands of the infamous Colombian "narco-traffickers" of the 1970s. This new history draws on actors and influences from around the globe across the first century of cocaine's existence. But ultimately, it is the long *Andean* nexus—in cocaine's nineteenth-century construction as a noble commodity, then twentieth-century redefinition as a criminal product—that proved key to its historical formation as a "good" or "bad" drug.

THE NEW HISTORY OF DRUGS AND LATIN AMERICA

Mind-altering and illicit drugs, along with their storied pasts, have long captured the imagination, but not until the 1960s brought the drug culture into the open did drug studies, especially medical or policy-oriented research, emerge as a field of growing inquiry in the United States. Only recently, however, has a "new drug history," if I may use that term, begun to be written. By the 1990s, trained historians began to displace medical amateurs and muckraking journalists in the search for new historical data and more rigorous interpretations of drugs, drug usage, and drug control regimes. Interdisciplinary currents exert a strong pull, especially of anthropology on history. Historians became more sensitive to ethnobotany's long insistence on the cultural and symbolic weight of intoxicants across human societies and the relative ways in which different societies embrace or reject altered states of consciousness. The unstable cultural boundaries between legal drugs (tobacco, alcohol) and illegal ones (cannabis, opiates), or between healing medicines and recreational ones (in the age of Prozac and Viagra), has compelled scholars to ask rigorously how such boundaries or categories were created and fixed in the first place. Raging present controversies about faltering and unjust U.S. drug prohibitions have also given an impetus to new historical interest as historians try to locate or test less punitive drug regimes in the past or grasp the political and cultural origins of this century-long social quagmire. A pathbreaking series of historical studies of early modern Europe has highlighted the centrality of colonial stimulants—tobacco, coffee, chocolate, tea, alcohol—in both the making of modern sensibilities and European capitalist expansion.[3] New studies of world commodities—spices, opium, cotton, Coca-Cola, beer, cod, salt—as a revealing microcosm of modern consumption and globalization have become a publishing industry, and legal or illegal "drug foods"[4] rank among the most universal of globally consumed goods. The rise of "social constructionism" across the social sciences and of cultural studies in the humanities have made the constitution of drug regimes an inviting area of research and analysis. For all these reasons, more and more scholars are embracing the history of drugs. Their work is altering perceptions of drugs and of our possible present and future relationships to them, and it is making notable contributions to European, Asian, and American history, in which drugs have played a notable and long-overlooked role.

Latin America is a critical terrain in the global history of drugs, but apart from diplomatic historians studying evolving U.S. drug policy toward the region, historians of drugs have not turned much attention there. Yet, as classical economic botanists noted decades ago, the vast majority of the world's known psychoactive substances — alkaloid-bearing plants, fungi, cacti, seeds, and vines, from peyote to *yage* — are American in origin, profoundly rooted in indigenous and shamanistic communities.[5] During the colonial period, some of these, such as tobacco and cacao (used for chocolate), quickly transformed into major exportable world commodities, becoming bulwarks of the Spanish and Portuguese empires. Newly imported drug plants, products of the so-called Columbian exchange, such as coffee and sugar (or its alcoholic derivative, rum), were added to this rich and lucrative Latin American psychoactive cornucopia. Along with silver coin, they were the products that most intimately connected Western consumers, or even the nascent working class, to the remote world of the Americas. By the nineteenth century, such habit-forming export commodities were crucial to the economies, societies, and revenues of many fledgling Latin American nations. In contrast, more regionally bounded drug cultures (such as those of yerba maté in Argentina, guarana in Brazil, mescal in Mexico, coca leaf in the Andes, or ganja in the Caribbean) were and are of special significance, involving many millions of local everyday users and deeply ingrained in national cultures.

Sometime in the middle of the twentieth century, in still murky transformations, illicit drugs like marijuana, heroin, and especially cocaine came to link certain marginalized zones of Latin America to the United States. Today, these linkages have created a booming underground economy — indeed, along with petroleum, arms, and tourism, drugs are one of modern history's most profitable and global of trades. Apart from its considerable economic role, the volatile drug trade adversely pervades the politics of many Latin American nations and has come to complicate, if not at times dominate, inter-American relations.

The economy of cocaine, by far, is the biggest and most entrenched of these inter-American drug economies — worth almost forty billion dollars annually in prohibition-inflated U.S. "street sales" alone, though coffee has a larger employment effect, from its legions of tropical dirt farmers to the urban subsistence Starbucks baristas in the north.[6] The ongoing

American "drug war" was launched amid the passions of the cocaine and crack cocaine boom of the 1980s, and cocaine remains its driving foreign nemesis. Based on the age-old native Andean coca plant and the countless thousands of peasants who cultivate it, the active sources of cocaine lie deeply rooted in the Andean region, in Peru, Bolivia, and in recent years Colombia. The traffic in cocaine remains overwhelmingly controlled by homegrown, successful, and eminently "Latin" entrepreneurs and middlemen. It is the one global drug culture based entirely on Latin American initiative, culture, and resources—hence, in many ways, all sensationalism about drugs aside, cocaine is now South America's most emblematic product.

How did it get that way? The multiple challenges of researching elusive, illicit drugs make this a daunting question. Despite its great notoriety—as an article of trafficking (Colombian "cartels") and of pleasure (in many nervous jokes)—cocaine is not well studied in its historical and particularly Andean historical settings. A few valuable studies exist, as noted in the historiographical essay at the end of this book, but despite these starts the history of cocaine in the Americas is far less developed than that, say, of the opiates in Asia and Europe.[7] It remains highly fragmented and scattered across the globe as pieces of a puzzle that cannot come together to explain cocaine's major transformations. This book, therefore, taking an essential Andean perspective, aims to firmly establish the drug's trajectory: cocaine's creation and spread as a world commodity (1850–1900), its halting redefinition as a global pariah drug (1900–45), and, finally, its metamorphosis between 1945 and 1975 into a booming international illicit pleasure drug, with worldwide reverberations today.

WRITING THE HISTORY OF COCAINE

My prior training and experience, along with the availability of fresh archives and new directions in drug history, have colored my approaches and methods in writing this book. I came to cocaine as an Andean specialist with a distinct curiosity about commodities: my previous books were about Peru's nineteenth-century guano trade, dried bird droppings coveted by European farmers, as strange and lucrative a commerce as the later world of cocaine. This interest in commodities has influenced my vision of cocaine's history and helped me to understand how a rich panoply of circumstances translates into a broader new conception of cocaine's Andean origins and its historical path from miracle drug to global drug menace.

The main contribution of this book lies in its systematic effort to tie together the disparate global threads of cocaine's history, using the hitherto unknown story of Andean cocaine as the central strand. Why focus on cocaine primarily from a perspective in Peruvian history? As readers will see, other sites played vital parts in cocaine's deeper history: Germany, the United States, France, Bolivia, and even the Netherlands, Japan, Java, Britain, Chile, and Cuba. But the varied global cocaine axes to and from the Andean region—and above all the tropics of eastern Peru—have played the longest, most continuous, and most decisive role in defining cocaine's historical shifts. As this book unfolds, I will show how events in, say, New York City (e.g., a blue-ribbon 1889 medical commission on cocaine, the city's bustling 1901 commodity markets for Trujillo coca leaf, gangs of roving cocaine fiends in 1911, Balarezo's busted 1949 smuggling ring, and the drug-induced dance culture of the 1970s) were all intimately linked to faraway actors from the coca fields of the Huallaga Valley below the town of Huánuco—and furthermore to the political offices of the Federal Bureau of Narcotics in Washington and the Government Palace in Lima. That Huánuco-Lima-Washington American axis is the key, in my argument, to illuminating cocaine's transmutations as a world drug commodity. It was in Peru that cocaine emerged as a dynamic nineteenth-century product, due in large part to local ideas and technological and business initiatives, and it was Peruvians of the mid-twentieth century (along with fellow South Americans) who, again taking faraway cues, reinvented their now-long-decayed national cocaine as the illicit world commodity it is today—decades before any glint of interest in the drug had emerged among would-be Colombian traffickers. Connecting these formative changes in the drug are a host of events, processes, and people, all implicated in one way or another with Andean cocaine.

Five larger methodological currents of this book deserve a formal preview. First, I privilege new findings. This book builds entirely new narratives about cocaine based on a mining of newly found archival documentation about the drug. A multitude of novel sources are employed, from obscure Peruvian medical journals of the 1880s to turn-of-the-century British pharmacy debates, dusty early League of Nations surveys, Amazonian property deeds, and specially declassified 1950s drug intelligence reports of the U.S. Federal Bureau of Narcotics (the predecessor of today's Drug Enforcement Agency, or DEA). This research, in Peru, the United States, and Europe, is often challenging, especially as it relates to underground cocaine after 1945, and it is fraught with interpretive dilemmas (e.g., deciphering truth from the controlling optic of police reports), but it is also surprising in how much it can alter received stories and pat analysis of the drug. Thus, readers may not encounter too much here about well-worn topics like Coca-Cola, Sigmund Freud, or Pablo Escobar, but they will understand more about the unseen events and processes that linked such disparate actors across the broad canvas of the drug's history.

Second, I bring a global perspective to bear on cocaine. For a host of reasons, drugs are, and have long been, among the most mobile and global of goods. Today, "international," "global," "beyond borders," or "trans-national" studies (pick your term) are all the rage in the social sciences, with good reason given the world's accelerated processes of globalization. A global perspective cannot, however, map everything, everywhere, that happens in a particular history. The best strategy is one that roots itself firmly in a specific cultural or social context — so-called glocal studies — and shows exactly how its larger worldly connections matter.[8] For example, in what ways, responding to German scientific agendas and pharmaceutical demand, did Andeans themselves work to mold cocaine's path as a global product? What happened, on the ground and underground, to concoct a thriving criminal cocaine culture decades after bureaucrats in Washington simply decreed the drug undesirable? Historians rarely follow such historical connections all the way up and down the line or back and forth in reciprocal fashion, though doing so can explain far more than simply focusing on a single side of a historical relationship. Thus, here readers will meet French coca enthusiasts, German chemical magnates, American medical men, plant explorers and prohibitionists, Dutch colonial planters, Japanese imperialists, Peruvian scientists and diplomats, tropical Andean modernizers, revolutionary Bolivian peasants, Cuban mafiosos, Harlem cocaine sniffers, and many other global actors. But the core of this book's analysis is grounded in a close, long-term regional study of the world's premier cocaine complex of greater Huánuco, Peru, the drug's little-known historical homeland and haven. This "glocal" site is used to articulate and integrate the bundle of global relationships at work in the emergence of cocaine as a legal and illegal commodity. Apart from this relational strategy, some analysis turns more on sustained comparisons: between the political economy of distinctive commodity chains or between the nationalist cocaine politics of Peru and the equally intense coca nationalism of neighboring Bolivia.

Third, I draw from recent advances of commodity studies. Like global studies, there are many contending varieties of commodity analysis, ranging from those that treat goods like so many soybeans in an abstract marketplace (price theory) to those that read changing forms of consumption as embedded social and symbolic practice (anthropological, historical). In drug studies, commodity or material perspectives are sorely needed for cooling down the burning and distorting passions that often surround mind-altering, contested, or forbidden goods. Much has been said lately about treating drugs as "mere" commodities in the ways they are built up and accepted like other exchangeable things and in the ways they acquire, carry, and convey meanings. Here, cocaine will be organized heuristically in a long series of "global commodity chains"—the spatial conception of production-to-consumption relationships introduced by global sociologist Immanuel Wallerstein.[9] With cocaine, however, I will draw out the political tensions between competing forms of commodity chains, which aid in the analysis of cocaine's transformations, and I will broaden the concept to encompass channels of noneconomic flows (of politics and law, of science and medicine, of notions of drug control, of illicitness itself), which are often as vital in defining goods as are their prices or cycles of production. This expanded focus on commodity flows has much in common with concepts like the "cultural biography" of goods and the "commodity ecumene" used by anthropologists of consumption.[10] I will also enter into a mysterious area of commodity studies, asking what happens to goods that are pushed into invisible and politically inflected illicit worlds.

Fourth, I take seriously the insights of "constructionism." It is an academic truism today that everything (even reality) is socially and politically constructed, so much so that the term is losing its specific meaning. In drug studies, the term was and still is highly useful—in denoting the impact that "set and setting," including huge historical contexts, have on the perceptions and even the cognitive or bodily effects of drugs. Drugs are absorbed through our complex social relationship with them, which is as vital as the active or addictive brain alkaloids within them. Historical constructionism reveals how drugs are "made," not born: made not just as constructed material commodities but in the culture-laden, internalized, ritualized, and contested ways they acquire their impassioned meanings and uses as heroic or menacing drugs, dreaded or desired drugs, foreign or domestic drugs, "hard" or "soft" drugs. Here, readers will encounter such forces and influences as national feelings, scientific certitudes, puritanical modernism, racial fantasies, cold war passions, and other emotions that become inscribed in goods, but especially in mind-altering drugs like cocaine. Historical representations, discourses or imaginings of cocaine, were sometimes as critical as its reality, and they often clashed across cultural and national boundaries.[11]

Fifth, I recognize the "agency" in the rise of cocaine. In the North American academy, scholars talk a lot today about agency, perhaps depressed about their own sense of helplessness in the world. People, and sometimes surprisingly lowly and anonymous folks, "make their own history," or so it is said. Indeed, this book underscores the ways in which Andeans acted as protagonists in the development of global cocaine through their ideas, beliefs, exertions, and activities. Thus, we will encounter local entrepreneurs and medical men who embraced cocaine with pride and made it into a widely available medicinal product; Peruvian diplomats and chemists who resisted, for many years, the outer world's changing pessimistic verdict on their drug; and Amazonian peasants and Pan-American smugglers who responded to its distant criminality by turning cocaine into their own illicit domain. New drug regimes were not simply imposed from abroad, even in the context of uneven or dependent dimensions of global power. Today, cocaine is often seen, with some irony, as one of Latin America's most successful homegrown exports—though it is hardly as profitable to host countries or peasant producers as many think—and it is often deployed as a derogative symbol of the Andean region. It is this regional agency, across generations, that helps to explain the autonomous and South American stamp of cocaine. That said, I sincerely hope this vibrant historical role is not confused with blaming Latin Americans once again for North America's intractable problems with drugs. Those are mostly problems of our own making.

Finally, allow me to lay out three observations about the limits of the book. First, this study focuses on modern cocaine and does not systematically deal with Andean coca leaf—a parallel topic wide open for historical research. I treat questions about coca where and when they intersect with cocaine's history while at the same time marking the vital distinction between the two "drugs," something some writers, following drug war pharmacology (the fallacy that chemistry determines drug outcomes), conflate or confuse. Coca, the dried leaf of the subtropical Andean shrub *Erythroxylon coca*, grown in the high *selva* region of the eastern Andes, has been embraced by indigenous peoples for thousands of years as a ritual and workaday stimulant. Anthropologists are still debating if coca's mastication by highland Indians is primarily for its mild energy kick or for its other complex alkaloids, vitamins, or myriad of physiological, spiritual, or symbolic properties.[12] If historically maligned by outsiders, including even twentieth-century United Nations drug control agencies, coca is a benign herb essential to Andean cultures, in its use analogous to that of tea in Asia. Coca must be carefully distinguished from one of its powerful alkaloids, cocaine, derived by German chemists in 1860 and first used medically, with most success as a local anesthetic, before emerging after 1890 (and again after 1970) as an intense recreational or stimulant drug of abuse in the United States and Europe. Cocaine use is potentially harmful, but the drug is not physically addicting like heroin or cigarettes. Andean coca use is local, while cocaine is for export, and the fact that they share one alkaloid of many does not make them comparable "drugs."

Second, though I am a recovering economic historian engaged with commodity studies, readers will find no concerted effort in this book to present systematic statistics about cocaine, whether in its legal phase (1860–1950) or its illicit phase (after 1950). Indeed, my background in economic history tells me that most of the numbers encountered globally about cocaine (say, those measuring coca harvests in nineteenth-century Bolivia or Japanese cocaine sales of the 1920s) are guesses, often bogus and uneducated ones, unworthy for marking macro trends or for undertaking sustained microeconomic analysis. Just as serious, official and unofficial figures about cocaine lack all consistency, confusing basic units of measure (pounds, kilos, hectares, ounces, grams, *cestos*, *arrobas*, *soles*, pounds sterling), confounding needed comparisons. This is not to mention the dearth of statistics and suspect statistic creation around underground cocaine in the years after 1950, including statistics derived from drug seizures or arrests for trafficking. Thus, readers will encounter plenty of numbers and even tables in the text, but they are mainly there for descriptive or illustrative value. For more on the statistical dilemmas and the data sources used here, readers can consult the quantitative appendix at the end of the book.

Third, the period after 1945, which the book treats as the era of the invention and spread of illicit cocaine, presents daunting challenges with sources, though I have found many fascinating and rich primary materials on the topic. By necessity, the chapters on this process build from fragmented international policing reports, primarily of the U.S. Federal Bureau of Narcotics and of the Bureau of Narcotics and Dangerous Drugs (BNDD), forerunners of the 1970s DEA, or from closely related United Nations or Interpol international drug control agencies. This means taking care, as much as possible, with their language and categories of drug "control," as well as with the inherently speculative, exaggerated nature of such documents, based as they are on a long, perfidious trail of suspects and informers. These documents offer problems of timing as well: police reports usually lag, probably by a few years, behind the emergence of illicit activities and spheres. Needless to say, cops are biased and low on certain analytical skills, though sensational press accounts of drugs, typically based on police leaks, make even worse sources.[13] Indeed, one could consider a reflexive or critical ethnography of the "drug archive" per se—how, for example, the FBN got its piecemeal information and (mis)interpreted it over the decades. So, while attempting to portray accurately early *narcotraficantes* and their trades, this book cannot tell a rounded story of their (under) world on their own cultural or personal terms, whatever those were. Yet, as historians as distinct as Richard Cobb and Carlo Ginzburg have suggested, policing or inquisition testimony often does lend critical clues to the real past men and women who inspired it, and the early antidrug crusaders who sketched these *narcos* were, in several senses, modern-day inquisitors of subversive substances.

COMING CHAPTERS

Chapter 1 explores the mid-nineteenth-century "invention," beyond the strictly chemical sense of the term, of cocaine from age-old Andean coca leaf. It looks at crosscurrents of world culture, science, desire, and demand that elevated cocaine into a coveted medical "good," in both meanings of the word, and particularly at the vivid Peruvian imaginings of coca and cocaine (including a nationalist cocaine science), which underpinned cocaine's creation as a national commodity. Chapter 2 focuses on the unstudied emergence of a legal Peruvian cocaine export boom in the era 1885–1905 based on national technologies around the region of Huánuco. This was among underdeveloped Peru's most dynamic early industrial experiments, imbued with a modernizing vision and discourse. And in global terms, this local industry swiftly resolved cocaine's initial supply bottleneck, by the 1890s allowing cocaine to become widely accessible and affordable for medical and popular use in industrialized countries, as well as for some precocious recreational uses. Chapter 3 sketches the shifting international circuits of commerce, science, and ideas evoked by cocaine by 1915. Apart from three initial Franco-, Germanic-, and North American–Peruvian commodity chains, and from adjacent Bolivia's distinctive regional cultural economy of coca, the drug diversified across the globe into rival Asian commercial circuits, promoted by Dutch and Japanese colonial powers in Java and Formosa. A remarkable multipolar interwar cocaine world emerged, and the tensions between these networks deeply affected Peru's national cocaine, as well as the longer global geopolitical fortunes of the drug.

Chapter 4 addresses the twentieth-century decline of Peru's national cocaine industry, buffeted by these international currents and rising world antidrug passions and politics. It explores an inward creative turn of regional elites, agronomists, engineers, diplomats, coca-leaf reformers, and scientists responding to the global and local predicaments of the drug. Legal cocaine survived as a legitimate if technologically backward industry until 1950 in Peru, a fact of great importance for its later history. Chapter 5 surveys the twentieth-century campaign, instigated mainly by the United States, to make cocaine into a proscribed pariah drug. This crusade was a radical turnabout of initial North American fervor for commercial coca and cocaine, and it harbored a complex of hidden actors, such as Coca-Cola interests. Here, the historic centrality of the U.S.-Peruvian cocaine axis comes to the foreground. This chapter also reveals how both Peruvians and Bolivians, with their own thinking and aspirations around the drug, reacted reluctantly to such pressures, which by the 1950s would culminate in a full worldwide prohibition regime around cocaine. Chapter 6 reveals the eruption, from the ashes of Peru's long legal industry, of an unprecedented flow of illicit cocaine after 1950, one of the ground-up responses of Andeans to cocaine's newly decreed criminality. Here, we see cocaine reglobalize, but this time as an illicit drug of the 1950s and 1960s swiftly spread by a new Pan-American trafficking class from its Peruvian origins to Bolivia, Chile, Cuba, and a host of other sites, including novel customers and consumers in the United States. Prior to 1970, Colombians had surprisingly little to do with this drug. Instead, the circuit was built by hundreds of anonymous Andean smugglers and "chemists" and politically structured by postwar U.S. anticommunist and antidrug campaigns in the region. Chapter 7 traces how cocaine's prior hidden history bequeathed after 1960 the cocaine we know today, based on a volatile social base in an Amazonian coca-capitalist peasantry, an energetic new Colombian entrepreneurial connection, and the 1970s political culture of the North American boom in cocaine consumption. The chapter closes with reflections on cocaine's revealed long Andean history, with its implications for studies of the historical formation of drug regimes and for our still-troubled relationship to Andean cocaine.

I

COCAINE RISING

1

IMAGINING COCA,
DISCOVERING COCAINE, 1850–1890

It was Karl Marx, in a foundational nineteenth-century text on commodities composed about the same time his compatriots were celebrating a new "miracle drug," *cocain*, who first stressed the mental life of things, that is, how market relationships are first constructed as a process within the human mind, enveloping ordinary goods in powerful, often paradoxical social illusions.[1] Drugs like cocaine, extraordinary goods that affect consciousness itself, are bound to excite the human imagination in even more passionate, fantastical, and mystifying ways.

This chapter examines historical discourses about coca leaf and cocaine from the Spanish colonial era through the mid-1880s, when both goods stood on the verge of their construction as world commodities. These shifting ideas were both a prelude to and a force in coca and cocaine's recognition and formation as marketable goods. The idiom for stimulants and intoxicants in the early modern world and beyond was primarily medical, in its varied guises, though by the nineteenth century coca and cocaine, especially in Peru, where the chapter ends, were also conceptualized in terms of nationalism and as potential national commodities. Underlying this protracted dialogue about coca and cocaine was a continual back-and-forth between Andean experiences, representations, and controversies and other debates emerging in Europe and later the United States—what today we might call "transnational" discourses.

I start here with an overview of coca and cocaine's genealogy from the conquest of the Incas in 1532 and of the circuits that emerged between Peru, Europe, and the United States in the realm of coca and cocaine science and medicine. Turning to the complex local responses from Peru in the nineteenth century, I examine a kind of elite scientific nationalism that sought to recuperate coca and claim cocaine as modern national subjects. The cocaine science of pharmacist Alfredo Bignon, Peru's little-known answer to Sigmund Freud, and Bignon's crucial contribution in the mid-1880s to cocaine's rise as a local and global commodity exemplified this republican scientific nationalism. Finally, in this chapter we will look at the tracts of Amazonian and commodity promoters, who also vied in this era for a new national commodity in coca and cocaine. This prior imaginary prepared cocaine's takeoff and boom as a legal commodity during the years 1885–1910.

With their entwined historical relationship, "coca" and "cocaine" must be defined and carefully distinguished for uninitiated readers. Coca is the dried, cured leaf of the subtropical Andean shrub *Erythroxylon*, which botanists now recognize in two domesticated species with four botanic varieties. The three-to-six-foot coca bush has been an Andean cultivar for at least five millennia, grown in the humid 500-to-2,000-meter *montaña* or *yungas* regions of today's eastern Peru and Bolivia, the ecological swath where the Amazon basin meets the foothills of the Andes. Coca leaf, with its sacred connotations, has been pivotal in Andean cultural history. Until recently, it was almost exclusively used by several millions of largely poor Quechua or Aymara Indians of the high sierra, although coca has now significantly generalized in Bolivia. The *chacchador* or *coquero*, the Peruvian terms ("coca chewers" is a poor translation), sucks rather than chews the wad for about an hour and often adds a powdered alkaline ash (the *llujt'a* or *ilipta*) to enhance its effects. It can also be taken in a tealike infusion and as a snuff by Amazonian groups. Coca is biochemically complex yet certainly benign in its use. Questions persist among ethnobotanists as to whether Indians seek minute doses of "cocaine" from using coca and about coca's prime functions in the Andes. Coca is a work-related stimulant, provides crucial vitamins, and is a digestive aid and salve for the high-altitude cold, hunger, and stress. It has many storied medicinal properties and aids physiological adaptation to high altitude, promoting enhanced glucose absorption, for instance. Coca use is seen as a ritual and spiritual act, as a cultural affirmation of community trust and ethnic solidarity, and as a coveted good of social exchange that integrates the scattered Andean ecological archipelago.[2] The notion that Indian use of coca is comparable to our workaday "coffee break" barely captures the depth of its meaning to Andean peoples, for coca's roles are so multifaceted and integral to indigenous identity. Yet, to cultural foreigners over the last half-millennium, coca leaf has also sparked alternately admiration and disdain. That coca is deeply indigenous and regional to the Andes (with modest outsider use only in parts of Argentina and Chile) has strongly affected its history.

Cocaine, by contrast, is a powerful stimulant, first isolated from coca in 1860, one of the leaf's fourteen known alkaloids. Like other stimulants, cocaine artificially ignites the brain's regulatory neurotransmitters, creating an instantaneous "rush," or sense of energy and euphoria, which peaks after about half an hour. Its specific pharmacological action (inhibiting dopamine uptake) is surprisingly similar to that of the common pediatric therapeutic drug Ritalin.[3] Cocaine, among other bodily effects, constricts and accelerates the cardiovascular system, which can endanger users with heart conditions. Its commonly used form is cocaine hydrochloride, HCl, which can be injected or smoked (in freebasing or as "crack") but is now usually snorted in small doses (20–30 milligrams), entering the bloodstream through mucus membranes of the nose. Cocaine has had many historic uses: in the nineteenth century as an experimental wonder drug, as the world's first true local surgical anesthetic, and in sundry commercial formulas; after 1970 mainly as an illicit recreational drug or drug of abuse. Illicit cocaine has a range of social roles. Users find it alluring for its energy, its pleasure, or as a pricey marker of glamour, sexuality, or success. Contrary to conventional wisdom, cocaine is not addictive in a strict physical sense; millions have taken it pleasurably without dire consequences, but many have fallen into personal or legal misery with the drug.[4]

Production of cocaine from coca leaf usually passes through two sites and stages: the first, controlled by local *cocaleros*, the coca-growing Amazonian peasants, pulverizes and leaches the leaf using kerosene and other simple solvents to make "coca paste" (or PBC, *pasta básica de cocaína*). This is sent on for refining into cocaine HCl in more sophisticated "labs" now run mainly by Colombians, who dominate the wholesale trade to consuming countries. These sites form the cornerstone of a globalized illicit drug economy worth upward of eighty billion dollars a year in risk-inflated prices. Some six hundred to eight hundred tons of cocaine are successfully smuggled annually to the drug's fifteen million or more eager aficionados of all classes and colors, primarily in the United States, Brazil, and western and eastern Europe. Since the late 1970s, layers of this business have become enveloped in notorious violence, reflecting the huge monetary stakes raised by global drug prohibition. The notion of controlling "cartels," however, is a misleading way of thinking about what now is a hypercompetitive and atomized enterprise. Overall, despite many billions spent on the U.S.-led drug war against Andean cocaine, its sources and consumers have only diversified in recent decades, though the number of American users (for demographic reasons) likely peaked in the early 1990s.

The differences between natural coca and chemical cocaine are hotly contested, with varied opinions infused by politics and ideology as well as science. As anthropologist Enrique Mayer vividly put it, comparing the experience of coca to cocaine is like traversing the Andes on "a donkey versus a supersonic jet." In the past, observers and critics sought to equate coca with cocaine—as coca's "drug" essence—whereas today, in the context of an alien and hostile drug war, it is vital to distinguish between the two, as in the currently popular Bolivian slogan "La coca no es droga."[5] Many of the differences lie in "set and setting," or the historical culture of use: cocaine culture, which practically anyone with the urge and cash can join, is famously hedonistic, risky, and individualistic, whereas coca is usually savored by Andean Indians to reinforce their shared traditional and community mores. Coca is bought and sold but historically integrated in a bounded regional circuit reproducing a cultural belt of highland "Andeanness"; cocaine, in its far briefer history, has become a rootless and ruthlessly global commodity. These two goods, coca and cocaine, have meshed in a shifting dialogical fashion, as sketched in the global historical and discursive survey ahead.

COCA AND COCAINE
IN THE *LONGUE DURÉE*, 1500–1850

Drug historian David T. Courtwright, building on a new wave of scholarship, has recently conceived of European capitalism's "psychoactive revolution" of the seventeenth and eighteenth centuries: an intense period of global expansion and lifestyle and consciousness change fueled by the assimilation and consumption of new colonial stimulant drugs such as tobacco, coffee, rum, tea, chocolate, and opium. As other scholars have beautifully illustrated for tobacco and chocolate, native American drug-food novelties of the sixteenth-century Columbian exchange, the acceptance of and desire for such goods was typically mediated by the medical theories of the age—Galenic, humoral, or materia medica. Medicine acted as a filter for and sometimes a barrier to new goods' attaining Europeanized status, first as colonial "creole" and then as civilized European modes of consumption.[6] Early modern medicine had the authority (if not the science) to stamp class and cultural meanings onto new intoxicants and the experience thereof, plant drugs that then quickly became world commodities and offered vast opportunities for commerce and profit.

Coca—the "divine plant of the Incas"—was an anomalous exception during Europe's psychoactive revolution. Not avidly absorbed into global trade like its alkaloidal cousins, coca was actively shunned during the sixteenth century. By 1700, coca had basically transformed into a regional commodity of limited range and a debased cultural artifact of the Andean realms of the Spanish American empire. It can be argued, perhaps, that coca was indirectly crucial to Europe's commercial revolutions because of the way it helped lubricate Spain's core colonial silver mining enterprise. By 1580, the leaf became a major consumable and stimulant for coerced Indian *mita* workers in the legendary silver mines of Potosí, and Peruvian silver swelled the world money supply and secured western Europe's ascension in the world economy. Paradoxically, there was to be a three-century lag in the metropolitan "discovery" of coca itself as a health good and tonic, and even then coca's properties remained controversial and shaded by cocaine, the alkaloid isolated in 1860. Only a full century later, as an *illicit* commodity, did cocaine attain its status as a major consumption good, one quite unlike coffee after all.

There are varied historical explanations for coca's early rejection by European colonialists and medical men. One is cultural: mastication of coca was aesthetically repulsive to Europeans, who had no comparable form or ritual of drug ingestion, and it was quickly judged an unredeemable indigenous vice. Another speculation is political: colonial officials, like the vanquished natives, deeply associated coca with defeated Andean gods, rituals, spirits, and the resistance of militant Incas. Because Incan culture and politics remained a live threat in the Andes, colonials had reason to dismiss coca's alleged energizing or healing powers as devilish witchcraft. Coca could not be co-opted by new ruling elites like the Jesuits, in contrast to, say, the *cacahuatl* (beverage chocolate) of the shattered and illegitimate Aztecs of Mexico.[7] Indeed, by the mid-sixteenth century, a full-fledged colonial "coca debate" was raging in the immense Viceroyalty of Peru. Powerful ecclesiastic "prohibitionists" (like Gerónimo de Loayza, archbishop of Lima; missionary Antonio Zuñiga; or the viceroy Marqués de Cañete, 1555–60), trying to outlaw its ruthless tropical production or root out its spreading use among Indian commoners, argued against relative pragmatists (like royal envoy Juan Matienzo, viceroy Francisco Toledo, and a few Jesuit allies such as José de Acosta and Bernabé Cobo), who, in intricate countermoves, attributed some powers to coca and accepted the inevitability of a limited Spanish coca trade. In this contentious context, there were no outright coca "boosters" on the European side. By 1600, however, the coca trade to Potosí alone was worth more than five hundred thousand pesos a year and had thus become a formidable colonial economic bloc. Under Spanish rule, the growing of coca and its sale to working migrants became "commoditized," to use an ungainly term, while coca's everyday use value in highland villages became an affirmation of surviving Andean values. In cultural terms, use of coca in Peru's highly segmented two-republics society was not creolized or "mestizo-ized" (as cacao quickly was in postconquest Mexico) but, to dominant elites, became instead a defining, lasting marker of a degraded subaltern "Indian" caste.

The fallout from the resolution of this Andean conflict was a negative and fuzzy image of coca abroad. Dr. Nicolás Monardes's canonical *Historia medicinal de los cosas que traen de las Indias* (Seville, 1580) barely broaches coca, although, tellingly, it waxes on about the medical properties of that American health plant, tobacco. Scant news about coca was transmitted outward through John Frampton's botanical bible *Joyfull News Out of the Newe World* (1596), which informed so many of the formative Pan-European medicinal debates. Significantly, little attempt registered to fit coca into the humoral system, which in contested or convoluted ways defined the other newfound stimulants and spices reaching Europe. Over time, outside the hermetically sealed Spanish American empire of the seventeenth century, coca became instead a fading fable of the conquest era, associated with Spanish obscurantism, pirates (who sometimes took up its use), or inherently deceitful Indians. It was an "El Dorado" of plants.[8] The mythical energy-producing leaf conjured up Indians performing impossible physical feats on empty stomachs in the style of Greek gods, an image hard to reconcile with their "primitive" or abject state. There was a highly practical factor at play as well: unlike processed tobacco, chocolate, or opium, coca leaf did not travel well, growing stale after months at sea, falling victim to alkaloid-killing rots. Indeed, any samples that reached Europe were deemed inert, adding to the scientific skepticism about the leaf's powers. So mythical was the coca plant that European botany lacked a credible depiction or classification — much less live specimens — until the eighteenth century.

Late in Peru's colonial period and at the start of the European Enlightenment, attitudes toward coca began to shift, sparking new curiosity about the plant. This was related to expanding new fields like botany or alkaloidal science after 1800 and to changing notions about the rationality of Indians. Spain's reformist Bourbons opened its formerly isolated empire to Enlightenment-style scientific expeditions (especially allied French missions), and after 1820 the new national states of the Andes — Peru, Bolivia, Ecuador — attracted a stream of influential foreign travelers and merchants, who went on to debate the region's scientific curiosities and untapped resources. This long story can be telescoped, beginning in 1708 with positive ruminations on coca's medicinal or nutritive value by Herman Boerhaave, the pioneering Dutch physician and organic chemist. In the 1730s and 1740s, Joseph de Jussieu, of the distinguished family of French botanists, pursued coca samples during scientific missions in Ecuador and the Bolivian Yungas, a journey that ended in personal disaster but provided the leaves needed for Jean-Baptiste Lamarck's botanical classification of the genus *Erythroxylon*. Spaniards Jorge Juan and Antonio de Ulloa, and then Baron von Humboldt himself (Europe's most eclectic Enlightenment scientist), took an active interest in coca, with von Humboldt both discovering and overstating the role of Indian "lime" (calcite) use in the potency of coca on his 1799 voyage to the Andes with French botanist Aimé Bonpland.

After 1825, when visitors descended from all over Europe to the now-independent American republics, coca became a favored, if highly exoticized, topic of traveler accounts. Visitors to Amazonian coca-growing areas inspired a series of prococa testimonials (about coca vitality and its role in Indian adaptability to harsh conditions), while skeptics denied coca's effects or deemed it a simple native vice like the orientals' betel or opium. These testimonials circulated in French, German, and English in a kind of intensifying nineteenth-century cacophony of coca. Swiss naturalist Johan Jacub von Tschudi, who made it to the *montaña* and interviewed sierran Indians on the sustenance of coca, engaged the German Eduard Poeppig, whose account of early 1830s presented the dark side of coca use.[9] Richard Spruce, the father of English ethnobotany, became fascinated with native Amazonian drugs in the 1850s, including *ipadu*, a coca snuff, and Dr. Paolo Mantegazza (an avant-garde Italian neurologist) lived in Peru's *montaña* and relayed his accounts of self-experimentation with coca, so exuberant that they sounded like descriptions of an early-day LSD "trip." By 1860, if curious about coca's attributes and pondering potential uses at home, experts still doubted coca's powers, because the dry coca leaf that made it to Europe or, now, the United States was invariably useless. Coca was also being swept into "modern" nineteenth-century neurological concerns about the relation between nervous energy (or spiritualist élan vital) and diseases, which superceded humoral discourse in shaping coca's medical roles.

The European (meaning principally greater German) "discovery" of alkaloidal cocaine in 1860, definitively isolated from leaf coca by Albert Niemann, a doctoral student in chemistry at Göttingen University, was far from a historical accident. Instead, *cocain* was the result of a deliberate, historically driven search for the "active principle" of coca, with multiple roots in advancing European sciences from 1800. The remarkable web of connections here explains why cocaine was a simultaneous discovery between 1855 and 1860. It is also true that urban Western culture of the mid-nineteenth century — a culture of quickening industrialization and the modernization of everyday life — offered a ready arena for the arrival of a new, miraculous energy-enhancing stimulant. Coffee, tea, sugar, and tobacco were already domesticated and too tame. The 1860 isolation of cocaine ended most speculation about the vitality of coca leaf, opening a new phase in this dialectical relation between herbal coca and scientific cocaine.

The quest for cocaine harks back to Boerhaave, who a century earlier hypothesized a "bitter" or "vital" essence of coca, offering clues for future Andean travelers. When German and French chemists perfected methods to derive the world's first alkaloids, not surprisingly, long-mythical essences were high on their to-do list, resulting in Wilhelm Sertürner's isolation of morphine from opium in 1805 and quinine from "Peru-bark" in 1820. Thus, the race was on for a magical stimulant with a tantalizing oral history. Von Tschudi's glowing reports on coca (including his own use of it) and continuing negations of the drug's power led Enrique Pizzi, an obscure Italian pharmacist working in La Paz, to toy in the mid-1850s with isolating coca's active principle as irrefutable proof. By 1857, Pizzi had come up with a substance that the connected von Tschudi took to one of Germany's leading pharmacologists, Dr. Friedrich Wöhler of Göttingen, famed for his synthesis of urea. Wöhler found nothing active in the compound after its transatlantic journey. Another late 1850s experimenter, Gaedke in Paris, inspired by Spruce and chemists who studied his leaves, suffered a similar setback with his odorous crystal "Erthroxyline." But Wöhler's curiosity was piqued, especially after Mantegazza's florid field reports of the 1850s, and he decided the problem was finding good coca. So in 1858 Wöhler contracted Dr. Karl Scherzer, the trade specialist of the Austrian frigate *Novara*, to fetch the freshest coca available explicitly for chemical analysis prior to the *Novara*'s scientific mission to the Pacific sponsored by Maximilian. Scherzer returned with a thirty-pound *cesto* of well-cured Bolivian coca, the largest sample yet seen in Europe.[10] Wöhler, in the German professorial fashion, delegated the job to his talented and short-lived doctoral assistant, Albert Niemann, who had already studied Spruce's coca specimens in Berlin. Applying alcohol, sulfuric acid, carbonate of soda, and ether, and using a textbook distillation technique, Niemann finally discovered *cocain* (constituting about 0.25 percent of the whole leaf), refining the method for his 1860 doctoral thesis at Göttingen. Within two years, Wilhelm Lossen, also of Göttingen, identified the chemical formula of cocaine hydrochloride, and many assays and tests followed.

With coca no longer shrouded in Andean legend, the next two decades sparked a whirlwind of experiments on cocaine, a rare and expensive drug still lacking a practical application, which it would only find as a local anesthetic after 1884. During this 1860–84 interregnum, the pioneering chemist Emmanuel Merck of Darmstadt (who had commercialized morphine) and a few others began making the drug in experimental batches. Researchers of this era tended to conflate coca and cocaine, enchanted by the physiological and neurological properties of stimulants, though a small group of herbalists also began a revalorization of leaf coca itself. The majority of cocaine's initial researchers were Germans, who dominated the rising fields of chemistry, biochemistry, pharmacology, and psychopharmacology: they included Schroff, Fronmüller, von Anrep, and Aschenbrandt, as well as assorted Frenchmen, Russians, Britons, and, as we will see, Peruvians. In their laboratory, animal, human, and self-experimentation on cocaine, all of them failed to recognize its noted "numbing" effect as an antidote to pain — a topic with another long genealogy in Western medicine. Cocaine, as American historian Joseph Spillane argues in his revisionist study, was the world's first "modern" drug: although plant-based, its discovery, profile, and applications all derived from evolving laboratory science and would be treated as such by modernizing pharmaceutical firms. Contrary to recent charges that early cocaine research got out of hand, most of it was cutting-edge and responsible science.

The most famous (at least now) of these late-nineteenth-century cocaine researchers was the young Austrian doctor Sigmund Freud. Freud would later attempt to cover up his early interest in drugs as his reputation took hold in the 1890s as the founder of psychoanalysis, a theory that has been linked to his cocaine "episode." Between July 1884 and July 1887, Freud, mesmerized by the "magic" of coca, his term for cocaine, and hoping to accelerate his career, published five essays now known as the "cocaine papers." Only one involved measurable experimentation, the rest being literature surveys based on Freud's access to the U.S. surgeon general's medical publication index. These essays and speculations reflected the influence of nascent French neurology, as well as Freud's own self-testing of the drug, acquired from Merck and, later, Parke, Davis and Company in Detroit. Freud was hardly alone: in the mid-1880s, there were hundreds of therapeutic and research notes circulating in European and American medical, dentistry, pharmacy, and chemistry journals about cocaine preparations and applications, exchanged across a spiraling international circuit including dozens of German scientists, as well as luminaries such as Britain's William Martindale and Robert Christison and Americans Edward Squibb, William Hammond, and William S. Halsted (a father of modern surgery). In a kind of "panacea" phase until the early 1890s, when the drug's clinical limits and dangers were absorbed, cocaine was tried or suggested for everything from labor pains to cholera, hysteria, hay fever, toothaches, and melancholy. Freud, in his landmark literature review, "Über Coca" (July 1884), covers existing classes of cocaine-coca therapy: as a generic stimulant (physical, mental, sexual); for all types of stomach and digestive ailments; for "cachexia" (wasting diseases such as anemia, syphilis, and typhus); for asthma; for anesthesia; and, to his regret, for treatment of alcohol and morphine habits.[11]

Freud's lasting impact was in getting his colleague Karl Köller, a Viennese ophthalmologist and anesthesia researcher, interested in the drug. In September 1884, Köller put together the clues and recognized cocaine's major and first proven value: as an effective local anesthetic. (Like the discovery of cocaine itself, his became a much-contested claim.) From the moment of Köller's 1884 announcement and demonstrations, cocaine revolutionized the global practice and possibilities of Western surgery. Hitherto impossible surgeries (on delicate areas like the eyes, throat, or genitals, or surgeries requiring the conscious cooperation of patients) were suddenly painless, if not easy. Cocaine would soon become deployed as a more general nerve block and in other sophisticated operations.[12] Köller's work inspired an even wider wave of applied medical research, and scarce cocaine, its price soaring, became an essential high-value commodity (the economic topic of chapter 2). Many German and French tracks led to Andean cocaine.

The decades after 1860 also saw renewed fascination with coca leaf and its incipient commerce, though cocaine's discovery often eclipsed coca.

Some traits of coca were now undeniable, given its known active principle, though German and other scientists preferred the precision, reliability, and sheer power of pure cocaine. A few ill effects of cocaine—its toxicity and later its controversial "habit"—were also projected onto the plant. The epicenter of coca's rediscovery was France, with its world-famous Vin Mariani of the 1860s. A burst of writings about coca emanated from France in 1860–62, soon after Niemann's isolation of cocaine. Angelo Mariani, from a long line of Corsican physicians and chemists, began experimenting in Paris with coca elixirs, finally perfecting his 1863 Bordeaux wine coca tincture. He named it "Vin Mariani a la Coca du Pérou" (although he used Bolivian leaf), and it was sold both as a "tonic stimulant for fatigued or overworked Body and Brain" and as a specific treatment for malaria, influenza, and all "wasting diseases." Mariani was a self-styled coca scholar steeped in a kind of transplanted or invented neo-Incan coca culture. Much has been written (on little research) about Mariani's astonishing commercial success, his Parisian "laboratories" and coca-leaf shrine, his prolific medical proselytizing, and above all about his innovative advertising campaigns, which recruited high-profile international celebrity and physician product endorsements in the Mariani albums.[13] What is notable here about Vin Mariani is the way it adeptly solved three of coca's historical problems in the West.[14] First, ingestion in a dignified

French perspective on the coca leaf, nineteenth century (Angelo Mariani, *Coca and Its Therapeutic Applications*, 2nd ed. [New York: J. N. Jaros, 1890], frontispiece)

wine superceded any associations with or need for repulsive coca chewing. Second, since alcohol actually enhances the impact of cocaine, Mariana's blend compensated for the degraded stimulant action of shipped leaf. Third, Mariani linked his concoction to idealized Incan "Mama-Coca" elites — symbolized as French-style noble savages — rather than uncouth Indians, and thus coca emerged as a salve for upper-class "brain workers." As a commodity (see chapter 2), Vin Mariani would leave a deep legacy in North America, where one of its local imitations reinvented itself in the mid-1880s as a health beverage called "Coca-Cola." Mariani's coca culture was explicitly proleaf and anticocaine, a drug he warned against in ersatz wines. Mariani also collaborated with his cousin Dr. Charles Fauvell, a noted Parisian throat specialist, who (among other clinical applications) used the blend to treat hoarse opera singers, adding to its acclaim and respectability. Cycling, another belle époque craze, also became a locus of Mariani coca culture. Moreover, advocated by Parisian sex researchers like Joseph Bain, coca wine was seen as the era's anti-Victorian aphrodisiac.

Across the channel, the Victorians also cultivated a keen interest in coca, although cocaine was readily available. Premier British botanists (Hooker, Spruce, and Markham) became engaged in *Erythroxylon* controversies, and the Royal Botanic Gardens at Kew mounted an active research and colonial dissemination program on the bush. Coca was broached as an early answer to England's social problem of the starving working class. English doctors prescribed various made-in-London coca wines and elixirs as the English went through their own bout of industrial-age "brain exhaustion." William Martindale (later president of the Pharmaceutical Society of Great Britain and editor of the long-standard *Extra Pharmacopoeia*) promoted coca for a range of illnesses and even saw it as a substitute for daily tea. The most famous British coca enthusiast was the Scottish medical man Sir Robert Christison, whose antifatigue experiments of the 1870s (scaling mountains like an Incan *chasqui* runner after chewing coca leaves) carried tremendous weight, since he was seventy-eight years old and then-president of the British Medical Association (BMA). In fact, the BMA continued to defend coca infusions long after their rejection by American counterparts.[15]

While the Germans admired cocaine and the French and British preferred coca, Americans were attracted to both with a special intensity. In mid-century North America, medical and popular cultures were particularly conducive to what became by the 1880s the country's "mania" for coca and cocaine. Two historical factors underlay American coca mania. First, Americans were — and remain — the world's most passionate consumers of all kinds of drugs, as cure-alls, mass market concoctions, and mind-altering substances. This national trait was exemplified during the nineteenth century by the country's astonishing level of whiskey drinking and the later proliferation of self-administered proprietary drugs, or patent medicines. Medical historian David Musto has diagnosed this drug culture as "the American disease," specifically as a deep cultural ambivalence with periodic swings between epochs of uninhibited drug use (most of the nineteenth century) and stern prohibitionist reactions (the first half of the twentieth).[16] An underlying factor in coca's American popularity was the diversity of the nineteenth-century American medical scene: rather than a monolithic and scientific profession — only consolidated with American Medical Association (AMA) victories after 1900 — there was a myriad of regional and competing schools of healers, doctors, and pharmacists, including herbalist forms of medicine (such as the homegrown Thomsonian botanical physicians), often drawing on Native American, frontier, and spiritualist — or what we now call "holistic"— health beliefs. These American "eclectics," who ran their own medical schools, were specially attracted to coca leaf after 1860, with a host of specific indications. For the most part, coca served as a broad antidote to the era's culturally diagnosed "neurasthenia"— so-called American nervousness (the title of neurologist George Beard's 1881 best-seller) — the rampant exhaustion and melancholic disorders of sedentary, civilized brain workers and their sensitive, anxiety-ridden women. Neurasthenia resembled what Continentals termed "hysteria," though today it would likely be thought of as a psychosomatic neurosis. Coca tonics, which might recharge burned-out brain function and "debilitated" nervous systems, were embraced as the primary cure — and, like many coca cures, they probably served as a feel-good placebo against pain, aches, or imaginary ills.[17]

The American romance with coca preceded cocaine and was magnified by its discovery until about 1900. Perhaps aroused by William H. Prescott's sympathetic pro-American portrayal of the Incas, the leaf was well-known in the United States, if hard to find before 1880. As early as 1865, New York physician William Searle secured a twenty-five-pound bale of disappointing leaf from Peru and initiated an active correspondence with medical colleagues there. Searle went on to compose an influential 1881 text declaring Andean coca the answer to Beard's neurasthenia. In another vein, a group of Philadelphia physicians in the mid-1870s, including coca-extract specialist Francis E. Stewart, employed coca-tobacco cigarettes as a salve against both sore throats and depression. Still another stream of medical discourse specified coca, and later cocaine, as life-giving substitutes against drug habits. The worrisome new notion of American "inebriety" derived from the country's heavy drinking and the silent southern scourge of post–Civil War morphine addiction. In a colorful example, a trade attaché in South America lauded coca in late-1880s pharmacy trade journals as the cure for the racial vice of northern "White People": whiskey. Two Kentucky physicians, W. H. Bentley (whose writings influenced Freud's view) and E. L. Palmer of the University of Louisville, treated opium and morphine users with coca infusions. As in Europe, confirmed coca doubters spoke out as well—such as prominent pharmacy figure Edward R. Squibb—and coca fever ran highest among doctors in peripheral zones outside the Northeast. The pioneer ethnobotanist Henry Hurd Rusby offered a scientific middle ground, carefully distinguishing in 1888 the curative values of "Coca at Home and Abroad"—its medicinal uses and potency being greater in the Andes before shipping.[18]

Thus, in the United States, instead of a race to find the alkaloid cocaine, there was a rush for ways to capture coca's essence, an effective elixir—a search brought home by Dr. Louis Elsberg's reports on French coca therapies. By 1880, Mariani had sent his brother-in-law Julius Jaros to open up a New York branch office. The Americanized Vin Mariani was an instantaneous hit, and Mariani's propaganda machine switched into English, warning of new, bogus American coca wines. The celebrated physician J. Leonard Corning wrote of Mariani wine, "It is the remedy *par excellence* against worry."[19] Detroit's Parke, Davis, soon to become Merck's chief American rival in cocaine, was still primarily an herbalist importer (like Cincinnati's Lloyd Brothers and many others), and it honed its fluid extracts of coca and an array of coca products in the early 1880s. By 1890, these additives became key not-so-secret ingredients in the proliferating patent medicines, such as popular Coca-Bola, a tobacco chew, or the strange-sounding (to us) Coca-Beef Tonic, which blended several of the era's health fads. Millions of Americans tried these remedies.

With the addition of African kola nut (caffeine) and the soda fountain health craze of the 1880s, the path was set for the popular craving for and wild commercial success of Coca-Cola. The drink was concocted in 1886 by Atlanta pharmacist John Pemberton as a dry version of his prior attempt at "Pemberton's French Wine Coca" (which he claimed was "superior" to Mariani's). Fluid extract of coca leaf was likely the most appealing of its secret "7-X" ingredients. Significantly, the scholarly Pemberton had been trained in a regional Thomsonian school, the southern Botanico Medical College of Georgia, and he was an admirer of Sir Robert Christison and a likely morphine addict himself (the result of his Civil War wounds).[20] The next chapter returns to Coca-Cola as the era's ur-American commodity, one with a profound impact on the Peruvian coca trade, although increasingly removed from its Franco-Peruvian cultural roots. After 1890, American herbalists continued to defend coca therapy even after edged out by cocaine and the proliferating critiques of patent medicine. The denouement of the American love-hate affair with coca leaf was epitomized by the classic study *History of Coca: "The Divine Plant" of the Incas* (1901) by the respected New York surgeon W. Golden Mortimer, a massively detailed, erudite defense of the virtues of medicinal coca (including invaluable surveys of coca-dispensing U.S. physicians). Mortimer took pains to distinguish coca from cocaine and rooted his work, as the title suggests, in neo-Incan history and imagery, à la Prescott and Mariani.[21]

During this era, the United States also became deeply entangled with the new drug cocaine through medical progress in the 1880s, via popular products in the 1890s, and spreading into recreational use by 1900. With the largest consumer market during the medical era, U.S. cocaine production (led by Parke, Davis and several German branch houses) soon rivaled Germany's. News of cocaine advances spread quickly to and across the United States. For example, in October 1884, the team of distinguished specialists treating former president Ulysses S. Grant (already an enthusiastic drinker of Vin Mariani) immediately adopted a cocaine solution for the excruciating pain of his terminal throat cancer, less than a month after Köller's Vienna breakthrough. The next years saw hundreds of research and medical publications and announcements about cocaine, some fostered by the active publicity medical gazettes of "ethical" (wholesale) pharmaceutical firms like Parke, Davis.

However, as recently shown in Spillane's study of cocaine medicine, these applications were neither indiscriminate nor faddish.[22] Cocaine research was eminently modern, since cocaine was among the first drugs whose physiological impact could be actually monitored and measured. In clinical practice, cocaine acquired four kinds of applications by the late 1880s. First was its generalization in surgery, especially as a local anesthetic in nose, throat, dental, and eye operations. Leading surgeons (like Johns Hopkins's founder, William Halsted, or J. Leonard Corning) developed whole new surgical fields based on cocaine. The second usage, parallel to coca therapy, was as a tonic and stimulant, an application steeped in the era's neurological science. Former surgeon general William Hammond, a neurologist, for example, injected severely depressed female patients with cocaine. It seemed to work well in an era long before the existence of pharmaceutical antidepressants. The third usage was in the treatment of opiate addiction—a usage that was soon recognized as problematic. The fourth use was for hay fever, asthma, and other respiratory ailments (whose symptoms cocaine certainly relieved), all still considered diseases of the nervous system. Within five years of Köller's discovery, medical opinion in the United States became fully aware of cocaine's well-debated dangers (such as its toxic side effects or the more debatable potential for "habit" formation), as detailed by a special 1889 commission of the staid New York Academy of Medicine.[23] Doctors quickly and discreetly restricted dosages and medical usage, narrowing cocaine's crucial role to that of a surgical anesthetic. Cocaine, however, had won a legitimate place in American medicine. What arose later—cocaine's mid-1890s spillover into patent medicines and rumored pleasure use—lay outside the realm of medical practice and was opposed by alarmed doctors, pharmacists, and the larger ethical pharmaceutical industry. Most felt that self-regulation, rather than federal prohibition, was the best cure for this problem.

Finally, after 1875, European powers (Britain, the Netherlands, and to a lesser extent France and Germany) began working on formal coca colonization schemes—a "botanical imperialism" that would transplant coca from the Andes and befit their expanding tropical colonies. In contrast, the United States aptly opted for a more informal sort of coca diplomacy. It focused on closer trade relations with and market intelligence from Peru and Bolivia, weak nations that would eventually fall into the U.S. sphere. These efforts were exemplified in an early (1877) navy "sanitary report" on coca, by State Department questionnaires (about the "difficulty" of obtaining the leaf) during the sharp mid-1880s coca scarcity, and by widely published 1886 coca reports of Consul-General Gibbs (from La Paz, and then from Lima). By the 1890s, consuls and attachés on the ground assumed an active stance helping Peruvians upgrade coca cultivation and packing, as well as gathering commercial intelligence about the new local cocaine industry. These were the first visible articulations of Americans to coca in the Andes in attempts to promote its expansion and linkages to North America. Like the Spanish coca debate of the sixteenth century, they were also a forgotten prelude to the later U.S. campaign, after 1915, to extirpate a by-then-unwanted diabolical plant.[24]

A PERUVIAN COCA SCIENCE

Far away, in Lima, Peru, these same worldly medical and cultural fascinations with coca and cocaine impinged on national elite attitudes toward Andean coca leaf, a reimagining integral to cocaine's later construction as a national commodity. Central to this process of coca vindication was the energetic cocaine research and writings of the obscure Franco-Peruvian pharmacist Alfredo Bignon between 1884 and 1887, the same years Freud was writing his own cocaine papers.[25] While Freud, as many note, personified the European cocaine zeitgeist of the mid-1880s, Bignon's research was part of a consolidating and now-forgotten nineteenth-century nationalist science around Peruvian coca and cocaine. Moreover, the technological advances from Bignon's "scientific excellence" (the idea that surprising nodes of innovation can spring from the periphery) led to Peru's late-1880s launch of cocaine as a world commodity.

Bignon was a prime mover in a wider and longer national movement around coca and cocaine. The timing should not suggest, however, that the Peruvian discovery of coca in its own backyard was a mere reflection of the cocaine mania sweeping the European and American world. The enhanced image of coca abroad after the 1840s, especially the discovery of its active principle in 1860, no doubt helped elevate coca's legitimacy at home. But Peruvians came up with their own, often complex responses to the drug. Scientific and other interest in coca was part of a broader awakening of a Peruvian scientific nationalism in the context of Peru's fragmented, unevenly forming, and weak postcolonial nation. Scientific nationalism was often articulated by educated immigrants (in striking cases like those of the naturalized Italian naturalist Antonio Raimondi or the Polish engineer Eduardo Habich), all deeply immersed in transatlantic intellectual currents. With Paris a pole of cultural and scientific fascination with coca, it was no accident that Francophone Peruvians like Bignon figured in local discoveries about coca, as would local Germans. Their interstitial roles complicate unidirectional models of scientific flows (from "core to periphery") as well as essentialized ideals of early Latin American national identity.

Generally, there were three prospective routes for the nationalist recuperation of coca's possibilities in Peru. A first possible path for coca was cultural or historical. In theory at least, Peruvian elites could have embraced coca leaf's centrality as a popular or indigenous marker of Peruvian identity and a cultural artifact or proof of Peru's long and authentic historic roots as a nation. In Peru, however, that avenue was largely blocked in the nineteenth century owing to the deep cultural divide between ruling urban elites on the coast and the coca-using sierran Indian majority, a schism increasingly construed as a racial hierarchy. Indeed, when nationalist-style *indigenismo* arrived vibrantly in the early twentieth century, most of its proponents were resolutely anticoca, viewing coca as a toxic and degenerating vice of Peru's *raza indígena*. Paradoxically, Andean coca nationalism of a neo-Incan kind was more commonly found overseas, among French coca wine connoisseurs or New York readers of Mortimer's *History of Coca*, a copy of which was dispatched to the Biblioteca Nacional in Lima.[26] In contrast, a cultural embrace of Andean coca proved more feasible among Bolivia's small literate class, given the leaf's spatial and social integration into the altiplano nation and strong elite stakes in *yungas* coca growing.

The second nationalist route was coca's potential as a national commodity, or, to use historian Arnold Bauer's term, coca as a "modernizing good."[27] In fact, this type of dreaming and writing about national coca became a virtual obsession after 1860, especially evident in revived schemes for Amazonian development (explored in promotional writings later in this chapter). Coca, as guano had been, was a natural monopoly for Peru, just waiting to be discovered as a marketable and lucrative commodity. Coca plantations could awaken the sleeping tropical riches of the savage eastern *ceja de la montaña* ("eyebrow of the jungle") lands of Peru, finally helping to bring those disconnected territories into the civilized nation. Following the devastation of Peru's coastal economy during the Pacific War (1879–81), such pleas for new and more national exports took on a desperate tone.

A third avenue was medical or scientific nationalism, which turned out to be perfectly suited for coca. By the 1850s, literate urban Peruvians gleaned that European science was confirming the value of one of Peru's untapped national resources, overcoming ancient prejudices on both sides of the Atlantic. Lima's medical elites, many of them ardent liberals and internationalists, had access to the latest in overseas research through their active mid-century medical societies and journals. Such *científicos* were among Peru's few real public intellectuals, and they were emissaries of a universalizing modernity. Modern metropolitan science could legitimate and nationalize Peru's gift to the world. Typical of these tropes was the notion that modern chemistry would transform the lowly Indian coca plant into that most exciting and useful of commodities: medicinal cocaine. This can be read as a metaphor for elitist Peruvian nationalism generally—the guided transformation of an inert, telluric, and buried raw material of (Incan) history into a superior and hybrid modern good.[28]

Alfredo Bignon was also part of a national coca movement dating to the independence era. Tellingly, when Peruvians spoke of coca in the 1880s, they often invoked this national scientific genealogy (sometimes even back to the "Inca" Garcilaso de la Vega) rather than refer to European discovery. The first in this line was Dr. José Hipólito Unánue, the towering scientific and political savant of Lima's Enlightenment Sociedad de Amantes del País salon, who went on to become a leading republican patriot and (among other posts) one of Peru's first finance ministers. Unánue's 1794 "Disertación sobre la coca" in *El Mercurio Peruano* surveyed the leaf's distribution and medicinal uses across Peru, extolling its centrality to the viceroyal economy and lauding coca as a future export to Europe. His thesis that use of lime in Indian coca preparations was the secret to its vitality was not only correct but influenced other investigators, including von Humboldt.[29] Unánue followed his Upper Peru (Bolivian) counterpart in *El Mercurio Peruano*, naturalist Pedro Crespo, a late-colonial functionary who strove to publicize *yungas* coca as a stimulant for enervated European sailors. Unánue's *disertación* continued to find readers after Peru's independence, resurfacing, for example, in 1837 in a scientific monthly in Cuzco, a traditional region of heavy coca use.

In October 1858, on a wave of coca news from abroad, an editorial, "La coca peruana," appeared in the pharmacology section of the *Gaceta Médica de Lima*, Peru's principal medical journal. Reacting to the Continental search for coca's alkaloid and its distillation, the unnamed editor (likely French-trained José Casimiro Ulloa, a vital figure in mid-century medicine and politics) flatly declares: "In our country the stimulant and tonic properties held by coca leaf (*erythroxylon coca*) are well-known, which is even widely used by the *raza indígena* as a daily food. . . . It is desirable to apply chemical processes to this indigenous plant, so that its applications become more beneficial and general in medical practice, still so confined to the narrow realm of Andean empiricism."[30] Ulloa's editorial was, in effect, a call for Peruvian scientific action.

That call was echoed in the remarkable career of Tomás Moreno y Maíz, a figure far less known than Unánue or Ulloa. Moreno y Maíz was a former Peruvian chief military surgeon who had migrated to Paris by the 1860s. He was also an associate of Bignon, likely from a period shared in the highland mining town of Cerro de Pasco, where they encountered coca firsthand. In 1862, two years after cocaine's isolation, amid soaring

French coca interest, Moreno y Maíz embarked on a series of experiments with Parisian rats to determine if cocaine could in fact substitute for food and water, as suggested by Indian lore about coca's power as a hunger suppressant. The rats died, probably because he failed to employ more nutritious infusions of coca, a result that dampened French coca mania. His first piece in 1862 for Peruvian readers, "De la coca," begins by noting that "Peru offers a wide and fertile field for studies . . . above all, the marvel of Coca, put to so many uses by our Indians." He continues, "This plant recently becoming so known in Europe, will be another source of wealth for Peru." In a response, Juan Copello, one of Lima's pioneering medical professors (an Italian-born blood researcher and later, with Luis Petriconi, a famed nationalist writer on Peru's economic crisis of the 1870s), wrote "Clamor coca," calling for scientific emulation with other locally known medicinal plants. Discussion of coca went hand in hand with campaigns for a more national reformed pharmacopoeia. Later, Moreno y Maíz was also credited with independent verification, from experiments on frogs, of cocaine's anesthetic qualities (like Freud, allegedly prior to Köller in 1884). Peruvian colleagues proudly cited him throughout the 1880s for that momentous discovery. Freud himself twice cited Moreno y Maíz (the accents of his name mangled) in his own "Über Coca," along with other French researchers, for "provid[ing] certain new facts about cocaine" and for disproving the so-called coca source of savings energy conservation hypothesis.[31]

Moreno y Maíz's works not only appeared in France, in the lingua franca of Peruvian medicine, but also, with a lag, in Spanish in Lima's medical gazettes. He became well-known in Lima solely on the basis of his cocaine research. In 1876, "Sobre el Erythroxylon Coca del Perú y sobre la 'cocaína,'" the "excellent thesis of our compatriot" completed in Paris in 1868 (translated by Dr. Enrique Elmore), appeared as a serial publication in the Gaceta Médica. It also came out in El Nacional, Lima's leading reform newspaper, no doubt to publicize coca's developmental promise. The thesis is a thirty-page compendium of extant historical, botanical, commercial, and pharmaceutical knowledge about both drugs, ending with depictions and analysis of Moreno y Maíz's dozen animal experiments (with hyperstimulated rats and frogs), most concerning cocaine's nerve action. Much like the young Freud, who also mingled in Paris with the pioneer neurologists of that avant-garde French science, he saw nerve and genital excitation as one. Yet in the preface to his 1868 thesis, Moreno y Maíz credits his fascination with coca not to Parisian trends but to his encounters with coca sustaining the highland Indian through daily toil. An expanded French version of the thesis came out as a ninety-one-page pamphlet in Paris. Moreno y Maíz lauds the stimulus of coca to research, not just to body and mind, particularly after isolation of its active ingredient in 1860.[32]

The same gazettes reproduce a stream of notes on coca from the French pharmacy and chemical press, as well as essays on still-fashionable hashish and opium. French medical currents predominated in Peru after Dr. Cayetano Heredia's revolutionary mid-century reorganization of the national medical curriculum, including the practice of sending students to Paris for final training and bringing eminent foreign scientists to Peru (among them refugees of 1848 such as Raimondi, republican Peru's foremost scientific light). To Peruvians, it must have seemed ironic to read this multitude of European coca specialists resorting to remote, ancient, and exaggerated hearsay about the Andean leaf. The fact that some *limeños* of "high respectability" (the choice phrase of visitor von Tschudi from the 1840s) privately partook of coca may have given them insight into and even an affection for the leaf. The tide of opinions flowed both ways. For example, Francophile Manuel A. Fuentes, Lima's prolific guano-age publicist and statistician, published an 1866 paean to coca in Paris, part of a lifelong attraction to the leaf. Besides enumerating in French coca's possible cures, Fuentes exclaims, "This plant could possibly become today a branch of exportation as advantageous to Peru as cacao, quinine, and guano."[33]

In March 1866, the first dramatic result appeared of earlier pleas for local research and recognition of coca: the Lima Faculty of Medicine thesis of Dr. José Antonio de Ríos, "La coca peruana," published in the *Gaceta Médica*. The thesis displays a standard compendium style, from its "Historical Summary" of Incan coca to its modern "Botanic Study." Ríos, in his own words, was driven "since starting medical studies by a vehement desire to know the national products that can be used to fight diseases, the benefits one sees in the Indians." He explained that "because its therapeutic action is insufficiently understood," coca was "destined to contribute huge services." A noted student of chemistry, Ríos was to serve two decades later with José Casimiro Ulloa in the country's Coca Commission of 1887–88, which also promoted Bignon's research. Dr. Miguel Colunga, one of two physicians on Ríos's 1866 thesis committee, also resurfaced two decades later on the same commission. In January 1868, Antonio Raimondi himself (who often wrote on economic botany) contributed an essay, "Elementos de botánica aplicada a la medicina y a la industria," weighing in on the era's great coca debate: the nature of the leaf's "excitant properties." Referring to cocaine, Raimondi distinguishes it from coffee and tea's already-recognized stimulant, caffeine. Other studies appeared in the Peruvian medical press, for example the detailed 1875 "Estudio sobre la coca" of *limeño* physician Eduardo Nuñez del Prado, which elaborates the material and medicinal uses of Bolivia's coca of the *yungas*.[34] Perhaps this was early commercial spying on Peru's only coca-growing rival. Along the way, Nuñez endorses Unánue's early insight about coca's eclectic nutritional value.

In short, Lima was bombarded with local coca studies, information, and controversies after mid-century, much of it with a French accent. Nationalist ideals of scientific analysis and exploitation of Andean medicinal plants and indigenous lore dominated this vibrant discussion. *Limeño* elites were in the process of elevating coca into a national good—in both senses of the word—often via the mediation of "scientific" modern cocaine. In December 1875, a new Sociedad de Medicina was inaugurated in Lima around the *Gaceta Médica*: among its founders was the pharmacist Alfredo Bignon, whose name had appeared in druggist ads as early as 1866.

In the larger political and social picture, Bignon's "cocaine papers" of 1884–87 arose during the associational revival and intraelite struggles that followed Peru's Pacific War with Chile (1879–81). This catastrophic event marked a painful divide between Peru's failed early republics and the national reconstruction that culminated in the Aristocratic Republic (1895–1919), the peak era of cocaine. As Peruvian medicine recovered from the war, it began to remake itself in more scientific fashion, stressing national and applied research. In Peru, exclusive medical societies served as a key site for elite "civilizing" and nationalizing discourses, often of a hygienic, social, or positivist bent. The white men debating the scientific merits of coca in these salons were some of Peru's most distinguished doctors and educators, whose esoteric research and discussions barely even filtered to Lima's broader news-reading public. By 1885, the original *Gaceta Médica*, which had folded in 1868, revived as an organ of the capital's two renovated medical societies, institutions integrated by the same group of physicians, professors, and professionals. One was the Academia Libre de Medicina de Lima (led by Ulloa), which evolved into Peru's French-styled Academia Nacional de Medicina. It put out its own short-lived research *boletín*, as well as a bimonthly journal, *El Monitor Médico* (1885–96). The other group, the Sociedad Médica Unión Fernandini, had a more pharmacy and syndicalist orientation and in 1885 launched *La Crónica Médica* (edited by

Both journals represented San Marcos University's Faculty of Medical Sciences and disseminated a mix of the latest foreign and national medical developments. From these circles, authorities convened specific bodies on cocaine: in early 1885, the Comisión de Cocaína of the Academia de Medicina gathered to evaluate cocaine-making techniques and therapies (the procedure followed with most new pharmacy formulas in Lima) and foster their use in national medicine. The commission recruited doctors D. L. Villar (president), Miguel Colunga, R. L. Flórez, Pedro Remy, and, as usual, Ulloa. In 1888, the government appointed a distinct university commission, this time casting a wider commercial lens on Peruvian coca leaf: La Comisión de Coca, staffed by Ulloa, Colunga (Raimondi's bota-nist heir), and José A. de Ríos, vice-dean of the faculty of medicine and author of that youthful 1860s coca thesis.[35] These commissions validated a national science. Bignon's research appeared not only as articles but as proceedings of the academy throughout 1885–87, which conjures up the image of a lively debate among this specialized audience as he read aloud his Lima cocaine papers.

BIGNON'S COCAINE PAPERS, 1884–1887

The wellspring of cocaine interest in nineteenth-century Peru lay in this nascent clique of medical scientists. Between 1885 and 1887, chemist Al-fredo Bignon, encouraged by *limeño* colleagues, conducted ten published investigations on cocaine and coca leaf, establishing a now-forgotten field of Peruvian cocaine science with broad nationalist and commercial overtones.[36] In a whirlwind of scientific energies that swiftly rose and fell, Bignon exemplified a precocious form of what medical historian Marcos Cueto dubs "scientific excellence on the periphery"—the modernist circles and innovative institutions of scientific research that evolved in *civilista* Peru after 1890.

Born in Paris in 1843 (to where he returned after 1900), Bignon was raised in Peru and trained in the Sección Farmacéutica of Lima's Faculty of Medicine, becoming one of the country's top pharmacists. He came from a family of druggists, including his brother as well as his father, Luis Bignon (a probable refugee of 1848), who by the late 1850s had become a pharmacy teacher in Lima before resettling in Chile. Bignon's own career began in the late 1860s with a *botica* in Cerro de Pasco—a highland center of miner "chewers" near the coca supply shed of Huánuco—where he is said to have started pursuing chemistry on his own. In 1872, Bignon returned to the capital after his father's death to run the thriving Droguería y Botica Francesa Alfredo Bignon on Calle Plateros, just off Lima's politically central Plaza de Armas. After the Pacific War, Bignon served as a professor of pharmacy and chemistry, becoming active in Lima's new Academy of Medicine. Childless (which perhaps explains his scientific productivity), Bignon toyed in other businesses as well, such as a local ham factory, and honed an eclectic range of scientific pursuits, such as metallurgy, as well as interests in social issues like alcoholism. As an educated European, Bignon was well-known in Lima's small world, "a friend of Raimondi, Ulloa, Castilla, Villar and other celebrities of the time." Like other cosmopolitans, Bignon left home for travels and study in Europe, including a course in industrial chemistry in Germany. His papers and comments were published and quoted abroad, and his cocaine methods and expertise were cited by leading American, British, and French chemists and coca specialists. Bignon, in short, belonged to that lively transnational network of cocaine researchers that swiftly crossed the globe during the 1880s. He was also a dedicated promoter of Peruvian research: beyond his own working example, he endowed a Bignon Chemistry Thesis Prize in the Faculty of Medicine. Despite his French roots, Bignon was, in the words of his sole chronicler, "a citizen of Peruvian science."[37]

Between late 1884 and early 1887, Bignon undertook nearly a dozen major published papers, studies, and experiments on cocaine—with laboratory equipment, on animals, or, in Freud's psychopharmacological fashion, on himself. His work attracted a circle of admiring peers. His discoveries occurred after hours, in the back room of the Plateros pharmacy, where Bignon allegedly tinkered with cocaine for years prior to 1884. Bignon's major achievement was a novel cost-saving kerosene precipitation method for production of cocaine from fresh coca leaf (as opposed to Niemann's original 1860 alkaloid hydrochloride from dried coca). This was a "crude cocaine," or cocaine sulfate, that he also strove strenuously to test, compare, and apply therapeutically. A modernist like his mentor Moreno y Maíz, Bignon strongly valorized the properties of cocaine over coca, which he deemed too inert or inexact for clinical use. Yet for a scientist, he was also unusually attuned to the notion that cocaine's therapeutic traits might vary with the salt of cocaine used or even its sources in distinct varieties of coca bush.

Bignon's intense cocaine phase (1884–87) began with the January 1885 publication of his new method for the extraction of cocaine from fresh coca. The backdrop was the rapid improvement and dissemination of cocaine-refining techniques: Niemann's textbook 1860 alkaloid isolation, Lossen's chemical analyses and the sophisticated 1890s German-patented "ecognine" extraction method for dried leaf, and others of Einhorn, Meyer, Hesse, Phieffer, Liebermann, and Castaing, as well as numerous assaying methods. In contrast to advanced laboratory techniques, Bignon's aim was cocaine's "easy and economical preparation in the same places as coca cultivation," a direct response to the cocaine shortages blocking usage globally in the mid-1880s. Bignon immediately requested the formula's examination by the specially appointed Lima Cocaine Commission. The commission's ten-page *informe* of March 1885, signed by Ulloa, is a deep reflection on the Peruvian scientific lineage of coca and cocaine from Unánue to Moreno y Maíz, the latter celebrated for discovering cocaine's anesthetic powers, as well as cocaine precursors in Indian calcite use. Among three accepted techniques for making cocaine, the committee lauded Bignon's for its sheer simplicity and its reductions of wasteful heating and pulverization. The breakthrough here was in the use of kerosene and soda ash as precipitants after a prolonged maceration of coca in lime. The staggered use of solvents required some eighty-seven hours (three and a half days) to produce viable cocaine. Bignon's method yielded a 60 percent cocaine sulfate, so-called crude cocaine, or *cocaína bruta* — one not as pure or soluble as the medicinal end product (cocaine HCl) processed with hydrochloric acids. Peru, flowing with petroleum from the new Zorritos field of the north, also manufactured bicarbonate of soda in Lima. The report stressed that in Peru, endowed with the raw materials, "one could establish a large-scale national industry, which could produce an invaluable article of export." Coca "indigenous to Peru with its rare and extraordinary properties exalted unto the fantastic" by countless foreign conquerors and travelers was now, thanks to Bignon, becoming a tangible reality.[38]

In July 1885, Bignon published "La cocaína y sus sales," a six-page comparative study of new varieties of cocaine that suggests that standard cocaine hydrochloride, in addition to being difficult to produce, was not necessarily the best anesthetic. Most of the testing Bignon performed on his own tongue, so it seems. In May 1886, Bignon presented his latest paper to the Academy of Medicine, "Acción fisiológica de la cocaína," a twenty-page research report based on his administration of varying dosages and drug formulas in experiments with *limeño* dogs (most of whom died in fits of nerve poisoning). From here, Bignon began to draw out larger theories of

INFORME

DE LA COMISION NOMBRADA PARA ESTUDIAR EL PROCEDIMIENTO
DEL SR. A. BIGNON, PARA EXTRAER LA COCAINA.

Comision: – Doctores D. L. Villar (Presidente)—M. F. Colunga—R. L.
Flórez—P. F. Remy – J. C. Ulloa (Secretario Relator.)

La coca, indígena del Perú, por sus raras y extraordina-
rias propiedades exaltadas hasta lo maravilloso, llamó desde la conquista la atencion de todos los nuevos pobladores
del imperio conquistado, así como el de todos los viajeros
y sábios que desde entónces han venido á explorar nues-
tras regiones.

Su verdadero estudio científico no fué hecho, sin em-
bargo, hasta que nuestro inmortal fundador de la medicina nacional, el Dr. D. Hipólito Unánue, publicó su céle-
bre disertacion sobre el *aspecto, cultivo y virtudes de la coca*,
que ha sido y es hasta hoy el fundamento de todas las investigaciones que se han hecho sobre esta singular planta,
cuyos efectos parecian asemejarse á los del té y del café.

Apesar de esto, la coca no figuraba en la Terapéutica,
hasta que, estudiada su composicion química y descubierto
por Niemann en 1850 uno de sus alcaloides, la *Cocaina*, se
comenzó á estudiar su accion fisiológica y terapéutica por
Mantegazza en 1857, Gosse en 1862, nuestro finado com-

Informe of commission to evaluate Bignon's cocaine method, 1885
(*Boletín de la Academia Libre de Medicina de Lima*, 1 [20 March 1885]: 77)

cocaine's action on the nervous system based on contemporary notions
of nerve conduction, building on decades-old findings of Moreno y Maíz.
Aware of cocaine's clinical dangers, Bignon judged the drug's toxicity an
indirect effect of its action. A parallel experiment appeared in *El Monitor
Médico*, in which Bignon used human urine samples and urea analysis to
trace cocaine absorption. Again, Bignon acknowledged the innovations
of Moreno y Maíz. In late 1886, Bignon forwarded a therapeutic note,
"Propiedades de la coca y de la cocaína," a strong statement of the medicinal superiority of cocaine over Indian coca leaf. Bignon, unlike earlier
national coca enthusiasts, found leaf itself neither tonic nor nutrient,

dismissing as folkloric claims of coca's medicinal value. In December of 1886, Bignon presented the academy with his most intricate paper to date: "Posología de la cocaína" (posology is the science of quantifying dosage), which made rigorous comparisons of the therapeutic qualities of cocaine salts and solutions using hypodermic needles, pills, and varied tinctures. Bignon concluded that his own impure cocaine sulfate contained "more energy for a lesser cost," revealing of neurological stimulation concerns beyond surgical anesthesia.[39]

Perhaps Bignon, like Freud, was a user himself, for his scientific output soon reached a frenetic pace.[40] In September of 1886, he published three different notes and experiments on the drug, weighing in on the era's running "botanical" coca controversies. The first, surprising in light of Bignon's aversion to natural coca, is largely botanical, "Sobre una nueva coca del norte del Perú," an analysis of the so-called Trujillo variety of *Erythroxylon coca*. He confirms its higher ratio of uncrystallizable (ecgonine) alkaloids: we now know this to be a separate species, *E. novogranatense*, with a greater diversity of alkaloids—perhaps one reason why northern Peruvian leaf has been long preferred for coca essences more than cocaine making. The second note, "Sobre el valor comparativo de las cocaínas," a collaboration with doctors José Antonio de Ríos, Juan C. Castillo, and R. L. Flórez, systematically compares the cocaine action of alkaloids derived from Peru's regional coca leaves, that is, the northern, central (Huánuco), and southern varieties.[41] Bignon's outlook was commercial again, and indeed these are trade varieties, not, as once widely believed, always congruent with true subspecies of the plant.

Such research could only have been performed by local scientists knowledgeable about Peruvian coca culture and provenance. A central concern here was odors left by residual coca alkaloids, a problem in syrups, additives, and salves but not injectable cocaine, and a possible factor in the long-standing consumer preference for Trujillo leaf—a taste that extended to later drinkers of Coca-Cola. Other *limeños*, such as the pharmacy teacher Manuel Velázquez, were perfecting marketable coca elixir formulas during the same years. Years later, the American coca crusader Mortimer would cite these distinctions of Bignon's to argue in favor of coca therapies, the opposite of Bignon's stance. This work on coca was soon joined by another detailed dog autopsy paper, "Estudio experimental del antagonismo de la estricnina y de la cocaína," a series of seven gruesome experiments to probe the neutralizing action between strychnine and cocaine and its therapeutic implications for such conditions as tetanus, epilepsy, and other so-called overexcitation disorders. Like American and European peers, including Freud, Bignon prescribed cocaine injections for nervous ailments like hysteria, epilepsy, and neurasthenia.[42]

In January 1888, Bignon presented still another "communication" to the academy, "Sobre la utilidad de la cocaína en el cólera," an exemplar of applied social medicine at a time when cholera epidemics still posed a threat in coastal Peru. A critique of articles by the Argentine doctor Lucindo del Castillo published in *La Nación* in Buenos Aires, Bignon's paper contests Castillo's therapeutic claims for coca tinctures alone, though acknowledging possible anesthetic benefits from the action of their cocaine.[43] This is a window into a scattering of original research about coca and cocaine across the Americas, with examples popping up in contemporary Chile, Argentina, and Mexico, in part because coca was a long-accepted item of the regional pharmacopoeia. Bignon was not alone in prescribing cocaine for symptoms of cholera in what were larger international controversies about cocaine's internal indications. But Bignon ends here by sharply assailing the "moral anesthesia produced on the spirit of doctors" (pun intended), referring to stubborn medical preferences for coca leaf over the measurable benefits of alkaloidal cocaine.[44] His polemical tone resembles Freud's famed swan song to cocaine, "Craving for and Fear of Cocaine" (July 1887), which also suggests that rising criticism of medicinal cocaine (and his own work on it) was psychological at its core. In April 1887, Bignon's final note on cocaine appeared, a succinct analysis titled "Soluciones de cocaína" on clinical uses for Vaseline-cocaine mixtures. While he would write no more about cocaine, Bignon continued to publish on other scientific topics, including translations of advances in alkaloid chemistry.[45]

Bignon's intellectual production on cocaine was so prodigious — more than a dozen major articles, communiqués, and notes over three years — that the academy ended up posting simple summaries for lay readers. What began with a simple patriotic or commercial motive, a made-for-Peru cocaine-making formula, ended in a wider scientific quest in chemistry, botany, physiology, neurology, and therapy. Granted, medical professionals, even working pharmacists, were not yet terribly specialized anywhere in the late nineteenth century (outside of Germany, doctoral programs in sciences were just starting up in the 1890s), allowing the social space for such maverick contributions. This pragmatic approach to discovery was noted by Bignon himself in an 1886 essay on therapeutic drugs. Although they worked in different veins of cocaine research, Bignon was actually twice as prolific as Freud — who published but five cursory cocaine papers

sense, as only one of Freud's self-testing or literature studies involved
external observation or measurement. Bignon was not only cited abroad
(albeit less profusely than Freud, who was a true cocaine publicist), but
translated excerpts of Bignon's Lima cocaine papers were also actually
published in major French, German, and U.S. journals, including even an
essay on cocaine dentistry not published at home.[46]

Bignon's working language and location in Peru may have been to his
scientific disadvantage, but he was not entirely isolated there. *La Crónica
Médica*, then Peru's leading medical journal, published other original studies of cocaine, as well as a stream of overseas clinical reports on cocaine's
utility in surgery, heart conditions, and even as a cure for insanity. The
journal's later editor, Dr. Almenara Butler, was a notable case, with his
own April 1885 report, "La cocaína en las quemadas," about his clinical
work saving young burn patients with cocaine-laced petroleum jelly bases.
Bignon's cowritten papers strikingly reveal a coterie of local working colleagues and the respect his research garnered in Lima. The members of
the academy's Cocaine Commission all became virtual experts on cocaine,
some with their own coca obsessions dating back decades. San Marcos
Medical School records show a smattering of Peruvian medical research on
coca and cocaine, including, for example, Eduardo Showing's 1884 thesis,
"La medicina tónica y sus aplicaciones terapéuticas" (Dr. Showing was
of one of coca-rich Huánuco's elite families); a medical thesis by Rodolfo
Mercado, "Aplicaciones higénicas y terapéuticas de la coca" (1894); and
one by Víctor Diez Canseco, "La raquicocainización en cirujía" (1902).[47]
Cocaine research was, however, petering out after 1887.

In sum, a strong current of scientific nationalism ran throughout this
mid-1880s episode. In a sense, Bignon's work was a precursor to the more
public (and better-known) scientific "coca debates" research that resurfaced
in Peru in the three decades after 1920, involving San Marcos medical
luminaries such as the anticoca crusader Carlos Gutiérrez-Noriega and Dr.
Carlos Monge Medrano, founder of Peru's school of highland Andean biology,
which proved more open to coca. In the 1880s, the keyword was coca and
cocaine as eminently "Peruvian" subjects for modern research — *trabajos
nacionales* in the idiom of Lima's medical journals. A July 1885 editorial of
El Monitor Médico, "La cocaína" (by J. C. Ulloa himself), boldly asserts that
"as the plant itself originates from Peru, where it is principally grown, its
study rightfully belongs to the *sabios peruanos*, who have at their reach the
observation of the effects caused by use of coca leaf, and have been best

able to study them." Study of coca combined "obligations of patriotism and science." Peruvian researchers, Ulloa wrote, "with their studies of coca and cocaine have opened to science new and broad horizons, and a duty of our fraternal patriotism was to reclaim this glory for its own sake and for the *patria*." The researchers' actual proximity to coca and firsthand experience of its use by Andean people gave would-be Peruvian scientists a privileged place in its study compared to far-off European counterparts. They were, so to speak, Humboldts *in situ* — lifting the veil over Peru's natural wonders still left by Spanish colonialism.[48]

It was a paradoxical nationalism, practiced by cultural binationals, the most cosmopolitan (and whitest) members of Peru's coastal elite, one invoking a dialectic between the local and traditional (coca) and the universal and scientifically modern (cocaine). Another hallmark of these *limeño* researchers' work is what is euphemistically called today "the industrialization of coca," the production of medicine as a national social calling. For example, Butler's burn study preached for affordable national medicines and wider access to modern treatment: "Peru is very sensitive, as the cradle of coca, to how steep such substances cost . . . and now has the good fortune of preparing cocaine itself. . . . With primary materials in our hands, it is so desirable to establish cocaine processing on a grander scale. Keeping the needed coca on our soil may stop the enormous flight of those who wish to intensify its export to Europe. . . . like quinine and now cocaine, *hijas de la República*, medicine ought to reach our sick at comfortable prices."[49] By the end of the nineteenth century, cocaine was a respectable daughter of the republic, thanks largely to Peru's adopted son Alfredo Bignon. It was soon to become — due to the application of the "Bignon method" — a new and prized national industry, with distant echoes of his chemistry still with us today.

IMAGINING AN AMAZONIAN GOOD

Before the mid-1880s, the medical and national prestige of coca was on the rise, along with the science of cocaine. Fascination with coca circled the globe, starting in Germany and France, popularizing the leaf as a tonic and cure even in the English-speaking world. But coca and cocaine remained almost mythical commodities of Peru. In 1877, after a decade-long campaign to diversify Peru's coastal economy, the sum of Peruvian coca exports came to only 7,955 kilos, worth less than eight thousand *soles*. Peru's annual trade-oriented *Memorias de Ministerio de Hacienda del Perú* barely spoke of coca. Mariani had to find his leaf in the remote Bolivian Yungas, later making a virtue out of necessity by stressing the drink's mild alkaloid content. Technical missions such as Juan Nystrom's of the late 1860s, sent to identify Andean exports or industrial possibilities in advance of new railways, evinced scant interest in coca, even when passing though coca lands like Cuzco's La Convención Valley. Nystrom, as a curiosity, only notes French coca mania and a reported "unabated enthusiasm" of European army officers for the drug's military possibilities. Agricultural surveys of the 1870s — even those written by Frenchmen, such as J. B. Martinet's classic 1877 *L'agriculture au Pérou* — elide coca as a commercial topic.[50] This negligence marks the whole mid-nineteenth-century catalog-like "resources of Peru" genre, as if coca were of but passing ethnographic interest, like exotic Indian foodstuffs *quinoa* or *oca*. Between the 1850s and 1880s, when coca, in part thanks to cocaine, became a medicinal reality in the Western and *limeño* gaze, it was still not a national or international good. In part, this was because the *montaña* of Peru, where most coca came from, was still an unimagined and inaccessible region of the nation in the eyes of coastal republican elites.

Mere fascination, or an eagerness to purchase it abroad, would not make coca into a viable commodity. Peruvians themselves had to rethink the place of coca regions and act on that, which they did in precisely the five-year period 1884–89. Three factors came together to nationalize the global interest in cocaine and transform it into a real good. First, in the aftermath of the Pacific War, the mono-exports (guano and nitrates) of coastal Peru were exhausted, destroyed, or forfeited, putting the state in dire need of exports to fund its recovery. The postwar Peruvian imagination turned to more broadly "national" possibilities and with new intensity cast an eye on the remote frontiers of the eastern Amazon, including coca's homeland in the *ceja de la montaña*. Secondly, coca, joined by industrializing cocaine, acquired an articulated role in scenarios of national renovation. The visibility of Bignon's cocaine science in Lima's Academia de Medicina helped spark that process. Finally, the state needed to embrace and validate these commercial possibilities, which it did, for example, with commissions to promote coca and cocaine as national commodities. Even as the ink dried on its proposals in 1889, Peru had already broken into and begun to shape world cocaine markets.

Peru and Bolivia's Pacific War with Chile was essentially, as many historians have argued, a war over exports. Victorious Chilean armies ransacked the country's coastal and urban centers, sealing the fate of Peru's already fading fertilizer export era of the nineteenth century. The painful national recovery of the 1880s was fitful and uncertain. Peru required more than a decade to reach its former economic levels and markers of modernization before entering a dynamic era of diversified and "autonomous" modern growth after 1895. Yet soon after the 1879 fiasco, one historian suggests, the roots of this diversity were already germinating in a Peruvian "developmental imagination." It manifested in a visible spatial shift. Promoters and *pensadores* could no longer focus their hopes and projects on a corrupt and devastated Lima or on the rubble of its littoral state. The task of building a new Peru necessarily decentered and stretched their imaginations to encompass Peru's vast regional spaces, untapped resources, and forgotten peoples. The first major voice in this inward regionalist thinking was Luis Esteves, a civilist party deputy and proindustrial writer, author of the country's first genuine economic history—a book written amid the traumas of the Pacific War in 1880. Esteves, a precocious *indigenista* (urban pro-Indian writer), no longer actually ignored coca, yet he approached the topic with a studied transitional ambivalence. Here was a rare Peruvian to write darkly about coca as an Indian *vicio*, analogous to the European habit of tobacco or Asian opium, when most elites still regarded Indian use of alien alcohol as a greater peril. And Esteves voiced skepticism, foreign fascination aside, about coca's commercial horizons: "With a pardon to all such prophecies, I don't see this plant's great future unless science discovers a useful application." His surveys touched briefly on coca, which through "modern chemistry" might finally find, he thought, its "profitable uses"; cocaine (which before 1884 had none) was not a motive. Esteves foresaw a shift of crops on *montaña* estates—but from the traditional vice of coca to modern commodities like coffee, cacao, and quinine.[51] Within a few years, Esteves's wariness of coca was obsolete. Peru's regional imaginary fixed on colonizing the tropical Amazon—and developing coca leaf—providing industrializing cocaine its national space.

Amazonia, especially the subtropical slopes of the *ceja de la montaña*, the lush, rain-drenched foothills of the eastern Andes, has always held a vibrant place in the Peruvian imaginary. It was a risky, unstable frontier (of savage imagined "Chunchos" Indians) and a land of fabled riches (from Spanish El Dorados to the alleged fecundity of its mild climes and soils). This area was the someday expansion valve of crowded coastal and Andean Peru, from republican European colonization schemes to the modernist "marginal highways" of the 1960s. It was also a site of strategic value where Peru, Brazil, and even the United States and European powers vied over paper dreams of an integrated fluvial-rail passage to link the Andes and Pacific to the Atlantic world, bringing forth the *montaña*'s legendary cornucopia.

Throughout the nineteenth century, the compact valleys and green eastern ridges in the two-thousand-to-six-thousand-foot range remained Peru and Bolivia's active coca zones—Chachapoyas, Huánuco, Huanta, La Convención, and the steep Bolivian Yungas—vestiges of once-organized colonial mission and planter enterprises of the sixteenth century, supplying mines and upland haciendas with their workers' daily chewing leaf, *vicio* or not, and oiling isolated local paths and rivers as these regions' only real currency of exchange. Estimates—and they are of the crudest sort—of coca commercialized for these internal ethnic market routes run about fifteen million pounds annually for Peru (and another ten million for Bolivia and five million for Ecuador and points north), always for the "eight-million" native users of the central Andes, to cite Clements Markham's variations on estimates by Poeppig, who had at least visited the humid zones. As a good imperial botanist, Markham immediately grasped in 1862 the significance of "Dr. Niemann's" newfound "active-principle of the coca leaf." Lieutenant William L. Herndon, a North American naval officer on a precocious mid-century "exploratory mission" of the Huallaga Valley, the long-sought gateway to the Amazon, marched by the tiny backwater of Tingo María and took notes on the valley's coca-covered slopes. The bush was a "great blessing" to Peru, at least to its hard-pressed Indians. Herndon's commodity gaze focused elsewhere: North American manifest destiny would help Peru with its slumbering Amazon riches, which he predicted "must mingle with the products of our Mississippi."[52]

In exactly 1862, Antonio Raimondi himself—republican Peru's greatest geographer and scientist—first confirmed the activities of a corresponding Sociedad de Patriotas de la Amazonas, which would bring roads, commerce, and (white) populations to places like Tingo María, a small spot he also noted in passing. In the meantime, Peru's few real colonizing experiments (like the Austrian peasants packed off to Amazonian Pozuzo, a hamlet to become a crucial site in the later Germanic-Peruvian development of cocaine) were deemed abject failures.[53] By 1885, Raimondi's colonizing association had become "proletarianized" and progressive, reincarnated as the Sociedad Obreros del Porvenir de la Amazonia (the Workers Society for the Amazon's Future). Its president, a "Dr." Mariano Martín Albornoz, elaborated its ambitious goals in his postwar pamphlet for colonization and immigration to the zone. Peru, according to this group, had to forcefully engage the Amazonian region to transform the nation's raw products into industrial commodities—thus the titular recourse to the social ideal of *obreros*. Such utopian industrial schemes were hardly unusual for Peru, nor was the idea of locating Peru's future in the east a new one. The novelty was the example cited alongside celebrated "Peru bark." Albornoz foresaw: "This should also take place with coca, being our production, and ours too the discovery of its highly important anesthetic properties [attributed not to Köller but to Moreno y Maíz's 1868 Paris thesis]. The factories where they will make these singular substances will not only bring a positive advantage to the country, and enrich the manufacturers, but provide an immense service to humanity. For in saving huge costs of transport of leafy plants, they could offer consumers at modest prices quinine sulfates and cocaine."[54] What better way to display pride in Peruvian science than by extolling Moreno y Maíz over Europe's Niemann, Köller, and Freud? Versions of such pro-Amazon texts went to press in other languages to lure in those improving colonists and capital. By the early 1890s, "colonization of *montaña* lands" was officially revived in Peru, elevated into a policy and a branch of Peru's new 1895 Ministry of Development (*fomento*).

When Carlos Lissón, the foremost sociologist of his age—Peru's analogue to Mexican *científico* Francisco Bulnes—sat down to compose his classic of Peruvian positivism, *Breves apuntes sobre la sociología del Perú en 1886*, he was barely aware of developments just underway (for example, the rocketing price of coca following Köller's 1884 anesthesia discovery). Yet his widely read book brims with optimistic predictions and prescriptions about a marriage of coca, science, Andean nature, and Amazonian development. After citing coca for its ancient role in the survival of the highland Indian, Lissón moves on to a more modern theme: "Today they demand it from Europe in grand quantities, which will only increase when it is adopted by their workers and soldiers. It will and must become a rich and strong natural article of exportation, which will profitably replace even sugar, which has never had rivals in its market.... We find here in the midst of our poverty, that Science has opened up a fountain of public wealth, giving value to one of our natural articles. To coca, as with our mines, we need to commit ourselves in order to overcome our misery, yet never forget our experience, now that we will provide all humanity with this good." Yet Lissón also warns of overconfidence. Peru must act quickly, he urges, to supply coca abundantly and cheaply, or risk repeating the infamous national saga of cinchona bark, coveted for its quinine prophylaxis against nineteenth-century malaria. That too was once a uniquely natural Andean "monopoly" (a concept that "science does not respect")—that is, until wily British and Dutch imperial agents transplanted and developed it themselves in the 1870s as an industrial-scale commercial drug. Still, Lissón held high expectations of coca during this miserable "economic present of the citizens." "Amidst the general devastation of our agriculture," Lissón went on, a capitalized Western "Science has come to reveal we have a treasure in our Coca." He predicted, "All the *cejas de montaña* of Peru will cultivate it, especially in Junín, Huánuco, and Cuzco which will have a railway to move it to Europe. Coca will inevitably spawn grand capitals when cultivated on such a vast scale, and thus provide us economic respectability and renown."[55] Thus, by the late 1880s, grandiose Peruvian hopes became invested in coca and scientific cocaine. As coca and cocaine transformed over the next decade into prospering national commodities, their glorification by liberal elites would also intensify.

Hopes in cocaine were also transnational, not merely nationalist, reflecting the era's rippling scientific and commercial currents. The movement for Amazonian development invoked global actors, shown, for example, in a guidebook put out by the consul general of Peru in Southampton, Britain, H. Guillaume, three years after the publication of Albornoz's 1885 colonization tract with the revealing English title of *The Amazon Provinces of Peru as a Field for European Emigration*. Guillaume was acting at the time in his role as "Delegate Member of 'La Sociedad Obreros del Porvenir de Amazonas del Perú.'" His alluring message about Peruvian coca was dressed in an orientalist and imperial discourse: coca from "the eastern slopes of the Andes, is, to the natives of that region what opium is to the Turks and betel to the Malays," he wrote. "It is not only a powerful stimulant, but also an aliment and a tonic."[56] Later, Guillaume projected a more scientific tone: "Another drug which has lately been fortunately discovered by medical science, viz, cocaine, an alkaloid of the coca plant...to which we are indebted to Peru. It is only quite recently, — within the past three years, — that the valuable properties of this drug have been recognized in this country as a local anesthetic.... It entirely superceded and dispenses with chloroform and other drugs, which are more or less of a dangerous nature. As a stimulant, the leaves of the coca plant are very remarkable."[57] In the end, despite the exertions of the Obreros del Porvenir de Amazonas, few European colonists arrived specifically for coca—though those that did mattered—and eventually imperial forces did transplant it elsewhere, repeating the national narrative of cinchona. Still, Peruvian visionaries of the 1880s had refurbished coca into a heroic commodity, which, in league with local science, would indeed build a national industry out of cocaine.

The apex of this promotional movement came with the report of the official Peruvian Comisión de Coca in the (Peruvian) spring of 1888. Whereas the 1885 Cocaine Commission focused exclusively on the science and pharmacy of cocaine, this time commercial aims predominated, reflecting a coming together of Amazonian coca and scientific cocaine as well as the now-beckoning markets. The 1888 Coca Commission, which was both government- and university-sponsored, was staffed by J. C. Ulloa (that epitome of Lima medical politics), Miguel Colunga (botanist and San Marcos University dean), and José Antonio de Ríos (author of Peru's first thesis on coca in 1866, now a distinguished vice dean of the Faculty of Medicine). Their official report of October 1888 zeroed in on promoting Peruvian coca, the only commodity of the era to merit its own special study mission.

The origins of the Coca Commission are obscure, but its result was a public campaign to foster Peruvian coca leaf, as well as Bignon's crude cocaine, as a mass-market export. Written by this team of national medical luminaries, all deeply familiar with their subject, the Coca Commission's recommendations were issued between July and October of 1888, just as the world coca boom accelerated. In contrast to Bignon's 1885 faith in medicinal cocaine (perhaps by now tarnished by reports of cocaine's dangers), the members of the commission insisted instead on a popular or social role for coca abroad. Like earlier researchers, the commission was infused with coca nationalism and the allure of commercial prospects. With a push by the Peruvian government and agriculture, coca, they claimed, "could replace tea and coffee itself, since science had revealed its tremendous advantages." Peru's men of science seemed overcome by their enthusiasm. But considering Pemberton's secret formula for his new health drink Coca-Cola (a mere toddler at two years old), coca would at least give coffee and tea a run for their money in the century to come.[58]

A July 1888 report to the rector of San Marcos University by Peru's minister of finance strongly seconded the practical implications of the Coca Commission's findings:

> The importance for the Republic of augmenting exports . . . the appreciation of coca leaves in European markets has sparked a considerable price rise, which has now oiled regular exporting of this good, to the

benefit of our farmers. The extension of consumption and hence demand for useful products depends on the depth of efforts made to popularize knowledge of their myriad applications.... The Ministry can now organize active propaganda [a neutral term in Spanish] to convert coca into a valuable article of export. Our farmers of the interior, invested in the coca bush, will no doubt, and with scant effort reap the benefits that come from wider use of this product.[59]

Peru's coca boom of the 1890s would prove them right about its national value as an export.

The formal "Informe sobre la coca" brings Peru's trail of nineteenth-century medical interest back full circle to the Andean coca bush. It offered a five-page survey of the "physiological and therapeutic effects of coca," its "hygienic properties" and "medical applications" (some skittishness aside), and ended with a programmatic list of "Means to Promote the Consumption and Uses of Coca." The *informe*'s preface emphatically reminds readers of the tradition of Peruvian research on coca, stating that Peruvian doctors, "so gratifying to patriotism and the pride of National Medicine ... in their studies of our land's privileged plant, ... revealed to the world of science the powerful and if you like marvelous properties of *la sagrada yerba de los Incas*."[60] Unánue, Moreno y Maíz, and even obscure Nuñez del Prado receive their due, but no mention is made of Bignon, despite his work on coca botany. Republican medicine, the report argues, had effectively reversed the Spanish conquest's ancient black legend of coca as "una planta diabólica."

The commission's survey of coca's physiological effects contests Bignon's stance (and that of much European science) that coca leaf is a mere vessel for cocaine. In a point-by-point examination, coca itself is deemed "energizing," affecting in multiple ways the human digestive, circulatory, muscular, and nervous systems. Mantegazza's and Espinoza's comparative studies of pulse rates prove coca's energy enhancement: tea, coffee, chocolate, yerba maté — the known stimulants — pale next to the measurable power of coca infusions. Even the chewing of coca, long reviled in European and *limeño* eyes, has positive bodily effects, such as the "enviable dental state" of Andean Indians, evidenced in the natives' disease-free gums.[61]

Ulloa and his colleagues did not make many commercial points about coca's medicinal potential, which was still controversial in Western medical circles. Nor did they recur to the North American obsession with coca as a nerve stimulant and cure for enervating neurasthenia, a sign perhaps of Lima's European medical heritage.[62] Instead, they focused on coca's "hygienic" powers, the broader contemporary category for health-related or socially prescribed consumption. Coca enjoys vast industrial applications, they maintained: It can help workers or farmers across the world adjust to and revitalize themselves under the demanding work regime of the new industrial order. As a prime example of its utility, coca seems to alleviate the effects of lead and mercury poisoning and thus merits a place in the diets of miners everywhere. Indeed, coca's "energizing and sustaining force" can revive "wasted," "weakened," and undernourished workers in every occupation. Coca is, in short, the perfect herb for capitalism—a role already played by coffee and tea by the eighteenth century.[63] This targeting of the industrial working classes, if not entirely new, went against the grain of much coca use in "industrial societies," in which it was mainly the privileged domain of nineteenth-century "brain workers" (the intellectual classes). The commission found only one marketing drawback to coca: its strange taste and odor, especially to the "razas blancas," though new infusions and imbibing methods could overcome that barrier.

The closing section of Peru's 1888 "Informe sobre la coca" lays out the "means to promote its consumption and exportation." The more "numer-ous the applications," the commissioners calculated, the brighter coca's future. They discussed better ways of taking coca: Mariani's booming liquor and "sus imitadores norte-americanos" (which included a nascent Coca-Cola), as well as new elixirs and tonics concocted in Lima. The boom in medicinal cocaine was sure to ebb, they thought, with its saturated medical uses and markets. Thus their call to actively promote economical commodity coca, and before others embraced it as their own crop: "There is no reason to doubt the possibility and feasibility of reaching this goal, recalling how analogous substances, cacao, coffee and teas, became taken above all as necessities of man, especially in the work of conserving, raising or renovating their force, which is the appeal of all types of stimulants."[64] They grasped their economic history in the roles of stimulant trades in the birth of European capitalism itself.

The commission ended its report with nine policy recommendations, though most were unneeded and unheeded in the heady age of coca: (1) publicize, in a world survey, the "hygienic qualities of coca" and the specific benefits of coca use; (2–3) publish this news in "thousands of copies in diverse languages" for business owners in Europe and the United States, for agricultural societies, ship captains, factory foremen, and so on, and for distribution by foreign consular agents (their clear target here was the working classes); (4) mandate Peruvian legations abroad to actively perform this "propaganda" on behalf of coca; (5) survey Peruvian coca farmers to gauge their delivery capacities during and after an intensified marketing campaign; (6) encourage planters to set up export "factories of *cocaína bruta*" on their own estates, tapping Bignon's invention; (7) establish national competitions for leaf quality and improved techniques in packing and shipping; and (8–9) cut customs duties on needed tools and chemicals to encourage industrial start-ups. All told, the projected Peruvian coca campaign of the late 1880s required a wisely invested ten thousand *soles*. Such a program promised to raise consumption, production, and export of "so precious an item of our agricultural field"—coca, the coming rival of coffee and tea.[65]

With a creative impulse of Peruvian science and *letrados*, coca had come a long way in the nineteenth century, from a colonial pariah habit of backward and remote Indians to an object of intense curiosity to consolidating national medicine to a raw material in Bignon's promising local variant of cocaine to an ideal good for a national conquest of the vast Peruvian Amazon to a great white hope of government export policy during Peru's recuperation from the Pacific War and other disasters of the nineteenth century. Coca and cocaine, at first through shifting imaginaries and then through formative Peruvian action, were in the throes of becoming genuine modern commodities, with their own projected national and social spaces.

The next chapter on Peru's legal commodity boom of the late nineteenth century will show how Peruvian coca exports took off in the 1890s, reaching millions of pounds by 1900, prompted largely by the global market itself, yet how coca ultimately failed to become a legitimate necessity of everyday working life in the West. Coca's rival turned out to be the rise of Peruvian crude cocaine during the same era, the direct outgrowth of Bignon's innovative cocaine science, specifically his economical new method for processing the leaf. In May 1886, the same year Carlos Lissón dreamed of Amazonian coca riches and Alfredo Bignon and his colleagues of better cocaine science, readers of London's main drug-trade journal, the *Chemist and Druggist*, may have missed a tiny item under "Materia Medica Notes": "Ten days ago a Hamburg firm received from Peru a consignment of cocaine prepared there from the fresh leaf, and which is, we understand,

the first commercial supply which has been received in Europe. It is now a common knowledge to pharmacists that in drying, and frequently in packing, the alkaloid level of the coca leaf is diminished. For this reason it was suggested, shortly after cocaine came into prominence, that the alkaloid should be prepared in Peru from the fresh leaves and exported in a crude state."[66] Peru's legal national cocaine industry had begun, rooted in Bignon's national science and the redemptive notions of nineteenth-century coca visionaries. It would leave its mark on the history and coming circuits of global cocaine.

2

MAKING A NATIONAL COMMODITY
Peruvian Crude Cocaine, 1885–1910

In the two decades after 1860, Peruvian pharmacists, medical authorities, promoters, and statesmen began recasting the possibilities of ancient Andean coca leaf and experimenting with its newfound derivative, cocaine. Between 1886 and 1900, a small group of national entrepreneurs, along with localized foreign capitalists, were able to transform these ideas, using local know-how and resources, into one of Peru's most dynamic exports during its recovery from the myriad catastrophes of the nineteenth century. This chapter reconstructs the rise of this new national commodity in Peru: industrial cocaine. By 1900, cocaine and commercialized coca leaf sales together had risen to be among the nation's top-earning exports. The triumphant transformation of cocaine, a model national commodity glorified by Peru's liberal spokesmen, remade remote tropical regions rarely touched by either the world economy or the Lima state.

The story of cocaine's emergence as a "miraculous" late-nineteenth-century drug is usually told in different terms and from very different sites. Cocaine is portrayed as the product of advancing European science and medicine in a timeless morality tale of a stupendous medical discovery gone awry. Another story focuses on cocaine as the result of an American cultural mania for popular cures and its anxiety-provoking spread to deviant "fiends." This chapter, however, goes to cocaine's creation as a classic export commodity rather than a drug per se, while stressing its roots as an Andean construction. This Andean angle on early cocaine opens new perspectives on the drug's local and global histories and their complex intersections. First, it shows an unsuspected wave of Peruvian enterprise — petty industrialists and colonizing planters relying on the 1880s spurt of local science — that molded a legitimate world commodity out of Peru's novel crude cocaine. For more than two decades, peripheral Peru became the world's unrivaled producer of cocaine, supplying the tons needed to meet new global appetites for the drug. Second, although bounded and absorbed by global forces, Peruvian initiative, or "agency," tangibly shaped world cocaine circuits and politics of the late nineteenth century by breaking the drug's supply logjam of the mid-1880s, deflecting the coca designs of world powers, and pushing aside rivals like Bolivia. Peruvians provided the stream of cheap cocaine that drove the drug's larger transformation from a scientific rarity into a medicinal necessity and panacea and then into a mass consumption good and even globalizing drug of abuse by 1900. Third, the legal Peruvian cocaine industry of the 1890s structured local regional political economies of cocaine (around central Amazonian Huánuco and northern La Libertad) and inspired national identification with the drug, both of which would affect the trajectory of cocaine in the twentieth century. Finally, in cultural and political terms, the modernity of cocaine, stamped in pharmaceutical centers like Germany and the United States, became magnified in the context of an underdeveloped and culturally fractured society like Peru's.[1] Peruvians celebrated cocaine as a national fusion of time-honored Andean traditions (Indian coca) with modern elite science, industrialism, and profit.

This chapter begins with an overview of cocaine's global commodity expansion in the 1890s. It then explores the first "industrialization of coca" in the capital city, Lima, through the application of Bignon's science after the Pacific War, as well as cocaine's dispersion to Peru's coca lands, from the Amazonian redoubt of Pozuzo to the highlands of the north. The story then moves to a thicker spatial and social analysis of what was to be the world's longest-standing cocaine complex: greater Huánuco and the verdant *montaña* of the Upper Huallaga Valley. Introduced by German and Croat pioneers in the 1890s, by 1905 the thriving cocaine industry became the domain of Huánuco's colorful political strongman, Augusto Durand. The chapter ends by looking at the turn-of-century ideational exuberance spun off by this peculiar national modernizing good.

FORMING A GLOBAL MARKET, 1885–1910

From the 1850s to 1885, despite swirling fascination, research, publicity, and speculation about the uses of Andean coca and cocaine, no world market existed in these products. They were not yet viable commodities. Emmanuel Merck of Darmstadt (whose firm came to dominate cocaine in the late nineteenth century) first made cocaine hydrochloride in 1862, two years after Niemann's isolation, but for two decades the alkaloid remained simply an experimental novelty. Even into the late 1870s, Merck refined fewer than 50 grams a year, using but 25 kilos of Peruvian coca; by the early 1880s, however, Merck was sending brochures to doctors to promote its sale. The chief commercial use of coca was Angelo Mariani's French Vin Mariani—founded in 1863, shortly after Merck first made cocaine—and much is said about the coca-laced Bordeaux beverage in cultural terms: about Mariani's audacious Incaic and art nouveau–styled publicity, his belle époque coca salon and laboratory at Neuilly on the Seine, his adoration and dissemination of the plant, the drink's fashionable clientele, its fit to the age of neurasthenia. Little, however, is known of its economic or commodity history. Vin Mariani was surely the main importer of Bolivian (and likely some Peruvian) coca leaf before 1885, taking in as much as 20,000 kilos a year and reexporting the bottled product throughout Europe and soon across the Atlantic. Mariani also diversified into coca tea, a pâté, and pastilles that actually contained doses of cocaine, though his eponymous coca wine remained an epoch-defining commodity for the rest of the century.[2] The endorsement albums, now collector's items, grew to thirteen volumes. By other routes, samples of coca also reached medical professionals and select consumers in the form of tonics and tinctures, as coca's reputability finally spread through the Western pharmacopoeia, medical catalogues, and pharmacy gazettes in France, Britain, Spain, and the United States. By 1880, coca leaf had found some profitable uses, though it was hardly a mass market good. Cocaine could make neither claim.

After Köller's late 1884 confirmation of cocaine's effectiveness for anesthesia (and related campaigns by Freud and Aschenbrandt on the drug's medical-hygienic possibilities), commercial cocaine took off rapidly, led by its revolutionary use in surgery and a storm of medical experimentation. The principal locus of world research, production, and distribution was Germany, with Emmanuel Merck paving the way, building on his company's previous experience with alkaloidal morphine and quinine. Pressures on supply and demand in 1884 sparked a dramatic fourfold spike in cocaine prices, as Merck immediately pumped its production to 30 kilos by 1885. Though prices soon plummeted to one mark per gram, at least thirteen German firms, mostly centered around Frankfurt, took up cocaine manufacturing as the era's pharmaceutical industry rapidly consolidated. Cocaine was a defining good in their scientific and commercial modernization. Merck's closest European rivals were Gehe and Company, Knoll and Company, I. D. Riedel, and the two branches of C. F. Boehringer and Sohn, though production lines also started up in countries like Britain (Burroughs-Wellcome) and France (Houdé, Midy) before migrating elsewhere. But commodity cocaine was born of crisis: in 1885, the two largest makers, Merck and Gehe, even suspended production — pushing prices and market panic higher — because of the sheer shortage of chemically active, quality imports of dried coca.[3] Over the next few years, pharmaceutical and chemical trade journals and experts on both sides of the Atlantic debated solutions to this coca supply crisis as the number of proposed medical uses for cocaine — now in its panacea stage — multiplied.

But Merck soon rebounded by finding the ideal solution to coca's scarcity: Peruvian crude cocaine, an odorous, yellowish, semirefined 50–80 percent sulfate-cocaine cake that shipped easily and retained full potency. Merck refined this into medicinal grade cocaine. Thus, by 1888, cocaine had became one of Merck's staple goods at 300 kilos (ten times its 1885 output), which rose to more than 600 kilos by 1894 and 1,500 kilos in the three years after 1900, reaching a 5,000-kilo peak in 1910. By 1900, Hamburg, the European drug entrepôt, took in more than 4,200 kilos of crude cocaine, and other German laboratories made an additional 565 kilos directly from leaf. In this way, cocaine became Merck's single most profitable drug line in the 1890s, three-quarters of it destined for reexport, helping fuel the company's astonishing growth and diversification into a global pharmaceutical giant. The firm opened its later independent U.S. branches in 1887 and by 1899 was making its quality Merck cocaine in Rahway, New Jersey.

Pharmaceutical firms in the United States quickly rose to meet the German challenge. By 1900, the United States was the world's major consumer market for cocaine — for widespread medical applications as well as patent medicines and other usage, including leakage to pleasure users. By 1900, almost a third of the world's cocaine was made in the United States, which consumed an even greater share of the era's booming coca-leaf beverages and concoctions. Three firms pioneered commodification of cocaine: McKesson and Robbins (a New York drug wholesaler and early coca importer), E. R. Squibb and Company (renowned for drug development more than sales), and Detroit's originally herbalist Parke, Davis and Company, which turned into an aggressive cocaine booster and Merck's direct American rival. Many German firms also shipped to the burgeoning U.S. market,

Merck factory at Darmstadt, late nineteenth century
(Merck, *E. Merck Darmstadt: A History of Chemical Achievement, 1827–1937*
[Darmstadt: Merck, n.d., ca. 1938], lithograph)

notably Boehringer and Merck. Parke, Davis sponsored its own *Therapeutic Gazette* and pharmacopoeia (the 240-page 1892 *Pharmacology of the Newer Materia Medica*), both overflowing with research about cocaine (some of it genuine and/or from the firm's innovative drug laboratory) and about herbal coca remedies, an enduring interest of the firm.[4] Like Mariani in France, Parke, Davis exemplified the new powers of mass advertising, here in an integrated pharmaceutical firm that captured about a tenth of the seemingly bottomless U.S. cocaine market of the 1890s. Other significant producers were Powers-Weightman-Rosengarten (Philadelphia), New York Quinine and Chemical Works (selling that kindred Andean byproduct), and Mallinckrodt Chemical (Saint Louis), which made for a stable core of six to eight cocaine makers and a clutch of smaller ones. In contrast to German firms, American companies for the most part continued to refine cocaine directly from coca leaf (save for Powers-Weightman-Rosengarten), whether because of the vibrant parallel American coca market, the bias toward manufacturing in 1890s drug tariffs, or their relative proximity to

Peru's northern coastline. Spillane estimates an overall U.S. cocaine market (imports from Germany plus domestic manufacture) of one to two tons by the late 1880s, climbing to two to four tons a year in the 1890s and to a soft peak of five to nine tons a year between 1900 and 1910.[5]

Behind this cocaine surge lay a differentiating market. As accepted medical usage, such as for dental or surgical anesthesia, and therapeutic nerve tonics hit their limits in the 1890s — due to recognition of side effects, medical debates about poisoning, and the development of substitutes like eucaine in 1895 — a newer kind of market emerged, prompted by so-called nonethical firms, that is, those advertising directly to consumers. At its extreme, a multitude of "patent" formulas featuring cocaine appeared. The popular cocaine-laced chewing paste Coca-Bola, launched by Philadelphia physician Charles L. Mitchell in 1886, was sold as a treatment for tobacco, alcohol, and opium habits. This form of commodity growth compensated for restraints on medical usage. By 1900, some patent medicines (such as snortable cocaine cures for hay fever, cough, cold, and flu) were slipping into a gray area of stimulant use, part of a massive and varied self-medication industry that reached the astonishing $100 million high-water mark in 1905. Until then, recent research shows, legal cocaine of the medical era had been a highly reputable "modern" American drug — emblematic of the newly integrated pharmaceutical firm exploiting the latest in scientific laboratories, known therapies, and a new medical press.

The era's related market in coca products merits its own description. While many physicians welcomed cocaine because it was more "scientific" or therapeutically precise than coca (still often criticized as inert), a vibrant popular international market also emerged in coca beverages, tonics, medicinal tinctures, cordials, cigarettes, and the like across this entire era. Already pronounced in France and Britain — where coca wines flourished after 1860 and mainstream medical opinion long distinguished coca's value — "coca mania" found its widest expressions and most intense boom market in the United States. Here, cultural preferences for herbal coca mattered, associated with the rampant phenomena of "American nervousness" and driven by a motley medical profession, including eclectics, regional pharmacists, and scores of promoters, such as confirmed herbalist import houses like Lloyd's of Cincinnati. Innumerable sellers of patent medicines threw coca into their formulas, sometimes substituting the cheaper cocaine after 1887. Besides being the antidote for neurasthenia, coca was consumed as a healthy alternative to the national American vice, drinking — and generally as one that cleared rather than clouded the mind.

Trade journal ad, 1890s (Originally Fitz Hugh Ludlow Memorial Library)

This romance with coca climaxed paradoxically in the age of legal cocaine, exemplified by Mortimer's *History of Coca: "The Divine Plant" of the Incas*, whose remarkable appendix survey of the landscape of American coca medicine found coca wines still favored in 1900 by 83 percent of physicians.[6] Much like the members of Peru's 1888 Coca Commission before him, Mortimer hoped that coca, once "better appreciated," would "come into general use in every household as a stimulant" as eighteenth-century tea and coffee had. Mariani's wine, another prominent example, won more than seven thousand physician "endorsements." Mariani—a true international commodity man—quickly grasped the American therapeutic market, opening on West Sixteenth Street a thriving New York branch and production facility by the 1880s run by his trusted brother-in-law Jaros. At least twenty flagrant imitations popped up by the early 1890s, which Mariani warned against in his special English-language publications.

One of them, Atlanta pharmacist John Pemberton's up-market Peruvian Wine Cola, permutated into an alcohol-free health beverage named Coca-Cola in 1886, with less than a quarter of Mariani's coca per dose. It soon took the South by storm, generating dozens of regional imitations of its own in the 1890s. Under Asa Candler's business direction and due in part to its early coca-related and sexualized advertising (the company claimed that it was good for the sexual organs), Coca-Cola raked in sales of $519,200 by 1900 (at the time, a great deal of money) and more than $10 million by 1910. Coke's success in bottling, franchising, and commoditizing the corner soda fountain venue, in combination with the tingling essence of coca, spawned scores of emulators with purposely confusing brand names, a few of whose products were heavily drugged. Despite some serious run-ins with antidrug authorities after the passage of the 1906 Food and Drug Act, Coca-Cola became the most famed of twentieth-century American world commodities, though few in today's consuming public (beyond historians) recall the origins of the current Atlanta firm in this Franco-Andean drug culture. Cocaine — but not its secret formula coca-leaf extract, "Merchandise No. 5" — was removed from Coca-Cola in 1903. Much like today's decaffeinated or diet beverages, a decocainized Vin Mariani also made an appearance. Thus, a thriving popular mass market in Andean coca products pervaded the era 1885–1910. In commercial terms, the question remains what portion of bulk U.S. coca imports went into the benign coca product craze rather than into distilling medicinal cocaine. Coca imports topped four hundred thousand tons by the mid-1890s, doubling to over eight hundred thousand tons in the years 1902–8; these imports came almost exclusively from Peru and were worth many hundreds of thousands of dollars. In addition to a relic "Bolivian" type, New York drug trade publications (which handled about a third of this bustling trade) early on distinguished between two branded varieties of Peruvian coca leaf: Huánuco leaf, used for cocaine, and northern Trujillo leaf, used for extracts and syrups — the latter clearly dominating the U.S. market by 1900.[7]

None of these worldly commodity booms — German or American, of medicinal cocaine or consumer coca — would have been feasible without a dynamic response by Andeans, from the Peruvian planters and peasants who planted, tended, and expanded coca fields in remote tropical valleys to the pharmacy and factory entrepreneurs who built a new industry from scratch after 1885 to supply locally developed crude cocaine to overseas drug magnates like Merck.

The numbers coming out of Peru by 1890 track this evolving trade from the ground up but are poor and jumbled ones, like the inconsistent and badly deployed statistics marking the history of cocaine everywhere.[8] They are collated here from fragmented, obscure Peruvian sources to define the trends needed to pursue sociohistorical questions about cocaine's rise and regional ramifications. Although sample lots of cocaine reportedly left Lima by late 1885 (and coca leaf in the mid-1870s), only by the year 1890 was enough Peruvian cocaine on the move to merit the collection of official statistics (see appendix, table A.3). Bear in mind that overall revenues are less dependable guides than output, given cocaine's initial price volatility and Peru's salad of used and reporting currencies — national *soles* (*S/*), "Peruvian pounds" (*Lp*; originally five *soles*, falling to a more stable ten *soles* over the period 1898–1930), or pounds sterling, dollars, francs, piastres, and German marks. Bulk measures of the two export goods — in pounds, ounces, kilos, *arrobas*, *quintales*, British tons, metric tons, or even *cestos* and seedlings — were equally diverse. (See appendix on these problems.) Crude cocaine was Peru's fastest-growing quantum export of the 1890s, a decade of swift export recovery overall from the Pacific War. Starting from a modest baseline, 1,700 kilos in 1890, cocaine exports tripled to four to five metric tons (i.e., 4,000 to 5,000 kilos) by the late 1890s. Cocaine exports peaked at 10,700 kilos in 1901, a 600 percent rise from 1890, before flattening to five to six metric tons by the years 1906–10. Sales passed increasingly through Lima's port of Callao, a sign of rising Huánuco cocaine, while coca leaf flowed primarily through northern Salaverry (near Trujillo in the department of La Libertad) and initially from the southern port of Mollendo, diverted from indigenous markets. The global political economy of cocaine in distinct commodity chains is analyzed ahead in chapter 3, but the broad trend of dramatic growth is clear from 1890 to 1910.

Coca leaf exports, on the other hand, by 1892 had expanded to 128,548 kilos (two-thirds to Germany, worth some *S/*120,000). The earliest known report, from 1877, put prewar coca exports under 5,000 kilos, worth *Lp*1,425 (then just over *S/*7,000), a value which nominally soared some fortyfold over the next two decades. Yet by 1892, the value of Peru's 3,300 kilos of exported cocaine, *S/*195,000, surpassed the total value of leaf exports. In 1891, Germany — mainly via the Hamburg drug emporium — took in about two-thirds (64 percent) of Peruvian cocaine production; that figure would rise to 82 percent in 1899 before receding to 60 percent in 1910 once rivals entered the field. In 1891, Americans bought 17 percent of Peru's cocaine (largely via New York), and they purchased the same portion in 1910, with Britain and later France the only other buyers of note. Coca started out similarly but diverged over time: by 1910, the U.S. market (with 85 percent) dominated, with Germany taking only 10 percent of Peruvian coca sales.[9] As we have seen, by the 1890s, top German firms had specialized in refining crude cocaine and in few coca concoctions, while key U.S. manufacturers mainly used baled leaf. The hegemony of coca in the United States also reflected the beverage boom after 1900, which used closer, cheaper, lower-quality Trujillo leaf. German cocaine sold virtually everywhere, including New York (by Merck, Boehringer, or Gehe), and Germany thus set the world price of the drug.

Measuring cocaine's development in terms of value or unit price is more difficult, and the data are not good enough to estimate the product's "returned value" (the impact of its export earnings on a host economy). Peru's real exchange rate depreciated by a radical 40 percent in the early 1890s, but a reversal of this trend after 1897 cut into export income. At its peak in 1900, cocaine fleetingly emerged as the country's fifth most remunerative export.[10] Yet, taken in context, cocaine never surpassed 4 percent of all Peruvian export revenues, and it fell to only 1.5 percent by 1907 as other commodities like sugar, rubber, and industrial minerals leapt ahead. However, cocaine earnings remained vital to specific regions, given cocaine's strong linkages to labor-intensive coca-growing activities.

Both cocaine and leaf prices proved volatile, hit by shortages, runs, stockpiling, and overseas speculation (usually in Hamburg), and with breakdowns of local transport due to civil wars, floods, and outbreaks of cholera and plague. Major price "advances" occurred in 1884–86 (spiking at more than 500 percent), the formative year of world cocaine markets. By late 1886, shortages eased, but sharp price swings recurred in 1887, 1891–92, and during Peru's Piérolist civil war of 1894–95. As crude cocaine flooded the market, the late 1890s brought a price depression, followed by a jump in demand by 1900 before the ongoing price slump from 1902 through 1910. Cocaine's value to Peru in 1910 was half that of 1900, and in "real" terms (corrected for local price inflation) even less. Yet year by year the gains from industrialized cocaine dwarfed those of raw coca by 30 to 100 percent margins, revealing the roles of value added and low raw material prices in the consolidating global drug industry. Still, bulk Peruvian coca sales for overseas cocaine makers or additives advanced steadily during this era, mainly to U.S. markets: from the three hundred tons of the early 1890s to a million or more kilos annually during the 1902–5 boom, halving to roughly five hundred tons by 1909–10 at its price nadir. By 1910, Peru's lawful coca and cocaine, products of these dramatic developments since 1885, entered a long, irreversible crisis, leaving the export marginal until the rise of illicit cocaine.

These shaky numbers actually conceal vital shifts in Peru's geographic poles of cocaine. The rapid evolution of the crude cocaine industry after 1885 passed through three regional or entrepreneurial paths en route to its apex in 1900–1905. The first phase, between 1885 and 1889, an offshoot of Bignon's cocaine science, was led by Lima pharmacy workshops geared to German consignment. In the second stage, 1890–95, pioneered by the remarkable Arnaldo Kitz, an emissary of Merck, the industry migrated inland to the Amazonian sources of coca, first rooting in the remote German Pozuzo colony. Cocaine soon dispersed across Peru's vast coca frontiers in about ten rustic workshops, north and south — the shift behind the dominance of crude cocaine profits over coca by the early 1890s. Third, after 1900, when cocaine exports peaked at over ten tons, the industry, with some two dozen factories, settled into defined regional spaces, integrated by two distinct commercial circuits. Northern Trujillo-branded leaf (from the highlands of La Libertad) was mainly sold for processing tonics in the United States. Trujillo hosted few cocaine plants and beyond 1910 was increasingly drawn into a kind of private network servicing Coca-Coca. The second circuit penetrated the Upper Huallaga Valley for its alkaloidal Huánuco leaf, coveted for its convertibility into cocaine. By 1900, most crude cocaine, exported through Callao to Europe, originated in Huánuco, where the trade was pioneered by immigrants before passing to the control of strongman Augusto Durand. Huánuco was destined to become a unique Andean haven for the culture, politics, and trade secrets of cocaine. Finally, to the far south in Bolivia, we must note the *yungas* Bolivian leaf circuit, explored in chapter 3, which after a brief era of sales for French coca wines (1860s–90s) turned inward to the nation's customary indigenous "chewing" trades. How did cocaine's regional complexes come into play, and what did they mean in the longer trajectory of the drug?

LIMA-CALLAO: BIRTH OF AN INDUSTRIAL GOOD

In the mid-1880s, rising interest in coca and cocaine manifested itself, as we have seen, in the remarkable research drive of pharmacist Alfredo Bignon, part of a revival in the national imaginary of Peruvian coca influenced by transnational fascination with modern cocaine. Bignon's scientific curiosity had, in fact, a significant and unrecognized impact: it spurred the rise of crude cocaine processing centers in Lima, which helped Peru to quickly capture its niche in global drug production. Coca and cocaine became Peruvian commodities.

Early signs of these pioneer products are ads for locally made cocaine appearing in Lima's medical and pharmacy journals. The first, not surprisingly, was Bignon's, whose simplified cocaine formula of 1884 was formally approved by the Academy of Medicine's ad hoc Cocaine Commission in 1885. Amid ads for imported drugs (including cocaine) and local elixirs of coca, in January 1885 Bignon's Droguería y Botica Francesa advertised in dramatic bold print its "Cocaína y sus Sales etc." in *El Monitor Médico*. Yet within months, by March of 1885, competition surfaced: Meyer and Hafemann's Droguería por Mayor — Botica Inglesa at 188 Espaderos was offering its own in-house cocaine, no doubt related to Meyer and Hafemann's "Commercial Relations in France, England, Germany and the U.S."[11] Six months later, in September 1885, there was nothing timid about their growing enterprise: a full-page display in *El Monitor Médico*, set in bold angles, boasts "COCAINA PURA Y SUS SALES — Preparados en su laboratorio químico por Meyer & Hafemann." These ads ran for months, distinguishing for buyers the pharmacy's many experimental varieties of cocaine: *muriato de cocaína* (*puro, cristalizada, blanca*), soluble *sulfato de cocaína, tanato de cocaína, salicilato de cocaína*, and, not least, *bromhidrato de cocaína*, which was alleged to blend all the desired therapeutic qualities. Lima medical retail sales aside, these batches went directly to buyers in Hamburg, who immediately seized upon easily refined crude cocaine sulfates.

El Monitor Médico heralded Meyer and Hafemann's samples from the "factories of her laboratories," duly presented in December 1885 for approval by the standing Cocaine Commission. A long letter to the editors tried to stem any controversy about the new "factory of cocaine." True, Meyer and Hafemann's method looked "almost identical" to Bignon's, but this was a remarkable case of simultaneous discovery, inspired by study of kerosene filtration of cinchona. Their method, however, eliminated altogether time-consuming leaf pulverization. As Meyer and Hafemann confessed, "When the miraculous properties of cocaine were revealed and this alkaloid won greater importance day by day with its varied medical applications, we proposed on this account to bring it here, convinced of getting better results using fresh leaf without a suffering overseas voyage."[12] The commercial lure of cocaine, if not its precise formula, was contagious in Lima.

Ad for Lima-made cocaine, Meyer and Hafemann Pharmacy, 1885
(*El Monitor Médico* 1/11 [15 November 1885])

In December 1885, less than a year after Bignon's moment of glory, the four-man Lima Cocaine Commission delivered another lengthy *informe*, this time on the six types of "cocaína y sus sales preparados por Meyer & Hafemann." The commission assayed chemical purity and therapeutic strengths, monitoring thirty-seven surgical operations ("without the least discomfort") on corneas and other delicate organs, and it also surveyed indications for hemorrhoids, second-degree burns, and gingivitis. Its members compared Lima cocaine to Merck crystals, certifying that Meyer and Hafemann's had "with little doubt" double the anesthetic "action." They hailed Meyer and Hafemann for "putting medicines in the reach of the sick, with uses justified in so many illnesses." Bignon had no recourse, since local formula committees simply evaluated medicines without awarding patents or monopolies. Moreover, Meyer and Hafemann were already deeply immersed in the export business. Vitally, they enjoyed direct relationships to German shippers and, by 1889, formal contractual arrangements with Merck himself.[13] For the German pharmacists and merchants of Lima, cocaine was no scientific hobby. In contrast, Bignon ceased publicizing his cocaine by the end of 1885.

What was the meaning of these developments? Peru's nascent cocaine makers of 1885–86 were a clutch of mainly German pharmacists and traders appropriating for gain Bignon's novel sulfate refining technique in the capital of Peruvian science, politics, and commerce. German merchants consigned the product, encouraging this shift from highly perishable, irregular, and bulky coca leaf to reliable, semiprocessed cocaine for the long voyage to Hamburg. This promised spectacular savings in transport costs alone, since some two hundred parts of fresh coca went into each kilo of crude cocaine. Peruvian coca passed overland across the central sierra; processing the leaf freshly in small pharmacy batches meant a further 13 to 15 percent retention of alkaloid. In a few years, artisanal workshops were attaining a product purity of 90 to 96 percent, a doubling of Bignon's level. As cocaine-making methods adapted to conditions outside Lima, Bignon-style leaf pulverization into a moist coca paste prevailed, which was then precipitated into a dried sulfurous cake similar to *pasta básica de cocaína* (the peasant staple of today's illicit drug trades). By 1889, Lima placed more than 1,700 kilos of cocaine sulfates abroad, breaking the bottleneck of global coca supply.[14]

The impact at the other end of the cocaine trade, in Germany, was immediate. The first recorded shipment of semiprocessed cocaine reached Hamburg in May 1886, no doubt from Meyer and Hafemann. In 1885–86, Merck had produced only 70 kilos of cocaine, using 18,396 kilos of Peruvian leaf, despite demand; two years later, it manufactured 300 kilos, using 375 kilos of Peru's crude cocaine instead — doing away completely with costly, unreliable leaf imports. By 1895, Merck's purchases of Peruvian crude cocaine surpassed 1,800 kilos.[15] Almost all German and other Continental firms followed suit by the 1890s; only American firms (notably Merck's competitor Parke, Davis) stuck with leaf imports for reasons related to tariffs, freight costs, and the broader American penchant for leaf coca. Merck's strategy triumphed: its lucrative refined cocaine hydrochloride, as we have seen, fueled the firm's formidable expansion in the 1890s. Lima's crude cocaine revolutionized the global price, availability, and popularity of the drug. Whereas the post-Köller cocaine scarcity of 1885 drove the price of Merck's cocaine up fourfold from six to twenty-three marks per gram (scaring away even Freud from his researches), the next few years brought a rapid price descent (and Freud carried on with complimentary Parke, Davis samples). In the United States, cocaine's broadest market, retail prices plummeted some fiftyfold, from one dollar a grain in 1884 (thirteen dollars per gram of Merck) to some two cents a grain in the 1890s.

the "gay 90s."

In fact, the German maneuvers here proved deliberate. Apart from contracts with binational pharmacist Meyer, we know that Merck sent its own agent on a mission to Lima—likely Arnaldo Kitz, the pivotal figure (with Bignon) in the creation of the early cocaine industry. Kitz and Company became Lima's busiest cocaine exporter of the 1890s, selling exclusively to Merck. Moreover, Kitz was to be the force behind the early 1890s push that moved the cocaine enterprise out of Peru's coastal capital and into coca's Amazonian homeland, where cocaine has stayed ever since. By the late 1890s, Merck relied on Kitz and Company (whose Lima factory refined a coca paste from Pozuzo) for roughly 1,800 kilos a year, a third of Peruvian output. One of Merck's closer rivals in the race for cocaine, C. F. Boehringer of Mannheim, also dispatched a chemist to Lima during the coca crunch of 1885–86, the staff doctoral student Louis Schaeffer. Unlike Merck, who outsourced for supply to Kitz, Boehringer tried erecting its own factory in Lima, but the project for unknown reasons failed, losing some one hundred thousand marks. The very same Schaeffer, in a remarkable jump, landed in New Jersey in the mid-1890s, carrying his arcane knowledge of coca processing north and there starting a company (later known as Maywood Chemical Works) that would supply Peruvian secret coca extracts to Coca-Cola over the next century.[16] Notably, none of these trained German drug specialists significantly altered Bignon's basic processing method or Peru's aromatic caked intermediate product.

By 1888, a German consul identified four cocaine makers in Lima, including nationals C. M. Schröder and J. Meyer. One pharmacy (probably Meyer's) held contracts to provide 70 kilos a month to Germany, roughly 840 kilos a year, a huge consignment in the novelty era of the drug.[17] Meyer (now sans Hafemann), along with German merchant houses like Prüss (and later his son), Schröder, and Dammert and Sons, carried on as cocaine exporters through the 1890s. Bernard Prüss, an early exporter, became Kitz's nearest rival when he opened one of Lima's larger cocaine complexes of the 1890s in the port city Callao. Germans dominated, though others joined too. An 1889 note on the boom tells how one of Lima's "largest and most successful" (still unidentified) cocaine makers began as a "bricklayer by occupation" before joining this "better and more promising trade for making money." In the 1890s, the French house of Pehovaz Frs. became cocaine makers as well as shippers. One Peruvian national—pharmacy professor Manuel Velázquez of the Antigua Botica Inglesa-Italiana, one of city's best-known druggists—started making cocaine. He was also a promoter of fluid coca extracts and elixirs, which, as we have seen, found their own modest consumer markets in Britain and France. Remy's Cuzco-made "coca elixir" also made it abroad, with sixty bottles going to London in 1892. On the other hand, a coca beer (patented by Carlos Boeschel in 1895) and coca chocolates remained local delicacies.[18]

The distillation of crude cocaine in pharmacies using Bignon's technique proved transitional, lasting about a decade. It paved the way for cocaine's shift to territories deep in the Andes. The rise of Lima's cottage industry was welcomed across the North Atlantic in German, British, and American drug trade journals of the late 1880s and early 1890s. Yet by 1900, observers counted only two running factories in Lima and one in Callao—these were Kitz, Pehovaz, and Prüss—of twenty-four nationwide.[19] By 1910, no cocaine factories stood in the capital, "the great factory of Prüss" the last to fall, though several exporters (Dammert, Pehovaz, Schröder, Kitz and Company, Prevost, and Grace) became trusted specialists in placing the drug abroad. Cocaine manufacture had migrated elsewhere in the Andes, closer to sources of coca supply.

While it was neither a massive nor a long-running business, cocaine making in Lima successfully launched a brand new world commodity. As a critical juncture, this had two longer-lasting (if ambiguous) implications for Peru's larger linkage to burgeoning world circuits of cocaine. One effect, a dampening of local autonomous drug science, reveals the limits to Peru's insertion in the global drug trade. The other, the braking effect on world coca colonization projects of the 1880s, reveals the opposite, namely, how Peruvian protagonists could forge a secure niche in the trade.

The first side of agency here requires a brief return to the saga of Alfredo Bignon and the circle of medical coca enthusiasts who made Lima a vibrant site of cocaine science in the mid-1880s. The Germans who remade Bignon's process into a workable industry were practical businessmen, not scientists. But that does not quite explain the rapid retreat of Peruvian initiatives. In mid-1887, Bignon suddenly abandoned his studies of cocaine, eventually retiring to Paris. Cocaine research practically dried up in Peru over the next decades. Nor did French or many nonhyphenated Peruvians fully participate in cocaine's emergence as a world commodity.

In fact, Bignon had been animated by commerce as much as nationalist science, hoping to make his fortune in cocaine, much as Freud had experimented with the drug out of personal ambition. In June 1885, in the middle of his most frenetic experiments on the drug, Bignon sailed

off for Europe, where he petitioned for and won a coveted ten-year official privilege, aided by his still-active friend Moreno y Maíz, to import
cocaine into France, one of the drug's better markets. In Paris, Bignon's
Lima cocaine samples were acclaimed by eminent French surgeons and
professors, such as Baumetz and Bardet in the Hospital Cochin. Bignon's
method also gained international publicity and endorsements from pharmacy and cocaine experts like Britain's William Martindale, and much of
his research was cited, published, and critiqued in the world of cocaine
science.[20]

Part of the reason for Bignon's abrupt withdrawal from the study of
cocaine is that he soon faced competition from the most powerful forces
in the emerging field of cocaine: well-financed Germans—the world's
dominant pharmaceutical and scientific bloc (Merck, Boehringer, Gehe,
Riedel, Knoll)—and activities of their agents and links to the Andes, *limeño*
pharmacists and businessmen like Hafemann and Kitz. Bignon's scope was
more limited: France had only a pair of modest cocaine makers, Houdé and
Midy. Most vitally, French medical and consumer culture still valorized
herbal coca-leaf extracts over cocaine science, as epitomized by the ever-
popular Vin Mariani. French-style medicine permeated Bignon's Peruvian
milieu and continued as the key style of medical practice in the twentieth
century, but more modern German research models and pharmaceutical
products were starting to supplant it worldwide.[21] Cocaine's dramatic
success as a truly modern drug exemplified that global cultural-scientific
conflict. Bignon and his *limeño* circle belonged to the wrong commodity
chain in the global race to commodify Andean cocaine.

Little is known about Bignon's personal denouement with his formula.
Nothing came of his French exporting scheme, and his pharmacy stopped
publicizing cocaine. The fact that by 1888 Bignon played no role whatsoever
in the official Peruvian Coca Commission was telling. Instead, Bignon
turned to other scientific pursuits, from alkaloid chemistry, vaccines, and
disinfectants to weather observation. In September 1886, still sharing his
cocaine research abroad, Bignon expressed his urge for a wider circle of
colleagues: "Resolving all of these questions . . . is not within the reach
of a single individual, and furthermore, many of them pertain to scientific regions that are well off-limits to me." The historical juncture was
quickly passing for lone artisanal scientific excellence. By the late 1880s,
Lima's medical journals were flooded with cocaine notes from overseas
clinicians and chemists, laboratory scientists joined in the most science-
driven phase of the North Atlantic industrial revolution.[22] Squibb's and

Merck's cocaine-making formulas became standard in the United States and Europe, with Peruvian crude reduced to a cost-saving raw material or chemical curiosity. By the early 1890s, American, German, and French medical-grade cocaine won market prestige in Lima over local pharmacy brands. Ironically, now the catchy pharmaceutical ads were for Frenchified imports like Pastillas Houdé and Cocaína Midy rather than for national cocaine. Bignon's own business illustrated this trend, for he too imported drugs. Decades after his return to France in 1900 (where he died), Lima's rebaptized Laboratorios Antigua Botica Francesa had evolved into one of Peru's main pharmaceutical importers.[23]

Moreover, cocaine, reports already suggested, was losing its heroic luster as a miracle drug of the 1880s. It was a drug with dangerous side effects and perhaps chilling social consequences. Thus, by the 1890s, Peruvian medical researchers, not only Bignon, actively turned to more pressing issues: epidemics, vaccines, sanitation, and other national social problems. Even in Peru, Bignon would later be ignored and discounted as prescientific by the 1920s generation of researchers, including Hermilio Valdizán, Carlos Enrique Paz Soldán, and later Carlos Gutiérrez-Noriega, who in their anticoca zeal did not regard fine distinctions between coca and cocaine or types of cocaine as serious pharmacology. In this brief window, an original national cocaine science had excelled on the periphery in Peru, soon superceded by a German-dominated commodity trade. Peruvians were left at the less lucrative, less innovative end of the world drug industry. Only in the two decades after 1915 would motley local "reformers" of the drug signal a revived national science of cocaine, disconnected from the first phase — and this time in dismal, derogatory, and derivative tones.[24]

The second, countervailing trend linking Lima's incipient cocaine (and Peruvian agency) to the world market helped Peru secure an enduring niche in the global drug trade. Lima's innovation shifted the perceptions and priorities of overseas drug interests and states, particularly in their varied projects for coca colonization, which might have pushed the industry elsewhere. With the cocaine price crunch and scarcity of 1884–86, worried metropolitan drug firms and imperial governments reacted in several ways. Britain from the Royal Botanic Gardens at Kew and its extension stations in colonial India, the Netherlands from Buitenzorg imperial gardens near Batavia, and France and Germany all launched colonial botanic experiments with coca to ensure steady supplies and new colonial revenues. As a rising star of modern pharmaceuticals, cocaine was strategically important. U.S. trade journals debated options such as coca growing "at home" or possible cocaine substitutes derived from chestnuts or benzoyl. Emblematic of the beckoning opportunities in this debate, Mark Twain recounted setting off on a youthful coca-growing get-rich-quick venture of his own, ending up instead working steamboats at the mouth of the Mississippi. U.S. authorities ordered the navy (linked to the surgeon general) and its Andean consuls to investigate and ensure reliable import channels from both Bolivia and Peru, by the 1890s advising local shippers and coca grow-ers.[25] Complicating matters, many drug manufacturers (save for confirmed herbalists) remained wary of coca imports, with their problematic freight costs, unstable quality and price, tendency to spoilage, poor Andean transit, and political disruptions of trade. Coca doubters persisted long after its active principle was known.

In the late 1880s, in little-known activities, European imperial agrono-mists began experimenting with coca as a colonial crop in an amazing array of places: the Dutch East Indies (Java, Sumatra, Madura); British India (Ceylon, Madras, Assam, Darjeeling, and other sites, plus Malaysia); Anglo, French, and German colonial Africa (Zanzibar, Togo, Cameroon, Nigeria, Sierra Leone, the Gold Coast, and even Portuguese São Tomé); and across the Caribbean (Jamaica, Guadalupe, Martinique, Trinidad, the Dominican Republic). Similarly, coca was promoted in Florida, California, Hawaii, Australia, Colombia, and Porfirian Mexico.[26] The bush sometimes thrived, since coca grows in the same climes and ecological niches as tea. Not discounting the depth of Andean peasant lore about its culture, coca is not so tricky to grow, even going feral (like a weed) in parts of India. Yet until about 1906, the expanding international coca and crude cocaine trade remained almost entirely in Peruvian hands. Even Bolivia, with an equal or greater store of received coca wisdom and about one-third of Peru's crop, receded from commercial coca export. Why wasn't coca appropriated by others, the fate suffered by Peru with Peru-bark?

The turning point in this puzzle was the Andean mission of Henry Hurd Rusby in the fall of 1884—just as Bignon was perfecting his method in Lima. An aspiring "pharmagognocist" (today's ethnobotany or economic botany) of later stature and influence, Rusby was ordered to Bolivia by George Davis of Parke, Davis and Company. His mandate was to personally "establish connections for obtaining supplies of [coca]," as well as collect valuable commercial data on locally used coca medicines and cures. He soon found himself, exactly like Bignon, busily experimenting with making "crude alkaloid in the coca region" (as well as varied fluid extracts) for its easier transshipment north. In one scary incident, endlessly retold in cocaine's anecdotal histories, Rusby accidentally blew up the makeshift experimental still in his wood-frame hotel room, almost burning down all of La Paz with it — the kind of chemical mishap that would become commonplace again during the later age of illicit cocaine. Rusby's twenty-thousand-pound, $250,000 special shipment of coca for Parke, Davis was also lost crossing Colombia amid a storied "revolution."

These adventures aside, Rusby soon put in print how coca's real options got defined "at home and abroad." In a widely read 1888 report, he noted how "factories . . . have now been established in the region of production, for the manufacture of crude or impure alkaloid, which is then shipped to Europe or North America for refining." In Rusby's expert opinion, Americans no longer really needed coca leaf (inert abroad anyway due to poor packing and shipping) or risky overseas chemical experiments, because the Peruvians themselves had fulfilled this role perfectly with the crude cocaine coming out of Lima. Rusby later distinguished himself as a professor of botany, physiology, and materia medica at Columbia and as chief of the U.S. Pharmacopoeia; indicative of the U.S. political reversal after 1905, he also became an outspoken foe of coca.[27]

Much of the American drug trade press (die-hard herbalists aside) shared Rusby's stance. In January 1885, just as Bignon's method appeared in an obscure Lima publication, the major trade journal *American Druggist* declared, "If ever there was an argument for manufacturing an article of this kind in its native country, such an argument is supplied in the case of coca." It called for large-scale processing of crude cocaine in South America "on the spot" (the same term applied by Austrian trade specialist Karl Scherzer decades before) as opposed to coca cultivation within U.S. borders, proposed for Florida or colonial Hawaii. Within months, the same journal carried good news from Lima, reporting on both Meyer and Hafemann's venture and Bignon's promotional trip to Paris. Two years later, duly impressed by real Lima cocaine, *American Druggist* reiterated its earlier view: "A large quantity of the cocaine on the market is prepared from the crude alkaloid imported from South America. There is not enough profit in extracting the alkaloid from the leaves in Europe [or in the United States]." By 1892, the journal noted, "Trade in coca leaves has lost much of its importance since crude cocaine commenced to be manufactured in Peru."[28] In an age of accelerating communication, news of *limeño* industrial strides quickly circled the globe.

A similar scenario unfolded in Britain. In 1889, London's authoritative *Chemist and Druggist* published a trade note called simply "Crude Cocaine":

"For more than a year past, crude cocaine has been sent from Peru to the States and Europe [i.e., Hamburg] in rapidly increasing quantities and of better and better quality. . . . During 1888, the quantities exported from Peru became very large, and the quality reached 90 to 96 percent. . . . It is highly probable that the importation of coca leaves into the States and Europe for the manufacture of cocaine is nearly at an end."[29] The last prediction was only complicated by national or firm loyalties to leaf. Unaware of Bignon's role, the *Chemist and Druggist* wrongly assumed Peru's "youthful industry" of cocaine exploited the Squibb process. Five years later, in 1894, legendary imperial botanist Clements R. Markham, the pioneer "Andeanist" who in the 1850s helped whisk cinchona seedlings out of Peru to sustain Britain's disease-ridden tropical empires, was invited to reflect on coca at London's commercial Imperial Institute. Markham, a president of the Royal Geographical Society, delivered a maverick "Uncommercial Coca-Lecture"—sounding much like Rusby, his slightly less imperious American peer. Markham marshaled statistics on the strides of crude cocaine. Already by 1892, Peru's coca exports had reached 128,548 kilos (worth S/120,000 Peruvian), but cocaine exports exceeded 3,300 kilos valued at S/195,000. Cocaine was thus more profitable than leaf. Markham, relieved, spoke out against mounting another colonial venture against Peru: "There is therefore no probability that coca-growing will ever become an industry in other countries."[30] Markham's intervention was likely enough to halt the expansion of the motley coca projects in British India. Of the Peruvian cocaine noted by Markham in 1892, all but 154 kilos actually went to Hamburg, where Merck had already abandoned leaf with the aid of his agents Meyer and Kitz in Lima. Other German drug firms would need coca until later in the decade, since Merck had cornered the initial supply of crude cocaine still made in Lima.

The crucial point here is that scientists and entrepreneurs in mid-1880s Lima, as historical actors, relieved the fundamental price and supply constraints of this new commodity. The early, ample provision of Peruvian-made cocaine enabled and convinced weighty metropolitan interests to specialize in refining and marketing the drug globally, to abandon a push for colonial coca plantations, and this shift likely drove more costly Bolivian leaf off overseas markets as well.[31] Peru maintained its coveted national monopoly on coca and crude cocaine and set some terms of its own integration into the world drug trade—though not the most prestigious or profitable niche assumed by firms like Merck. Had major powers—Britain, Germany, or the United States—acted otherwise, that is, had they moved into significant coca-cocaine ventures by the 1890s, as they had earlier done with tea and opium, the goods' twentieth-century trajectories might have looked quite different, perhaps allowing for a more diverse and legitimate global enterprise, with globally traded coca leaf (at least) less subject to a single nation's antidrug passions.

COCAINE "ON THE SPOT": AMAZONIAN COCA

The revolutionary technology and commodification of cocaine first issued from Lima pharmacies in the mid-1880s, but by the latter part of the decade the enterprise had swiftly dispersed across Peru. Cocaine production emerged as a true agro-industrial activity rooted near sources of fresh coca across the Andes in Amazonia, starting with Kitz in the German outpost of Pozuzo and spreading out to the rest of coca country. With a clear economic motive — it was far easier, surer, and cheaper to trek brown sulfate bricks over the Andes than perishable bales of dry leaf — this shift led by 1900 to the industry's focus around the eastern town of Huánuco, cocaine's historical haven.

After 1885, coca began to flow out of Peruvian ports — from Salaverry in the north through Lima-Callao and Mollendo in the far south. More than a thousand bales of leaves made it to Hamburg in 1886; a British consul in the south noted, "Coca is the only new article here, around which demand is developing for the fabrication of cocaine, now used in surgical operations to alleviate pain."[32] By the mid-1890s, coca was thriving commercially in the warm districts of Otuzco, Huamachuco, Huánuco, Tarma, Huanta, and Cuzco, largely through the intensification of plots and plantations oriented to local indigenous or miner markets. Huánuco had become the major outpost of commercial coca by the late 1890s, though its leaf plantations hark to before the eighteenth century. In 1889, Huánuco's prefect publicized cultivation of coca, encouraged by foreign coca agents and merchants, the exhortations of the 1888 national Coca Commission, and the propaganda of the Sociedad Obreros del Porvenir de Amazonas. By 1895, a special office of the newly formed Peruvian Ministry of Promotion focused efforts on the "Colonización y Tierras de Montaña," the high jungles of eastern Peru long idealized for riches but crippled by their lack of roads and *brazos* (exploitable peasant labor). Land claims under the aegis of this office usually cited "coca" as their motive, and a few noted "cocaine."

Coca grew across the *montaña* and even in a few sierran valleys, but the capital of Peruvian cocaine throughout the twentieth century was to be greater Huánuco Province, which literally sits above the sprawling, wild Upper Huallaga River Valley, whose waterway is a tributary of the Amazon. The central Amazon's long entanglements with cocaine date to pioneer Arnaldo Kitz and the jungle village of Pozuzo. In 1888, Kitz undertook a purposeful trek to Pozuzo, armed with a vision and a formula—Bignon's, adapted for rustic conditions—for making cocaine on a major scale.

Pozuzo, as Peruvian schoolchildren know, is the legendary "lost colony" of Austrian Tyrolean peasants (from near Italy) of the late 1850s who ended up in one of the most inaccessible spots of the Peruvian Amazon. It was a fiasco of liberal Peru's obsessive attempts to bring industrious farmers to the unstable nation. Pozuzo is still a haunting place to visit, isolated by a long and bumpy cloud forest "road," with hewn triangular wooden peasant houses and hex signs, its misplaced blondes racing on motorbikes alongside colorful Ashanti and Shipibo mates. By the late nineteenth century, Pozuzo, with several hundred penurious survivors (565 in 1888, in 98 families), was synonymous with past liberal folly—with "whitening" colonization schemes, with Europeans abandoned and "degenerating" in the diseased tropics. Pozuzo was also off the map. Not accessible by a straight road via Peru's central Tarma-Chanchamayo Pass, Pozuzo's sole outlet to the world was still a jungle path through thick forests along branches of the Huallaga to its higher Andean district capital of Huánuco, about 125 kilometers away—a hiking distance of several days. Pozuzo was known for its fertile outcrop, Pampa Hermosa, yet aside from the dreams of a newly arrived town leader, Fr. Luis Egg, the town had few prospects. Even Pozuzo's cattle seemed "very backwards," as if, like their herders, they had decayed in the sweltering heat.[33]

Within fifteen years, a government report of 1904 on the central *selva* confirmed dramatic changes in Pozuzo thanks to the efforts of Kitz: "The chief industry of the German colony is the fabrication of cocaine and cultivation of coca, as these are the only products that can sustain the enormous toll of transport to Lima."[34] Pampa Hermosa had been put to good use. Remote and tiny Pozuzo was now a key link in a long chain of historical Austro-German interest in coca and cocaine: from Humboldt and then the Germanic travelers of the early republic through Scherzer and the coca-collecting *Novara* voyage of the mid-1850s to that leaf's use in alkaloid-seeking experiments by Wöhler and Niemann at Göttingen down to Merck's Darmstadt firm, which hired Kitz. Poeppig, the noted coca writer-traveler of the 1830s, penned a later tract on the "Germans lost in the South American jungle." Scherzer, an early advocate of Pozuzo, also precociously predicted a year after cocaine's birth, in 1861, that "the means will surely and easily be found for extracting *on the spot* the active principle of coca, as it is being at present done by industrious Yankees in Ecuador, with the cinchona."[35] The means was found by Kitz, following Bignon's footsteps and those of the German druggists of Lima.

The record on Arnaldo Kitz is scarce. He sold his cocaine exclusively to Emmanuel Merck and more than likely landed in Peru as his personal emissary. He first shows up outside Huánuco by 1886 — year one of the world cocaine squeeze — to purchase the Tulumayo property for a mere S/2,000. The property consisted of a huge expanse of jungle near Tingo María. It was sold by his heirs in 1904, later becoming a key site in cocaine's twentieth-century saga. Kitz dabbled, not surprisingly, in other tropical commodities, such as wild rubber. In January 1888, a Peruvian supreme resolution granted Kitz and two partners land rights in Pozuzo's Chantabamba *montaña*. So, by 1890, Kitz made his way out to the "lost" Austrians, *on the spot*, and found there a desperate German-speaking community ready to embrace his scheme. Stories still circulate of itinerant "Germans" in the jungle revealing the secrets of cocaine.[36] Kitz was a Johnny Appleseed of cocaine — or, better put, its Fitzcarraldo.

Kitz's formula became Pozuzo's economic lifeline, and by the early 1890s Pozuzo emerged as the world's prime source of crude cocaine. A detailed description of Kitz's operations, including a crude sketch of his cocaine factory, survives from the turn of the century. Kitz's personal Hacienda Victoria was a "large extension planted in coca," with some seven hundred thousand bushes rendering yearly more than nine hundred *arrobas* (some twenty-three thousand pounds). The German peasants supplied an equal share of fresh leaf for the town's factory. The elongated workshop, built out of two lanes of locally hewed wooden barrels and piping, used hauled-in petroleum, carbonate of soda, and chlorine (ingredients likely acquired from Cerro de Pasco mining companies) to leach and dissolve the cocaine by hand and chemically; it was then purified with sulfuric acid and pressed into a crude paste. This simple and light product was ferried across the Andes by pack mule through Huánuco for further refining in Kitz and Company's Lima offices before shipment to Merck. In Lima, Kitz quickly became a respected businessman, socializing with the city's worldly elite. There is also evidence of Kitz's run-ins with Huánuco authorities, who were keen to impose hotly disputed "coca taxes" on his transiting

Scene from the Austrian Amazonian colony of Pozuzo, ca. 1900
(Carlos B. Cisneros, *Atlas del Perú: Político, minero, agrícola, industrial y comercial....* [Lima: Imprenta Gil, 1900], 72)

cocaine.[37] He won these battles on the grounds that crude cocaine was a distinct product, one officially fostered by the Peruvian state.

After 1893, Kitz transferred the firm's main operations to Huánuco and Lima. By 1904, well after his departure, sales of cocaine from Pozuzo amounted to only 10 to 12 kilograms monthly, about 120 to 140 kilos a year. Even this dwindling cash flow sustained the "decrepit" community: some twenty to thirty workers tended the factory in 1904 and labored on their allotted coca and subsistence plots. Kitz repaired the town's bridges and paid the village priest. Huánuco cocaine surpassed them by 1900, yet *pozuzeños* still paid homage to their departed ally from afar: "Establishment of the factory was tremendously beneficial to the colony. . . . its founder, Sr. Kitz is remembered with affection and respect, after having lent such indispensable services to the Germans of Pozuzo."[38] By 1910, only memories flickered of Kitz's project: Pozuzo, lost again, hobbled along with coffee, rubber, and timber, its fleeting prosperity of cocaine over.

In Lima, Kitz married into a prominent family, the Dibós, whose patriarch was a mayor of Lima. He died childless in Huánuco in July 1896, the likely price of his years in the insalubrious tropics. Kitz and Company carried on as a working merchant house into the early twentieth century, fronted by his last partner, Carlos Knoll. Until his demise, this celebrated father of Peruvian cocaine and solid member of the Chamber of Commerce used the Lima offices to purify his crude cocaine paste from Pozuzo before shipping it on his account to Hamburg and up the Rhine to Merck. Kitz cocaine was the only Peruvian "brand" truly known abroad, cited as such in Mortimer's *History of Coca*.

Kitz left a firsthand, if ornery, sketch of himself in early 1891, when A. J. Dougherty, the U.S. consul in Callao, tried to interview him about cocaine supplies amid ongoing scarcity concerns. (He got better results with cocaine makers Prüss and Plejo, the latter of whom was visiting from Huánuco and talkative about his favorite product.) Kitz noted to Dougherty that the value of cocaine had again soared on world markets (from 200 to 250 marks per kilo) due to the breakdown of sierra transport during the latest of Peru's civil wars. Yet he reiterated his will to sell his wares exclusively in Germany, where in any case Kitz held long-term contracts with Merck. Queried on prices and competitors, Kitz tersely replied, "I have my own method of manufacture, and that is my own secret, as well as the cost to me of the manufacture." Kitz was even annoyed by the consul's note taking, yet he still managed to implicate his chief rival, Prüss and Company, in shady deals. Prüss, on the other hand, welcomed Dougherty into his workshop in Callao and opened his ledger books to the prying consul.[39] Kitz, to the end, was a loyal agent of the German commodity sphere.

Pozuzo was not the only place where backwoods cocaine workshops popped up in Peru, though, significantly, none appeared in coca-rich Bolivia. At the 1900–1905 height of Peruvian crude cocaine exporting, Alejandro Garland, one of Peru's leading economic lights, proudly reported no fewer than twenty-one such factories. Secondhand sources stretch this number to twenty-five or thirty. By 1900, about a third of Peru's swelling national coca crop likely went into cocaine making or related coca exports. Coca's industrialization was national in scope, from Peru's far north to the far south. Garland sketched this dispersion: "In Cajamarca there is a small installation on the Hacienda 'Marcamachay' (Cajatambo Province), and two others in the Department of La Libertad. Huánuco Department counts on 12 installations including the existing one in the Pozuzo Montaña. In the mountains of Huanta there are also two established workshops, not to mention the two factories of Lima, one in Callao and another pair in Cuzco." It was Garland who crowned cocaine "the essentially" and "exclusively Peruvian industry." The coca plant, he noted, had failed "to acclimatize outside of Peru," despite known attempts at transfer, and Indian Bolivia, with its vibrant local demand for leaf, had failed to industrialize it. To Garland, "nature" and Peruvian ingenuity made cocaine a Peruvian monopoly, able to serve the entire world's needs.[40]

This emulation of Pozuzo can be glimpsed through a thicket of local records. Even in the remote southern Andes, immigrants joined with rustic *hacendados* to exploit new opportunities in coca and cocaine. The prefect of Huanta in 1903 noted, for instance, an unheard-of burst of coca sales (some 740 *arrobas*) not only to Huanta's traditional upland mining pole of Huancavelica but "as well to the United States, by a Society recently organized by Juan Ichantequi and company of this *plaza*." Area coca was also used in making Remy's coca elixir in Cuzco. A few years later, the sub-prefect of Ayacucho reported "a new factory for cocaine now constituted . . . in the zone called 'Machinte' where all roads into the jungle end." Three neighboring valleys developed into the department's coca zone, harvesting fifty thousand *arrobas* of leaf yearly "superior in quality to that obtained in other departments, such as Huánuco." Bragging rights were also on the rise. Cuzco's tropical hinterlands, which raised 1.5 million kilos of coca in 1898, hosted three factories at its peak, one at Santa Ana in the Urubamba Valley, sending both coca and cocaine out of the southern port of Mollendo during the 1890s. However, with the post-1910 crisis of Peruvian cocaine, the tropical south — Huanta, Ayacucho, and the newly colonized lowland valleys of Cuzco such as La Convención — receded from cocaine (the last factory closed by 1911) and redirected their leaf sales to expanding southern Indian coca marts, edging out the former Bolivian coca.[41]

On the opposite end of Peru, the northern coca pole of La Libertad and parts of eastern Cajamarca and Chachapoyas played a distinctive role. Their activity in the 1890s consolidated a world market for branded Trujillo leaf, with lasting ties to U.S. beverage makers (notably Coca-Cola) and a few steadfast cocaine magnates of the twentieth century. Two northern areas saw early commercial coca farming: the Maranón Amazonian region east of the Andes (Huamachuco and Cajabamba) and especially the Otuzco province of La Libertad in the upper reaches of the Pacific-flowing Moche and Chicama river system that lies slightly west of the main Andean cordillera. Both zones historically supplied coca to miners at Hualgayoc and other small mines. Otuzco coca, from the *E. novogranatense* plant, became the only leaf exported from Pacific slopes, growing at a five-hundred-to-two-thousand-meter niche; this microclimate, in combination with the area's singular sun-drenched irrigated leaf culture, may explain some Trujillo characteristics, such as its thin, long, paler, "tea-like" leaf.

By the 1890s, Otuzco, benefiting from the soaring export prices of Huánuco leaf, became the premium northern coca. Transport costs for leaf proved appreciably lower than from the usual Amazonian regions, since bales did not even cross the high Andes, and the northern port of Salaverry was a cheaper, faster route to New York or Hamburg. A local survey of 1896 calculated new Otuzco investments in *cocales* (coca plantings) in the lands later known as Sacamanca. Nine districts or haciendas had 2.7 million young bushes on line for an annual crop of 4,700 *quintales*, about 200,000 pounds. Led by Huayabamba (600,000 plants) and then Las Compas and Campín, the most productive districts had over a hundred coca planters between them. Coca had become Otuzco's second most profitable economic pursuit.

Reports also specified a motive in the forward move to cocaine refining. Venerable northern merchant clans like A. Goicochea and Company and the German house of Ludowig hurt local coca planters by buying up local coca low at auction to skim the high profits in transshipment to Lima. According to one 1897 press account, the upstarts "Genaro Risco, owner of a farm at Huasyobamba, and José Antonio Delfin at Cayanchal, intend[ed] to establish a manufactory of cocaine on their property so as to be independent of that intolerable and ruinous monopoly, and inaugurate a wholesome trade competition." They were also acting on prices: cocaine in Lima fetched 60 *centavos* a gram, which meant that 15 to 20 *soles* of coca would render 180 *soles* of cocaine — "a handsome profit," it was said, for local farmers.[42] Many details are lost, but the story didn't end well, as processed cocaine also became a mainstay of the north's commercial oligarchy.

By the early 1900s, the clans invested in cocaine making and leaf exports were those of Teofilo Vergel and Alfredo Pinillos Hoyle in urban Trujillo and Gustavo Prados in the highlands. The first two were closely aligned with the Goicochea and Acharán commercial houses, the monopolists of lore. Pinillos, a leading old merchant and landowner, was a political figure active in the Peruvian Chamber of Deputies who lucratively managed the colonial Goicochea interests later known as Pinillos, Goicochea y Cia. His son would become the exclusive supplier from Otuzco haciendas for Coca-Coca's secret Merchandise No. 5 syrup for much of the next century. Located at Bolívar 718, the Pinillos-Ayllon cocaine factory was a pride of Trujillo commerce and industry.[43]

Teofilo S. Vergel, "a gentleman widely connected in the commercial circuits of the north and the whole Republic," was the north's other principal cocaine *empresario*. A fine description survives of his electrified multiproduct factory, initiated in 1914 (a late date for cocaine, the result of surging prewar German demand) on Calle Progreso 812 with sixteen employees and chemists. A depiction of the factory reads, "The Factory of Cocaine processes 600 pounds daily of coca, with a monthly cocaine production of 60 kilos, exported for sale in Europe." Such a modern plant, with its annual 720-kilo capacity, was formidable for Peru. Pinillos and the others drifted in and out of the cocaine trade after 1910, bolstered in the Trujillo coca circuit by their long-term contracts with Coca-Cola and its trading partner, Maywood Chemical of New Jersey.[44] Vergel held on to become one of Peru's most vocal regional advocates for cocaine through the 1930s.

HUÁNUCO: CROATS AND COCAINE, 1890–1905

By the mid-1890s, Pozuzo's cocaine trail led to Huánuco proper. This was to become the world capital of Peru's legal cocaine industry, lasting until 1949, when the Peruvian military, to appease overseas drug warriors, ended the drug's legal phase. Anticipating the 1960s and 1970s, it would be the tropical Upper Huallaga river zones tied up with Huánuco's cocaine complex — notably Tingo María, the coca paste capital of the 1980s — that birthed the *illicit* trade which made "cocaine" a household word in our times. Huánuco's crude cocaine industry passed through four stages, each led by distinctive actors. First, the "industrialization of coca" (still a euphemism for cocaine) in the 1890s was propelled by an unlikely group of Croatian immigrants in the tropics, who made Huánuco the world's major cocaine zone by 1900–1905. Second, the period 1905–20 saw the mature industry fall under the control of the enterprising regional caudillo, Augusto Durand. The third and fourth stages (followed in subsequent chapters) saw cocaine's steady decline of the 1920s–50s, resisted by its next leader, Andrés A. Soberón, and its aftermath in the birth of illicit cocaine after 1960 in the Huallaga Valley, the main corridor in the rise of the Colombian drug traffickers. Cocaine and Huánuco have had a close, long-term relationship.

Cocaine gravitated to the Upper Huallaga for many reasons, including a long history of coca culture dating to colonial or precolonial times (ethnobotanists believe domesticated *Erythroxylon coca* originated here in the central Amazon), the exertions of modern coca colonizers, and above all the weight of Huánuco's historical geography. In Huánuco Province, the capital town of Huánuco proper sits squarely between a typically cool sierran social economy above (of haciendas, flocks, and small mines) and the semitropical frontier zones of the Amazon basin below.[45] After independence, Huánuco emerged as Peru's gateway via the navigable Huallaga river system, with eight major tributaries, into the country's nominally national Amazon territories. Communications from coastal Lima to Huánuco were, for republican Peru, relatively good: the road passed through the mine country of La Oroya and Cerro de Pasco, making it the direct route to the high *montaña* jungle (six to eight days, cut in half by 1900 by the vertiginous railhead to La Oroya). "Sumamente bueno" ran one description of the road, a true rarity in Peru.[46] Moreover, alternative routes to the central Amazon via Jauja and Chanchamayo became blocked for most of the century, as resurgent Chuncho Indians in those frontiers wiped out and scared off European settlers. After the Pacific War, large swaths of that land, finally pacified, were ceded to the British Peruvian Corporation (to pay off Peru's crippling nineteenth-century foreign debt) and related Italian colonists. Both groups opted to plant familiar coffee and cacao over exotic Andean coca, for example in Oxapampa, even though the latter included German refugees from Pozuzo. Further south in Huanta, rebels also commandeered ancient coca lowlands, part of a general Amazonian frontier recession that made Huánuco coca the country's most accessible, particularly for export.

In the poetic prose of Esteban Pavletich, the town's later literary and political renegade, "Huánuco constitutes the nexus, the confluence, the nest, the union between the two vastest and prolific Peruvian regionalisms—the sierra and the *montaña*."[47] This confluence has sparked many historical dreams of conquest, or, put differently, of "regional development."

Descending into the hot and humid hills below temperate Huánuco (some 1,925 meters above sea level), well-off *vecinos* (townsmen) had long kept a foothold in plantations or land claims in the scattered, densely forested *montaña*, as well as in a gamut of highland mining, farming, and trading pursuits. But coca, introduced by colonial Franciscan settlements, was for many reasons always the most tradable and monetized of regional special-ties (sugarcane rums and coffee and, later, wild rubber, timber, and tea were others). "Nothing is sold from this valley but coca," navy lieutenant William L. Herndon noticed at mid-century from Chinchao while on a remarkable North American scientific mission with a commercial aim to stake out Peru's eastern gateway to the Amazon. Coca held on throughout Peru's depressed nineteenth century by satisfying appetites of miners for chewing leaf at the nearby Cerro de Pasco silver district, Peru's largest clutch of surviving mines. Raimondi reconnoitered the zone in 1860 and noted its coca yield of 25,000 *arrobas* (275,000 kilograms), 81 percent for mastication in Cerro de Pasco, Tarma, and Jauja. In 1874, before it became an export, some five hundred mules plied about 50,000 *arrobas* of coca a year up to the mines and highland Indian villages, oiling two-thirds of Huánuco's estimated monetary transactions of S/600,000.[48]

Certain of these *montaña* lands — *quebradas*, subtropical river ravines with ridges in the five-hundred-to-seventeen-hundred-meter range — were legendary for their coca, even to faraway armchair observers of Peru. Twelve kilometers downstream from Huánuco town, itself cut by the rushing headwaters of the Huallaga, the tropics began, and sharply drop-ping Andean verticality forms compact niche valleys perfect for coca. The first *cocales* appear in Santa María de Valle, where many townsmen held farms. But the best known and most continuously exploited was the narrow Montaña de Chinchao. Chinchao and the fecund microclimate of Derrepente, with its four annual harvests, gave a year-round supply of leaf. Its haciendas, such as Cassapi and Mesapata, and settlement Acomayo, lay about 60 kilometers below Huánuco — a few days' hike. Panao, an Indian village off this path, had smallholder coca, coveted coca muleteers, and inevitable conflicts with greedy outsiders, labor contractors, and mestizo colonists. Further downstream, 145 kilometers below Huánuco, at 617 meters, lay the beautifully set fluvial outpost of Tingo María (sub-province of Pachitea, population 100 in 1900). Chiguangala was Tingo's working coca field, along with the unexploited riverbank Tulumayo, with its mas-sive three-hundred-thousand-*hector* forested hacienda, Pampayacu, the one briefly owned by Kitz. Tulumayo, still controlled by the Portuguese

Martín family (assimilated later as the "Martínez"), was to be a key site of contending interests over the next century of cocaine history. In the late nineteenth century, it also marked the Amazonian agricultural frontier, little used except by the itinerant rubber trappers and rain forest tribes who ranged here in the 1890s.[49] Pozuzo, to the southeast, was known for coca, as we have seen, but was too remote for leaf to travel well, in contrast to an accessible stretch of the northeastern sub-province of Huamalíes, Monzón, some 110 kilometers upstream on its tributary from Tingo María, a four-day journey from Huánuco. Verdant Monzón, of the vast middle Huallaga regions, would be coca's active frontier by 1900. But well into the twentieth century, the Chinchao—with the Durand clan's famed Éxito factory and sprawling San Carlos hacienda at its core—remained the most intensely exploited coca zone in all Peru.

Travelers descending the Huallaga Valley from Huánuco invariably remarked on this regional specialty, its trade, rites, and rhythms of cultivation, traditional processing, and local uses, all of which seemed so exotic to intrigued Westerners before 1900. Von Tschudi himself passed the San Carlos hacienda in the 1840s. One of the best depictions of the coca lands, published in English by J. L. W. Thudichum in 1885 (amid soaring fascination with cocaine), compiled the sightings of earlier visitors, particularly German Poeppig (1837) and Austrian von Tschudi (1838–42), translating in effect the German gaze on coca. "The coca of Huánuco is the most celebrated of Peru," Thudichum affirms from London. He continues: "Nearly the whole produce came from the Quebrada of Chinchao. From the highest point at which the plant does yet succeed [Challana farm, near Carpis Pass] to Cuchero, the last inhabited place, there were about forty plantations on a line of five geographical miles." These were not opulent places: they were "termed 'Haciendas,' but contain[ed] no buildings except the miserable huts which the South American does not term Casas but 'Ranchos.'" Yet Chinchao outposts were profitable. A typical *cocal* investment was *Lp*2,500 (still at 5 *soles*), which by the second year cleared a *Lp*1,700 profit. After six years of maturing bushes, a coca farm yielded owners an impressive 45 percent annual return on capital. Thudichum had a typical Protestant slant on the pre-boom Peruvian landowners: "The planter has never to fear failure of harvest, or sudden sinking of the prices of the leaves; loss by rain is rare. If few planters grow rich, this is caused by their idleness and their profligate way of life." Plantations averaged twelve workers, mainly *enganchados* (peasants "hooked" by debt, whether lowland Indians or highland migrants), plus the owners, peddlers, and

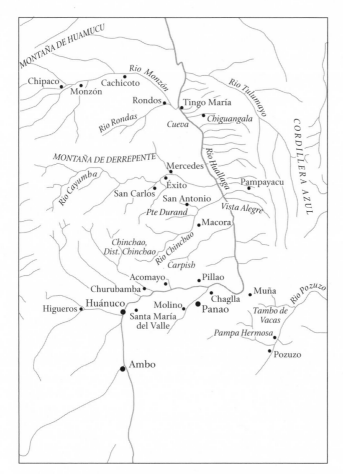

MAP 2.1. The Huánuco-Huallaga Cocaine Region, 1930s

Source: Modified from "Red Vial del Departamento de Huánuco," from Perú, Servicio Técnico de Puentes y Caminos (Lima: Ministerio de Fomento, 1936).

their families. "About 5,000 people live in this small district on the results of coca alone," Thudichum reported.[50] Coca lands were notorious for their unhealthy and coercive labor regimes, later the target of *indigenista* reform invectives. Coca growing was an ethnically segmented activity. Of a population of 2,505 in 1877, the Chinchao had only 94 self-identified "whites," mostly planters and merchants, and 1,795 Indians, presumably the vast majority of its 838 *agricultores* and 613 *jornalero* day laborers. Trusting the country's first true national census, all of Huánuco Department (with its three provinces, Dos de Mayo, Huamalíes, and Huánuco) hosted only 78,991 souls in 1877—under 4 per square kilometer, taking into account its uncharted jungle. It was still Indian-dominated, with mixed settlers bunched in the core Huánuco Province. The head town of Huánuco, famed for its refreshing springlike climate, had only 5,263 town dwellers, who thrived largely from the control of regional commerce and from sales and levies on coca passing up from Chinchao and Monzón plantations.[51] Its leading citizens were those somnolent planters.

By the 1880s, "Huánuco coca" (including a locally dubbed "Monzón" leaf) was coca with a pedigree, the most coveted in foreign markets, then expanding for medicines and concoctions like Vin Mariani. In the swirl of botanical controversies around *Erythroxylon coca*, the single coca plant famously reproduced and disseminated across the British Empire from nineteenth-century Kew Gardens was the alleged gift to science of the bishop of Huánuco, though modern botany disputes this provenance.[52] Huánuco leaf—tellingly termed "Peruvian" leaf among buyers—was usually described as dark green, glossy, thick, and "bitter and aromatic," indicative of high alkaloid content. *E. coca* contains fourteen complex alkaloids, and—in addition to the genetic variety—climate, horticultural methods, and drying, packing, and shipping practices can vary its cocaine content. As testing arrived late in the nineteenth century, observers discerned that Huánuco leaf produced twice as much cocaine alkaloid as its Andean competitors—upward of 0.75 percent—and it was thus avidly sought by makers of cocaine. Bignon demonstrated its higher crystallization ratio (85 to 90 percent, meaning less cocaine in ecgonine form); modern ethnobotany confirms its high cocaine ratio but mainly attributes this to its growth in relatively high sites like Chinchao.[53]

After the Pacific War ended in 1881, and visibly after 1889, the coca trade awoke. That year, prefect Ramón Freire (a later owner of the Tulumayo tract) added an instructive "Cultivo de la coca" guide to his annual report, urging coca cultivation and export from Chinchao-Derrepente. It also appeared in Peru's governmental *Registro oficial*. Land registers reveal a stirring land market in the 1890s, as Huánuco families traded, speculated, consolidated, and mortgaged themselves in *montaña* plots. A few outsiders moved in, too: colonizers from other parts of Peru and abroad took advantage of liberal new "tierras de montaña" laws, which gave away tropical lands to anyone who could prove or simply claim an economic or populating intent. In the 1890s, land petitions on the Huallaga or Monzón frontier invariably invoked the lure of coca.[54]

New decrees to tax this bustling regional trade multiplied, and just as quickly "exemptions" were granted (in 1887, 1890, and 1892) for coca that was put straight into cocaine making. Huánuco's population doubled in two decades to over 145,000 by 1896, concentrated in coca lands and along coca trading routes. Local fortunes were made by merchants close to Huánuco's Impuesto de la Coca, helping to overcome the region's long-felt scarcity of capital. This colonial-style coca toll, auctioned to private collectors for substantial cash advances, paid for some 60 percent of town revenues by 1900 and was plowed into municipal projects as well as road upkeep to the coca ravines. This local fiscal network became a visible source of accumulation and clientelistic influence by figures like Juan Plejo, Juan Boyanovich, and Augusto and Juan Durand, allowing them to contract coca with advances of loans to farmers below, assuring their leaf supplies and reinvesting profits in their cocaine factories. Related political posts were captured by the planters and their friends. Indeed, there are few signs of local competition or family rivalries in Huánuco, as close marriage and business collusion characterized its coalescing society of coca. The regional politics of coca gave Huánuco its own robust political identity, often in rebellion against a distant central state in Lima.

By 1900, its height of activity, the entire department boasted some three thousand coca growers, though the coca elite, with some thirty to forty intermarried families, were rooted in Chinchao and Derrepente. Certain of their *apellidos* lasted for generations in coca: Repetto, Ramírez, Sara LaFosse, Funegra, Lambruschini, Cavalíe, Malpartida, Mori, Ampudia. Around 1900, Prefect Huapaya found these zones harvesting 1,265,000 kilos of leaf, 110,000 *arrobas* of the 121,934 provincial total. They also shipped out 918 kilos of cocaine (a low estimate for the time) at a going price of 200 *soles* per kilo. Authorities collected S/58,000 in coca taxes for the town coffers. There were three working factories in Chinchao alone, bringing to the outback the province's first telephones and electricity, and one in Huánuco City. Huánuco now hosted half the nation's cocaine plants, and, as coca pioneers spread into Monzón, even more rustic workshops. No wonder the prefect could reflect in 1900, despite a decade of volatile cocaine prices and unsettling regional politics, that Huánuco was now a "rich section of Peru," adding, "This local industry is so valuable because of a strong demand for the article, and the praiseworthy men who invest themselves here are giving it, every day, a broader and broader reach." By 1905, a new prefect reckoned that export of "this alkaloid" was worth "more than a million *soles*." Despite perennial *huanuqueño* gripes about bad roads ("suedo-caminos") and labor shortages, he said, "Our industries have acquired a grand development and importance." National officials in

Lima also extolled coca's role. In 1905, Peru's minister of finance mused, "It is not yet possible to say the degree of importance cultivation of this precious bush will reach, but we surely can say its future is grand."[55]

The little-known protagonists of Huánuco's industrialized coca were immigrant Croats—among the first Juan Plejo in 1891, then José Más (a Spaniard, in fact), followed by Salvador Nesanovich. By the late 1890s, they were joined by fellow "Austro-Húngaro" or "Yugo-Slavo" cocaine makers: Juan Boyanovich, the brothers Manuel and Estevan Marinovich, plus the merchant Montero brothers, Juan Languasco, and three of the Durand brothers, Augusto, Gregorio, and Juan (see appendix, table A.3). Evidence suggests that Arnaldo Kitz, who after leaving Pozuzo landed in Huánuco in the early 1890s, lent his techniques to the Croats, who had originally entered Peru as skilled miners at Cerro de Pasco. Croats commingled with the suffering Germans of Pozuzo; a few trekked on to Monzón; others set up installations on tropical haciendas, veritable agroindustrial complexes, and, by 1900, workshops in the city center. The pioneers bartered and borrowed with merchant houses and emerging banks in Lima: Dammert, Grace, Banco Italiano, Banco Alemán Transatlántico.[56] Maybe their foreign accent (as well as technical skills) lent these men just the social respectability needed to differentiate "modern" export cocaine from Peru's timeworn upland coca peddling. In 1897, "Austriácos" (a term then referring to immigrants from most of southeastern Europe) were one of six groups of people, all of European extraction, given the status of "whites" in Huánuco Province, where some two thousand of them were outnumbered by ten times as many "Indians." By 1910, the Croats had become integral members of the regional elite, and their unusual (for Peru) last names still grace Huánuco commerce.

Huánuco property deeds and legal records trace specific Croat careers. "Juan Antonio" Plejo, for example, entered the area around 1891 and by 1892 was arranging massive coca purchases for his running factory. He related his operations with gusto to the inquisitive U.S. consul in 1891, lauding "the best leaves," Huánuco's, as his best-kept trade secret. Each kilo cost roughly eighteen to twenty *libras peruanas* to produce. By 1893, Plejo joined with the German merchant Schreiber in another factory, the first in Monzón. By the mid-1890s, Plejo was multiplying his capital by administrating the Ramo de Coca impost, an activity that sparked many complaints and suits. In 1912, Plejo also drew national attention from the famed muckraking Lima *indigenista* Pedro S. Zulen, who denounced Plejo's *cocal* Santo Toribio for "Esclavitud en Huánuco"—for "abusing" the

Indians of Panao, especially José Laurencio, whom Plejo refused to pay for contracted land improvements. By the teens, his factory faltered, though the Plejo family thrived into the 1920s, with a well-endowed 250-hectare coca hacienda, Santa Rosa de Quie, next door to the Durand factory.[57]

Salvador Nesanovich—who exhibited his cocaine and coca at world expositions, garnering a bronze medal at the 1904 Saint Louis fair—had a modest start in the early 1890s in Chinchao with his hacienda-workshop San Antonio. Nesanovich appears to have been a close partner, coca supplier, and agent of the Durands, with whom he co-rented farms and sometimes plants in the early 1900s. By then, Nesanovich, who also ran a copper mine, was well-off, able to raise in a 1902 partnership *S*/14,000 to branch into a new plant in Monzón. In 1909, he brokered another deal for a Derrepente factory. As with most of the founding Croats, low prices in the teens forced him to sell off land and workshops. Estevan Marinovich (and a brother, Manuel) joined the group later, tied to the fortunes of the Durand family. Born in 1865 in "Austro-Húngaro," Marinovich owned a factory by 1905 and by 1910 two factories, Paltos and Ascensión, as well as Derrepente *fundos*, one later sold to Augusto Durand. In 1911, he signed on to a massive cocaine deal with Emiliano Wiese, the Lima banker, arranged by Durand, who then bought one of his factories for *Lp*5,700. In 1917–18, the Marinoviches were among the main participants in Durand's last venture, a made-in-Huánuco "Sindicato de Cocaína." Like all the Croat pioneers (and fleeting others), their glory days were over by the 1920s, when they sold out to Durand or his successor, Soberón, and moved on to less risky trades. Croats (like other diasporas discussed ahead) show up in later acts of cocaine's history: a faction of Bolivia's landed elite of lowland Santa Cruz were also Croats, drawn into another sort of cocaine trade by the 1960s. This demonstrates, as the earlier diaspora of French and Germans of Lima also does, the vital role of cultural-technical diasporas as active agents of peripheral country trade, legal or illegal.[58]

At the peak of legal Peruvian cocaine, a surviving 1902 Huánuco "Administración de la Coca" tax register provides a picture of the structure of cocaine's regional trade network. Huánuco, the gateway on the main road out of central Peru's high *selva*, ran a "guía" coca transit tax, which, given leaf's bulk, provided a reliable revenue and record. At the retail level, scores of modest, anonymous coca farmers and itinerant traders (plying internal coca circuits) paid small imposts on a weekly basis. There were also more established merchants: Montero Brothers, Tello, or the Chinese house of Wing and Wing Chang (a new ethnic presence in sierra coca

Crude cocaine factory, Monzón, ca. 1900 (Marie Robinson Wright, *The Old and the New Peru* [Philadelphia: George Barrie and Sons, 1908], 446)

sales), warehousers and wholesalers to Lima of export-grade Huánuco leaf. In Lima-Callao, German, British, and American merchants consigned overseas sales of coca and, from Huánuco, crude cocaine, dispatched by German houses like Prüss and Dammert. The tax book depicts the cocaine makers themselves: from the small nearby workshops of Más and Languasco, registering 4–8 kilos weekly with authorities, to the dominant and distant producers Kitz and Company (with his deliveries from Pozuzo), Nesanovich and Marinovich (out of Monzón), and Plejo. These firms paid monthly taxes on substantial transshipments, 14–80 kilos of cocaine each, to Lima. In 1902, Salvador Nesanovich was the reigning regional industrialist, selling more than 600 kilos, eclipsing the fading Kitz and

Plejo concerns.[59] He made at least 7 percent of the 8,209 kilos of crude cocaine Peru officially placed overseas that year. The same coca levy that multiplied Croat fortunes in the 1890s would sustain Huánuco's public services for decades to come.

Crude cocaine was a success story in Peruvian terms, with its integrating regional pole of coca, the meteoric rise of exportable cocaine, and the displacement of competitors (even some world powers). Peru had a virtual world monopoly on the product by 1900. But the industry relied on a fairly simple and static technology. Kitz and others had adopted the Bignon formula to jungle conditions, using local materials and Peruvian chemicals. It was a good technology for 1890s Peru, well adapted to coca's remote geography. Almost all equipment was locally hewed, down to wooden piping and cisterns, making it an "appropriate" indigenous technology. A few practical improvements ensued—notably by the well-capitalized Augusto Durand after 1900—but the technique of these so-called factories (workshops) barely changed over time. Cocaine sulfates, through local praxis and lore, reached 80–94 percent purity, improving on Bignon's results. Most workshops ran on a part-time or intermittent basis, adapting to price spikes, shortages, direct orders from abroad, or the arrival of a fresh local delivery of leaf. Extraction of the drug involved a three-stage process of maceration, precipitation, and purification, and it minimized the use of modern inputs like kerosene and recycled bicarbonate of soda. Workshops required only three to five workers, who shipped out small batches of cocaine in carefully weighed bricks or in tin cans. Indicative of its low productivity, the process still used two hundred kilos of coca to produce each kilo of cocaine, at a production cost of £11. No one put up laboratories in Huánuco to test or update these routines, neither in coca culture, harvests, and drying nor in the Bignon-Kitz pulverization and leaching process.

This technological lag may have been due to the high costs of ferrying machinery or technicians over the Andes, to cocaine's volatile price, or to a Peruvian sense of low commercial rivalry or, by 1905, of saturated markets. A larger thread linking the 1880s to the 1980s is that the initial innovation, spread, and then long stagnation of this peculiar technology for producing crude cocaine sulfates conserved it as an entrenched *huanuqueño* regional specialty. Under pressure later in the 1950s, this local practice, or *metis*, was transferred to peasants and ad hoc chemists as *pasta básica de cocaína* (PBC, or coca paste), a key input in today's world traffic in illicit cocaine.

A few descriptions and early photos survive of Huánuco's jungle instal-lations, though most date from after 1905, when critics were already taking aim at the now-outmoded Bignon-Kitz method. By 1903, calls issued from Lima to upgrade to distillation of pure cocaine hydrochloride (HCl) or to adopt advanced European ecgonine alkaloid methods, surveyed in the official *Boletín de Fomento* by Pedro Paulet, one of Peru's top civil engineers. Alfredo Rabines, in the *Engineer* of London in 1911, detailed Peruvian procedures, adding: "The extraction of cocaine from the leaves of the coca plant as carried out upcountry in Peru is not by any means an up-to-date process. It is, however, the only method available to the farmers at the present time, as owing to distance."[60] Peruvians thus knew of overseas advances in cocaine efficiency and that better and surer profits pertained to the metropolitan pharmaceutical firms that refined and distributed medicinal cocaine globally. In this sense, this Peruvian industry had adapted all too well to the local opportunity niche offered by the global division of labor in scientific medicine and the German commodity chain that governed its heights.

There was a similar scrutiny of national coca cultivation, which had swiftly expanded to meet commercial opportunities during the 1890s yet had barely improved as an industrial crop. Peruvians held to age-old routines in cultivation, pruning, weeding, pest control, harvesting, dry-ing, and baling, despite formal advice from coca agricultural pamphlets. This was logical: ignored by colonial authorities, Peruvian (and Bolivian) peasants and backwoods *hacendados* were the bearers of all accumulated wisdom on the coca bush, European botanical experimenters aside. Coca was quickly transformed into a specialized input for cocaine. Cultivation intensified in places like the Chinchao, and extensive growth occurred along frontiers. But few *cocales* adopted "modern" or scientific practices in rotation, pruning, fertilization, seed selection, or soil testing, although improvements registered in drying and shipping techniques, encouraged by foreign merchants. Roads into coca zones remained primitive, seasonal, and few and far between. The effect was that Peru's established *cocales* (especially the cocaine-bearing ones near Huánuco) simply aged—deplet-ing soils, productivity, and their own long-term commercial prospects. In Peru, coca remained essentially a peasant crop—"left to the devices of the Indians until very recent times"—which posed a social obstacle to change, though with its own safety valve of local peasant leaf consump-tion. Even the larger commercial coca haciendas used archaic indirect labor systems, such as colonizing contracts or sharecropping, in order to attract (or exploit) scarce labor in the forbidding *montaña*. It was like the paradox of crude cocaine: what served well—peasant knowledge—did not easily progress.[61]

By 1905, during coca's commercial apex, Peruvians were becoming aware of these problems. Calls for agrarian change sounded from newly minted "national" agronomists (e.g., Carlos Bües or Alberto Martín Lynch) anxious to make coca more scientific for cocaine, that is, to give it a higher alkaloid content. There were also isolated improvements, such as the introduction of mechanical leaf driers by Durand on his model Éxito farm-factory; Durand even sponsored Taylorist labor studies of coca there. In 1912, Peru's national agrarian monthly, *La Riqueza Agrícola*, surveyed the "abandoned state" of Peruvian coca culture. Throughout the 1910s, coca critiques intensified from Lima and from informed *huanuqueños* such as Mario Durand and Manuel Vinelli, and as low-quality leaf slipped into local uses, a new national critique deplored the Indian "coca habit."[62] For after 1905, Peruvian coca had taken a crisis blow from unexpected quarters: the far more modern, productive, and scientific coca plantations taking off in Dutch Java. These elite assaults on cocaine empiricism, and local coca use, are examined fully in chapter 4 on cocaine's devolution of the twentieth century.

AUGUSTO DURAND: THE CAUDILLO OF COCAINE

After 1905, almost everything about Huánuco, including its cocaine, revolved around one central figure: Don Augusto Durand, the unrivaled commercial leader, financier, and spokesman—or, best put, the caudillo—of the Peruvian cocaine industry. Durand, still known as one of the key political actors of turn-of-the-century Peru, is not much recalled for his industrialism. Yet, as a 1923 obituary recounted, Durand "developed the country's cocaine industry on his Huánuco farms, having become one of the leading if not the world's largest producer of this alkaloid.... he brought to his farms the most modern advances of science, industry and mechanics. The first telephone, telegraph, rail, and first automobile reached his *montaña* lands."[63]

Augusto Durand Fernández de Maldonado has a multifaceted place in Peruvian and Huánuco lore as regional strongman, inveterate "revolutionist," political animal, self-proclaimed "moral caudillo," founder and *jefe* of the maverick Liberal Party, diplomat, journalist and owner of the Lima daily *La Prensa*, hero of Nicolás de Piérola's Revolution of 1895, and then president of Congress. After 1910, Durand emerged as the implacable foe of Augusto B. Leguía, who persecuted and finally eliminated Durand during his eleven-year Oncenio dictatorship (1919–30). Born in Huánuco in 1862, "Dr." Durand took a law degree at San Marcos with a thesis on "the people's right to rebel." He returned home to agricultural pursuits in the late 1880s before taking a sojourn to the United States and Europe during the height of cocaine fever there. A key fighter in the 1895 revolution that ushered in Peru's formative Aristocratic Republic (1895–1919), Durand continued to irk Lima authorities. Indeed, he again headed revolts against Lima in 1908 and 1914, earning exile abroad in 1907–8, 1911–12, and the early 1920s. After 1900, the Durand name dominated political life in Huánuco. Not just Augusto but also his brothers, Juan and Gregorio, all officials and businessmen, gathered a passionate clientele among militants drawn to the autonomy program of Durand's Liberal Party. Durand is a legendary figure, though not universally admired. Esteban Pavletich, a later Croat-*huanuqueño* rebel, immortalized Durand as the consummate *gamonal* (brutal Andean landowner), the fictionalized "Dr. Aníbal Morand" in his celebrated protest novel *No se suicidan los muertos* (The Dead Can't Kill Themselves), wherein the action is set on Chinchao cocaine hacienda Triunfo.[64]

There are two puzzles in Durand's relationship to cocaine. Were his interests in cocaine and coca largely a function of politics—a financial base to launch his political adventures? And did the industry suffer or gain from his politicized leadership? At the least, Durand's strong role suggests the depth of the ties between the cocaine industry and Peru's elitist Aristocratic Republic. In a larger political sense, it highlights coca's special historical role in fueling and funding local politics of the eastern Andes, vast spaces weakly integrated into the Peruvian state at Lima.[65] Coca circuits have exerted this kind of power during colonial rebellions, from Túpac Amaru's of the 1780s to that of Huanta's peasant royalists of the 1830s, from Huánuco as a stronghold of modern Aprista insurrectionists of the 1930s–40s to the fierce Maoist "narco-terroristas" of the 1990s Upper Huallaga.

Politics aside, the Durand name barely shows up in cocaine business prior to 1905, though Augusto had been farming coca since 1888. It is likely that Huánuco's Croats bequeathed Durand a developed field, which he would organize, articulate, and project on a grander scale—similar to the relation found a century later of Colombian traffickers to their still-anonymous 1950s Andean *narco* predecessors. In addition to a string of

Dr. Augusto Durand,
caudillo of cocaine
(William B. Parker,
Peruvians of To-day
[Lima: Hispanic Society
of Americas, 1919], 340)

estates straddling every ecological niche of Huánuco, the family had held the Derrepente San Carlos hacienda since 1846, which passed to Augusto in 1893. After 1905, its annex, Éxito ("Success") was host to Peru's principal cocaine installation. San Carlos was the productive jewel of the Chinchao, one of its few progressively managed estates. Local archives show the four Durand brothers (and then myriad offspring) as consummate deal makers, mobilizing banking capital, coca supplies, mortgages, and commercial, political, and familial linkages with the Croats, notably Nesanovich. After 1900, Durand also became synonymous with the "improver"—the cocaine magnate embracing progressive change, with San Carlos–Éxito held up as the model for all visitors, reporters, and reformers on the topic of Peruvian cocaine. Durand publicized his venture by inviting technical experts to use San Carlos as their base of operations. After 1910, it was Durand the consolidator: snapping up and uniting failing smaller plants with schemes to prop up falling cocaine markets, including grandiose plans in 1911 and 1918 for seller cartels.[66] Durand became the spokesman for a regional progress energized by cocaine and other tropical exports, freed from the dictates of Lima. Yet his was a kind of absentee leadership, broken by Durand's frequent political forays, though exiles abroad also helped Durand's larger business connections. Finally, with Durand hounded by Leguía, the 1920s family business hobbled on as the Negociación A. Durand (under his widow, Emilia, and Croatian manager Alfredo Mastrókola), slowly divested of former glories. Legal cocaine, its leadership passing to Soberón, entered its steady twentieth-century decline, taking Huánuco with it.

Huánuco's long-running paper, *El Huallaga*, sheds light on these developments. Just after 1900, cocaine's zenith, Huánuco underwent a political transition from control by Lima's imposed, often hostile prefects to a regional hegemony by kinsmen and partisans of Durand. By 1904, brother Juan Durand became Huánuco's activist mayor, and Augusto president of the provincial Sociedad Agrícola, as the "organic intellectual" of the *hacendado* class. Their brother, Gregorio, would soon head the Junta Departamental. Mayor Durand was an urban mobilizer of area coca fortunes, his political machine rooted in regional redistribution of surpluses generated by the Impuesto de la Coca. Durand rationalized the tax system and extended its scope beyond its mandated role for building Chinchao roads and funding local services, making it into a means of managing the regional cocaine network. Juan Durand, "his name alone the guarantee of progress," steered the helm of local politics through the 1910s.[67]

The Durands were also seeking to expand their economic base in line with greater Huánuco's. In 1903, Juan Durand, who besides being a *político* was one of Peru's most prolific geographers, published a call from the Chamber of Deputies for a trans-Andean railway scheme to link the Huallaga (i.e., Peru's Amazon basin) to the Pacific, not coincidentally via Huánuco City. A favored Durand cause here was the treasure found along the way, especially in the tropical belt of Chinchao y Derrepente — by now with seventy haciendas, 49,000 inhabitants, and "more than 18,000 day laborers," available at only "20–40 *centavos* a task"— suggesting the elite had resolved by now its historic labor problem. The zone hosted "the leading coca haciendas in the Universe . . . and its biggest concentration of factories." The Durand family complex, San Carlos, merited praise, as it was delivering over a thousand *arrobas* (twenty-five thousand pounds) monthly of top-notch leaf. At a hundred thousand pounds a year, this was a sixth of Huánuco's coca supply, and worth its exact weight in *soles*. Coca, according to Durand, could underwrite a "million-dollar *Trust*," the basis for a lasting regional prosperity linked by rivers and rails.[68] In

1909, with coca prices retreating and Amazon rubber beginning to boom, Juan Durand published another treatise on "los gomales de la región de Monzón," whose rubber wealth (and virgin timber) are measured by their proximity to San Carlos's elastic boundaries.

The biggest local news during the Aristocratic Republic was always clan chief Augusto Durand's comings and goings — literally on the road from Lima or figuratively in the shifting politics of the Liberal Party in the capital. The local press reveled in his profuse speeches, his every arcane political move. For Durand, in and out of jail and embroiled in high-stakes conflict with Leguía, this was cocaine's moment of glory. By 1910, Éxito was Peru's dominant factory, with Durand amassing the workshops of his neighbors, Cocheros and Ascensión in 1911 alone. A *Lp*9,940 Banco Wiese loan funded Durand's consolidation spree, assisted by local ally Marinovich. Durand's next project was even bolder: as cocaine prices dropped after 1910, the "indefatigable" caudillo unveiled in October 1911 his "Grand Trust de Cocaína." Formed in Europe against the "unscrupulous business" of Hamburg, the syndicate aimed to expend "5 million *soles* to buy up all the coca of Peru, put up new cocaine factories in the zones of production, and raise the price of this product." Some plan was unfolding: reports claimed "the majority [90 percent] of coca producers in the Department have celebrated contracts with Durand to sell him their coca...receiving advances for three years of crops...true protection for the workers of coca." This project, analogies to misnamed modern drug "cartels" aside, is best seen as an active response from peripheral Peru to the cocaine buyer syndicates that had arisen by 1910 among German pharmaceutical firms, and later across Europe.[69] Given the modest quantities in global circuits — under ten metric tons — cocaine prices were frequently and easily fixed by a clutch of large firms. Durand's campaign, if stymied by the world war, showed his clan's determination to leverage transnational links and local buying power in its attempts to steer the now-beleaguered industry of Huánuco. Harder to fathom is whether Durand was exploiting his political acumen to salvage cocaine or if the region's chief industry was instead mortgaged to fund his political career. This was not the last of Durand's pecuniary schemes for cocaine — a global one followed the war in 1918 — but it did mark the fading of the Durand-Croat alliance. Durand's audacious efforts clearly count as local "agency" in the logic of global drug trades.

By 1919, the erstwhile chief of global cocaine was being hunted down by Leguía's forces — through a botched ambush that year in Chinchao, army raids on the coca haciendas, and finally Don Augusto's scandalous political murder in April 1923, which sent many of the Huánuco Durands into exile. Cocaine, once Huánuco's guiding star, was left floundering in the 1920s, increasingly marginal in markets, technology, politics, and international prestige.

THE GLORIFICATION OF MODERN COCAINE

By 1915, after three decades, Peru's boom in legal cocaine was over. Sparked by overseas excitement about the drug, it began with tinkering Lima pharmacists and national promoters of the Amazon, spread out with Kitz's industrializing march to jungle Pozuzo, and migrated with enterprising Croats to central Huánuco until absorbed after 1900 into Durand's cocaine kingdom. After 1915, cocaine would devolve into a struggling regional culture, subject to new Peruvian debates on reforming national cocaine and to rising global controversies about menacing drugs.

Before its fall from grace, cocaine won very good press in Peru, lending the drug a modern, nationalist, and progressive image that would only haltingly fade during the twentieth century. This profitable new Peruvian commodity incarnated long-held fantasies of nineteenth-century liberals, medical men, and Amazonia boosters. To be sure, cocaine had not quite fulfilled the 1888 Ulloa commission's hopes of replacing "tea and coffee" on Western tables and work breaks, but it had conquered its best market. Nor had cocaine kept Peru's local science advancing, as Bignon and associates wished. But cocaine was the economic lifeblood of provinces like Huánuco, bringing the untamed jungle into the nation and establishing a lasting foothold in the north. It was the commodity that epitomized the liberal, autonomous, diversified, export-led modernization that economic historian Rosemary Thorp has termed "the rise [and fall] of a local developmental effort"[70] in early-twentieth-century Peru, tied into the restitution of modern Peruvian elite politics under the Aristocratic Republic. Cocaine sparked admiration because it had been developed due to a private entrepreneurial drive, without recourse to clumsy governmental action or archaic protection. Cocaine met long-delayed Peruvian desires for industry of its own and for a form of agro-processing suitable to this essentially agrarian country.

Moreover, in the broadest national or ideological sense, cocaine seemed to confirm the happy marriage of Peruvian history and tradition (el Perú profundo of Incan and indigenous coca cultures) with the strides of modern and universalist science and medicine (refined cocaine and its miraculous worldly utility). As Peru's truly hybrid gift to the world, cocaine became emblematic of the creole elites' insecure, fragmented, and contested modernist vision of Peruvian national identity. It was a "modernizing good." Furthermore, cocaine was applauded for its unique Peruvian-ness: no other nation could produce it, or so it seemed, given the country's natural coca monopoly (at first shared with backwardly Indian Bolivia) and the market-capturing local innovation of making crude cocaine in Peru. Cocaine seemed like a more honestly earned and serious product than the accidental and now-derided rentier monopolies in guano fertilizer of the nineteenth century or Spain's colonial silver—Peru's classic "false prosperities."[71] Such optimism about cocaine bred a Peruvian complacency to harsher realities: the cocaine sector's technical lags, its possible migration elsewhere (as happened with Peru-bark to colonial Asia), and the swift downturn in coca and cocaine's moral and economic stock after 1905 (particularly in the United States, once its own consumer and medical affair with the leaf and powder ended).

The prototypical voice for modern cocaine was Alejandro Garland—one of Peru's premier economists, officials, and publicists of the Aristocratic Republic. In 1896, Garland proclaimed cocaine's essential liberalism against other "artificial" industries, calling coca the "appropriate product of our soil and our own climate" and asking, "What protection has been demanded by the fabrication industry of cocaine?" His liberal economic stance was echoed by José M. Rodríguez, another leading industrial and trade specialist. Garland judged cocaine one of the top four "new" exports driving Peru's long-sought diversification. The same year, economic essayist José Clavero lauded liberal coca as one of the exemplary "treasures" of Peru: "Coca, a precious plant with Peruvian origins, of Cuzco, Huánuco and other interior lands, has grand applications in industry and science.... the paternal protection of the government will not deprive the world of its benefits." A decade later, at cocaine's apex in 1905, Garland returned to cocaine to celebrate its exemplary progress: "This new industry, so essentially Peruvian, has acquired a grand development in the past years.... Peruvian exportation of cocaine amply satisfies world demand.... it seems that Nature itself wished to conserve this plant for Bolivia and Peru." Coca was "a plant we must justifiably classify as miraculous." If sales of crude cocaine seemed to be peaking abroad, Garland envisaged unlimited prospects for coca sales for booming cola beverages and for export of Peruvian-made coca elixirs, bitters, and even wines. Sociologist Carlos Lissón's uplifting vision of coca from the decade before had come true: Peru had found a traditional good "that modern science makes into a huge article of commerce with portentous therapeutic applications."[72]

Across the nation, in literary salons and chambers of commerce, cocaine's prestige ran high. *Arequipeño* writer Percy Gibson counterposed cocaine to the coca habit of Indians: "Coca sustains the Indian's moral cadaver and his bestial body . . . but coca can convert into a reason for national industry and a fount of the country's riches." These modernist tropes about coca leaf and purifying cocaine would resonate in Peru for decades to come, though in time splitting into the dichotomy "good" cocaine, "bad" coca, the inverse of today's indigenous rights slogan. Cocaine's positive image persisted well beyond its time, for example, mirrored by economic essayist Eduardo Chocano: "Coca[,] the 'divine plant of the Incas' . . . who can ignore this ever-useful product, whose modern and unlimited scientific and industrial application provides such wide benefits? Coca[,] a bush so supremely and exclusively Peruvian, as if to say that nature has a special effort here . . . to make our country an original gift, or better put, at once so peculiar and useful."[73] Cocaine was a peculiarly Peruvian success story between 1885 and 1910 — the fruit of many local ideals and initiatives — and this legal commodity boom left its mark on the worldly saga of the Andean drug.

In 1910, legal Peruvian cocaine reached the end of its boom output and national honor. By 1915, it had fallen into full crisis — with the rise of new cocaine commodity chains rivaling the Germanic and American ones that had nurtured Peru's plantations and crude cocaine workshops. Most surprisingly, American demands for both drugs dwindled due to new antidrug laws designed to curb the sale of popular coca products and suppress the dreaded cocaine fiend. By 1920, diplomats began to project the U.S. anticocaine message onto the global stage, adding to Peruvian anxieties about coca leaf and the racial degeneracy of the country's Indian masses. Cocaine was no longer a legitimate or heroic world commodity. Peruvian cocaine, which stirred such high hopes at the advent of the century, entered a prolonged struggle — for markets, for nationalist rescue, and for lost honor — and withdrew into being a regional specialty of Huánuco, cocaine's historic haven. The next three chapters take on all of these topics.

II

COCAINE FALLING

COCAINE ENCHAINED

Global Commodity Circuits, 1890s–1930s

This chapter serves as a kind of bridge — or analytical interregnum — between cocaine's nineteenth-century formation as a global commodity and its commercial decline and eventual demise as a licit commodity during the first half of the twentieth century. Instead of building from archival detail, as in most of the book, in this chapter I adopt a more synthetic and explicit political economy and commodity perspective on cocaine. Specifically, I place cocaine's historic rise and fall in the context of global commodity chains as a way to portray and analyze the intrinsically global origins and ramifications of modern drugs such as cocaine.

The "commodity chain," a sociological conception first developed by so-called world systems theorists in the 1980s, is a heuristic or analytical tool that considers goods in the light of their global connectedness. Commodity chains are used to trace the discrete social and spatial networks that connect distant producers of commodities all the way through intermediaries and to consumers.[1] In terms of analytical work, commodity chains bring together in a single linked process the geographically segregated (and naturalized) worlds of supply and demand, zones of production and consumption that often exhibit highly distinct social relations and national cultures. More recently, commodity chain approaches have been exploited more generally, as I intend to do here with cocaine, to help bridge the gap between national units of analysis and the transnational, or to bridge the categorical separation of domains of material culture, commerce, and consumption. Commodity chains, for example, can be broadened conceptually to show how movements of goods are accompanied and facilitated by flows of culture, science, politics, prestige, and other immaterial exchanges. Thus, commodity chains converge with growing academic interest in the "social life of things"—the constructionist idea that goods are not just objects but rather that they possess deeper and often hidden relational histories and meanings.[2] Finally, in global commodity chains, world markets are rarely "free" in the conventional economic or policy sense. Rather, they are socially structured or segmented and infused by unequal levels of power. Commodity chains capture power differentials between actors in the "core" and "periphery" of the world and, by recognizing the agency in reciprocal flows, move beyond the deterministic spirit of once-popular (Latin American) dependency theory.

Andean coca leaf and industrializing cocaine offer a striking historical case for thinking about commodity chains. As we saw in chapter 2, neither existed as a significant commodity until the late nineteenth century, which allowed us to closely observe their complex sociohistorical transformations into marketable and exportable goods. As I will stress here, coca and cocaine, rather than entering into undifferentiated, abstract world markets, became organized into extended and distinctive transnational commodity networks, and these (especially via the tensions between rival chains) carry analytical significance for understanding cocaine's shifting long-term fortunes and politics. Such long-distance chains highlight how transnational forces interacted with local conditions in the development of cocaine—specific poles relating to varying coca-cocaine zones, defined regional product spheres even within the remote Andes.

The purpose here is to show the utility of thinking about coca and cocaine in distinct global commodity chains over long historical periods. As such, this chapter presents much of the book's larger quantitative data to illustrate the shape of these changing commodity movements, though these data do not easily lend themselves to robust aggregates or comparisons.[3] This chapter also delays discussion of illicit tastes and trades in cocaine, which, save for a turn-of-the-century eruption, were modest enough to have had a negligible impact on world cocaine production before 1950. Chapters 6 and 7 examine the birth of today's illicit chains of cocaine during the 1950s, 1960s, and 1970s.

The chapter is divided into two parts and periods. The first, 1860–1910, reviews in synthetic world commodity terms what we have seen so far about the creation of early Andean networks of coca and cocaine. Two major commercial chains linked nascent Andean coca to overseas markets—the German/European-Andean circuit and the U.S.-Andean circuit—along with minor French and British nodes of science and culture. This section also analyzes Bolivian coca, the key comparison case for understanding the retention of a regional, rather than globalized and industrialized, coca commodity chain. The second part looks ahead to the decades 1910–50, the era of mounting political and market constraints on coca and cocaine, related in part to rising international narcotics control. In this period, three commodity chains arose that worked to marginalize existing Andean cocaine, which had been closely tied to the declining German chain: a managed U.S. hemispheric network, a Dutch-European colonial network, and a Japanese Pan-Asian network. These new commodity chains, which crumbled during World War II, were a prelude to the illicit cocaine circuits that were to reintegrate the eastern Andes to the outside world by the 1970s.

THE GERMAN-ANDEAN CONNECTION

With deep roots in Andean cultural history, coca did not become an exportable commodity until the late nineteenth century. Global nineteenth-century commercial and scientific revolutions sparked a renewed interest in and appreciation for coca and for its alkaloid cocaine isolated in 1860. As seen in the preceding chapters, many of these signals emanated from abroad yet provoked dynamic responses in the Andes. Much had to change for coca to become a world commodity: Its scientific, medical, and ethnic prestige had to rise (in Peru and Bolivia as well as in Europe and North America). It needed "modern" uses, outlets, and spokesmen, and to become the focus of merchants, planters, colonizing labor, capitalists, shippers, consumers, and governments. These conditions all came together quickly after 1850 as European science settled the previously debatable question of coca's stimulant power, as industrializing societies searched for and developed new health stimulants (such as Vin Mariani and Coca-Cola) and embraced modern medical marvels (cocaine as local anesthetic and medicinal drug after 1885), and as Andean elites and nations vied for new export goods to speed their recovery from their republican-era economic fiascos.

Broadly speaking, the first impulse to the commodification of Andean coca and cocaine came from Germanic Europe (and to a lesser extent France) in the mid-nineteenth century; by 1900, Germany was the driving research and producing interest in cocaine. These influences were felt deeply in Peru, the largest exporter, and in how Peruvians organized the initial coca trades.

Interest in coca as a modern stimulant was awakened by the development of German alkaloid science. Andean traveler reports of early-nineteenth-century scientists von Humboldt (1801–3) and later Poeppig (1827–32) and von Tschudi (1838–40) sparked a global race to discover coca's active principle. Germany's leading chemists were involved: Wöhler (a founder of modern organic chemistry) personally arranged for the delivery of bulk samples of rare fresh coca by Karl Scherzer of the 1850s scientific mission of the Austrian frigate *Novara*, which finally acquired enough Bolivian leaf for German experimentation. Wöhler's student in Göttingen, Niemann, immediately used this coca in his laboratory isolation of "cocain" in 1860, beating out the other aspirants. In the following decades, Austrian medical men, most famously Freud in the mid-1880s, played the key early role in researching and fostering cocaine's medical uses.

The turning point was Freud's colleague Karl Köller's 1884 verification of cocaine's anesthetic powers, suggesting its first clinical use. As the first truly effective local anesthetic, cocaine swiftly revolutionized the possibilities and progress of Western surgery. Germans dominated the international controversies that soon spiraled around cocaine's scientific and medical properties and applications (and their ethical dimensions); Lossen, Lewin, Aschenbrandt, Ehlenmeyer, Hesse, Schroff, and others entered into these debates. All of them used the scarce medicinal cocaine hydrochloride made by E. Merck of Darmstadt, which following Niemann's discovery became the drug's sole world supplier based on modest but now regular imports of dried Peruvian and Bolivian leaf.[4] A pan-European interest in coca had steadily awakened since the 1850s, leading after 1885 into a frenzied decade-long boom. Cocaine was eminently German and modern: it epitomized the new applied German laboratory sciences, such as pharmacology and biochemistry, that were to push medicine into research-based allopathic models, and it related to the scientifically driven second industrial revolution.[5] Of Western powers, latecomer German industrialization was more science-intensive, larger-scale, and statist, rather than linked to agricultural traditions or newer colonial market ventures. Yet German verification of coca's usefulness via cocaine also spurred medical and commercial interest in coca leaf infusions among more herbalist and eclectic medical circles in France, Britain, and the United States, feeding into distinctive commodity chains there.

German interests and the port of Hamburg dominated the economic field. Merck enjoyed the experience, Andean connections, and product prestige, though it produced modest quantities, less than a kilo of cocaine a year before 1884. After cocaine's adoption in surgery, production soared to over five hundred kilos annually in 1890, fifteen hundred in 1898, and to more than twenty-four hundred kilos by 1902. Merck produced about a quarter of world cocaine, and for the decade after 1885 cocaine was the firm's single most profitable product line. More than a dozen German firms followed Merck into cocaine, among them Gehe, Riedel, and Boehringer, along with overseas branch houses. Hamburg auctions set the world price of coca. Merck's turning point came in 1884–86, at the advent of surgical and medical usage, when cocaine prices and output jumped five and twenty times, respectively. This spike caused a much-debated crisis in global coca supply. Merck's strategy, using agents sent to Lima, was to encourage nascent Peruvian suppliers of the semiprocessed sulfate cake known as crude cocaine. Crude cocaine could be shipped more efficiently and at lower cost than poor-quality dried leaf, and it was processed into medicinal-grade cocaine in Germany for Merck's burgeoning global sales network. It also fit the German scientific preference for modern cocaine. By 1900, almost all German imports — more than six thousand kilos yearly at its peak in 1903–5, worth nearly £100,000 — arrived in this form, making coca leaf obsolete for German manufacturers save for Farbwerke, which used the German ecgonine extraction method. German success promoting crude cocaine was, as argued in the last chapter, also a pivotal reason for the abandonment by the 1890s of rival colonial coca projects of the British in India or the Americans in Rusby's Parke, Davis mission.[6] By then, domestic national cocaine processing had spread to Britain, France, Switzerland (Hoffman-LaRoche for export), and smaller sites in Italy, the Balkans, Finland, Poland, and Russia.

The German turn to crude cocaine was also too successful: with world production in excess of fifteen metric tons by the early 1900s, medicinal markets were saturated and began to leak into nonmedicinal exports and uses. Merck soon successfully diversified into many other drug lines, although in 1913 it still registered an output of nearly nine thousand kilos of cocaine by tapping into the new coca supply routes from Asia. As cocaine profits and prospects slipped, by 1906 the clutch of German cocaine-making firms swiftly formed a cocaine syndicate with monopsonistic buying, cartel-pricing agreements, and strong organizational and regulatory ties to the German state. By 1911, the year of the first Hague antinarcotics convention, a secretive cocaine cartel involving most European export producers was formed in Basle. By the eve of the world war, which sparked military stockpiling of the drug, the European cocaine network was no longer primarily market driven.

A decisive factor defining the European network as a separate commodity chain is how European (largely German) interests entered and

TABLE 3.1 Merck Cocaine Production and Imports of Coca and Cocaine, 1879–1918

Year	Merck Production (kg)	Peruvian Coca (kg)	Peruvian Crude Cocaine (kg)	Dutch Java Coca (kg)	Crude Cocaine of Java Leaf (kg)
1879–80	0.05	25			
1880–81	0.05	25			
1881–82	0.09	58			
1882–83	0.30	138			
1883–84	1.41	655			
1884–85	30	8,655			
1885–86	70	18,396			
1886–87	257	3,629	389		
1887–88	300		375		
1888–89	303		350		
1889–90	511		595		
1890–91	557		585		
1891–92	436		434		
1892–93	505		558		
1893–94	626		656		
1894–95	645		683		
1895–96	791		1,081		
1896–97	831		870		
1897–98	1,509		1,819		
1898–99	1,553		1,832		
1899–1900	1,564		1,695		
1900–1901	1,418		1,991		
1901–2	1,886		2,116		
1902–3	2,454		2,745		
1903–4	2,157		2,821		
1904–5	2,426		2,885		
1905–6	2,469		2,487	58,967	323
1907	1,881		953	94,018	1,647
1908	3,642		1,634	220,429	3,721
1909	4,183		1,239	238,066	3,972
1910	5,241		3,151	186,127	3,183
1911	4,681		2,072	261,254	4,080
1912	6,049		1,384	422,776	6,552
1913	8,683		1,226	724,189	10,683
1914	6,212		791	487,245	7,295
1915	265			203,972	2,966
1916	447			68,380	829
1917	1,246				
1918	1,738			6,744	72

Source: See appendix.

shaped Peruvian economic space. In the 1860s and 1870s, as we have seen, Peruvian medical and national spokesmen—men such as Fuentes, Moreno y Maíz, Ulloa, and Ríos—overcame traditional elite prejudices and began seriously to reevaluate native coca as a now-marketable good. For a host of cultural and institutional reasons, French medicine was the standard in Peru, and the major post–Pacific War Peruvian actor in this circuit, the remarkable Alfredo Bignon, was a naturalized Frenchman in Lima, though he shared the German penchant for cocaine. But commercial developments, which made Peru by 1890 the monopoly supplier of both world coca and cocaine, followed German cues and connections (and some emerging American coca trends). Between 1884 and 1887, Bignon's experiments on cocaine in Lima—mirroring Freud's on the European side of the cocaine chain—perfected his simplified method for distilling crude cocaine, which was promoted by Lima medical circles and by official Peruvian commissions. But by 1886, German pharmacists in the capital—figures like Meyer and Hafemann—emerged as the dynamic cocaine processors, sending their product on to Hamburg via local German merchant houses like Prüss and Schröder.[7] Boehringer also sent a chemist to Lima with the same plan. The Franco-Peruvian circuit was outflanked by German commercial science, and metropolitan firms like Merck, once Bignon's innovation had generalized, had no use for Peruvian science.

It was Arnaldo Kitz, a German merchant arriving in Lima as a commercial agent for Merck, who went further to the source of supply: the eastern Andes. By 1890, Kitz had marched off to isolated Pozuzo, home of an 1850s Austrian peasant colony, to set up the region's first working cocaine factory. Scherzer, who advocated for Pozuzo, had predicted in 1861, within a year of cocaine's isolation, "extracting *on the spot* the active principle of coca."[8] In producing areas, Bignon's invention soon became known as the "Kitz formula." By 1892, Peru's crude cocaine earnings surpassed revenues from coca leaf. In the mid-1890s, Kitz shifted operations from the jungle to nearby Huánuco, with its fertile Chinchao *montaña* estates and its prized cocaine-making leaf. For the next six decades, this district remained the Andean capital of cocaine, delivering virtually all of its output to Germany until World War II. Much Peruvian enthusiasm went into colonizing and industrializing *montaña* coca lands from 1885 through 1910 with the help of Croatian immigrants, drawing in thousands of peasant workers and sharecroppers. By 1900, greater Huánuco Province was home to a dozen cocaine manufactories, more than half the country's total, with a regional elite rooted in coca and cocaine, dominated by the regional boss, Augusto

Durand. Durand drew on links to "German" finance (e.g., Banco Wiese or Banco Alemán Transatlántico in Lima) but also focused regional resistance, in his cartel schemes, to by-then-monopolistic German domination. These complex local structures of production — particularly the commercialized core Huánuco zone — were oriented to and connected over thousands of miles to German pharmaceutical concerns, and they would remain so, despite cocaine's sinking fortunes, until the eve of World War II.

Around 1901, which was, in the eyes of German consuls in Lima, Peru's zenith of legal cocaine, total production peaked at 10,700 kilos of crude cocaine, which required the processing of some 1,600 metric tons of raw coca leaf. Peru still also exported 610 tons of coca leaf (more than half of that northern Trujillo leaf to the United States), for a national export of 2,200 tons. Huánuco coca, used more for cocaine, fetched a premium price. As usual, these numbers do not quite add up, but following traditional estimates of 15 million pounds of Peruvian coca overall, the export boom likely left about three-quarters of national coca in indigenous circuits, much of that leaf grown in the *cuzqueño* south.[9] Together, and fleetingly, coca and cocaine were Peru's fourth-highest export earner, and they continued to excite the developmental imagination of liberal national elites. Some 97 percent of Peru's crude cocaine flowed to Hamburg just as German imports were peaking between 1905 and 1914.

Along with Germanic alkaloid cocaine, medical, commercial, and popular fascination grew with herbal coca leaf. Also a global movement, "coca mania" was particularly pronounced in France and Britain (and reached its height later in the United States), and it had distinctive cultural roots and associations, some with imported Andean accents. In 1863, as we have seen, Angelo Mariani launched his remarkably successful Vin Mariani coca-Bordeaux elixir, which swept the world with its sophisticated marketing and health campaigns. Between 1863 and 1885, before the surge of cocaine, Mariani became the largest buyer of Andean coca, mostly from Bolivia. Parisian awe for and medical opinions on coca filtered to Peru via shared institutional cultures and transcultural figures like the Peruvian scientist Dr. Tomás Moreno y Maíz (who settled in Paris in the 1850s) and Bignon in Lima. Despite this flowering half-century cult around coca, and despite some serious cocaine research, the French cocaine industry remained small, consisting of producer firms Midy, Houdé, and later Roques, with modest national consumption.[10] It would be hard to characterize French involvement in coca and cocaine as a commodity chain; if it was one, it was a faint one defined by one central commodity, Vin Mariani.

Influential British botanists, pharmacists, and medical men, famously Spruce, Martindale, and Christison, also fixed on coca as a health and workday stimulant. They would long defend coca tonics and medicine on their own therapeutic terms, as seen in the slant of medical and pharmacy journals like the *Chemist and Druggist* and the *British Medical Journal*. Domestic coca wines and herbal concoctions thrived in London, which had, like France, vibrant plant-based materia medica pharmacy traditions. With the mid-1880s cocaine boom, however, the Royal Botanic Gardens at Kew, which had worked wonders with Amazonian cinchona and rubber and which had a historic tie to coca dating to its 1840s director, pioneer coca botanist Sir William Hooker, began a crash program of coca research and colonial botanical experiments in India, Malaysia, Jamaica, Guiana, West Africa, and elsewhere — as did the Dutch, French, and even, fleetingly, the Germans in Africa. At home, medicinal-grade cocaine was made by Burroughs, another Andean plant explorer, and later by May and Baker. Although coca took well to places like Madras, by the 1890s it was discouraged as a colonial crop, save for the purpose of making coca elixirs from Ceylon. Clements Markham, the tropical commodity imperialist who knew Peru well, came down against commercial coca, eclipsed by the rapid success of the German-Peruvian crude cocaine nexus. By the 1920s, Indian coca was a relic, as were British consumer coca goods. Thus, Britain, still the world's reigning economic power, never became a force in global coca-cocaine: in short, it was a commodity chain that never unfolded. If it had, creating a vested British colonial stake in cocaine, the drug's twentieth-century trajectory might have been different.[11]

The German-Peruvian chain thrived also, perhaps, at the expense of Bolivia's possibilities in modern coca. Bolivia, with its deep-rooted and robust Andean coca culture, did participate in the initial commodification of coca after 1860, but it ultimately differed from Peru in two respects: it never became a substantial exporter of the leaf abroad, nor was Bolivian coca industrialized into cocaine.[12] In short, Bolivia was never subsumed into global commodity chains. Instead, Bolivia's *yungas* coca zones nurtured a supraregional leaf circuit extending into northern Chile and Argentina for "traditional" indigenous and "modern" worker (migrants, miner) usage. Bolivia became a protagonist in global cocaine only after the 1952 revolution, when it would be a pioneer site of illicit coca-cocaine capitalism. Comparison study of the "Pan-Bolivian" regional circuit sheds light on neighboring Peru's distinctive and particular commodity linkages.

Nineteenth-century observers routinely sized up Bolivia's coca crop at half of Peru's: 7 million pounds, versus Peru's 15 million of "30 million pounds" across the whole Andes. This is a crude and misleading guess dating to the 1790s, shortly after Upper Peru (Bolivia) was carved out of the Spanish Viceroyalty of Peru by colonial fiat. Though few hard facts are known about Bolivia's coca before 1900, between 1850 and 1950, production likely ranged from 2.2 to 4 million kilograms a year. Bolivian coca differed from Peru's in two major respects. First, Bolivian coca enjoyed greater postcolonial continuity. The bush thrived in the warm *yungas* ravines of the Río Beni watershed just east of La Paz, high microclimates akin to the Peruvian *montaña*, and, on a lesser scale, in the *yungas* of Cochabamba. Bolivian coca suffered less postcolonial disruption and geographic constriction than Peru's, which was wracked by the devastating late-colonial Túpac Amaru revolts, as well as by insurgent Amazonian Indians before 1860. Second, in geographic terms, Bolivian coca proved more central to integrating Bolivian national spaces than Peruvian coca. In Peru, coca held on in weakly linked, remote Amazonian watersheds and the Indian sierra, both zones of Peru largely off the map for postcolonial Peruvian elites and national authority clustered on the coast around Lima, Trujillo, and Arequipa. In Bolivia, the *yungas* lay next door to La Paz, the country's new altiplano capital. About a third of Bolivia's 1 to 1.8 million nineteenth-century inhabitants nestled in that department. Indeed, coca, for Indian communities or miners at Oruro or Potosí, was the one product that linked the fractured economic and social spaces of Bolivia, especially the north-south axis between La Paz and Potosí-Sucre, in the long era between the fall of colonial silver and the rise of tin mining later in the century. Mining was for export, and coca was a trade closely linked to mines that animated Bolivia's weak national market.[13]

Moreover, the coca culture of the *yungas*, if more diverse in land tenure than assumed (with a mix of large haciendas, farmers, and fifty-eight active coca-growing *ayllu* indigenous communities), still enjoyed the strong participation of the national elite. Major families and lobbies were invested in the leaf, and as far as the culture of coca usage, Bolivians of all walks knew and embraced coca. La Paz, with only forty thousand souls in 1885, was "nine-tenths Indian," at least in Rusby's American gaze, which meant open coca use even in the capital. Coca's centrality was epitomized by the formation in 1830, just after independence, of the Bolivian Sociedad de Propietarios de Yungas (SPY), led by dynasties like the Gamarra, Iturralde, Romecí, and Ascarrunz families. It become one of Bolivia's longest-standing and most decisive political associations, followed by regional branches in

Cochabamba (1897) and the lowland Chapare. The Gamarra family alone owned seven coca estates, including five of the country's largest. This translated directly into political influence: *yungas* landlords contributed a third of turn-of-the-century ruling Liberal Party members, articulating coca with the central state.[14] Thus, in contrast with Peru (where coca interlaced elite families only in a few remote provinces), no major political or cultural controversies erupted around coca, at least until the 1940s, despite Bolivia's sharp ethnic divides and structures of domination. In Bolivia, no upper-class medical movement was needed to resuscitate coca as a viable national good, because it already was one, and core Bolivian elites, including diplomats at international drug conventions, would vigorously defend coca use throughout the early twentieth century in an era when Peruvian science began to view coca, if not cocaine, as a racial vice. Thus, Bolivians barely suffered Peru's various shifting schisms — spatial, social, economic, medical — between "traditional" (i.e., backward) coca and "modern" (i.e., scientific) cocaine.

The key unanswered questions are why Bolivian coca did not join in the regularized commodity chains to the United States or Europe that formed in the 1880s and 1890s and why Bolivian coca resisted industrialization. In other words, why did Bolivian coca stay bounded in a regional leaf circuit? Bolivia perhaps can be considered as a link in the early but fading nineteenth-century French coca chain. Opportunities presented themselves: small irregular shipments did come from Bolivia, such as the 1860s coca leaf purchases that got Vin Mariani off the ground, or indeed the early batch gathered for Niemann's isolation of cocaine. Statistics on further 1860–1890s exports are hard to come by. In the mid-1880s, the *yungas* figured prominently in Rusby's and consular scouting reports for U.S. drug firms.[15] The U.S. consul general in La Paz cited a figure of "5 per cent" (i.e., 170,500 kilos) of Bolivia's "7,500,000 pound" crop as shipped to the United States and Europe (and 40 percent for Argentina, Chile, and Peru combined). This figure exaggerates, since records of Bolivia's exports to Europe for Vin Mariani in 1885 reveal only 22,000 kilos at the height of that trade before declining to less than 10 percent of Europe's leaf imports over the next decade. New York and London drug buyers recognized a branded "Bolivian" leaf (although it was actually from the same bush as Huánuco's), which enjoyed a quality and price premium, though after 1900 France was its sole market. And Bolivian leaf, as later events would show, was just as viable for making cocaine. Even into the 1920s, long after overseas sales withered, Bolivians could dispatch up to

40,000 kilos on special demand for French elixir makers. In the 1950s, firms like New Jersey Merck and even Coca-Cola intermittently scouted Bolivian Indian markets, or at least threatened to use them as a bargaining chip against established Peruvian suppliers. Nor were close-by Chilean or Argentine consumers of the leaf good alternatives, as officials there sporadically banned coca imports.

I can speculate about the reasons why a legitimate Bolivian coca export chain never developed in the late nineteenth and early twentieth centuries, but research is still needed to explain Bolivia's apparent coca involution. Geography alone was a big factor: within Bolivia, *yungas* estates lay close to their core traditional consumers (the "Aymara race") and, compared to those of Peruvian growers, faced far higher transport costs down to the coast and abroad. Overseas buyers invariably cited Bolivia's high transport costs in explaining their choice of Peruvian leaf. Thus, except during acute shortages, relative prices favored Bolivia's healthy domestic leaf market. The obstacles occasioned by Bolivia's loss of its Pacific ports to Chile following defeat in the Pacific War worsened these shipping difficulties. In sociological terms, the mercantile elite who plied coca were virtually all Bolivian and were themselves embedded in the regional coca networks. In Peru, merchants, especially near coastal ports, were just as oriented to European products and markets, particularly the émigré houses (German, French, and British) that became leading coca consignees. Bolivia also faced constraints generating a coca surplus. Bolivia's geography of coca, fixed historically by the intensely cultivated, narrow *yungas*, had likely reached its productive limit by the mid-nineteenth century, with no active frontier. Indeed, until the 1910s, over nine-tenths of Bolivia's two-to-three-million-kilo crops issued out of the terraced *yungas* of La Paz.[16] (In 1913, the *yungas* portion of the crop was recorded at 97 percent, mostly from Nor y Sud Yungas and Inquisivi, with only 3 percent from Cochabamba and Santa Cruz.) Opening new coca zones in lower-altitude Amazonia below the *yungas* would have required impossible investments in roads and willing colonizers. In contrast, Peruvian coca zones enjoyed room for expansion, as farmers were actively recuperating coca frontiers lost to Amazonian natives and political breakdowns since the 1780s. Peru expanded its capacity quickly to meet overseas demand in the 1880s and 1890s. Bolivia's coca transformation, accompanied by a new politics of coca, would wait until the 1940s and 1950s, first with the rapid growth of the Cochabamba's *yungas*, then with the explosion of a new-style peasant coca in Amazonian Chapare, Beni, and Santa Cruz after the 1952 revolution.

TABLE 3.2 Bolivian Coca Production and Exports, 1900–1942

Year	Production (kg)	Exports[a] (kg)
1900		347,128
1901		255,718
1902		156,095
1903		211,595
1904		—
1905		216,853
1906		—
1907		—
1908		97,576
1909		163,586
1910		195,000
1911		252,276
1912		96,197
1913		81,550
1914		347,700
1915		389,300
1916		331,900
1917		362,548
1918		355,151
1919		413,100
1920		365,300
1921		373,053
1922		315,053
1923		342,606
1924		376,042
1925	2,355,200	388,802
1926	3,439,730	438,000
1927	3,671,950	360,000
1928	3,420,617	399,000
1929	3,309,010	433,000
1930	3,067,050	44,700
1931	3,282,744	407,000
1932	2,852,184	347,000
1933	3,392,293	336,000
1934	3,177,302	205,000
1935	3,140,052	340,200
1936	2,677,000	—
1937		—
1938		—
1939		447,000
1940		469,000
1941		382,000
1942		373,000

Sources: See appendix.

[a] Primarily to Argentina and Chile.

To say what Bolivian coca did not become — a starting link in a global commodity chain — does little justice to the dynamic regional circuit that continued to thrive and has long produced a feisty nationalist politics of coca (still evident today in current president Evo Morales, former head of the national coca growers' union). Nor does it explain coca's delayed industrialization except to say that German-Peruvians got there first and fast cornered the market in crude cocaine. We have a fine panorama of Bolivian "liberal coca" as it looked around 1900, broader than what remains for Peru because the Bolivian state and local bodies always held a greater stake in coca (its stablest source of tax revenue) and thus in censuses and record keeping. In 1902 — the peak of the legal world coca-cocaine trade — there were 167 active haciendas in the *yungas* supplying about a fifth of the national crop. Dozens of Indian *ayllus* also commercialized coca, employing time-honored forms of community labor exchange. Some 28 percent of Bolivian leaf was still consumed around the exhausted mining pole of Potosí.[17] Scarcely any *yungas* coca — less than 0.01 percent of recorded crops — exited the Andes overseas through the port of Mollendo. Yet a busy class of national merchants and muleteers plied it across Bolivia, and about 10 percent of the harvest (a low count of 156,000 kilos in 1902) moved into northern Argentina, mainly for Bolivian migrant sugar workers and their counterparts in Salta, Tucumán, and points south. About a tenth of those exports flowed to Chilean nitrate workers and other miners in the northern deserts taken from Bolivia and Peru in the Pacific War. By 1902, cross-border sales to southern Peru's indigenous zones had dried up as Peru's own coca plantations crept south. These coca routes were essential to Bolivian finances (underwriting 42 percent of La Paz's treasury), to upkeep of roads and local commercial life, and to bridging the country's vertiginous ecological and ethnic niches, but they had a negligible impact beyond the Andes. Much would have to change — as it did dramatically in the 1950s — for Bolivian coca to finally link up with global commodity chains.

THE U.S.-ANDEAN CHAIN

To grasp the Andean circuits firmly, we need to draw out another coca commodity chain: the one between the United States and Peru. North American interest in coca and cocaine grew after 1860, explosively after 1884. In contrast to Germany's cocaine, however, the U.S. chain also had a pronounced medical, cultural, and political-economic bias toward coca leaf. In 1900, Americans were the world's largest, most avid consumers and boosters of both substances, by then seemingly domesticated, all-American goods. By 1910, however, American attitudes and policies had dramatically turned against coca and cocaine alike, and the United States began its long global campaign to banish cocaine. In the broadest perspective, U.S. relationships to coca must be seen as a part of expanding informal U.S. influence in the Andean region, and, as this book argues, the United States exerted the decisive influence on the drug's longer history.

North American fascination with coca leaf, sparked by the European coca movement, took on distinctive tones. As we have seen, by the 1870s, American doctors, pharmacists, and entrepreneurs were actively discovering coca. Mariani's firm opened its most successful branch office in New York, accelerating the spiraling growth in Americans' taste for the herb. Leading American physicians, such as William S. Searle, traded notes and coca samples with their Peruvian counterparts. Coca soon became among the most widespread additives in popular remedies and tonics, prescribed for a vast range of conditions and ills, real and imagined. Most of these maladies were related to neurasthenia, the American condition of brain or "nerve exhaustion" linked to fast-paced urban life.[18] Thus, coca began as a brain worker's salve, though by the 1890s its use was spreading across (or down) the social (and racial) spectrum, and its commercial preparations included concoctions spiked with pure cocaine instead of coca leaf extracts. Pioneer American drug firms, such as Parke, Davis, at first specialized in coca medicines. While scores of respectable U.S. physicians experimented with, wrote on, and debated the merits of coca (and later cocaine), coca's appeal derived mainly from the herbalist or Thomsonian eclectic healer tradition, a lively native alternative to rising, often European-inspired, allopathic medicine. The Gilded Age romance with coca resounds in W. Golden Mortimer's classic 1901 *History of Coca: "The Divine Plant" of the Incas* (which argued at length for the therapeutic singularity and superiority of coca leaf) and in Mark Twain's tale of his youthful quest to fulfill the American dream by making a fortune in coca. The age of American coca lives on in our national soft drink, Coca-Cola, launched in 1886 by Atlanta pharmacist John S. Pemberton as a dry southern imitation of Mariani's health beverage.[19] Within a decade, Coca-Cola was a pathbreaking commodity, and the company was a burgeoning buyer of the leaf. By the early 1900s, Americans imported six hundred to a thousand metric tons of coca annually, mainly for such popular markets. New York was coca leaf's world entrepôt, as Hamburg was of cocaine.

TABLE 3.3 U.S. Coca Imports and Cocaine, 1882–1931

Year	Coca Imports (tons)	Total Cocaine[a] (tons)	Year	Coca Imports (tons)	Total Cocaine (tons)
1882	30	0.19	1907	758	5.52
1883	4	0.03	1908	317	2.10
1884	25	0.16	1909	550	4.45
1885	191	1.20	1910	354	7.70
1886	253	1.59	1911	613	3.97
1887	201	1.31	1912	590	3.75
1888	241	1.59	1913	588	3.80
1889	147	1.38	1914	356	2.33
1890	56	0.85	1915	524	3.29
1891	37	0.83	1916	474	3.07
1892	121	1.82	1917	317	2.60
1893	331	4.19	1918	530	3.58
1894	155	2.98	1919	512	3.81
1895	234	2.90	1920	452	3.18
1896	419	3.67	1921	153	1.16
1897	479	3.58	1922	17	0.33
1898	230	2.37	1923	151	1.03
1899	167	1.67	1924	111	0.69
1900	539	4.55	1925	50	0.31
1901	696	5.57	1926	131	0.81
1902	891	8.21	1927	132	0.83
1903	997	8.58	1928	118	0.74
1904	685	5.32	1929	120	0.75
1905	951	6.11	1930	111	0.69
1906	1,325	8.46	1931	179	1.11

Sources: See appendix.

[a] "Cocaine" is aggregate of imports and U.S. production but may overstate total because of imports of beverage coca leaf.

The United States actively promoted initial Andean coca trades and left an early mark there. In 1877, Peru exported only eight thousand kilograms of coca, apart from Bolivia's modest sales. During the 1884–87 coca scarcity, coca supply and domestic growing proposals were hotly discussed in American pharmacy journals. Parke, Davis sent its company ethnobotanist, Henry Hurd Rusby—a towering figure in American pharmacy—on a vital coca mission to Bolivia to scout out new supplies, processing methods, and native coca therapies.[20] The U.S. Navy, in cooperation with the surgeon general and consuls in La Paz and Lima, worked to identify and secure coca supply routes from the Andes. In the 1890s, U.S. commercial attachés in Lima pursued contacts with local cocaine makers (including the German Kitz) but mainly aided Peruvian merchants to upgrade their coca-shipping and leaf-drying practices. Peruvian producers responded to these cues and market signals, more than doubling their coca exports during the 1890s.

American physicians and pharmaceutical companies also welcomed the 1884 discovery of cocaine as an anesthetic and expanded its gamut of modern medical uses, though they realized soon enough the drug's potential dangers, limits, and lures. By the mid-1890s, major U.S. firms — among them Parke, Davis, Schieffelin, Mallinckrodt, and Merck — competed vigorously with German suppliers.[21] By 1900, they were refining a total of five to six metric tons of cocaine per year, about a third of world supply. Total U.S. consumption, including domestically refined cocaine and European imports, peaked around nine tons in 1903, or about two-thirds of all global usage. Even 1890s tariff politics entered into play: new high, effective tariffs on cocaine, which allowed herbal coca to enter the country for free, strongly favored home production of cocaine from leaf imports. Peruvian crude cocaine processors recognized this complex bias, and European branch firms (like Merck in Rahway, New Jersey) adapted by refining coca in the United States. Due to the consumer taste for coca — soaring after 1900 with Coca-Cola's spectacular national market successes and its many "cola" imitators — and the country's relative proximity to the Andes, which allowed import of fresher, cheaper leaf, the United States never made the switch to imports of Peruvian crude cocaine.

After 1900, U.S. buyers focused increasingly on the distinctive northern Peruvian coca leaf circuit of La Libertad instead of Huánuco's *montaña* cocaine lands, Cuzco's Indian leaf markets, or the leaf of remoter Bolivia. Grown under drier conditions west of the Andean escarpment, "Trujillo"-branded leaf was deemed more flavorful and less odorous, and thus best for tonics, such as the secret Merchandise No. 5 in Coca-Cola. Transport costs for bulky leaf shipped via the nearer northern port of Salaverry to New York proved lower than anywhere else in the Andes. Thus, La Libertad's Otuzco and Sacamanca districts evolved into the long-term supply shed of leaf (after 1903 specially decocainized) for Coca-Cola, organized by oligarchic regional merchant notables such as the Goicocheas and Pinillos with ongoing ties to American contract buyers. In a remarkable twist across commodity chains, the man charged with taking the cocaine out of Coca-Cola (and whose family firm carried this skill into the 1960s) was Louis Schaeffer, who left Peru after his 1880s cocaine mission for Boehringer to set up shop as a maker of American coca syrups in Maywood, New Jersey. In short, the German and North American chains developed around different cultural, medical, business, and political principles and even articulated to distinguishable spatial poles and social networks within the Andes.[22]

Finally, one need note the first surge of American anticocainism. A long story itself—told here in chapter 5—growing American disillusionment with cocaine (and, less rationally, coca) was a reaction to early enthusiasm for the drug. Cocaine became a symptom of the ambivalent love-hate "American disease" (to borrow David Musto's term) of drugs as both a cultural cure-all and scourge.[23] By 1900, dominant medical and governmental opinion had begun to turn against unregulated cocaine, along with alcohol and true narcotics, due to anxieties about the spread of drug "fiends" and underclass illicit use. By 1915, the United States had become a lonely crusader in world anticocainism, starting out by portraying rival Germany as a kind of evil drug empire. Domestic coca and cocaine controls, legally erected between 1906 and 1922, worked many paradoxical effects, some still with us today, such as the banning of harmless consumer coca. As the supply and demand for cocaine became regulated and reduced through an intricate system of coca controls, the outcome was a high degree of state–pharmaceutical firm cooperation in defining the trade and in defining U.S. interests in or against coca. By the 1920s, only two New Jersey firms—the Americanized Merck and Coca-Cola partner Maywood Chemical—dealt with coca and cocaine, and the business assumed a monopolistic form. In many ways, drug legislation institutionalized for cocaine control purposes the long American favoritism toward leaf imports. The effect was a centralized and state-governed coca chain—in that sense, not so different from the cartelized European chain of cocaine.

GLOBAL COCA UNDER PRESSURE, CA. 1905–1910

By 1905–10, licit cocaine's apogee, two distinctive coca commodity chains articulated with the Andes increasingly linked to two differing products and zones within Peru. Since 1860, interest in cocaine had swiftly circled the world: scientific flows surfaced in Germany, Austria, Switzerland, France, Britain, Italy, Russia, Japan, the United States, Peru, and Argentina. As a consumer item, or even as a newly discovered pleasure drug, cocaine soon enough sparked local drug scenes and panics in India, Australia, Egypt, Holland, France, Germany, Russia, England, Chile, Cuba, and especially in American cities and across the American South. Two sets of documents from the era speak eloquently to the global reach of cocaine commodity chains after their two decades of expansion and to the political tensions already rising along their links. One, from 1909–10, is a detailed memorandum on cocaine issued by the British Foreign Office and colonial Imperial Institute — produced at the behest of the Chinese sovereigns. It informs them about this exotic and "pernicious" Western drug, which Chinese officials feared might soon come to replace their opium scourge of the nineteenth century. The memo offers details on the "bodily effects" of the drug, the sources of commercial leaf supplies (in Peru and increasingly Java), and the abandoned colonial growing experiments elsewhere. It lays out Peru's strictly bifurcated trade pattern through export series of coca leaf to the United States (2,650,141 pounds worth $488,545 in 1905–6) and of crude cocaine to Europe via Hamburg (6,313 kilos for £108,600 in 1906). The Imperial Institute still saw coca prospects in Ceylon, then peaking at 24,000 kilos, but strictly for English coca preparations. The Foreign Office reviews the known habits of "cocainists"— in American jargon, the cocaine fiend — cocaine's formal ban in China, and the new Poisons Acts at home and their legal ramifications in the colonies, as Britain already had a worrisome cocaine problem in India. To British specialists, cocaine was a global drug with a markedly ambiguous profile.[24]

The second set of global documents consists of the reports of Eduardo Higginson, the distinguished Peruvian consul general in New York, as he closely observes the coca trade's reversals in the leaf's key port during the critical juncture 1904–12. While marshaling market statistics and business advice for suppliers in Peru, in 1904 Higginson gloats about the spectacular growth of "refreshing and invigorating soda beverages [i.e., Coca-Cola]" in the United States, which offset the bias of U.S. tariffs hurting Peruvian cocaine makers. As coca was Peru's product alone, the consul assures readers of the prospects of continual growth in the coca leaf business. Yet midway through his tenure, in 1907 (the same year Finance Minister Garland lauded cocaine as "the essentially Peruvian industry"), Higginson's reports suddenly turn sour. He notes the alarming new anticocaine laws and passions in the United States and a sharp 50 percent drop in coca imports through New York. He calls on Peruvians to form a "trust" (a then-popular term in the United States) to handle this volatile market, something we know national cocaine magnate Augusto Durand actually tried. By 1912, Higginson's coca reports read like the postmortem of Peruvian coca. He relays more bad news about the new Asian competitors who are undercutting Peruvian prospects; Peru's sole salvation in the business, he recommends, is to move quickly into fine-grade "elaborated cocaine."[25] As such intricately transnational documents attest, not only was cocaine by 1910 a truly global commodity, it was one already rife with global contradictions.

DIVVYING UP GLOBAL COCA, 1910–1950

The four decades after 1910 represent cocaine's declining middle age between the drug's licit peak and its global source- and end-market prohibition after 1950. From production of more than fifteen tons in 1905, global use likely halved by 1930; by 1950, the United Nations set legal world medicinal needs for cocaine at under two metric tons. Three factors drove this steady fall: a narrowing of medical usage due to newly discovered alternative anesthetics and to changing medical opinion, anticocaine laws and campaigns by states and other international bodies (efforts focused on fighting "narcotics"), and market retreat and diversification on the part of vulnerable cocaine makers and coca planters. During this era, cocaine's steady decline was not buffered by the rise of illicit cocaine following scattered episodes of the recreational use of surplus pharmaceutical stocks from the teens to the early 1920s. The United States, cocaine's largest consumer market, initiated trade restrictions with the 1906 creation of the Food and Drug Administration, created a putative federal ban in the 1914 Harrison Act, and instituted a fully operative import control system by 1922. Less successfully, Americans also pushed for global cocaine controls at the Hague Conventions of 1912–14 and successive Geneva-based League of Nations conventions after 1924.

Yet rather than vanish, cocaine divided into a trio of politically constructed and geographically segmented global commodity chains. The first was a Dutch colonial Javan-European chain, which by 1915 unexpectedly displaced Peruvian producers from many former markets. The second was Japan's state-promoted Pan-Asian circuit, launched in the 1920s in response to League and industrial imperatives. The third chain was the lingering U.S.-Andean nexus, increasingly tied to corporate privilege (mainly of Coca-Cola) and government drug control (under Harry Anslinger's new Federal Bureau of Narcotics) and, on the Peruvian end, dividing into coca and cocaine circuits imbued with nationalist and statist hopes of rescue.[26]

This market devolution is what one might expect of such a politicized and declining commodity. The global market for coca and cocaine, built in the prior period, ceased to exist. Beneath the shifting commodity chains, cocaine's status as a commodity per se was being gradually reversed.

THE DUTCH COLONIAL COCA BOOM, 1905–1930

The speedy Dutch rise to prominence in world coca trades took the drug world by surprise, especially the Peruvians, who in 1900 still saw themselves as modern heirs of an Incan birthright to the global coca market. In 1904, Dutch Java (the island now part of Indonesia) exported only twenty-six tons of coca leaf; this soared to eight hundred tons in 1912 and an industrial supply of seventeen hundred tons in 1920, glutting the world market for coca. The Dutch built an especially productive and integrated industrial cocaine regime, yet it was dismantled by decree almost as quickly as it arose.

The Dutch scientific-commercial stake in coca dates to the 1850s, like most European interest, starting with botanist J. K. Hasskarl. Serious coca planting began in the mid-1880s as coca botanical transplant experiments spread among colonial powers. Dutch authorities initially rebuffed coca projects, allegedly wary of the corruption of colonial natives already suffering under the controversial drug auctioning system known as "opium farming." One Dutch advantage was fortuitous: the abnormally high-alkaloid coca bush that Javan, Maduran, and Sumatran planters obtained from the colonial botanical gardens at Buitenzorg near Batavia descended from a strand of Peruvian *Erythroxylon novogranatense* acquired from Kew or a botanical firm in Belgium. It contained twice the cocaine content of quality Huánuco leaf (up to 1.5–2 percent), but in a hard-to-refine crystallized ecgonine form, useless for herbal coca products.[27] With Peru's rapid entry into crude cocaine after 1889, not much European interest was evinced in Javan coca; only about five hundred acres came into cultivation, and small lots reached European buyers in the 1890s.

After 1900, several factors suddenly focused Dutch interest in coca, spurred on by national botanical and chemical specialists like Willem Burck, Maurits Greshoff, A. W. K. (Anna) de Jong, and Emma Reens. Dutch "moral" qualms about further drug crops evaporated as the Dutch now drove to dominate the field in mercantilist fashion. One factor was the establishment in 1900 of Amsterdam's large Nederlandsch Cocainefabriek (Netherlands Cocaine Factory, or NCF), subsidized by the state bank.

The NCF freely pirated advanced German patents for ecgonine cocaine extraction, an efficient method for extracting cocaine from dried leaf still monopolized in Germany by Farbwerke. The NCF soon dwarfed its two smaller domestic rivals dating to the mid-1890s. The second factor was concerted investments in plantation productivity and leaf quality. Dutch advisers and planters proved especially good at systematic seed selection and high alkaloid retention through uniform leaf harvesting, baling, and shipping techniques, supported by local government laboratory testing. Despite urging by de Jong and others, the Dutch did not refine exportable crude cocaine or establish a more modern cocaine factory in Java; the teens were too late in cocaine's product cycle to make this a worthwhile venture. Pliable cheap Javanese field labor, an easier plantation geography near to shipping, four annual handpicked harvests of young leaves, economies of scale, technical rationalization, rotation, and intercropping with colonial rubber and tea projects all helped Javan efficiency surpass the geographically constrained and haphazard peasant-style coca culture of the Andes. By 1911, some 44 plantations captured a quarter of the world coca market, making Amsterdam into the world's most active coca marketplace. Coca filtered through Amsterdam into a high-margin, fully integrated cocaine industry, and Javan leaf also came to supply 40 percent of Hamburg's coca needs with the generalization of ecgonine refining methods throughout Europe.

The global trade disruptions of World War I brought even more European reliance on this new coca corridor. At the peak of Javan production in the early 1920s, more than 120 plantations plied coca from Java.[28] All of it was for industrial export refining, as no local consumption of coca (chewing) or other uses were found for this kind of leaf. Dutch industrial-grade coca also made it to Japan, Belgium, France, and even to the United States. In the 1920s, impressed by such high-alkaloid, quality leaf, even New Jersey Merck bypassed the unreliable Andes. The company acquired its own Javan plantation, Tjitembong, a vertically run, factorylike property that performed well into the 1930s. Three world "cores" of cocaine now uneasily coexisted: Darmstadt, northern New Jersey, and Amsterdam, with an expanded NCF becoming the biggest single producer.[29] Together, they dramatically cut prospects for Peruvian coca, which was virtually wiped out of European markets between 1908 and 1915, and for crude cocaine, banned in the United States and now confined to a shrinking, politically risky German refining sector. Hamburg imports of Peruvian cocaine halved to under four thousand kilos by 1911, and overall export values plummeted

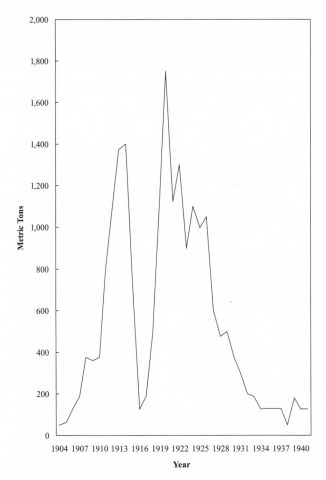

FIGURE 3.1 The Rise and Fall of Java Coca Leaf, 1904–1940
Source: See appendix.

by some 95 percent by the 1920s. Peruvians watched these developments haplessly, without the time, capital, or technical expertise to mount a response.

Almost as dramatic as its rise was the dismantling of the Dutch cocaine network. By 1920, Javan coca basically satisfied the whole of world cocaine demand, estimated at twelve tons. After the war, prices plummeted once again, and revenues fluctuated wildly throughout the 1920s. To diversify, the NCF even began making novocaine, cocaine's new, fully synthetic substitute. Authorities erected price controls to manage the surplus. Assisted by the League of Nations (interested for drug control purposes), a new formalized European cocaine syndicate was formed in

1924 with eight firms called the European Convention of Cocaine Producers. It encompassed the NCF and the three largest German makers, with only small domestic French, British, German, and Russian firms left outside its jurisdiction. At first, this meant more planned purchases from Java, but it also meant steadily declining cocaine quotas, in accordance with the 1925 Geneva Convention on Opium and Other Drugs. A Dutch national Association of Coca Producers was also formed, which soon worked to downsize itself and diversify into alternative colonial crops.[30] In the late 1920s, Dutch production shrank systematically. From 1929 through 1931, in contradictory political moves, the Netherlands opted to comply fully with the coca-cocaine export controls of the League's Geneva Manufacturing Limitation Accord (despite unease with U.S. drug crusading and in a fiscal move to favor colonial opium interests). The Dutch were evolving into model international citizens, although it helped their effort that their coca, unlike that in core Andean coca zones, played a small part in Javan commercial and cultural life. With an inconsequential home market, NCF output withered to 250–300 kilos annually (the allotted tenth of recognized world markets), and Javan coca fell under 200,000 kilos.

Japan's invasion of Java during World War II mortally disrupted the vestiges of the corridor, and the subsequent U.S. liberation/occupation led to the explicitly mandated destruction of remaining coca planting in Java. Notably, just as in the case of Japanese coca, discussed below, the absence of an autonomous or coca-using peasantry (as well as the powers of colonial-style fiat) made it easy, once willed politically, to permanently eradicate a modern-style coca complex. By 1946, only a few aging patches of Indonesian coca bush remained. The Dutch coca-cocaine chain had been a brief but spectacular political marriage of colonialist state, scientific industry, and commercial planters — and a historical reminder that even today coca might escape the Andes for other tropical realms if pressures warrant.

JAPANESE IMPERIAL COCAINE

The even-less-appreciated Japanese cocaine network of the 1920s and 1930s may have been spurred by the Dutch example, as well as a series of intriguing chain crossings. By the 1930s, Japan was one of the largest producers and purveyors of cocaine to east and south Asia, though the statistics (and licitness) of this state-sanctioned trade remain clouded in controversy.

Initial Japanese involvements with coca and cocaine were entwined with Western initiatives and influences. Jokichi Takamine, a brilliant, cosmopolitan Japanese chemist (still known for his 1894 discovery of adrenaline), had worked for Parke, Davis in the 1890s, the firm's cocaine heyday, and he brought this expertise back to Japan's Sankyo Pharmaceuticals, becoming its president in 1913. Sankyo enjoyed strong early links to American pharmaceutical interests, notably Johnson and Johnson. The firm emerged as a major cocaine producer by the early 1920s, contracting for large lots of crude cocaine from colonial Formosa (Taiwan). Powerful and diversifying Japanese sugar interests in Formosa had begun investing in coca in the teens, though some processors began by purchasing Javan and Peruvian coca and crude cocaine until Japan achieved self-sufficiency in coca in the 1930s. Another formidable figure in this story was Hajime Hoshi, who also trained in the United States (including obtaining, in 1901, a Columbia journalism degree) before founding Hoshi Pharmaceuticals in 1911. Hoshi founded the national pharmacy school that later became Hoshi University and as a member of the Diet became a national political figure. In 1917, in remarkable chain-jumping that caught some international attention, Hoshi Pharmaceuticals acquired an immense jungle coca tract in the middle of Peru's Huallaga Valley. The 225-square-mile Tulumayo property and its Pampayacu plantation, that key site in cocaine history once owned by Kitz, was a source of coca, crude cocaine, cinchona, and also of knowledge about this business.[31] Other Japanese companies ran plantations in Dutch Java. A further global push came from a handful of German drug firms, which, following the initial institution of export controls on cocaine and opiates in 1912, began using Japanese companies for transshipments, especially to forbidden Chinese markets, from the 1910s through the 1920s. With the European cocaine surplus fed by the Dutch entry into the field, these transfers became substantial: some years saw more than four thousand pounds of cocaine passing through Japan in this semilicit trade.

Japan's role in narcotic economies in general has been read in two contrary ways, and international warnings sounded from the start. In one sense, the cocaine trade fit Japan's Asian-oriented industrialization process and expansive trade sphere. Starting during World War I, Japan sought self-sufficiency in the face of disrupted trades, and close relations of the state with large firms was a basic feature of Japanese business culture. The development of an integrated pharmaceuticals industry represented an important sign of scientific modernization. Japan—which had escaped

TABLE 3.4 Japanese Cocaine Imports, Cocaine Production, and Colonial Coca, 1910–1939

Year	Cocaine Imports (kg)	Formosa Coca (kg)	Cocaine Production (kg)
1910	421		
1911	579		
1912	1,229		
1913	1,484		
1914	1,694		
1915	1,942		
1916	2,224		
1917	2,559		
1918	1,296		
1919	1,201		835
1920	3,331		1,823
1921	2,074		2,326
1922	238		3,717
1923	115		3,469
1924			
1925			
1926		49,884	
1927		68,596	
1928		129,050	
1929		164,397	
1930		178,939	
1931		159,838	
1932		105,938	
1933		103,386	
1934		108,521	
1935		102,409/133,901	900
1936		94,781/94,781	900
1937		73,927/141,453	896
1938		83,634/65,464	900
1939		78,668/139,144	900

Sources: See appendix.

Note: Years 1935–39, conflicting figures of Friman/Musto.

domestic drug scares and barely had any drug regulation—did not share in the novel Western ideal of demarcating illicit and licit substances, propagated in the interwar era by the League of Nations. For Japan, drug exports were a normal and necessary business. A second view, rooted in U.S. and League concerns of the 1920s and in testimony at the Tokyo war crimes trials, considers Japan's involvement in drugs extraordinary or nefarious.[32] In this view, the Japanese relied on deliberate deception of Western drug control bodies and on militarist or imperialist profiteering in illicit sales across Asia. Without subscribing to Japan-bashing conspiracy theories, we can at least conceive of the Japanese commodity chain as emerging from the shadows of growing League jurisdiction over narcotics. This increasingly autonomous Asian coca-cocaine network thrived from 1920 through 1945.

By 1920, Japan itself produced more than four thousand pounds of cocaine a year, which then doubled to eight thousand pounds by 1922. Official figures for the 1930s show production at just under two thousand pounds, but some historians and contemporary League officials consider these numbers doctored for external consumption. (This is a hard charge to prove, though Steven B. Karch has tried to using putative estimates of coca alkaloid capacity.)[33] Exports across Asia officially dropped to negligible levels, though complaints registered over Japanese firms and reporting procedures, and cases emerged of deliberate smuggling, as evidenced by the proliferation of falsely branded "Fujitsuru" and "Taiwan Governor" cocaine vials in India and by the trickle of illegal cocaine infiltrating China via Amboy, Shanghai, and Singapore. The Japanese also likely engaged in covert strategic stockpiling of medicinal drugs for modern total warfare, the same role handled for the United States by FBN chief Anslinger. Other specialists have noted growing diplomatic cooperation between Japan and international drug officials, at least until the invasions of Manchuria and China, when colonial opiates became a global issue and Japan became a League pariah. The firms making cocaine and morphine were among Japan's largest, including Hoshi, Sankyo, Takeda, Koto, Dai Nippon, and Shiongo Pharmaceuticals, and they enjoyed growing links to major trading trusts (such as Mitsui and Mitsubishi) and to interlocking governmental, colonial, and high military officials. In 1934, Formosa's Kagi district was said to have kept 694 acres under intensive coca cultivation (by Shoyaku and Hoshi). Earlier plots on Iwo Jima and Okinawa were abandoned, but leaf harvests averaged three hundred thousand pounds per year in the late 1930s. Peruvian imports officially ended in 1938, as Peru nationalized Nisei-managed Tulumayo.

During World War II, Japan's entire pharmaceutical industry, self-sufficient in an imperial state, came under the wartime jurisdiction of the Japanese state. At the time, seven firms were making cocaine, a number surpassed only in Germany. In that sense, if cocaine was marketed for nonmedical purposes across occupied Asia—and the evidence on this question mainly concerns opiates—the state would have borne responsibility. In any case, Taiwan's coca was uprooted by war and the entire drug sector reorganized, without its cocaine, under the U.S. occupation of Japan in 1945. The industry's prior marketing practices became scrutinized at the postwar Tokyo war crimes tribunals. But no local coca use had emerged among agriculturalists, leaving few obstacles to its complete eradication. An autonomous two-decades-old sphere of cocaine production abruptly disappeared—again showing that in the absence of a coca peasantry (and with military efficiency), cocaine could be contained.

THE U.S.-ANDEAN CHAIN, 1910–1950

The U.S.-Andean chain, despite these rivals and its own commercial decline, proved the most resilient and decisive in the long-term histories of coca and cocaine. Coca and cocaine as modern commodities were born in 1890s Peru, with the United States the defining consumer market; from 1910 through the 1940s, modern U.S. anticocaine policies incubated in this peculiar relationship. And in the 1950s through the 1970s, when illicit cocaine finally erupted, the cold war chain that reinvented itself in this form began in eastern Peru and worked its way, famously, to Miami and Hollywood. Despite cocaine's shrinking commercial importance, this was the drug's most historically loaded chain, operating within an expanding informal American sphere.

Aggregate statistics, as reported from Peru, show that coca trades, over-whelmingly with the United States, fell from, on average, 584,000 kilos for 1909–13 to 242,000 for 1919–23 to 128,000 for 1929–33 before climbing to the 140,000–180,000 range for wartime usage in the early 1940s. Crude cocaine exports, mainly from greater Huánuco, fell from over 10 metric tons at their peak (1905–6, mainly to Germany) to 1 ton (i.e., 1,000 kilos) in 1927 before fluctuating around the 200–900 kilo range during the 1930s. In the 1920s, crude cocaine was strictly prohibited by U.S. law, though Peruvians found modest new buyers in Japan and France. By the mid-1930s, Germany was Peru's sole cocaine relationship, one threatened by world politics. With their volatile prices, coca and cocaine export values had collapsed some 95 percent from their peak in 1900–1905 to under S/200,000. It was a shattering fall, given the fervent early national hopes for cocaine. Economically, coca and cocaine remained significant for Peru only in regional terms.

TABLE 3.5 Peruvian Exports of Coca and Crude
Cocaine, 1877–1933

Year	Coca (kg)	Cocaine (kg)
1877	8,000	
1888	29,000	1,730
1890	6,677	930
1891	128,543	3,215
1892	377,762	4,550
1897	494,000	4,200
1898	406,718	4,346
1899	312,112	4,500
1900	565,730	7,745
1901	610,100	10,688
1902	933,284	8,268
1903	1,026,000	10,000
1904	911,000	9,500
1905	1,489,598	6,788
1906	1,210,652	5,914
1907	654,103	6,057
1909	496,328	5,266
1910	495,729	5,524
1911	768,017	5,434
1912	769,751	2,944
1913	392,918	3,267
1914	477,648	979
1915	393,404	1,353
1916	265,834	1,576
1917	306,535	1,896
1918	167,449	2,967
1919	385,583	596
1920	453,067	1,637
1921	87,849	157
1922	124,357	778
1923	190,000	192
1924	169,850	967
1925	216,714	621
1926	204,209	1,048
1927	142,797	980
1928	150,092	625
1929	101,273	236
1930	191,609	—
1931	169,524	246
1932	96,647	420
1933	85,721	918

Source: See appendix.

Note: No data available for years 1893–96 and 1908.

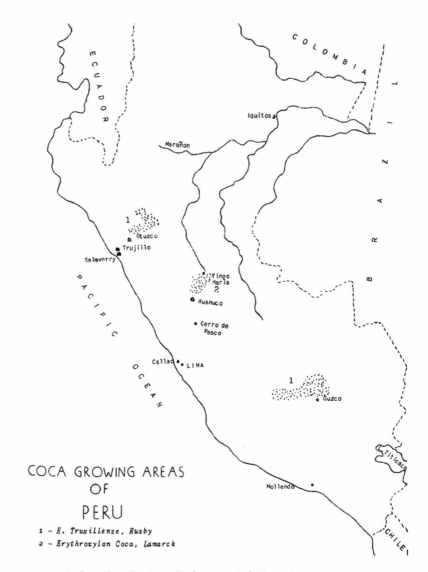

MAP 3.1 Andean Coca Regions, Early Twentieth Century
Source: Emile R. Pilli, "The Coca Industry in Peru," report for Merck, New Jersey, 1943, 6.

Surveying those internal regions reveals the reconfiguration of Peruvian coca and cocaine circuits in relation to larger commodity chains. Bolivian coca, loosened from global ties, reverted after 1900 to trade entirely within a regional nexus. The notable fact is that as Peruvian cocaine fell under market and legal stress it neither modernized itself into a fully integrated industry (as nationalists called for) nor converted into an illicit export chain, which did not emerge anywhere until the 1950s.

Peru's largest shift was also a reconcentration of coca leaf back into the home market of traditional users. During the late 1890s boom, as much as a quarter of Peruvian coca flowed into export-related channels, though that figure is hard to substantiate; by the 1930s, the tradables share was far smaller, at 2–3 percent in good estimates. In part, this market involution reflected the steady demographic advance of Peru's rural folk (i.e., mainly Indians) and their accelerating labor migrations during the twentieth century. Coca production for this internal circuit soared from under 4.8 million tons in the mid-1920s to 5.4 by 1930 to over 6 by 1940 to 8–11 million tons during the 1950s. Regionally, this reflected a moving coca frontier, fostered by national agronomists, toward newer tropical regions of the south, especially Cuzco's La Convención and Lares valleys, close to the indigenous zones known as the "mancha india," which previously took in Bolivian coca. In the early 1940s, in a crude guess, one U.S. expert put Peru's entire leaf crop at 6,840,000 pounds, with 6,000,000 used by the nation's two million male chewers. (Females, who certainly also used it, somehow did not count.) Peru's three chief coca circuits were defined as northern (La Libertad, for export cola extracts), at 1,600,000 pounds, or 16.5 percent of total crop; central (greater Huánuco, for crude cocaine and central sierra leaf trades), at 2,240,000 pounds, or 33 percent; and southern (mainly Cuzco), at 3 million pounds, or 47 percent, for indigenous use.[34] Even the specialists jumbled coca numbers, in this case confusing even pounds and kilos. In terms of regional networks, northern Otuzco or Sacamanca growers remained tied into the powerful Pinillos export clan, which worked exclusively for Maywood, Coca-Cola's trade agent, and routinely bought two-thirds of local crops. Huánuco's chief commodity, depressed and backward, remained crude cocaine, helping its traditional elite hold their ground. By the 1930s, as roads improved, Chinese merchants plied provincial coca trades upland to Junín, and peasant-driven coca frontiers advanced downstream on Tingo María's jungles. Some six to ten crude cocaine workshops, still using Kitz's technique of the 1890s, worked the industry, mainly part-time, largely on demand. After Durand, a new regional magnate, merchant Andrés A. Soberón, rose to the fore, keeping ties to German consigners and lenders but also eyeing other markets, even the closed U.S. market for cocaine. Observers found Cuzco's southern hot zone of colonizing estates less noteworthy, with its low-alkaloid domestic leaf, despite campaigns to improve its coca culture.

Peruvian cocaine politics after 1910, treated at length in the chapters to follow, also related to developments at the other end of the chain.

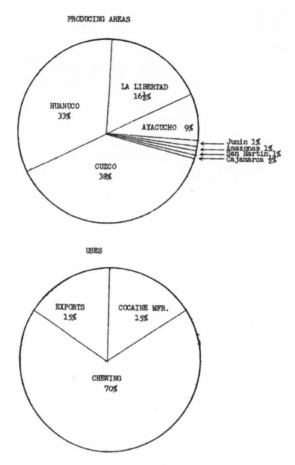

FIGURE 3.2 Peruvian Coca Regions and Coca Uses, ca. 1940
Source: See appendix.

Growing world anticocainism filtered to Peru, in a great turnabout from 1905–25, via science, politics, and markets. In medical science, the new idea of cocaine as a poisonous, addictive narcotic paradoxically mutated in Peru into growing anticoca sentiments that perceived coca as backward or harmful to national development. Combined with racism against the country's Indian majority, this attitude fueled a novel anticoca hygienics movement by the 1930s, with the goal to constrict coca use. Ironically, cocaine, with no local abusers, was still considered a modern, or at least neutral, Western good. Peruvian officials ignored pressures from the United States and the League to restrict cocaine and coca after 1920, avoiding or foot-dragging at international drug forums. Officials, defending Huánuco's livelihood, felt that global antidrug campaigns discriminated against the Peruvian nation. Bolivian officials, in contrast, had no cocaine trade and thus nothing to avoid, becoming outspoken defenders of their national leaf in 1920s Geneva. By the mid-1920s, Peruvian health officials embraced a few modern (i.e., U.S.-style) narcotics controls, but only in the mid-1940s did regulation spread into policing, a prelude to the criminalization of cocaine making in 1948–49. Meanwhile, during the 1930s, a vociferous countermovement arose, led by the elite Dr. Carlos Enrique Paz Soldán, to nationalize the entire industry of coca and cocaine as a modernized state monopoly, in open defiance of encroaching global constraints on cocaine.[35] Paz Soldán was appalled by Peru's falling fortunes, as well as by spreading Indian coca use. The idea, which gathered some state support, was for Peru to face the world as the sole sanctioned exporter of this medicinal necessity. Thus, market and political pressures flowing along the U.S.-Andean chain led to a schizoid and increasingly statist discourse on coca and cocaine. Global commodity segmentation worked in contradictory ways.

The United States still managed the far end of this hemispheric chain (save for a withered Hamburg entrepôt until World War II), instituting mounting controls to seal out cocaine. The chief features of the U.S. cocaine circuit were specialization in coca and decocainized coca syrup, closely supervised monopolies in cocaine processing, a total and largely functional prohibition on nonmedicinal cocaine and coca in the domestic market, and an intensifying global campaign against still-licit coca and cocaine elsewhere. The elusive goal of global prohibition was reached only after World War II with the destruction of the three extant chains — Dutch, Japanese, and German — and the full entry of Peru (and, after a delay, Bolivia) into the U.S. sphere of cold war interests.

The United States had been the world capital of coca and cocaine usage and a pioneer in its popular abuse, and after 1910 U.S. officials worked passionately to reverse that state of affairs. There is little question that illicit (as well as medicinal) use of cocaine largely dried up in the United States after 1920, though the reasons remain unclear. Popular coca products were banned and disappeared, with the notable exception of thriving cocaine-free Coca-Cola. One factor was a political economy of control that emerged out of the previous North American penchant for coca leaf and, by 1920, the concentration of coca handling in just two firms, New Jersey Merck and nearby Maywood Chemical. Rather than regulate thousands of pharmacists, dentists, and physicians at the retail level, officials pinched cocaine at the top. By 1920, these two firms had become intimate intermediaries of the nascent federal antidrug bureaucracy, trading intelligence and favors and ensuring that only supervised bulk coca leaf entered the single port of New York. Every detail of the distillation process — of Merchandise No. 5 (Coca-Cola's decocainized extract made by Maywood from Trujillo leaf) and of Merck's high-grade medicinal cocaine — was tightly regulated by the FBN. For a time, this system functioned well, hastening the disappearance of illicit cocaine in the 1920s as well as helping to ensure the monopoly successes of Coca-Cola against soft drink competitors and its monopsony with Peruvian coca dealers. Maywood focused exclusively on northern Peru, forging a closed corporate and family commodity circuit with the Pinillos clan and even winning coca its own congressionally sanctioned judicial status as "special-leaf imports." As the volume of legal and illegal cocaine shrank and consumer addiction to Coca-Cola rose, these special nonmedicinal imports grew to make up a larger and larger portion of Peruvian exports. By World War II, the United States consumed twice as much coca in beverages — more than two hundred thousand kilos annually — than was used in making residual medicinal cocaine, which had fallen to under a thousand kilos a year. By the mid-1920s, a well-diversified Merck, the monopoly U.S. cocaine maker, turned to leaf from its own Java plantations, in effect building its own in-house, state-approved coca-cocaine commodity chain. Merck looked to Peru only during and after the war; by the mid-1950s, seeing little use in continued manufacturing, it gave up making cocaine and simply bought and distributed Maywood's Coca-Cola cocaine residue.[36] In effect, all American cocaine became a by-product of the Coca-Cola chain, or empire.

American cocaine politics abroad (explored in chapter 5) were a sideshow of a general antinarcotics diplomacy in which the United States, with few colonial interests, became the driving force behind erecting a world system of cocaine prohibitions via successive Geneva conventions of the League of Nations. The first target was the Germans, then the Japanese, and finally errant Peru and Bolivia. In some sense, this campaign slowly worked, by defining and reducing "legitimate" cocaine spheres after 1920. It also backfired, for example by sparking the expansive shadow chain emanating out of Japan. Broadly, the interwar era presents a paradox in standard thinking about drug control: the era with a diversity of licit global cocaine chains and coexisting legal regimes around the drug was the least troublesome in terms of cocaine's status as an active social problem, especially in the United States. Moreover, the United States still exerted little or no limiting control at the periphery—in coca source areas like Peru—though American diplomats had set the goal of limiting cocaine at the source as early as 1915. These tolerant circumstances gave no incentive to illicit trade. In the 1920s and 1930s, to pressure Peru and back Coca-Cola, officials began taking a deep interest in Peruvian coca and cocaine, cultivating an FBN–State Department drug intelligence web in Peru facilitated by Maywood and Coca-Cola officials and contacts. Slowly, North American notions of modern drug control filtered to Peru, though Peruvians (and to a greater degree Bolivians) resisted imported anticoca ideals. FBN records reveal little direct American meddling in Andean drug policies prior to World War II, though a good deal thereafter. In a larger sense, however, the United States structured the options available for the Andes in this realm—by its ban on cocaine imports, by curtailing world markets, and by blocking national schemes of drug control.[37]

By the end of this era in World War II, the future of licit world cocaine chains looked grim. In 1942, New Jersey Merck sent chemist Emile Pilli on a special mission to investigate the decrepit Peruvian industry as war cut off the firm's Asian leaf supply. His fifty-page report, "The Coca Industry of Peru," a classic of industrial espionage, surveys firsthand Peru's three main coca-growing and cocaine zones. Merck eyed some of Peru's 6.6-million-pound crop, which Pilli fleshes out in terms of uses (coca chewing now an official worry), cropping, labor, climate, harvests, drying, sales, exports, and distribution networks. His cocaine survey stresses the rapidly changing situation of Huánuco, with its severed German and Japanese ties, exhausted soils, backward workshops, and nascent jungle frontier. As a pragmatic business, Merck judged postwar market prospects to be poor and vied for modernized links to coca growers and even a U.S.-sanctioned local production of "pure salts" of cocaine hydrochloride. Illicit cocaine was still an unforeseen specter, as was now-archaic hemispheric boosterism of Pan-American Union Commodity of Commerce pamphlets like "Coca: A Plant of the Andes," last issued in 1928. But suspicious premonitions were being raised in a stream of new intelligence reports about Peruvian cocaine (like that from consul William Burdett's 1931 drug inspection tour of Huánuco) and in the antinarcotics-colored required American "Coca Reports" on the Andean crop and custom.[38]

This intensifying U.S. optic on Peru, rather than on rival global cocaine chains, was indicative of dramatic shifts underway during World War II. The last worldwide accounting of cocaine registered in the mid-1930s, when the League of Nations, under State Department prodding, attempted to assess the globalized factory production of all aboveboard narcotic drugs. For global cocaine, it counted ten small export crude co-caine factories across Peru; only Merck and Maywood in the purposely constricted U.S. home market; Amsterdam's centralized NCF factory (with its range of cocaine derivatives); six diversified German plants under the Nazi regime (Boehringer, Hoffman-LaRoche, Knoll, E. Merck, Riedel, and Chininfabrik, several in exports); and four authorized domestic and export firms in imperial Japan, plus a related pair of colonial factories like the Shinei plant of the Taiwan Drug Manufacturing Company for crude and refined cocaine. Home-market coca alkaloid lines persisted in such scattered places as Argentina, Belgium, France (two), Britain, Brazil (for coca extracts), Poland, Finland, Russia, Switzerland (some for export), and Czechoslovakia.[39] With thirty-six plants by this count, the number of firms refining the drug had shrunk considerably since 1910; a third of them belonged to Germany and Japan, or more than half (twenty-two) in a grouping that included Germany, Japan, and Peru's crude cocaine workshops. The League's dream was to erect a formal universal regime around all remnant drug manufacturing, carefully managing from the metropolitan core of the commodity chain the progressive extinction of medicinal cocaine and then eradicating the tropical coca fields at the other end in the Andes, Java, and Taiwan. This never happened: the dislocation of cocaine's commodity circuits during World War II and the birth of a new, illicit one in the decades to follow raised and then dashed hopes for ending cocaine's status as a modern commodity.

During the world war — a significant turning point for commodity chains in general — the United States closed Peru's outlets to Japan and Germany, and the Japanese invasion put Java off the map. Cocaine's most modern circuits, those with high-tech plantations and large factories, were destroyed once and for all. American concerns about and surveillance of the drug fell on Peru just as state-to-state ally ties intensified during the world conflict, continuing into the subsequent cold war. The Andean cocaine network became strategically defined within broader bellicose understandings of licit and contraband trades. By 1945, even wary Peruvian officials grasped the need for restrictions and the long-hobbled Huánuco industry's hopeless prospects under postwar U.S. hegemony. As an anticoca consensus gathered at the new American-inspired United Nations drug agencies, Peru rushed to outlaw cocaine making in 1947–49 and to begin loose regulation of the Indian coca bush under a national monopoly, a

process delayed in Bolivia due to coca nationalism, its Axis tilt, and the
1952 revolution. By 1950, the U.S.-Andean commodity chain, born a century
before and the last survivor of its kind, came to an end — at least in its
licit market phase.

CONCLUDING WITH CHAINS

This synthetic transitional chapter sketched the commodity chains developed and traveled by licit coca and cocaine during cocaine's rise and
demise as a modern global drug between 1860 and 1950. These were not
just interconnected markets of supply and demand but institutionalized
and embedded channels for the flow of science and medicine, political
ideas and influences, and varied attempts at monopoly and control.[40]
They were segmented by changing cultural tastes for coca-cocaine and by
shifting colonial and neocolonial spheres. They reflected diverse levels and
forms of international power as well, between the multitude of unequal
actors and relationships at play in the growing, processing, marketing,
regulation, and use and misuse of these substances. In several senses, over
the long run these commodity chains, and the tensions along and between
them, helped construct the initial nineteenth-century market legitimacy
of coca and cocaine, and in reverse they would structure the commodity's
progressive criminality over the twentieth century. These global relational
dynamics permeate the rest of Andean cocaine's unfolding story.

As I will show in chapters ahead, after a protracted era of decline and
constraint until 1950, commodity chains of coca and cocaine became after
1950 both more and less market-driven phenomena, and this may indeed
reflect, as cynics may suggest, a revenge of the coca periphery. Andean
cocaine, outlawed by authorities at all levels of the chain, escaped state
oversight and forged its own underground spaces and linkages, the work
of a changing cast of criminalized agents. It was governmental and international prohibitions that pushed cocaine radically into unregulated
illicit markets. One intriguing plot of the story is that once cocaine was
made illegal on a global scale, cold war circuits of illicit cocaine basically
reverted to their original geographic spaces in the eastern Amazon and
to their long links with the United States. The 1970s jungle *pasta básica*
of cocaine was still Peru's old 1890s crude cocaine sulfate, but now it was
being forwarded to criminal refiners in Colombia and vendors in Miami
rather than to Merck in Darmstadt.

4

WITHERING COCAINE
Peruvian Responses, 1910–1945

COCAINE'S PERUVIAN CRISES

The last chapter sketched the global commodity networks of cocaine that had coalesced by 1920 and whose tensions and competition ended for coca's homeland the buoyant era during which Peruvians had built the export commodity cocaine and dominated its world supply. After 1910, legal Peruvian cocaine tumbled into a deep economic crisis from which it would never rebound. Shaken by the sudden explosion of the Asian colonial cocaine circuits, its possibilities were also constrained after 1915 by a new politics of anticocainism: the antinarcotics political economy of the United States, shrinking medicinal usage, and delegitimization by the restrictions of advancing international antidrug conventions after 1912 (the topic of the next chapter). In less than a decade, cocaine was transformed from one of liberal Peru's national modernizing hopes to a stagnant technological relic of clans in remote Huánuco.

This chapter explores how that three-and-a-half-decade period of global commodity decline (1910–45) was felt in Peru, as cocaine transformed from a heroic nationalist commodity into a limping regional good during a long, revealing pause before cocaine's reconfiguration after 1945 as an illicit export good. I look at the tepid entrepreneurial reactions to cocaine's crisis and the more creative Peruvian responses in a variety of projects, ideas, and debates — agrarian, industrial, sanitary, legal, and governmental — to revive or defend the dying industry, which climaxed in the vociferous 1930s prococaine campaigns of Dr. Carlos Enrique Paz Soldán. Declining commodities, as much as rising ones, can excite the national imagination and become laden with enduring symbolic passions and value. While all of these responses arose in relation to cocaine's more glowing past, they tended to offer defensive or statist solutions to the commodity's impasse. None of them succeeded in saving legal national cocaine except in postponing the inevitable. Yet it was precisely the atavistic survival of small-scale cocaine, rooted and valued in a regional coca culture, that was to make eastern Peru the incubator of world illicit cocaine after 1945.

The decline of cocaine in Peru occurred in a dialectic with the distinct saga of Andean coca leaf, a subject that has won greater scholarly attention than Peruvian cocaine.[1] Because of that richer historiography on modern Andean "coca debates," this chapter focuses on the social imaginary of Peruvian cocaine, coca's alter ego, often lost amid writings on coca leaf. In the nineteenth century, the scientific aura of alkaloidal cocaine helped awaken a broad Peruvian elite interest in and identification with Andean coca leaf. In the early twentieth century, coca leaf survived, embedded in its ethnic economy, with at least two million daily users among high-land Indians, but literate Peruvian elites began to exhibit what I would call "scientific schizophrenia" about coca. By the 1910s, vocal Peruvian *indigenistas* (urban-based, pro-Indian reformers) began again to accent the negative and backward in the coca habit. The driving idea was that coca chewing inured Indians to their dismal plight and exploitation by whites (including the oppressive working conditions in the *gamonal*-run coca plantations of Huánuco).[2] It was a paradoxical idea, coming as it did during Peru's first modern age of national Indian restiveness and rebellion, and perhaps serving as a denial of growing Indian agency. Ironically, the anticocaine message and nascent addiction models emanating from Western medicine were translated in Peru through a coarse filter of elite prejudices into anticoca feelings and campaigns. Cocaine, despite its faltering profits, remained a modern product; age-old Indian coca was surely not. In contrast, in neighboring Bolivia, where national elite families held *yungas* plantations and where the nation's urban and state society was spatially and ethnically integrated by indigenous coca trades, anticoca sentiments came much later, and timidly, among national modernizers. In Peru, where coast and sierra entailed separate cultural worlds (not to mention the exotic and distant coca *montaña*), the chasm between traditional coca leaf and modern cocaine grew ever wider. Coca's imaginary suffered from Peru's tripartite archetypal division into coast, highlands, and jungle.

Early-twentieth-century reformers, starting in the 1910s with the pioneer social psychologist Hermilio Valdizán, began to attribute indigenous passivity and other perceived defects to coca use. To Valdizán, who hailed from Huánuco, coca bred a socially induced mass mental disorder. To a rising generation of social observers and public health advocates, the coca vice became both a cause and a symptom of the Indians' patent "racial degeneration," as these observers put it in the rising idiom of modern Latin American eugenics and hygienics. By the 1920s, this idea had evolved into a full-flung medical model, tested and broadcast by a school of San Marcos medical professors, unknowing pharmacology heirs of Bignon, in a kind of dismal national coca science.[3] In the eyes of medical authorities such as Carlos Ricketts, Carlos Enrique Paz Soldán, and, in the next decades, Carlos Gutiérrez-Noriega and Luis Sáenz, coca use was an alarming "toxico-manía"—a mass poisoning, a mass addiction—of the Peruvian highlander. Coca was cocaine, the bad drug now profiled by overseas pharmacology and policemen. All kinds of ills, from malnutrition to low intelligence and borderline insanity, were "scientifically" attributed to coca through bogus measurements of cocaine levels in the Indian bloodstream in research often abetted by U.S. scientific bodies. Such research projected an image of coca that was the obverse, in a peripheral site, of the French-inspired healthful and spiritually uplifting image coca enjoyed in the late nineteenth century (shared by eminent Peruvians like those of the 1888 Coca Commission) or prior American notions of coca as a cure for ailing modernity. It hardly mattered that this was poor science, usually supported by population-biased experiments or observations among poorly nourished, illiterate, deviant, and chronically ill coca-chewing indigenous inmates of prisons, mental institutions, and army barracks. By the 1920s, such research had begun to translate into various hygienic projects to actually restrict Indian coca usage and culture.

In time, this dismal science, shared by Left and Right, was vigorously contested by the nationalist 1940s and 1950s Andean biology school of Dr. Carlos Monge Medrano of the same San Marcos University, which began to argue that coca usage was an environmental adaptation of highland Indians, with positive physiological and medical implications worthy of serious biomedical research.[4] Until then—and indeed until coca's full, post-1970s ethnographic and scientific vindication—modern pharmacological reductionism, the notion that coca leaf mimicked cocaine, came out in Peru as anticoca fervor. In some sense, "modernizing" anticoca activists were right, even if their science and cultural politics were dubious: if coca leaf was essential to indigenous identity, its eradication would speed Indian assimilation into a coastal nation. Since cocaine remained an elite export commodity, with scant local abuse, it largely escaped negative connotations until it was fully criminalized in the 1950s.[5]

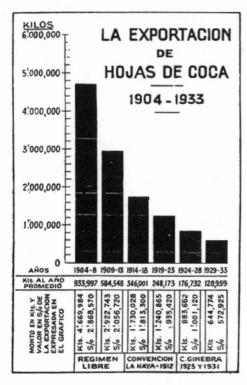
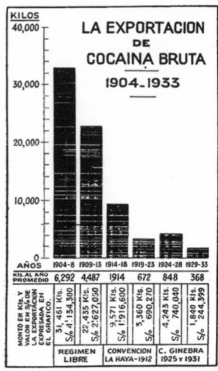

FIGURE 4.1 The Decline of Peruvian Coca and Cocaine, 1904–1933

Source: See appendix.

Note: The two captions in Paz Soldán's chart read "Exports of Coca Leaf, 1904–1933," and "Exports of Crude Cocaine, 1904–1933."

The personification of this national schism between coca (as adversary) and cocaine (as advocate) was Dr. Paz Soldán, whose nationalist schemes for cocaine are addressed below. Paz Soldán, in the course of these 1930s polemics, also left one of the sharpest portrayals of the fall of Peru's turn-of-the-century cocaine exports, starkly visualized in four-year averages.

Whereas cocaine exports of over 31,461 kilos (thirty-one tons) brought Peru over S/4,000,000 (about $2 million) in the four-year span 1904–8, these revenues halved by 1909–13, with sharp price drops, and continued to slide. After a spurt in medicinal demand during World War I, the bottom fell out of Peru's market. From 1919 through 1923, Peru sold only 672 kilos a year on average, dropping to 368 kilos between 1929 and 1933. By then, cocaine sales, mainly from remnant factories of Huánuco to Germany,

France, and Japan, earned Peru less than *S*/100,000 a year — a 94 percent fall since their peak in 1904–8. Figuring in the era's inflation and Peru's weakening *sol*, this meant that sales of cocaine brought in only about $35,000 a year. Coca exports, buoyed by U.S. demand for northern leaf for Coca-Cola syrup and southern leaf for Chilean workers, fell less violently. Whereas in 1904–8, on average 934,000 kilos of leaf earned *S*/2,868,570, by 1919–23 this figure had fallen to 248,173 kilos worth *S*/935,420; by the Depression (1929–33), coca exports averaged 128,959 kilos for earnings of *S*/527,925 — an 82 percent revenue fall since their peak in 1904–8. Over time, the economic roles of coca and cocaine had reversed: in 1904–8, cocaine revenues were about twice coca's, but by 1929–33, coca earnings were double those of cocaine.[6] Huánuco, with its cocaine leaf, suffered the most from this shift, though both commodities turned into minor items of national export.

A remarkable Peruvian prism on cocaine's decline is the dispatches of Eduardo Higginson, Peru's consul general in New York, who chronicled the fortunes of Peruvian coca and cocaine, among other commodities, from 1904 to the eve of World War I. Published in Peru's *Bulletin of Foreign Affairs* and the agricultural journal *La Riqueza Agrícola*, this transnational news from coca's main foreign port surely caught the eye of national coca brokers and cocaine makers. Even as Lima officials professed enthusiasm for coca and cocaine (the country's fourth export earner in 1904–5), Higginson already noted weaknesses in their overseas markets. In his initial 1904 report, he underscored the negative influence of the 1896 protective tariffs for American pharmaceutical firms: "High duties are not allowing [Peruvian cocaine] to compete with the U.S.-manufactured [drugs]." Peruvian cocaine swiftly diverted to Hamburg, earning over 1.6 million marks there in 1905 in the drug's global price-setting market. Higginson was a firm believer in Peruvian coca's world monopoly, and he thus saw good prospects for coca as a raw material for protected U.S. cocaine manufacturing. "Bad luck" plagued coca transplant schemes, leading him to believe that the Peruvian product would "never face any important competition in any market." Moreover, the recent commercial conquests of American "*vino medicinal* . . . with cola [Coca-Cola] for refreshing invigorating carbonated drinks, with huge consumption in hot weather" seemed to ensure coca's glorious future. "I have faith in this important product, whose demand keeps growing and growing," he wrote. Higginson endorsed a bifurcated market — cocaine for Europe, coca for Americans — offering suppliers industrial tips from the Ministry of Promotion.[7]

Just two years later, in 1906, Higginson's coca optimism was waning, overshadowed by the Amazonian rubber boom. (Like cinchona and coca, rubber was a native product that Peru failed to hold onto against colonial rivals.) Progressive-era events clouded coca's future. A New York "trust" of coca buyers and big cocaine makers was now working in concert to push down coca costs. In 1906, this "important Peruvian product" fetched some $223,000 on U.S. markets; in 1907, coca earned less than $73,000 in city markets, falling to eighth among Peru's exports, behind even straw hats. Higginson also relayed a first sign of American anticocainism in the 1906 Pure Food and Drug Act, the "governmental decree that orders all drugs and medical preparations to reveal their ingredients." Cocaine, found in "most" patent formulas, was deemed "dangerous to health," and its consumption halved within the year. Higginson warned his countrymen of "very strong measures against the abuse of cocaine" ahead. Still, as the sole supplier, Peru might have acted to stop deep revenue falls, as he implored Peruvian exporters to create their own price-sustaining "combination."[8]

Even that option had faded by 1912, the year of the Hague International Opium Convention. In 1911, coca sales for New York chemical plants bottomed out at $66,000. Higginson surveyed the five firms still making cocaine (of which only Merck, Mallinckrodt, and Schaeffer — i.e., Maywood Chemical Works — would stay in the field). The swift, unanticipated competition of Dutch Javan coca, now selling in New York, was an even greater shock. Peru was losing what Higginson called its national "privilege": "The leaf which is cultivated now in Java is superior to that of Peruvian origin.... Java's production keeps augmenting, threatening our whole industry since it can soon supply all world demand." Peruvian consuls in Amsterdam and Hamburg, who witnessed the fall of those markets, echoed his opinion. By 1914, a Peruvian consul, M. D. Derteano in Hong Kong, laid out the details of Java's meteoric success story from 1905 through 1913. Coca's fall was irrevocable and had been solidified by the continental coca "syndicates." In his final words on the subject, Higginson endorsed a crash program in Peru. To compete at all, Peru's planters had to swiftly modernize, improving coca stocks, soils, productivity, and transport — a Herculean task under coca's Andean social organization. Like ill-named Peru-bark, coca leaf was a lost cause. "Perhaps it would be most beneficial to develop manufacturing of cocaine, as some agriculturalists have established in Peru, seeking the best market for finished products," Higginson remarked.[9] He urged a move up the modern industrial ladder

from raw coca leaf and semi-industrial crude cocaine to lucrative crystal
cocaine hydrochloride, a message that was to remain a running motif of
Peru's cocaine industry reformers until the 1950s. Peruvian entrepreneurs
would never achieve this, in a larger historical sense leaving the task to
enterprising Colombians in the age of illicit cocaine age after 1970.

REFORMING COCAINE

As Peru's share of crude cocaine on world markets fell after 1910, calls
intensified to reform the foundations of the national cocaine enterprise.
Technicians quickly grasped that reliance on the locally designed Bignon-
Kitz method committed Peruvian workshops to an obsolete technology
in the rapidly changing pharmaceutical world. Peru made the simplest
intermediate, crude cocaine rather than the marketable medicinal cocaine
(cocaine hydrochloride or ecgonine-refined alkaloid) of laboratory science.
Reformers still touted cocaine as a modern national good, but their aim
was adaptive, without the agency or innovation of Bignon's 1880s national
science. Cocaine reformism shared in broader twentieth-century ideals
of industrial development and calls for national protection of the drug
against world adversaries. By the 1930s, this became a state centralizing
project to rescue a dying industry, dramatically urged on by Paz Soldán.

Like Peruvian elite coca prohibition, modernizing visions for cocaine,
for complex reasons, never took hold. The industry remained (in the modernizers' term) "rudimentary," based on Bignon's precipitation processes
to its very end in the late 1940s, when such jungle-adaptive techniques
facilitated cocaine's disappearance underground. Had a modernized cocaine sector emerged in this period and remained a legal or manageable
outlet for Andean peasant coca, it might have offered some alternative to
the illicit coca-cocaine economy that arose in the 1960s. A more modern
or consolidated industry would also have been easier to control, or even
dismantle if need be. If historically moot, these reformist visions richly
reveal cocaine as a declining good.

Awareness of Peru's technological lag in cocaine making was evident
before the crisis hit. In 1903, to take the earliest known case, Pedro Paulet,
another Peruvian chemist with European connections, former head of the
technical National School of Arts, published a compendium of cocaine
extraction techniques in Peru's official *Bulletin of the Ministry of Promotion*.
Paulet rigorously compared cocaine extraction methods that moved beyond
Bignon's two-decades-old formula, though crediting him with the country's

ability to "fabricate alkaloid in the same places that produce coca, taking into account how remote these areas are from industrial centers." Paulet showed Peruvian teachers and investors how to make pure crystallized hydrochloride of cocaine (the most profitable medicinal product); cocaine via the multistep ecgonine-refining process, which the Germans and Dutch applied to Asian coca; and the "industrial preparation of Libermann and Giesels." He also offered updates on assays of coca and cocaine and the latest therapeutic dosages. Paulet did not prescribe a course for Peru's industry, but he laid out techniques to capture wasted residual cocaine and the valuable precursor, ecgonine. This was the essay Higginson urged Peruvian refiners to heed. But the sheer success of Peru's industry at this point, still thriving in the crude cocaine business, precluded innovation. In 1911, engineer Alfredo Rabines published a succinct essay, "The Production of Cocaine in Peru," in two English-language journals (London's *Engineer* and Lima's *Peru To-Day*), illustrating the three-step precipitation processes used in three-man Peruvian workshops, that is, the Bignon-Kitz method. Rabines injected his own hopes while sketching a now clearly "wasteful" and "crude" technology: "No doubt when the means of communication are improved the method of extraction will also improve." His suggestion was to shift refining out of its remote jungle bases, thus reversing the direction of Kitz's original move.[10]

In 1913, another Franco-Peruvian scientist, Emmanuel Pozzi-Escot, a professor at the School of Medicine at San Marcos University—a contract post that placed him in Peru's tiny scientific elite—published research titled "The Peruvian Cocaine Industry (Coca Culture, Extraction of Cocaine)" in a pair of French pharmacy and agricultural journals. Cocaine, to Pozzi-Escot, who paraphrased Minister Garland, was still the *produit essentiellement national*. However, Andean coca was now thriving in French Indochina, Oceania, and Ceylon, and it was facing challenges from German import monopolies and medical synthetics. This daunting "crisis" for Peruvian agriculture, Pozzi-Escot insisted, could only be overcome by application of real "agronomy" and "chemistry." In contrast to Asian coca, his survey of Peruvian coca culture across regions and varieties showed a crop stuck in "the times of the viceroyalty." The extraction of cocaine was worse—"le procédé du pharmacien français Bignon"—deemed "excellent thirty years ago when knowledge of cocaine's properties was rudimentary and sale prices allowed all kinds of mistakes." Pozzi-Escot advised Peruvians to think of coca not as a cocaine-bearing plant but as an "ecgonine engine" that could provide higher output in a simpler series of steps.[11]

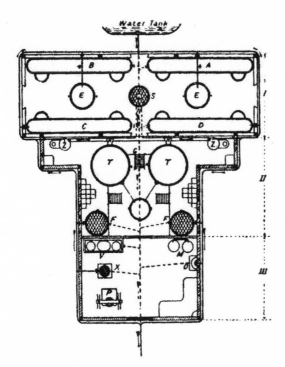

Layout of equipment in Peruvian cocaine workshop,
ca. 1910 (Alfredo Rabines, "The Production of Cocaine
in Peru," *Peru To-Day* [Lima], 3 September 1911, 32)

In the same era, Peru's first scientific national agronomy arose that
zeroed in on reform of coca practices, though trade pamphlets extolling
coca and improved leaf date to the 1890s.[12] Coca, in most cost calculations,
constituted some two-thirds of the final cost of export cocaine, the high
bulk ratio behind the Amazonian location of factories. Since efficient
Asianlike coca practices were the goal of scientific agronomists, they assumed that Peru's increased coca output could be absorbed by indigenous
coquero populations, who consumed about four to six million kilos of
leaf annually. Peru's new prococa agronomists, most of them naturalized
foreigners, yearned for higher coca output and government support for
growers, and thus were out of sync with the nation's new medical anticoca
movement.

The two leading coca specialists from 1910 through 1950 were Carlos
Bües and Alberto Martín Lynch. In 1911, Peru's Ministry of Promotion
released a thirty-nine-page pamphlet by Bües, "La coca: Apuntes sobre

la planta, beneficio, enfermidades y aplicación." Bües relied on German sources for coca's medicinal properties, noting its possible "abuse" before introducing a survey of coca derivatives. Bües saw open vistas for upgrading Peruvian coca practices, a crop grown without fertilizer or systematic pruning, hampered by labor shortages in sparsely populated tropics. The chief method of leaf drying was still exposure to sunlight in the open air. Planters in colonial India had experimented on coca with tea driers, an innovation applied only on one Peruvian hacienda, Durand's. Bües scrutinized transport and harvesting costs, U.S. coca outlets, and what he termed "enemies of the bush," coca's unstudied fungi and insect pests (a topic pursued later by his German peer, Johannes Wille, at Lima's La Molina Agrarian University in the 1930s). Even with the rise of Java coca and U.S. anticocainism, Bües remained bullish on the crop: "I maintain my faith in the future of this important product, for which demand will increase to the degree that its production improves." Coca represented an "*industria nacional* capable of wider extension and worthy of paternal care," he insisted.[13]

Bües made a career out of the plant: some twenty-four years later, he published another detailed coca survey, "La coca en el Perú" (1935), this time under Peru's Dirección de Agricultura y Ganadería for the Third Pan-American Scientific Congress. Here, Bües carefully charted the impact of Javan competition, as well as the internal shifts in Peruvian coca production to the southern valley of La Convención, an area oriented to Indian villagers rather than export cocaine, though he noted some Japanese pharmaceutical interest in Cuzco leaf. Bües compared production costs of several La Convención *cocales* with those of "industrial" Huánuco, making good use of the rich data left by "that sacrificing and notable public man, Augusto Durand" (d. 1923) from his farm-factory, Éxito, in the Derrepente. Amid statistics on coca's steady twentieth-century decline, Bües admitted that the export field had been reduced to the United States for extracts or leaf for Chilean miners. He offered no specific productivity plan: perhaps coca's involution into a noncompetitive domestic crop like Bolivia's was patently clear on these colonizing frontiers.[14]

Bües's coca doppelgänger was Alberto Martín Lynch, whose first agronomic treatise appeared in Peru's private-sector promotional journal *La Riqueza Agrícola* in 1912, enhanced by modern photography. Lynch, who conducted research in the cocaine *montaña* of Chinchao, also facilitated by Durand, had a clear industrial orientation, working on measures to compare and boost the alkaloid ratio of Peruvian leaf. In his estimation,

Javan leaf averaged 1.5 percent cocaine, occasionally peaking at 2.4 percent; Peru's top leaf contained 0.6–1 percent alkaloid. Peruvian routines, such as clear-burning fields, were wasting coca's high-nitrogen soil: "In time, the proverbial fertility of *montaña* lands will be a myth." In fact, some Huánuco zones did become exhausted by the 1930s, a factor in the opening of the Huallaga Valley below. Like Bües, Lynch nurtured a long interest in coca: another of his coca studies appeared some forty years later in 1952, when he was still lamenting Peru's lack of proper fertilization and ignorance of the country's "mosaic" of coca varietals. Another Huánuco coca reform study in 1912–13 by C. Deneumostier (director of the National School of Agriculture and Veterinary Science) and H. Jacob (professor of agronomic engineering) noted the "critical period for cocaine in the world market" while advocating "rational and scientific" coca cultivation in seed selection, planting, and weeding. An editorial note to a separate study by Jacob bemoans "the alarming state of abandonment" of Peruvian coca compared to the "official energies invested in an exotic cultivar" in Java.[15] Peru was not the only promoter of coca long after the bush lost political favor: recall that the Pan-American Union in Washington was still reprinting its colorful English-language pamphlet "Coca: A Plant of the Andes" in 1928 as part of its investor-oriented Commodities of Commerce series.

With such a set of exotic *apellidos*, agronomy in Peru might seem the domain of itinerant European *técnicos* — perhaps a reason why coca reforms fell on deaf ears among rustic planters and peasants on the far side of the Andes. Peru's anticoca medical science was in this sense more "national." But there were also prococa cries from local voices, indeed straight from the leaf's homeland. In 1918, for example, Manuel Vinelli, an aspiring chemist from Huánuco, presented his San Marcos thesis, "A Contribution to the Study of Coca," which concerned, in a familiar nationalist trope, "one of our industries which has its birthplace in Peru." Vinelli championed a more "scientific agriculture" that could raise the alkaloidal potency of diverse subspecies of *Erythroxylon*, even through better climate zoning and soils. Such knowledge was useful in "making plantations of this leaf for industrial purposes." What followed was an academic survey, reminiscent of nineteenth-century coca theses, of history, botany, geography, and particularly coca's "chemical composition," which rounded up previous studies of alkaloidal levels (including an encomium to Bignon's oeuvre) and drug purities attained by diverse cocaine-making formulas. Vinelli embraced coca reforms broached by earlier writers like Lynch, such as seed selection for alkaloidal level and intensive cultivation. Vinelli, who went on to have a noted career in chemistry, also pitched a plea to the university on behalf of Peruvian science: "I believe, Señor Decano, that one of the branches of industrial chemistry whose establishment in Peru can lag no longer is that concerning the extraction and purification of widely used alkaloids — and especially those found in the country's national flora."[16] Cocaine nationalism had not quite expired in Peru, despite the antidrug storm raging outside the Andes.

A rarer form of testimony comes from Mario A. Durand, scion of the Huánuco cocaine clan, still the world's largest producers, who put together a 1916 pamphlet on the secrets of coca cultivation and refining. Durand was a local "organic intellectual" of cocaine, not a trained agronomist or chemist. This detailed primer, "Coca: Dos palabras," serially published in *El Huallaga* (Huánuco's chief newspaper), starts with a flowery paean to "all work that ennobles man" and has a rough, practical tone. Readers learn about coca's ancient and honorable pedigree, its climatic preferences, the Monzón frontier, leaf quality and price fluctuations, values of commercial varieties, Peruvian leaf's superiority to Bolivian product, marketable applications, and the exporters. Durand then turns to the plantation, including building materials for wooden factories, harvests, leaf pressing and shrinkage, drying areas, export wrapping, cocaine assaying and refining methods, and even the regulation of lax factory labor. The dilemmas of coca and cocaine are conveyed through an intensely local lens. Durand's focus is upholding the quality of Huánuco's branded commercial leaf, which some sellers adulterated with poor leaf from other zones. His sharpest concerns are such issues as export taxes, seasonally irregular coca supplies, and the region's dismal road network. The pamphlet was likely written around 1910, before coca's definitive commercial crisis (coca and cocaine were still generating "more than 2 million *soles*"), though Durand saw the threat of rising Javan competition.[17] There is, however, in over twenty pages little in the way of cocaine or coca science, suggesting that, left to their own devices, the *hacendado* — "industrialists" of Huánuco — would not have done much to upgrade their antiquated techniques or sliding competitive position. We will see what they tried further along.

The key historical question is why none of these many cocaine and coca reform projects, save for southern coca colonization, took hold. Generally, one can surmise that cocaine's depressed commercial prospects stifled change. Unlike Bignon's timely innovation of the 1880s, which was quickly seized upon by other entrepreneurs, neither the government nor intrepid investors would now risk effort or scarce capital in a losing venture. From a global angle, the two chief markets for Peruvian cocaine were structured as if to stifle change, particularly industrial upgrading to refining medicinal cocaine HCl. Monopsonistic German pharmaceuticals, which took in most of Peru's crude cocaine between 1910 and 1940, were profiting, however narrowly now, from the reigning division of labor, which made them the processors and distributors of a Peruvian raw material. If faced with competition, they could easily have switched sourcing to Java. The United States, on the other hand — the power casting a longer commercial and political shadow over the Andes — explicitly prevented imports of all kinds of cocaine (rather than coca), a ban finalized in the 1922 Jones-Miller Act. U.S. officials were also increasingly wary of cocaine fabrication on antinarcotics grounds. Peruvian analysts grasped that cocaine's market share was basically fixed by politics, lending no incentive for larger output. There was, in short, no extant market pole for Peru to modernize its industry around, despite domestic support for its promotion.

Huánuco's cocaine clans may also have resisted upgrading because it would have invited greater state intervention, for example, to regulate a product with illegal possibilities. Coca cultivation, the drug's key cost factor, was most stymied by land tenure: few "modernizing" *hacendados* in the labor-tight conditions of the Peruvian *montaña* could afford to restructure coca production, which was governed by a mix of peasant sharecropping and *enganche* indentured labor. Steep coca terrain defied transformation of its flexible peasant "patches" into labor-intensive plantations like Java's. Low-productivity frontier expansion through road building was among the few options. Yet even if coca became twice as cheap in Peru or factories twice as efficient processing it, such changes would not have made up for the revenue falls suffered since the early 1900s.

Some of these limits to the cocaine political economy surfaced during Peru's most mobilizing prococaine campaign, waged by Paz Soldán during the 1930s, for a state-run world cocaine monopoly. But Peruvian fantasies of the industrialization of coca never quite died, merging by the 1940s into modern national industrializing ideologies, such as import substitution of the sort advocated by the Economic Commission for Latin America (CEPAL). Two exemplary industrial projects suffice to illustrate the tenacity of these fantasies. In November 1938, agronomist Federico Luzio published "Tecnología: La fabricación de cocaína en Huánuco," a technical survey of coca culture in Monzón, Chinchao, and Derrepente and of the "extraction procedures, the same used in Huánuco since 1890 by the German chemist Sr. Arnaldo Kitts [*sic*]." Luzio presents a detailed breakdown of cost structures in crude cocaine processing. Huánuco was now making eight hundred to a thousand kilos yearly, mostly in Soberón's factory, but desires to double output were hampered by the decayed state of older *cocales*. Luzio was indignant: "Bear in mind that this is an industry capable of doing much more." Luzio's "Analysis of Afflicting Difficulties" discounts widespread complaints that League of Nations conventions were limiting Peru's exports. Rather, he diagnoses domestic obstacles, such as poor land conservation and lack of fertilization and pruning—exactly the critiques voiced over the prior quarter-century. Luzio envisions as he ends a kind of migration of science to the land: "a small laboratory" on each hacienda to determine the peak moment of alkaloid harvest or selection of seed. "From an industrial and chemical perspective," Luzio insists, Peru was a simple producer of raw materials; even if it sold some alkaloids, the market demanded the ability to produce crystallized cocaine hydrochloride, "cocaine for immediate medical use." He suggests "a factory under the control of the Government and its Organs of Control." Peru's private sector had failed over three decades to transform itself, forcing cocaine reformers like Luzio to call on national authorities to do the job. In 1937 and 1938, officials unveiled plans for a sanctioned Cóndor factory in Lima to create experimental batches of cocaine HCl amid ongoing pressures for state monopolization.[18]

By World War II, which stirred industrial hopes across Latin America, cocaine was read as a metaphor for the larger "industrial problem of Peru." In October 1943, chemist Dante Binda presented his essay "La cocaína: Problema industrial en el Perú" to the Second Peruvian Congress of Chemistry (the same congress, not coincidently, that saw the first and only historical survey about Bignon). Binda's industrializing polemic contains little chemistry. Long facing rivals, the crude cocaine business, he argues, "has felt an ever more obvious shrinking of our country's industry, creating serious problems not only for industrialists, but for our workers and agriculturalists." This was not entirely true, as Binda himself shows, for the war, while closing old German and Japanese cocaine markets, also sparked by 1942 a rise in emergency sales to the Allies. The key problem, as Binda amply documents, was outdated technology: "The procedure used today for extracting alkaloid from coca is almost exactly the same as that used by the French chemist Bignon more or less 60 years ago." Peru was missing an opportunity, since cocaine hydrochloride sold for three thousand dollars a kilo, ten times the going price of crude cocaine. Like

Luzio, Binda argues for state initiative and control, which he adroitly links to projects to preempt possible illicit trades in the drug: "A need exists to put up a factory for cocaine hydrochloride in our territory, and the moment could not be better; it would give life to an agonizing industry, helping to solve a range of socioeconomic problems, and is consistent with the government's policy of exploiting what our own soil provides." Binda's technical note ends on a classical trope of Latin American economic nationalism, one resonating in Peru since the century before: "We must abandon our deeply rooted custom of selling primary materials in exchange for products created from the same materials; it would be difficult to find a more obvious case [than cocaine]."[19] Whatever real obstacles afflicted legal cocaine, until its end it remained a magnet for Peruvian nationalists.

COCAINE AT HOME:
ENTREPRENEURIAL RESPONSES

By the 1890s, Peru's cocaine industry had sprouted in many corners of the country — Lima, Pozuzo, Trujillo, Cuzco, and Huanta, as well as Huánuco — peaking in 1900–1905 with a reported twenty-four working cocaine refiners and exports reaching ten tons of cocaine yearly. By the early 1900s, cocaine's capital was centered in Huánuco under the business leadership of the national firebrand, Augusto Durand. In response to the dramatic price falls after 1905 and the bad news of consuls like Higginson, several entrepreneurial reactions ensued, including attempts at developing regional cartels and monopolies, encouraging crop diversification, pushing frontier development, and searching for new overseas markets, though not revamping technology or creating illicit markets. Nothing was able to restore the product's bygone prosperity. Still, as factories closed elsewhere, cocaine remained the regional mainstay of Huánuco, its main families, its municipal funding, and its politics, as the business shifted from domination by the Durands and Croats to the up-and-coming Soberóns in the decades after 1920.

The extended Durand family, led by the daring political caudillo, journalist, and entrepreneur Augusto, achieved its sway over cocaine during the commodity's buoyant phase from 1895 through 1905. Durand was a centralizer, mobilizing business and familial alliances with the Croatian cocaine makers, such as Nesanovich, Boyanovich, and Plejo, and with landowners as a coca broker, which underwrote the family's hold on Huánuco's municipal politics. Durand used his cocaine enterprise to

TABLE 4.1 Peruvian Cocaine and Coca Exports, 1910–1950

Year	Cocaine (kg)	To Germany (kg)	Coca Exports (kg)	To United States (kg)	Internal Crop (kg)
1910	5, 524	4,271	495,729	277,044	ca. 2,800,000–3,300,000
1911	5,434	5,106	768,017	467,143	—
1912	2,944	2,729	769,751	423,936	
1913	3,267	2,449	392,918	144,323	
1914	979	732/791	477,648	330,066	
1915	1,353		393,404	273,677	
1916	1,575		265,834	98,799	
1917	1,896		306,535	153,417	
1918	3,766		286,607	135,362	
1919	596		385,583	· 175,891	
1920	1,637		453,067	197,677	
1921	157		87,849	10,015	
1922	778/882	402	124,357	43,548	
1923	192		190,009	93,737	
1924	967/1,534		169,850		
1925	621	3,378	216,714	42,457/72,000	
1926	1,048/1,850	2,400	204,000	61,292	4,800,000
1927	980/1,610	2,500	148,000	84,377/114,000	5,000,000
1928	625	3,590	150,000	56,108/110,000	5,200,000
1929	236	2,100	101,000	51,503/61,000	5,400,000
1930		1,100	191,609	67,623/89,000	5,400,000
1931	246	1,000	169,524	165,629/221,000	5,000,000
1932	420	245[a]	96,647	67,652/101,000	4,800,000
1933	918/368		85,721	58,899/81,000	4,484,759
1934	962		69,639	62,703/85,000	4,667,285
1935	670	399[b]	94,559	76,003/110,000	4,645,848
1936	900		174,745	· 137,140/171,000	4,921,176
1937	300/1,322	327	187,000	155,584/189,000	5,292,903
1938	100/1,298		275,622	199,187/208,000	5,845,545
1939	300/1,194		308,982	244,515/263,000	5,903,428
1940	600/1,690		347,522	281,400/352,000	6,336,497
1941	1,000/2,264		433,222	370,413/420,000	6,444,240
1942	2,790/2,825		465,500	390,500/360,000	6,805,228
1943	1,198		458,600	447,395	6,674,018
1944	99		251,154	202,057	6,890,278
1945	1,605		426,620	316,224	7,095,420
1946	930/1,153		247,417	228,782	7,415,239
1947	863/893		371,937	315,237	7,407,586
1948	1,276/1,008		335,008/300,000	289,375	7,604,736
1949	383		107,739	142,078	7,560,942
1950	315		155,857	112,742	7,925,990

Sources: See appendix.

[a] Huánuco cocaine only.

[b] Six months only.

finance his political empire, which included the left-wing Liberal Party and ownership of the opposition newspaper *La Prensa* in Lima.[20] After 1910, Durand's response to cocaine's crisis was threefold, involving modest diversification, modernization, and further attempts to stabilize prices via a regional cocaine trust.

Diversification was evident in his brother and fellow *político* Juan Durand's 1909 campaign to open new frontier zones through road building and railways down the Huallaga into the Amazon in pursuit of the era's fleeting wild rubber boom. Some coca cultivation in fact followed the rubber tappers, for example to Monzón.[21] Durand was also the only *hacendado* to have embraced—or who could afford to embrace—productive innovations, for instance drying furnaces for uniform leaf installed in his much-admired San Carlos estate. Cartel schemes show Durand's awareness of his initial market power, often financed by sizeable bank loans from political allies. But they also reveal his miscomprehension of the structural shift in world cocaine markets: prices would never recover to 1890s levels, especially in light of Javan competition. Nonetheless, after his first failed 1904 trust, Durand tried twice more. In 1911, he announced a new Gran Trust de Cocaína, formed in Europe with rumored loans of five million *soles* to buy up "all of Peru's coca" through paid delivery contracts and to build more, not fewer, factories in the field. Rival or failed factories fell into family hands. In 1917, Durand tried again after a business trip to Argentina with the Sindicato de Cocaína, financed by Buenos Aires banker José Didero, which extended buy-up deals across the region.[22] It was probably hard to resist the willpower of Durand or his ready cash. Results were, however, not readily seen, as cocaine prices dipped sharply again after 1919. Durand was likely using these loans, and the mortgage of the Huánuco industry, to fuel his other activities, including his political adventures.

Politics was both Durand's lifeblood and his downfall. After 1919, he was relentlessly persecuted by the strong-arm Oncenio regime of Augusto B. Leguía (1919–30), long his nemesis. Leguía sent troops marauding across Durand family lands in the *montaña*. In April 1923, Leguía infamously had Durand assassinated, and much of the politically harassed family fled to Lima or abroad. Local political entanglements, as much as Asian rivals and metropolitan anticocaine laws, brought down Durand's cocaine emporium. Éxito and a phalanx of kindred properties in Derrepente limped on for two decades as the family trust of Negociación A. Durand, managed by the "Viuda de Durand" (Emilia) and a Croatian son-in-law, Alfredo Mastrókola. The family name still evinced pride: ads for Éxito in the 1920s boasted

A Huánuco cocaine maker, 1920s (William E. Dunn, *Peru: A Commercial and Industrial Handbook* [Washington, D.C.: U.S. Department of Commerce, Bureau of Foreign and Domestic Commerce, 1925], 142)

of Rosa Durand (among other farm enterprises) as the "Propietaria de la Mejor Fábrica de Cocaína del Departamento."[23]

Cocaine devolved into a part-time pursuit for the Durands, with at best seasonal rhythms, though Éxito, surviving into the 1940s, remained Peru's longest-running such factory, serving as the desperate family's cash cow. The family concertedly diversified from coca, and by the 1930s San Carlos had become well-known as a tea plantation. The Negociación was still one of Huánuco's major coca concerns after World War II, though bit by bit the *montaña* properties were sold off to support the scattered but illustrious Durand family, which today has no ties left to Huánuco.

To assess the challenges facing cocaine makers like the Durands and Soberóns, an analysis of the shaky industry was prepared in 1926 by engineer Jorge Hohagen, a renowned public servant (then chief of exports at customs) and a *huanuqueño* himself. Peruvian coca exports had slipped from a postwar spike in 1920 (453,000 kilos) to less than half that by 1925 (216,000). Most went to Chile, earning less than *Lp*20,000 (*S*/100,000). With the United States out of the picture, cocaine exports narrowed to Germany, Japan, and France, dropping from 133,000 ounces worth over *Lp*120,000 in 1918 to 21,000 ounces earning under *Lp*18,000 in 1925. Prices dipped by more than half between 1918 and 1921, bottoming out in 1923 at 2.69 *soles* per ounce. After studying changes in European demand, Hohagen stresses the small scale of Peruvian cocaine making, describing "pequeñas oficinas" (workshops) with three to five workers in leaching operations putting out about a kilo a day. He also details the costs of the typical operation, probably based on Éxito records. Using a ton of leaf for 5 kilos of 84–94 percent crude cocaine meant a 200–1 coca input ratio, a fairly high estimate. Each kilo cost about 15 *soles* to process, a third of which went to labor, a third to four chemical inputs, and a third to amortize a factory. Hohagen, perhaps working on a "valued-added" basis, did not compute coca costs, but coca itself came to a low 45 percent of expenditures in his overall accounting. Shipping a kilo to Germany in effect doubled cocaine's cost margin. All told, each kilo sold cost *Lp*11 (55 *soles*) to produce and ship, whereas the buying price in Hamburg was *Lp*20 — still allowing, after all the struggle involved, a decent profit.[24]

Based on this cursory analysis using Hohagen's shaky figures, cocaine remained a profitable if intrinsically small-scale enterprise, even with the drug's depressed price. Cocaine's challenge was a highly uncertain, stagnant market, with nowhere to place additional product. A U.S. report on the sector in 1928, quoting Peru's first official report on the industry that year, listed an aggregate capacity among all national factories at about 3,000 kilos, though it failed to note that Peru had not actually sold that much cocaine for nearly twenty years. The size of the consuming market was governed by encircling restrictions rather than by relative prices or cost factors in making cocaine.[25] This may help explain, in a strictly economic sense, why owners shied away from innovation in Huánuco, especially technological advances that relied on economies of scale. With greater factory size, output, or efficiency, prices would have dropped, and no compensating increased revenues would have followed unless the sector was strictly controlled by a price-fixing monopoly. This remained the drug's dilemma until new, high-price markets opened up, that is, the novel illicit demand beyond the 1950s.

By the mid-1920s, leadership of Huánuco cocaine had passed to the merchant Andrés Avelino Soberón, with his Obraje factory and "Huánuco"-brand crude cocaine. Between 1925 and the late 1940s, Soberón's factory was the one constant of the area's ailing cocaine industry, as other makers revolved in and out. The five Soberón brothers, some tied to the Durands by marriage, never became wealthy from cocaine. Like Durand, they spread themselves across all the area's ecological niches, from dairy farming to small mining ventures with foreign investors. Curiously unlike Durand, they were not involved with farming *montaña* coca per se. They were also politically active, notably in the rebellious Peruvian APRA (Alianza Popular Revolucionaria Americana) Party, an incipient force in national peripheries like Huánuco and a local heir to Durand's Liberal Party. Soberón chaired the 1930s Junta Departamental de Desocupados, a leftist lobby; his son and most active partner in cocaine, Walter Gustavo, became Huánuco's Aprista mayor in the 1940s. Cocaine has enjoyed a long association with the Peruvian Left, relating to the region's off-center political circuits. Andrés Soberón led a stubborn if sensible campaign to find new and diverse overseas markets for cocaine in the three decades after 1920, including Japan and, fruitlessly, the United States. In his quest, he was the last of a dying breed of legal cocaine makers.

Soberón was born in Huánuco around 1883. A seasoned merchant, he entered the cocaine business in 1918, and archives reveal his earlier connections with Durand, during the 1917 price spike of World War I. In one of the deals from Durand's last *sindicato*, Soberón acquired (with brother Manuel) the Machay farm-factory in Chinchao, financed by the Banco del Perú y Londrés, a future partner. He was first in business with one of the last Croat cocaine makers, Juan Milosovich, from whom he likely learned his craft. By the mid-1920s, Soberón had set up his factory on the Quinta Obraje, a block-sized walled house and garden acquired in 1919, creating an industrial presence in the town proper. It had an annual capacity of six hundred kilos using the slow, six-barrel Bignon-Kitz precipitation method. Peru's 1928 Public Health Department survey of drug factories put Soberón's production at four hundred kilos yearly, still trailing the Durands, though smaller producers also marketed through Soberón's firm. During the 1930s, Soberón repeatedly mortgaged the enterprise to keep it afloat, usually to his sisters and brothers. He and his brother Walter seemed unusually devoted to cocaine; in 1932, Soberón was the first to apply for a Peruvian cocaine license. Like the Durands, Soberón stressed his high-quality "Huánuco" product, advertising the "gold medal" won at the 1930 Ibero-American fair in Spain. In one of his advances to American drug firms, offering up to fifty kilos a month, he boasted, "The cocaine I manufacture is better in quality and percentage than similar cocaine obtainable here."[26] Because of his marketing savvy, Soberón sold cocaine for other factories—by the 1930s even for Éxito and Pampayacu.

In this way, Soberón became cocaine's dominant force in Peru, accounting for at least half the total crude cocaine exported between the

1920s and the 1940s. Soberón worked principally through Dammert, a Peruvian-German middleman dating to the 1890s boom, but also directly contracted shipments to Japan. He boldly wired American firms and officials (to their dismay), trying to crack their ban on Peruvian crude cocaine imports. Tragedy also struck the family concern: in 1938, one of Soberón's sons (Augusto, an engineer) died in a horrifying industrial accident while processing cocaine without a mask. Yet Soberón pressed on. After the war, with bleak prospects ahead, Soberón was the one regional cocaine maker still delivering exports. In 1949, he was the last Peruvian cocaine maker to close shop when the industry was outlawed, packing a final seventy-seven kilos to Lima and leaving a rich inventory of the tools of his trade. Some sources suggest that in his Lima retirement, Soberón's interest in cocaine even extended into the illicit era of the 1950s.[27]

One of few direct portraits of Soberón (and of the industry per se during its long depression) is the testimony of a U.S. consul in Lima, William C. Burdett, who in April 1932 undertook a challenging trip to Huánuco to meet Soberón. Burdett was investigating Soberón's offers to sell sulfate of cocaine, this time to New Jersey Merck, as part of the larger, evolving U.S. effort at drug surveillance in Peru. Burdett casts a skeptical lens on Peruvian law and initiatives to regulate the drug industry. He surveys coca exports to the United States and the exporters applying for cocaine licenses, at that point only Soberón, the Durands, and Trujillo's Ayllon.[28] Burdett reveals how the slumped industry—now in *the* Depression—exported only on demand, with no regular contracts. In 1932, Soberón filled such a special shipment to Osaka's Shionogi and Company, similar to one of Ayllon to Biedermann in Bremen. "The drug," Burdett describes, "as exported from Peru, is about 86% grade and is obtained by a process of kerosene and sulphuric acid precipitation." Burdett recounts his high-altitude rail and road journey to cocaine's remote capital in Huánuco, nestled amid seven-thousand-foot mountains, "which can only be reached from the outside world by the route described." He repeats lore that "the leaves grown in the surrounding mountains carry a cocaine percentage higher than those grown in other parts of Peru." He introduces Soberón: "[Soberón] is a comparatively wealthy Peruvian, about 50 years of age, and was born in Huánuco but makes business trips to Lima. In addition to the cocaine factory he owns mines and lands. He, of course, professed a faithful obedience to all Peruvian laws and regulations concerning his business." Burdett paid a personal visit to Obraje, then refining little over a kilo a day, half its capacity. Soberón deflected the blame for illegal marketing to the United States, claiming "his business has always been with Germany, France, and Japan."[29] Burdett's twenty-page report also surveys drug imports, the coca habit, the coca bush, and its harvest and circuits around Huánuco. He ends with an ominous warning about drug traffic, a "danger more potential than actual," but prophetic in light of later 1950s FBN charges against Soberón. Yet Burdett's jaundiced view of the industry was still rare. Until the 1930s, when commercial guides to Peru touched on cocaine, which they often did, they portrayed the industry as a kind of exotic or fossilized part of the Amazonian scenery. Instead of being described in menacing tropes, it was seen as quaintly out of touch with the larger world.[30]

Soberón was not the only cocaine maker left in Huánuco. The early 1920s saw the last active Croats fade away, perhaps as clients of Durand's commercial machine, which collapsed with his murder in 1923. (Twentieth-century cocaine makers are shown in the appendix, table A.4.) Some old-timers carried on for a decade, such as the regional merchant house of Montero Brothers. By the late 1920s, as factories elsewhere in Peru receded, some 80 percent of national cocaine was said to originate in the Huánuco *montaña* between the Chinchao and Monzón Rivers. During the late 1930s, responding to cocaine politics in 1936–38 and stirring prewar demand, the number of individuals trying their hands at cocaine multiplied; these were often ex-employees of older workshops, mainly marketing their small shipments via Soberón. A League list of licensed Peruvian factories in 1936 counts eight in Huánuco. Fortunato Rada worked his modest venture in Monzón, Huánuco's traditional coca frontier. Carlos Baroli, an Italian immigrant, tried his luck in the late 1930s in Chinchao, as did his partner Ascencio Orfanides, as well as Enrique Martín and the Ramírezes of coca-growing clans. Fernando Gallardo and Víctor Funegra had short-lived workshops. José Roncagliolo ran the Bolívar plant, one of the few to outlast the war. A unique experiment was Julio Barranchea's Cóndor factory, established in 1937 not in Huánuco but in Lima using leaf sent specially overland from Chinchao. Two years later, however, the Cóndor trademark had relocated back to Huánuco under new management, with the Lima factory left to the state. There are early 1940s reports of efforts by Chinese merchants to enter and consolidate the industry, led by Julio Chan Waiy and his incorporated Inca factory. Soberón resisted and survived the takeover bid. Shipments spiked in 1939 as German and Japanese houses bought up cocaine ahead of demand, at times surreptitiously, pushing national cocaine revenues above coca's for the first time since 1918. Still, even with the medicinal demands of World War II, when exports peaked at nearly three thousand kilos in 1943 (a third of earlier levels), the sector only employed 17 full-time workers, as enumerated by Peru's 1940 census. Yet some 4,562 men and 607 women labored in the *cocales* around Huánuco, not to mention muleteers and other brokers. Nearby factories took in nearly half the area's leaf. Respectable Huánuco families like the Repettos, Malatestas, Maldonados, Figueroas, Ampudios, Castillos, Ramírezes, Lambruschinis, and Durands still formed the core planter class, rooted in the *montaña* of Chinchao, Derrepente, and Chiguangala.[31]

The global Japanese stake in industrial cocaine, and Japan's colonial coca complex in 1920s–30s Formosa, was sketched in the last chapter. For Peru, the impact was felt dramatically in the form of chain-crossing Japanese investors and their agents in the heart of the Huallaga region, starting during the wartime drug shortage of the teens. U.S.-trained chemist Hajime Hoshi was a global figure in cocaine and a political force in Japan. Between 1917 and 1919, his expanding Tokyo firm, Hoshi Pharmaceuticals, Sankyo's main cocaine rival, bought up a huge swath of land near the jungle hamlet of Tingo María, the so-called Tulumayo tract at the junction of the Tulumayo and Huallaga rivers. This ill-defined territory of over 300,000 hectares (about 225 square kilometers, or 1.2 million acres), some of it abutting the Chinchao Valley and on the other side extending to Pozuzo, hosted a dozen scattered coca *fundos*. It enjoys an uncanny centrality in the history of cocaine, including past ownership by Kitz and Durand. Peruvian officials, notwithstanding a racial ambivalence, welcomed the Japanese during the early twentieth century, as they had embraced the prior Germans of Pozuzo, as a wave of industrious (non-Indian) *colonos* who could help develop the Amazon.[32] Starting in 1917, the Durands and kindred Martín clans sold Tulumayo piecemeal to the K.K.K.K., Hoshi's Japanese consortium, a purchase that raised some international concern. By the 1920s, its fertile plantations, such as Pampayacu, run by naturalized Nisei-Peruvians like the Saitos, Oshis, and Sawadas, sent coca leaf, cinchona, and scientific know-how about coca culture back to Japan before Formosa, where Hoshi also put up plantations, became a self-reliant drug colony in the 1930s. In the mid-1930s, Pampayacu alone rendered 46,000 kilos of coca, second in the region only to the Durands' San Carlos estate. By the late 1920s, a crude cocaine plant run by Masao Sawada was also operating there, in and out of service over the next decade.

In 1937–38, Hoshi's Tulumayo tract was suddenly nationalized by Peru, a move abetted by the United States in a prewar campaign to counter

Japanese influence and resources in the Americas. Indeed, since the 1920s, U.S. officials had kept watch on Japanese drug activities, one of their first surveillance steps in the Huallaga. The expropriation, which occurred amid rising anti-Japanese fervor in Peru as well as rising land values as the first roads reached the lower jungle, was long contested in Peruvian courts via Hoshi's legal agent, Sawada, to no avail. After 1937, the land reverted to the Peruvian state, and it would play a key role in the postwar development of the Huallaga Valley, and later of illicit cocaine.[33] With the case in limbo, the area's Nisei community, by now, like the Croatians, part of the Huánuco elite, distanced itself from Hoshi, claiming its own rights in the tract, and took care of the blacklisted "Japanese factory." Sawada and others stayed, becoming active at war's end in Tingo María real estate. The direct Japanese role here stood in the way of Soberón's quest to expand Huánuco's cocaine markets, as Hoshi's vertical organization captured local cocaine or, later, replaced it with colonial cocaine from Formosa.

Finally, while Peru's cocaine producers after 1900 clustered around Huánuco and factories in Lima and the south closed by 1915, northerners continued to play a secondary role, mainly in the surviving Trujillo enterprises of Martín Ayllon and Teofilo Vergel. The northern coca circuit of Peru, controlled by merchant-*político* Alfredo Pinillos, was tied into the highland Otuzco coca region of eastern La Libertad, especially the conglomerated Sacamanca farms, known for their flavorful extract leaf. Pinillos's operation gained a near world monopoly on sales of "special leaf" for Coca-Cola via the port of Salaverry and Maywood Chemical. This became after 1910 an essentially separate circuit from both Huánuco and the newer haciendas of Cuzco. In the north, despite ample capacity to process it, cocaine remained an elite sideline, discouraged by steady sales of leaf to Maywood, biases about alkaloidal content, and the prestige and connections of Huánuco's producers, who cornered most European orders. The north's robust commodity linkage to the U.S. market must have also constrained cocaine sales.[34] Yet two northern factories stayed on line, sporadically at least; indeed, during the depths of the early 1920s cocaine slump, their sales briefly rivaled those of Soberón. Ayllon was a partner with the coca monopolist Pinillos. Gustavo Prados, the active manager of Ayllon's main Sacamanca hacienda, at times managed an in situ plant. In the 1920s, Genaro Risco at Hacienda Huayobamba and the Chinese Chon Fan reputedly made cocaine. Vergel's workshop sat within a larger sixteen-man merchant industrial enterprise. A detailed 1921 portrait remains of his fully electrified plant (something unheard of in Huánuco), reputed to use six hundred pounds of coca daily making sixty kilos a month for European sales. Vergel was a connected "caballero" of northern commerce and, like Pinillos, busy in Goodyear vulcanization and distribution, a good alternative to risky cocaine. He would rise to defend cocaine interests in the mid-1930s more vocally than Soberón, who kept a low profile during the era's cocaine debates. The two factories continued to be listed in local business guides but with the minute market became part-timers after 1925. Vergel and Ayllon's operations survived until criminalization in 1949, when some of these owners' kin fell into trouble with the new laws.[35]

In the two decades after 1920, the men who ran Peru's struggling cocaine industry looked very different from the intrepid innovators sought by Lima's outspoken coca reformists and cocaine nationalists, and from the determined cocaine pioneers of the 1880s and 1890s. Their last hope was to slog on, mainly by manipulation of local politics or in a frustrated search for market share in what was a politically bounded, stagnant cocaine world. Huánuco, in particular, became a regional haven for Peru's depressed culture of low-tech cocaine. However, the mere survival these rustic workshops, leftovers of Bignon's and Kitz's heroic age of legal cocaine, would prove vital in cocaine's longer transformation as a world commodity.

NATIONALIZING COCAINE: PAZ SOLDÁN OF THE 1930S

Debates over cocaine's decline and the drug's possible future came to a head in Peru during the 1930s. The driving figure in this controversy, Dr. Carlos Enrique Paz Soldán, opened his crusade with a fiery prococaine polemic in 1929: a call to resist emerging global drug controls, and their marginalization of national cocaine, through a protective state-run Estanco de la Cocaína y la Coca. The sinuous national and transnational politics of this cocaine campaign would climax in the mid-1930s. This dramatic yet little-known episode merits close analysis for two reasons: first, it reveals the array of national political and social forces that could be stirred around declining Peruvian cocaine, and second, it reveals much about the global actors and constraints then working against national or alternative projects for the drug.

Paz Soldán was the scion of one of Lima's most distinguished intellectual and political families, a cosmopolitan if eccentric twentieth-century ana-logue to José Casimiro Ulloa. During the 1920s, he served on the directive committee of the Pan-American Sanitary Union in Washington, where he made a name as a progressive in public debates over the racial politics of the Pan-American eugenics movement, a lifelong interest. Paz Soldán was founder and director of the hygienics Instituto de Medicina Social at San Marcos University and editor of the prominent medical journal *La Reforma Médica*, which advocated European-style social medicine in Peru. He was also an apparent early elite sympathizer with the nascent APRA Party—the northern, leftist, anti-imperialist social movement of caudillo Víctor Raúl Haya de la Torre that convulsed Peruvian politics from the 1930s to the 1960s, and which intersects at several points with the saga of cocaine. His personal crusade on behalf of cocaine was born of association with (as he put it) "mi amigo Ignacio Antonio Pagador y Gómez de Léon, descendiente de Don Quijote."[36]

Paz Soldán's writings touched a range of themes circling Peruvian cocaine since the turn of the century, along with global political influences of the 1930s. These include the scientific admiration of "modern" cocaine, cocaine as an agro-industrial answer to regional backwardness, statist control of drugs and industrial planning, the drug as a nationalist magnet for anti-imperialism, and, not least, his stark contrast of cocaine to Peru's traditional and maligned Indian coca habit. Social medicine, the left-leaning public health movement he embodied in Peru, still shared the hygienic and eugenic concerns of Latin American elites. In the context of global cocaine, Paz Soldán's crusade of the 1930s marked a challenge, or perhaps even an alternative, to the rising external models of drug control championed by the United States and the League of Nations. Here, Western notions of causality get inverted: rather than cocaine problems of the West stemming from Peru's surplus coca leaf, a classic supply perspective on drugs, restrictions and plummeting Western demands for cocaine were driving Peru's spreading national health emergency of coca. American orthodoxies of market control were reversed as well: the Peruvian state could manage such abuse by its guided social monopolization of world cocaine trades. Paz Soldán urged Peru, through technology and state action, to retake its monopoly position lost to rival commodity networks since the teens.

Paz Soldán pursued this cause in scores of 1930s pamphlets, editorials, essays in the professional *La Reforma Médica*, and public debates in the press. His 1929 manifesto, in Peru's highbrow *El Mercurio Peruano*, was "El problema médico-social de la coca en el Perú," which was anticoca in an *indigenista* vein. But Paz Soldán links that discourse closely to cocaine. In the West, cocaine abuse exploded around World War I, which he attributes to the unhindered rise of Japanese cocaine. Yet Peru also suffered from an unbridled national "toxicomanía," the "cocamanía" of the "degenerating" Indian race, left to chew the now-surplus coca crops. It was an argument Paz Soldán would try to wield with statistical precision in years to come. Paz Soldán underscores Peruvian interests and reasons of state, ignored by the international drug conventions that Peru never attended to. He musters data to dramatize Peru's collapsed share of world cocaine markets, now one-twentieth the scale of the turn of the century. In broad strokes, Paz Soldán links each market collapse to successive world drug regimes at The Hague and Geneva, conventions he portrays, not unrealistically, as forums for industrial nations to protect their own national manufacturing interests. League "quotas" on cocaine were deforming Peru's regional industry and oppressing its natives. "The coca producers of Peru, without organization or solid means of defense, are clandestinely exploited by the giant international trusts," he says, in a tone redolent of Haya de la Torre's early anti-imperialism.[37]

Paz Soldán's global solution was a state "estanco," a form of Spanish colonial political revenue monopoly: "The Peruvian Monopoly of Cocaine would be a type of Chamber of Commerce and at the same time an organ capable of regulating production, controlling consumption, and working—decisively—around the whole problem." What Paz Soldán pictures in his crude charts is a gigantic corporate body with four articulating sections or functions, or, in his capitalized political idiom, "LA FRENTE NACIONAL DE LA INDUSTRIA COCALERA DEL PERU." First was a bureau for "technical and chemical studies," which would erect factories to manufacture refined salts of cocaine and even substitutes like novocaine. Next was a bureau of "indigenous cocainism" to conduct studies and campaigns on the problem, using Peru's cocaine revenues to "redeem the indigenous population." Third was an office for "Propaganda, Education, and Toxicomanía Assistance," presumably to prevent modern forms of drug abuse and addiction. The fourth section dealt with "Administration, Statistics, Consumption, Prices, and International Conventions," in effect setting the terms for Peruvian cocaine to recapture world medicinal markets. In Paz Soldán's wide sociomedical vision, "science" and "control" were closely entwined.[38] The first step was to wrestle back nearby South American cocaine HCl markets from German firms, then the world.

Paz Soldán refined the project of a state-regulated modernized cocaine industry over the next decade in ever-starker salvationist terms. In 1934

ESQUEMA DE LA ORGANIZACION
DEL ESTANCO DE LA COCAINA.

CONVENCIONES INTERNACIONALES SOBRE NARCÓTICOS.

EXPORTACION Y VENTA AL EXTRANJERO DE COCAINA

VENTAS INTERIORES DE COCAINA PARA USOS MEDICINALES.

VIGILANCIA DEL TRAFICO ILICITO.
SECCION VENTA DE COCAINA

ESTANCO

| SECCION ADMINISTRA-TIVA- ESTADISTICAS PRODUCCION- CONSUMO CONVENIOS INTERNACION | SECCION TECNICA OBTENCION PRODUCTOS DERIVADOS ... | USINA CENTRAL DE FABRICACION DE COCAINA PURA Y CRISTALIZADA. | SECCION DE ESTUDIOS MEDICO SOCIALES SOBRE COCAINISMO INDIGENA ... | SECCION DE PROPAGANDA -EDUCACION Y ASIS TENCIA - COCAINO-Y ... MANOS ... |

NACIONAL DE LA COCAINA.
SECCION COMPRAS Y SELECCION
SECCION RECAUDACION DE IMPUESTOS.

CONTROL SOBRE LA OBTENCION DE LA COCAINA BRUTA.

LABORATORIOS REGIONALES

ESTACIONES AGRICOLAS

CONTROL SOBRE LA PRODUCCION Y CULTIVO DE LA COCA.

ECONOMIA AGRICOLA de la COCA PERUANA.

Paz Soldán's national cocaine *estanco* scheme, 1929 (Carlos Enrique Paz Soldán, "El problema médico-social de la coca en el Perú," *El Mercurio Peruano* [Lima] 19/135–36 [November–December 1929]: 600)

essays in *La Reforma Médica*, he lambastes "the inexorable ruin of the Peruvian coca industry by the international blockade of markets," referring to the 1931 Geneva accord, which Peru had signed in 1932 under little-known circumstances. Because of that pact, eight thousand tons of Peruvian coca leaf was silently killing the nation's Indians. Yet, Paz Soldán insists, as the world's leading "producer of excellent coca, Peru has the duty to exploit its native plant." The sole route around these restraints were "giant manufactories of pure cocaine," a path to "equality with·German, French, Dutch, Swiss, Italian manufactures": "PERU SHOULD ENJOY"—the caps are his—"MODERN FACTORIES IN ITS OWN TERRITORY TRANSFORMING THE NATIVE AND ABUNDANT COCA OF ANDEAN VALLEYS INTO NOBLE PRODUCTS OF MEDICINE AND INDUSTRY." Paz Soldán rails against Peru's acceding to the Geneva Convention without a proper defense of cocaine, calling this move the "R.I.P." of an established industry, leaving in its wake Indian "racial degeneration" and "spiritual death." Paz Soldán's defense of modern cocaine contrasts with cocaineless Bolivia's mid-1920s diplomatic effort to defend indigenous coca leaf usage in international forums.

The scant scholarship on Paz Soldán's campaign, abstracted from this cocaine militance, lumps him as an *indigenista* ally of the coca-phobic conservative *arequipeño* Dr. Carlos Ricketts.[39] In late 1929, Ricketts, then a congressional deputy, introduced a coca *estanco* bill to Peru's Congress as a means to eradicate the highland vice of coca chewing, a political outgrowth of the anticoca medical movement brewing since the 1910s. The bill died during a two-year ordeal of regime shifts and challenges from regional coca lobbies, notably the coca growers of Huánuco. Yet Paz Soldán, with his heavy social medicine and at times left-wing accent, was a world apart from Ricketts. He was an industrial modernist who personified the growing chasm in Peru between scientific cocaine (still understood as noble) and Indian coca (deemed bad for social development). Instead of coastal anticocaism, Paz Soldán drew on social public health ideals, and, along with the later Andean biology school of Dr. Carlos Monge Medrano, his respected San Marcos colleague, he would influence national and international coca control of the early 1950s.

Paz Soldán's crusade swiftly had sharp, if obscured, international repercussions in the secret maze of U.S. and global politicking that by now enveloped Peruvian coca politics and drug control. On 21 September 1930, the *New York Herald* announced, "League Drug Crusader Believed Slain by Poison." The report told of the mysterious case of Spanish diplomat Antonio Pagador, killed by his daily glass of milk, allegedly poisoned by trafficking interests during a private mission in Chile. The State Department and FBN subscribed to a deeper version of events, linking Pagador to the Peruvian *estanco* scheme. According to their sources, Pagador, a veteran player in League antiopium politics, was locked in negotiations for "installation of a plant in Lima, Peru, for the manufacture of cocaine out of coca leaves under the auspices of the Peruvian government." His collaborator, Purdue professor of chemistry R. Norris Shreve, joined because "it offered a means for the controllable manufacture of this essential local anaesthetic." The idea, following Paz Soldán, was to use the enterprise to curtail native coca consumption and exports to the West. New York's Schieffelin Drug Company (a politically connected former coca importer) was to become sole "world agent" for a Peruvian monopoly of cocaine hydrochloride. The disillusioned Shreve believed that Pagador was murdered by agents of British, German, or Swiss drug firms, from whom "illegal traffic in cocaine originates."[40]

This global conspiracy theory was never substantiated, but evidence does exist of a monopoly plan that had the secret blessing of the League and President Leguía. By 1930, talks in Lima had even pinpointed a factory site. Peru's finance minister, Fernando Fuchs, was negotiating with Pagador about a monopoly deal worth a reported "$1 million" in annual revenues, a substantial sum at the onset of the Depression. In a January 1930 speech marking Peru's patriotic "Homenaje al Huánuco," Leguía personally lauded cocaine, in contrast to that national "menace," coca chewing: "Cocaine and its derivatives are of great use in medicine." Next, in the topsy-turvy course of Peruvian politics, the 1930 fall of Leguía's regime doomed the Pagador project, taking Ricketts's coca monopoly down with it. In another twist, rumors flew that Pagador had discovered the plan was a fraud, a front for "illicit traffic," and "washed his hands of it," adding another layer of suspects in the case. Pagador's influence, including his camaraderie with Paz Soldán, ran deep in world drug control circles. Over the next few years, Eugene Schaeffer of Maywood Chemical Company, a presence in Lima, would try to get Peru talking again to the League "to protect their Legitimate sale of coca," but without the lure of the 1929 *estanco*. The State Department had opposed Pagador's project all along on the simple ground that no cocaine could legally enter U.S. ports. The United States in effect blocked the one coveted scheme of Peruvian drug control — Paz Soldán's national monopoly of cocaine.[41]

As the 1930s Depression unfolded, Paz Soldán's initiative sent waves across Peruvian society, including, for the first and last time openly, mobilization of the national agrarian and regional interests tied to cocaine. During the 1930s, virtually any source of local employment or revenue seemed worthy, and nationalist cocaine protests became endorsed by the upper echelons of the Peruvian state. The politics of this mobilization were often puzzling. Apart from the underground Peruvian politics of *aprismo* and *indigenismo*, corporatist, popular front, unilateralist, and nationalist motifs like Paz Soldán's enjoyed the international prestige of the political Right and Left alike. Paz Soldán's grand "Alianza Nacional" fitfully emerged, even among businessmen. In May 1933, Teofilo Vergel, the respectable Trujillo merchant, began campaigning in the local paper *La Industria* for a "national industry"— his cocaine factory — against what he cast as the "monopolies" and "restrictions" of the League. The Lima press picked up his pronouncements, and reports filtered to a watchful FBN in Washington. In 1934, Paz Soldán stepped up his cocaine crusade from his *La Reforma Médica*, and President Benavides promised action, if only to calm Aprista unrest. In 1935, the official *Boletín de Agricultura y Ganadería* published the agronomy text of long-active Carlos Bües, "La coca en el

Perú," which framed the global problem of coca decline, apart from highly local soil conditions, in terms remarkably similar to Paz Soldán's.[42]

The banner year for prococaine agitation was 1936, fueled by rumors about the impending Geneva talks on "illicit traffic." Paz Soldán's coup was convincing Peru's Sociedad Nacional Agraria (SNA), the powerful lobby for big coastal sugar and cotton, to adopt the coca question in the name of national landed interests. The SNA sponsored a massively appended thirty-five-page report, *La coca peruana: Memorandum sobre su situación actual*, by none other than Paz Soldán. It was his usual plan, more convincingly argued, with all the APRA-inspired "National Alliance" slogans edited out, as befit Peru's conservative landed class. The booklet decries "unjust international pacts" and glorifies coca as "Peru's special gift to the world." In fine detail, Paz Soldán dissects the sinking regional economies of coca and cocaine, surveying global prospects for refined cocaine. He ends on a call for Peru's unilateral "denunciation" of the 1931 Geneva Convention.[43] Echoes of his memorandum would make it to Geneva and back again.

La Vida Agrícola, Peru's agricultural mouthpiece, soon took up the cause. Its dramatic March 1936 editorial, "La coca en peligro," endorsed the SNA's protest petition to the Consejo Superior de Salubridad (Peru's drug supervision board). The editorial disputed the policy of "imperiling" coca and cocaine by signing drug treaties: "We hope this opportunity is not lost. The dangers to coca are not new. Disgracefully, until now Peru has not paid this problem serious attention... [which is] not simply a defense of its obvious rights as millennial grower of coca." Questioning the state's passivity since 1912 in the face of international anticocainism, *La Vida Agrícola* argued that suppression of legal cocaine imparted "a serious blow to critical regions of the country." This protectionist furor forced President Benavides to issue another supreme decree in March 1936, this one aimed at "remedying this situation and defining clearly the action the State should adopt toward one of Peru's most autochthonous industries." It mandated the creation of a national "study commission" with members drawn from the ministries of health and finance, the SNA, and representatives of the coca and cocaine sectors. It was to prepare a "defense of the national interests" for Geneva as well as new domestic restrictions on Indian coca use—the dual program long advocated by Paz Soldán. Throughout the year, *La Vida Agrícola* pushed the issue by, for example, serializing the SNA memorandum.[44]

Although it is hard to ascertain if the study commission actually met, the SNA duly appointed its two delegates, Hernando de Lavalle and Jorge

Souza. Simultaneously, Vergel launched a new round of missives from the north, printed in Peru's leading Lima dailies *El Comercio* and *La Prensa*, before descending on Lima as a regional delegate. Vergel decried the "50%" drop in coca crops suffered by Trujillo and Otuzco provinces and pledged to win back markets "displaced by the foreign boycott." The U.S. Embassy monitored these events with alarm. In a June 1936 confidential memo, "Subject: The Approaching Narcotics Conference Interests Peru," U.S. officials fretted over Paz Soldán's influence. Peru, they thought, might follow Bolivia's resistant lead or Turkey's defense of opium, the latter of which had resulted in state-run morphine factories set up against European will. Peru's foreign minister was talking to Bolivia about a common coca policy. Peru, U.S. officials worried, might seek the vacant seat on the League's Opium Advisory Committee (OAC). The Peruvian Congress had voted to "demand" a larger cocaine export quota from the League and was planning an official delegation "ensuring that future Conventions not be detrimental to Peru's coca growers." The Peruvian delegate, Enrique Trujillo Bravo, had his credentials and views checked. Follow-up U.S. reports assessed the political climate: Peru had grave doubts now about signing the Geneva accords, as its exports suffered "without [Peru's] having taken part in the discussions, and without insisting on her rights as the oldest coca producer in the world."[45] U.S. officials feared rising drug protectionism in Peru, which might result in a policy quite different from American-style drug control.

Some of the pronouncements seem more ambivalent, signs of political contradictions around national indigenous coca use and export cocaine. Reports implied that, along with foreign powers, the private Peruvian owners and operators of cocaine factories were wary of Paz Soldán's monopoly campaign. Their ostensible leader in Huánuco, Soberón, stayed conspicuously silent on the whole issue. They allegedly wanted intervention "endeavoring to reconquer the export market," but hardly nationalization. As always, calls for larger "export quotas" came with warnings to "restrict the consumption of narcotics," that is, coca. Liberal *El Comercio* went about quoting illiberal Paz Soldán verbatim in its 1936 editorials: Peru, like Mexico, must take its place in the League "to support and assert the rights of Peru for a larger exportation of cocaine," the paper declared, concluding, "Peru is vitally invested."[46] Few doubted the shaky premise, in a ruined global economy, that a big cocaine market was somewhere out there.

As historians now know, the 1936 OAC Illicit Drug Trafficking Conference in Geneva about the illicit traffic in dangerous drugs was doomed from the start, a "noble failure." Hit by political defections, the League was fading into irrelevance as clashing industrial nations geared up for war. Bitter infighting marked the proceedings, and no moves were taken around limitation of raw materials or their trade. Indeed, coca had been quietly shelved as an official concern two years before, and the League made no attempt to impose specific cocaine export quotas, the deep Peruvian fear. A Peruvian observer sat mutely through the Geneva sessions. But the country offered little cooperation save for delivering a list of eight "Licensed factories" and notes on opium dens.[47] In 1938, the League's OAC would nominally add Peru to its ranks, with no perceptible impact prior to the arrival of a new postwar order.

The denouement of this transnational controversy came with the 1938 visit of the OAC's general secretary, Eric Ekstrand, to Lima. It was a Latin American PR junket for a beleaguered League, replete with upbeat reports of cooperation on every front. Yet Ekstrand's tour ended in Peru in an open debate with the followers of Paz Soldán. He arrived in Lima in May 1938 and held planned meetings with top officials from Public Health and Foreign Affairs aimed at Peru's formal signing of the 1925 and 1936 accords. Ekstrand reported that "much stress was laid on the advantages, from the standpoint of active cooperation with the League of Nations, of arranging for all important documents," referring to accounting long ignored by Peru. He met with the head of the SNA, which he called "an important centre of information" that did not "make itself in any way responsible for the views expressed by authors whose works it published," a veiled reference to Paz Soldán. Ekstrand did manage to tease out of Peru its first drug report since a note of the early 1920s, and the Ministry of Foreign Affairs and U.S. Embassy lauded the visit, along with novel proposals for drug limitation.[48]

The ministry also published Ekstrand's extended official response to Paz Soldán, "Memoria del director: Sobre el libro 'La Coca Peruana.'" In it, Ekstrand argued that the core legal premise of Paz Soldán's long 1930s polemic, that League conventions somehow shackled Peru with drug "export quotas," was "in error." Peruvians ought not view this issue so conflictively, the general secretary argued. Ekstrand graciously added that "some of the measures suggested by Sr. Paz Soldán . . . are well in line with existing informal conventions regarding opium [i.e., the idea of state monopolies]" while denying any intentions for "a plan of limits on the legitimate trade of coca." Thus, League failures at control were turned into political virtues in Peru. "Once this misunderstanding is relieved, Sr. Paz Soldán will realize that his country can freely at any time become a manufacturer," Ekstrand held, and it could place for sale whatever cocaine the market would bear. Cocaine's troubles did not derive from a "conspiracy of industrialized nations" but from "free competition among competing world factories." Like Turkey, Peru could have a "Frente Nacional de la Industria de la Coca, the modern factory making all end products of coca, under direction of the state." Peru, stated Ekstrand, had no reason "to crusade for justice: it was already assured by existing international conventions."[49]

Ekstrand's San Marcos address, delivered on Paz Soldán's home turf, was just as conciliatory. As recounted by *La Revista Agrícola*, he said that "these issues have great interest among us, as producers of coca and crude cocaine, and because of public 'erroneous concepts' that League control harms legitimate Peruvian producers." Soon, everyone seemed to back down from or claim victories in the 1930s struggles over cocaine. The SNA distanced itself from Paz Soldán, boasting that *its* efforts had "stopped" outside forces from restricting national cocaine. Ekstrand spoke of a glorious reception in Peru, even though he returned empty-handed. In his own next round of writings, Paz Soldán abandoned the cause of cocaine for a tirade against the "Slavery of Indian Cocaism," as well as anti-Japanese racial polemics, leaving Peru's industrial dreams to others. Despite his often shrill postures, Paz Soldán remained an elder statesman of Peruvian social medicine in the 1950s.[50] Like Freud's, his cocaine episode was quietly forgotten by posterity.

Well in retreat as a commodity, cocaine could still excite political passions in the 1930s going beyond the long-voiced concerns of Peruvian *técnicos* and university reformers. In this realm of ideas, the modernist and nationalist allures of cocaine outlived the drug's actual importance to Peru. If Paz Soldán's ambitious national project failed in the end, it was an episode that nonetheless exposed all the complex and contradictory local and global interests surrounding Peruvian cocaine by the 1930s.

REGULATING COCAINE

Peruvian governments tried to deflect U.S. and League of Nations anticocaine pressures after 1910. Although overarching state control (à la Paz Soldán) did not succeed, after 1920 authorities did gradually begin to regulate the sector by means relating to national sanitary projects, local taxation, and, by the late 1930s, with an eye on the threat of contraband from remote drug factories. The model was medical, specifically managed by Peru's Bureau of Health or through self-policing by boards of local notables instead of by the centralized antinarcotics bodies arising in other parts of the globe. The turn to policing cocaine, a corollary of its criminalization, would only arrive after World War II, as Peru embraced the punitive international drug regime.

Cocaine was initially a model liberal product, entailing little governmental intervention despite the drug's semiofficial promotion of the late nineteenth century. By 1900, cocaine resembled other taxable goods, if affected by varied local coca imposts (including a Huánuco tax on "extracción de la cocaína") that supported most of the region's paltry public services.[51] Indeed, if the Peruvian state had taxed and regulated these products more stringently, as Bolivians did with *yungas* coca, more would be known about the contours of their initial production and trade. By the 1910s, revenues from cocaine were a minor source of the industry's legitimacy with the state; by the 1920s, cocaine and its inputs became tax exempt due to the industry's precarious condition.

Coca leaf had become a matter of heated medical and policy debates by the 1920s, but the same cannot be said of narcotics and specifically not of cocaine, which had no users or abusers to speak of in Peru. Law 4428, President Leguía's supreme decree of late 1921, placed basic import-export controls on cocaine, along with most other pharmaceutical products. By the mid-to-late 1920s, prescription-like controls became formalized by a Sección de Narcóticos of the Dirección de Salubridad Pública. By 1927, this board had assumed responsibility for gathering statistics on cocaine factories, which were explicitly prohibited from selling cocaine within national markets. Local pharmacies were supplied with carefully cataloged imported pharmaceutical cocaine HCl. The goals here signaled emerging concerns with hygienic and sanitary issues, though the Peruvian state was still too feeble to consistently promote public health. In 1927, the eminent researcher Dr. Sebastian Lorente, head of Leguía's nascent public health system of the 1920s, along with Dr. Baltazar Caravedo, prepared a report on "toxicomanía" in Peru for the Eighth Pan-American Sanitary Conference, held in Lima likely at Paz Soldán's behest. Lorente and Caravedo tallied the challenges of modern *toxicomanía* (a term encompassing drug manias and addiction), but they argued that Peru's long Incan history and the place of coca in Peruvian society ill fit such categories (though other local medical authorities increasingly believed that Peru fit the mold). Lorente and Caravedo deemed coca the Indian's "panacea universal"; as such, its use was not an easy habit to legislate away. Instead, the nation's public health menace was opium smoking among the Chinese community, the era's typical Pan-American racial scapegoat. Opium presented a foreign threat to a healthy national *raza* as it filtered from decadent "dens" into urban life, democratizing among "the elegant, journalists, pseudo-intellectuals, artists, and all those who seek from intoxicants their true inspiration." Opiates drove Leguía's narcotics law, and over the next decades Peru would see periodic police sweeps of opium-smoking scenes. Opium was sold through a government monopoly (founded in 1887 and reorganized in 1921), violated at times by illicit poppy patches. The Lorente-Caravedo report is notable both for its lack of concern about cocaine as an abusable or contraband drug, though Peruvians were well aware of its ill repute elsewhere, and for the authors' insistence on health "prophylaxis" (drug education) rather than police or punitive approaches to drugs.[52] This path showed the imprint of Peruvian social medicine.

Varied centralizing projects to regulate coca and cocaine surfaced in the late 1920s and the 1930s, including the larger monopoly schemes, but few new actual controls were put in place, despite the passage of a dozen amending decrees on narcotics between 1923 and 1935. Sporadic reports from the Bureau of Public Health (still in the Ministry of Promotion and/or Public Works) began to put out charts of data on cocaine exports specifying their who, when, and where. The best was a small census of the entire cocaine industry, including a declaration of each factory's capacity, published in early 1928 in the wake of the Lorente-Caravedo report and quickly passed on to U.S. officials. Another decade would pass before the next survey. Controls mainly stayed at the local level. In this, Peruvians were ignoring the pressuring advice of North American and League of Nations functionaries, who advocated specific cocaine restraints, sent Peru samples of model repressive laws, and at times kept a closer watch on local cocaine than did Peruvian officials. Consul Burdett's 1932 inspection tour of Huánuco was a case in point. While engaging Soberón, who lawfully renewed his cocaine license that year, he sized up the Peruvian system of control: "Factories producing cocaine are required by the Office of Narcotics to produce their books for frequent inspection by what is known as the Departmental Pharmaceutical Delegation.... This delegation exercises only perfunctory control[,] and in an isolated village such as Huánuco it would certainly be composed of friends of the cocaine manufacturers." Burdett remained dubious of Peru's will to curb smuggling. Health officials confided to him their reluctance during the Depression to curtail "any industry which shows a profit, regardless of its nature."[53]

Enforced licensing requirements were in fact a new means of control, likely inspired by the League of Nations format, along with export declarations and improved delegation reporting procedures. By mid-1932, six cocaine licenses had been issued, four in Huánuco and two in Trujillo, with names and other details released in the press by Peru's director of health, Enrique R. Rubín, who came from a family with Huánuco ties. These pharmacy boards actively functioned in 1930s Huánuco, as revealed each time cocaine factories requested permits via the prefect and Pharmacy Delegation to fill export orders, typically in fifty-to-one-hundred-kilo lots, via Lima. All cocaine had to pass, with stamped *guías* (passes), to the laboratory of the Bureau of Public Health in Lima, which handled exports with a small group of registered export firms such as Dammert, Nonomiya Shoten, Stone, and Gratry. Nothing suggests circumvention of the process, as cocaine lacked illicit demand or smuggling circuits. Peru's surviving clutch of cocaine makers seemed to quietly police themselves. In 1936, Peru prepared a nineteen-page listing of its antidrug laws for the U.S. Embassy, including inspection procedures and fines, which was relayed to FBN offices in Washington. In November 1937, new rules were issued for transit of coca leaves to Lima for the projected Cóndor factory, the same year Peru opened a hospital ward for drug addicts in the capital. By 1939, the same Dr. Caravedo (a pioneer psychiatrist and editor of the *Archivos Peruanos de Higiene Mental*) appeared more taken by U.S.-style medical treatment of addicts. Depression-era price controls on basic medicines were also part of the state's slow advance, as the Bureau of Health was merged into the growing governmental apparatus dedicated to "work" and "social security."[54]

World War II marked a crucial transition here. The Peruvian state quickly expanded and militarized a slew of bureaucratic functions. Shortages of imported medicines spurred tighter control and vigilance, and the United States, ever more active in Peruvian affairs, spied on Peruvian officials and exerted higher standards of accounting. For the first time, rumors of "contraband," or illicit sales, began to fly. These, however, had mainly to do with illegal sales to Axis powers, a true temptation for Peruvian cocaine makers, who had long relied on German and Japanese markets for their output and who much wanted to (but could not) sell legally to the United States. Now, U.S. and Peruvian officials together closely monitored such suspicious sales, including those to allegedly neutral Spanish, Swiss, Chilean, and Argentine clients. In March 1939, two "German subjects" (Otto Lietzenmayer and Berthold Feuchtuger) were dramatically seized by Lima's police intendant while setting up a small cocaine lab, with four hundred grams of finished drugs, in Miraflores, one of Lima's flashy new neighborhoods. Sales were registered to German merchants in Chile and even increased to Russia during its brief Nazi alliance. Wary U.S. officials felt that half of Peruvian cocaine stocks entered what they termed "clandestine channels." In December 1939, by supreme resolution, Peru suspended new cocaine licenses pending review to "guarantee the licit elaboration of this substance." One Huánuco cocaine maker, Víctor Funegra, suspected of "irregularities," fell under the British "Statutory List" of economic warfare, having long exported with now-proscribed Adolf Dammert. Authorities also scrutinized Soberón's neutral trade. War discourse and practices marked a vital legal transition in cocaine's status to the illicit.[55]

In July 1941, the official gazette announced Peru's first true antinar-cotics policing decree, aptly entitled "Strict Control over the Traffic of *Estupefacientes* [Narcotics]." Police, in conjunction with the Bureau of Health, were mandated to investigate all instances of illegal drug use or sale. The decree spelled out the boundaries of "tráfico ilícito" for the first time. War meanings transmuted into wider understandings of illicit behavior. A July 1943 decree shored up reporting and pharmacy controls over scarce narcotics. A confidential U.S. report in 1943 suggested that the Peruvian government was looking into means to "improve the ef-fectiveness of their control over the production of cocaine" among its eight to ten licensed producers. As early as 1941, rumors surfaced of a state cocaine HCl production plan related to the monopoly schemes of the 1930s. A May 1944 decree announced Peru's intent to test cocaine HCl production at the Bureau of Health lab for needed domestic medicinal use, though samples were long delayed. Another 1944 decree centralized the work of "Control de Narcóticos" from local pharmacy boards to the capital's Bureau of Health and called for a "reorganization of control of drugs." Carlos Ávalos, who began working within the Bureau of Health in the mid-1930s, became in effect Peru's first narcotics expert and drug cop, and after the war he would take charge of a narcotics squad, later centralized in the Peruvian Investigative Police (PIP), in cooperation with the American FBN. One of Ávalos's chief wartime tasks was police ration-ing of medicines like codeine. After 1945, a new hybrid journal, *Revista de Sanidad de la Policía*, appeared in Lima, edited by Dr. Luis Sáenz, a career anticoca scientist. It merged medical with policing concerns, including applied chemistry for narcotics detection. In March 1945, the press sounded an alarm about Peruvian youth and illegal drugs (without publishing any specifics) in a call for stringent laws. Observers believed the state would simply forcibly relocate the cocaine industry to Lima, an act tantamount to nationalization.[56]

However, prior to 1945, the degree of direct state control over cocaine was slight, informed by hopes of an export revival and perceived priorities of public health. Save for war contraband, cocaine was not yet a matter for the police and military, as it would swiftly become in 1947–50 when national cocaine, caught in a vortex of cold war international politics, finally became criminalized in Peru.

LEGAL COCAINE, CA. 1940S

The key fact of cocaine's trajectory after its 1910 peak was the sheer survival of Peruvian cocaine and its techniques, however primitive and crippled after decades as a declining commodity. The story of Peruvian cocaine contrasts with that of Bolivia, which never industrialized coca, as well as with those of the more sophisticated Dutch, Japanese, and German cocaine industries. Slim hopes remained of revival as a regional or state-run industry adapted to an encroaching world antinarcotics order. World War II marked the point of no return for legal cocaine: warfare devastated Peru's competing coca-cocaine circuits, which fell under strict U.S. occupation after 1945, and shut off Huánuco's last markets in Germany and Japan. The war, which briefly stimulated demand for cocaine and coca, put the American focus on allied Peru and on this semistrategic good. Cocaine's postwar options narrowed. The new antidrug bodies of the United Nations, unlike the defunct OAC, pursued a clear U.S. agenda and launched a 1947–50 commission that directly challenged Andean coca. The UN cut licit world cocaine quotas to four tons and then to fifteen hundred kilos by 1950. Peru's relic legal industry was doomed.

A remarkable view of where Peruvian cocaine stood at its final crossroad is provided by a secret 1943 wartime report, "The Coca Industry in Peru," prepared by chemist Emile Pilli for his employers at Merck in Rahway, New Jersey.[57] This is a gem of industrial espionage, if tarnished at times by its bad math. Much like Rusby's Parke, Davis–sponsored Andean journey of the 1880s, Pilli's mission was to scout Peru for scarce supplies of coca leaf. Pilli was responsible for a strategic commodity of Merck, the sole dedicated U.S. cocaine refiner, after the loss of its plantations following the Japanese invasion of Java. At fifty pages, Pilli's rare unpublished monograph is the most sweeping look ever at Peruvian legal cocaine.

Pilli's report begins with coca's "Historical" origins, covered with a slight *indigenista* accent, and a botanical survey that sticks to descriptive commercial (rather than old varietal) distinctions between "Huánuco" and "Trujillo" leaf. Pilli is wary of extant coca classifications, which still lacked reliable chemical analyses, a problem going back to the days of Bignon. The next section maps "Producing Areas" of Peru's three principal coca zones: the central area (Huánuco, at 34.5 percent of national coca), the northern area (Otuzco and La Libertad, at 19 percent), and the southern area (Cuzco and Ayacucho, at 46.5 percent, mainly of Cuzco origin). Pilli also offers less reliable data on the coca consumed in the cocaine sector. He estimates 1 million pounds of leaf were going into "Exports" (15 percent, presumably with leaf for Chile), 1 million for "Manufacture of Cocaine" (15 percent), and 4.64 million pounds "Used for Chewing" (70 percent). Misled by unit confusions, this is a gross overestimate of the production of industrial coca, exemplary of errors among even the best of specialists. Cocaine leaf in fact hovered at 2–3 percent of totals. After 1915, Peru's copious southern coca was flowing into indigenous circuits. Tables of leaf exports show a recent doubling of Coca-Cola-related U.S. sales, but war-inflated coca exports in 1942 (465,500 kilos) were still half the peak of 1904–8.[58]

The next sections of Pilli's monograph dissect the planting and harvesting of coca in Peru, starting with "Terrain, Soil, Climate" (lowland soils coming on line did not yield as fine a leaf as traditional thirty-five-hundred-foot clay soils) and "Cultivation" (the planting cycle of unirrigated and unterraced *cocales*). A topical survey of "Harvesting" is followed by a digression on coca lichens, a customary but still mysterious means of gauging the age of a coca bush. A section on "Crops" probes the conditions for optimal leaf output and, not surprisingly, bemoans Peru's poor scientific culture of coca. It was still unknown whether younger or older plants, or those at higher or lower elevations, bore the most alkaloid—the same questions that had plagued Lynch thirty years before. Peru had about nine to ten thousand acres in coca, in broken hilly plots rather than manageable fields, for a total of 13–14 million plants—not far above the guesses of a century before. Coca was thriving in the warmer lower valleys east of Huánuco, now approaching Tingo María thanks to road building in the

been dominated by open-air fanning. After 1935, in coca's one technological leap, large Huánuco planters adopted indoor furnace drying (a Javan
technique first used by Durand) that was, like jute baling, still regulated
by "rule-of-thumb." Much coca was saved from rain and rot, yielding the
uniform leaf desired by Indian chewers.[59] Pilli's is the most intimate look
at Peruvian coca culture since Mario Durand's in 1916.

In "Sales and Distribution," Pilli next turns to commercial questions,
the analysis of which was his overriding mission in Peru. He separates
his analysis by coca's three trade zones. In the north, Merck appeared
locked out: the Pinillos clan had maintained, through exclusive contracts
with Merck rival Maywood, a three-decade hold over regional coca sales.
Prado's Cayanchal, with a 180,000-pound output, was among the top
four growers and the zone's most quality-conscious supplier. Northern
farmers mixed leaf indiscriminately in Maywood's lots, including 5–6
percent "foreign matter" that was then cleaned up by Pinillos. With soaring Coca-Cola demand and little new planting under way, Pilli expected a
regional shortage only worsened by war transport bottlenecks.[60] Yet Pilli
still managed to land an undisclosed new Merck delivery contract with
the old cocaine hand Prados.

Turning to the coca circuits of Huánuco, Pilli reveals a rarely discussed
development: the rise of Chinese coca traders. Imported as coerced coastal
laborers in the nineteenth century, they began to disperse throughout Peru,
by 1900 reaching Huánuco as small-time brokers of coffee and coca. By
the 1940s, Pilli was averring that "While over 80% of the coca produced in
Huánuco is grown by Peruvians, about 90% of the distribution and sales
is in the hands of Chinese nationals."[61] Only 3 percent of regional coca
originated in the disputed Japanese Pampayacu plantation, still in the
name of blacklisted Hoshi. Pilli untangles a maze of Chinese deals that
had captured coca markets through ownership of Hacienda Santo Toribio,
leases of Durand properties, monetary advances, intimidation of small
farmers, and formation of the Sociedad Industrial y Comercial Inca, a large
crude cocaine venture. Leading figures in this group were the wealthy
Augusto Kuan Weng, his brother-in-law Julio Chan Waiy, Tasy Long y Cia,
and Alfonso Tanjun, a Lima community leader. Waiy was said to drive this
organization and to exert "a powerful influence on the cocaine market of
the world." Recalling Durand's strategy of 1904–18, Waiy was leaning on
Soberón to sell out (a deal so far "refused") and negotiating a takeover of

the old Éxito plant. Waiy's "ambitious plan" included the formation of a new 1942 corporation, funded by Lima's Chinese investors, that aimed to raise cocaine prices in England and Russia, that is, a regional "trust" designed "to manipulate the global market at will." Despite Pilli's hand in commercial intelligence, other records (e.g., Huánuco tax registers and business guides) are more ambiguous about the Chinese role, which in any case proved short-lived, over by the end of the war.[62] Pilli's concern reflected his goal of diverting more Huánuco leaf to exports via Callao, which was blocked by Waiy's objections to overseas leaf sales. Waiy had intervened to stop Merck's unprecedented request for 500,000 pounds of Peruvian leaf. Brokers at home, Pilli suggests, knew little of coca's thorny Peruvian markets.

Pilli's main focus was Huánuco, given Merck's interest in cocaine. Forty-three percent of Huánuco coca went into making crude cocaine, and, as Pilli notes, cocaine was still the life force of regional commercial life. He continues with a roundup of the region's commercial varietals, demarcated as in Durand's time: Chinchao or Chiguangala coca, Derrepente, Monzón, Tingo María, and Pillao, as well as leaf-packing grades (top-quality *prensa*, hand-packed *pulso*, leftover *huanta*, and low-potency *coñupo*). Chinchao was the closest and oldest coca district of Huánuco, starting fifty kilometers east of the city at Carpi, "considered the best in all of Peru" for cocaine making.[63] But Pilli the chemist wonders if Chinchao leaf truly contained more alkaloid, a belief never proven by assays. He suspects that his contracted northern leaf was its equivalent. Monzón and Tingo María marked coca's frontier, the latter "recently open to colonization." One Tingo planter, José Prato, was working to harvest 60,000–100,000 pounds by 1943 entirely for cocaine, a precocious feat given the zone's later centrality in the illicit cocaine boom of the 1970s. As Pilli closes his study of Huánuco, he turns to "Production" and confirms the fears of Peru's early agronomists: "The production of coca in the Huánuco district is less than what it was some twenty-five years ago. This reduction has been due largely by [sic] the poor care given to the plantations with the resulting dying of the plant." The main culprit was chronic erosion. Some Chinchao farms had lost half their bushes, with some ridges now barren. Diversion of five thousand hands of scarce labor into road building also stymied planters. Yet in Pilli's list of major Huánuco planters, the old families still reigned: Repetto (Hacienda San Miguel), "Japanese" Pampayacu, Tello (of Pipish), Malatesta (of Vilcabamba), Ramírez (of Bellavista), and the relic estates of Gregorio Durand and the Figueroas. The regional crop was 2.1–2.4

million pounds, still led at 150,000 pounds by the Negociación A. Durand.
But small farmers now contributed 1 million pounds, at less than 10,000
each, a group which was to multiply after 1945 as the Huallaga became
an official zone of colonization.

Leaving Huánuco, Pilli left pithier impressions of Trujillo coca (the
diverse grades of Otuzco leaf used for Maywood extract) and Cuzco coca
(38 percent of Peru's crop, from dozens of often huge plantations, largely
for Indian consumers). Huánuco cocaine makers actively shunned the
abundant southern leaf as inferior in quality. Pilli includes here a de rigueur,
if clumsy, digression on "Coca Chewing," that timeless fascination of
outside observers. He takes coca to be an exclusively male "habit" of two
million Indians, a poor basis for calculating its use, and covers such tourist
topics as lime additives. In Paz Soldán fashion, Pilli muses on the effects
of 20,000 pounds of cocaine entering the indigenous bloodstream yearly,
"4.5gms" per capita. Citing U.S. authorities who asserted that Indians must
exhibit the long-term symptoms of cocaine poisoning, Pilli admits that
such signs were barely noticeable among Peru's already "dull" Indians.

The final quarter of Pilli's commissioned study is devoted to the future
of Peru's "Crude Cocaine Manufacturing." After three decades of neglect,
the business lay in shambles. The nadir, with only 368 kilos sold, was 1933,
though lend-lease orders had later briefly lifted sales to around 3,000 kilos.
"Cocaine manufacturing establishments in Peru gradually closed, until today
[1942], there are only five licensed manufactures," Pilli remarks. These
included the Sociedad Industrial y Comercial Inca (the Chinese trust),
Huánuco (Soberón), Monzón (Rada), Éxito (ex-Durand), and three others
off line. Pilli observes no tangible technological progress: "The method of
manufacture used at present is identically the same as introduced in Peru
in 1890 by a German, Mr. Arnaldo Kitts [*sic*], and with slight modifications,
employed by all manufactures. Equipment consists of a battery of tubs or
barrels constructed of cedar arranged either in a straight row or in two
rows of three barrels each." He proceeds with a familiar description of
the eight-tank sulfuric acid and kerosene leaching process. Two kilos a
day were squeezed from each 600 pounds of leaves. After six days' time,
workers pressed and stacked "snow white" cakes of crude cocaine to dry.
Pilli explains: "The process is rudimentary. No laboratories are maintained
and there is absolutely no control at any point in the extraction process"
prior to the product's being forwarded to the Bureau of Public Health in
Lima for a final assay. Peru's cocaine was usually 90–93 percent grade,
with 10–15 percent in ecgonine form.[64]

Pilli, a professional chemist in New Jersey, was struck by the industry's apparent aversion to chemistry, especially to optimize leaf alkaloid extraction. He writes: "In all of Peru there is not one person thoroughly familiar with the subject. True, the planter knows how it is planted, harvested and dried, but knows nothing about alkaloid contents. The manufacturer of cocaine knows something about the method which he follows. He knows that certain results are automatically obtained if this or that operation is performed, but knows nothing about alkaloid contents." This was the gist of his workshop interviews. The rare times Peruvians reported high yields Pilli attributes to their having accidentally "coordinated" their haphazard techniques. After juggling coca use ratios of manufacturers (starting with Chinchao *pulso primera*) and his own fieldwork, Pilli decided that "all the data and information in Peru, gained through a half-century of cocaine manufacture, may be misleading." His own Trujillo leaf tested highest at over 1 percent alkaloid. Pilli was, as expected, obsessed with efficiency. He enumerates every site where "losses" of alkaloid occurred, from washed leaves to discarded carbonate sulfate solution. And like other analysts since the 1910s, Pilli sized up the industry's cost effectiveness. In Huánuco, a kilo of 90 percent crude cocaine cost 217.15 *soles* ($33.40) to make: the thirteen *arrobas* of coca remained the costliest input (182 *soles*, or 84 percent of cost), with other materials (12 percent), wages (less than 2 percent), and managerial "supervision" (above 2 percent) making up the remainder of the cost. Save for sodium carbonate, all of cocaine's inputs were Peruvian. This was the cost basis for sales to England, where May and Baker's war prices fluctuated between £15 and £20. Ultimately, for Pilli, these rustic work sites were simply not modern enough: "The terms 'plant' and 'factory' have been applied in this report to the cocaine manufacturing establishments in Peru. . . . our conception of the word 'factory' perhaps gives a false perception. More often than not, these establishments are but adjuncts to residences or living quarters of the owner. . . . There is not one instance where a building has been erected, or an old building remodeled for the purpose of serving as a cocaine manufacturing establishment."[65]

Pilli's conclusion, "The Future of the Coca Industry"—"the outcome of which is almost certain"—is understandably gloomy. He laments the decrepit plantations of Chinchao, which "as a coca-growing area," he predicts, would "pass into the pages of history." The opening of Tingo María seemed promising: "In the not distant future this area will become an important coca growing district in Peru," he guesses, though its low-altitude leaf had yet to be appreciated. In the north, pressures mounted on aging *cocales* from "the ever increasing demand from the Maywood Chemical Works." Merck's purchasing mission was imperiled by tight coca supplies and shipping. Regulation of the industry from Lima was "very loose," suggesting a possibility (already occurring, so Pilli had heard) of contraband drug surfacing for sale on the streets. "The government realizes this," he notes, and had moved to put stronger curbs in place, with the idea of ultimately bringing all cocaine manufacturing, by decree, into a manageable Lima location.

Aware of Peru's constraints under international convention, Pilli, like the national technicians before him, focuses on the industry's defining limit: "Factories engaged in the extraction of cocaine alkaloids from the leaf, can only produce those alkaloids in a crude form and market the same as 'crude cocaine.'" Pilli purposely ventures beyond his "present report" to speculate, "The time is most favorable for those engaged in the manufacture of cocaine to begin the manufacture of cocaine salts [cocaine HCl]." Laws would need adjusting, and "competent personnel" would have to be recruited "either by the present manufacturers, or by foreign capital, once it realizes the possibilities here offered." Pilli seems to have known that a decade of debates and official concerns had unleashed "strong forces at work whose object it is to nationalize the coca industry," what he calls the "Stanco" plan. "Peru has ambitions of becoming a dominant nation in the production of cocaine," he notes. The United States could approach Peruvian cocaine by means similar to its strategic purchases of quinine, by formal "agreements" or "the establishment in Peru of cocaine extraction plants sponsored and financed by the United States government," ending its half-century ban on cocaine imports. This latter option would portend, argues this Merck scientist, "the ultimate elimination of cocaine manufacturing in the United States." Thus, Pilli saw beyond the narrowly defined interests of his employer and U.S. homeland.[66]

Cocaine in 1943 was a moribund though surviving legal industry in Peru, its last global redoubt. National alternatives to its decline had been clearly voiced but not implemented during the 1930s Depression. It is difficult to say if this juncture represented a lost opportunity for the creation of a modernized national cocaine industry or even a viable alternative to later imported repressive models of drug control. Perhaps over the long run, a revived and well-regulated industry may have prevented Peruvian cocaine from moving underground and swayed coca-growing peasants from entering into illicit commerce. Pilli's intelligence report raises two larger questions about Peru's stymied commodity in the postwar era. First, would the United States, now paramount in world drug affairs and ever more dominant in Andean states, ever consent to a small Peruvian cocaine industry modernized in the statist form envisioned by technocrats? This was an idea with long support and resonance, especially in the capital of Lima. Second, while Pilli was a keen observer, he failed to see one future for this languishing industry, that of illicit cocaine. Perhaps this future was not quite thinkable at the time, given the dearth of Andean expertise in drug smuggling and the extinction of American coke fiends in the early 1900s. After its stagnant middle age, dramatic changes lay ahead for Peruvian cocaine—though these changes were mediated, as seen in the next chapter, by the twentieth-century saga of missionary drug control from the United States.

5

ANTICOCAINE

From Reluctance to Global Prohibitions, 1910–1950

In this chapter, I trace the global anticocaine movement born in the early twentieth century, which culminated at mid-century in a full-blown global prohibition around cocaine—a regime restricting producing regions in the Andes as well as production, medical usage, and illicit use in consuming sites such as the United States. The rise of twentieth-century narcotics control is the subject of a vast literature not only because this system's paradoxical legacies still plague us today, but also because the campaign to ban menacing drugs was one of the first models of internationalized norms and policing institutions. That scholarship, however, barely distinguishes the fate of cocaine from those of genuine narcotics (such as morphine, heroin, or opium) with which the drug is often conflated and confused. Moreover, few studies of drug control are genuinely transnational or constructionist, connecting the political and legal aims and ideals of would-be drug controllers in metropolitan sites like Washington and Geneva with the realities and reactions at the other end of the drug commodity spectrum in places like Peru and Bolivia. Yet in order for a prohibition regime to actually be built and work its effects, it must be absorbed and accepted by actors and institutions on the political periphery. In fact, the initial American quest for containment of cocaine provoked resistance, both passive and active, so that the construction of a global prohibition system was long delayed until mid-century (1949–61). Besides affecting the timing of the global drug control regime, the objections from the Andean side of the political chain help illustrate some possible historical alternatives to prohibition or to the illicit drug trade that followed it in the 1960s.

My arguments here have two peculiarities, in part because the topic and its store of official documentation are so large as to defy synthesis. First, for analytical economy, I have artificially separated issues of anticocainism from illicit cocaine per se, which I cover in later chapters. But readers should know that an early, shadowy era of cocaine use accompanied the rise of anticocaine passions and laws in the United States (1900–1920) and elsewhere, and that later nascent networks of illicit trafficking from South America began in the same years as the consolidation of global cocaine prohibitions (1950–65). Both of these contexts suggest thorny chicken-and-egg questions of which provoked which, the new laws or the shifting uses of drugs. Second, I will focus here on the origins of and projection of anticocainism from the United States and its export to and reception in Peru. It is already clear that other world-historical cocaine sites existed, with differing ideas about the drug: notably Germany, the Netherlands, Japan, and, for coca, Bolivia. Elevation of cocaine into a world menace, however, was a predominantly American quest in the first half of the twentieth century, one colored by the informal projection of U.S. power. The stubborn persistence of cocaine as a commodity in Peru despite global efforts to deconstruct or decommodify the drug proved crucial to the rise of illicit cocaine in the postwar world.

These long-term developments also suggest a paradoxical periodization for cocaine history in terms of policy outcomes. From 1910 through 1945, the United States proved adept at containing cocaine within its own borders and among its own citizens, with few objections, but the U.S. policing regime failed when diplomats tried to foist its ideals on the rest of the world. In effect, a "multipolar" cocaine world prevailed during the first half of the century, with a diversity of cocaine production sites, cultures, and uses. Yet during this era, cocaine remained a minor social problem that did not generate sizeable, dynamic, or lasting cross-border trafficking circuits. From 1945 to 1965, when the United States finally attained its long-standing goal of instituting a global anticocaine hegemony encompassing the last coca-growing zones of Peru and Bolivia, the reverse occurred: the birth and spread of illicit cocaine, which quickly spiraled into today's global economy of cocaine. Moreover, before the 1940s, the United States refrained from direct meddling in Peruvian drug policy, and thereafter it aggressively intervened against cocaine. These paradoxes may look like the result of classic sociological "labeling" (the idea that as you call people criminals or deviants, they start to act that way), but they also suggest real and even huge unintended social consequences of global cocaine prohibitions.[1] But before we reach that broad idea, there is new history to tread through.

The first part of this chapter excavates the origins of North American anticocainism, including the ban on domestic coca use, a dramatic turnabout for the country that before 1905 had been the leaf's major promoter and consumer. It also sketches the U.S. political economy of coca and cocaine that structured prohibitions after 1914 and eased repression of these goods after 1920. The next section unearths the drug politics of Coca-Cola, which served as a longtime but discreet mediator of U.S. cocaine policy at home and abroad. The third part examines the export of U.S. anticocainism from 1914 through 1940 as this policy filtered into drug congresses and League of Nations bodies, and it looks at the elusive reactions of producing nations Peru and Bolivia. After analyzing the antidrug pressures exerted against Peruvian cocaine during the interwar era, the chapter closes on the post–World War II triumph of U.S.-style prohibitions within the rising United Nations drug order and the translocal politics of this pyrrhic global victory.

ORIGINS AND STRUCTURE OF U.S. ANTICOCAINISM, 1900–1940

Between the late 1890s and the 1920s, a dramatic turnabout in medical thought, popular mores, and policies made coca and cocaine into pariah drugs on the American scene. The absolutist zeal of American anticocainism became the driving force, when applied to international antidrug politics after 1912, behind the unfolding global prohibition regime that was eventually to envelop all facets of cocaine by the 1950s. U.S. anticocainism arose from state and local initiatives starting as early as 1887 in Oregon and adopted by all forty-eight states by 1914. At the federal level, the Pure Food and Drug Act of 1906 charged the FDA with labeling and regulating noxious drugs and additives in consumer medicines. The Harrison Narcotics Tax Act of 1914 imposed a drug tracking tax and was used as the foundation of a national punitive prohibition regime. The 1922 Jones-Miller Act finally closed U.S. borders to cocaine and strictly regulated residual coca imports.

The widespread enthusiasm for and use of coca and cocaine in late-nineteenth-century America makes this reversal very puzzling. The shift was similar to those accompanying the embrace or rejection of medical and other goods generally, albeit a process charged by intense social desires and fears. What are not very convincing are attempts to see the progression of drug policy history as a Whiggish reform — that is, the notion that drugs were successfully banned when science awoke to their medical or social dangers. Such explanations cannot account for why some drugs inspired backlash over others—the coca versus tobacco question—or, in this instance, why benign coca became targeted along with perilous cocaine. Nor do they explain the reasons for or timing of the historically novel decision to regulate from above the bodily intake of modern citizens. American cocaine prohibitions surely related to the larger Western, Victorian, and industrial modernity that sought, for still dimly grasped reasons (including enhanced work discipline and the marking of new class, race, and gender boundaries), to delimit the "nonmedical" use of psychoactive or habit-forming substances. But even this generality is puzzling, given cocaine's initial association with scientific modernity and coca's special role as the antidote to exuberant modernization.[2] In contrast, alcohol and tobacco differed in their earlier commercial and cultural embrace in the West, which left large, self-conscious user constituencies, as well as states fiscally dependent on their trade. Similar anticocainism sprang up in other areas of the industrial world: in the Netherlands, it came enveloped in medicalizing professional ideals; in Germany, it was tethered by the corporatist ties between chemical firms and the state; and in Britain, it expressed itself in a wartime racial "drug panic." None of these anticocaine movements, however, had the strength, durability, or global ambition of American anticocaine politics.

The reversal of American passion for cocaine has been seen in two major ways: as synonymous with turn-of-the-century efforts to ban narcotics and rationally limit antisocial behavior, which included the antialcohol and antitobacco "inebriety" movement, or, alternatively, as a missionary crusade fueled by social irrationalities like racism. David Musto analyzes cocaine within his broad cultural frame of "the American disease," which describes the ever-ambivalent "love-hate" relationship of drug-infested Americans with drug highs and drug cures and the losses of collective memory as history's pendulum shifts for and against different chemicals. Americans, led by medical authorities, were thus reacting against their earlier unbridled enthusiasm for cocaine, in time forgetting the drug altogether, including its learned social dangers. Insofar as Musto differentiates cocaine from dominant antinarcotics discourse, he stresses the growing fear of drugs of the criminal "lower classes," analogous to the downward mobility of once-respectable American opiate "habitués." Cocaine only became deviant by the late 1890s with the popular adoption of drug sniffing over former "brain worker" use via medical injection.[3]

Who was using, or was imagined to be, proved crucial in such "symbolic crusades." Part of the passion of U.S. anticocaine politics came from representations of the drug as a particularly American vice, one that directly bred criminals and criminality. As many writers note, anticocainism was specially spurred on by American racism after 1900, a campaign born with the New Orleans and Atlanta race riots that equated cocaine use with uppity southern blacks and race-mixing drug parties — potent fantasies during the formative years of Jim Crow.[4] Prohibition was born of panic. Race-mongering became blatantly political in later efforts to get southern Democrats and even overseas Anglo-Saxon allies onto the bandwagon of federal drug legislation. Similarly, Lester Grinspoon and James Bakalar, who focus on cocaine, highlight racism against African Americans in cocaine's demonization in the first decade of the twentieth century, along with disdain for fringe groups like pimps, prostitutes, and day laborers. Such public passions combined with anticocaine warnings and polemics, accumulating since the mid-1880s, by disillusioned medical men from Europe and the United States. Power also intervened in how professionalizing guilds of pharmacists and the rising AMA sought to limit rival medical currents or patent-drug buyers from direct access to medicinal commodities like cocaine or coca.

A new interpretation, anchored in Joseph Spillane's research on American cocaine, lends a more nuanced sociopolitical rationality to this puzzling shift. To Spillane, American medical science had never gone overboard treating cocaine as a panacea; rather, by the 1890s, cocaine's indications were well-defined and limited. Physicians and most pharmacists sought responsibly to rein in the drug's usage after early recognition of its clinical dangers and recreational possibilities. The plethora of local cocaine laws in the United States attests to both the drug's specificity and concerns about its dangers. Nor did modern American pharmaceutical companies promiscuously push cocaine onto unwary consumers by 1900. The swelling popular market resulted from the broader American tradition of patent medicine sellers and the benign mania for coca tonics, concoctions, and cures, as well as from cocaine's plummeting price. After 1900, "shadow markets" for cocaine had already sprouted in cities among "tenderloin" district underclasses of thieves, prostitutes, and gangs. This reality, along with the often frightful manic appearance of chronic cocaine users, fed into the construction of a discrete new social type: the "cocaine fiend," an exaggeration based on small truths magnified. Racism was surely at play — as was a lively initial cocaine culture among African Americans — but cocaine anxieties were broader. Above all, anticocainism won credence as part of the advancing American Progressive movement: the drug was read as a cautionary tale about the unbridled power and greed of American pharmaceutical firms, which after all had first promoted it. Cocaine served as a key symbol for corporate reform in the name of the duped American consumer. Most manufacturers and wholesalers of American cocaine, and the pharmaceutical and pharmacy lobbies, actually joined the crusade in order to maintain their clean image against small-time spoilers hawking cocaine, in a typical corporate infiltration of Progressive-era regulation. Many of the same firms conveniently made cocaine substitutes, such as eucaine and procaine. The crusade's deeply principled politics, marking no distinctions between high- and low-potency goods, made safe, popular coca goods disappear from the market, a rationality carried to absurd lengths in related Bureau of Chemistry trials against decocainized Coca-Cola in 1909–11. Indeed, the FDA act hit coca more than cocaine: in its first two years, the number of coca products fell from more than twelve hundred to about three hundred. In the United States, few objections registered to antidrug legislation, which quietly passed (despite skirmishes over use of federal powers), since drug users themselves exercised little voice, unlike boisterous drinkers of alcohol. So what began as a rational medical regulatory movement ended, following further permutations by the 1920s, as one of the world's most punitive antidrug regimes.[5]

Beyond these initial political passions, a structured political economy took hold within the rising U.S. system of cocaine prohibitions, one linked by the 1920s to a defined foreign policy for cocaine. This structure had four main pillars: the long American preference for coca imports, the centralization of cocaine makers, the collaboration of pharmaceutical interests with drug controllers, and the political mediation of Coca-Cola's leaf circuit to the Andes. I will argue here that such structures eased the turn to prohibitions policy and helped cocaine prohibitions to work domestically during the long stretch up to World War II.

The first pillar was the specialization of U.S. cocaine and coca commerce by 1900 in the importation of coca leaf. This reflected established medical and consumer tastes for natural coca and extracts, proliferating patent goods, relative proximity to leaf exporters in Peru, and the consequences of ad valorem taxes on imported cocaine derived from chemical industry tariff struggles of the 1890s. Tariffs favored production of cocaine from duty-free leaf rather than from crude cocaine as in Germany, a bias even Peruvian industrial spokesmen decried.[6] By 1900, U.S. coca purchases averaged 500–1,000 tons of coca annually, mostly Trujillo leaf, with imports peaking in 1907. Little crude cocaine entered the country — only 134 kilos in 1903 — mainly for use by a single firm, Philadelphia's Powers-Weightman-Rosengarten. Booming consumer wants for coca-flavored soft drinks, a massive business by 1905, also fueled this trend. Over time, an ever-larger share of American leaf imports went into beverage usage rather than medicinal cocaine.

This import favoritism for raw coca leaf was effectively absorbed into U.S. drug policy. The 1922 Jones-Miller Act flatly banned all cocaine imports into the United States, whether German medicinal grade or Peruvian crude. Authorities believed that such imports stood a strong chance of becoming contraband: as a high-value, low-weight product, cocaine is easy to smuggle, something known all too well today. This ban also sanctified the monopoly of domestic cocaine manufacture. Bulky coca, on the other hand, was easy to track and register at customs offices, just as it was vanishing from the domestic pharmacy and consumer market. The 1930 Porter Act tightened this structure by placing management of coca inspection routines firmly in the hands of the newly formed Federal Bureau of Narcotics. The FBN rarely authorized special licenses to import or handle coca. Thus, the United States, year after year, could clearly report to international authorities at the League of Nations that it imported no cocaine and strictly controlled its foreign coca. This edifice of commercial control predated outright prohibition and was visible in the first official U.S. *Traffic in Opium and Other Dangerous Drugs* reports of the mid-1920s.

At the same time, in a second development, the number of American firms manufacturing cocaine steadily dropped, a concentration that simplified and aided control of the drug. In 1900, eight major U.S. firms — drug wholesalers, pharmaceuticals, and chemical companies — vied for the high-margin, booming cocaine market: Parke, Davis; Squibb; Mallinckrodt; McKesson and Robbins; Scheiffelin and Company; Powers-Weightman-Rosengarten; New York Quinine and Chemical Works; and the New Jersey branch of Merck. With a tariff rent and dwindling markets after 1914, the number of working U.S. cocaine makers shrank to three by 1920, and it was down to two by 1930. Merck in Rahway, New Jersey, nationalized in the 1910s, dominated the field, absorbing several competitors after Mallinckrodt abandoned cocaine. Maywood Chemical in nearby Maywood, New Jersey, made medicinal cocaine only as a byproduct of production of its special flavoring for Coca-Cola, and the firm passed this cocaine along for distribution. No doubt, cocaine's pariah status after 1905 speeded the process of industrial concentration, as the drug's legal outlets shrank owing to informal local bans prior to criminalization and its production became risky or disreputable for drug firms. Cocaine's medicinal roles continued to narrow, replaced by substitutes, and legitimate world "need" quotas were later set ever lower by the League of Nations, from six thousand kilos in the 1920s (half of earlier known levels) to under two thousand kilos after World War II. This concentration culminated in 1948, when the United States officially halted imports of coca leaf from Peru, its last source, for medicinal purposes, and Merck ceased making cocaine from leaf.[7] This left Maywood as the country's last maker of cocaine, which it sold to Merck for refining and distribution, and all of this cocaine came from the residues of leaf used for Merchandise No. 5, Maywood's secret extract produced for Coca-Cola. By the 1950s, a relic American cocaine industry was both a monopoly and a literal by-product of "Coke."

The secret of this pyramid structure was its focus on imports of coca leaf, funneled through the pair of firms at the top. This pattern merged into emerging cocaine controls between 1914 and 1930. The country's few narcotics officials, rather than directly oversee tens of thousands of dentists, chemists, and doctors — as they tried to do in the 1910s — turned to close regulatory links with the import/manufacturing/distributing firms at the top, which in turn helped foster and police a shrinking domestic sphere of legal cocaine usage. This proved far simpler than trying to manage the 136 proprietary medicines still containing cocaine in 1919, much less forty-three thousand dentists licensed to use it nationally. Once-popular coca also fell under bans due to fears that criminal elements might distill it into illicit cocaine, an unlikely prospect given that 120–180 pounds were needed to make each pound of the drug. Few protested that the consumption of harmless coca products might fend off use of harder drugs like cocaine. Thus, coca prohibition complemented broader drug controls. Treasury, customs, and FBN officers could track registered bales of leaf handled by trusted intermediaries while closing profit stimuli and gateways from imports of cocaine.[8] By the 1920s, the United States took in only about fifty thousand kilos of leaf annually for cocaine per se, mainly from Merck's Javan plantation. The Jones-Miller Act also banned U.S. firms from exporting cocaine, simplifying surveillance and precluding the shadow trades (and anticontrol lobby) that plagued state–drug firm relationships in Europe. By 1930, bureaucratized walls surrounded coca imports, managed by an informal top-down political compact between the FBN director, Harry J. Anslinger (1930–62), and the two firms, Merck and

Maywood, that brought closely watched leaf through the single sanctioned port of New York.

The third pillar of cocaine's political economy of control was the ability of actively involved companies to facilitate state actions. Major pharmaceutical firms and professional associations, the ethical wholesaler firms in medical markets, rallied to or spearheaded calls for reform of unregulated American cocaine after 1900 in efforts to mute public criticism of sales practices and shift the blame for the social problem of cocaine. The deviant fiend, pleasure, or criminal user, and urban cocaine-dealing "combinations," or gangs — for example, the notorious West Side "Hudson Dusters," who thrived in New York in the 1910s — were attributed instead to unscrupulous proprietary, mail-order, direct advertising business, or so-called Jew-pharmacists. At each step to prohibition, the government relied heavily on drug firms for inside trade information and for legal-institutional advice. In 1909, 1913, 1914, 1917, and 1922, the Treasury and State departments convened consultative conferences with manufacturers to shore up the new narcotics regime.[9] The Harrison Act, the basis for today's "war on drugs," passed without a whisper thanks to industry collaboration, unlike the earlier, failed Foster Bill. A 1913 congressional memorandum on the Harrison Act noted "the new cocaine evil which threatens this country" and a stiffer 1909 "prohibitory" tax on cocaine. It went on to laud "a vast amount of reliable evidence... furnished by the importers and manufacturers, pharmacy and policy officials." The memorandum continued: "It would be impossible for the illicit dealer under a prohibitory tariff to import his supplies from abroad, and they have expressed their willingness under law to account for the sale of their product. There can be no doubt of the earnestness of the American manufacturers of cocaine to control the illicit traffic."[10] Americans were pragmatic, harnessing the concentrated power of corporate partners to mediate drug control, in this case to abrogate the consumer rights of allegedly duped drug users. U.S. drug control was a subset of other forms of Progressive-era corporate self-regulation, much like the corporatist cartel model adopted by the German state to manage commercial cocaine.

Manufacturers met with drug control officialdom in periodic drug trade conferences, haggling over supply quotas and control measures. Detailed notes of such meetings survive for 1917 and 1922. At the first, pharmaceutical executives still expressed doubts about the perceived "toxicity" and "addictiveness" of cocaine, but these reservations gave way by the latter meetings to a businesslike give-and-take relationship. In the late

1910s, the United States was in the last throes of a dramatized cocaine scare, played up by claims of health officials that "75 percent" of import coca somehow vanished into criminal channels. By the late 1920s, federal officials declared their airtight sealing out of contaminating cocaine. By 1930, the new chief of the FBN, Harry Anslinger, was in constant contact and on a first-name basis with top Merck and Maywood executives about cocaine, having forged a personal and political relationship with these two firms that would carry over three decades — until the eve of another era, that of the explosive drug culture of the 1960s.[11]

COCA-COLA POLITICS, 1910–1950S

Much has been written on the business and cultural history of that emblematic commodity Coca-Cola, but almost nothing is said in these writings about its ongoing relationship to Andean coca leaf, much less the company's hidden influence on U.S. drug control and transnational cocaine politics with the Andes. Newly opened archives help trace such developments, restoring continuity between Coca-Cola's roots in nineteenth-century American coca culture and the post-prohibition era.[12] The key was Coca-Cola's long-term compact, via the intermediary Maywood Chemical Company, with the Federal Bureau of Narcotics, predecessor to the DEA.

Like other corporate actors in drug policy, Atlanta's Coca-Cola Company underwent a perceptible conversion between 1900 and 1920 from a passionate target of drug reformers into a government ally. The original Coca-Cola concept and recipe, concocted by Atlanta pharmacist John Pemberton in 1886, was born directly out of the era's buoyant American coca culture, company denials notwithstanding. Without fluid extract of Peruvian coca — coded as "F. E. Coco" (fluid extract of coca) in the formula — Coca-Cola would never have attracted the masses to drugstore soda fountains. After 1900, the firm's pioneering business practices, such as its bottler distribution system and bold advertising, amplified its success nationally. By 1914, hundreds of imitators thrived throughout the states with patchwork kola and coca brand names — "Kola-Coca" in one clumsy example — while others, such as a drink called simply "Dope," capitalized on the popular soft drink's drug connotations. Despite Coca-Cola's economic triumph, critics, many of them Progressive social reformers, still equated its refreshment with "dope" and associated Coke jingles with drug abuse. Critics also exploited Jim Crow fears, with sensational tales of "Negroes" hopped up on soda fountain binges.[13] Coca-Cola was hardly the cause of southern racial or drug problems, but to preempt further negative publicity its famed president, Asa G. Candler, quietly withdrew cocaine from the product in 1903.

It was then that Coca-Cola first teamed up with Schaeffer Alkaloid Works of Maywood, New Jersey, a small but expert concern. In a remarkable set of worldly connections, the firm's founder and namesake, German-born chemist Dr. Louis Schaeffer, had been sent in the mid-1880s as a young doctoral student by Mannheim's Boehringer and Sons to Lima on a failed mission to set up a local cocaine factory for the firm. Schaeffer gleaned much about Peruvian coca and, reassigned by Boehringer, landed a decade later in New Jersey. By 1899, after quitting over a patent dispute, he had used his extract formulas to build a durable family business. As Maywood Chemical Works, his factory passed to his son, Eugene, and later to other clan members until 1959, when it was sold as a subsidiary to Chicago's Fortune 500 Stepan Chemical Corporation.[14] For briskly expanding Coca-Cola back in 1903, it was politic to discreetly farm out the controversial business of cocaine extraction to an independent operation. Soon, in addition to manufacturing other alkaloid extracts, Schaeffer specialized in the production of the top secret decocainized leaf fluid dubbed "Merchandise No. 5" since it was the fifth of the so-called 7-X mystery ingredients in Coke syrup sold and sent by the barrel to bottlers across the land. Maywood's partnership with the Coca-Cola Company would last out the twentieth century.

This decocainizing reform was not enough. In 1906, the FDA's chief chemist, Harvey W. Wiley, to the chagrin of President Roosevelt, began a heated pursuit of Coca-Cola following populist muckraking attacks on coca- and caffeine-laced patent medicines. In 1907, the drink was pulled off army bases. Ironically, the climactic second federal show trial of Coca-Cola, held in Chattanooga, Tennessee, in 1911–12, hinged on charges of consumer fraud: namely, that Coke willfully duped consumers by boasting the c-word in its name, though it no longer contained coca. Coca-Cola won the case despite expert testimony against it by luminaries such as Columbia University's H. H. Rusby, who two decades before had been the premiere American specialist on coca leaf botany and medicine and later became editor-in-chief of the U.S. Pharmacopeia. Key testimony, including Schaeffer's, hinged on the nature of Merchandise No. 5 and its secret decocainized coca extract, which Rusby used in extreme doses to kill rabbits.[15] Even after Wiley's defeat, zealous antidrug lobbies targeted Coca-Cola, such as the pre-Prohibition Women's Christian Temperance

Union. Cranks and later foreign critics of "Coca-Cola imperialism" continued to attribute the drink's popularity to a concealed habit-forming dose of cocaine. Coca-Cola executives wrestled with the prospect of jettisoning the trace coca flavoring as not worth this trouble but kept it due to their alleged "cult of the formula."

By the passage of the Harrison Act in 1914, the tide had turned, and Coca-Cola was becoming a key government ally in the fight against foreign drug menaces. By 1917, remaining suits against the firm were settled out of court. In part, this warming relationship embodied the era's spirit of corporate regulation and the externalization of drug threats as the United States joined in the new global antidrug forums. In part, it reflected the cultural prominence of Coca-Cola, on its way to becoming a shining symbol of American capitalism and lifestyles—a shift that required a collective amnesia, abetted by the firm, about its Franco-Peruvian drug origins. The Coca-Cola Company's unique needs in the coca trade loomed large, so it strove to refurbish its image in official circles as it branched out in national and, by the 1920s, overseas markets.

By now, Coca-Cola employed a stable of busy lawyers. Section 6 of the Harrison Act was brokered by Eugene Brokmeyer, powerful lobbyist for the National Association of Retail Druggists and friend of Hamilton Wright, the first American drug diplomat. The Harrison Act thus explicitly exempted Merchandise No. 5 ("de-cocainized coca leaves or preparations made therefrom, or to any other preparations of coca leaves that do not contain cocaine") from the law's reach. Journalists like J. Leyden White leveled withering attacks against this privilege, playing on popular belief that Coca-Cola still contained cocaine: "Even the drug trade knows but little of this mysterious 'Merchandise No.5' for which the 'joker' was placed in the Harrison Law.... The corporation claims that Merchandise No. 5 is used exclusively for 'FLAVOR.' We are faced with the fact that one of the most vital and ethically revolutionary enactments of the U.S. congress carries a 'joker' to preserve the TASTE of a so-called soft-drink." White surmised that "Merchandise No.5 imparts a narcotic effect, a cocaine effect to those who imbibe it though Coca-Cola, [which is] the only narcotic whose distribution is not restricted under the Harrison law." Such outcries forced the Treasury Department, the first body charged with revenue drug enforcement, to undertake in 1915 regular chemical inspections of Coca-Cola syrup production at Schaeffer Alkaloid Works. Schaeffer had an early sideline selling cocaine extracted while making flavoring, which by 1930 the FBN, leaving nothing to chance, ordered incinerated. After the passage of the 1922 Jones-Miller Act, devised in consultation with drug firms, the making of New Jersey Merchandise No. 5 evolved into a ritually regulated act.[16]

By 1930, every annual report of the Federal Bureau of Narcotics contained a conspicuous rider devoted to Merchandise No. 5. In part, this served foreign consumption: the commissioner's annual *Traffic in Opium and Other Dangerous Drugs* statement was a national report to the League of Nations and later UN narcotics agencies. Coca presented a political dilemma, given the zealous American role in drug crusades as the chief global antagonist to cocaine. Domestic politics and good-old-boy agreements oiled this bureaucratic pact, revealed in meetings between Colonel Levi Nutt (Anslinger's predecessor), Stuart Fuller (antidrug chief at State), and Coca-Cola and Maywood executives. The United States, the 1930 report stated, allowed no imports of cocaine, ecgonine, or their salts, and it prohibited domestic cultivation of coca. But it did allow a unique legal provision for imports of so-called nonmedicinal coca. The FBN commissioner was authorized to issue special import permits, a power that was updated in 1924 and 1930. "The purpose of this provision was to permit manufacture from this additional coca leaves of a non-narcotic flavoring extract," one report explained, but all "excess alkaloid" was destroyed "under the supervision of an authorized representative of the Commissioner." With no mention of Coca-Cola's specific interests, reports reiterated the meticulous U.S. control regime, entailing "continuous personal observation of factory operation during the entire process. . . . by a representative of the Commissioner of Narcotics who is furnished samples of all products at various steps in the operation." Labs reported directly to the commissioner. Not only alkaloid but "spent leaves themselves" had to be "destroyed by the manufacturers, by *incineration*," in Anslinger's presence. In practice, an FBN chemist and a narcotics inspector "were stationed at the factory of this manufacturer [Maywood] to observe and check the process and to witness the destruction" at taxpayer expense.[17]

Spurred by Stephen G. Porter, chair of the House Foreign Affairs Committee, Coca-Cola lobbied for the 1930 Porter Act, which sanctified inspection procedures. Anslinger swiftly doubled the leaf quota, granting Maywood purchase rights to 120,000 pounds of "Peruvian variety" coca in coming terms. FBN statistics show a rising curve after 1930 of designated "special" or "non-medicinal" leaves: by 1938, 107,000 kilos of "non-medicinal" leaf accounted for over half of coca imports, while the rest were for Merck cocaine. By the early 1940s, Maywood's share exceeded 200,000 kilos a year, twice the leaf used for cocaine. The Maywood circuit extended abroad to Peruvian leaf growers in La Libertad, the area long coveted for its elixir and beverage coca.[18] Cemented by alliances and long-term buying contracts with politician Alfredo Pinillos, the network reached its apex during the 1930s, a surprisingly robust era in Coca-Cola's global reach. Company officials conducted inspection tours of the Sacamanca farms, which in good years accounted for 15 percent of Peru's coca exports. Over time, officially sanctioned Merchandise No. 5 dwarfed the legal U.S. cocaine-making enterprise.

Over four decades from 1920 to the 1960s, a political pact reigned between Coca-Cola and the FBN on coca and related cocaine issues, a relationship richly documented in FBN files. In this area, the personnel and practices of Maywood and Coca-Cola became indistinguishable. The implications of the FBN's relationship with Coca-Cola spanned domestic and foreign drug control and, if more hidden from sight, were comparable to the quasi-official role that United Fruit Company played policing the Caribbean in the U.S. banana commodity chain. Maywood embodied the managed U.S. coca trade structure that limited imports to bulk leaf. It gave the Treasury and FBN access, data, and aid on all coca-related operations; it enforced and profited from the full U.S. ban on cocaine imports. Maywood officials frequently spied and informed on errant coca sellers and buyers. Coca-Cola and Maywood tapped their overseas clients to gather data about coca crops or policy changes coveted by Anslinger, who became highly knowledgeable about Peruvian cocaine. Maywood worked to persuade the Peruvian state of the wisdom of U.S.-style drug policies, while Coca-Cola lawyers participated in world drug conferences and Andean missions, offering technical advice and political intelligence on evolving coca issues. As Harold Hirsch, the famed Coca-Cola vice president, framed the larger relationship in 1933, "This Company has at all times in good faith cooperated with the Narcotic Bureau of the Treasury and will be pleased to continue to so cooperate with that Bureau and the Department of State both at home and abroad." In the pre-1950s era, before the FBN and State Department began to meddle themselves in Peruvian drugs, such corporate mediation was crucial, though not always successful.[19]

In return, the Anslinger-era FBN paid rapt, consistent attention to Coca-Cola needs at home and abroad. The chief task of the FBN was to certify to the public and critics that Coca-Cola was a drug-free drink. Anslinger backed the firm in home markets, helping to stifle irksome "cola" competition, in part because his job of drug control benefited from a simpler

TABLE 5.1 U.S. Coca: Medicinal and Special Imports, 1925–1959

Year	Total Imports	Coca Leaves Medicinal[a] (kg)	Nonmedicinal[b] (kg)
1925	72,254	72,254	
1926	133,347	133,347	
1927	114,594	114,594	
1928	110,667	110,667	
1929	61,617	61,617	
1930	89,699	89,699	
1931	221,235	122,748	98,486
1932	101,624	101,624	
1933	81,699	81,699	
1934	85,551	81,070	4,480
1935	110,330	94,468	15,861
1936	171,389	101,855	69,533
1937	189,598	101,384	88,213
1938	208,581	101,041	107,540
1939	263,814	123,138	140,676
1940	352,200	146,189	206,011
1941	420,388	127,484	292,904
1942	360,655	89,849	270,806
1943	447,395	207,408	239,987
1944	202,057	67,555	134,501
1945	316,224	45,359	270,865
1946	228,782	90,718	138,063
1947	315,237	180,183	135,053
1948	289,375	289,375	
1949	142,078	142,078	
1950	112,742	112,742	
1951	130,849	130,849	
1952	112,354	112,354	
1953	150,183	150,183	
1954	125,392	125,392	
1955	141,290	141,290	
1956	184,095	184,095	

Source: See appendix.

Note: Cola leaf not clearly separated before 1930; separate reporting but not imports cease after 1947.

[a] Imported for extraction of Merck cocaine.

[b] Imported for Maywood manufacture of non-narcotic flavoring extracts.

business structure. Since the coca craze of the 1890s, a string of U.S. firms and chemists had continued to claim formulas and rights for coca extracts, which they were eager to offer to rival soft drink manufacturers. The FBN worked to keep such coca men as Saul Penick and Sadtler and Sons out of the field, often by drug harassment, in effect policing the Maywood extract monopoly. Over time, most patent-era cola imitations folded, a trend broken only in the 1960s by the breakout of coca-less Pepsi. Abroad, the U.S. government also certified to the world, and prying drug agencies, that Coca-Cola syrup was definitively not a narcotic substance — a recurring rumor across the globe even into the 1950s, for example among nationalists in France and Egypt. The FBN opposed statist coca projects, perhaps because such projects were at odds with its larger control goal of ensuring cheap leaf supplies. Peru's de facto world monopoly in extract leaf could have steeply raised the costs of Coca-Cola in a world set on limiting coca crops, unlike the competitive Java-flooded market in cocaine-grade coca. The FBN facilitated strategic good status for Maywood and allocated it scarce shipping during World War II, a dramatic era for Coca-Cola's global expansion. By the 1960s, the agency even began secret projects to prepare the firm for an era without Andean leaf (which never materialized, due to resurgent coca nativism and illicit cocaine). Only by the mid-1950s did FBN concern with cocaine traffic finally eclipse its services to Coca-Cola. Yet as postwar debates mounted on coca's future, the FBN wrote Coca-Cola needs into new treaties, leaving a still visible imprint on the 1961 Single Convention.[20] In short, for decades, the FBN did its best to protect and promote Coca-Cola's global market conquests, along the way muddying U.S. drug diplomacy with countries like Peru.

The mediation of Coca-Cola and Maywood was one cornerstone of a political economy that involved the extinction of popular coca products, a flattening of drug imports, and a corporate alliance with the nascent U.S. drug bureaucracy. These ad hoc arrangements appear to have worked surprisingly well, at least for the five decades until the 1960s. Possibilities for both licit and illicit cocaine trades quickly receded in the 1920s, with few incentives for contraband imports (the telling exception being diverted vials of European medical-grade cocaine). In the years just following the passage of the Harrison Act, the United States was still gripped in a cocaine scare. Officials brandished wild figures of "a million addicts" in the country, giving prominence to the control of cocaine over that of heroin. By 1932, however, authorities deemed underground cocaine a mere "rivulet" compared to the unleashed dam perceived in the 1910s.

A late 1930s survey of 1,592 addicts in the New York region, that former cocaine haven, turned up just 2 habitual users of the drug. By World War II, the FBN was declaring sales of illicit cocaine "without significance," in fact too scant to even fulfill obligatory reports on street prices. Narcotics officers also successfully steered the reduction of U.S. medicinal cocaine allowances from their peak of around ten metric tons before 1910 to under a ton a year by the 1930s. Historians have not accounted for how and why illicit cocaine receded in the aftermath of prohibitions, and no doubt many social and cultural factors intervened, as former aficionados died or switched to other vices.[21] Cocaine's disappearance was trumpeted as a lasting triumph of early drug control—quite a premature claim from today's vantage point. In effect, during the interwar period, U.S. borders became sealed to cocaine, unlike drug evils heroin and marijuana, even as cocaine was openly produced and traded in varied sites around the world, including Peru.

EXPORTING PROHIBITION: THE UNITED STATES, THE LEAGUE, AND THE ANDES, 1910–1940

While cocaine and coca prohibitions took hold with relative ease within the United States (the nation generating anticocaine fervor), their export abroad proved more halting and problematic. After 1909, as the United States joined in the new array of international narcotics meetings, treaties, and institutions, attempts to place cocaine high on the agenda did not succeed either in the big-power League of Nations or through influence over small powers like Peru and Bolivia. From the very start, American diplomats homed in on ideals of limitation at the source, including Andean coca leaf and cocaine, to no avail. Their impotence, paradoxically, helped postpone the social dilemmas of illicit cocaine until after World War II.

The genesis of the international drug control complex has gained scholarly attention since the 1960s, but no research has appeared that concentrates specifically on cocaine. In part, this is because little was said or done about cocaine. Cocaine, as a stimulant, became lost in the wider categorical construction of a global "narcotics" menace, in which the relation of cocaine to coca leaf (when considered at all) was distorted through the lens of morphine. The United States played an ambiguous role in early global drug politics.[22] Here was the world's most adamant, idealistic, and, as many claimed, bullying antidrug power, unconstrained by the realpolitik of possessing drug-growing or drug-using colonies or by core chemical interests, as Britain, Germany, Switzerland, the Netherlands, and France were constrained. Coca-Cola, which mediated rather than dictated American goals, was the closest thing to a sheltered U.S. coca lobby. Thus, American positions at antidrug conventions and in the League of Nations after 1920 proved absolutist. Initial drug diplomats Bishop Brent and Hamilton Wright boldly demanded comprehensive drug bans, from Third World drug plant sources to end-use manufacturing firms — the so-called American plan for the rapid elimination of all production not serving medicinal and scientific needs. Americans also strove to criminalize, rather than medicalize, the condition of drug addicts everywhere. However, after Wilson's larger 1919–21 League of Nations ratification failure, an uncompromising United States remained estranged from League politics. It was unable to flex its informal might in drug diplomacy until the United Nations fully embraced the American vision, with its special sensitivity to cocaine, right after World War II.

These dynamics played out starting with the 1909 Shanghai Opium Commission, a result of U.S. anticolonial zeal after encountering opiates in the newly acquired Philippines. The first 1911 Hague conference, at American behest, recruited twelve nations and eluded the imposition of substantive controls. The second and third Hague International Opium Conventions of 1913–14 broadened the range of participants and targeted drugs. But wrangling over instituting even national drug restrictions deadlocked the British, Germans, and French. The Harrison Act, moved through Congress in 1914 to meet U.S. treaty obligations, received its impetus from Wright's crusade for an American antidrug foreign policy. After World War I, the number of ratifying parties grew on paper to sixteen, as the Treaty of Versailles appended the prior drug conventions. Henceforth, the scene of debates — and there were many — shifted to Geneva and the set of bodies formed around the League of Nations' Opium Advisory Committee and the later Permanent Central Opium Board (PCOB). Behind the scenes, missionaries like Elizabeth Washburn Wright (Hamilton's widow), Stuart Fuller of the State Department's Far Eastern desk, and the FBN's Anslinger after 1930 advanced American agendas, adopted by a few converted allies like Britain and Canada. The first and second Geneva Opium Conferences (1924–25) collapsed when U.S. delegates walked out dramatically after failing to win their way on raw-material controls. The third Geneva Conference on the Limitation of Manufacture of Narcotic Drugs in 1931 marked a shift to pragmatic industrial controls, over time garnering fifty-seven signatories for a system of import-export and needs

A fourth meeting, the 1936 Conference for the Suppression of the Illicit
Trade in Dangerous Drugs, reflected its titular concern: delegates drew
up penalty structures, but given the League's decay and the coming war,
nothing came of it. The United States, just as in 1925, refused to back
flimsy controls.

The outcomes of World War II, however, shifted the balance of drug
crusades toward the United States with the breakup of colonial spheres
and the crushing of obstructionists and defector nations Germany and
Japan. Propagandistic tales of global "red" drug-pushing aside, a little-
noted implicit antidrug consensus united the puritanical United States,
the Leninist Soviet Union, and, after 1949, the new pariah state of "red"
China (the People's Republic of China), even amid their escalating cold war
tensions. The United States held clear sway over reborn United Nations
drug agencies, notably the Commission on Narcotic Drugs (CND). The UN,
anxious to stem another postwar drug resurgence, swiftly embraced the
international raw materials eradication program championed by Washington
since the 1910s.[23] U.S. hegemony thus sparked the first global offensive
against cocaine and coca, now reduced to just two world sites within
American reach: Peru and Bolivia, states that had hitherto managed to
evade controls. In 1949, Peru banned free enterprise cocaine and embraced
schemes to curtail coca; Bolivia, straying from U.S. designs during the
war and 1952 revolution, lagged until 1961. Triumph finally came, after a
decade of talks, in the 1961 UN Single Convention on Narcotic Drugs, the
binding universal and comprehensive antidrug regime that rationalized
the maze of earlier treaties and institutionalized campaigns against coca
and cocaine. This antidrug edifice took a half-century to build and still
reigns, despite today's skepticism about its prospects and its definition
of success with coca and cocaine.

How did cocaine even become part of a global drug agenda dominated by opiate politics? How did cocaine relate to the interwar League
campaigns? How did source nations like Peru and Bolivia react, and did
their compliance or resistance affect the emerging system of prohibitions
against cocaine? This section addresses these questions from the thick
legacy of printed materials left by would-be League drug controllers.

A key disjuncture at the genesis of the international drug movement
was between the U.S. struggle with cocaine, more infamous than opiates
during the anxious clampdown of the teens, and the larger campaign born
against opiates in Asia. Cocaine panics erupted elsewhere in the 1910s

and 1920s in Britain, Germany, France, Australia, Russia, and India, but without the force to propel drug policies, which in these countries mainly concerned colonial trades or opium smoking in Chinese enclaves. By the mid-1920s, another disjuncture arose when the United States seemingly resolved its first bout with illicit cocaine yet continued, less urgently, to press for a universal ban on the drug and its raw materials. These conditions weakened moral imperatives for global controls on cocaine, an uncertainty that eased the abstention of faraway nations like Peru and Bolivia. Thus, until 1945, metropolitan drug control debates and treaties stuck to the problem and discourse of opiates.

Indeed, cocaine almost failed to make it into initial drug conventions and might have ended up like cannabis, delayed until later in the century. Hamilton Wright and his peers proved adept at exploiting racism and cocaine dread at home to rush through national drug laws, using cocaine horror stories collected by Wright himself from a 1909 national survey of police chiefs. It was overkill given the broader, decisive Progressive critique of cocaine. But U.S. diplomats were reluctant to complicate or clutter a precarious international crusade. Wright's personal Hague Convention letter books from the 1911–14 period reveal exertions to extend colonial opium politics to a European antimorphine crusade to encompass modern drug manufacturing powers. Cocaine as a global menace entered here as a political ploy. The British, playing their best to avoid comprehensive drug initiatives, brought cocaine to the table to incite their nemesis, Germany, a country expected to block any agreement that hurt its key pharmaceutical cocaine sector. For a complex of reasons, however, including intensifying state involvement with a saturated cocaine industry, the Germans actually embraced the idea of regulation, turning the proposal around to impose strict limits on cocaine. German wariness then focused on the sticky problem of treaty nonsignatories. So by 1913, American diplomats felt free to fight cocaine as symbolic of their universal drug campaign, one without artificial distinctions between drugs or national borders.[24] Wright also goaded on the Anglican bishops leading the movement with news of cocaine's effects on the "Negroes" of the American South. Bewildered Chinese delegates wondered aloud about this new Western drug: if Eastern opium were banned, so must cocaine be, both for balance and to ensure the drug did not fill the void left for China's millions of recovering opiate addicts. Chinese sovereignty was a raison d'être of the drug crusade, so such objections counted, even if interrupted by the war. Emergency wartime drug controls, such as the Defence of the Realm Act in Britain and the decrees of the German War Ministry Health Department, specified cocaine and persisted given anxieties about a postwar drug epidemic. Once tacked on to the list of world drug dangers, cocaine stayed, folded into successive conventions after Versailles.

Until the mid-1940s, however, cocaine was not a serious object of international debate or control, much less covered by working prohibitions. Instead, it was part of a larger bureaucratic drug accounting scheme deployed by the League of Nations. Cocaine was a category governed only by analogy to tightening opiate restrictions in the mazelike League system. The American shadow over a body it did not join only made cocaine's status more ambiguous.

For the United States, cocaine's nemesis and the champion of cutting off drugs at their source, the problem of the Andes arose immediately. During the Hague meetings of 1911–13, the State Department relied on the Netherlands to round up support from Latin America and was keen to win Peruvian ratification. Peru's mysterious failure to sign convention documents became a festering complaint. President Wilson's official 1913 Hague Convention report noted Peruvian intransigence: "When the conference assembled.... American diplomatic representatives met with a hearty response from the Latin American nations, and by the end of 1912, all of the Latin American states except Peru had notified the U.S. that they had signed or would be pleased to sign the International Opium Convention, or paid high complements to this Government for its initiative and continuous leadership in a high purpose."[25] "Except Peru" marked a conspicuous absence in the age of American dollar diplomacy, and failure to sign on to the convention was surely not an oversight of Peru's well-trained diplomatic corps.

In private communiqués, American annoyance was explained: Peru would not sign, or even respond, due to its entrenched "interests in coca." In early 1912, Wright dashed off a last-ditch plea to Peruvian foreign minister Francisco Pezet: "We learned from our representative at Lima that the Peruvian Government preferred to remain non-committal in regard to the Convention. That Peru should hesitate to commit itself to so important an instrument did not wholly surprise us, for this Government has been aware of the peculiar interest of Peru in the market and economic side of cocaine questions. Yet, at the same time it has been felt that Peru could, as several other nations have done, join in the international movement for the suppression of the abuses connected with the opium and cocaine traffic, without injuring her real interests." While counseling compliance for appearance's sake, Wright hoped to embarrass Peru's upper-class diplomats: "Otherwise, Peru of all the Latin American States, will be in the position of having excluded herself from an important international Conference, representing nearly every Civilized nation of the globe." Bolivia provoked similar, if less urgent, protests. Dutch minutes of 1913 relate the same story of deflected appeals. Peru cited "economic difficulties" as its reason for not sending a delegate, though it had diplomats working throughout the continent.[26] Peru's stance, in one opinion, had repercussions beyond coca, having inspired abstention by poppy-growing states in the Balkans, leading to the 1912 impasse behind the call for a second Hague conference. Peru finally signed on Hague principles in 1921 via Versailles, but its role remained nominal.[27]

By the mid-1920s, American perceptions of Peruvian intentions had hardened. Congressional documents for the 1924 Porter Resolution, which called for forceful action at the upcoming Geneva limitations conference, branded Peru a delinquent producer of coca, even though Peruvian coca was by all extant standards perfectly legal. Congress also trotted out Wright's decade-old missive on Peru's treaty truancy. A legal discourse arose about responsibility for source drugs in Peru and Bolivia: "[Their] production is controllable by virtue of sovereign power of those governments . . . over exportation and production. The production of coca leaves—from which cocaine is extracted—in Peru, Bolivia, and the Netherlands' possession of Java, is likewise vastly in excess of the quantity required from which an adequate supply of cocaine for medicinal and scientific purposes could be contained." Between awkward errors of fact, this basic notion located the source of the cocaine evil in distant excess supplies of coca, an argument that Peruvians like Paz Soldán were later to turn on its head in their defense of the drug. This trope befit the excess production supply focus of early U.S. drug diplomacy. By the mid-1920s, Peru evoked American disdain as a coca country and peddler of crude cocaine for wily Germany and Japan. Peru ignored all calls for the conference and never signed the 1925 accord, a refusal that mirrored the U.S. boycott after the failed 1925 American bid for full raw material controls.[28] Indeed, after their Geneva fiasco, U.S. envoys reportedly dissuaded Latin American nations from signing the weak accord so as not to award it hemispheric legitimacy.

By 1925, however, American anxiety about cocaine, Peruvian or otherwise, was receding. The drug's noticeable use had faded to now-marginal racial sites like Hollywood or jazz scenes. Malfunctioning alcohol prohibition and nascent heroin trades seemed far more troubling issues. Stringent domestic and corporate surveillance of coca and cocaine appeared to be working. The United States still needed to overcome its ignorance of Andean cocaine, and it started doing so. Both nations became estranged from the League of Nations and its drug control schemes for distinct political reasons, making the League an unlikely tool in the U.S. ideal of stamping out hemispheric cocaine. The League, U.S. sniping aside, turned to efforts against drug manufacturing powers.

What role did the League play in advancing restrictions on cocaine, and how did coca source countries like Peru and Bolivia respond? The genesis of international narcotics institutions (the Opium Advisory Committee and the Permanent Opium Control Board) has produced several good studies and many participant apologetics but little that is specific to cocaine.[29] Historians wading into the outpouring of printed materials from League drug bodies during the 1920s and 1930s (debates, annual reports, conference preparatory documents, statistics, decrees, correspondence) are swamped in reportage. Cocaine's inclusion here was a nod to external U.S. pressures. It was also, I contend, an essentially fictitious system, put on paper to parallel the League's antiopiate drive. Officials at times invoked a drug category called "cocaine," but they lacked genuine knowledge of the drug or any defined anticocaine policy. League record keeping and quotas for cocaine, although resulting in beautiful rounded figures, were fictive estimates of the drug's production and of demand for it. To functionaries in Geneva, in the absence of data, a country and its drugs simply fell off the map. The abstention of major global actors in cocaine, especially the Andean states, from participation in the control regime was the weakest link in this theoretical control edifice, though the subterfuge of nations like Japan did not help either. Andean responses were purposeful: Peru consistently ignored League cocaine initiatives, and Bolivia rose in spirited defense of indigenous coca. The League was not only powerless but blinded about cocaine.

Coca and cocaine never ranked high on the League agenda. Its documentary maze reveals profuse discussions and debates of the OAC, obsessive exercises to set up a global statistical apparatus, and cryptic political intrigues around the 1924–25, 1930–31, and 1935–36 Geneva conferences, as well as other stillborn drug control schemes. In this world of bureaucratic politics, opium, morphine, and heroin, as well as obscure drugs like khat, powder caffeine, and newfound synthetics, overwhelmingly dominated. The League's rare forays into cocaine related to industrial world drug syndicates; the Dutch-German cartel of the mid-1920s, which officials hoped might systematically lower global production; import-export tracking for transparency in international trades; technical aid for governments interested in erecting national drug laws; Dutch reports on Java; deepening concerns with Japanese activities; and schemes to replace medicinal cocaine with new synthetics.

About once a decade, a League committee would launch a short-lived campaign to bring Peru and Bolivia under the rubric of "raw materials" or "coca leaf" control, as seen in preparations for both the 1924–25 and the 1933–34 limitation conferences. The template officials applied to cocaine was the relation of poppy to raw opium to manufactured morphine. A "Questionnaire Regarding the Coca-Leaf" was devised and randomly mailed out, and high-sounding policy committees convened, such as the Committee C on coca at the 1924 Geneva conference. Bureaucratic responses flowed in from such sites as Iceland and Madagascar ("The Coca Plant is not grown in Iceland"), translated into French, and charted, gaps and all, adding nothing to knowledge of the drugs. For the 1924 talks, W. G. van Wettun, a veteran Dutch drug diplomat, drew up an intricate twenty-nine-part document titled "Draft Treaty Relating to the Coca Leaf," which managed to avoid all mention of the Andean countries. In the mid-1930s, a primitive coca eradication program was drafted. But nothing came of such schemes, nor could it without the participation of coca-growing states. In both instances, officials met a wall of Peruvian abstention and Bolivian resistance, and they quietly separated and shelved coca projects in favor of more pressing opium politics. More unanswered inquiries and invitations went out, as did admonitions, like those in 1934 and 1937, to involve the Latin Americans, embodied by OAC head Ekstrand's 1938 goodwill tour of the region.[30]

Critics, especially Americans, attacked League pretensions about cocaine as a sham, though a useful one for keeping the world aware of a lurking menace. A 1928 broadside of the Geneva-based, American-funded Anti-Opium Information Bureau cut through League fictions by raising the provocative topic of "Strange Omissions: Crude Cocaine"—a reference to the export's freedom from all regulation. The author questioned official amnesia about a substance "derived from the coca leaf grown in Peru and Bolivia and injurious to the addict as the refined drug" yet never "amongst the substances of which must be limited." He sardonically suggested that "excavations in Peru and the Free Port of Hamburg" were "expected to reveal . . . huge deposits of crude cocaine to which it may be claimed the Convention should not apply."[31] In the League's truncated perspective,

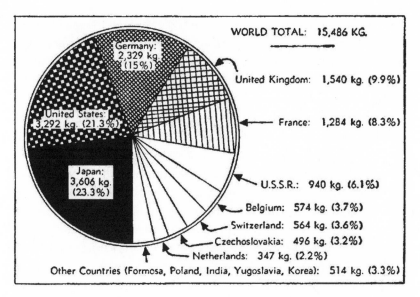

WORLD TOTAL: 15,486 KG.

Germany: 2,329 kg. (15%)

United States: 3,292 kg. (21.3%)

Japan: 3,606 kg. (23.3%)

United Kingdom: 1,540 kg. (9.9%)

France: 1,284 kg. (8.3%)

U.S.S.R.: 940 kg. (6.1%)

Belgium: 574 kg. (3.7%)

Switzerland: 564 kg. (3.6%)

Czechoslovakia: 496 kg. (3.2%)

Netherlands: 347 kg. (2.2%)

Other Countries (Formosa, Poland, India, Yugoslavia, Korea): 514 kg. (3.3%)

FIGURE 5.1 League of Nations World Cocaine Accounts, Mid-1930s
Source: See appendix.

only ecgonine-derived cocaine from Dutch Java leaf counted in quotas that seemed to award syndicates of colonial planters and European drug firms. Nor could the United States, despite its informal sway, compel Andean participation in the League efforts or controls.

Peru's main response to the League was to ignore it, with occasional offerings to placate pressing officials. From its inception in 1922, the OAC, like the Americans before, lamented the absence of communications with and attendance from Peru, which soon became a yearly plaint. Drug conventions, reporting, and controls remained voluntary activities. After signing the Versailles Treaty and its Hague principles, Peru dropped out of the League in the mid-1920s to protest perceived favoritism toward Chile in the Tacna-Arica border dispute. Peru's Bureau of Health (and agricultural department) supplied a two-page report on the 1922 coca crop, a requested list of the country's cocaine factories and registered opium dens in 1928, and another list in 1936, always with vague promises of delivering more in the future. Internal records of the Peruvian Ministry of Foreign Affairs register the archived messages and invitations from the League.[32]

With the rise of a Depression-era nationalist prococaine bloc, Peru debated the merits of continuing to ignore the League amid rumors of secret drug accords and impending cocaine export quotas. A Peruvian observer, Enrique Trujillo Bravo, mutely sat through the 1936 Geneva sessions that had already abandoned any action on coca. As seen in the last chapter, Ekstrand's 1938 OAC mission to Lima underscored the problem of Peru's absence for the League.[33] He pursued meetings with health officials, the Ministry of Foreign Affairs, and agrarian lobbies in a struggle for formal signing of the 1925 and 1936 accords. Ekstrand debated Paz Soldán's positions and nodded to Peru's right to a cocaine monopoly, against U.S. objections; this move was celebrated in Lima as a victory against foreign coercion. Peru then joined the OAC, but no perceptible change resulted, save that by 1940 the Ministry of Foreign Affairs was answering circulars. Peru effectively never recognized League sovereignty, a situation only reversed with the advent of the United Nations. The political meaning of Peru's protracted foot-dragging is harder to ascertain, though it might be understood as a weak power's strategy to protect its embattled national cocaine. Peru operated what was effectively passive resistance to the League's drug control program, stymieing League efforts and keeping Peru off the map of global controls.

In contrast to Peru, little Bolivia opted for outright resistance, as it engaged in active, if intermittent, participation in global drug forums. Bolivia's bold but unknown prococa stance during the League's fleeting raw material debates of the mid-1920s stemmed from lobbying by its elite coca growers' association, the Sociedad de Propietarios de Yungas. Bolivia, which had no national cocaine industry, also provoked fewer outside suspicions. But the SPY immediately grasped the threat posed to indigenous coca by League debates and inquiries about the leaf. Bolivia had precipitously signed the 1912 Opium Convention and provided a few early 1920s coca export statistics. By 1923, however, the SPY was alerting Bolivia's Ministry of Foreign Affairs of the need to oppose League efforts to label coca an international narcotic and the forced adoption of national anticoca laws.[34] Like Peru's 1888 Coca Commission, the SPY urged the opposite: a defense of the healthful properties of Bolivia's superior coca leaf and its prospects in export commerce. Great pains were taken to distinguish coca leaf and its local usage from cocaine, which the SPY argued was not easily obtained from quality *yungas* leaf. Bolivia was decades out of step with, or ahead of, world opinion. Bolivian elites were not only heavily invested in coca but sincerely racist in their belief that the nation's enervated Indians needed coca's stimulus.

In mid-1924, at the second Geneva conference on raw materials, with its short-lived Committee C on coca leaf, a lone Bolivian delegate showed up. Peru had claimed it could not send anyone "at such short notice." In June, the League registered an official letter of protest from the Sociedad de Propietarios de Yungas, which Bolivia's delegate, Arturo Pinto-Escalier, entered as official testimony in August. The SPY memo stressed coca's benign cultural essentiality to the Bolivian Indian. Coca was not the addictive narcotic imagined by the League, and it was also no "danger to society" like alkaloidal cocaine. In any case, the SPY insisted, coveted *yungas* coca was too valuable to waste on cocaine. Rather than attack the leaf, the SPY advised, the League should appoint a "Delegation of Scientists" to Bolivia for a firsthand study of coca.

Pinto-Escalier's own 12 August defense of coca chiefly concerned Bolivia's Indians and the role of coca from the Incas to modern tin mines. His authoritative source was none other than W. Golden Mortimer's 1901 *History of Coca* (the title of which Pinto-Escalier mistranscribed), in a fascinating case of global textual circulation across the transition to exported American anticocaism. Pinto-Escalier denies any "pernicious" health effects of coca—long-chewing Indians enjoy special longevity, he maintains—and argues that if Bolivia lost this "restorer of energy," labor would simply grind to a halt among high-altitude Indians, as early Spaniards learned. He cites Mortimer's lore that Indians carefully select the least bitter (less alkaloidal) sweet leaves, a point today's coca anthropologists support. Bolivian Indians were not on cocaine. Nor did Bolivia's numerated exports to neighboring lands go into making cocaine. Bolivian coca had "no morally corrupting influence," Pinto-Escalier insists. Quite the opposite: for the native population, it was a moralizing force. Later sessions found Pinto-Escalier rising to spontaneously debate the coca question, with U.S. delegate Stephen Porter (chairman of the House Foreign Affairs Committee) advocating the opposite view of the United States. Elaborating on his earlier memo, the Bolivian ended with the striking claim that "production of coca-leaf in Bolivia is an exceptional one.... my Government, to its great regret, would be unable to accept any measure tending to prevent the use of coca leaf in conformity with the established customs of Bolivia."[35] Transcripts register applause for the speech. These interventions still resonate as a forgotten precursor to president Evo Morales's dramatic defense of coca to the United Nations assembly eight decades later in September 2006. Andean reluctance was enough, it seems, to frustrate the American convention plan to limit "excess" coca in 1924.

In 1927 and 1932, the Bolivian Congress reiterated that the country would not "restrict the cultivation of coca...nor prohibit the use of the coca leaves among the indigenous population," a direct challenge to League pretensions. Bolivians continued to shield coca against imagined threats during the 1930s, though some intellectuals were now starting to fret about the Indian and coca. The spy refused to submit its data for League reporting and hoped to regain Bolivia's lost regional coca markets and actually extend local consumption. In 1932, it commissioned a flowery anti-League defense of coca by Dr. Nicanor T. Fernández. Its title alone spoke volumes: "Marvelous Properties and Qualities of Coca — Opinions of Prestigious Doctors and Naturalists." State decrees sanctioned coca through brands and licensing. In 1933, Adolfo Costa du Reis, Bolivia's envoy to the League, sought "advice from industrialists and landowners of the Yungas" on new steps to shield coca. The spy expressed contempt for the League's perceptions and initiatives. During Ekstrand's 1938 tour, he found Bolivian authorities "of two divergent views," and they were still ambivalent a decade later when the un visited La Paz. Bolivia's resistance contrasts with cocaine-making Peru, which, in Lima's muddled elite anticoca politics, found that its only practical path was to ignore League authority.[36] Bolivia's reaction also had internal repercussions. Unlike Peru's slow addition of hygienic drug regulation from the 1920s and acrimonious national coca debate, Bolivia's weak state refrained from taking steps to regulate drugs prior to 1961, when it finally succumbed to a new wave of American pressures.

The League, in turn, seems to have ignored Bolivia's challenge during the 1930s, another case of letting its problems slide off the map. The social place of coca leaf in Bolivian culture, then as now, defied drug control syllogisms. In Latin America, ironically, only passionately anticoca Colombia (which had scant coca) and a few Caribbean colonial outposts joined on any regular basis in League antidrug deliberations. Yet League actions mattered. The League was a global showcase that placed drug control permanently on the world agenda. By reflexively associating cocaine with narcotics, over time it advanced the American cause of delegitimizing the drug. Shrinking League medicinal quotas for cocaine to under five tons by the 1930s furthered this goal, so long as barriers failed to spark shadow trades. If a state opted to submit to League designs, the impact was dramatic. The Netherlands, as an internationalist strategy in the 1920s, employed the League certificate system to dismantle its large, if then unprofitable, colonial coca-cocaine enterprise. Even countries that preserved autonomy, such as Weimar and later Nazi Germany, could follow League drug principles, and few could claim the League was beholden to

American ambition. At the other extreme was Japan, which launched its colonial drug empire in the shadow of League controls and remained a controversial pharmaceutical power throughout the 1930s, even if it never dealt cocaine on the scale imagined.[37]

The most revealing feature of this interwar cocaine world was the multiplicity of cocaine sites and legal regimes, the obverse of the staunch American plan of uniform prohibition, which would have criminalized everyone from leaf farmers to casual illicit users. This League weakness, or global tolerance, actually worked to preclude the rise of interwar cocaine trafficking, as it kept profit incentives down. Cocaine reached its low ebb as a social problem, particularly in the United States. Only the rapid success of American pressures after World War II would transform cocaine into a novel and highly dynamic illicit commodity.

THE UNITED STATES VERSUS PERUVIAN COCAINE

If the League of Nations proved feeble on cocaine, what impact did direct American pressures have against Andean sources like Peru? Newly opened country archives of the FBN shed light on four aspects of this question. First, despite the concerns evinced about delinquent coca nations at the advent of its drug crusade, the United States did not or could not meddle in Peruvian (much less Bolivian) drug policy, in part due to the sheer paucity of local policy apparatus. The diffusion of overseas drug science was more decisive in this era, a process seen in the medicalized *toxicomanía* discourse during Peru's 1920s–40s national coca debate, which was slowly turning coca into a drug. Second, archives reveal the ongoing mediation of Coca-Cola and Maywood in Peru, which had a moderating influence on prohibitionist U.S. officials—a role to recede only with the rise of concerns about cocaine traffic in the 1950s. Third, a tangible U.S. impact on Peruvian drug policy was U.S. blockage, via structures of trade, of the viability of alternative drug control schemes, in particular the modernizing national cocaine monopoly envisioned by Peruvian experts of the 1930s. Finally, in contrast to the League's blinders on global cocaine, the United States sharpened its powers of surveillance and intelligence over Peruvian cocaine, and over Andean coca writ large. By World War II, the FBN had acquired a realistic picture of the drug it was set to suppress.

Drug surveillance was the central development of the interwar era: an informal imperial gaze of U.S. officials working to assess Peru's possible drug threat. Unlike the League, the Americans had agents on the ground in Peru, including consular and embassy officials, customs men, and coca buyers for Maywood and Merck, and these agents routinely passed trade and political information to the FBN and the State Department. Before specialized drug agents were stationed in Latin America starting in the late 1940s, regulations charged consular officials with making reports on dangerous narcotics, which in Peru spurred a regular flow of information on first cocaine and then coca.[38] After 1930, Anslinger's FBN perfected its own data collection skills, often as leverage against rival agencies. As reports multiplied, agents stored and analyzed names and numbers, sometimes abetted by Peruvian health and police officials. Such a watchful U.S. eye made sense. Officials distrusted League capabilities and initiatives, fully aware of their inability to gather evidence on source country resisters like Peru. Peru nominally belonged within the American sphere, as did its problematic cocaine. Although Peru suffered no punitive action for exporting drugs, since by the 1920s the American cocaine scare had passed into remission, officials routinely voiced their dismay about this sleeping menace.

Concerted efforts began by the mid-1920s to grasp the local contexts of coca and cocaine. By the mid-1930s, routinized U.S. narcotics intelligence capacity had outstripped that of the League, and likely of Peru's own government. During the war-torn 1940s and beyond, drug surveillance became aligned with incipient forms of inter-American state-to-state co-operation. An official disclosed a unique tool in this effort in the 1920s, during the administration of the pro-U.S. Leguía regime: American firms assumed management of Peru's customs house and patriotically reported on any suspicious port-side narcotics activities. The terms of the 1922 Jones-Miller Act also exerted political pressures: like the controversial congressional drug certification process today, it banned drug exports to any nonsignatory or rogue nation of the Hague conventions. This tool was blunted in Peru, which bought most of its pharmaceuticals from Europe under the 1920s Gratry contract. Rather than restrict Peru, officials on the scene began to focus on drug intelligence.

These informational reports are impressive, offering a bonanza for historians. Consuls systematically collated copies of all Peruvian narcotics-sanitary legislation by 1922 and every change in decrees to come. In 1923, the United States began prying into the interests of rival countries, notably Japan, in Peruvian coca and "coca-cake" (crude cocaine), amassing files on Huallaga land purchases and their Nisei agents. The year 1924 marked the first of the Peruvian "Reports on Coca," carefully prepared at the Lima embassy for State Department recipients using an array of statistical sources. Unlike the modest nineteenth-century U.S. coca reports, these reports are not commercial but forensic portraits of a perceived foe. Annual coca export briefs followed. In 1928, with the aid of Peru's fledgling Bureau of Health, the country was encompassed in a global U.S. census of narcotics manufactures outside of League self-reporting, providing the first comprehensive data set on Huánuco and Trujillo factories. Throughout the 1920s and 1930s, the supplies of coca to Maywood and Coca-Cola and any policy or political threats to them aroused deep curiosity and concern.[39] Merck, which procured industrial coca in Java, carried less weight. In 1932, regular "Reports on Cocaine" came on line, the first being a report on the 1932 consular mission to Huánuco. Shipments of "raw cocaine" also merited multiple and yearly reports. In contrast to Peru, the United States seemed less intent on tracking Bolivia, despite its lively coca politics. One obligatory nine-page "Coca Leaf in Bolivia" report appeared in 1933, as well as a fragmented memo on *yungas* leaf in 1937. Until the 1950s burst of illicit labs, the pivotal U.S. concern about Bolivia was its diversion of cocaine to Axis powers during World War II.[40]

The 1932 mission merits closer examination for what it says about the interests and mentality of evolving drug surveillance. In April 1932, William C. Burdett, a U.S. consul in Lima, ventured across the Andes on an investigation of Huánuco cocaine, responding to Soberón's letter campaign to U.S. firms offering samples of cocaine sulfates. For the newly empowered Federal Bureau of Narcotics, his twenty-page report amounted to a narcotics inspection tour of Peru's far-flung cocaine district. Burdett cast a jaundiced eye on all Peruvian efforts and laws to oversee the drug industry. His survey lays out the bare facts of coca exports, cocaine licenses, sporadic shipments to Japanese and German firms, production processes, drug purity, the geography and cocaine culture of remote Huánuco, and a lively sketch of Soberón and his business, including a guided tour of his Obraje factory. Burdett puts Soberón's predicament in its context: "Huánuco was long the center of the Peruvian cocaine industry.... The only one [factory] being worked at the time of my visit is that owned by the firm of Andrés Soberón.... He, of course, professed a faithful obedience to all Peruvian laws and regulations concerning his business." Burdett injects his doubts about Soberón's last disclaimer in light of Peru's temptingly corrupt business climate. When questioned, Soberón insisted he solicited U.S. orders in ignorance of the country's 1922 legal ban on cocaine imports. His usual outlets were in Germany, France, and Japan, but he confessed to the consul that he "was seeking new markets in view of the large potential cocaine production in Huánuco." Burdett continues: "I gathered that Mr. Soberón would not be adverse to selling cocaine to American buyers whenever he can do so without incurring risk of fines."[41] This supposition was right, for Soberón would keep trying to break into the U.S. drug market, with special intensity when World War II closed his old markets. Burdett's choice words raised the specter of excess drug production, in the American imaginary the long-dreaded cause of illicit traffic.

Moving beyond Soberón himself, Burdett turns to the coca bush and its harvest, packing, and circuits around Huánuco, as well as to the conflictive topic of coca chewing, stressing that to locals, "foreigners do not differentiate between coca and cocaine whose effects on the system are entirely dissimilar." He returns to end his report on a menacing note: while "there are no more grounds for suspecting Mr. Soberón of complicity in illicit traffic in narcotics," smuggling would be easy given the zone's physical isolation and the moral weakness of Peruvian public servants, including those in public health, during the "chaotic situation" of the 1930s. Burdett reassures officials at home that American drug firms lacked all interest in "unrefined and insoluble" crude cocaine, the result of their long political economy. In effect, then, cocaine policed itself with respect to U.S. borders. To the American gaze in 1932, illicit cocaine remained thus a "danger more potential than actual"—a prophetic word on market-hungry producers like Soberón.[42]

For the remainder of the 1930s, perceptions congealed of Peruvians as congenitally corrupt, and thus a latent drug threat—a stance at odds with the growing cooperation from Peru's nascent drug apparatus. Intelligence mounted on factious Peruvian drug politics, with diplomatic mail filled with press clippings of local opinion flowing back to Washington. Paz Soldán's crusade and related intrigues gained in-depth coverage. Officials began interviewing knowledgeable Peruvian health, police, and diplomatic figures. These discussions confirm a local awareness of anticocainism, though Peruvians tended to blame northern drug users rather than coca planters or crude cocaine refiners for problems. An FBN version of international tag began with every Peruvian attempt to send cocaine ads or samples to Merck, Maywood, or former cocaine makers: U.S. firms would relay such messages to Anslinger, whose agents had the Lima embassy sternly warn the offending Peruvian sellers.[43] In 1936, at the height of Peru's cocaine debate, officials liberally cooperated with the United States by completing an elaborate official U.S. questionnaire on drug laws and practices. At thirty pages, this surpassed in scope all the data Peru had ever supplied to the League put together. By the late 1930s, signs multiplied of strategic collaboration, with yearly reports filed on Peruvian cocaine "stocks" and sales and intelligence on any drug ties to Axis powers Germany and Japan or any rumored wayward commerce. This scrutiny intensified during the war, a key juncture in defining illicit trades and controls, exemplified in Merck chemist Emile Pilli's industrial espionage field study "The Coca Industry in Peru."

Yet throughout this relation until the 1940s, there was no recognizable American effort in Lima or Washington to coerce or convince Peru about cocaine. Washington simply became better equipped to size up the potential, productive and political, of Peruvian cocaine. To be sure, officials expressed contempt for lax Peruvian attitudes and practice in private, but this was rarely communicated or leaked. Unsuccessful forays to change Peruvian policies were invariably the work of private intermediaries, such as Maywood executives. Such caution transpired in a context of aggressive American diplomacy on other fronts, such as commercial policy, which assailed Japanese textile dumping in Peru. There was much U.S. hand-wringing about Peru's continuing official opium monopoly for ethnic Chinese, more in some years than about the rustic cocaine makers of Huánuco. In 1938, Anslinger induced *El Comercio*, Lima's leading daily, to publish translations of his infamous "Marihuana: Deadly Assassin of Youth" campaign, without much local resonance. In short, until 1945, there was no specific U.S. foreign policy to export drug prohibitions to Peru, beyond a busy gathering of intelligence. Peruvian records show that Washington's stance was known but easily overlooked. Unknown is whether this low profile with Peru reflected the dearth of cocaine within U.S. borders — Anslinger's exemplar of triumphant hard-line drug control — or jurisdictional conflicts with the prudent State Department.

The second fixture of U.S. drug policy toward Peru, beyond an ever-wider gaze, was the mediating role of Coca-Cola and its energetic partner in Peru, Maywood Chemical — a pact that, as we have already seen, also worked in domestic control. Behind the scenes in Peru, the activities of Coca-Cola and Maywood extended well into the postwar decades. In contrast, Bolivia, which had no pharmaceutical or outside commercial interest in its leaf, saw no active foreigners in coca politics. Maywood's overseas role had four facets.[44] First, Coca-Cola served to maintain the broader U.S. system of control, based on a regulated monopsonistic import of coca leaf and an absolute ban on imported cocaine. Second, the firm used its informal networks and contacts to collect some of the drug intelligence described above, especially spying about sensitive political matters. Third, Coca-Cola/Maywood tried to sway Peruvian policies, sometimes at the behest of the FBN, in matters affecting the availability and price of beverage coca, which made up a growing share of leaf sales from Peru. Finally, Coca-Cola, as the major legitimate American user of coca, was a moderating or muddling force on U.S. policy, since the firm, however private its corporate view, stood in the way of the extreme official demonization of coca and any projected eradication of coca leaf. This was a looming unstated tension in the nexus, since Coca-Cola/Maywood were doing much to please the FBN, and vice versa, in Peru.

An active presence in Peru since the 1910s, Maywood's compact with the FBN in overseas coca policy was dramatized in a complex episode that unfolded in Lima between 1928 and 1933. It originated in a secret Coca-Cola project, linked to the firm's global ambitions, to outsource expanding production of Merchandise No. 5 from New Jersey to Peru, closer to Maywood's coca suppliers. When news of the project leaked, however, it sparked alarm among global antidrug forces. The episode ended in a dramatic early 1933 burning of surplus cocaine, supervised in Lima by Maywood president Eugene Schaeffer, the founder's son. These fires marked a symbolic end to the venture but in a larger sense sealed Coca-Cola's loyalty and centrality to the hemispheric anticocaine political economy.

The "preliminary experimental" factory went up in 1928 and 1929 in Callao, Lima's port, just before the regulations of the Porter Act took effect. In this joint venture initiated by Coca-Cola, Maywood disguised the project with a dummy firm, the Rohawa Company, licensed by Leguía's dictatorship, which aided many American enterprises of the 1920s. Only two trial batches of Merchandise No. 5 were ever made in Lima. The first run of 1928 reduced 9,600 pounds of leaf into 4,800 pounds of "Coca Extract," and, apart from destroyed by-products, some 18 kilos of cocaine were sold by a Coca-Cola broker to French pharmaceutical buyers. In 1929, chemists cooked up a far larger batch of extract, 24,106 pounds, which left Coca-Cola in uneasy possession of 79.5 kilos of Peruvian cocaine.[45] In both instances, the coveted merchandise was shipped out in carefully enumerated hundred-gallon drums via Germany to local Canadian bottlers. Coca-Cola viewed this as a critical project, anticipating crippling syrup shortages as its overseas business briskly expanded during the 1920s and, in the 1930s, under the new Coca-Cola Export Corporation.

There were obvious advantages to making this product in Peru, which had fresher leaf and lower transport costs — the same factors that induced the innovation of crude cocaine in the 1880s. Yet it was also a political risk, both for Coca-Cola and for American drug diplomacy. Company officers later denied even having "contemplated" supplying the U.S. home market with imported extract in violation of the Jones-Miller Act, much less tinkering with cocaine. But in mid-1929, that option was in fact lobbied for by top Coca-Cola executives to Levi Nutt (head of the pre-FBN Narcotics Bureau), who pressed for import permits on the technicality that decocainized coca was a narcotic-free substance. An FDA memo of March 1930 objected due to qualms about another detail: the *cocaine*. What, FDA officials wondered, did Coca-Cola actually do with the cocaine by-product from Peru? With Americans the staunchest world foe of the drug, the possibility of cocaine being sold internationally by a visible U.S. firm making the drug overseas had enormous potential for political fallout. The controversy spiraled as the Porter Bill, crowning Anslinger's FBN and new coca controls, came under congressional debate.[46] Alarm spread to Canada, whose H. L. Sharman, chief of the Narcotics Division, was a staunch U.S. ally on global drug issues. The PCOB exposed a traffic of "essence of coca leaf" between Canada, Germany, and Peru, unleashing a formal inquiry and protest. By 1933, the issue had drug hands Sharman, Anslinger, and Fuller up in arms, as well as outgoing Secretary of State Stimson, who demanded an end to the scheme of "Maywood Chemical Works Lmd. at Callao." The project was left with one last defender, Coca-Cola's chief attorney, Eugene Brokmeyer, an expert on Merchandise No. 5 since 1914.[47]

In early 1933, five years after the plant went up, telegrams bounced between Coca-Cola, the Lima embassy, and top drug officials. Brokmeyer sent company regrets for embarrassing the State Department in its global antidrug efforts and pledged its strict adherence to the system of supervised coca operations in New Jersey, just bolstered by the Porter Act. On 16 February 1933, a South American cable arrived in Washington: "COCAINE BURNED TODAY AMERICAN CONSULATE." Schaeffer had personally performed a symbolic cocaine incineration for Coca-Cola, overseen by U.S. and Peruvian drug officials, while shutting down the risky operation. In Fuller's words, there was no longer "cocaine loose." This veiled act sanctified the Coca-Cola role in American drug control, even if another covert deal allowed the plant to be simply mothballed in case of emergency shortages. The larger system funneling coca via the United States held fast.[48]

Coca-Cola's role and cocaine diplomacy with Peru suffered some fallout. To impress his company's loyalty upon the FBN, Schaeffer, who stayed on in Lima, launched a private campaign in March 1933 using highly political partner Pinillos to sway Peru to join in the upcoming Geneva drug talks. Schaeffer was walking the same streets, now against cocaine, that his German cocaine-making father, Louis, had as a youth in the mid-1880s. He warned cabinet ministers that if Peru failed to join League pacts, it would "lose the business and revenue from the legitimate sale of coca."[49] This presaged Maywood's later coca diplomacy, which stalled purchases as a means of FBN arm-twisting. Not much came of this bold effort, which took the drug-shy U.S. Embassy by surprise, given the complexity of Peru's relations to League politics. In a later, related episode in 1940, Anslinger actually called off H. J. Hartung, ever-active Maywood vice president, from raising questions about the Geneva convention on a forthcoming Peru visit. But Anslinger did request that he fetch the FBN some new coca statistics.

For American policy, as well as for cheap coca, Maywood also worked during the 1930s against the state monopoly in coca advocated by local experts and crusaders like Paz Soldán for national drug control. This made sense, for the proposed Peruvian monopoly in cocaine hydrochloride and coca aimed to produce its own export extracts and significantly raise coca prices, and it would have run up against the U.S. ban on imported cocaine. Peru's de facto monopoly in Trujillo-type extract leaf could have easily hiked the costs of making and drinking Coca-Cola. Maywood's local extract venture, from 1928 through 1933, occurred precisely during the rise of Peru's Depression-era efforts to nationalize the industry. Thus, shutting down the factory was also a way of persuading Peruvian officials that no future lay in exports of extracts or medicinal cocaine.[50]

The 1930s, perhaps not by accident, became a surprisingly buoyant time for Coca-Cola and Maywood Chemical and for their intimate partnership with the FBN. Coca-Cola managed to double its corporate revenues during the depths of the Depression, and Maywood doubled its intake of Peruvian coca by 1940. The FBN redoubled efforts to enforce a domestic monopoly on coca essence, which was linked to Maywood's unique "special leaf" coca pipeline from Peru. Maywood disclosed to the FBN not only its own coca operations but also any signs of unsolicited Peruvian marketers or sales. The FBN, wielding special import permits and threats of narcotics harassment, discouraged all mid-1930s coca syrup rivals (Yukon Club Kola, Better Kola, and so forth) attracted by the strangely booming cola business. As the world war neared, State Department and FBN cables of 1937–38 show officials debating how to best sustain Coca-Cola's leaf supplies amid rising tensions.[51] Anslinger politicked to allocate scarce shipping to haul Peruvian coca to New Jersey rather than permit operation of the secret extract plant. The war would sharply expand Coca-Cola's global influence and bring the United States directly into Peruvian drug policy.

Finally, long-standing market ideologies and structures underlay U.S. influence, especially in derailing the mobilizing 1930s *estanco* project for Peruvian regulation of cocaine. U.S. drug policies generally have suffered from their awkward position between prohibition (the extreme of negating a commodity's existence) and the free-market fervor pervading other fields of the imperium. But in much of the world, and invisibly in Maywood's coca monopoly at home, statist controlling solutions dominated. The League tapped European cocaine syndicates to rein in pharmaceutical markets and sanctioned the breakaway opium monopolies of states like Turkey and Bulgaria.[52] In Peru, the drive to nationalize coca and cocaine, which erupted in 1929–33 and reared its head until the late 1940s, had many sources: anti-*coquero indigenistas*, relic cocaine interests, and modernizing national chemists, agronomists, and medical authorities like Paz Soldán. Along with progressive sanitary legislation, it was the one acceptable Peruvian model of control, unlike the external barriers and imposed quotas that infuriated nationalists. A working monopoly might have managed, over the long run, to reduce cocaine exports as well as keep the coca peasantry within legitimate visible realms of commerce, unlike outright criminalization of cocaine or cultural discrimination against Andean coca leaf.[53] Eventually, these ideas, squeezed through a filter of war statism and prohibitions, materialized in the ENACO (Empresa Nacional de Coca, or National Coca Company) coca agency of the 1950s, a pale imitation of its initial vision. Without resources from medicinal sales, it lacked the capacity to oversee the sector by the 1960s. In some ways, its coca statistics and plans were as make-believe as those of the defunct League of Nations.

As with other drug policy matters in Peru, official U.S. opposition to the national monopoly scheme was discreet but decisive. Time after time, in 1930, 1933, 1936, and 1940, American officials evinced their instinctive dismay at the idea, from the Pagador League scheme to Paz Soldán's long crusade to ministerial war planning. It was unthinkable to help Peru find its own way and means to drug control. After all, a monopoly would need to break into the tightly policed, banned American drug market. Yet, unseen by Peruvian actors, the most entrenched American interest in the relation, Coca-Cola, adamantly opposed the monopoly on grounds of self-interest and supported a structure for the coca trade that made it unfeasible. In 1940, Maywood even enlisted its man Pinillos again to help block impending moves toward a wartime coca *estanco*.[54] When ENACO came into being in the 1950s, by default, UN teams that hoped to transform it into a functional arm of drug control lamented the obstacles put forth by the United States. In effect, U.S. beliefs and informal pressures stifled one of the few institutions that might have kept illicit drugs at bay.

During the interwar era, with the cocaine threat at home dwindling, the United States did not try to export cocaine prohibitions to Peru, much less Bolivia, which lay way off its radar. Instead, U.S. drug agencies honed their intelligence capabilities and scrutiny of declining Peruvian cocaine, allowed Coca-Cola/Maywood to mediate for its control system, and quietly blocked local alternatives to prohibitions and to the chaos of illicit cocaine. Forceful American intervention came only after the shifts of World War II, and with these changes, Andean prohibition.

FROM GLOBAL WAR TO
WAR ON COCAINE, 1940–1950S

I can only suggest the complexity of the social, political, and global processes that closed cocaine's long life as a licit national commodity in Peru — in short, the inauguration of a truly universal prohibition regime around cocaine. World War II set the stage by irrevocably tipping the global balance against Peruvian cocaine, tightening U.S.-Peruvian ties, and defining illegitimate trading. In its wake, in rapid telescoped fashion from 1947 through 1950, Peru's legal factories became criminalized under a strict new antidrug regime, and coca fell under monopoly and United Nations purview, all with Peruvian approval. Anticocaine policies came together during the long 1950s (1950–64), spurred by cold war politics, the global march to the 1961 Single Convention, a U.S. secret war on cocaine, and police cooperation against the first outbreaks of illicit coke, the new Andean product of these repressive years.

World War II changed the basic terms for Peru and the United States around cocaine. In the largest sense, the war for the first time forced distant South America into direct working relations with the United States. Historians working the vast archive of U.S.–Latin American relations sense

this sea change in state-to-state ties in the sheer expansion of documentation and bureaucratic surveillance. For the first time, Peru systematically
began to absorb and mimic U.S. models of drug control, though not in ways
that suggest measures forced on the country from afar. Peru's last options
for cultivating alternative markets were shattered on 7 December 1941.
Axis outlets abruptly closed for good. In response to Soberón's market
scramble of the late 1930s, a Japanese query for cocaine, ironically, arrived
on 4 December 1941, duly noted by U.S. and now-watchful Peruvian drug
authorities. These changes transpired just as rival cocaine circuits flowing out of Java, Formosa, and Japan became cut off from the West and
later destroyed, though none of these sites had ever spawned entrenched
local coca use. In 1945, U.S. occupations ensued of the two major cocaine
producers, Germany and Japan, and Allied and UN officials put narcotics
control along American lines high on their list of reforms. Only the United
States came out with postwar cocaine capacity, and this capacity was
geared to lower world use; moreover, it still refused to absorb Peruvian
cocaine. No room was left for cocaine commodity chains autonomous of
U.S. control.[55]

For the duration of the conflict, cocaine became a curiously unrecognized
strategic commodity in U.S.-Peruvian ties. Cocaine, as Peruvian officials
noted, was crucial for the modern battlefield and its mass civilian casualty
fronts and was demanded as such by the Allies, which tripled Peru's exports
to over three thousand kilos by 1943. Yet unlike cacao, barbasco (an Amazon
insecticide), cotton, cinchona, copper, or other crucial goods, cocaine
was never covered under any bilateral price or quantity pact of the War
Commodities Board, though there were tacit supply understandings. In
1942, Peru's minister of finance, Davíd Dasso, suggested giving a legitimate
status to cocaine, but he was strongly rebuffed by Washington because of
implied Peruvian drug mischief. Signs point to high-stakes politics here,
manipulated by Anslinger with Coca-Cola to maintain the status quo on
Peruvian cocaine in secret deals and trade-offs worthy of *Catch-22*'s Milo
Minderbinder. Anslinger worked to mold Peruvian actions by wielding
threats to cut the country off from hoarded wartime stocks of medicinal
morphine and cocaine. Just prior to the war, Anslinger approved pilot
projects for Maywood to grow coca domestically in case of disruptions in
Puerto Rico or Hawaii; Merck eyed sites in Costa Rica.[56] Yet, in an explicit
deal, Anslinger, who lost sleep over the alkaloid in imported coca seeds,
abandoned the scheme on Peru's pledge to suppress new poppy planting
and assure Maywood steady and ample coca supplies. While Coca-Cola

did not win the war per se, its expansion among GIs on the fronts made it seem that way. Imports of "special leaf" doubled during the conflict, aided by a heroic 50 percent exemption of duties. In contrast to coca, officials rigorously upheld the cocaine ban at U.S. borders, emergency or not, repeatedly rebuking Peruvian producers, especially the pleading Soberón, for approaching American buyers.[57] Instead, Anslinger and the State Department brokered circuitous covert deals with Russia and Britain to sell the leftover Peruvian drugs from the proscribed markets of Hamburg and Osaka.

Good-neighbor ties with the north meant enhanced reporting and a collaborative watch, for example, on cocaine stocks readied for the Allies or their foes. With intergovernmental access came real spying. During the war, officials first began talking of illicit commerce, which one political report put at fully "one-third" of all cocaine produced—presumably unlicensed production. Beyond numeric conjecture was the way the concept of "illicit" grew out of the global contest itself. It was first defined, articulated, and enforced in terms of suspected shipments to Germany and Japan and in the command language of war. Loyalties got checked, with our drugs perceived to be "legit" and theirs not. For Peruvian producers, this presented a real dilemma, for Germans and Japanese had been their sole customers and personal business ties before the commencement of hostilities. To American, British, and militarizing Peruvian authorities, all the cocaine produced for these clients now was suspicious "contraband" to be prevented from delivery. Even before 1941, a harsh crackdown hit non-nationals in cocaine, resulting in the dramatic expropriation of Japanese Huallaga properties in 1937, police raids on a German home lab in Miraflores in 1939, and the exile of longtime Nisei agents in Huánuco.[58] The label of "illicit" stuck and shifted until by war's end it had definite meanings that had been blurred before. Much of this vocabulary drew from the lingo of intelligence operations and secret wars. In 1939–42, intelligence reports flooded in, especially from the British, of impending cocaine shipments, now pegged as "smuggling" via Spain, Italy, Argentina, Bolivia, and Switzerland—neutrals everyone knew abetted the other side. Secret intercepts and diversions verged on drug busts, though now no one burned the captured cocaine. A discourse of "drug wars" derived from war itself and would intensify in the coming cold war.

All this subterranean activity around cocaine in dimly discernible ways added to the new wave of restraints on the drug traced in chapter 4. These partly served to stem strategic thefts during wartime scarcity and rationing of medicines. For the first time, openly articulated and diplomatically blunt admonitions concerning lax Peruvian controls came out of the FBN, Federal Bureau of Investigation (FBI), State Department, and the embassy in Lima. In Peru, the police edged themselves into the realm of drugs and were quicker to join forces abroad than diplomatic arms of the state. Narcotics became demedicalized, shifted from pharmacy boards to the police. In 1939, authorities placed new limits on Lima's Cóndor factory; in 1940, they suspended new factory licenses; in 1941, strict transit controls, which legally defined "tráfico ilícito," expanded to cocaine throughout the country; in 1942–43, official notices laid the ground for a state monopoly; and in 1944, the government began production trials of pharmaceutical cocaine in Lima Bureau of Health labs to offset import shortages. For the first time, locked in struggle with the Nazis, the British jumped into cocaine. Throughout 1942, diplomatic notes flew about a novel British scheme to curtail Peruvian production by rationing the imported soda ash used to refine crude cocaine: in today's terms, this was an attempt to control "precursor" chemicals.[59] Cooperation pacts multiplied between the United States and Peru. A portent of things to come was the 1942 accord creating the U.S.-sponsored Tropical Agricultural Station, the largest in the Americas, crucial to the worldwide struggle for tropical commodities. Its location in tiny Tingo María allowed officials to parcel out adjacent seized Tulumayo lands to land-hungry colonists. This put U.S. agents — or agronomists at least — right in the middle of prime Huallaga coca territory, although dispatches avoided mention of the bush.

The war also heightened Peruvian anticocaism, with its ambivalent relation to cocaine. It was as if Paz Soldán's two sides had split into warring camps, as his later writings after 1939 became less corporatist and stridently anticoca. In general, anticocaism thrived under the militarization of public health. On one side was Carlos Monge Medrano's and Alberto Hurtado's San Marcos Institute of Andean Biology, founded in 1931, which became state sponsored in 1940. Its charter had called for scientific study of coca in high-altitude societies, and by 1946 its researchers, rejecting addiction and degeneration ideas, began to articulate the physiological and neurological logic behind the continuing use of coca by so-called Andean man. Despite Monge Medrano's *indigenista*-inspired ideal of Andean man, the Rockefeller Foundation supported the institute as a site of experimental professional science in Peru, preferable to the eclectic European social medicine style of Paz Soldán, and the institute enjoyed linkages with a host of elite U.S. institutions. Ever distrustful of its views on coca, the embassy monitored the institute's progress. Monge Medrano would head the postwar Peruvian team of the 1948–50 UN Commission of Enquiry on the Coca Leaf. On the other extreme, Dr. Luis Sáenz, a medical officer in the Guardia Civil, published *La coca: Estudio médico-social de la gran toxicomanía peruana* (1938), which, as its title foretold, reduced all coca use to a toxic mass addiction of Peru's Indian nation.[60] This side also absorbed scientific training and support from the north. This was the era that bequeathed the short-lived but dismal anticoca science of Gutiérrez-Noriega, which helped to unite the long-separated politics of coca and cocaine. Both were equally dangerous to the nation. The Peruvian military police published some of these works and entered medical territory with its own 1940s sanitary journal. Small anticoca steps were taken, like banning coca chewing in barracks and prisons, the places where Gutiérrez had found most of his deviant, malnourished, and degenerate *coquero* population. Amid the war in 1943, longtime coca agitator Carlos Ricketts and Sáenz founded Peru's homegrown Anticocainism League, which would rail against national coca and cocaine far and wide into the cold war, accusing foes, even Peruvian governments, of foot-dragging for the benefit of their international cocaine-mafia-communist allies.

Finally, during the war, Peru began working with the League's Opium Advisory Committee, or at least its exiled shell in Princeton. In 1940, Peru formally announced to the League its enlarged production for export, followed by a lapse in reporting until 1944, when officials prepared and mailed coca and cocaine statistics for the Allied cause. There was another reporting gap until 1950. Although Peru had nominally joined the OAC in 1938, the League's invitation to become a sitting member remained unrealized, despite Anslinger's frequent nudging, passed on by Maywood's Vice President Hartung on the scene.[61] Maywood's heavy local presence during Coca-Cola's global war effort may have helped to delay the League-approved Peruvian *estanco* proclaimed by wartime statist decrees. In a departure from Peru's long history of avoidance, the postwar UN Commission on Narcotic Drugs was established with Peru as a permanent sitting member.

At war's end, legal cocaine came to its last crossroad, as Peru faced the United States alone on the global stage. Former German, Dutch, and Japanese cocaine networks now lay physically demolished by warfare or under U.S. occupation. The United States had no need for, nor legal leeway for, imports. Only France and Britain bought Peru's crude cocaine, and this in tiny lots. Cocaine's pent-up modernizing hopes had no outlet, although Peru's capacity to produce, and its surplus stocks, had swollen during the war. The newly formed UN swiftly assumed and revived campaigns for international drug control, operational by 1947 in the Economic and Social Council's Commission on Narcotic Drugs. In contrast to the League, the CND fell under American tutelage and influence, with Anslinger himself playing a direct role. Scant international opposition registered; even the new archenemy, communist states, tacitly backed UN antidrug militance for reasons related to their own peculiar ideologies. These facts alone assured cocaine's place on the international agenda and spelled far stricter quotas for meeting world medicinal and scientific needs. By the 1950s, these fell to fifteen hundred kilos, less than half the allowances inflated in the 1930s for German and Japanese interests, and purchases of Peruvian crude cocaine dwindled to under four hundred kilos by the late 1940s.

For the first time, officials launched a serious drive to define coca leaf as the raw material of cocaine control, unlike earlier 1920s–30s efforts deflected from a weak League. The broader-based CND voiced deep concerns about another postwar breakdown of drug controls, projecting a spiral of drug abuse from wartime surplus drug stocks, restless veterans, and new international gangs. In the United States, postwar anxieties surfaced about reported drug use among alienated urban minorities, bohemians, and youth.[62] In 1948, regulating cocaine also became even simpler, as the FBN abolished nonmedicinal leaf imports. As Merck ceased making the drug, Maywood's new cocaine monopoly, from the residual of its Coca-Cola extract, was semantically dubbed "medicinal." For the first time, Peru lay within the solidifying apparatus of world drug control. Cocaine was no longer flowing within the context of a multipolar world with a diversity of opinions on its place and prospects. U.S. officials had long held an abolitionist stance toward legal cocaine: thus, the postwar years offered them a perfect opportunity to see that through. Drug policy "imperialism," if that term fits, was no coordinated conspiracy, but it was certainly overdetermined.

Thus, within two years of war's end, long-held Peruvian reluctance and resistance about national cocaine crumbled. Authorities moved abruptly, helped by a 1947 turn to a militarized cold war regime, an international scandal about illicit coke smuggling in 1949, and a well-timed visit by the new UN Commission of Enquiry on the Coca Leaf. A swift march of decrees charted the new prohibition regime. Peru's supreme resolution of April 1947 instituted stricter cocaine factory transit controls; each factory was to lie within two kilometers of a "chief town" and, more remarkably, was to modernize by installing "a small laboratory operated by a pharmaceutical chemist responsible for control of production and appropriate statistical data." In a July 1947 resolution, the Peruvian state convened an interministerial panel "to study the question of the industrialization of coca and problems connected with its commerce and Peru's international obligations." The panel endorsed a monopoly. A December 1947 decree-law established the crude cocaine monopoly, which by June 1948 was operated by a state-run factory of the Ministry of Public Health with "exclusive rights to manufacture, export, and sell cocaine and its salts and derivatives." In August 1948, a Lima control board subsumed all older local coca taxes. In March 1949, Peru's penal code on drug production and trafficking was radically revised to accord with international norms. Simultaneously, the state revoked all existing licenses for legal cocaine manufacture. In April 1949, Peru appointed a chief of the Department of Narcotics, a post directly responsible to the UN. Police also shut down the last factories. In June 1949, officials announced an *estanco* of Peruvian coca, which by August had gained sole rights for leaf export. From September to October 1949, a national commission called for comprehensive study of coca in collaboration with the visiting UN coca mission. In January 1950, Peru defined the juridical-medical status of addicts. By July 1950, authorities had canceled leftover private cocaine contracts, directing all proceeds from the "industrialization of coca" and crude cocaine exports into agencies for "narcotics control" and new programs of "addict treatment." New institutions, congealing at a slower pace, had come full circle, enveloping cocaine in a sphere of illegality. And on the ground from 1948 through 1950, cocaine became swiftly criminalized by scores of arrests and seizures led by a fully operational national narcotics squad, the Peruvian army, and drug agents swooping in from the United States.[63]

Politics, big and small, drove cocaine prohibition. Besides the expanding narcotics police, no Peruvian lobby directly profited from criminalization. But cocaine's larger transformations of the 1950s would closely follow the course of the cold war in Latin America as the drug carved out its new underground currents. After a brief political opening until 1947, the United States expected new loyalty from its hemispheric client states, including accordance with its policies on drugs. Political operators like Anslinger made drugs part of the global anticommunist struggle, blurring the reality that communist regimes abhorred drugs. Peru's quick moves to outlaw cocaine coincided with a sharp political transition: the broad democratic postwar regime of José Luis Bustamante (1945–48), which included a political pact with the long-proscribed APRA Party of charismatic leftist Haya de la Torre, was overthrown by General Manuel Odría in October 1948. Both regimes, in the spirit of the times, sought to curb drugs; Bustamante, reflecting *indigenismo*, invited in the UN coca mission and embraced the *estanco* as a national industrial project. But Odría characteristically declared a militarist campaign of suppression against cocaine.

Odría, the kind of anticommunist economic liberal Washington adored during the 1950s, was in part trying to curry favor with, or aid from, the United States, which had initially supported Bustamante's democratizing front and a mellowing APRA. The general soon found a vociferous ally in Anslinger. Odría's crusade was also fueled by his implacable internal war against APRA, which counted more than four thousand arrests effected under his emergency Law of Internal Security. The repression forced Haya de la Torre into his legendary years of refuge in Lima's Colombian Embassy. The coup had begun in October 1948 after militant young Apristas staged a failed, bloody naval uprising in Callao, which served as a dramatic pretext for Odría's rightist putsch and the torrent of measures against the Left. In a Byzantine round of political accusations, Odría's *junta militar* began to vociferously denounce the drug money behind APRA's aborted 1948 revolution. Allegedly, sympathizers among the Balarezo gang of New York cocaine smugglers, busted in 1949, funded the revolt, among them acquaintances of Haya de la Torre's brother. APRA, which itself had little coca policy, hotly denied the fabricated charges, creating alarm among prudent State Department career officers. Nonetheless, tales of drug corruption helped justify Odría's housecleaning against APRA and Bustamante and let him claim, at least, that he had Washington's blessing. It also gave a special military fervor, efficiency, and discourse to Odría's local war on drugs, with tactical victories illustrated in the trafficker mug shots adorning Lima's dailies in May 1949, months before any U.S. move against Balarezo.[64] The scores of arrests in unprecedented nationwide drug sweeps, including raids on a few legal cocaine makers, were casualties of Odría's crackdown on subversion, which entailed more than 80 drug-related arrests in 1949 and 110 in 1950–51. It helped that Huánuco, typical of peripheral Peru, was an Aprista party stronghold. Soberón's son Walter was the town's APRA mayor, making Odría's reprisals a rerun of Leguía's 1920s war against the rebellious Durands, intensified with drug war anticommunism.

The triumph of prohibitions coincides and connects with two close-knit developments: the birth of illicit cocaine in Peru and the 1947 advent of a decades-long U.S. secret war to stamp it out. This problem presents an unavoidable chicken-and-egg dilemma, although the longer trail of evidence affirms that the main impact of prohibition and antidrug police activities was only to speedily disperse illicit coke across and beyond the Andes. This story also marks the debut of aggressive meddling by U.S. drug agencies in Peruvian politics, spurred on by the urgency to wipe out cocaine, a feat that U.S. officials believed fully possible. By the late 1940s, police forces shouldered a larger role in Peru's control of drugs, and FBN drug agents and even Interpol joined in to aid Peru's narcotics squad. It was small stuff in terms of agents or budgets, but it signaled a new working antidrug alliance between the two states, one pushing Peru to full criminalization.

Smuggling of illicit cocaine from the Andes began in the immediate postwar years with the drying up of legitimate markets for Peruvian cocaine. The pioneers were typical "ant smugglers," Peruvian and Chilean sailors concealing a few vials of the drug, at first from Callao on Grace Line ships heading to Havana and New York. By 1948–49, the traffic attained a regularity and scale revealed in the arrests of the Balarezo gang, which involved dozens of accomplices and an alleged street value in the millions. Within two years of escalating FBN counterdrug activity, cocaine, wiped out by Peruvian forces in Huánuco, spread further afield to bases in northern Chile and revolutionary Bolivia, with underground supply lines stretching across the hemisphere, nurtured by small-time Pan-American mobsters. After decades of absence, a cocaine menace — a forgotten "White Goddess" of the Andes, as *Time* dubbed it in 1949 — was back on the American radar, if only detectable in the ounces or pounds found at borders. To Anslinger, the certified source of troubles was Peru, confirming American assumptions held since 1912.[65]

Newly released FBN papers reveal the start of a concerted multinational campaign against cocaine even before the sensational New York drug scare of August–November 1949. These interventions quickened Peru's push to prohibition. In late 1948, Salvadore Peña, a dedicated New York customs detective, worked a two-month undercover assignment against so-called Latin cocaine and came up with an elaborate plan to stem the trade with police counterpunches and diplomatic pressures inside South America. By mid-1949, the FBN's leading district commissioner, New York's Garland Williams, a seasoned ex–Office of Strategic Services (OSS) officer, along with ace agent James C. Ryan, filed a series of reports linking unregulated cocaine in Peru to the streets of New York. The FBN dispatched Ryan, after a quick Berlitz Spanish course, on a fall 1949 Latin American tour, with several extensions. He received a warm reception from his Peruvian counterparts, particularly Carlos Ávalos, long-apprenticed pioneer of narcotics vigilance in Peru, now busily employed by the Odría regime. Ávalos had befriended Anslinger while attending earlier UN meetings in Lake Success, New York. Captain Mier y Terán, chief of the Peruvian Investigative Police, Peru's FBI, and a repressive anticommunist Odría stalwart, proved particularly responsive. His counterpart in Washington, J. Edgar Hoover, joined in the investigations. During 1949 and 1950, these agents set up cross-border sting operations, culled witnesses, and arranged extraditions. This was no longer a one-sided gaze but a network of penetrating ties and intelligence sharing between U.S. narcotics agencies and like-thinking Peruvian counterparts, revealed in scores of letters, cables, and memos of the FBN, FBI, and State Department.[66] Informal relations became permanent relationships that reinforced the ethos and walls of drug prohibition. Once cocaine was defined as a simple criminal matter, internationalist cops saw eye to eye about it. During this formative episode, Anslinger also tapped anonymous tips from a network of American citizens in Peru, who denounced suspicious "cocaine labs" in Pucallpa, Trujillo, and beyond. One of these informants, a mysterious and angry-toned "Frank of Lima," claimed to be an agent of the newfound Central Intelligence Agency (CIA).

Arguably, such policing relationships proved more decisive to prohibitions than diplomatic maneuvers. Anslinger, as usual, made many propagandistic claims for his efforts in the press, including Lima's, as well as serious diplomatic gaffes, such as propagating the volatile drug slander against Haya de la Torre. One businesslike meeting at the State Department with Peruvian Ambassador Berckemeyer became inflated in Anslinger's triumphant later narrative: "Your Commissioner went to the Peruvian ambassador and succeeded in having the President of Peru close all the factories. In six months there was a phenomenal change in the prevalence of cocaine addiction — it had almost disappeared again."[67] On the contrary, the real news this time was that illicit cocaine did not disappear but rather after 1950 became the elusive mouse in a cat-and-mouse game with FBN agents that would only escalate over the next decade.

FBN agents dispersed across the Americas on longer and longer missions, some quite daring, most quite futile — actions going far beyond the pre-1940s surveillance regime. No matter how aggressive the pursuit, cocaine slipped away to spawn new sites, routes, smuggling tactics, and groups. In the mid-1950s, covert U.S. operations against cocaine were buttressed by intelligence and Andean drug raids conducted by Interpol under UN auspices. By 1960, the task required a wider hemispheric intelligence web on cocaine. With hundreds of busts annually, cocaine had emerged as the FBN's chief concern in the Americas, though it was never publicized as such. By the early 1960s, this apparatus expanded again to include long-term postings of specialized drug agents in the region (men like Thomas Dugan, William Durkin, Wayland Speer, and James Daniels), the systematic recruitment of local undercover operatives, and police cocaine seminars and training fellowships in the United States. Apart from attempts to break up smuggling rings and preempt shipments, the long-range U.S. strategy soon fixed on the hoary notion that cocaine would go away only if coca supplies were dried up. Coca eradication transformed from a mere theoretical possibility into an urgent political goal. These ideas and activities intensified during three panicky inter-American anticocaine police summits, disguised between 1960 and 1964 as UN "coca congresses," which treated coca leaf as an element of emerging criminal circuits.[68] Hemispheric policing relations, even if backfiring and ballooning into illicit networks, became the sinews of the new prohibitionist regime.

Another critical transnational development in Peru's route to prohibition was the 1948–50 UN Commission of Enquiry on the Coca Leaf. Not only did this sustained multinational study group provide much-needed ideological legitimacy for the first anticoca measures in the Andes, but, vitally, it did so with the willful acquiescence of the Peruvian and, to a lesser extent, Bolivian states. In a longer transnational historical arc, the commission replayed the role of nineteenth-century medical currents in awakening coca interest, but this time in reverse, to sway national elites now willing to embrace strong anticoca views. Publicity from the mission indelibly linked the national dilemma of coca, with some added local nuance, to the global criminal problem of drugs, the final step in bringing coca leaf into the closed circle of prohibition. In contrast to past League efforts, the mission worked to make Peru into an active participant in the international drug regime.

The new CND had already jump-started discussions of coca, but impetus for the mission came in an April 1947 request of Peru's UN delegate, Carlos Holquín, for a scientific "field survey" to determine once and for all the "harmfulness" of coca. Peru was asking in effect for international political arbitration of its long-standing unresolved national debate, the dispute between medical scientists with a research agenda informed by an addiction-degeneration view of coca leaf use and the rising Andean biology school, which by the postwar years had consolidated its scientific vision of coca leaf use as a benign or useful adaptation of Andean man to high-altitude environments. By July 1947, with the collaboration of the Interim Commission of the World Health Organization, officials prepared coca questionnaires and detailed preparatory studies. American scientists dispatched to the Institute of Andean Biology in Lima relayed their frustrated efforts there to find negative things to say about coca.[69]

Despite this scientific ambiguity, the new UN body had already assumed the bolder task of conducting a survey for "limiting and curtailing" cultivation of coca leaf. In mid-1949, just as coke trafficking exploded into the Peruvian and American news, the UN announced its plan for a September–October crash "field trip" to Peru and Bolivia. Behind the scenes of this five-year internationalized coca controversy, Peru also called upon the related monthlong UN Mission of Experts for the Reorganization of the Narcotics Administration in Peru, known as the Logan Mission, which strictly dealt with curtailing cocaine. The report of the March 1948 Logan Mission, which has disappeared, strongly supported the pace and form of Odría's course of criminalization. The experts advised the creation of a stronger, independent antinarcotics bureau and an end to all private manufacture; heeding multilateral opinion, it also backed the new monopoly on crude cocaine, which Peru eagerly broadened to coca with the 1950 formation of ENACO. State production and marketing of cocaine became an arm of the coca control monopoly. Further hidden was Anslinger's spying and prying to push the upcoming coca mission in a prohibitionist direction.[70] This was not difficult, for his old friend Howard B. Fonda, vice president of Burroughs-Wellcome and Company, headed the group, mailing back "Dear Harry" letters replete with tip-offs for locating illegal factories of cocaine. Maywood's Hartung also sat in on sensitive CND coca leaf sessions, and Anslinger worked to ensure that the mission's recommendations did nothing to infringe on Coca-Cola privileges.

The eight-man Commission of Enquiry on the Coca Leaf embarked in September 1949 on its extensive three-month itinerary in Peru and Bolivia, including site visits to growing areas in Huánuco and Tingo María. Its members received much local assistance. Peru formed its own National Coca Commission to complement its work, led by Andean-man scientist Dr. Carlos Monge Medrano and filled out with an eclectic range of ten luminaries, including the busy national narcotics chief, Ávalos. One wonders whether members knew of the body's 1888 prococa predecessor and namesake. The UN mission landed in Lima just one month after the police breakup of the Balarezo gang, that other monument to growing U.S.-

Peruvian collaboration. The timing of those New York arrests, engineered by the FBN's ex-intelligence officer, Garland Williams, sent a clear, urgent message to the UN team about the intimate ties between illicit cocaine and coca leaf and between the Andes and drug threats to the rest of the world. Fonda's Russian delegate, reputedly drunk for most of the trip, was the easiest to persuade.

The commission's 169-page, twenty-chapter published report of May 1950 covers enormous ground, from the living conditions of Andean Indians to high-altitude science to the botany, chemistry, cultivation, taxation, and control of the leaf. Its UNESCO-style universalism was incompatible with the local Andean-man thesis of indispensable highland coca use. Yet its recommendations, steeped in a vague UN postwar social and developmentalist discourse about the "vicious circle" of poverty and coca chewing, satisfied no one. On the one hand, the commission had jumped to a foregone policy recommendation of "gradual suppression" of the coca bush over ten to fifteen years via crop substitution by healthier foodstuffs such as coffee, tea, rice, and citrus fruit. Thinking about coca had come full circle since Peruvian promotional yearnings of the 1880s, with imported alkaloidal plants like coffee now set to replace native coca. Chewing would inevitably wither away through the uplift and modernization of squalid Indian lifestyles.[71] The UN had yet to discover "culture" (indigenous or otherwise) as an obstacle to or an ally in its vision: no anthropologists sat on a panel staffed by chemists, drug executives, antidrug officials, and physiology professors. Anslinger, who saw coca leaf as simply another bad drug and Indians as simple addicts, found this all too wishy-washy, an opinion shared by Peru's hard-line prohibitionists like the doomed Gutiérrez-Noriega (soon to perish in a car wreck overseas), whose research the mission cited profusely. Yet the achievement of a UN antileaf consensus made the report a watershed for coca discourse in the Andes and beyond. While it is easy to overstate the power and agency of this one 1949 UN mission, it did lead toward the goals established in the 1961 UN Single Convention: to uproot coca globally under a then-delayed twenty-five-year timetable.

Reactions to the report sputtered in. The Peruvian press passionately debated its contents, though mainly accepting its basic terms, such as "the problem" of coca. In early 1951, Peru's own Commission for Study of the Coca Problem put out a twelve-page "counter-reply" to the UN team. Monge Medrano's disjointed self-styled "polemic" had few substantive objections to UN aims but insisted that "the science" was still missing to assess coca's effects on "man," Andean or not. It was the same vexing question behind Peru's original call for the mission in 1947. With its personalized tone, the reply read like a proposal for more funding of Monge Medrano's institutional research. Over the next few years, Peruvian delegates to the CND objected to pushing ahead with the limitation program if coca's harmful effects had yet to be proven, an objection widely interpreted as more stalling.[72]

No matter, the crucial development was that coca leaf was officially and fully problematized now in Peru, as etched into the titles of official commissions and writings. The mission assured Peru's ongoing cooperation with the total international drug regime, for example in compiling genuine statistics and national reports for UN consumption. Peru's forty-eight-page missive for 1950 is a mine of real information, followed by coca reports of the Peruvian Bureau of Health, though even with ENACO to help, Peru could not replicate a full national report until 1955. Bolivia, on the other hand, seriously lagged in joining the prohibitionist club, whether due to ideological purity, its war-era Axis tilt, or the revolutionary chaos starting to sweep the nation. Since 1932, Bolivia had sent drug agencies one curt 1943 report, and the nation was not active on the CND. In 1949, Bolivia lent its cooperation to the UN tour, adopting an official stance to "concur" with any Peruvian objections, presumably because of Peru's established coca science. Yet behind the scenes the coca-growing SPY renewed its decades-long protest that "Bolivian Coca is Not a Narcotic." This time, however, Bolivia's Foreign Ministry did not relay the SPY's vital message to the UN itself.[73]

Such objections were unthinkable in Odría's Peru of the 1950s, now a pillar of repressive prohibition. The last counterweight, legal Huánuco cocaine exporters, was banished. Despite scientific misgivings about coca, Peru's denigrated and remote Indian coca users had never held weight with the Lima state. U.S. drug policing and a control discourse were now integral to the Peruvian polity. It had taken a long, circuitous route to overcome Peruvian reluctance since 1910.

THE 1950S DENOUEMENT

The 1950s marked a denouement of the 1949–50 Peruvian prohibitions process before two vital benchmarks of 1961: the UN Single Convention, which institutionalized cocaine and coca into a universal drug regime, and Bolivia's belated consent to the antidrug campaign. The emergence of illicit cocaine in the 1950s, spurred by Peru's crackdown on legal cocaine, became the covert driving force of U.S. policy and began to overshadow other traditional concerns, interests, and actors in cocaine. The United States and Peru routinized their working antidrug relationships, which operated via FBN assistance and local policing, without much fanfare or diplomacy. But the early success of this repressive alliance in 1949–50 displaced the now-mobile drug, mainly to Bolivia, Chile, and Cuba, thus demanding the erection of a wider series of repressive hemispheric policing and political networking against the spiraling menace. The secret war against cocaine heated up, informed and channeled by the Pan-American cold war. Bolivia, with the collapse of its feeble state during the 1952 revolution, became the drug's next battleground, across time-honored Andean leaf zones that had never industrialized coca. Bolivia would only accept drug prohibition following mounting political pressures and scandals about cocaine traffic amid the postrevolutionary state's early 1960s reshaping under American tutelage. Yet at the same conjuncture, the hemispheric impact of the Cuban Revolution of 1959–61 dashed any early hopes of containing cocaine.

In Peru, the long-coveted state monopoly, part of ENACO, was set to go by late 1950. Peru was finally making genuine cocaine hydrochloride in a rundown government facility called the Fiscal Laboratories for the Industrialization of Coca, which could export legally from Lima around the globe.[74] The FBN swiftly sent in inspectors to spy on and snipe at the project. By the mid-1950s, its output was five to six hundred kilos, a fifth of World War II exports and one-twentieth the turn-of-the-century legal peak. It had few real prospects without an open U.S. market. ENACO management of and incentives for Peru's coca-growing peasantry also proved tenuous: despite the UN coca campaign of 1950, Peruvian coca crops, like Bolivia's, grew substantially over the next decade. Crops hit eleven thousand tons and entered remote areas as the land under coca cultivation doubled to over sixteen thousand hectares. Peru's monopoly never came close to its nationalist ideal of drug control.

For Coca-Cola, the 1950s proved its quintessential epoch in American culture, and the firm enjoyed a virtually symbiotic political relation with Anslinger. Maywood was among the first to protest Peru's monopoly, especially its pricing, yet it managed to continue its long northern supply compact with Pinillos. But Coca-Cola had greater coca concerns to cope with throughout the 1950s: keeping Anslinger attentive, as the FBN turned its focus to the threat of illicit cocaine; fostering tolerance of the leaf's virtues amid rising world anticoca fervor; struggles with global anti-

American nationalists, who revived early anti-Coke narcotic polemics; and ensuring Coca-Cola's permanent coca niche in the drawn-out negotiations around the 1961 Single Convention.[75] Anslinger's activism helped achieve the latter, though overall the gradualism and compromises of the treaty, a capstone of his long internationalist career, disappointed the aging FBN chief. The challenge of Coca-Cola politics was to reconcile the openly aggressive U.S. anticoca stance, which broached no local exceptions, with this hidden American corporate privilege. After Anslinger's retirement in 1961, the restructured U.S. drug administration, the Bureau of Narcotics and Dangerous Drugs, even helped Maywood embark on the top-secret and short-lived mid-1960s "ALAKEA" project, which planned to cultivate extract coca in Hawaii. It was insurance against expectations of post–Single Convention limits on Andean coca, though it went against the grain of the long-standing American prohibitions pact and, like the 1929–34 Lima extract factory episode, was a big risk to drug diplomacy. Maywood continued as the nation's sole provider of medicinal cocaine, all now a byproduct of decocainizing the Coca-Cola — and American — empires.

But that long tightly managed trickle of legal American cocaine would be drowned out as an official preoccupation when after 1960 all dams broke against a flood of illicit cocaine from the Andes, the topic of the next two chapters.

III

ILLICIT COCAINE

6

BIRTH OF THE *NARCOS*
Pan-American Illicit Networks, 1945–1965

Between 1947 and 1964, a wholly new class of international cocaine traffickers swiftly arose, formed by little-known Peruvians, Bolivians, Cubans, Chileans, Mexicans, Brazilians, and Argentines. These men—and often daring young women—while pursued by overseas drug agents, pioneered the business of illicit cocaine, a drug whose small-scale production in eastern Peru had remained aboveboard until the late 1940s. After 1945, commodity cocaine, vestige of a heroic bygone age, was entering its final stage of decline, constricted as it was by the global effects of World War II and closely watched by U.S. and UN drug controllers. Despite some suspicions to the contrary, not since the teens had cocaine existed as an illicit drug. It had never been trafficked across borders from distant producers to global consumers, and never directly out of coca's homeland in the Andes. By 1950, however, a handful of couriers were smuggling it by the ounce from Peru; by the mid-1960s, this flow topped hundreds of kilos yearly, linking up thousands of coca farmers of the eastern Andes to crude labs, organized trafficking rings, and a bustling retailer diaspora in consuming hotspots like New York and Miami. The Colombians of the 1970s, the Pablo Escobars who were to leverage this network into one of hundreds of tons worth untold billions, are today notorious. Yet historians have yet to uncover their modest predecessors or the actual origins of Colombia's role, much less cocaine's passage from persecuted commodity to illicit world good.

In this chapter, I focus on these first, "pre-Colombian" *narcos* as the historical midwives of cocaine's transition from a vestigial legal good to a dynamic illicit one. Highlighting these mobilizing middlemen means this chapter cannot do justice to the social history of coca-growing peasants, colonizing migrants who by the mid-1960s also became a force in the emerging economy of cocaine. Nor do I directly analyze U.S. anticocaine policies or activities, the secret war against the drug launched in 1947, or the era's changing North American drug tastes and demand, though all impinged on cocaine's rise.[1] Yet even this close-up lens on pioneer *narcos* cannot easily convey a rounded sense of their underworld, especially on their own personal or cultural terms. By necessity, this new narrative about early traffickers derives from scores of fragmented international policing reports, mainly of the Federal Bureau of Narcotics and later the BNDD. In exploiting these reports, I try to move beyond, as much as possible, their official categories and language of drug control, as well as their speculative biases based on a trail of suspects and informers whose evidence was exaggerated in police eyes. I hope, however, as diverse schools of historical analysis suggest, that such inquisitional policing testimony can lend critical clues to the real past men and women who inspired these forensic portraits.[2]

In this chapter, I trace out the middlemen—"traffickers"—and cocaine makers—"chemists"—who emerged transnationally between coca-growing peasants and cocaine-hunting drug agents in the postwar decades. They constituted a new class, articulating via newly clandestine markets the highly localized conditions for drug trades in the context of the new obstacles and incentives planted by foreign and state judicial interests. This smuggling class came together across a vast expanse of shifting geographies through transnational networking, shared learning experiences, and the invention of new tools of the trade. Its stream of cross-border activities overflowed cocaine's remote historical outpost in the eastern Andes in a surge of local agency that was to transform the global drug trades. Its actions constructed, in other words, a new kind of international commodity out of cocaine. In larger political terms, cocaine's new transnational geographies also belonged to the cold war history of the Americas, as rising political tensions of the era structured the major spaces for and movements of illicit activities. Illicit cocaine thus emerged after a century of history within vying global commodity formations as a Pan-American product of the high cold war, propelled outward by a related series of cold war events and developments.[3]

To observe these political roots, I divide the postwar decades of cocaine's resurgence (1945–65) into two clear stages: 1947–59 and 1959–65. Illicit cocaine began on one end with the advent of the cold war and the stepped-up international campaign to extend coca-cocaine prohibitions to

the Andes. Illicit cocaine surfaced in eastern Peru in 1947–49 as anticommunist regimes suppressed this long-legitimate local industry; run out of
Peru, it incubated after 1952 amid the revolutionary chaos of neighboring
Bolivia. Loose smuggler corridors sprang up across Chile, Cuba, Brazil,
Argentina, and via Latin American cities with urban drug scenes. Initial
cocaine trafficking resembled the criminologists' spontaneous "disorganized crime" or petty "ant trades," taking root in the gray area between
legitimate and criminal commerce and dependent on older Andean coca
circuits.[4] In the second phase, from 1959 through 1965, cocaine consolidated
itself into more systematic growing, processing, and smuggling circuits.
Its watershed was the 1959 Cuban Revolution, which sent now-practiced
Cuban drug mafias across the Americas, including into the United States.
When Bolivia, then cocaine's incubator, finally fell under U.S.-style drug
control, coca-growing peasants flooded into lowland jungles, lending the
export a new, unstoppable social base. By 1965, at the height of U.S.-backed
modernizing regimes in the region, a commodity chain built by unsung
chemists and smugglers tied peasants to distant pleasure users in the
north.

This chapter revolves around those shifting transnational geographies
of illicit cocaine. It begins with the politics of cocaine in Peru during the
drug's final turn from lingering regional commodity to illicit coke after
World War II. The next part turns to the emerging *narco* corridors crossing
the borders of 1950s Chile, Cuba, Argentina, Brazil, and Mexico, and, by
1960, cocaine's migration from the Andes through a new Pan-American
smuggling class. The chapter ends on Bolivia's revolutionary merger of
peasant coca and cocaine, prelude to illicit cocaine's startling takeoff after
1965.

PERU: BIRTH PANGS OF THE ILLICIT

The lush *montaña* of eastern Peru below the town of Huánuco, botanic
cradle of the coca plant, was for six decades after 1890 the capital of Peru's
commercial cocaine industry. The same site became, after 1950, the seedbed
of the illicit cocaine that would famously flourish there during the 1980s. By
1947, Peru's clutch of surviving cocaine makers, led by Andrés A. Soberón,
saw few prospects ahead due to encroaching anticocaine politics and law.
Thus, Soberón ended his thirty-year quest to save the region's industry.
In May of 1949, after drying a final seventy-seven-kilo load, he threw in
the towel, officially closing his Huánuco factory. At the same time, his son

Walter, Huánuco's mayor, resigned from the hounded left-wing Peruvian APRA Party. Soberón retired to Lima, ceding his equipment to the new state lab at the Ministry of Public Health.[5] As cocaine making became off-limits, another option arose: petty drug smuggling up the Pacific Coast.

These local changes were the outcome of global shifts in the history of cocaine stretching back to the turn of the century, when Huánuco had placed on world markets ten tons of crude cocaine using its own simple technologies. Advancing world legal restrictions on cocaine—the missionary movement spearheaded by the United States since 1911 described in chapter 5—were finally taking effect. U.S. officials had had a difficult time convincing the rest of the world of the evils of cocaine and of producers and refiners such as Peru, Bolivia, Germany, Japan, and Dutch Java. By the mid-1920s, anticocaine strictures existed on paper in League of Nations conventions and in early U.S. aspirations to stem cocaine at its coca raw material source. Little came of these crusades save for a slow but steady global delegitimation of cocaine, long resisted in Peru, where it still enjoyed the status of a scientific, or at least embattled national, good. Until 1945, a multipolar cocaine world prevailed, with distinctive legal drug regimes coexisting in various corners of the globe. World War II ended the tolerance of cocaine: warfare obliterated the relic circuits of Europe and Asia, and the United Nations, closer to American drug ideals, immediately put control of coca and cocaine production high on its agenda. In 1947–50, the UN mobilized for pliable cold war regimes in Peru and Bolivia its visiting Commission of Enquiry on the Coca Leaf, which brought home to these holdout nations the need to ban cocaine and rein in the cultivation and chewing of native coca. By 1950, Peru, under highly politicized circumstances, had outlawed private cocaine and issued a range of punitive drug controls; Bolivia, rocked by revolution, took another decade to comply with the U.S. campaign to close cocaine's last legal spaces.

What is striking about that fading multipolar world was the scant impulse it gave to illicit cocaine between 1920 and 1945. Unlike heroin, international smuggling markets and routes never arose for cocaine after both "heroic drugs" fell under global bans after 1915. This is most remarkable, given that the recreational uses of cocaine had in fact been early and widely appreciated, given the ease of smuggling this lightweight powder, and given that during the interwar period itself cocaine was legally and loosely made in a variety of sites around the globe, from Peru, Germany, and Holland to Japan. Paradoxically, it was lack of direct repressive pressure against these producers, or against depressed yet legitimate sales outlets, that kept incentives low for illicit cocaine trades.

Illicit cocaine has a genealogy, but its trail is situated mainly outside of the Andes. Recreational use and abuse of cocaine erupted as early as the 1890s, especially in the United States, where the drug became readily available, injected, imbibed, and sniffed. By 1905, the cocaine fiend had become a frightful menace of public caricature, especially when racialized as the notorious cocaine-frenzied "Negro" in the Jim Crow South. Cocaine subcultures thrived in the "tenderloin" underworld among fast-living prostitutes and thieves in southern plantations and ports, as well as among higher-class artistic sets. The scandalized press coverage, pharmacy and medical journal editorials, and police reports attest to the thousands of early cocaine users. In the United States, this culture of cocaine peaked in the 1910s, fed by cocaine gangs, "combinations" like New York's legendary ferocious West Side Hudson Dusters, mail-order sales of snortable high-potency asthma cures, and shady pharmacists, most of them allegedly Jews. This visibly deviant consumption lent a special emotive force to U.S. anticocaine initiatives beginning even before the 1906 Food and Drug Act in a wave of local and state anticocaine laws. Cocaine lovers also proved abundant in Europe, famously so in London's West End theater district, among the Parisian prostitutes of Montmartre, in decadent artistic or upper-class circles in Berlin, and in sailor paradises like Rotterdam and Hamburg. Such pleasure use even reached faraway outposts like colonial India and Buenos Aires, where by the 1920s tango bars became legendary coke dens.[6]

For reasons that are still only dimly understood, North American illicit cocaine rapidly receded in the 1920s. Early drug controllers gained a quick foothold in the regulation of medicinal retailers and dentists, from whom most cocaine leakage had occurred. Respectable wholesale pharmaceutical firms policed themselves.[7] The United States also erected a tight political economy of cocaine control: no cocaine was imported after 1922, and by 1930 only two firms manufactured the drug from leaf, New Jersey Merck and nearby Maywood Chemical, working diligently with the emerging drug authorities of the FBN. No major underworld figures pursued possibilities here, perhaps distracted by timely profit-making opportunities in alcohol prohibition after 1919. Rumor had Arnold Rothstein, the era's colorful New York gangster, looking into the cocaine business but investing in heroin and baseball instead. Chronic cocaine users did not live long, and since cocaine is not in fact terribly addictive, its users may have soon converted to other sins. By 1924, the pioneer drug treatment specialist Lawrence Kolb found only 7 cocaine users in a sample study of 150 U.S. addicts. In time, cocaine faded into a drug of folkloric status in the culture, a nostalgic note of blues men or the fleshpots of early Hollywood, though tiny seizures of medicinal cocaine continued through the 1920s. The half-century hiatus in American popular cocaine use from 1920 through 1970 has been read as a users' "great drought," or, alternatively, as a period of social amnesia about the drug's perils. The vanishing of cocaine contrasts with the rise of more addictive morphine and heroin, both of which by the 1920s and 1930s were developing small but steady international illicit routes from Asia to Europe and the United States and whose use would expand among American youth and minorities by the 1950s.[8]

In Europe, however, where anticocaine fervor ran fainter, cocaine subcultures persisted, exemplified in the decadent nightlife of Weimar Germany and even reputably among the upper echelons of the Nazi regime. Coca wines became decocainized and slowly emptied from pharmacy shelves, though potent Tónica Kola still graced Spanish shops into the 1940s. In Europe, the pattern was clear: all illicit cocaine originated in localized diversions of medicine-grade drugs, usually branded vials of Merck or Hoffman–LaRoche, with periodic thefts organized from Italy or the Low Countries. In Spain and parts of Latin America, as a vestige of this pharmaceutical era, "merca" continues to be slang for cocaine. The Dutch Naarden pharmaceutical affair, the most dramatic of the late 1920s, exposed some 90 kilos of cocaine destined for shadow sales in Asia, yet the drug was dwarfed by the 3,000 kilos of heroin and 950 kilos of morphine involved in the scandal. In the Far East, rumors persisted of officially sanctioned trafficking by the Japanese in Manchuria and India during the 1930s, when Japanese military-industrial officials stopped providing accurate drug production figures to the League. Proof of forced sales, however, exists only for opiates. India was a known destination for interwar Japanese cocaine, smuggled in by sailors and spreading out along the colony's railroads. The drug became popular even among artisans in Calcutta and Delhi and was taken orally like betel by the despised "cocaine eaters." Authorities seized a startling 205 kilos at cocaine's Indian height in 1930, but India was the exception to shriveling worldwide use. In the postwar years, the newly launched Interpol noted a burst of cocaine use in Europe traced to abandoned Wehrmacht stocks, scavenged and run by gangs of displaced Polish-Jewish refugees.[9] Japan's defeat marked the definitive end to Asian illicit cocaine.

Almost everywhere in the world — whether smuggled across the Pacific from Japan, along the Mexican border, across the straits of Malay, in contraband Merck vials via Panama, among Egyptian highbrows or returning Russian World War I veterans and Moscow waifs, from corrupt Italian drug firms, by sailors in Valparaíso, in Argentine brothels and upscale touristic Cuba — stories are told about isolated cases and scattered cocaine use from leaky pharmacies or of the escapades of lone smugglers. By nature, such drug sources and sites were finite, irregular, disconnected, and quickly ran dry, unable to stimulate an ongoing cocaine culture. Pure cocaine became a great rarity, if ever found always blending into other drug use, as told in oral histories of aging addicts. The original early-century culture of recreational cocaine had died, the dearth of cocaine an ancient lament of American blues songs from the 1920s. Nowhere prior to 1950 did active networks come together that linked coca growers to illegal refiners of cocaine to long-distance smugglers and active user markets, that is, to an illicit commodity chain with true possibilities of growth.

The annual drug reports of the FBN can provide a variety of time series portraits for the United States, though, like all official seizure-based narratives, these are portraits that ignore the drugs that got away. Bear in mind that today's DEA claims to interdict about 25–30 percent of all illegal drugs. By the 1933 FBN report, *Traffic in Opium and Other Dangerous Drugs*, Harry Anslinger said of cocaine, referring to the teens: "The stream of illicit traffic at present is a rivulet compared to the river which was emptying into the country for a long period of years." In the early 1930s, agents seized only 4 to 160 ounces yearly nationwide (see appendix, table A.5). By the late 1930s, even that rivulet had dried up, "so small as to be without significance," according to the 1938 FBN report. During World War II, authorities deemed illicit cocaine a "negligible factor in the illicit narcotic traffic." In 1943, this meant there was apparently "no cocaine on the market," although a mere 5 ounces surfaced in 1942 before receding to 2 in 1944. Anecdotal finds indicate a scattering of minuscule diversions of European and Japanese medicinal cocaine. In the early 1930s, the FBN was still tracking leftovers of two 1922 lots of French Roques Pharmacy hydrochloride; some nine hundred quarter-ounce vials eventually showed up, mostly via Nogales, Texas. In 1936, officials found eleven bottles (120 grams) of Hoffman-LaRoche cocaine on an unlucky "Panamanian Negro" in the Canal Zone, soon sentenced to five years. In 1938, vials of May and Baker cocaine, usually refined from Peruvian sulfates, made their way from Montreal to New York in the publicized Celli-Ignari case. In 1940, two sailors arriving from Asia tried to sneak in Japanese cocaine. This was all classic anthill smuggling of what travelers could opportunely stuff in their pockets.[10]

Anslinger seemed to gloat about cocaine's defeat as living proof of what tough leadership could do about drugs, just as he was turning to that "killer drug," marijuana, in the mid-1930s. As table A.5 in the appendix illustrates, illicit cocaine hit the radar screen only in the postwar era, ratcheting above the one-kilo mark in the late 1940s, the ten-kilo mark in 1962, and then to over one hundred kilos seized by 1970 before tons of "snow" began to fall upon U.S. shores by the mid-seventies. This new, post-1947 trail was the path of modern cocaine, a sign of its invention by South American *narcos*.

There is even less prehistory of cocaine smuggling from the Andes. Huánuco archives offer a few hints of small-time contraband activities by hard-pressed cocaine merchants, but none are quite believable, organized, or significant. One cocaine old-timer I interviewed in Huánuco recalled the 1943 arrests of Anatolio Gómez and "Tacho" Herrera, who allegedly drove stolen cocaine over the mountains to Lima. There was a 1934 FBN case of a Loyola student who "accidentally" mailed an envelope north of Peruvian cocaine and stories of drugs with fake Bolivian labels. During the 1930s and 1940s, the most-wanted Peruvian drug suspect was actually Carlos Fernández Bácula, a disreputable Peruvian diplomat stationed in Europe from a distinguished family with Huánuco and Aprista connections. Bácula, who frequently misused his diplomatic pouch, however, was moving French heroin rather than native products of Peru. In the mid-1950s, after various arrests, he retired to Chile, where the FBN investigated him, to no avail, for any link to the newly erupting Andean cocaine trade. In fact, he is the sole Andean listed in the infamous State Department "Name File" of interwar drug traffickers. Not one of hundreds of such suspects dealt with cocaine. Moreover, the League of Nations authority responsible for shutting down illegal narcotics labs, which carried out some fifty-four operations in the middle years 1920–36, never identified a single cocaine lab. In 1943, Peruvian envoys in Panama were said to be moving narcotics, diamonds, and "Peruvian women to Panama to . . . a life of prostitution," but cocaine was not specifically indicated. In 1939, in a war-related incident, police took in a pair of Germans setting up a cocaine lab in a Lima suburb. During the war, as discussed earlier, "contraband" Peruvian cocaine—that is, that diverted toward Axis powers—became closely tracked through

Argentina and Spain. This was a crucial transition for defining the limits of approved drug commerce, of licit and illicit trades.[11]

The first documented case of South American cocaine smuggling dates from 1939. Undercover officers on Brooklyn's Sixteenth Street pier nabbed Ramón Urbina, a Chilean sailor, after he offered his Puerto Rican partner a 250-gram sample of cocaine carried from Chile. The evidence flew overboard during an ensuing scuffle with crewmen of the *Copiapó*, but Urbina later pled guilty and received two and a half years. The next incident, eight years later, revealed more of a trend. In October 1947, Peruvian informants warned that the *Santa Cecilia*, a Grace Line ship, had cocaine aboard. Police seized steward Ralph Roland in Weehawken, New Jersey, "in possession of slightly over a pound of cocaine." Betrayed, he confessed that "Peru was wide open for purchase of cocaine" from customs agents in Callao. Two months later, Alfonso Ojen, a naturalized American ship's waiter, was arrested in Callao harbor with "2 bottles containing 14.4gms cocaine" hidden in his bunk. Ojen's steamer, the *Santa Margarita*, sailed on to Brooklyn, where he was questioned by FBN agents, who were unable to trace his source. FBN reports of 1945–47 collate eight such ship seizures of probable "Peruvian origin." Something new was afoot.[12]

In December 1948, Salvadore C. Peña, a New York customs agent, filed a confidential memo to the FBN based on a special "two-month undercover operation." In this dirty work, he had befriended "various Latin traffickers and smugglers." They confirmed prevalent suspicions of "*dangerously increasing smuggling of cocaine into the United States*." Peña claimed to have witnessed "the open trafficking in cocaine especially among the extensive Puerto Rican, Cuban and Spanish population in New York City." The report, a masterpiece of its genre, warts and all, merits excerpting for its sketch of the sailor-driven drug circuit:

> SOURCE The principal and easiest source of supply for cocaine is located at El Callao, Peru, and at Valparaíso, Chile.... principle [*sic*] ports of call for boats making the South American run . . . it is believed the coca leaves produced in Peru are processed on a large scale, possibly with the under-cover protection of corrupted officials.
>
> INTERMEDIARY DISTRIBUTING POINTS The loads of contraband cocaine secured by the traffickers at Peru, Chile and Bolivia are sometimes brought directly to the United States when the boats make a direct run, or if the contraband is transferred to other boats at Bilbao

[Panama] and Havana.... Information secured from seamen supplied names and addresses of some of the traffickers handling loads of cocaine at Havana...and at Callao.

SMUGGLING When the boats arrive...loads of cocaine are brought ashore, especially in the port of New York, by longshoremen...because longshoremen are not searched going through customs.... Cocaine is also smuggled on passenger planes, some traffickers make special trips by car to Miami, where they received their loads, 2 or 3 kilos at a time.

CONSPIRACY Generally a group of Puerto Ricans or Cubans get together and pool several thousand dollars which are given to a seaman going to South America.... The price usually paid at the source is from $200 to $250 per gram of pure cocaine. The retail price in New York is from $250 to $300 per ounce, cut cocaine.... The peddling of this cocaine...is usually uptown among the Puerto Rican, Negro and Cuban section of New York and around the bars and the Latin night clubs around the Times Square area.[13]

Thus, by 1948, cocaine was moving beyond individual smuggling, as Peña details in credible terms a loose diaspora of "Latin" cocaine smugglers from Callao to Havana into New York. What is absent from his account is any description of the refining of Peruvian crude cocaine into powder cocaine or examination of the origins of this new Latin taste for the drug, which at the same time was starting to spread among the New York bebop jazz scene. Peña notes the difficulty, lacking informers, of cracking such mobile groups. He did draw up a plan, which involved sending Spanish-speaking undercover agents to Peru "acquainted with the idiosyncrasies of the Latins," by which he meant the corruptibility of local officials. A four-month mission to Peru, Chile, Bolivia, Panama, and Cuba would gather the data necessary to bring in diplomatic sanctions against the trade. The problem could be blocked at its mysterious source, akin to operations against Prohibition runners in 1920s Cuba and traffickers of opiates in 1940s Mexico. Whether or not Agent Peña got that assignment, within months dramatic cocaine busts — from the Huallaga to Harlem — became front-page news.

The sensational August 1949 arrests of the so-called Balarezo gang was the first modern international cocaine scare. On 20 August, the *New York Daily Mirror* headline read: "SMASH BIGGEST DOPE RING HERE: Seize Leader in City; Peru Jails 80...Tied to Peru Revolt." Even *Time* played

Eduardo Balarezo, pioneer
Peruvian cocaine trafficker,
1949 (U.S. National Archives,
RG59, Department of State,
Decimal Files, 823.114,
Narcotics/Peru, Enclosures,
October 1949)

up the affair. Balarezo, forty-nine, a naturalized U.S. citizen, was a ship steward for Grace Line with a host of contacts in New York and Lima. Born in Lambayeque in 1900, Balarezo was described in Peru as a bow-legged *zambo* (a mixed-race black). He had resided several years in New York, reputedly even crossing paths with the crime boss "Lucky" Luciano. After officers raided nine houses, he was picked up while boarding a boat to Italy. According to the federal prosecutor who arrested Balarezo and six accomplices, Balarezo began smuggling cocaine in 1946. His business expanded in 1947, and by 1949 he was moving some "50 kilos of pure cocaine" a month, worth a reported $5 million, focused on the "Harlem district" and using two couriers named Edelstein and González. This was surely the Grace Line circuit sketched by Peña in 1948. Only thirteen kilos were captured in New York, however, said to possess an adulterated street value of $154,000 per kilo. Balarezo owned a mansion in Great River, Long Island, cavorted with Peruvian dignitaries, acquired a young mistress, and easily posted a $100,000 bond. In Peru, the sweeping arrests, including that of Balarezo's wife, Carmen, were engineered by Odría's trusted PIP chief, Captain Mier y Terán, who had spent two months in New York solidifying leads. Among those detained were "prominent Peruvian businessmen, one of them a known Customs official."[14]

The FBN depicted its target as an "International Cocaine Smuggling Ring" with some fifty links across New York and Puerto Rico. It took less than a month to convict Balarezo, who received five years and a $10,000 fine, and others with the testimony of turncoat Geraldo Tapías Chocano.

In a crossover from cold war politics, Balarezo's high-profile prosecutor was Joseph Martin, who at the same time was leading the prosecution of Alger Hiss. FBN director Anslinger waxed triumphant for years: "The suppression of this traffic has averted a serious crime wave," he claimed, and he wrote glowingly of his action in his various drug-fighting books. The scope of the operation, from New York to Callao and Huánuco, led by New York narcotics agent Garland H. Williams, Anslinger's top field manager, revealed new forms of U.S.-Peruvian cooperation crucial to fight cross-border trades, involving on Peru's end the nation's first active drug squad. FBN threat magnification aside, this business had clearly moved beyond the work of solitary sailors.

In Peru, however, the scandal over illegal drugs was eclipsed by its politics: the claim that Balarezo was an Aprista militant and ally of APRA chief Haya de la Torre, who had funneled $50,000 in drug money to the failed 1948 naval uprising that had led to Odría's coup. Fed by FBN leaks from Williams, the conservative anti-APRA Peruvian regime and press reveled in this political conflation of narcotics, "Communism" (i.e., the moderating APRA Party), and Haya de la Torre, then holed up in Lima's Colombian Embassy. Drugs, arms, and contraband imports, all traded by a sinister APRA "cell" in customs, became the focus of Odría's outcry against the "Régimen de los Apristas," the former Bustamante government. Odría's persecution of the Left intensified in 1949. Peru demanded extradition as Balarezo reputedly bragged of killing seven loyalists himself during the 1948 mutiny. For its part, "el Partido del Pueblo" vehemently denied any connection to drugs, and soon APRA, outlawed in Peru, launched a hemispheric press campaign to clear its name. Alarmed State Department officials and Harold Tittelman, ambassador to Peru, distanced themselves from the FBN. Not only was the evidence of Haya de la Torre's link through his brother to Balarezo in New York suspect, but starting in the mid-1940s prudent American officials were quietly courting Haya and APRA as possible anticommunist allies.

Diplomatic historian Glenn Dorn has recently untangled the Byzantine partisan politics of the affair. The contradictory and fabricated APRA drug charges, in his assessment, were invented by anticommunist PIP chief Mier y Terán and broadcast in New York by the seasoned ex–OSS officer Williams.[15] Anslinger jumped into this fray not only to invigorate his new anticocaine campaign with cold war passion but also to forge a working antidrug relationship with Odría. Peru was still not a strong ally on drugs. The State Department, on the other hand, enjoyed delicate ties to

publication of the case's internal documents and spreading anti-American
protests, it demanded retractions from Anslinger and Odría's ambassador.
Outgunned, in April 1950 Anslinger quietly withdrew, yet never formally
rescinded, the APRA drug charges.

A key question, apart from the actual scale of the trade, is where
Balarezo's group got its cocaine. Where did illicit cocaine first spring up
in the Andes? In a zeal to criminalize the entire industry, American reports
cast suspicion upon a reported "eighteen" legal or unregistered cocaine
factories. Williams spoke of two large plants in Huánuco producing $2
million in cocaine a year, as well as a chemist who he said "may" work
in "basements" converting the area's sulfate-cake staple, crude cocaine,
into saleable cocaine hydrochloride. Williams's claims about the capacity
of Peruvian cocaine were wildly inflated, as was most evidence filtered
through informers. Sources named for Balarezo included Orestes Rodríguez
of Ferreñafe, husband of Alicia Martínez, a young go-between for her
uncles, the de la Torre, and Balarezo; Martínez was a possible FBN plant.
A Julio Vázquez reportedly sold three kilos to the group in early 1949. In
mid-1949, Hoover's FBI zeroed in on Gustavo Prados, a long-known worker
in northern cocaine plants and frequent visitor to New York who began
supplying detailed accounts of the industry. One lead, Héctor Pizarro, had
brothers said to run a cocaine lab in Amazonian Pucallpa. Sales moved
via "El Chino" Morales, a notorious figure in later drug rap sheets. Peru's
leading daily, *El Comercio* (Lima), printed similar sorts of accusations.[16]

Odría used such news to tighten the screws against both APRA, with
some four thousand political detainees by 1949, and cocaine. In April
1949, Peru's last nine licensed cocaine factories closed for good under
special antinarcotics decrees. Mass roundups followed under Peru's new
antisubversive Law of Internal Security. From late April through late May
1949, well before the breakup of the Balarezo gang, the military mounted
drug sweeps from Lambayeque, Huánuco, and Huancayo to Lima. Mug
shots of the *narcos* ran in Lima dailies, which hailed the offensive and "the
timely decrees of the Junta Militar." Authorities uncovered five "clandestine
factories" in varied parts of the country. Peru's 1950 narcotics report to the
UN detailed those arrested and convicted for cocaine running, though it
is hard to tell, given the political hysteria and legal ambiguity of the drug,
who was truly a trafficker. That said, the seventy-plus cocaine-related
arrests listed for 1949–50 suggest a number of possible cocaine sources:
the northern Ayllon clan; Soberón's associate in Lima, Guillermo Carter

Silva ("a chemist with a clandestine laboratory"); and the eight-man gang of Morales and the Panamanian businessman José Steel. The UN also names Julio Vázquez and six others linked to Balarezo, notably supplier Orestes Rodríguez, whose getaway imperiled the criminal case in Peru. A driver, Pedro García Céspedes, was picked up in Huánuco in June 1949 with cocaine refined in Chorrillos. Leandro Ferreyra, caught on the New York route, pointed to Rodríguez's "clandestine factory" in Ferreñafe for "drugs sold to the crews of Grace Line Vessels of Cuban, U.S., Panamanian and Porto-Rican [sic] nationality." Even without any captured goods, Ferreyra got five years and a $16,000 fine. Other cases included that of Cuban José Flaifel Moubarack, a highly active courier of the 1950s; a local French prostitute, Angela Pasqüero; and a Peruvian laundress, the last two presumably small-time users.[17]

Some ties surfaced between the former legal cocaine industry and newly illicit cocaine. By definition, legal businesses of the 1940s became illegal ones, but this remained a gray area of commerce until Odría's mid-1949 and 1950–51 dragnets, which netted another 110 drug arrests. Some families, like the venerable Durand clan, had long since diversified from cocaine, becoming prominent in national public life. Several recognizable "chemists" and minor figures were among the scores arrested, unfairly or not. Some may have viewed stocks of cocaine as hard-won severance pay when the industry stopped and tried to pawn them on the black market. Others unwittingly sold legally registered cocaine to traffickers. García Céspedes's crude cocaine came from Huánuco. Soberón, after retiring in mid-1949, was charged in 1950 with supplying chemist Carter Silva and sentenced to six months and a twenty-thousand-*soles* fine. Known figures in illicit sales — Prados, who was tracked by the FBI in New York, and Rodríguez — had worked the legal sector.[18] By the mid-1950s, Peruvians engaged in legal cocaine surfaced in new Bolivian exploits. The tropics beyond Huánuco made for easy escape, so Peru's military campaign against cocaine, inflamed by hatred of APRA, simply scattered its seeds.

Local archives fill a few gaps. For example, reports from the Huánuco Prefecture show that in July 1948, after state plans to monopolize the industry began to take shape, José Roncagliolo, owner of the Bolívar crude cocaine factory, registered to dispatch cocaine to the Health Ministry in Lima, consigning twenty-one kilos to one César Balarezo, a possible relation of Eduardo Balarezo's or a pseudonym. (A Balarezo clan resided in Huánuco.) In northern Peru, an anonymous tip in August 1948 denounced the "Fabricación de Cocaína Clandestina" on the Sacamanca hacienda, whose license may have lapsed. The owner's sons, Ricardo and Santiago Martín Ayllon, engaged in suspicious behavior: there was cocaine stashed under farm goods in transit to Trujillo, buyers and couriers in Lima and Bolivia, and visits to the Hotel Bolívar, Lima's watering place for foreigners. The informer duly listed addresses for all the principals. Authorities seized forty-four kilos, despite rumors that the Ayllons had official protection. In April 1948, this cocaine lair became front-page news in Peru. Sixty-year-old Santiago Ayllon, long invested in legal cocaine, received eighteen months from the National Executive Council in 1950, his sons and accomplices lesser terms.[19]

The most remarkable allegation, from the FBN itself, concerned Huánuco cocaine patriarch Andrés Avelino Soberón, dedicated to this trade since 1917. If at all true, the allegation would make Soberón, then sixty-eight, the "Johnny Coca-Seed" of South American cocaine. In mid-1949, Odría's men closed the last of Huánuco's factories, yet a number of those implicated later that year as illicit refiners of cocaine paste acquired their stock there. Soberón, now retired, was soon picked up along with other merchants and, despite his pleas of innocence, sentenced.

Not much was heard of Soberón until 1953, when a U.S. agent posted a series of secret reports via Ecuador about the advent of cocaine manufacturing in Bolivia. He charged that the cocaine sold freely at nightclubs and restaurants in downtown Lima, especially Silvio Canata Podestá's at Manco Capac 590, originated with Andrés and Walter Soberón. The operation seemed sizable: "paste" (presumably crude cocaine) was manufactured in twenty-five-to-fifty-kilogram lots stored "in an isolated area some 40 miles northeast of Huánuco." The Soberóns, given their arrest record, worked discreetly. Most dramatic was the agent's claim that the Soberóns were "responsible for the operation of a clandestine cocaine laboratory in Bolivia," having "sent two cocaine manufacturing experts to the country in 1951." Nelson Alfred López, an FBN agent in Lima assigned with Carlos Ávalos, head of the Peruvian narcotics squad, soon launched an inquiry. He reported that following the 1949–50 crackdown, cocaine, "known in Peru as PICHICATA," became a staple at Lima hot spots like the Embassy Club, Penguino, and Negro Negro. The agents then ventured, much like consul Burnett had in 1932, the six-hundred-mile round trip to Huánuco to interview former mayor Walter Soberón. Posing as members of "a large Chicago syndicate," they overcame Walter's misgivings, leading to a night ride to a jungle gathering of the Soberón clan. There, the hosts unveiled "a sort of hot-house" with "a platform about two feet high and covered with leaves and jute," on which López "was shown 28 bricks of a dark yellow paste purported to be cocaine paste." Soberón demanded an all-or-nothing deal for the drug cache. Later, for a delivery plan, agent López contacted one Raúl Wissmar, as usual in Lima's Hotel Bolívar, "a Peruvian about 32 years old," to act "as future liaison man with Soberón." Agents mingled in Huánuco, where locals blamed the Soberóns for the town's troubles. A storekeeper recounted local rumors of "two expert workers," Álvaro Salvatierra and Uvalde Recavarren, sent to Cochabamba or La Paz, Bolivia, in a scheme shielded by a Czech diplomat in Bolivia or Patiño tin operatives. This amazing exposé ended by recounting Soberón's earlier offer to the Ministry of Health to unload "one ton" of cocaine and warnings of high protection in Peru's regime.[20]

I am still unsure what to make of these documents, given the unreliability of much FBN analysis. Little came of them. Soberón was not rearrested, and the family pursued an exemplary life in Lima. Perhaps political protection was at work, as several Peruvian officials were later implicated in aiding traffickers. Perhaps Soberón, bitter over his 1950 persecution, sold off some aging cocaine stocks, since an actual Huallaga factory sounds terribly risky. As for the link to Bolivia, it is during this period that illicit cocaine labs began to pop up in that country's clandestine industrialization of coca, but setting up such labs did not require much technical prowess. Peruvians and Bolivians meshed in Bolivia during the 1950s, as did numerous Cuban and Chilean smugglers. Such links are circumstantial, yet if they were real, Odría's cocaine war had wide repercussions.

For the rest of the 1950s, repressive Peru was no longer the center of illicit cocaine making. But Peru had already played the decisive role of transforming its moribund regional culture of crude cocaine sulfates into a new class of marketable product: the illicit "cocaine paste" of would-be international drug smugglers. Interested Cuban mafia men continued to scout Peru, and repeat arrests and allegations registered, suggesting the formation of a few criminal careers in cocaine. At least a dozen colorful policing reports of fleeting labs and trafficking, mainly toward Brazil, issued from Peru in the decade 1951–61.[21] But it was not until the early 1960s, following the Bolivian and Cuban revolutions, that illicit cocaine begin to return in force to eastern Peru, in Tingo María, Uchiza, and Pucallpa, and this time became dispersed and socially entrenched as roads and peasant agriculture advanced into the Huallaga Valley. In Peru, petty smuggling from fading factories of the 1940s was crushed with military efficacy by 1950, fanned by the cold war passions of cocaine's first Pan-American trafficking scandals. Suppression of legal cocaine swiftly dispersed the trade across borders, with revolutionary Bolivia poised to be the next site of cocaine's evolution as an illicit drug. Before examining that key 1950s development, I want to turn to the protagonists and spaces of the new pathways north of illicit cocaine: in Chile, Cuba, Mexico, and beyond.

CHILE: COCAINE CLANS

Chile, with Cuba, was the major and now-forgotten transit route for illicit cocaine throughout the 1950s. Indeed, the Chilean corridor, linked to Bolivia, sporadically grew until the early 1970s, when the 1973 coup finally propelled the cocaine trade to Colombia. Chile's northern outposts, Tarapacá, Antofagasta, and Arica, far from the capital, bordered Peru and served as Bolivia's outlet to the sea. Valparaíso sailor clubs had long offered cocaine and other delicacies, and Valparaíso was a port of call for the Grace Line freighters that plied the Pacific coast to the United States.

As early as 1945–47, the FBN speculated from seizures that Chile was the source of the cocaine being smuggled to New York. It was not until the early 1950s, with Peru's role in cocaine fading and Bolivia in turmoil, that Chilean *narcos* moved beyond courier roles to emerge on their own as risk-taking *empresarios*. Newly founded Bolivian labs sent cocaine sulfates or even pressed coca down the sierra to Arica for refining and smuggling. Authorities complained that the traditional Bolivian coca route (a leaf trade banned in 1957) for workers in northern mining camps facilitated illicit trade.

By the mid-1950s, Chilean and American authorities clearly identified the multitudinous Huasaff-Harb clan as the dominant force of the Bolivian trade, a position the group kept until a major international bust in 1966. (There were many spellings of this family's name, including Huasoff, Huasof, and Harv, yet one race, "Arabian," in U.S. consular classification.) César Harb, his wife, and their four sons formed the nucleus of this labeled "syndicate," starting out with the sailor circuit of the late 1940s. In 1952, they reputedly built their first two cocaine labs in northern Chile. Rubén Sacre Huasaff, the eldest son, became the chief refiner, based in Antofagasta and Valparaíso. Luisa Huasaff Harb, his aunt, frequently visited ostensible relatives in Connecticut; Amanda, another sister, was the "owner-manager of the most renowned house of prostitution in Valparaíso," according to a detailed 1959 exposé in *Vistazo*, with "interests in her right in the traffic of cocaine." The piece called the Huasaffs "the Borgias of cocaine." The article noted Amanda's son René Harb Huasaff as another large "dope distributor," adding, "It is through Arica that the cocaine of the Pacific Coast is exported." The family enjoyed direct family ties in Bolivia, where Amanda's brother Ramis had settled. The ring operated with the complicity of pharmacists and compromised Chilean police. Indeed, family members eluded arrest for many years due to tip-offs from the federal police, among whom they found an ally in Carlos Jiménez García, the sub-prefect of investigations.[22] Exports complemented a flourishing domestic pleasure market, with cocaine "available in most night spots in Santiago" from local celebrities such as the Cuban bongo drummer known as "Jimmy." In Chile, it was said "no hay fiesta sin cocaína." The Huasaffs typically used women, overlooked in border searches, as couriers from Bolivia, although two exceptions were nabbed in 1959. The clan's Bolivian connection was no small fish: Luis Gayán Contador, a Chilean-born friend of Amanda's brother Ramis in Bolivia, who had risen remarkably after the 1952 revolution to become chief of the National Identification Service, or political police, under Paz Estenssoro. His business, involving cross-border protection rackets, scandalized Bolivia in the early 1960s. Leftist *Vistazo* described the racket:

> All cocaine is sent to Arica, from there it goes to the north, diverting only what is necessary for Santiago.... the raw material arrived in ... Santiago's airport, in police envelopes, marked confidential. Other detectives ... were involved in the handling of these raw materials. The cocaine also arrived by other methods, including automobiles and passenger aircraft. Bolivian cocaine is yellow and of a disagreeable odor [as sulfates]. After treatment it acquires a white, almost metallic color. It is then mixed with boric acid and bi-carbonate so that a kilo of pure cocaine is converted into three of "Pichicata" [Peruvian term]. One package of cocaine contains a gram.

That same year, 1959, Chile accounted for half of cocaine seizures at U.S. borders, some 985 grams alone found on the hapless Humberto Figueroa and Jesse Colson. Within Chile, Interpol reported the capture of 1.2 kilos from a seven-man Santiago team tellingly composed of five Chileans, a Cuban, and a Bolivian. Authorities rounded up more Bolivian-Chilean traders in 1960 and 1961, and in 1962 they recovered 288 kilos of coca from a "public highway, on a donkey's back," plus 800 kilos of leaf netted during a police raid in Arica. That year, a courier named Williams was convicted for possession of a kilo of Chilean coke found in a New York safety deposit box. A 1962 UN report quoted Chilean health authorities about the growing   263

Birth of the Narcos

trend, with six cocaine HCl seizures totaling 3 kilos between June and July 1960: "Illicit traffic in Chile is much greater than previously thought.... our efforts must be continued and steadily intensified."[23]

Ramis Harb, self-described "hijo de árabes," later testified about the routes of this family enterprise. The clan initially piggybacked on the well-trod Panama-Cuba-U.S. route. By 1952, Ramis was ferrying cocaine from Bolivia directly to Mexico "on his own account," where he carefully placed one-to-two-kilo packets in safety deposit boxes of the National Financiera and Banco Mercantil of Monterrey. He owned more than three Mexican passports. Under assumed names, he would personally deliver the cocaine or send it by courier to his New York contact, Enrique Sierra.[24]

Members of the Huasaff-Harb clan were arrested at least twice during the 1960s after the downfall of their police protector, Jiménez, in 1959. Their prosecution, however, mainly served to disperse cocaine into a more competitive enterprise employing hundreds of Chileans. After 1960, ever more cocaine moved via Mexico. In early 1963, a women ensnared in Mexico with four kilos from Arica led police, in the words of Antofagasta's consul, to "the house of Huasaff[,] a complete laboratory for processing of cocaine." The police report described what they found: "The center of distribution activities was a restaurant known as 'El Pollo Cojo' [The Lame Chicken].... Huasaff declared that the drug laboratory was a legacy of his father and that he had not been involved in the drug traffic for years." Those last words suggest the spirit of a true family enterprise. Captured records showed evidence of the family's many forays to Bolivia. "A peculiar fact of the case" was the defense of the group by Arica's departmental attorney.[25] The Huasaffs' last stand came in June of 1966, when the core of the clan was caught with a "large clandestine laboratory" following a botched late 1964 bid to run ten kilos through Kennedy Airport using the mule Juanita Bradbie. Six convicted New York codefendants, including Sybil Horowitz, revealed the family's burgeoning U.S. network. A massive sting in Chile soon brought down Luisa Huasaff, her husband, René Harb Huasaff, Ramis, and his live-in companion.

Chileans had evolved from part-time smugglers into the heads of organized international drug rings, with emulators across the Andes by the mid-1960s. In 1966, the UN, reviewing local police reports, counted more than 460 Chilean cocaine runners, with more arrests to come in 1967. Breaking the Huasaff clan had opened a floodgate. Officials tagged the mid-1960s Chilean corridor as one of three thriving cocaine routes to the

United States (along with Peru-Panama-Mexico and Bolivia-Brazil–the Caribbean). Bustling border barter trades laundered drug profits, helping sellers survive the turbulent 1960s and early 1970s. UN experts dubbed Chile "an important producer of cocaine" with a dozen significant "organizations." The politically tinged 1970 Squella-Avendaño affair starred a former air force officer running some $10 million in cocaine to Miami. Yet despite rising political tensions with the United States, and despite the tendency of officials to read drugs in the optic of anticommunism, a congressional report of 1973 still lauded the cooperation of the Allende regime in the drug fight.[26] Chile's path in democracy and drugs was broken by the coup of September 1973, which pushed the cocaine traffic out of the divided country toward Colombia, where it would blossom in coming years.

CUBA: COCAINE CULTURE, COCAINE EXILES

Cuba was the hub for the development of international cocaine traffic and tastes for the drug during the 1950s, a role that is better known than Chile's. Havana was among the first postwar global sin capitals, with roots in Prohibition as a site where offshore U.S. gangsters rubbed shoulders with their Latin counterparts from Chile, Panama, Argentina, and Mexico amid the readily corrupted regimes of Grau (1944–48), Prío (1948–52), and Batista (1952–58). Havana's notorious gambling and pleasure clubs, and its freewheeling prostitution industry, became the era's pioneer test markets of cocaine. The spreading modern taste for cocaine, including that of curious American tourists, was a Cuban invention, worthy of its own cultural history. A vibrant new Pan-American "mambo" cocaine culture superseded the relic blues inflection of prior recreational cocaine.[27] By 1950, Cuban couriers were venturing out in search of cocaine's ingredients; by the mid-1950s, Cuban labs prepared Andean cocaine for distribution in the United States and beyond. The 1959 revolution, by forcing the flight of Cuban drug dealers, marked a sea change for cocaine. The FBN declared Communist Cuba the bête noire of cocaine then breaching U.S. borders, but the real problem was its underground capitalist diaspora seeking havens from Mexico to Miami.

Cuban traffickers, such as Abelardo Martínez del Rey, were scouting Peru by 1948–52, and as opportunities arose in revolutionary Bolivian paste they quickly shifted their operations there. By the mid-1950s, Havana had emerged as the capital of this inter-American cocaine culture and commerce. In 1954, Cuba saw two major seizures of over three kilos. Mi onlico estate near Havana housed a lab where police seized "prepared cocaine," raw cocaine, coca, a false-bottom suitcase, and "ether, camphor, acetone and laboratory apparatus such as test-tubes and fake labels marked Merck." Chemist Carlos Aulet Curbelo, age fifty, got away, but police later apprehended accomplices, including Oscar Méndez Pérez in Brooklyn, who received five years. A 1956 seizure of 2.7 kilos in New York originated in Cuba. By now, Interpol regarded Cuba as the main staging point for Bolivian cocaine entering the United States. In 1957, alarms sounded with the seizure of more than 12 kilos of coke in Cuba, an enormous haul for the time. In 1958, police came upon a "clandestine laboratory" with 700 grams of finished cocaine HCl at the Residencia Fontanar in Havana. The "possessor and chemist" was José Ríos Benze, alias "El Gallego Ríos." However, Cuba's most talked-about traffickers were two Lebanese merchants with long records and a history of jail time served in the opiate trades: José Flaifel Moubarak; his father, Nicolás Flaifel Yapur; and José Gabriel Pérez Fernández. Flaifel Moubarak was implicated in varied Peruvian cocaine rings of the early 1950s and later Bolivian schemes. The members of the extended González clan (Esther, Armando, Miguel, and Ramón among them) also threw themselves into cocaine and by 1960 dispersed to Guatemala, Mexico, and the United States. Bolivia's colorful trafficker, Blanca Ibáñez de Sánchez, worked her La Paz–New York route with regular pit stops in Cuba until her arrests after 1959. In 1958, a mysterious Bolivian, probably Ibáñez, bribed her way out of Cuba after being caught with twenty-six kilos. Andean police archives of the 1950s sketch the comings and goings of Cuban buyers, the core intermediaries of the trade: Miguel González, Gustavo Portella, Abelardo Martínez del Rey, José Ara, Régulo Escalona, and Manuel Méndez Marfa, all with trademark Cuban aliases, to name a few.[28]

It is hard to say how much organization there was to this new transnational crime. Few signs point to direct intervention by the North American mafia figures in Havana. It seems that the traffic in cocaine was a strictly Cuban or Hispano-American affair of tough, homegrown smuggling outfits, perhaps following the example of foreign heroin dealers. The first year of visible Andean contraband, 1947, was also the year of "Lucky" Luciano's postwar effort to settle offshore in Cuba before FBN pressures forced him out due to his alleged ties to heroin interests. During the Balarezo case, Anslinger was desperate to link the two flows. Meyer Lansky and company flooded 1950s Havana, friendly with the locals until both the revolution and the development of a new capitalist paradise in Las Vegas drew them away. Cocaine was a natural sideline to the other entertainments of Batista's Cuba—gambling, cigars, women, and great Cuban music. Oral and mafia histories relate a similar tale: the vanguard role of Cuban nationals, including those living in the United States, in promoting cocaine, in part as a result of the FBI assault on domestic mobsters after the 1951 Senate Kefauver Committee investigations. Later, during the 1960s, the U.S. mafia peacefully ceded domestic coke retailing to well-connected Cubans. This was a transition as portentous for drug traffic as the previous 1930s–40s ethnic shift from predominantly Jewish gangs to Italian gangsters had been for mafia history. Officials pictured the Cubans in a "highly-organized" trade: "Cocaine traffic in the United States is almost exclusively by Cuban nationals residing and operating in New York City. These violators cause large quantities of cocaine to be delivered through professional couriers, mostly passengers on commercial airliners, directly from Havana to New York. . . . Cuban Traffickers in New York City then distribute the cocaine to other ethnical groups [sic: African Americans?] . . . and interstate to criminal associates in Chicago, Detroit . . . and other large metropolitan cities."[29]

Castro's 1959 revolution marked a noticeable spike in the quantity of cocaine seized in the United States, which rose to six kilos and three in Cuba, more than the previous half-decade combined. Smuggling routes scattered invisibly across the Caribbean basin. Cubans fled to Argentina for secure bases, and some were arrested transferring labs in Mexico. The core of this new professional international cocaine trafficking class was composed of Cuban exiles. In 1959, police netted no less than eleven Cuban cocaine smugglers with their signature "false-bottom suitcases." The revolution revived the once-rival Chile-Mexico corridor of the 1960s. By 1962, Miami had become a second U.S. port for cocaine—not surprisingly, given the city's large exile population—which included gangsters taking what they could from the island. The FBN reported two dramatic seizures that year, from Gabriella Giralt and eight others, with over 5.5 kilos kept in Miami and Key West safe houses. Pioneer distributors throughout the United States, such as New York's Felix Martínez, a.k.a. "Cubuche," and his brother-in-law Miguel Uzquiano, were Cuban nationals. Tied in with Mexican gangster Botano Zeijo, Martínez used a clothing firm as cover for heroin and cocaine sales from Chile, rising to become "a major distributor of narcotics in the New York area."[30]

The FBN was fully aware of this dispersing stimulus of Cuba's revolution, detailed in a special "Cocaine Traffic" memo of November 1961. Its collation of twenty-four major cocaine suspects underscored the Cuban role: "In most of our cases, where we are able to trace the cocaine back to the source of supply in South America, there is usually a Cuban involved somewhere along the line.... It appears that the Cubans are taking over as middlemen... smuggling the cocaine into this country." Cubans reportedly managed all cocaine coming into New York, the principal growth market, as "the only people able to bring cocaine into this country in any quantity or regularity." In Central America, which in FBN geography included Mexico, the FBN believed that "laboratories" were "being set up by Cubans who left Cuba because of the Revolution." The memo noted widening circuits of cocaine from Peru, Bolivia, Brazil, and Ecuador connected by this Cuban diaspora. The list of two dozen prime cocaine suspects in the Americas included Bolivians at the source, followed by a parade of prominent Cubans: Antonio Martínez Rodríguez, or "El Teniente," "a well-known trafficker of drugs in big scale," sighted in Lima in the 1950s; his brother Jorge; Mack and Modina Piedras, "Cuban functionaries of the regime of Batista"; Cristóbal Pérez, thirty-seven, of Havana; José H. Rodríguez at the Sevilla Hotel; a woman, Angélica García; Aulet Curbelo, the escaped early chemist; Dr. José Regalado, alias "Pepín"; Markos Cárdenas Xiquez; and Humberto Bermúdez Pérez, the last two "known traffickers of drugs." Even as late as 1962, the FBN sensed there were "important fugitives...reported to be living in Cuba at this time and evidently continuing in the cocaine traffic," including Louis Binker (a key target of their investigations), William Irizarry, Eduardo Berry, and Ramiro Infanzón. The latter group tapped seamen and women to sneak cocaine north. A second 1962 FBN report on the "Trafficking of Cocaine Hydrochloride" affirmed the drug's "dormancy" and then "gradual rise until 1959, when it spurt[ed] upwards at an alarming rate" due to the building of the Cuban-Bolivian corridor. The FBN had no less than forty-three ongoing Cuban-related investigations ranging from "California to New York and Michigan."[31] Nothing here suggests support or planning by U.S. mobsters—that is, this was a national diasporic project.

As it had done with the 1949 scandal with APRA, the FBN tried to paint "Communist" Cuba as a cocaine lover's paradise, in contradiction of its own evidence. In one theory, Batista's flight allowed relatives of ex-president Prío to reopen his old drug emporium. Just months after his triumph in March 1959, Castro felt compelled to answer Anslinger's inflammatory charges that Havana was "full of cocaine coming up from Bolivia" and Lebanese heroin. To the U.S. demand to deport American and other "hoodlums,"

Castro shot back in *La Prensa Libre* (Havana): "We are not only disposed to deport the gangsters but to shoot them. Send us that list and they will see.... Evidently the Commissioner has not heard that there has been a Revolution here and gangsterism, racketeerism, interventionism, and similar things have stopped.... We shall handle these affairs here with our own means and all can rest assured that Cuba will not again become a center for narcotics traffic as in the past."[32] By the 1961 Inter-American Coca Consultative Congress in Rio, U.S. officials like BNDD administrator Charles Siragusa spent much of their time tracking and complaining about "Communist" propaganda and influence, such as the warm reception given to Cuban delegate Dr. Miguel Uriquen Bravo. Within a year, diplomacy collapsed with U.S. rejection of the "Cuban Note on Narcotics," which was an official Cuban protest after the Bay of Pigs that ongoing FBN charges formed part of a "dirty" U.S. plot to prepare the invasion and "discredit the socialist Revolution in Cuba." Among the final acts of his thirty-year reign, Anslinger did launch an aggressive disinformation campaign about Cuban cocaine. "Dope Pours into Cuba" read one of his press leaks about a fourteen-kilo find, which actually occurred in Mexico. Anslinger alleged that Cuba was using cocaine to raise "vast sums" and to drug its dissidents, a practice he termed "Narcotics for psychotics." He boldly claimed that "Communist agents" smuggled two million dollars monthly into New York. More likely, Cuban émigrés in this business were fueling the other side, the rightist anti-Castro exile movement, just as they were to do with the Nicaraguan contras decades later. Anslinger, his usefulness over, retired shortly thereafter.[33] The Cuban Revolution marked a turning point in cocaine's history in which it was dispersed to widely scattered markets by a new Pan-American class of career traffickers.

ARGENTINA: MAFIAS OF COCAINE

Argentina of the venal post-Peronist years resembled Chile as an outlet for Bolivian cocaine of the 1950s–60s, but with notable differences from its neighbor. Buenos Aires had long hosted overseas smuggling networks of Italian and Jewish mobsters, whose wares included narcotics. A national tradition of cocaine use had also taken root in the popular tango clubs, a site of urban cocaine culture since the 1920s. Rosario's mafia made it the "Chicago of Argentina." Northern provinces like Salta and Tucumán, geographically and culturally tied to Bolivia, had sizeable regional coca-using communities. By the mid-1950s, cocaine dragnets and scandals implicated

Argentines, who to some extent shared in airborne smuggling of cocaine until the early 1970s.

In Argentina, the trade was not dominated by a clan, and its most striking characteristic was the sheer number of participants. A UN report of 1964, "Illicit Traffic in Cocaine," from the third meeting of the panicky Inter-American Consultative Group on Coca Leaf Problems, targeted Argentina. Organized thefts from pharmacies had historically sufficed for domestic use, since Argentina had its own pharmaceutical cocaine-processing facilities. After 1952, the UN group noted, supplies flowed out from Bolivia: "Federal Police have come to the conclusion that illicit traffic always uses the same route, i.e. via Santa Cruz, Yacuiba, Salta, Tucman [*sic*], Córdoba and Buenos Aires, by train and Lorry and also by using port and airport facilities. It appears that Argentina is a victim country and not a transit country." The report records thirty-eight cocaine arrests in 1962. A year later, fifty-six people were "implicated in cocaine traffic cases," with 3.29 kilos seized on their way to heavily adulterated domestic retail sales; in Salta, a freshly refined cache of 848 grams surfaced at the Bolivian border. The Bolivian drug connection lit scandals among northern governors and police. Officials also worried about coca leaf chewing in Indian Salta and Jujuy, where even the middle class indulged in coca, and with quickened postwar migration, coca markets spread into Buenos Aires. The UN quoted the "greatly exaggerated" report of an early 1960s Geneva expert who put the city's number of "cocaine addicts" (i.e., coca users) at twenty thousand, though it was agreed that "Buenos Aires [had] become the largest centre in South America for this narcotic drug."[34]

Interpol eyed Argentina as a smuggling entrepôt rather than a self-described drug victim. In 1959, it cited two seizures amounting to half a kilo in a mushrooming trade involving Bolivians, Cubans, and "one female trafficker," probably Ibáñez. The most dramatic discovery was of a "clandestine laboratory" for refining Bolivian sulfates in Ituzaingo, Buenos Aires Province, replete with flasks, acids, and "ten litres of a macerated substance." The lab was clearly export-oriented: according to Interpol, "a person had arrived from Havana (Cuba) in order to set up a drug trafficking organization in Buenos Aires." Those arrested included Lucho Aguillera, an "industrial chemist" from Santa Cruz; the soon-released Cuban Lara Duboe Osmara, who led police to the factory; the ubiquitous Bolivian trafficker Blanca Ibáñez Herrera (Sánchez), "supplier of the product dealt with in the laboratory"; and her accomplice from Oruro, Junto Alba Medina, as well as three foreign traffickers "for whom the cocaine was intended." In 1960, someone tipped off police to methods of smuggling narcotics and cocaine north aboard Braniff flights, along with "watch parts . . . concealed behind the decalage doors or plates on the plane." In 1961, authorities found 2.5 kilos with six traffickers, including "2 Poles," in a Buenos Aires flat converted into a "clandestine laboratory" by the Bolivian Vicente López. Arrests continued in 1962, mainly on highways, such as the arrest of a lorry driver ferrying 890 kilos of coca leaf that was not necessarily destined for cocaine. For 1963, Interpol detailed six more seizures in Argentina of cocaine stashed, among other places, "under a motor-car chassis" and "in a chimney." In 1964, Milton Trigo Paz, a Bolivian, was intercepted in Miami in transit to New York via Buenos Aires with twenty-six plastic bags containing 840 grams of 77 percent pure cocaine taped inside a "plastic girdle." By the late 1960s, airport arrests show opportunistic Argentines moving drugs via commercial airline flights to Miami and Europe.[35] Argentina's post-1966 military regimes dampened this trade, and, like that of other South American mules, their role was taken up by Colombians after 1970.

BRAZIL: COCAINE ACROSS THE AMAZON

Brazil shared a long, porous, and still uncharted western border with lowland Bolivia and Peru. In the 1950s, fluvial and land routes for smuggling cocaine arose from Bolivia's new paste zones of Chapare and Santa Cruz. With lively cocaine scenes in Rio and São Paulo and the Brazilian police's vociferous antidrug postures, Brazil was seen by the early 1960s as a key cocaine transit space. Cocaine surged during late-1950s developmentalist moves into the interior and the Goulart era of weakened central authority from 1961 through 1964.

In 1958, Brazilian authorities issued a special UN report on "traffic in cocaine supplied by illicit manufacturers in Peru and Bolivia." Cocaine flew to interior Matto Grosso for overland passage to Rio; most of it was siphoned off internally, but some was smuggled for reexport via Dutch Guyana (Surinam). Seizures rose from 3.7 kilos in 1958 to 8.4 in 1959. By the early 1960s, further UN studies suggested that smuggling routes had split and dispersed "as a result of the action taken by Brazilian authorities." It continued: "Cocaine produced in some 20 clandestine factories in Bolivia and Peru came for the most part from Santa Cruz de la Sierra, Cochabamba, La Paz, Roboré (Bolivia) and from Iquitos, Lima, Fazenda

Upini, [and] Sao Camiri (Peru)." The report noted that "the traffickers tend to pass through Corumba" and ten other enumerated border posts. Apart from a Bolivian land and Peruvian river route, smugglers had opened a bypass via Buenos Aires across Paraguay.[36]

Police spun rich smuggling stories about these illicit trails. For example, in Rio in May 1961, "the trafficker Alfredo Bello, Brazilian, owner of several gaming houses and gambling dens, was arrested and 200gm of cocaine were seized at his residence." He carried checks from other sellers, mainly Japanese and Syrian-Brazilians, to buy Bolivian cocaine at Londrina for US$3.90 a gram. A Bolivian smuggler "known as Jorgihno" brought coke into Brazil via Matto Grosso. Five of his cohorts included "Paulo Santiago Fernández de Lima, *alias* 'Chicken Stew,' owner of night clubs in Brasilia" and a TV performer, Luiz Wanderley. The police report noted: "Jorgihno and the Japanese are the main links for the sale and distribution of cocaine in south Brazil... and also work with Josefina Galvano, 'the spook,' a Bolivian, who is undoubtedly the brains of the gang and has been living at Santa Cruz de la Sierra since she left Brazil." In May 1961, police identified a loose international gang in Caias composed of "Magnaldi, Peruvian, a gambler owner of a nightclub at Copacabana; a certain Jesuisino, partner of a woman known as Dora, who keeps a gambling den at Copacabana, the singer[s] Nelson Goncalves and Roberto Luna." On the Amazon route, they netted Genaro Masulo, an accountant for Amazonas State, and Fabio García de Freites, a Brazilian businessman, with 1.5 kilos in Manaus. In trying to trace its source, police reported: "Genaro states that he was in contact with a Syrian in Manaus who introduced him to a presumed seller of fish in the Manaus market who trafficked in Narcotic drug." Cocaine originated in Iquitos, Peru, and was sent downriver to São Paulo by José Loureiro of the Manaus Municipal Aquarium. A mysterious "Abraim" had put up the Iquitos lab "and hired one of the most expert chemists of Pará, in charge of the conversion of large quantities of cocaine."[37] This collage of hedonistic demimonde ethnic traders and Amazon smugglers filled the blotters of police always on alert against Brazil's sin-loving countrymen.

The international police soon also joined in the watch. In 1960, the organizers of the first joint UN- and U.S.-sponsored Inter-American Conference on the Illicit Traffic in Coca-Leaf and Cocaine purposely chose Rio as their meeting place. Brazil produced negligible coca, but its hard-line antidrug discourse won it this privilege. The conference, the first in a series of increasingly shrill police meetings to combat cocaine, tried to find ways to link supposed coca-leaf problems to the burgeoning problem of illicit cocaine. Indeed, by the late 1950s, U.S. drug agents had jumped into action in Brazil. In a semifictionalized 1959 account, *Undercover Agent—Narcotics: The Dramatic Story of the World's Secret War against Drug Racketeers*, FBN agent Derek Agnew includes a racy chapter on the "Amazon Drama," complete with speedboat chases on the Upper Amazon. His real-life assignment in 1956–58 focused on the Corumba rail crossing from Bolivia and a hidden Rio lab; he helped local police crack an "extensive traffic in cocaine involving Peru, Bolivia and Brazil," including twenty-three trafficker arrests. The story came alive with Cuban gangsters, riotous Frenchmen, fast launches, and a lumbering Amazon contraband boat, *La Belle France*. Agnew, in his self-described "secret war" against the drug, spoke of the "promise of rich harvests to come," a cryptic reference to even larger operations, or perhaps to cocaine's bountiful future in Brazil.[38]

Despite this crackdown, by 1963 Brazilian authorities were voicing their "genuine alarm" about a "cocaine addiction" with which they could not cope. Seizures shot to 3.4 kilos in 1962, mainly in São Paulo, and in Bahia, Paraná, and Guanabara states. By now, Brazilian police had mapped out two meandering cross-border flows, of which they reported: "The most important of these routes starts in Peru, follows the Amazon from São Paulo de Olivenca to Manaus in Brazil and continues to Paraimaribo, which is a free port." From here, traffickers shipped cocaine to Italy or the United States via the West Indies. The second route police sketched began in La Paz, Cochabamba, and Santa Cruz, Bolivia, and wove through Paraguay and through Misiones, Argentina, for sites across Brazil. Federal police soon seized four more Amazonian craft for "illicit trading of every description." With Bolivian rumors of "500kg of cocaine smuggled into the Brazilian town of Corumba for onward dispatch to Rio, São Paulo and European countries," a problem of "serious proportions" seemed to be "daily growing worse."[39]

Brazil continued to serve as one of three main flows of cocaine through the 1960s but was never to become the massive channel sources predicted, as cocaine drove north through Colombia and Mexico instead. The antileft authoritarian 1964 regime, like the later Chilean coup, blunted the potential of Brazil's freewheeling traffickers. Only in the 1990s did cocaine return in force to Brazil, with new Atlantic transshipment routes and within the country's vast slums and pleasure spots, making Brazil today the world's second leading consumption market for the drug.

MEXICO, PANAMA, ECUADOR, COLOMBIA:
MODEST STARTS

The FBN flagged Mexico, Panama, Ecuador, and Colombia as minor transit points for early cocaine. Mexico's role proved more significant than the others', with efforts to test new smuggling routes into the United States and, by the late 1950s, cocaine projects of Cuban and native mafia. Panama, with its prime location as meeting ground of foreigners, was always a suspected zone of smuggling activity. U.S. officials distrusted the country's "Arab gold"—that is, its Middle Eastern merchants—and worried openly about the vulnerable nation's grasping presidential clans, nightclubs, and the stopovers by Pan-American Airlines. In one intricate 1961 scheme, corrupt Peruvian officers exchanged arms and drugs via Panama with a group of disaffected Cubans. In the mid-sixties, the BNDD judged a Panamanian undercover agent working on its behalf, one Rubén Blades—clearly the salsa singer's father—as one of the country's only honest cops. Ecuador, with no coca culture of its own, was a known transit and trading post for cocaine smugglers, and Ecuadorians served as Andean regional couriers. Colombia, on the other hand, barely merits mention as a transit point during this period. The country's overzealous coca reports overshadowed the only two known smuggler groups, one from Cali nabbed in Brooklyn in 1961 and others caught in 1966. During the late 1950s, the scions of a respected Medellín family, the Herrán Olazaga twins, Tomás and Rafael, were implicated in narcotics smuggling, albeit mainly of heroin, in a complex affair reminiscent of Peru's rogue Bácula clan. A few historians hint at Colombia's long interest in cocaine, but the evidence shows only episodic offshoots of Cuban projects rather than revealing any emergent trafficking network. Prior to 1970–75, Colombian entrepreneurs overlooked their locational potential in the new Andean cocaine trades in favor of traditional Caribbean pursuits in contraband and, by the 1960s, Santa Marta marijuana, that is, "Colombian Gold." Thus, prior to cocaine's dramatic 1970s shift to Colombia, global policing and study missions of the 1960s left the country entirely off official mapping of cocaine routes and trouble spots.[40]

Early Mexican developments were more portentous. Mexico enjoyed venerable smuggling traditions and a border traffic with the United States in liquor and opiates, and it had a legendary official tolerance for graft. A local taste for cocaine had taken hold by the 1940s, mainly in upscale brothels using medicinal-grade drugs diverted by the same Middle Eastern national mafia behind Mexico's heroin trade.[41] By 1952, long-range traffickers, such as the Chilean Huasaff-Harbs, free of Cuban ties, quietly exploited Mexico as their safe house en route to the United States. Of the scores of drug couriers dispatched by air through Mexico, authorities nabbed only those smugglers armed with an insufficient *mordida* (bribe). Heroin and cocaine traveled together. "El Chino" Morales and Régulo Escalona, early Cubans in Peru, carried this mix via Mexican safety deposit boxes in 1955. By the late 1950s, more trade was washing up from Cuba, encouraging Mexican attempts to process cocaine in HCl labs by locals tapping Cuban expertise to diversify from heroin, then under stiff U.S. pressure. The 1955 arrest of Cubans Méndez Marfa and Miguel González in New York, who were holding Bolivian cocaine, spotlighted Mexico's new role. In 1956, 2.7 kilos of Bolivian-Cuban coke traversed Mexico before being intercepted in New York. Agents arrested Roberto Rodríguez in Chicago in 1958 trying to unload 190 grams bought in Villa Acuña, Mexico.

In September 1959, a new type of discovery shook Mexico: "two clandestine laboratories installed in dwelling houses" in Mexico City, along with 6.2 kilos of cocaine, were discovered following the arrests of four Cubans and eleven Mexican nationals, including five women. Raw materials had been flown directly from Bolivia. That year, cocaine seizures soared across the region, with the moves to Mexico reflecting Cuba's new inhospitality for gangster-capitalists. In 1960, in a spectacular case, a cocaine lab in Cuernavaca blew up — an occupational hazard among novice refiners — obliterating all but 74 grams of evidence. The FBN fingered the five Cuban González brothers, arrested with 1.5 kilos, though one had perished in the cocaine inferno. The next year, authorities detained four Mexican cocaine smugglers. By January 1963, sourcing had branched out to Peru: two Mexican women, María Garrido Cruz and her friend, were hauled in near the airport in possession of more than 4 kilos. Police also stopped Panamanian and Ecuadorian drug runners crossing Mexico. That year, an ambitious U.S. sting operation busted "El Lobo," Francisco Samayoa, and two Cubans who had conspired to ferry Mexican cocaine to New York. In June 1960, clues from Mérida, a city but minutes by air from Cuba, led police to a large Mexico City factory with 7 kilos in process, run by a team of Mexicans with four Cubans, including again Méndez Marfa. The 1961 FBN memo detailing the hemisphere's top Cuban-Bolivian traffickers clarified this Havana-to-Mexico shift. Agents analyzed cases like those of Ramón González and Nilda Gómez, Cubans who fled to Guatemala before landing in Mexico. Not only were Cubans "taking over as middlemen and smuggling the cocaine into this country [the U.S.]," but "laboratories were being set up by Cubans who left Cuba because of the revolution."[42] Castro's moralization at home gave a boost to Mexican vice.

By 1965, Mexico had reached a new plateau of national entrepreneurship, which emerged after the collapse of the Chilean Huasaff-Harb clan, whose members had long used Mexican routes after their Arica arrests. In a turbulent early escapade, police set up for arrest Jorge Asaf y Bala, Mexico's most notorious homegrown *turco* mobster (but no known relation to the Chilean Huasaffs). Asaf y Bala, long suspected of making Havana-Mexico cocaine deals, confided to undercover agents his desire to break into this drug, hoping to use his ties with such local underworld figures as José Mayawak Mayer, Manual Sharfin Pérez, and Salvador Escasi. After Asaf y Bala barely eluded arrest with fourteen kilos in 1964, U.S. agents applied pressure on his family for his cooperation. A year later, authorities caught Asaf y Bala with two false-bottomed suitcases from Lima. Asaf y Bala had hired Ecuadorian chemist Julio Rubeiro Moreno to set up a lab "located near the U.S. Embassy" in the Zona Rosa.[43] With four kilos, it was the largest Mexican take yet, but Asaf y Bala and associates, no doubt protected, slipped away again. Mexicans were confidently taking this business into their own hands, having mastered the lucrative trade from Cubans in flight. The trend persisted throughout the 1960s, along with burgeoning exports of nationally sown marijuana. By the mid-1960s, the Andes-Mexico route was one of three penciled in on BNDD maps of cocaine aimed at the underbelly of the United States, and it was a hidden prelude to the infamous Sinaloan drug lords of the 1980s.

BOLIVIA:
REVOLUTIONIZING COCAINE

Like Peru, Bolivia has a venerable tradition of coca, cultivated in the lush, steep *yungas* ravines east of La Paz and Cochabamba. Here, coca was socially integrated into a pan-altiplano community of Indians, proletarian miners, and even urban elites. The vociferous Sociedad de Proprietarios de Yungas, led by the Gamarra family, was among the country's oldest and most able political lobbies. Unlike in Peru, however, Bolivian coca leaf never industrialized at the turn of the century due to geographic adversity or perhaps to the pull of the Indian market itself. No local precedent existed for cocaine making or illicit sales, although *yungas* leaf had a good alkaloid content. After 1950, following the displacement of Peru's legal and illicit trade in 1947–50, Bolivia rapidly transformed over the next decade and a half into the major incubating site for illicit cocaine, a development that passed through discernable phases. The Bolivian national revolution of 1952 and the sinuous U.S. cold war politics to reverse it, victorious in 1964, provided a fertile ground for new illicit activities in drugs. The revolution, which abolished the national army, ushered in an era of statelessness.[44] The country lacked elementary narcotics laws or drug police until the 1960s, making it a perfect climate for propagating a new drug culture. Already dirt poor, Bolivia fell into deep economic turmoil during the 1950s. Revolution broke the traditional rural order: groups like the SPY lost power, and during the 1953 agrarian reform invading peasants displaced coca's *yungas* elites. Other landless peasants began to settle in new lowland colonization zones in the Chapare, east of Cochabamba, and in remote Santa Cruz and Beni provinces. By 1960, a reconstituted Bolivian state, propped up by U.S. foreign aid, began promoting the development of these tropical regions as a social safety valve. The ironic result of these processes was to provide illicit cocaine a new and dynamic social base and social space in the new coca districts of Bolivia's lowlands. I will narrate these developments in several stages: the 1949–55 arrival from the outside of illicit cocaine; the rise of a mid-1950s national cocaine circuit, exemplified by smuggler Blanca Ibáñez and the paste labs of La Paz and Cochabamba; the tipping-point drug-related political scandals and repression of 1961; and the early 1960s birth of coca capitalism.

In Bolivia, the birth of a cocaine culture was sparked by external actors and influences. In the early 1950s, the FBN raised the specter that Andrés Soberón, the former leader of Peru's Huánuco cocaine industry, was sending operatives and chemists into a safe haven in Bolivia. Initial drug arrests and rumors invoked the Peruvian crackdown, which sent Cuban and other smugglers scrambling for new sources of coca supplies. There were many suspect foreigners at work: Peruvians and Peruvian-Croatian chemists, exiled Germans and Jews, and above all the Chilean Arabs of the Huasaff-Harb clan, strategically positioned within Bolivia.

In March 1950, the FBN's Garland Williams wrote Anslinger from the New York office about "Rumors of Illegal Narcotic Activity in Bolivia." Williams asserted, "Cocaine traffic is now originating in Bolivia under the direction of Peruvian traffickers who receive payment for the drugs in Lima, Peru, and Callao, and there afterwards arrange for the drugs to be distributed from Bolivia to Chilean ports." Odría's Peru had proven too risky, so remnants of the Pacific coast merchant marine gangs now recruited sailors in Callao to pick up the Bolivian goods in Antofagasta. Peruvian police seemed delighted to deflect attention to Bolivia's new role. FBN intelligence followed on the heels of the first reported Bolivian cocaine deal, an incident at the Hotel Nacional in Obrajes, a suburb of La Paz, involving a Peruvian, Jaime Florentino, and an Argentine, Alberto Robinson. The pair was freed when the powder turned out to be processing soda. The Bolivian press also alluded to cocaine-laden letters posted to Buenos Aires, a form of trade originating in an aging government cache of 116 kilos seized from Germans in 1941. New Jersey gangster Michael Tremontona, it was said, had bought a Cochabamba alcohol plant as cover for processing cocaine. The Czech consulate also fell under suspicion. A mid-1950 report, which even the FBN admitted might have contained "considerable fabrication," had "communist" agents sending cocaine to Argentina and Brazil, men soon reidentified as "bohemians" instead. By mid-1950, U.S. authorities officially labeled Bolivia the principal source of cocaine entering the United States.[45]

A year later, the trademarks of Chilean traffickers appeared. Published reports of Chilean police officer Luis Brun confirmed the rerouting of the Peruvian corridor of 1947–48. "Chile is the base of the traffic with Bolivia," Brun announced, an opinion echoed in another exposé in *La Razón* (Buenos Aires). Bolivian police, who denied any cocaine making on their turf, began working with the Chilean authorities. In October 1951, the first Chileans were arrested in La Paz: they were "Siro-Libanés," including chemist Said Harb, linked to "Mrs. Huasaaf, owner of the Hotel Savoy at Valparaíso," who supplied sailors of the Santos Line. According to these sources, the decommissioned lab produced "approximately 100 kilos of cocaine per month"—a major scale if true—including hydrochloride. The Chileans "Rames, Ruben and Harbe," however, soon escaped under Bolivia's flimsy narcotics laws, a recurring event over the next decade. Two years later, authorities discovered in typical fashion a related lab in Cochabamba when it burst into flames. The chemist died, and two injured workers, including Judith Polini, were hospitalized "under police control." Yet police soon retracted the report that the gang was affiliated with Antonio N. Harb, depicting it instead as composed of "Ecuadorians." In a similar move, the implicating cocaine, apart from a hundred kilos of pressed coca, was reclassified as legal sulfates of soda.[46]

As the revolution unfolded after 1952, opportunities opened up in drugs too. The Huasaff-Harb clan worked Bolivia continuously during the decade despite their intermittent arrests in both countries. A key to their success was the protection offered by Luis Gayán Contador, a well-placed Chilean who had fought for Bolivia during the 1930s Chaco War. After the revolution, Gayán naturalized himself and swiftly rose under Paz Estenssoro to become chief of Bolivia's political National Identification Police, later heading both the border and La Paz police forces. The 1951 police source denying the presence of cocaine in Bolivia was Gayán. Amanda Huasaff's brother Ramis Harb in La Paz knew Gayán intimately, and his activities would later spark an international cocaine scandal among the revolutionary *políticos*.

In August 1953, not even Gayán could stem the arrests of a gang involving Rubén Sacre Huasaff (a "Chilean of Arab origin"), José Luis Harb (nominally Bolivian), and six Bolivians of mainly German extraction. Authorities believed it to be the revived 1951 gang, working in Bolivia from 1949. The press pictured its labs as "well-equipped," inaugurating a 1950s genre based on forensic photos of confiscated drug-refining apparatus. The Huasaff connection was clear. Authorities seized a Peruvian journalist, Carlos Camacho, instrumental in exposing the gang, for his engagement in "political activities" and for being a *narco* himself — all the handiwork of Gayán. La Paz newspapers protested with a call for stricter narcotics laws. Police stumbled upon another lab on Calle Chaco belonging to Davíd Fernández with sixty bags of sulfates and two abandoned suitcases of crude cocaine.[47] Again, a Bolivian judge let the presumed traffickers go. In May 1954, Captain Manuel Suárez sought FBI aid to jail an international group from Cuba, Chile, Argentina, Peru, and Panama, now "out on bail and operating as before from the factory that was previously raided." Police raided the group again. Interrogations produced links with the Huasaff Ramis Harb and military officer Carlos Zembrano.

By 1955, Sam Levine, a U.S. undercover drug agent of later renown, was working to arouse South American editors about the hemispheric threat posed by Bolivian cocaine. In New York, Cuban cocaine was traced to Bolivian leaf and graft, a conclusion also certified by Interpol. The FBN's annual report of 1955 featured Bolivian cocaine: the largest jump in seizures since Peru's in 1949 came with the detention at La Guardia airport of Cuban Régulo Escalona (over a kilo) and the notorious Cuban traffickers Marfa and González (over three kilos).[48]

The typical ring of the 1950s was composed of a mixture of Bolivians and varied cosmopolitan figures. In 1957–58, the FBN identified a Greek national, Karambelas, as "an important cocaine smuggling trafficker," ferrying the drugs between his restaurant in Esquintla, Guatemala, and contacts at the Greek consulate in La Paz. Argentine Jews often served as couriers, like León Fruscher, Itzchak Hercovici, Salomo Funtowitcz, and Leib Witz, the latter caught in Brazil with Bolivian coke in June 1959, or the Polish émigrés Zelda and Hersh Freifeld, later nabbed in New York. So did Bolivian-based Germans such as Puttkammer, Wallschllaeger, Netzeler, Bornemann, and Bosch. Jewish traders and refugees had performed a pioneering role in the rise of global drug smuggling since the 1920s in Shanghai, Turkey, and the United States. They were well placed to pass illicit goods across transborder communities. One wonders if these contrasting diasporas in Bolivia of Nazi war criminals and "Hotel Bolivia" holocaust survivors ever crossed paths around drugs. With its active refugee underworld, La Paz became known as the Shanghai of South America, while the revolution scene attracted its share of sociotourists like the young Argentine motor-cyclist "Che" Guevara. Most accounts still featured scattered Peruvians and organized Chileans at the core of the cocaine trade. For example, in July 1957, a Dutchman took "five kilograms of cocaine" from Bolivia to a "warehouse on the square of Iquique." In early 1956, authorities named five suspects after a dramatic raid on a La Paz lab, including José Salgado, a "Chilean national, the chemist who operated the factory." The U.S. attaché noted his ties to "the Chilean group which has operated here on and off for some time."[49]

In 1958, Bolivia's cocaine trade was continuing its growth, having reached "30 kilos a month" in the guess of a senior official in the Ministry of Government. Officials found five kilos in another "rude factory" in a Los Obrajes suburb, this one run by Cuban Rosa Peña with two Bolivians, notably the chemist Raúl Bosch. The FBN even knew that "the traffic in cocaine between Bolivia and Cuba [was] handled primarily by women who enter the country as tourists and who smuggle the drugs in small handbags with false bottoms." In May, police raided the "largest" cocaine operation yet in La Paz, hidden in Isías Díaz's shampoo factory and oper-ated by a Peruvian with four locals.[50] The Peruvian chemist was Renaldo Marinovich, a refugee from the Croat clan of Huánuco cocaine.

By the late 1950s, however, a native Bolivian trafficking group had arisen, exemplified by the legendary female trafficker Blanca Ibáñez de Sánchez (also known as "Delicia Herrera"—like "Blanca," surely a tantalizing alias). Born in Riberalta around 1930 to a "well-placed" family, her La Paz home faced the *El Diario* offices on Loayza Street. Her State Department visa photos reveal an elegant, well-attired white woman. Ibáñez became an energetic entrepreneur, rising from the ranks of Cuban apprenticeship as a female mule. It was typical in the 1950s to tap women as mules, as customs agents were still unaccustomed to check the luggage or orifices of well-heeled Latin women. Ibáñez established a home base in the modest Star Hotel, owned with her husband in La Paz, from which she allegedly ran her own "cocaine laboratory" in secret locations in Cochabamba, Santa Cruz, and "elsewhere." She bragged of a purification lab in Havana. By her own account, she began by buying up coca harvests from "Peruvian Indians" as a guest in Lima's Hotel Azúcar. Ibáñez became the courier's courier, frequently passing through Argentina, Brazil, and Havana en route to New York. In 1958, she began to bypass her Cuban sponsors, traveling directly into the United States, an upward mobility the FBN pinned on "ruthless greed." She ultimately failed in this first bid when her novice Cuban street contacts bilked her. In 1961, her lover and middleman, the Cuban gangster Juan Suárez, also turned against her after his arrest. Ibáñez was often trailed and arrested between 1956 and 1961, leaving decent information behind for historians in criminal files.[51] One 1958 investigation sketched Ibáñez's personal network in New York. Among the detained were four local Hispanics, taken by police for dealing to "Negroes" at such dives as the El Prado Bar on Eighth Avenue and Fifty-First Street on the West Side. Her partner was the nervous and talkative Louis Schemel, who to avoid jail and keep a U.S. passport promised authorities to "locate cocaine laboratories in South America." Schemel betrayed Ibáñez despite her offer to cover his legal expenses and her assurances of her ability to "fix anything." The FBN now assigned special agent Frank Martin specifically to trap Ibáñez. In 1959, she was arrested in Argentina with seven accomplices as the supplier of Bolivian sulfates to a lab in Buenos Aires Province with links to Cuba. She quickly fixed her way out. In Cuba, the ex-president's brother, Francisco Prío, reputedly protected Ibáñez, who regularly exchanged her coke at Havana's airport for identical suitcases of cash.

In April 1960, Ibáñez was haggling with a U.S. undercover agent in La Paz over a deal to unload five kilos for twenty thousand dollars. Negotiations played out for a year as the offer, involving two partners—the Bolivian Ebar Franco and a Chilean, Victoria Torres—doubled in size. Agents planned to trap her in Mexico, as Ibáñez was now wary of U.S. travel. In a novel joint U.S.-Peruvian-Bolivian operation following the Rio police summit, officials eagerly plotted to put Ibáñez away, since she had "in the

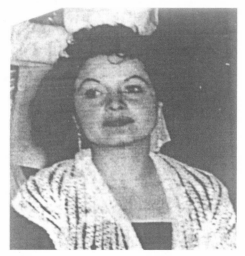

Blanca Ibáñez de Sánchez, Bolivian drug trafficker, ca. 1960 (U.S. National Archives, RG59, Department of State, Decimal Files, 411.24342/2–761, "Narcotics Trafficker Blanca Ibáñez de Sanchez," 6 April 1961)

past delivered large quantities of cocaine to other narcotics traffickers in New York City." "This woman has access to a cocaine laboratory," reports ominously noted, and was "head of a group of international traffickers." Bolivian carabineros joined in the action. But as told in a "Bolivia — Blanca Ibáñez" section of the 1960 FBN report, Ibáñez and most of her gang got away after a dramatic May 1960 armed street scuffle with dozens of aroused bystanders in a poorly lit slum. Officials later snared accomplices and seized the Star Hotel where the deal was hatched, as well as Ibáñez's "automobile service, wash-center," and other properties kept under various names.[52] It is unclear if this La Paz empire was used to finance cocaine smuggling or vice versa.

A month later, as if to taunt her pursuers, Ibáñez dropped a note at the embassy protesting her innocence and expressing curiosity about the "two American gangsters" talked about in the failed sting. Agents despaired of ever capturing Ibáñez after this narrow escape. In 1961, she topped the secret U.S. most-wanted list of twenty-four major cocaine dealers; Bolivians called hers South America's "most important gang" and signed on to Rio's new drug laws in part to trap her. Yet a "reliable source" found Ibáñez had "too many connections in the government to be held or tried for cocaine trafficking."[53] Then partnered with Miami-based Bolivians Alfredo Alipaz and Carlos Bosch, her possible chemist, she reportedly ran U.S. borders via Panama under false names. Blanca Ibáñez was an intriguing autonomous figure in early cocaine trades who then completely faded from sight, though her legacy of national cocaine remained.

The fall of Bolivia's ailing oligarchic state after 1952 and mounting U.S. intervention in the wavering revolution gave a political cast to the rise of cocaine. In contrast to other cold war conflicts, the United States proved unusually willing to work with the Revolutionary Nationalist Movement (MNR) regime, if mainly to undermine its left wing. Exiled Bolivian conservatives, for U.S. consumption, associated the revolution with "Communistic" cocaine sold for illicit funds to spread revolutionary arms, a powerful specter of communist drug contagion, particularly after the Cuban Revolution inflamed inter-American relations. As a new industry, cocaine likely did attract some political protection. By the early 1960s, these charges provoked drug scandals in the regime, the most flagrant against fiery leftist labor leader and MNR vice president Juan Lechín in mid-1961. If never proven, the accusations prompted Lechín's exit from politics and Bolivia's first antinarcotics drive, both prime American objectives in Bolivia.

By the mid-1950s, rumor already tied national political figures to cocaine, including Gayán, Lechín, and Colonel Carlos de Zembrano, a Cochabamba revolutionary tracked as a military attaché in Mexico — the latter suspected, among others stationed abroad, of misusing his diplomatic pouch. Whether true or not, such charges became common after 1952 as regime foes worked to discredit the MNR with drugs in the style of Odría's anticommunist campaign against APRA in 1949. In 1955, FBN sources, after the arrest of Cuban traffickers Méndez Marfa and González in New York, revealed that their six-pound stash was "produced in [a] laboratory on [a] farm near La Paz" that was "allegedly owned by [the] brother of [the] man who was president of Bolivia in 1954–55 [Paz Estenssoro]."[54] Beechcraft freely took off for São Paulo using a private runway. One "conspirator" was the "well-known violator" Ramis Harb. It is not hard to imagine cornered Cubans feeding such juicy clues to FBN interrogators.

The 1961 scandal began with a roundup of suspected Argentine smugglers. From Buenos Aires, *La Razón* charged "high Bolivian officials" with "complicity in the drug trade"— news filtered through Argentine provincial politics. The central figure was none other than Colonel Luis Gayán, the Chilean-born accomplice of the Huasaff-Harbs and, despite repeated exposés, chief of police in La Paz. Officials of the YPFB state petroleum firm and Vice President Lechín were also implicated, an idea U.S. embassy officials labored to prove. MNR loyalists in Congress rejected Lechín's resignation, though Gayán was suspended from duty and a parliamentary commission convened.

Gayán, from preventative detention, gave his dramatic commission testimony on 21 September 1961. Over four hours, he named "50 persons" engaged in cocaine manufacture and trade. Seventy other witnesses were called, just as the Bolivian Congress began study of unprecedented antidrug legislation. The crisis was fanned by exiled prerevolutionary president Enrique Herzog, who denounced Lechín's dealings in Brazil and Argentina, which he would return to document if only given "guarantees" of safety. Walter Guevara, ex-minister of government, joined this chorus. Meanwhile, the rightist press brought out anti-MNR tracts on "Anti-comunismo y cocaína." Behind the scenes, the U.S. Embassy, aided by the FBI, FBN, and an ardent informant, Ovidio Pozo, traced Lechín's travels to New York, where he lodged at the exclusive University Club in early 1961, revealing an unseemly relationship with the wealthy widow Corina Gruenbaum of the despised Bolivian *rosca* tin interests. Lechín, though a "professed communist of the Marxist-Leninist school," had put his two children (of whom he was "said to be very fond") in a New York State boarding school — hardly a punishable offense. His personal secretary, Mario Abdallah, was rumored to have had a hand in cocaine from the mid-1950s; Lechín, from a *turco* family himself (Oquendo), was likely tainted by such ethnic associations.[55]

Across the border in Córdova and Salta, roundups intensified with the detention of Argentine dealer Isaac Goldberg and Ciro Mercado Terrazas in Santa Cruz. On 14 November, the Bolivian commission, after interviewing Argentine officials and prisoners, released its first report, anticipating a "sensation" ahead. U.S. diplomats thought the report, if mainly old news, showed "a picture of a large narcotics net operating between Bolivia and Argentina," though it named only two acting officials, Gayán and José Requeña of the state petroleum firm. The commission highlighted, however, Bolivia's newest industry. Coca processing occurred in "Santa Cruz, Yacuiba, Villamonte, Chapare, and the Yungas" before passing through small border posts toward Salta and Buenos Aires, where it was refined into pure cocaine in the factory of Luis González. The commission backed Bolivia's immediate adhesion to antidrug measures: joining Interpol and signing the new UN Single Convention, which committed Bolivia, a largely prococa nation, to coca limitation and to drug laws, narcotics bureaus, and foreign training and assistance. By November 1961, President Paz approved Bolivia's first public anticoca decree, which intended to launch a UN coca substitution program. Markets for coca reportedly plummeted after the report, and "many cocaine factories in Bolivia and Argentina closed." Even the partisan U.S. vice consul, Samuel Karp, admitted that if this last news were true, thousands of Bolivians would be out of work in the *yungas*, bringing pressures to relax the drug repression. "Once the Commission has finished its work and the publicity has died down, narcotics operations in Bolivia would return to 'normal,'" he predicted.[56] By 1961, in short, job creation in the coca-cocaine sector was affecting Bolivia's national political dynamic.

Scholars of the Bolivian revolution, such as James Dunkerley, believe that accusations against Lechín, who left political life in September 1961 amid the scandal, were false, although Lechín was "careless" in his personal associations. Not only local right-wing foes but likely also the CIA station chief drove the affair to isolate Lechín's left-wing MNR faction from President Paz, who was quickly sliding into the U.S. orbit. Aid to Bolivia, including that for policing and lowland development, jumped some 600 percent between 1960 and 1964, turning the tiny nation into the hemisphere's highest per capita recipient, a showcase for the new anticommunist Alliance for Progress. An overlooked part of this story, making this episode Bolivia's version of Odría's offensive in Peru the decade before, was the de facto criminalization of tolerated cocaine trades. By 1962, Bolivia finally joined the global prohibitions regime, a U.S. goal since the 1940s, and quieted its prococa stance. Pressure on Bolivia came to a head after the 1961 Ibáñez fiasco, drug seizures at U.S. borders, and the 1961 BNDD survey of cocaine routes, which dramatized the new range of inter-American cocaine merchants. That helped prompt the first UN Inter-American Coca Leaf Consultative Seminars, a March 1960 anticocaine police summit in Rio where Bolivia first requested aid. The second meeting, specifically relabeled as being for "Inter-American Narcotics Control," occurred within days of the enactment of Bolivia's first drug laws in late 1961. The U.S. delegates who ran the affairs praised these moves, because Bolivia long had one of the laxest legal drug regimes in the hemisphere, based on simple regulatory health fines. The third Lima conference of 1963 saw Bolivia assume an active role.[57]

The embrace of prohibitions hardly meant the end of Bolivia's cocaine industry. In November 1961, at the climax of the MNR affair, a raid occurred in Santa Cruz City against "a large net of cocaine manufacturers and consumers." Among seven detainees was Emilio Harb, from that pioneer family in cocaine's dissemination. In March 1962, authorities smashed a major German-Bolivian smuggling ring, now bereft of protection, that had operated through Argentina to New York and Miami, its couriers

traveling with cocaine tucked in money belts.[58] The known ringleader,
Raúl Bosch, got away, along with an American accomplice, Donald Burt.
More BNDD traps were set from New York for ever-suspect officials, for
example one "Guichi," identified in 1964 as a close aide to President Paz.
The Bolivian police, meanwhile, claimed their officers had learned to
literally "smell out" labs using only their noses, at least in La Paz. Signs
pointed elsewhere: cocaine was swiftly spreading to distant Amazon sites,
becoming more elusive than urban labs or mules on scheduled ships and
planes.

By the 1961 scandal, cocaine was already taking root in lowland Santa
Cruz, a zone opened by a rising regional bourgeoisie in cotton, sawmills,
and cattle enterprises. Reminiscent of Huánuco, immigrant Croats rose
to prominence in the local elite, some of whom decades later would be
active in Roberto Suárez's rightist "mafia cruzeña" linked to drug buyers in
Medellín. The first road, to promote rice cultivation, reached Santa Cruz
in 1954. In an ironic link to cold war struggles, the hilly jungles between
Santa Cruz and Chapare were precisely where Ernesto "Che" Guevara,
another Argentine-Cuban connection, mounted his fated 1966–67 guerrilla
foco at Nancahuazú. Coca was also infiltrating the area, a poor choice for a
liberation war given the region's sparse and conservative *colono* peasantry.
A local *hacendado* kept mum about Guevara's activities to get in on the
mysterious visitors' supposed cocaine enterprise.[59] The first army unit to
encounter Che's guerrillas was surveying coca fields.

U.S. archives contain voluminous material about the 1960s explosion
of cocaine in Santa Cruz. By the early 1960s, illicit cocaine, born in crude
labs and of smugglers in the 1950s, still reliant on Indian market coca, was
flexing enough muscle to bring a new social force to bear in its future:
displaced highland peasants, a movement also starting to stir in Peru.
The 1964 anticommunist coup and the U.S.-backed Barrientos regime
(1964–69), with its "Pacto-militar-campesino," marked not only the official
end of Bolivia's revolution but a quickened transition to a socially rooted
economy of coca and cocaine. This shift was markedly spatial, notable for
the bypassing of the old *yungas* near highland cities for new coca fields in
lowland Santa Cruz, Beni, and Chapare.

By the 1960s, the Amazon had become the country's prime coca leaf
zone, and much of coca's expansion intersected with illicit cocaine. These
developments forced Bolivian and U.S. officials into panicky guesswork
about the size of the problem: they put cocaine production at 30 kilos a
month, employing 48 small sulfate labs, 23,500 hectares of bush, or maybe

12,000 tons of leaf. One tally put 10,000 tons of leaf in illicit circuits, though Bolivia's official crop came to only 1,500 tons. Coca yields had dipped after the 1953 agrarian reform, but Bolivia soon overtook Peru, this time by the labor of anonymous frontier campesinos with scant ties to the state rather than politically ensconced *yungas* oligarchs. By 1962, believable estimates had half of Bolivian leaf rerouted to "nontraditional" use, that is, to illicit cocaine. To the satisfaction of the Inter-American Coca Leaf Congress, Bolivian authorities seized "approximately 140kg" of this contraband in 1960–61. Yet that year, Brazil's illicit traffic report for the Rio summit found a strong cross-border drug flow out of Santa Cruz, plus a trickle down the Amazon from Peru. UN narcotics missions toured the region in 1964 and 1966, with site visits to the hot Santa Cruz border. By 1965, Interpol, which tallied sixty to seventy cocaine arrests and twenty seizures worldwide in the mid-1960s, began operating in Santa Cruz alongside the BNDD in stings and the training of Bolivian agents. The epicenter was Santa Cruz Province, though smugglers, including remnants of the Harb clan, fanned out all across Bolivia. Pursuing the trend, the U.S. consular office at Cochabamba, closest to the action, began writing regular briefs in mid-1964 on Santa Cruz antidrug operations. In 1966 alone, Consul McVickers reported twenty-five major cocaine busts, mostly in the wilds between Santa Cruz and Brazil.[60]

By the mid-1960s, these cocaine-related arrests in Santa Cruz accelerated to one every few days, a sign of the rapid seeding of coca bush. Moreover, the U.S.-Bolivian crackdown on Santa Cruz was hiking incentives far across borders for Peruvian peasant farmers in the Huallaga Valley, who began streaming into similar pursuits at an unprecedented pace by the mid-1960s. In June 1967, as a fatigued Che slogged from clash to clash with CIA-led patrols, the BNDD lent Interpol a "list of persons, believed to be Bolivians, who . . . have been engaged in the illicit growing, manufacturing or marketing of coca and cocaine."[61] This single national list contained hundreds of names. Cocaine was the new Andean revolution.

INTO THE FLOOD

This chapter has pieced together the rise of illicit cocaine after World War II as the product of cold war politics, encroaching world cocaine prohibitions, and a whole new breed of Andean entrepreneur. By 1950, cocaine's illicit sphere was forming, a fitting end to the legal commodity's protracted period of constriction and decline. Global and historical forces unleashed this transformation, but the main protagonists of the unprecedented illicit trade were local *narco* middlemen, some with links to traditional cocaine. At first opportunistic, irregular, and small-scale, by the mid-1960s cocaine's newest "commodity chain" was lengthy, socially rooted, and systematized, well-known to authorities if still kept out of the public eye.

In cocaine's longer cycle since 1860 in distinctive global commodity chains, it is notable that illicit cocaine was born in, and returned to, a long-term nexus between the United States and the Andes. This had something to do, no doubt, with the historical staying power and long experience of Peru's original cocaine-making clique in Huánuco, without equals in global cocaine. The *huanuqueños* possessed a rudimentary local technology suited to illicit transfer and use, a remote regional cocaine culture, and ties to peasants with autonomous coca-growing traditions. After 1950, the truly novel development was coca's industrialization in nearby Bolivia, which unlike Peru had never passed through an era of licit cocaine, and after 1960 its embrace there by illicit popular producers. The other innovation was the articulation of these two zones to a newly evolving international trafficking class, at first based out of key urban test markets in Chile and Cuba. Early repression, like later repression, seemed only to disperse cocaine to more and better-suited places and to add to these traffickers' capabilities, specialization, organizational learning, competitive adaptation, and tricks of trade. Perhaps illicit cocaine might have erupted and spread in any case, but the initial repression of the 1950s ensured that it did, there and then.[62]

In comparative and global terms, this trafficking economy of cocaine in the Americas paralleled the Eurasian one of illicit morphine and heroin that had reared its head two decades before during the 1920s, one that also restructured after World War II. As with many new industries, small-scale cooperation, spirited competition, and a kind of Pan-American networking seemed to prevail around newly illicit cocaine. Only later did violence and coercion enter the equation with the drug's cartelization and the hostile takeovers of the 1970s. Yet unlike heroin, early cocaine trafficking was not built and managed by a hierarchical transnational criminal class like the mafia but rather by a loose, diverse, and independent diaspora of Latin American ethnic traders, elite gadflies, political refugees, and petty criminals blazing the new corridors north.[63] It is often remarked with irony that even with its long and storied history of exports, cocaine is among Latin America's most successful and indigenous export

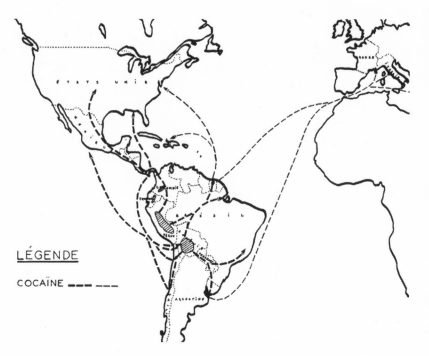

Pan-American cocaine routes, mid-1960s (U.S. National Archives, RG170 [BNDD], Box 54 [old Box 10], "Conferences and Commissions, United Nations Latin American Study Tour," 1966)

industries. It remains an "American" industry and is still running strong despite heavy pressures against it and opportunities for coca to migrate to other corners of the world. Perhaps this bottom-up local agency worked to preclude cocaine's later domination by overseas criminal or outside, control-minded institutions. It rooted itself deeply, beyond the reach of international policing or empires, first as a Pan-American project of local entrepreneurs and second, after the mid-1960s, married to a stubbornly entrenched regional peasant economy of coca. Politics as much as profit gave life to illicit cocaine, a drug entangled in transnational relationships as much as local circumstance.

What happened to these pioneering *narcos* of the 1950s and 1960s remains a mystery—even for flamboyant figures like Blanca Ibáñez. Clearly, they left a legacy for the next generation in the creation of illicit cocaine as a transnational good. The historical challenge is establishing direct, concrete links between the modest groups and sinuous illicit geographies uncovered here and the infamous Colombian *narcotraficantes* of the 1970s, who would personify, concentrate, and magnify the cocaine enterprise over the next decades.

Looking ahead, it is notable that cold war politics, along with the increasingly militant foreign drug policies of the United States, remained a constant in cocaine's illicit transformation, including the dramatic shift to Colombian leadership in the early 1970s. After 1964, cocaine's transition to a boom product was accelerated by the polarizing Andean politics of the 1960s (Barrientos in Bolivia; Belaúnde to Velasco in Peru; Frei to Allende in Chile), which produced unstable statist regimes fraught with cold war tensions. These Andean modernizing projects of Left and Right practically invited peasants to flood into the country's choicest coca zones as a politically cheap U.S.-styled developmental alternative to conflictive agrarian reforms. In Bolivia, the landed class of Santa Cruz became on the side local kingpins of the 1970s drug trade. In Peru, the early 1970s collapse of the leftist Velasco military experiment, as detailed in the next chapter, left thousands of colonized peasant families stranded in the jungles of the Huallaga with no effective state loyalties. Cocaine embedded itself in a dispossessed coca peasantry. By 1973, both Peru and Bolivia, politically and economically bankrupt, fell into profound chaos, an Andean disaster that would deepen with the 1982 world debt crisis and propel cocaine capitalism over the final decades of the twentieth century. Elsewhere in South America, new-style antileft military regimes, so-called bureaucratic authoritarianism in Brazil (1964) and Argentina (1966), hampered the freestyle, scattered hemispheric drug running of the early 1960s. This made the longstanding corridor from Chile, at the apex of Chilean democracy, cocaine's major highway to the United States until the impact of the nation's cold war 1973 coup steered cocaine to its future in Colombia. Fueled by these spiraling Andean crises, cocaine became the region's great, or only, boom industry of the late twentieth century.

THE DRUG BOOM (1965–1975)
AND BEYOND

Reflecting on cocaine's long journey over time, from its heroic commercial and nationalist origins in the nineteenth century through its contested decline as a legal commodity during the first half of the twentieth century to its politics-driven shift underground after World War II, here I focus on three changes that would unleash the drug's illicit boom by the 1960s and 1970s. These were, first, the collapse of postwar development schemes for Peru's Huallaga Valley, which brought a coca peasantry into the active intensification of illicit cocaine; second, the linkage in the early 1970s of this Andean cocaine capitalism, via cold war events in Chile, to a rapidly rising class of Colombian *narcotraficantes*, men who would lead cocaine to new markets and entrepreneurial heights; and, finally, the Nixon-era revolution of politics and culture that underlay the vast new demand for cocaine in post-1960s North America. Together, these three shifts of the 1960s and 1970s would transform the legacy of Peru's historical crude cocaine and the modest smuggling of early *narcos* into the massive and socially destructive South American drug bonanza of the 1970s and beyond. As with cocaine's earlier transformations, the transnational processes behind the boom were as much political constructs as inevitabilities. I will also, at the end of this chapter, broach the subject of cocaine's global changes since 1975, changes that are now primarily propelled by the escalating late-twentieth-century war waged by the United States against Andean cocaine, and I will consider the lessons that can be gleaned from a long-term study of drug commodities like cocaine.

The subsequent story of illicit cocaine in Peru stems from coca's modern surge beyond Huánuco's traditional tropical hinterlands in Chinchao, Derrepente, and Monzón, deep into the wilds of the Upper Huallaga Valley. This site was to become central to the world cocaine boom of the 1970s–90s. At the boom's height in the 1980s, the Huallaga supplied over half of the world's illicit coca crop and coca paste. Ironically, previous U.S. interventions inadvertently helped to shape the environment that created an intransigent peasant base for the illicit economy of cocaine.

The starting point of this peasant movement was 1937, although many specifics remain murky. That year, the Peruvian state, with the strategic-minded goading of the United States, seized the immense Japanese-owned Tulumayo tract acquired by Hoshi in 1917–19, some 300,000 hectares near Tingo María at the junction of the Tulumayo and Huallaga rivers. This particular swath of rain forest has an uncanny centrality in the world history of cocaine as a meeting place of German (Kitz), Peruvian (Durand), Japanese (Hoshi), and now American interests in the drug and, later, those of nascent 1970s *narcotraficantes*. Peruvian Nisei like the Saitos, Oshis, and Sawadas had worked its many *fundos*, foremost among them Pampayacu, delivering coca leaf, crude cocaine, cinchona bark, and knowledge of coca culture back to Japan during the 1920s and 1930s. In the mid-1930s, Pampayacu rendered some forty-six thousand kilos of coca, making it second in the region only to the Durand family estate of Éxito. After 1937, three-quarters of this land reverted directly to the Peruvian state, though Hoshi fruitlessly contested its war-related expropriation for years in Peruvian courts.[1]

In the same era, the military government of General Oscar Benavides, in a 1930s-style public works campaign, finally pushed the Lima-Huánuco road over the high Carpish Pass. By 1938, the road reached the forested banks of the storied Huallaga River below, 680 meters above sea level at the tiny hamlet of Tingo María — known as "La bella durmiente" despite consisting of little more than sixty crude huts at the time. Tulumayo lands quickly became commercially valued and coveted. In the 1950s, diesel bulldozers pushed the jungle road on to isolated eastern Pucallpa on the shore of the Ucayali, a river fully navigable into the Amazon. During the 1960s, these roads would become incorporated into Peru's ambitious national project of a unified Carretera Marginal de la Selva running along the entire Peruvian *montaña*. A supreme decree of 1938 had first established the "official colonization zone" of Tingo María, which conveniently was

able to use nationalized Tulumayo for its main land base, as well as 12.5
kilometer margins along the new road. The "official" in this designation
signaled governmental hopes for an orderly process of settlement in a
labor-short process of frontier expansion into an area infamous for its
unsettling *enganche* coercion of Indian workers. The whole Huallaga region
may have hosted as few as twelve thousand permanent inhabitants into
the 1920s. The established *hacendado* class of Huánuco, from the 1930s
mainly divesting themselves of coca leaf—often switching to its ecological
twin, tea—would not be the dominant force in this new frontier. Modern
jungle colonization by small farmers promised a revolution in land use
in Peru's central *ceja de montaña*. Yet it was a development program sim-
mering in the *limeño* imagination since the colonial period, which deemed
the Huallaga the gateway to Peru's long-awaited economic conquest of
the sparsely populated Amazonia and a bridge to the Amazon River and
Atlantic basin.[2] This was a strategic vision seconded in the long-forgotten
Huallaga scouting mission of American naval officer William L. Herndon
in the 1850s.

The United States jumped directly into this regional matrix during
World War II, the conflict which intensified hitherto lax U.S.-Andean state-
to-state relations, including those around drugs. Authorities "blacklisted"
remaining Japanese coca and cocaine interests. In April 1942, the United
States established, in league with the Peruvian government, the Estación
Experimental Agrícola de Tingo María. In the postwar years, it would
become the largest U.S.-sponsored tropical research station in the Western
Hemisphere, the type of technical outreach project long coveted by local
elites. The station was closely identified with Peruvian plans to colonize,
with allegedly surplus highland peasants, the Upper Huallaga and thus
finally exploit the region's vaunted "50-million acres" and its presumed
hidden riches. Beyond cementing a wartime alliance with Peru, the U.S.
goal was to replace at breakneck speed, with Peruvian-grown strategic
commodities, the rubber and quinine plantations overrun by Japanese
forces in Southeast Asia, products critical to the global war effort. The
long gestation period of these crops and unreliable transportation facilities
mitigated against that plan. After the war, however, the new U.S. presence
remained, quickly folded into Truman's cold war Point Four technical
assistance programs, and the complex became a magnet across Peru for
peasant migrants. In 1950, just as cocaine was being repressed as a legal
commodity 135 kilometers up the road around Huánuco, the station covered
625 acres and had sixty technicians and skilled staff, including seven U.S.

Department of Agriculture scientists and agronomists, some evidently not pleased to be assigned there. The model Italian farming colony, Saipai, was also a new pole in local agriculture. The population around Tingo María, in the newly demarcated province of Leoncio Prado, soared from 11,600 in 1940 to 45,200 in 1961 at 11 percent per annum, making Leoncio Prado the country's fastest-growing province. Station administrators immersed themselves in projects to disseminate more realistic commercial products, especially tea, as well as coffee, citrus fruit, tropical oils, the insecticide *cube*, lumber, and, as they abetted tropical deforestation, cattle grazing. In 1949, the official colonization zone with its six hundred plots extended over more than 3,000 hectares. The U.S. station expanded by the early 1960s into the lands of the Tulumayo Project, dedicated to cattle raising on hilly ex–rain forest land, before being incorporated when it ended into Peru's newly founded regional agrarian university, now the Universidad Nacional Agraria de la Selva. While colonial Huánuco City was falling into disrepair, Tingo María enjoyed not only a new university but many credit banks and other modern amenities, including a state-run Hotel de Turistas to one day lure tourists to its scenic wonders.[3]

This intriguing transnational embrace can be followed in the station's official reports, which included elaborate sociological studies of colonists, photographic essays, and well-presented station newsletters archived by the Department of Agriculture throughout the 1950s. The North American agronomists, with sound scientific and economic training, seemed more aware than their Peruvian counterparts of the limits of tropical agriculture, having extensively mapped the typically fragile tropical soils at their disposal. They also nonchalantly noted the continuing presence of coca in the region, including that planted by incoming settlers, as a peasant crop more ecologically resilient and commercially suitable for the Upper and Middle Huallaga than the ones they were experimenting with and promoting. "Coca continues to be the main crop," one agronomist confessed in the 1940s, and, more precisely, it covered 11 percent of the colonists' official acreage. During the war, officials on the ground briefly treated coca as a strategic crop, though agronomists had little knowledge base, nor need, to aid peasants in its culture. In their view, for example, coca allegedly had no "known pests" as a byproduct of its strong alkaloids (or, more likely — since it actually does have pests — of foreign ignorance). Peruvian agronomists begrudgingly admitted that "coca plays a very important role in the regional economy," but they disliked the bush's erosive effect on steep hillsides. The exhaustion of historical coca lands, such as those of Chinchao, was clearly another factor in migration down the Huallaga. José Prato was among the few commercial planters active in the 1940s near Tingo María, aiming to deliver some fifty thousand pounds of dried leaf yearly to the crude cocaine factories above. Transplanting coca was a tradition integral to migrant peasant strategies. The leaf was easily sold to upland communities, supposedly now channeled via the new ENACO monopoly to Indians who consumed some eight million tons of leaf in the 1950s, a third of which originated from the central *montaña*. The land put to coca doubled in Peru during the 1950s from 8,000 to 16,000 hectares, yet the crop itself expanded more slowly, from about eight to nine million tons, a sign of coca's low productivity and social role as an extensive peasant activity.[4]

The turbulent 1960s are harder to track.[5] The population of the Upper Huallaga grew on average 7.8 percent a year, reaching 10 percent in some estimates, still Peru's fastest rate. Changing demographics and massive new upland peasant unrest in the central and southern sierra, including a dramatic wave of campesino land seizures and guerrilla movements in the early 1960s, fueled the movement of colonists into the jungle. This was a vastly different social phenomenon than that of the urban-based elite *hacendado* class that directed coca's commodity expansion in turn-of-the-century Huánuco. In 1962, the United States coordinated a large-scale agrarian survey of the underutilized region. During the U.S.-backed reformist regime of Fernando Belaúnde Terry (1964–68), the development of the central Amazon became the president's personal quest. "La conquista del Perú por los peruanos," the nationalist modernizing slogan he popularized in a book of that title, was a conquest to be effected mainly by frenetic road building, including a "Bolivarian highway" that was to link eastern Bolivia, Peru, Ecuador, and Colombia. Peru's national plans of the 1960s aimed to bring a staggering half-million settlers down to the tropics. In this ideal, officials envisioned the Huallaga as the country's fertile future breadbasket. As Peruvian agriculture of the coast and sierra stagnated at mid-century, national officials sensed a dire need for land, yet this was an ecologically misplaced dream, since few crops actually thrive in the *montaña* without fast exhausting its thin, hilly soil. The fantasy was also eminently social: to somehow relieve Peru's festering land and ethnic conflicts in the sierra without recourse to a politically charged agrarian reform.

Untold thousands migrated to the region during the 1960s, now more spontaneously, without the official stamp of the state. The Huallaga's population leapt to over 92,000.[6] Support for tropical agricultural projects also internationalized during this apex of global development modernism: these included the 1966 Inter-American Development Bank project to colonize the expanses below Tingo María, similar to the bank's other 1964 plan for Bolivia's Chapare, all the way to Tocache. Planners made Aucuyacu, a later cocaine hotspot, into a hub for colonist services. With the overthrow of Belaúnde's faltering project in 1968 by the leftist military regime of general Juan Alvarado Velasco, the military instituted a radical national agrarian reform, accompanied by many florid and ambitious promises of social services and national integration for the peasantry. The military intensified investments in the Huallaga, and regional hopes reached their climax here. A national narrative of migration to the Huallaga even became immortalized in one of Peru's first feature films, Armando Robles Godoy's 1970 *The Green Wall*, about one family's fatal disillusion with the oppressive jungle and with Peru's oppressively bureaucratic state.

By 1972–73, the Velasco regime had itself fallen into disarray. The vertical-run state that had expanded so wildly, with few loyal followers, was now drowning in international debt and retracting itself, leaving thousands of poor peasant cultivators bereft of social services and attachments in the Huallaga. For example, a Velasco-created state lumber cooperative in Tingo María collapsed, leaving hundreds of workers to fend for themselves, many of whom went into coca-related activities. Agricultural credits suddenly vanished. In less than a generation, the province, with as many as 200,000 by 1972, had gone from labor-starved to overflowing with impoverished workers.[7] False promises of tropical development, of the founding of a veritable peasant paradise, fed deep regional resentments. The same retreat of the Peruvian state after raising expectations generally has been cited as a factor in Peru's later revolutionary upheaval, born in Andean Ayacucho with Sendero Luminoso. In the Huallaga, the safety valve of peasant illicit coca was to relieve only some of that social tension. The reversion to the leaf, which flourishes in this perfect coca environment, was likely already underway, with an estimated 5,000 hectares in coca by the early 1970s. But after 1973, amid the regional power vacuum, a stampede to coca ensued. Even prior to 1970, U.S. officials spoke in hushed tones of the return of illicit cocaine to Peru after the drug's 1950s flight to Bolivia. Reports sporadically named Tingo María and points downstream in antilab operations even during the quiet 1950s. By the 1960s, the burst of activity by restless autonomous peasants had become hard to ignore, as processes at work in Peru's jungles echoed the migratory, political, and market shifts underway in faraway Bolivia's Chapare and Santa Cruz (as later in Colombia's Caquetá rainforest) or even responded to reverberations from Bolivia's crackdown on drugs after 1964. A U.S. report on Peruvian cocaine in August 1971 affirmed that "the majority of clandestine laboratories are in the Department of Huánuco in Northeast Peru" and that "light aircraft and small ships which ply the coast of Peru are reported to be used to smuggle cocaine and coca paste into Arica, Chile, and other adjacent countries." This was the same Chilean conduit serving lowland Bolivia. By 1972, U.S. officials were speculating that some 25,000 Peruvian families survived from coca growing and that already "an estimated 100 clandestine mobile labs produce 'pasta.'" Amid the collapse of Peruvian central authority—the nationalist Velasco government opposed by the United States—U.S. field reports began to exhibit panic, or, in officialese, great "urgency," about cocaine. A State Department telegram of 1970 detailed an "emergency" aid program of just one hundred thousand dollars for the PIP, Peru's FBI, to simply continue paying for salaries and supplies for local drug suppression. The year 1973 marks the end of declassified U.S. reports, just as cocaine erupted from below in the Huallaga.[8]

By 1974, the whole Huánuco region was abuzz with rumors about the birth of a locally grown *narco* class. This date coincides, significantly, with the first systematic forays of Colombian traffickers into the region, after the first year of Pinochet's rule in Chile and his clampdown on long-established long-distance drug smuggling routes. The Huallaga was indeed a "gateway," not to the Amazon sea but, with light aircraft, to the isolated border smuggling post of Leticia, the fluvial town where Peru, Brazil, and Colombia conveniently meet, and from there to the new traffickers of central Colombia. In this wholly new circuit, Huallaga peasants, paste makers, chemists, and the local *narcos* bringing them together sat far closer to the Colombian frontier and thus had a clear geographic advantage over the distant Bolivian coca competition, despite Bolivia's head start in peasant coca capitalism. *La Trinchera* (Huánuco), a regional newspaper, documented the birth of the Huallaga *narcos*. In June 1974, the PIP captured four young men in Huánuco, labeled as *narcotraficantes*, all from the Morales family, with 530 grams of *pasta básica de cocaína*. Through the filter of confessions, we learn how cocaine was processed near kilometer eighty of the Tingo María–Pucallpa highway.[9] In July 1974, the Guardia Civil made another bust, this time at the house of María Figueroa and the aptly named *fundo* El Progreso, with 20 kilos of cocaine and all the tools and residues of the trade. Their chemist was Juan Trujillo Velázquez. In

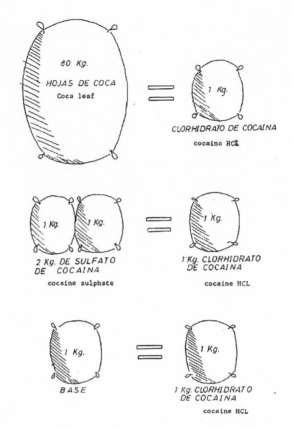

Pasta básica de cocaína commodity chain, a policing view, mid-1960s (U.S. National Archives, RG170 [BNDD], Box 54 [old Box 10], "Conferences and Commissions, United Nations Latin American Study Tour," 1966)

February 1975, *La Trinchera* ran a story titled "Capturan Narcotraficantes con 450 Mil en Pasta." Authorities suspected an "international ring" behind this 212-kilo find, though those held hailed only from Monzón and Huanas. In March 1975, another impressive find occurred at the Tingo María highway checkpoint. The paper published "Detectan Laboratorios de Cocaína" about the September 1975 demise of a five-man band led by Juan González, thirty-four, of the Santo Tomás farm in Tingo María.

In November 1975, two large confiscations, one of nearly 30 kilos, registered in Huánuco, both of which involved plastic-lined *pozos* — improvised processing pits, the cheap and mobile technology familiar to drug journalists and DEA agents today. This enhancement of the production

process's strategic mobility was perhaps the one major improvement on
the Kitz-Bignon on-site cocaine formula of the nineteenth century. The
simple chemical ingredients — cement lime, kerosene, and household solvents — were all common trade goods on a development frontier. There
are many and fairly flexible methods for making cocaine. Yet it was no
accident that peasant *pasta básica de cocaína* (and its watery relation, "coca
paste"), the main fixture of the Huallaga's furtive new export economy,
mimicked the homegrown formulas, processes, and ingredients of Peruvian
crude cocaine (cocaine sulfates or *cocaína bruta*) introduced to this region
by Arnaldo Kitz in the early 1890s. Indeed, the great historical secret of
the Huallaga is how this simple technique, inherited from Peru's long-
depressed, technologically stagnant national cocaine industry in nearby
Huánuco, could be easily transferred to and eagerly adopted by even illiterate
working peasants.[10] In a larger genealogical sense, the story of modern
Andean cocaine was inscribed by the formula for crude cocaine. It was
heroically invented by pharmacist Alfredo Bignon, profitably deployed
in the jungle by the itinerant Kitz, promoted as a world commodity by
the regional strongman Augusto Durand, and stubbornly guarded in its
declining years by merchant Andrés A. Soberón before being passed on
to underground chemists whose names are known only from police files
and to even more faceless peasant migrants after 1950.

 La Trinchera editorialized in late 1975: "The clandestine manufacturing
of cocaine in our Department has intensified notably over the last few
years, to such a point to be considered the world center, after Bolivia, of
this activity." The paper demanded a firm response: "*Los narcotraficantes*
cannot coexist in the heart of our society; as a latent danger, we must bring
down an iron fist."[11] Yet Peru's crisis of governance, which was to endure
for decades to come, combined with the local crisis of a restless atomized
peasantry with cultural roots in coca, made it too late to contain cocaine.
The same processes had unfolded a decade earlier across the Amazon in
lowland Bolivia, where colonizing peasants, breaking traditional ties to
landlords in stateless times, had found refuge in coca. By 1979, the Huallaga had an estimated 33,000 hectares in illicit coca, already three times
more than Bolivian land dedicated to coca, and this figure was growing
all the time. Cocaine had become socially entrenched in this popular illicit sphere with scarcely a directing class of its own. For such reasons,
Peruvian cocaine capitalism was essentially unstoppable, in contrast to
the colonial Asian coca circuits so easily dismantled by authorities and
forgotten after World War II.

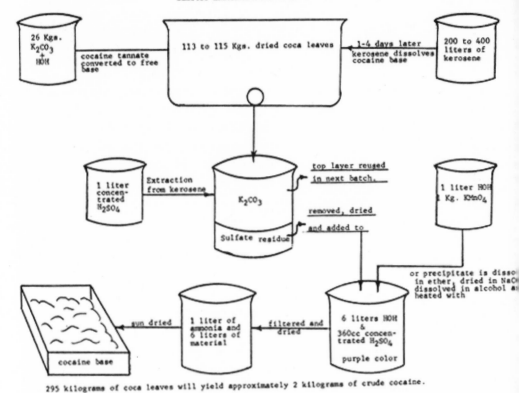

ILLICIT EXTRACTION OF COCAINE BASE

26 Kgs. K₂CO₃ + HOH

cocaine tannate converted to free base

113 to 115 Kgs. dried coca leaves

1-4 days later kerosene dissolves cocaine base

200 to 400 liters of kerosene

Extraction from kerosene

1 liter concentrated H₂SO₄

K₂CO₃

Sulfate residue

top layer reused in next batch.

removed, dried and added to

1 liter HOH 1 Kg. KMnO₄

or precipitate is dissolved in ether, dried in NaCl dissolved in alcohol and heated with

cocaine base

sun dried

1 liter of ammonia and 6 liters of material

filtered and dried

6 liters HOH & 360cc concentrated H₂SO₄

purple color

295 kilograms of coca leaves will yield approximately 2 kilograms of crude cocaine.

Illicit crude cocaine diagram, Drug Enforcement Administration, 1970s ("*Erythroxylon Coca*: A Lecture by John T. Maher," typescript, Drug Enforcement Administration, National Training Institute, September 1976, plate II, 43)

By the late 1970s, the Upper Huallaga, where Kitz once roamed, was the base of a triangle linked to the swiftly consolidating international trafficking class from Medellín — the so-called Colombian drug cartels — and from them to a rising breed of luxury cocaine users in the United States. The Huallaga become "developed," as it were, as a sea of green peasant coca, peaking at about 120,000 hectares around 1990 and supporting as many as 60,000 *cocalero* farmers making and selling their historically rich *pasta básica de cocaína*. Beautiful and sleepy Tingo María woke up to become cocaine's legendary Wild West, dollar-flooded boomtown. Just two actors remained in the unresolved riddle of illicit cocaine: the Colombians and the Americans to the north.

One of the great historical mysteries about modern cocaine trafficking is how it finally passed into the hands of the now-infamous Colombian drug lords of the 1980s and changed, through their expansive business practices, into one of history's richest and most volatile illicit trades. Drugs in Colombia have attracted an endless stream of journalism, sensationalism, and drug war mythology — producing, among other things, the misleadingly centralized and nonmarket concept of "cartel" itself — but little research has seriously plumbed the historical origins of the trade. It may be a dangerous research assignment. A few historians gingerly suggest that Colombian mafiosi evinced early interest in drug peddling, but I argue otherwise: the modern cocaine trade was systematically established in the period 1945–70 by Peruvians and Bolivians, and mainly via Chilean and Cuban mediation. Prior to the 1970s, Colombian meddling proved episodic without building into anything resembling the full cocaine commodity chain that had emerged in eastern Peru and Bolivia by the late 1960s. The resilience of Andean coca peasant capitalism over the next quarter century at the base of the global illicit trade, rather than coca from Colombia itself, was the fossil print of cocaine's evolutionary path.[12] Until the mid-1990s, Peruvian and Bolivian campesinos dominated coca growing and traded their *pasta básica de cocaína* in a clear international division of labor in which Colombians refined it into cocaine hydrochloride and aggressively managed its sale into the United States. The transition to Colombian middlemen came in the period 1970–75, hastened by the wave of right-wing military regimes strangling the other smuggling routes and urban cocaine scenes across South America, most dramatically the dictatorship that followed the Chilean coup of 1973, which closed the drug's most traveled conduit north.

Colombians brought a number of sociological advantages to their new guiding role. As economist Francisco Thoumi has argued, Colombia's penchant for this trade was not primarily economic (not the result of classical comparative advantage) or locational per se, though Colombia's fractured geography and station midway to the United States soon helped. Rather, in Colombia, sociopolitical conditions were ripe: the nation possessed a state that was historically weak and illegitimate due to incessant regional strife since the La Violencia civil war of the 1950s, combined, unlike in Peru and Bolivia, with assertively "modern" economic elites. Many Colombians had deep, hands-on experience in regional contraband trades, as well as experience with the practical uses of violence. By the 1960s, the northern Caribbean coast, like the Sierra Nevada de Santa Marta, had became a prime site for smuggling of "Colombian gold" marijuana overseas, building upon prior cigarette and contraband appliance trades. The wily *marimberos* who moved it pioneered the smuggling techniques later adopted and amplified by national cocaine traffickers.[13]

Yet the Department of Antioquía, where Medellín lies, nestled in mountainous north-central Colombia, as well as the southwest boomtown of Cali, were both socially and geographically removed from the coast and from the Amazonian portals where cocaine paste first began to appear. What Antioquía, and its capital city of Medellín in particular, was endowed with, as every Colombian schoolchild knows, was the "entrepreneurial spirit" exemplified in the national myth of *antioqueños* as a lost "white" race, reputedly Israelites. As one historian recently argued, the cocaine trade jolted Medellín from its traditional mores, yet the city significantly was until the 1960s Colombia's most modern industrial heartland.[14] However, with textile factories in sharp decline and many former workers fleeing to such far-off places as Miami and Queens, its hard-pressed middle class was ready for a newly ambitious economic activity.

BNDD archives reveal Colombian experiments smuggling cocaine starting around 1970, typically linked to Panamanian or other, older stopovers in the trades. For example, in December 1970, Enrique Jaramillo-Gutiérrez (forty-one, "a native of Columbia [*sic*] South America") was arrested at customs in Honolulu after a sinuous journey through Mexico City to Australia and back. In October 1970, U.S. agents interrogated three Colombians, Elmer Castillo, Pedro Rodríguez, and Efraín Cuero-Giron, who were returning home loaded with cash after carrying three kilos of coke obtained from Dunaldo Millias in Buenaventura, Colombia, for sale in New York from nearby Hoboken, New Jersey. That same month, authorities seized fifty-four pounds of cocaine from two Colombians at Washington's Dulles airport, Bravo González (b. Caldas, 1935) and María Aldaña Conde (Bogotá, 1931), traveling via Guatemala under false passports. These spiraling years in the cocaine trade, 1965–73, were remarkable for a freewheeling, dispersed style of cocaine smuggling. Cocaine-related arrests radiated from virtually every possible site and nationality in the Americas, incriminating Peruvians, Bolivians, Argentines, Panamanians, Mexicans, and now this trickle of Colombians. Moreover, Leticia and similar Amazonian border posts like Macoa and Ipiales, the hub for most transshipments to Medellín, Bogotá, and Cali during the 1970s, already hosted a few recognized *narcos*, notably the brothers Camilo and Wilson Rivera, amply known in Bolivian circles, and their relation Verónica Rivera de Vargas, a.k.a. "La Reina de la Coca." Their specialties were small jungle landing strips and ephemeral Amazonian airline companies.[15]

Yet not until 1973 did a noticeable Colombian ascent occur, then sparked by the dramatic cold war events in Chile. One DEA-related source relates that in the years just prior to the 1973 Chilean coup, seasoned Chilean smugglers were already working to "layer" their heavily exposed business by taking on the more anonymous Colombians as couriers and mules. By 1970, after the fall of the Huasaffs, Chile developed a new "cocaine brotherhood" with locally renowned leaders such as female trafficker Ruth Galdames ("La Yuyiyo") and interlopers like the Uruguayan mobster Adolfo Sobosky. During these years, Chilean police won guarded respect from U.S. authorities for containing the "vice" domestically and for their vast inside knowledge of the galloping international trade, still based in the north near Bolivian supply lines. A few months after the bloody coup of 11 September 1973 that destroyed elected president Salvador Allende's "democratic road to socialism," a resourceful "DEA official" quickly convinced General Pinochet to jail or expel the country's top nineteen cocaine traffickers. The basis for this move was the argument that illicit drug monies might just be used by a regrouping underground Left to threaten state security. These actions sent other traffickers scurrying, some to Argentina, where the military would also soon assume power. Sobosky and five others later pled guilty in the United States. The efficient and eager-to-please Pinochet, through his new chief carabinero, Luis Fontaine, had summarily shut down what was quantified as a two-hundred-kilo-a-month export enterprise, including a major laboratory of the two Álamos brothers, Olmedo and Guillermo, at the Mirasol seaside resort. The military promptly accused the defunct socialist regime of having masterminded the whole trade to siphon off illicit funds, a script that could have come right out of General Odría's Peru in 1948. A year after the coup, the dictator forced Rafael Alarcón, the country's tainted former narcotics chief, onto a plane for a drug trial in New York. Indeed, for good measure, the junta expelled all four previous narcotics heads since 1969 for abetting the traffic and was implicated in the political assassination of Luis Sanguinetti, Allende's chief of customs inspection.[16]

So ended a long era in which one Bolivian drug agent crowned Chileans "the best chemists" of South America, the group that had taught Bolivian coca peasants everything they knew. One irony here was that much later, in the years prior to his death in 2006, the humiliated Pinochet was himself accused, among other crimes, of resorting to selling cocaine by the late 1970s, refined at the Talagante army chemical plant, both to fund his overseas anticommunist terror network, Plan Cóndor, and to enlarge his family fortune abroad.[17] The greater historical irony is that Chile's political earthquake of 1973 swiftly disrupted cocaine routing, sending it in the other, more logical direction: north through Leticia, Colombia. With thousands of Peruvian and Bolivian peasants already busy at work in the business of producing *pasta básica*, Colombians eagerly took the opportunity international politics handed them.

The illustrious figures of Colombian drug lore reveal clear sociological aptitudes for the trade. Whoever first ran shipments through Leticia made the golden and swiftly emulated discovery of the possibilities of transshipment to the north. Published accounts portray the 1970s as a chaotic age littered with the comings and goings of scores of new *narcos*. Cocaine activities spiraled in Colombia. Colombians quickly broke loose of secondary roles under Chilean and Cuban traffickers. By 1973, one report put twelve hundred kilos a year already passing through Leticia. Shrewd businessmen like Benjamín Herrera, Alberto Bravo, Jaime Caicido, and, famously, Pablo Escobar and Carlos Lehder became Schumpeterian heroes of this wholesale cocaine trade.[18] Still, little is known about that rapid 1970–75 shift, when Colombians began flying in with cash to pick up cheap coca paste directly from Bolivian and Peruvian peasants. They quickly branched into the streets of Queens, Miami, and Los Angeles, pushing out local Cuban competitors with a merciless new level of violence, driving to unimaginable heights the Pan-American networks built by hundreds of Andean and Cuban *narcos* since the 1950s. Few, if any, of the pre-Colombian *narcos* probably continued on in this far more competitive, and more risky, market. As a paragon of this Colombian entrepreneurial zeal, Gilberto Rodríguez-Orjuela, the notorious "chess player" of the clan from Cali — a young, burgeoning city in the hot lands of southwestern Colombia — built up a highly profitable Colombian chain of discount pharmacies. In fact, his legitimate drug business captured a third of national sales in exactly the same years he was breaking into illicit drug exports. His cocaine was secreted in bulky wood exports out the Pacific port of Buenaventura. Swift profits drew Gilberto's brothers, one an Avianca flight supervisor, from legitimate jobs to the more lucrative cocaine trade. Diversion of venal union-funded banks and money laundering in Chrysler dealerships became tools in the Rodríquez family's strategy of accumulation. Benjamín Herrera of Cali, who plied heroin before cocaine, enjoyed a large organization, with Carlos Álvarez his trusted head chemist. It reputedly enlisted some ninety-two cousins and kin by 1975, with sales topping fourteen million dollars a year in New York City alone. With the complicity of airport police, the Herreras hired couriers disguised as students for the final leg of the journey. González Rodríguez Gacha was a former emerald trader, another high-value, low-weight commodity perfect for contraband. Eduardo Dávila hailed from the Santa Marta marijuana district and enjoyed the cooperation of Colombian antidrug squads. Carlos Lehder, the neo-Nazi from Quindío, Armenia, also dabbled in marijuana and learned about cocaine in an American jail cell in the early 1970s before establishing his infamous Colombia-Bahamas-Florida cocaine island-hopping corridor. Lesser-known *narcos*, traveling tortuously long bus routes to Peru and Bolivia for their first pickups, began to build up illicit capital and scale by reinvesting the fortunes of a few good runs.[19]

Pablo Escobar's is now the best-documented career. His grandfather was a storied *antioqueño* smuggler, yet his own formation was solidly middle class, marked by adoration of his schoolteacher mother, fervent Catholicism, and a typical Medellín leftist university education. His juvenile escapades in the 1960s involved organized car theft and dabbling in Caribbean contraband, especially American cigarettes, with his pal Alberto Prieto, the "Marlboro Man." His brother Roberto recalled that the inspiration for Pablo's move into innocent-sounding cocaine "traqueteo" (low-level trafficking) came from another buddy, "El Cucaracha" (the cockroach). Pablo's cousin Gustavo was his trusted partner. Around 1974, working for a shadowy *padrino*, Escobar used a rickety stolen Renault to ferry his initial load of five kilos over the Andes, building in secret compartments and switching cars at the borders to elude authorities. At first, he recruited simple mules for transfers to the United States, the eternal trick of the trade. Escobar reinvested his windfalls from the going delivery price of sixty thousand dollars per kilo before expanding with a veritable fleet of trucks and planes. Escobar's business quickly went wholesale, and he began employing Air Commanders and surplus commercial 727s that could ship ten thousand kilos north in a single foray. Escobar's innovations reinforced the dramatic 1970s slide in peasant producer and final consumer prices for cocaine. Escobar was ambitious: he tapped the large "paisa" diaspora abroad and swiftly outgunned — sometimes literally, tapping *sicarios*, or drug hit men — the established network of Cuban dealers in Miami and New York, ending their decade-long pioneering role and creating in effect a ruthlessly enforced sales oligopoly in the United States. Violence, such as the kidnapping of would-be competitors, became a regional business norm. By the mid-1970s, Escobar had already survived many run-ins with, arrests by, and miraculous escapes from local authorities and the Departamento Administrativo de Seguridad (DAS), the national security police. His brother Roberto has depicted their constantly fluid and ever-more-inventive smuggling techniques of the 1970s as a lucrative "3 to five years" ahead of tardy DEA efforts to block them.[20] Escobar's later exploits, built from this mid-1970s foundation, included bold political involvements, philanthropic works, ostentatious spending, and his eventual 1993 martyrdom, all of which made Escobar a global celebrity. The Ochoas, also of Medellín, forged a parallel route north, eventually ending up with their legendary cocaine-processing megacomplex, Tranquilandia. A third initial Colombian organization, the Bravos, fielded some 150 couriers and brokers in greater New York alone by the mid-1970s.

For a trade that barely registered in 1972, the Colombians' initial buildup was quickly achieved, basically by amplifying preexisting Andean coca capitalism and refining imported peasant *pasta básica de cocaína*. By 1975, Colombians were ferrying an estimated four tons of cocaine to New York City and Miami a year. The country allegedly had "60 to 80 major criminal organizations" competing in the trade, each with 50–100 members who shielded their consolidating business leadership. By the late 1970s, this multitude of rising Colombian traffickers had factionalized into the fabled rival regional clans of Medellín, Central, and Cali (del Valle), which by 1980 were collectively responsible for the more than one hundred tons of cocaine a year reputed to enter the United States.[21]

THE REVIVAL OF NORTH AMERICAN COCAINE

The shift to a culture of illicit cocaine in the U.S. market of the early 1970s is another topic that still begs for scholarly research, despite the fact that, like the origins of Colombian traffickers, it is a notorious episode in contemporary history. Changes in drug consumption of the 1970s left a profound mark on our history and politics, including the declaration of a punitive "drug war" that makes the United States the world's leading nation in incarceration at home and puts it on an ongoing war footing against the Andes abroad. It is also crucial to reconnect the long history of drug supply from the Andes, which this book necessarily focuses on, with the story of demand. Drug use does not emerge out of a vacuum created by easier availability in a kind of naive Say's law (supply creates its own demand) of addict-creating "pushers." In the interpretation I develop here, it was the political regime of cold warrior Richard M. Nixon (1968–74) that bequeathed the destructive age of American cocaine of the 1970s and 1980s. Like the South American supply of cocaine, North American drug demand was politically constructed.

Recreational cocaine usage in the United States was inching upward throughout the 1960s as enhanced supplies from Cuban mafia exiles helped the nascent postwar cocaine culture slowly break out of its racial or Latinized 1950s ghetto. By 1968, popular white rock singers, with the help of a few older "folkies," were dusting off and covering nostalgic old black cocaine ditties from the 1920s, a portent of the cultural revival of cocaine. Yet that year, domestic seizures still came to a mere 14 kilos of the 559 kilos of narcotics seized overall in the United States. Cocaine, in the words of one BNDD official, remained in "rather short supply." The Nixon years were the decisive turning point, as cocaine seized at U.S. borders rose exponentially, from 26 pounds in 1967 to 52 pounds in 1969 to 436 pounds in 1971, reaching an overall sevenfold increase by 1974. In 1970, the quantity of cocaine uncovered in the United States first exceeded that of heroin, the ostensible foe of Nixon's cranked-up anticrime "war on drugs." Simultaneous drug sweeps conducted across ten cities in 1970 as a kind of mini-war on cocaine netted 178 arrests, described by the BNDD as part of "the largest cocaine smuggling ring ever uncovered in the United States." It proved bigger than the Balarezo episode of 1949, but unlike in 1949, Nixon's crackdown made no dent in the growing trade. The opiate-passing mark also registered with drug busts on the streets of New York, still the world trendsetter of drug use. Police made 874 arrests for sale or possession of cocaine in 1970, which rose to 1,100 in 1971. New York had an estimated six thousand regular cocaine users in 1970, and some 19 percent of all drug aficionados had now tried it. By 1972, when reliable survey data was first gathered, hundreds of thousands of young people had experimented with the drug, including 10.4 percent of all American college students.[22]

Nixon's drug war would include launching in 1973 the outsized new drug agency, the Drug Enforcement Administration, an internationalized bureaucracy with domestic powers that have been associated with Nixon's project of fostering a larger repressive state. Nixon and Henry Kissinger's short-sighted foreign policies did not help here. The green light given to right-wing military regimes in Chile, Brazil, and Argentina inadvertently worked to funnel the trade into willing Colombian hands. Even the Cuban exiles secretly working for Nixon, like the illegal White House "plumbers" who sparked the Watergate scandal, rubbed shoulders with the right-ist Cuban cocaine-running organizations of the 1960s. Miami became a booming port of entry for cocaine under Nixon's watch. Nixon's drug policy, sometimes applauded for its social realism, embraced a wholesale utilization of methadone clinics to stem the politicized urban crime wave associated with the African American heroin problem, which had multiplied some ten times during the 1960s, and to calm fears of soaring drug abuse by disgruntled returning Vietnam veterans.[23]

All these strategies essentially backfired into the spread of cocaine. As the mythic white drug culture of the sixties, based on an open embrace of marijuana and hallucinogens, was still expanding up and down the social ladder, Nixon concentrated his legendary political ire against harmless marijuana. This was probably due to the drug's intimate association with the expressive youth culture protesting his continuing anticommunist war in Vietnam. In the fall of 1969, Nixon launched his controversial Operation Intercept against Mexican marijuana border smuggling, with a subsequent aerial spraying of Mexican hemp fields. A palpable marijuana shortage hit American youth, which was eventually to spur the massive domestic marijuana cottage industry the United States has today. In the short run, however, this harassment mainly accelerated the rise of the recently rediscovered drug cocaine.[24] Perceptive drug dealers — including Colombians, familiar with marijuana prospects from their own endeavors in the field — saw this as the perfect opportunity to market pricey, more concentrated substances like cocaine, in an unsurprising effect of the repression of bulky and mild drugs. Cocaine, still perceived as a harmless "soft" or gourmet drug, nonaddicting like marijuana, was easy to sell, especially in a climate where few believed the dire warnings of government drug propaganda anymore because of its dishonest approach to cannabis. Even the legitimate new grassroots campaign against amphetamine — with the contagious slogan "speed kills" — piqued interest in cocaine, for cocaine was seen as an apt substitute by the nation's army of speed freaks. Evidence suggests that another locus of spiraling cocaine use was Nixon's model East Coast methadone clinics. Edgy addicts sought out cocaine to alleviate the numbing effect of their therapy, or they simply switched their pleasures.[25] The dramatic cracking of the 1960s "French Connection" heroin pipeline, immortalized in the Gene Hackman film of the same title, along with Nixon's pyrrhic victory of a Turkish poppy ban in 1972, drove sellers and buyers to cocaine. It was, conveniently, a Western Hemisphere drug not in the hands of the Corsican or Italian mob.

All these signs of cocaine's rebirth alarmed world drug authorities, for in official eyes cocaine had vanished as a pleasure drug in the 1920s and rarely crossed borders. In late 1966, the UN convened an emergency mission to study what it tellingly termed "Points of Convergence of the Illicit Traffic in Coca Leaf and Cocaine in Latin America," mobilizing drug agents from Argentina, Bolivia, Brazil, Chile, Colombia, Ecuador, Peru, the United States, and Interpol. The resulting report offers a rich testimony on the emerging trade. The UN was concerned with the "heavy" processing of cocaine now spreading across Peru, the three well-formed supply lines from Bolivia, and the hundreds of Chileans plying cocaine to the north. Drug agents in the field, ever more of them, reported incidents on a daily basis. Chile's role, predictably, was read as sign of an ongoing communist cocaine conspiracy, especially after the election of the socialist Allende in 1970, which deeply disturbed Nixon.[26] The BNDD launched its own Cocaine Project in 1968 focused on the social causes of a rightly named new Andean "drug economy," which it located in peasant poverty. By 1972, the BNDD drew up a bolder "Narcotics Control Action Plan," which targeted Latin American cocaine. Faraway cocaine busts made small news in the *New York Times*. In 1971, as Nixon's drug war heated up, congressional hearings on "International Aspects of the Narcotics Problem" first brought cocaine into the public eye. By 1973, Congress had ordained another study mission on "The World Narcotics Problem: The Latin American Perspective," which took a global view of the expanding Pan-American cocaine economy just prior to the entry of the Colombians. By 1979, the boom had entered full swing as illicit cocaine flows reached the one-hundred-ton mark. The published House hearings on the problem were simply billed *Cocaine: A Major Drug of the Seventies.*[27]

At home, U.S. drug authorities appeared confused and divided by cocaine. Lacking a forceful drug czar like Anslinger, they were perhaps still regrouping after a history of overreactions to drug menaces that now evoked incredulity. On the one hand, the BNDD responded with covert overseas "international attack" operations to crush the South American cocaine trade, such as Operation Condor in 1971, which, needless to say, fell short of its aims. On the other hand, cocaine remained an officially declared low-priority DEA problem well into the 1970s. In April 1974, the newly formed DEA appointed an eight-man Federal Cocaine Policy Task Force to look into the drug's "potential hazard to society." The resulting report reviewed the scant data on users, cocaine's "colorful past," and the "divergent opinions" of the enforcement and "treatment community," which had yet to see a demand to cure cocaine addiction. A presidential "White Paper on Drug Abuse" in 1975 awarded cocaine a "low priority"—below every other drug except then-tolerated marijuana—because, it averred, "cocaine does not result in serious consequences such as crime, hospital emergency room admissions, or death." As late as 1977, under president Jimmy Carter, a specially commissioned National Institute on Drug Abuse (NIDA) monograph on the drug found that "cocaine as typically used in the United States at present poses only a limited hazard." Cocaine slipped in under the 1970s radar, probably because many experts still perceived it to be a soft drug of elites.[28]

When cocaine reentered American culture as an upscale drug in the early 1970s, there were powerful cultural elements in the American turn to cocaine beyond what Dr. David Musto has diagnosed as a mass cultural amnesia about its social and bodily dangers. This is a topic for a genuine adept of cultural studies (which I am not), one that deserves the studied attention usually lavished on the romanticized 1960s drug culture.[29] For one thing, the extent of illicit drug use actually peaked in the United States during the 1970s. Unlike the oft-politicized or underground 1960s drug culture, which, to invoke a huge generality, erupted in defiance of a conformist cold war corporate culture, the emergent drug cultures of the 1970s proved far more accommodating to the mainstream of American capitalism. The subversive act of breaking the law became for many more in the 1970s just another call for consumer rights. Cocaine reemerged as a glamorous and, now in multiple senses, "whitened" good: its earliest and seemingly unabashed proponents, spreading the good news about coke, hailed from Hollywood and the commercialized world of white rock music. Cocaine became a staple of both Hollywood films and the actual process of filmmaking, starting with the famous opening scene of the 1969 fall-of-the-counterculture parable *Easy Rider*. Rock stars and celebrities constituted the model moneyed and opinion-forming brain worker professions of the late twentieth century, and for them coke become a required stress reliever and work-focusing aid. The youthful countercultural music rag *Rolling Stone* soon crowned cocaine "the drug of the 70s." The staid *New York Times* dubbed it "the champagne" of drugs, opinions seconded by middlebrow coverage of the cocaine phenomenon in *Newsweek* and *Time*.[30] By Nixon's abbreviated second term, the hippie archetype, with its natural, low-key, toke-sharing alternative to consumption society, was definitely out, and outspoken anticapitalist drug radicals like Timothy Leary and Abbie Hoffman were on the lam. Few icons of the passing age made the cocaine-fueled transition. Jerry Garcia moved from hippie roots music to all-night jams, and the folkie-revolutionary Jefferson Airplane managed a hedonistic reincarnation as the warp-speed Jefferson Starship.

The new cocaine culture, to invoke the worst clichés of the time, was about individual hoarding and conspicuous consumption. Cocaine abetted the youthful political escapism and related cultural excess generated during the later Nixon years. No culture — since I cannot use the words "music" or "dance" to describe it — was more closely associated with cocaine than the beat of mid-1970s disco, with all of its manic and easy sexual connotations. New York's celebrated club Studio 54 became a pulsating temple of cocaine culture in the later 1970s, an all-night, every night party of celebrity sex, drugs, and disco balls, a drug scene presaged in Andy Warhol's decadent amphetamine and heroin-driven anti-1960s. Superficiality, success, and money were back in, and cocaine intensified and highlighted all their sensations and delusions. Cocaine, in part owing to its sheer expense, shared an clear affinity with the energized get-rich-quick American entrepreneurialism of the 1970s, exemplified by the saga of fast-living luxury-automaker-turned-cocaine-importer John DeLorean. By the end of the decade, the drug had become a staple of Wall Street's nonstop "bright lights, big city" lifestyle. The 1970s hatched the so-called yuppies, the inverted hippies, individualistic big-spender hipsters of the next "me generation" in the Reagan decade of the 1980s — nurtured, I would suspect, as an elite cultural class on South American cocaine.

In part, this style of high consumption was a spillover from the actual big business of distributing cocaine and the scores of overnight entrepreneurs it spawned.[31] Early on in the boom, amateur American fortune hunters rushed in: ninety-three foreigners were caught with the drug at Bogotá's airport in 1973 alone. By the mid-1970s, Colombian exporters were being met onshore in Cartegena and Baranquilla by an ambitious new class of American coke promoters, instant millionaires like Zachary Swan; the improbably named Max Mermelstein, an adviser and partner to Medellín drug lords; and the flamboyant early dealer George Jung, immortalized by Johnny Depp in the Hollywood film *Blow*. As a regional culture, the American South came back into the picture, particularly cocaine-drenched South Florida, overrun by adventurous Cuban and Colombian drug runners — bottled for popular consumption in television's later *Miami Vice* — and Texas, which also had a long border with Latin America and was home to memory-impaired party animals like the young George W. Bush. Even oppressed rust belt ghetto dwellers shared in this great American hustling bonanza of the 1970s. The antipolitical black cult of "Superfly"—a moniker for fine cocaine—was born in 1971, replete with gold chains, spoons, sexy "foxes," and, after 1973, a string of inspirational hit movies about antihero street dealers. Cocaine signified, in short, the passing of the more political, peace-loving, and introspective drug culture of the 1960s, or at least its representation as such, and indeed served as a chemical accelerant of this cultural-economic shift. Along with the sensory-deadening quaaludes of the 1970s, cocaine led to a more aggressive consumption culture, more in tune with the longer, violence-prone American tradition of alcohol use.

By the late 1970s, the plummeting price of cocaine and its wide social acceptability made it a drug of choice among the American business class and even the white middle class (no needles necessary), particularly in major cities and up and down the California coast. In 1977, cocaine enjoyed an estimated 4.1 million regular users in the United States, including a tenth of the up-and-coming generation of people aged eighteen to twenty-five. By the 1980s, the deepening slide in cocaine prices, an unwitting effect of continuously upping the ante against South American traffickers, combined with the drug's market saturation, led to cocaine's diversification into low-income African American retail markets: the crack boom, fueled by cocaine repackaged in a cheaper, smokable "freebase" form.[32] Amid the politics of American urban decay, the whole political and cultural narrative about cocaine became enveloped in renewed racial hysteria, colored by horrifically escalating domestic and foreign "drug-related" violence. The script needed rewriting, and cocaine was reinvented once again as a downwardly mobile, menacing hard drug.

COCAINE'S HISTORICAL PRESENT

Cocaine is still very much with us, in continuously shifting guises. Let me end this history by placing cocaine's contemporary consumption into its broadest global contexts, those connecting the Andes to the outer world. This relationship is deeply affected by the foreign drug wars of the United States. With a fairly steady demand, American cocaine lovers still spend in street prices about thirty-eight billion dollars on cocaine each year, a princely sum among drugs, amounting to some two-thirds of all illegal drug expenditures in the United States. This is why cocaine has remained the motive force behind America's permanent antidrug campaign, a crusade ambivalently supported by the American people, including its failure-ridden policy of interdiction and suppression abroad.

As American cocaine suppression heated up after 1980, huge new and segmented retail markets were discovered within the country, ranging from "middle America" and ghetto crack to the local turfs of Dominican and L.A. street gangs. By 1986, twenty-two million Americans, one in eleven, had tasted cocaine, including fully one-third of young people. In the Reagan-era United States, as retailing groups fought it out over market shares, cocaine became associated with ruthless urban violence and degradation — whether one blamed foreign cocaine itself, the system of drug prohibition, or the deplorable social conditions of neglected American cities as the root of such mayhem. U.S. prison populations swelled to three times their initial size between 1980 and 1994, putting a larger proportion of U.S. nationals in prison than the citizens of any other nation on earth; most of that increase was the result of draconian anticrack drug laws aimed at poor youth. By 1995, more young black men were in prison than in college.

In the Andes, where this story began, coca frontiers for illicit exporting via Colombia spread massively into the deep jungle recesses of the Huallaga Valley and Bolivia's Chapare as the Peruvian and Bolivian states both succumbed to severe political-economic meltdowns after 1980. Further steps against cocaine — including full-scale militarizing eradication campaigns since the Reagan-Bush drug wars were openly declared in 1982 — led to spiraling growth in cocaine production and entrepreneurial and political violence. The Huallaga, with its atomized, alienated, and harassed *cocalero* peasantry, became a major breeding ground and haven for brutal Sendero Luminoso guerrillas and their rival Túpac Amaru army. In Bolivia, in contrast, coca peasants unionized and peacefully struggled for their long-term recognition in national politics. Cocaine underwent dramatic price drops and reached higher street purity as astute Colombian middlemen overinvested ahead of demand for the lucrative drug to meet the rising risks of interdiction. Between 1982 and 1986 alone, production of illicit coca doubled. During the 1980s, the price of cocaine to dealers in Florida dropped from around sixty thousand to fifteen thousand dollars a kilo. This long-term slide was precisely the opposite of the one clear central strategic objective of the DEA: to steeply raise the buying price of cocaine so as to deter consumer use. The geography of illicit commodity chains shifted as well. The well-known mid-1980s rerouting of smuggling from cocaine's main and embattled Medellín-Miami corridor to a Cali–northern Mexican route obeyed the ballooning effect of drug suppression.

By the early 1990s, illicit cocaine commanded an estimated productive capacity in the range of a thousand metric tons in networks mobilizing literally hundreds of thousands of employees along the line—farmers, processors, guards, money launderers, officials on the take, smugglers, enforcers, street dealers, and rehab counselors—with millions of avid consumers worldwide and revenues ranging from fifty to a hundred billion dollars annually.[33] This chain is mirrored by a now-permanent antidrug bureaucracy and armies, supporting many thousands more with their annual expenditures in the tens of billions. Cocaine's productive capacity is some one hundred times greater than Peru's peak legal cocaine output in 1900 and, measured in terms of its prohibition price premium, is among the most lucrative commodity flows in world history. Since the late 1970s, the coca crop sown for illicit export has dwarfed domestic use of low-potency leaf for the first time in coca's long history. Cocaine's is also the most dramatic commodity network ever trailblazed by Latin American peasants and businessmen themselves, and while it is perhaps comparable in some ways to global coffee culture, it raises serious questions about why such a lucrative exporting success story, gross inequities and all, is found only in the region's illicit commerce. The violence-ridden American crack boom of the late 1980s and early 1990s has now subsided due to changing urban demographics, racial incarceration policies, and rival drugs like methamphetamine. Yet 7 million, or half of the world's 14 million regular cocaine users, remain North Americans (compared to the 3.5 million Europeans who indulge), white and black, rich and poor, who altogether snort up some 250–300 tons of it yearly. Well over 25 million Americans have tried cocaine. Unlike in the wilder 1970s and 1980s, resilient cocaine users seem to have settled into more contained use of the drug. They far surpass in numbers the surviving, or perhaps thriving, indigenous *coqueros* of the Andes, who now likely number around 6–8 million. In Peru, only 10 percent of coca sown is for legal or "traditional" usage, while the rest goes for cocaine. Interestingly, as cocaine's prestige fell after 1980, even in the Andes (where the drug became associated with rampant violence and corruption, as well as novel, risky smoking of local *basuca* PBC mix), coca's stock has dramatically risen, accompanied by a new identity-affirming ethnic politics of the sacred leaf.[34] To chew coca is now to be proudly Quechua or Aymara. Especially in Bolivia, this is a sign of the legitimate peasant politics of coca: organized growers who managed to lift one of their own, Evo Morales, into the national presidency in late 2005. There is now not only ritual coca use but informal usage among *mestizos* and a growing list of commercial Peruvian and Bolivian coca concoctions, including teas, toothpaste, and liquors. Yet, Coca-Cola's exception aside, there are no legally permitted international exports of such products under the UN 1961 convention, despite renewed interest in this area.

The current stage of global cocaine suppression, starting in the mid-1990s, has largely run illegal coca out of eastern Peru and Bolivia after crackdowns on coca peasants and cocaine flights ordered by the discredited Fujimori-Montesinos dictatorship and under Bolivia's U.S.-funded Plan Dignidad. Coca largely shifted into southeastern Colombia itself, the Putumayo and Caquetá jungle frontiers violently contested by leftist guerrillas and right-wing paramilitaries, but its overall quantity has not diminished. This move was an unprecedented development, an Andean coca capitalism divorced from indigenous coca traditions, which barely exist in Colombia. Indeed, the cultivar itself is a new *Erythroxylon* hybrid, likely a mixture of Peruvian varieties. Colombians, invigorated by the repressive breakup of the short-lived regional cartels by the early 1990s, including the targeted assassination of Escobar in 1993 and the bloody extradition of other cocaine notables, became more adaptable, competitive businessmen during the 1990s. They now have spawned hundreds of cell-like groups, flexibly built upon an integrated national agroexporter coca-cocaine enterprise, and they have even diversified into high-grade poppy and heroin (until a post–9/11 Afghanistan retook that field). Colombia's improved coca strains enjoy higher alkaloid content, and cocaine processing has become more efficient. Transshipment continues to flee Mexico, which after defeat of the systematically venal Party of the Institutional Revolution (PRI) in 2000 became less hospitable to politically connected drug lords, and is returning to dispersed Caribbean sites, including chronically impoverished and unstable Haiti.[35] These chains continue to unfold under a highly focused five-billion-dollar, militarizing U.S.-led drive against Colombian coca, the controversial Plan Colombia. Recent reports suggest that overall Colombian cocaine capacity peaked around 2001, and the DEA even claims its first success, in 2007–8, in raising the drug's wholesale price. But coca planting is quietly and quickly returning to Peru and Bolivia, where eradication policies left a deep scar in peasant unrest and anti-American politics, particularly in Bolivia, where coca has always held firm as an honorable national good. Steeper cocaine prices, if true and sustained, will only accelerate this movement back to coca's historic homeland. Dramatic new air links are being forged through Brazil, with its vast slums and pleasure spots, which by 2005 had become the world's second largest consumer of cocaine; across sub-Saharan Africa into burgeoning markets in Europe, where prices continue their slide; and among the capitalist nouveaux riches of the former Soviet empire. Illicit cocaine — goaded on by foolhardy drug policies — could end up replicating the geography of early-twentieth-century commodity coca, globalized to exotic locales like Indonesia, Taiwan, or West Africa. Cocaine's history is long and sinuous — and certainly not over.

AFTERTHOUGHTS: FROM COCA TO COCAINE

In concluding this book, I want to highlight for analysis and interpretation several of the key layers of cocaine's Andean narrative and the connections between these levels of cocaine history. These intertwined stories are the ones that, in my mind, reveal the vital implications of cocaine's complicated past and their links to the drug's problematic present.

In the first place, in a broad sense this has been the story of cocaine's construction and then delegitimation and deconstruction as a global commodity. Coca and cocaine were essentially new goods in 1860, with no prior international history, although coca has long autochthonous regional roots in the Andes. By the 1890s, both goods had been defined as and built into recognized, thriving world commodities, mobilized by and mobilizing a circuit of many thousands of peasants, planters, industrialists, and merchants, along with wider distribution, medical, and consumer networks abroad. Commodified cocaine required and also displaced commercial coca leaf, which after 1910, for a variety of reasons, ceased to be an active global commodity save in the specialized circuit of the emblematic American beverage Coca-Cola. Coca reverted to its long role as a Andean territorial or cultural good. After 1910, Peruvian cocaine, the target of mounting restrictions, became a fallen and depressed commodity, bereft of alternative outlets, reduced mainly to a regional mainstay of greater Huánuco. Cocaine was being slowly decertified as a legitimate commodity. After 1950, cocaine became reworked again through a series of different pressures and new boundaries, ideals, and social networks into an illegal good, although one drawing from its legal past. Illicit cocaine became a mobile shadow commodity, deftly moving between, around, and outside of the strictures of conventional commerce and states. This analysis

leaves open the question of why one of South America's most successful,
autonomous native commodities, cocaine, which today sustains millions
of people and so strongly colors the region, is an illicit one.

A second long thread in cocaine's commodity history is a peculiar
technology: the making of crude cocaine sulfates. Actually invented in
Peru during the brilliant cocaine research episode of pharmacist Alfredo
Bignon, this applied technique allowed cocaine to be produced cheaply
from fresh leaf with simple-to-use ingredients. Crude cocaine enabled
Peru to swiftly claim its place as a key semi-industrial site in the global
drug industry (against would-be colonialist or Bolivian trade rivals), and
it allowed cocaine manufacturing to rapidly migrate to and bloom in the
right tropical coca regions of the Amazon. As a semiprocessed input for
pharmaceutical-grade cocaine, however, crude cocaine also placed Peru
near the bottom of a global drug pyramid dominated by modern European
pharmaceutical firms. For a variety of reasons after 1900, Peruvians tena-
ciously clung to this now-native lore, embedded in the artisanal routines
of rustic Huánuco, defying the attempts by Lima experts and reformers to
upgrade or upstream Peru's national cocaine industry. This same relative
backwardness, however, made crude cocaine the perfect good for filtering
underground into an illicit cocaine industry after 1950, with its mobile
know-how easily passed on to informal chemists and itinerant peasants.
Coca and cocaine industries emerged elsewhere across the early-twentieth-
century world—highly modern ones in colonial southeast Asia—but only
Peru's coca complex generated and made this historic transition to illicit
cocaine, precisely because of its regional low-tech sulfate tradition. Indeed,
the family resemblance of crude cocaine, Amazonian peasant-mashed coca
paste, and *pasta básica de cocaína*—the chief inputs into today's shadow
economy of cocaine—is hardly accidental. And the hierarchical structure
of today's cocaine's global trade—dominated by sophisticated Colombian
refiners of cocaine hydrochloride and Colombian wholesaler smugglers
rather than the Eurocentric Merck organization of a century ago—is also
a visible legacy of this dualistic technological genealogy. As also seen
in this study, an intriguing foil to the path of Peruvian technology was
the underground trail of American coca politics emanating from another
kind of coca refining formula: Coca-Cola's Merchandise No. 5 flavoring
extract.

Third, the location or regionality of cocaine was both a research strategy
(as an in-depth "glocal" case study) and a central finding of this book. As a
modern good during a previous age of globalization, cocaine in one form

or another rapidly dispersed to every corner of the late-nineteenth-century world. Yet the drug's long-term incubator, through all of its key changes, was one particular region: the tropics around Huánuco, Peru, adjacent to the ancient coca fields of the Derrepente-Chinchao *montaña*. This region, for peculiar ecological, botanical, historical, and geographic reasons, came to serve by the final decade of the nineteenth century as the capital of the Peruvian cocaine industry, supplying most of the world's renowned German-refined cocaine. Cocaine was not only this strategic and remote area's chief economic pursuit but also the glue of its entrenched political networks and strong autonomist identities. For six decades, through ups and largely downs, Huánuco clung to its locally hewn crude cocaine. No other spot in the world matched this continuity or resiliency with the drug, making Huánuco by World War II a unique haven for the survival of cocaine's cultures of production. So again, it was hardly coincidental that the final momentous transition to illicit cocaine was birthed in greater Huánuco, and, apart from Bolivia's energetic transitional role during the 1950s, the Upper Huallaga would propel the rise of the Colombian *narcotraficantes* during the 1970s and 1980s boom as illicit development fled downstream with migrating peasants. More industrialized Asian and European cocaine complexes, in contrast, did not spawn illicit drug spheres when dismantled. Perhaps this was due to the effectiveness of formal colonial fiat versus the merely informal U.S. antidrug pressures exerted in the Andes, or to the remote geography of the central Amazon, or perhaps it was because only in the Andes did cocaine coincide with an entrenched and coca-valorizing peasantry, peasants who began to actively colonize illicit coca frontiers after 1950. Cocaine, of course, is once again an extremely global drug, yet glocally tied to specific social geographies.

Fourth, beyond a specific *metis* (locally embedded practical knowledge) and specific cocaine homeland, Peruvian and more generally peopled activity proved vital in how cocaine actually evolved.[36] It may seem strange to claim agency in a drug-gone-bad story—to claim that the cocaine industry was founded and honed on the periphery, precisely the sorts of claims stereotyped South Americans might wish to avoid today. Yet this agency is still worth noting. A local scientific community of excellence literally invented crude cocaine. Bicultural entrepreneurs quickly adapted it to local conditions in eastern Peru, and their exporting success broke the drug's supply logjam of the 1880s and thus helped structure the international distribution of turn-of-the-century cocaine production. Indeed, Peru's overproduction of crude cocaine (from a strictly productionist perspective) is what dramatically drove down world cocaine prices and helped the new drug spread well beyond its defined, legitimate medical uses in the West. During cocaine's protracted twentieth-century retrenchment, local elites safeguarded their traditional regional concoction, and national elites and the Peruvian state defied, or at least successfully evaded, the intensifying anticocaine crusade emanating from the United States until the aftermath of World War II irrevocably shifted the scales. Bolivian elites did essentially the same with their national coca leaf. A few critics even posed alternative national visions and projects to U.S.-style source prohibitions, alternatives that in hindsight might have worked to forestall the birth of illicit cocaine. In the postwar period, some Huánuco notables, including possibly their leader, Andrés Avelino Soberón, became protagonists in making cocaine illicit and dispersing it far and wide. The vital shift here (besides making active Schumpeterian entrepreneurs out of pioneer hemispheric drug traffickers) was a class one: now, illicit cocaine was embraced and developed by displaced and desperate peasants in eastern Peru and lowland Bolivia, often coca users themselves, a group far more autonomous of the state and resilient to external pressures than the previous landed elites of legal coca. This group was joined in the illicit trade by a host of homegrown petty criminals, businessmen, ethnic traders, bohemians, and hedonists from Chile and Cuba to Rio and Miami who created and propagated a new Latin-inflected cultural taste for cocaine in many Latin American cities, especially Havana, during the 1950s. This was a new trade invented, as it were, wholly in the South, which is probably one reason for its continuing vitality and perseverance against any outside would-be controllers, whether foreign mafia rings or the rule makers of metropolitan states and policing organizations. If such peripheral sites and actors had much to do with the making of cocaine in the first place, perhaps their renewed agency (or conscious resistance) can help undo the global drug conflict that has enveloped this drug since the 1980s.

Part of this action, or agency, in the fifth place, was the various ways in which Peruvians and others imagined and thought about cocaine: cocaine-producing cultures. Mid-century Peruvian *pensadores* and scientists, reacting to European cues, resuscitated and nationalized debased colonial coca leaf as Peruvian. Development of cocaine, even its local science, became a modernizing nationalist imperative. At the height of the commodity boom, cocaine was upheld by core national elites as a heroic, liberal, and perhaps most of all Peruvian good. Later, as cocaine's stock fell after 1910 in the West, Peruvian elites began to exhibit a shifting and locally colored schizophrenia about the two drugs: coca became decried as a backward, degenerating, and dangerous drug for the national Indian, while cocaine retained some of its modernist gleam, worthy of protection by the state. Needless to say, neither approach was good science. Bolivia, lacking industrialized cocaine until much later, inculcated more socially integrative prococa ideals, some of which have emerged vibrantly again in the current political cycle — vibrantly enough for president Evo Morales to openly challenge longstanding world drug orthodoxy. It is hard to say how these ideals and passions affected cocaine's illicit phase, though these ideological initiatives make it difficult to simply regard mid-twentieth-century drug suppression as an easy one-sided imposition or imperialist plot. Peru, perhaps out of principle, only belatedly joined the international crusade to extirpate the drug around 1948–50, when coastal elites converted to kindred pro-U.S. cold war beliefs, though one wing of Peruvian highland medicine again marked its symbolic dissent to the radical modernist 1950s ideal abroad of extirpating local coca use and culture. Bolivia lagged even further — until the early 1960s — in official drug control. While cocaine traffickers are not easily pictured as proud nationalists (though this phenomena is not unknown in Colombia), by the 1980s sectors of the Peruvian state selectively ignored U.S. imperatives against cocaine traffic — a kind of nationalist autonomy mixed with rampant corruption and fiscal survivalism — and have rarely pursued their role in the drug war with gusto. Meanwhile, since the 1980s, coca's nationalist stock has again been restored, largely due to late-twentieth-century ethnic or anthropological politics, and Andean governments even flirt with a few commercial possibilities for coca, still against the letter of the reigning UN 1961 Single Convention. In another ironic twist, the modern and progressive image of early-twentieth-century cocaine is now long extinct due to the drug's associations with hyperviolent drug lords, atavistically clad in a veritably medieval (i.e., premarket) discourse about crusades of good against evil.

Sixth, if cocaine can be thought of as a highly localized and highly impassioned commodity culture, it was also structured by global flows and structures, in other words, by a distant global political economy. This book has tapped the sociological concept of global commodity chains to organize and illuminate these complex bundles of transnational relationships. As seen in chapter 3, commodity chains, if broadened to encompass flows of culture, politics, power, law, and science, are not only apt descriptors of cocaine's segmented world markets and hierarchical production ladders, but shifts in commodity chains also help to explain the turning points in cocaine history and how global forces manifested themselves regionally on the ground. Cocaine triumphed in the late nineteenth century out of competing commercial-scientific linkages of German, Franco-British, and U.S. interest and scientific interests in coca and cocaine. If first swayed by French medicine, Peru's local development of crude cocaine was strongly tied in with the German pharmaceutical commodity sphere and its local agents, though by 1910 the North Americans had carved out their own regional supply and consumption chain around northern Peru beverage coca. Peruvian autonomy became limited by Peru's niches within these chains. In the early twentieth century, European dominance and commercial chains slowly waned, while Peru faced two sharp new competitors in the state-supported, colonial-style cocaine commodity chains erected by the Dutch and Japanese across Asia. The more informal-style U.S. sphere of influence, then turning toward restrictive drug control, constrained Peruvian options and was politicized by the monopolistic structure of the Progressive-era cocaine industry, as well as by the complications of Coca-Cola's privileged place in U.S. foreign policy. Peru's industry withered but survived. This multipolar interwar cocaine world, with legal production of cocaine in diverse sites and cultures, also precluded incentives for cocaine going illicit. (Recreational use of the drug was a widely known practice as early as the 1890s.) World War II, by wiping out the remnants of the Asian and German chains and by ensuring American ascendance in global drug policy, doomed Peru's legal industry. The United States, with its established political economy of coca as well as its militant ideology of cutting off drugs at their source, did not even envisage the solution of co-opting Peru's relic industry into a U.S. commodity chain, which might have safely funneled Peru's surplus drugs to select American firms. Instead, U.S. dominance meant the "export of prohibitions"—to apply Ethan Nadelmann's critical term—and with it, in reaction, the jerry-built hemispheric consolidation of an illicit chain in Andean cocaine, in place by the mid-1960s.[37] This new corridor, soon to be one of the most lucrative commodity chains in world history, reverted to cocaine's original spaces, linking Andean peasants via new Colombian middlemen to cocaine's once-more-thriving consumer markets in the United States. Thus, a kind of amplified commodity chain model helps explain cocaine's key historical shifts.

Finally, if diverse global and local forces came into play during cocaine's rise and fall as a legal good, the longest-running and most decisive relationship was that between the United States and the eastern Andes.

This relationship has been fraught with conflict and paradox from start to present.[38] North Americans have long enjoyed a vibrant national drug culture, in multiple senses of the term, and by the late nineteenth century they had became the world's major consumers and boosters of both coca and cocaine. By 1900, coca was as American as Coca-Cola. U.S. commercial agents actively promoted both goods in trade, though the messy politics of the American drug industry shut Peru's crude cocaine out of the relationship. By 1910, the United States, in a dramatic turnabout, had become zealously anticoca and anticocaine and began to lead its long and lonely crusade to ban the two drugs across the globe. Americans buried their own coca culture, in the process denying the Andean heritage of their beloved national soft drink. Yet until the 1940s, U.S. influence over big powers and small Andean states alike on this issue was minimal: few were alarmed about cocaine, though its usage and legitimacy waned. Slowly, the dismal American science and politics of cocaine filtered to places like Peru, helping to color, for example, its twentieth-century national coca debate, and U.S. powers of surveillance projected onto cocaine outdid even the Peruvian state's own capacity for and interest in control. World War II marked the first intensification of direct state-to-state hemispheric relationships, and it carried directly over into drug policy. As we have seen, Peru's move to criminalize and militarize cocaine after the war, infused by rising American cold war politics, met U.S. expectations.

Yet the greatest paradoxes were to follow: the secret cat-and-mouse game of incipient U.S. interdiction and escalating illicit cocaine, the inability of the United States to offer Peru (or later Bolivia) working solutions to the "problem" of cocaine, the contributions of modernist U.S.-led tropical development schemes to cocaine's spectacular growth in the Huallaga Valley and the Bolivian lowlands, the dispersal effects of cold war interventions in key drug entrepôts like Cuba and Chile, the skyrocketing incentives U.S. politicians gave to illicit cocaine by declaring an essentially political war on foreign drugs and against a menacing new domestic drug culture in the late 1960s. By the 1970s, a once-mythic pleasure drug, cocaine (like the nineteenth-century's mythical Incan coca bush), had returned in force as the real gourmet choice of Hollywood and Wall Street, helping to define a contagious new drug culture of the late twentieth century while also giving livelihood to some of the poorest and most marginal farmers of the far-off Andes. Cocaine's was, and is, a trans-American drug culture. Indeed, this book suggests that it is this sustained North American relationship with South American cocaine and coca (the sole drug-plant culture seeded and rooted in the Western Hemisphere) that was central to the longer development of U.S. drug policy in the Americas, instead of those policies emerging in relation to postwar Mexican opiates and marijuana, as often previously assumed.[39]

I hope, to conclude, that this book can make a modest contribution to the methods of the new and expanding field of archival drug history — a field that, despite Latin America's being a core zone of world drug culture and economy, has barely begun for the region. The subject of Andean cocaine has been viewed here through a dizzying array of lenses: as a long-term object of commodity formation; as a history of science, technology, and medicine; in terms of inspiring ideas and grassroots agency; as a microscopic regional social study; as an exercise in global political economy; and in terms of long-term transnational political relationships. Reduced to its essentials, this diverse kit of historical tools represents an attempt to bring closer what may be called objective "structuralist" and interpretive "culturalist" sensibilities and to closely connect local and global scales of analysis, inspired by some vibrant historiographical currents among historians of the Americas. Because of their contested nature as commodities, drugs offer historians an especially promising realm for this form of analysis — one integrating material development with its representation and commodities with the passions they arouse.

History can inform politics, so it is worth noting that at the start of the twenty-first century we find ourselves still deeply mired in a hemispheric drug war against cocaine. This costly and seemingly endless war — secretly initiated in 1947, openly declared and intensified under Nixon in the late 1960s, and dramatically escalated against powder cocaine, African American crack smokers, and Andean peasant producers during the Reagan years of the 1980s — has now lasted four decades. If dated to 1906–14, the genesis of American antidrug and anticocaine policy during the Progressive era, the duration of this war is approaching the century mark. The term "paradoxical" barely captures the contradictions, illogic, futility, and harmfulness of this war against both the Andes and domestic minorities. Drug control (that contradiction in terms) is an extreme example of what sociologist Robert K. Merton termed the "unintended consequences of social action," wherein the blowback effects of policy actually overwhelm any rationally considered goals. This seems especially the case when projected into the imponderables of distant and different societies. Ironically, the aim of American drug policy since 1914, which has been to cut drugs off at the source, has produced a paradox dramatically revealed in this history of cocaine.[40] Since the late 1940s, repression against incipient cocaine in the Andes has only backfired, fostering by the early 1970s its opposite: a true and aggressive cocaine "epidemic," or, to invoke another Mertonism, drug policy as a "self-fulfilling prophecy."[41] Its main impact since the 1980s has been to balloon and scatter illicit production and smuggling to new sites (now concentrated in southeastern Colombia) and contribute to the wealth and tactical sophistication of drug traffickers and to the moral and political decay of Andean states. The U.S. drug war has brought the street price of the drug to record lows, the precise opposite of its stated central aim, and has pushed drug abuse in new and perilous directions, such as domestic methamphetamine. It has spawned horrifying violence and human rights degradations at home and abroad and is now globalizing cocaine culture to such disparate places as Russia and Brazil. What is largely forgotten in this ongoing mayhem, and about the unyielding prohibitionist system behind it, is the longer entanglement between the United States and the Andes around cocaine that, through a sinuous course, has led to this disastrous warring relationship with the Andean commodity of cocaine. Like other destructive relationships, it seems driven by passions and detritus of the past. Perhaps any light this book has shed on that long relationship may someday help to heal it.

APPENDIX

Quantifying Cocaine

Readers may have sensed a kind of cliometric tension in this book: I frequently lament the poor quality, unreliability, and inutility of existing historical statistics for cocaine, or even their sheer absence, but the book also relies on a fair number of tables and even some new numbers. This appendix serves two purposes for the curious specialist reader: first, it discusses some methodological problems with historical statistics about cocaine and how certain choices were made, and second, it lays out the sources used for statistical data about the commodity.

Although I was once an economic historian with training in quantitative methods, this book does not undertake a systematic statistical study of cocaine. Indeed, that past training tells me that most of the global numbers encountered about cocaine are at best guesses, or often even bogus numbers, unworthy for marking many trends or for sustained economic analysis. This is true for both the legal (1885–1950) and illicit (1950–present) phases of cocaine history and whether the context and sources are metropolitan states with developed statistical capacities or relatively weak ones like Peru. My quantitative skepticism has four main sources.

First, legal coca and cocaine (in contrast to opiates in many sites) was not subject to systematic taxation or controlled in public monopolies at least until the 1950s ENACO, and even then dubiously. Indeed, for this reason, some early Bolivian statistics from coca leaf levies (collected by the organized Sociedad de Propietarios de Yungas) are better than Peru's, where coca went largely untaxed at the national level. Local government taxes were varied and ephemeral. Private data from pharmaceutical firms, merchant houses, and coca plantations are highly scattered or unavailable and not robust enough for reconstructing substitute aggregates. In chapter 5, another problem was raised of the possibility of fictitious cocaine statistic gathering by or for specialized bodies of the League of Nations between 1920 and 1940. Many — I cannot say what exact percentage — of the numbers about cocaine repeated by travelers, thesis writers, and trade consuls, and recycled in historical texts, are speculation, some educated, others not.

Second, official and unofficial figures about cocaine suffer from a bewildering lack of basic unit consistency. They arbitrarily confuse or switch units without reliable clues to the menagerie of measures and values used (which include pounds, kilos, tons, tonnes, metric tons, hectares, acres, ounces, grams, *quintales*, *cestos*, *arrobas*, seedlings, *soles* [S/], Peruvian pounds [*Lp*], pounds sterling, piastres, francs, marks, and U.S. dollars), which confounds the creation of national aggregates and genuine international comparisons, even if strong exchange rate data existed for places like Peru and Bolivia. Historians have picked up sloppily on these bad numbers, compounding the original problems.

Third, there is an obvious dearth of statistics, or even suspect official statistic creation, when it comes to illicit cocaine of the decades after 1950. There are, for example, good reasons to distrust statistics derived from drug seizures and trafficking arrests. Even in the prior interwar era, several countries, notably Japan, were widely suspected of fabricating medicinal cocaine reports sent to the League of Nations, as a cover for other shadow trades. There is even today deep controversy about the size of the far more obvious world cocaine economy and the utility of statistics (from seizures, informers, or other dubious sources and methods) deployed by official control agencies such as the DEA and United Nations International Drug Control Programme. This problem was more acute during the nascent era of cocaine trafficking (1950–70), before the trade or its suppression were regularized. Apart from faulty methodologies, political factors act both to underplay and to exaggerate the scale of illicit activities. Drug traffickers and coca-growing peasants themselves had an innate interest in elusive and deceptive behavior and have yet to release better statistics.[1] Organizations like the FBN and DEA have their own vested interests related to the political cycle. As in more qualitative aspects of drug trading (and the ways of portraying dealers), it is a nearly impossible to decipher what is going on from the other side.

Finally, there are pitfalls to even noble attempts to rectify the weakness of historical drug statistics. The distinguished historian of drugs

David Musto, for example, has shown this in his recent quantitative work "International Traffic in Coca through the Early Twentieth Century," a team effort to piece together global statistics on licit coca trades between the 1890s and 1940s. Musto's group thoroughly scoured official national and partial League of Nations statistics to chart cocaine and coca source exports from Peru, Bolivia, Java, and Formosa in search of world consumption trends. To formulate these new cocaine aggregates, Musto, a medical doctor by training, employs an ill-defined "Cocaine Equivalent," which likely reflects the "pharmaco-centric" bias of reducing coca leaf itself to its cocaine alkaloid content. This exercise thereby erases the historical regional trades in coca leaf for traditional uses (for example, that from Bolivia) or for commercial coca preparations, such as North American beverage syrups from northern Peru—quite substantial in the case of twentieth-century Coca-Cola. It ends up exaggerating turn-of-the-century world cocaine production and use, as well as missing the distinctive social and cultural significance of coca trades (something this book has tried to capture using the concept of commodity chains). However, the biggest trend Musto notes—an American peak usage in the teens and in Europe in the 1920s (probably inflated by German reexports)—may not be that wrong.[2] These criticisms in mind, I do use some of Musto's figures, sparingly, in chapter 3.

In sum, with such faulty historical statistics on cocaine, what should historians do? It would be a futile and draining task to try to recreate more reliable numbers about cocaine—or at least a life's work for a devoted cliometrician. Existing statistics are so fundamentally flawed that a recent university thesis on global cocaine history (by the Finnish geographer Jyri Soininen), mining the extant secondary sources, devotes much space to a running, rigorous, and often humorous critique of implausible or inconsistent cocaine statistics—including a few deployed by this author in earlier publications.[3] However, as with all faint, slanted, or fragmentary qualitative data, historians must learn to adapt, choose, and compromise among imperfect sources, which are often the sole window available into a foggy past. Quantitative data differ mainly in their spurious impression of scientific precision. Thus, my background in commodity studies convinces me that some statistics are usable here, albeit for limited ends and with the above-stated cautions and caveats. Readers encounter statistics, prices, numbers, and tables throughout the book, but they are mainly used for descriptive or illustrative purposes, or to demonstrate general trends: that is, how observers of the time depicted cocaine, sometimes numerically, whether right or wrong. Some charts (placed in the appendix) were built from scratch for special uses, explained along with their sources below.

The problem of currency units and exchange rates was broached above, so an approximate guide is appended here. During most of this era, Peruvian exports were typically denominated by the *libra peruana* (Peruvian pound, *Lp*), a unit that originally denoted five *soles* and was sometimes used synonymously with the British pound sterling (£). Apart from the array of other foreign currencies, dollars emerged as expected as a unit of account after the 1920s. Peru's post–Pacific War hyperinflation (not to mention that of the 1980s) and the 40 percent devaluation of the *sol* after Peru switched from the silver to the gold standard in 1897 prevent long-term comparisons of real *Lp* values. Carlos Boloña's published 1981 Oxford D.Phil. thesis has the best collation and calculations of nominal exchange rates; posted below is a summary of his long-term figures (sampled on a five-year basis) to help guide any monetarily-inclined readers throughout the text.

TABLE A.1   Sample Peruvian Exchange Rates, 1875–1965

Year	Sol/£	Sol/US$
1875	5.71	—
1885	6.49	1.33
1890	6.37	1.31
1895	9.97	2.04
1900	9.78	2.06
1905	9.86	2.06
1910	9.90	2.06
1915	10.87	2.36
1920	8.33	2.18
1925	12.26	2.50
1930	13.78	2.83
1935	20.48	4.19
1940	23.42	6.17
1945	26.06	6.50
1950	41.85	14.85
1955	52.80	19.00
1960	73.76	26.30
1965	75.16	26.82

Source: See Boloña, *Políticas arancelarias*, table A.3.4-9 (295), for yearly averages, or illustration A-6 for twentieth-century devaluations against U.S. dollar. Boloña himself notes data discrepancies.

textual tables, figures, and charts. I employ the source abbreviations system
used in the notes.

CHAPTER 2

Table A.2 below, used as a reference in chapter 2, was collated from obscure
Peruvian source fragments for the earliest trends to verify or complement
Musto estimates. Cocaine lots from Lima get reported as early as 1885, and
some coca leaf from the mid-1870s, but only by 1890 was enough Peruvian
cocaine on the move to merit accounting at customs. Many but not all
of these figures originate from the *Memorias de Ministerio de Hacienda del
Perú* (*MHP*). Total output or export quantum serve as a better guide than
revenues, given the drug's price volatility, unstable exchange rates, and
Peru's mix of currency units — national *soles* (*S/*), "Peruvian pounds" (*Lp*;
falling from five *soles* to around ten *soles* for the period 1898–1930), and
pounds sterling, dollars, or francs. But bulk measures of the two goods
(pounds, kilos, *arrobas*, tons) were also indicated inconsistently.

TABLE A.2 Coca and Cocaine Exports from Peru, 1888–1910

Year	Coca (kg)	Value	Reported Markets	Cocaine (kg)	Value
1888	28,660	S/369,361	Germany		S/100,000
1889			Europe	1,730	
1890				1,730	Lp366,000
1891	128,543	Lp241,473	Germany, U.S., U.K., France	3,215	Lp643,000
1892	388,465	Lp574,396 S/287,199		4,550	Lp910,000 S/455,000
1893	390,955	Lp707,792		2,357	Lp471,800
1894	372,360	Lp706,586		4,716	Lp943,200
1895				3,407	Lp600,940 S/681,400
1896	898,875	S/287,199			S/455,050
1897	494,000	$542,046 Lp54,204		4,206	$631,002 Lp63,102

(continued)

Appendix

TABLE A.2 (*continued*)

Year	Coca (kg)	Value	Reported Markets	Cocaine (kg)	Value
1898	408,000	Lp22,437		4,350	Lp65,197 (or £)
1899	312,000	Lp17,359 (or £)		4,500	Lp66,507 (or £)
1900	566,000	Lp33,943		7,750	Lp116,178
1901	610,000 (2,100 metric tons)	Lp36,614		10,700 (10,688)[a]	S/1,500,000 Lp160,322
1902	933,286	Lp62,895		8,209	Lp103,360
1903	1,042,900	Lp69,875		7,800	Lp97,506
1904	911,236	Lp61,053 £27,337		7,528	Lp94,000 £112,920
1905	1,330,841	Lp89,836		6,778	Lp116,590
1906		Lp68,299		5,914	Lp79,071
1907		Lp24,856			Lp66,630
1908					
1909	496,328	Lp19,614 (or £)	Germany, U.S., U.K.	5,266	Lp60,287 (or £)
1910	495,729	Lp20,337		5,524	Lp69,151

Sources: ODR, 26 Oct. 1889; Renoz, *Pérou* (1897), 66–67 (1890–1895); BAR, 1897, 545; *Geographical and Statistical Synopsis* (1899), 29, 61; CD, 24 Oct. 1896, 22 May 1897, 9 April 1904; Garland, *Reseña industrial* (1905), 144 (1897–1904); Maúrtua, *Porvenir del Perú* (1911), table "Valor de las exportaciones" (1877, 1897–1909); *Bulletin of the Pan-American Union*, 1914, "Commerce of Peru for 1913" (1909–10), 971.

Notes: Exchange rate: *soles* per £, approx. 9–10, 1895–1910; *soles* per $US, approx. 2–2.2. S/=*soles*, Lp=*libras peruanas*, £=pound sterling, $=U.S. dollars.

[a] Reported from German consular reports; 2,100 metric tons refers to all national coca.

The purpose of the following table, table A.3, followed up by the twentieth-century table 4.4 for chapter 4, is to analyze the emergence and shifting location of the entrepreneurial groups involved in industrial cocaine. If it is valuable for identifying these trends in the book, I nonetheless make no claim of precision here, because ownership was often unstable, sources are scattered, and until workshops came to be officially licensed in the late 1920s, Peru had nothing approaching a national census of cocaine workshops.

TABLE A.3 Reported Cocaine Factories by Region, Peru, 1885–1920s

Years	Coast (Lima-Callao)	East Central (Huánuco/Monzón)	Amazonia (Pozuzo)	North (Trujillo/Otuzco Cajamarca)	South (Cuzco, Huanta, Ayacucho)	Total (Peru)
1885–89	A. Bignon, J. Meyer, Hafemann, C. M. Schröder		A. Kitz			4–5
Early 1890s	Meyer, B. Prüss	Kitz and Cia, J. Plejo, S. Nesanovich	Kitz			6–8
Late 1890s	Kitz and Cia, Pehovaz Frs., Prüss, Velázquez	Plejo, Nesanovich, Montero/Fisci, J. Más	Kitz and Cia	J. A. Delfín, G. Risco	"Machinte," Santa Ana	10–12
Early 1900s	3 2 Lima, 1 Callao	11 Kitz and Cia, Nesanovich, Plejo, M. Marinovich, Montero Bros., Más, J. Languasco, 3 Monzón	1 Kitz and Cia	3 2 Trujillo, 1 Cajatambo	4 2 Cuzco, 2 Huanta	21 (Garland)
1914	0	A. Durand, R. Marinovich, E. Marinovich, Montero Bros., Nesanovich, Plejo	0	T. Vergel, J. Pinillos/Ayllon	0	30 (Vivian)
Early 1920s	0	A. A. Soberón, Neg. A. Durand, J. Boyanovich, Plejo, Montero Bros., J. Ibérico, G. Minoja, Milosovich, J. Beráun	0	Pinillos, Vergel	0	11

Sources: Late 1880s: Lima medical journals (e.g., *MM*, 1885–89) and overseas drug journals (*CD*, May 1886, Aug. 1889, Dec. 1890; *AD*, Jan. 1886, July 1889, and others).

1890s: NA, RG59, M155, Callao, vol. 13, April 1891; *CD*, May 1897; *AD*, March 1897; Clavero, *Tesoro* (1896), 47; Renoz, *Pérou* (1897), 66–7; "Cocaine," *BAR*, 1897, 545; ARH, Prot. (various); BNP, MR, MP, Huánuco.

Early 1900s: ARH, Municipalidad, "Impuesto de la coca," 1902, and Prot.; *CD*, Oct. 1904; Garland, *Reseña industrial*, 1902 ed., 31, and 1905 ed., 43; Garland, *Perú en 1906*, 213; Cisneros, *Frutos de paz* (1908), 19, 243.

1914–1920s: ARH, Prot.; ANP, H-6-1074, Matrícula de Huánuco, 1918; Vivian, *Peru and Development* (1914) 173; Walger, "Coca Distribution" (1914/17), 131–37; *Guía comercial* (1921), 451.

Note: Name spellings can differ. Contemporary estimates of numbers and listed names do not necessarily match.

This chapter on cocaine's commodity chains presents most of the global trends in cocaine and coca exports and production over the long term. For the reasons discussed above, I try not to depend wholly on Musto's official source aggregations, which conflate distinctive trades.

TABLE 3.1. Merck Cocaine Production and Imports of Coca and Crude Cocaine, 1879–1918

Source: Friman, "Germany and Cocaine," tables 4.1–4.2 (from Merck Darmstadt papers). A few of these figures were amended on advice from researcher Jyri Soininen (e-com., Helinski, Sept. 2007). Merck crude cocaine was made from Java leaf but not produced in Java.

TABLE 3.2. Bolivian Coca Production and Exports, 1900–1942

Sources: Musto, "International Traffic in Coca," table 7 (exports); Soux, *Coca liberal*, table 29 (corrections and interpolations of Musto exports); Canelas Orellana and Canelas Zanner, *Bolivia*, 105, production, 1925–36. Note that twentieth-century Bolivian "exports" are largely regional flows to north Argentina (up to 90 percent), Chile, or southern Peru, not overseas sales.

TABLE 3.3. U.S. Coca Imports and Cocaine, 1882–1931

Source: This table was compiled from two bar graphs prepared by Spillane for *Cocaine*: figure 3.5 (61) and figure 3.8 (64). Spillane's graphs derive from intensive research on imports lists in New York's ODR extrapolated to national statistics, and they are consistent with other sources. The aggregate cocaine figures—a good proxy for U.S. consumption—combine drug imports and U.S. production from leaf, but they may overstate totals, as they include leaf going into beverages at a time of growing use in Coca-Cola and other coca products.

FIGURE 3.1. The Rise and Fall of Java Coca Leaf, 1904–1940

Source: Adapted from de Kort, "Doctors, Diplomats, and Businessmen," figure 6.1. De Kort's striking graph was based on archival work in annual reports of the Dutch colonial Association of Coca Producers, primary research that appears in his 1995 Erasmus University dissertation. I prefer it to the slightly different Java export figures in Musto ("International Traffic in Coca," table 5), though Dutch reporting on Java was better than most official sources.

TABLE 3.4. Japanese Cocaine Imports, Cocaine Production, and Colonial Coca, 1910–1939
Sources: Friman, *Narco-Diplomacy*, tables 3 and 4 (42, 43; converted from pounds); Musto, "International Traffic in Coca," table 8.

TABLE 3.5. Peruvian Exports of Coca and Crude Cocaine, 1877–1933
Source: Musto, "International Traffic in Coca," from table 6, minus his "cocaine equivalents."

FIGURE 3.2. Peruvian Coca Regions and Coca Uses, ca. 1940
Source: Scanned from Pilli, "Coca Industry," 8. Pilli's study is a unique research monograph commissioned by New Jersey Merck during World War II.

CHAPTER 4

FIGURE 4.1. The Decline of Peruvian Coca and Cocaine, 1904–1933
Source: Reprinted from Paz Soldán, *Coca peruana*, 9, 11. The numbers in this chart look crude, but they illustrate a dramatic trend from a Peruvian perspective.

TABLE 4.1. Peruvian Cocaine and Coca Exports, 1910–1950
Sources: Cross-checked from Bües, "La coca en el Perú," 54–56 (1910–23); Hohagen, *Sumario sobre exportaciones*, "Coca" and "Cocaína," 77–85 (1918–26); Friman, *Narco-Diplomacy*, table 1, 1925–31 (Germany); ARH, lgs., 1932–38; *VA*, March 1936 (1924–35); *Perú en marcha*, table 18 (1926–42); Pilli, "Coca Industry," 7, 18–19 (1925–42); *Anuario Estadística del Perú* (Lima, 1950) (1933–50); FBN, *TODD*, 1961, table 11 (U.S. coca, 1925–50); UN, E/CN.7/242, 1952 (1946–50); LN, PCOB, E/OB/L (1937–46, 1946–48). Romano, "Coca buena," table 2, 301, provides some interpolations (1943–45). These export reports are more consistent than the pre-1910 series but still suffer from a few gaps, errors, and omissions. Major remaining discrepancies are (for cocaine, 1930s) between official Peruvian statistics (e.g., *Perú en marcha*) and PCOB reports and ARH lgs.; and (for coca exports to United States, 1920s–30s), between Pilli and *TODD*, 1961.

Table A.4 below is the chronological continuation and analytical complement of table A.3 for chapter 2. Some of these factories were ephemeral, part-time, or had revolving owners, but the data are probably more precise than those for the earlier chart.

TABLE A.4 Active Cocaine Factories in Peru, 1920–1950

Years	Lima	Huánuco	Monzón	Trujillo
Early 1920s		Soberón, Neg. A. Durand, Boyanovich, Plejo, Montero Bros.		Pinillos, Vergel, Chan Fan, G. Risco
1928–32		Neg. A. Durand, Neg. Japonesa ("Saito"), Soberón, Montero Bros., J. Ibérico, G. Minoja, Milosovich, Beráun	F. Rada ("Monzón")	Pinillos, Vergel "Manufacturers," Ayllon Bros. ("Sacamanca")
Mid-1930s		Soberón ("Huánuco"), A. Durand ("Éxito"), M. Sawada ("Pampayacu")	Rada	
1936		8 Soberón, Durand, Sara Lafosse, F. Gallardo, C. Baroli, E. Martín, Sawada, A. Orfanides, J. Roncagliolo ("Bolívar")		
1938	J. Barranchea ("Cóndor")	Soberón, Durand, Faroli, Martín, Pampayacu, E. Sara, A. Ramírez, Sawada	F. Rada (?)	Vergel, M. Ayllon ("Sacamanca"), G. Prados (?)
1940–43	M. Revilla ("Cóndor")	17 workers (1940 census): Chan Waiy ("Inca"), Soberón ("Huánuco"), Neg. Durand ("Éxito"), V. Funegra (?), Revilla ("La Victoria")	Rada, Pretel Vidal ("Monzón")	Pinillos, Vergel, Prados
1946–47		Soberón, Waiy, Durand ("Éxito"), Funegra ("Bolívar")		
1949		Soberón, Roncagliolo		
1950		"Japonesa," Baroli, Soberón		

Sources: Early 1920s: Guía comercial (1921), 451; ARH, Prot. (various).

1928: GL (1928), 309, 491; NA, RG170, Box 18, World Narcotics Factories, Nov. 1928 (orig. BSP, Feb. 1928, "Productores de la Cocaína," 158).

Early 1930s: GL (1932), 388, 463; NA, RG59, DF823.144. Aug. 1932 (Rubín report).

Mid-late 1930s: GL (1938), 455; ARH, lgs. (cocaine gías); BSP, June 1935 (Ávalos report); LN report, Oct. 1936, in NA, RG170, Box 18.

Early 1940s: GL (1942), 43; Pilli, "Coca Industry," 39–40; NA, RG59, DF823.144, "Cocaine Stocks," Dec. 1941; ANP, H-6-406, Censo Nacional de Población, 1940, vol. 1, table 83.

Postwar 1940s: ARH, lgs. (various); GL (1949), 291, 375 (also 1951).

Note: Spelling of names can differ. Factory names are in quotation marks.

After 1922, records of FBN-regulated coca imports into the United States became a reliable, standardized statistical source. ("Special Imports," a category largely discontinued after 1948, refers to leaf used for Coca-Cola's Merchandise No. 5 flavoring.) Most American coca came from Peru, specifically Trujillo, save for Merck's Javan plantation leaf of the 1920s and 1930s. A harder question to clarify is what proportion of leaf imports *before* 1920 had gone into coca products versus cocaine.

TABLE 5.1. U.S. Coca: Medicinal and Special Imports, 1925–1959
Source: FBN, TODD, 1961 report, adapted from cumulative table 11.

FIGURE 5.1. League of Nations World Cocaine Accounts, Mid-1930s
Source: LN, PCOB, C.24.M.24.1944.XI, "Pre-War Production of Drugs and Their Raw Materials" (1944), diagram 6 (1934–37). This chart illustrates the fictive nature of League of Nations cocaine accounts that lacked Andean and other types of data.

CHAPTER 6

After 1945, the book traces the spread of illicit cocaine, despite daunting source problems, which I tried to quantify crudely in table A.5 below. An array of primary materials do exist, including international policing reports of the U.S. Federal Bureau of Narcotics and BNDD, forerunners of the DEA, and related United Nations or Interpol drug control agencies. Apart from speculation here, seizures provide a partial, scattered, and inconsistent glimpse at smuggling, with the lingering question of how much they correspond to the real underground flow of drugs. (Today's far larger, more experienced DEA claims to interdict about 25–30 percent of drugs entering the United States.) These early documents, and their biased lens of drug control, are intrinsically guesswork and sometimes exaggerated, based on confessions of suspects, luck, and opportunistic informers. Timing is problematic, because without systematic intelligence (via embedded informers), police reports lagged behind the actual emergence of illicit activities and networks, likely by a few years. This type of evidence, combined with dense qualitative reports, does give a feel for the rising curve of illicit cocaine but cannot be read literally.

TABLE A.5 Cocaine Smuggling: Reported Seizures, 1935–1970s

Year	FBN/BNDD	U.S. Borders	U.S. Total	Interpol (global)	Seizures	Arrests
1935	582g/1.9kg	2.2kg/78oz			150–170 yr	
1936	196g/252g	277g/2oz	725g			
1937						
1938	306g	111g	417g			
1939	58g	50g	108g			
1940	115g	7.484kg-Ja	7.683kg			
1941			425g			
1942			121g			
1943			236g			
1944	2oz		56g			
1945			702g			
1946			1.25kg			
1947			36oz (?)			
1948			5.95kg			
1949	8.16kg (?)		13.63kg			57
1950			1.56kg			80-Pe
1951			2.12kg			110-Pe
1952			1.32kg			
1953	10oz	3oz	13oz			
1954	29oz		814g/42oz	3.8kg	9	
1955			5.62kg-2.7lbs	10.2kg-Pe 3.7kg	8	25
1956			284g/10oz	250g	2	7
1957		680g-Ec	822g	2kg + 7kg, Pe	4	10
1958	570g	1.77kg-Mx	2.34kg	12kg-Cu 2.3kg	7	27
1959	2.09kg	3.9kg-Ch, Ec	6.70kg	15.98kg	15	72
1960	2.66kg/6 lbs[a]	1.63kg-Bl, Cu	2.68kg	3.4kg/4kg	6	18
1961	4lbs	Bl, Pe, Pn	4.62kg	12.3kg/10kg	24	76
1962	19lbs/8.8kg	Bl, Cu, Pe	10.64kg	2.9kg+	20	67
1963	15lbs/6.9kg	Mx, Bl, Ar	8.3kg	10.7kg+	20	70
1964	18lbs	Bl, Ch, Ec	23.56kg			
1965	18lbs	Mx, Pe		17.4kg		
1966	19lbs/8.72kg	2.5kg-Ch, Pe	11.25kg	30.6kg-41.9kg		
1967	28lbs/12kg	8.5kg-Pe, Bl, Ch	20.54k	15.5-20.5kg[b]		
1968	63lbs					
1969	57lbs					
1970	364lbs	376kg Ch	731lbs (?)		137[d] (border)	
1971	436lbs	165.6lbs	280kg/601kg	782lbs[c]	239[d] (border)	
1972	295lbs[c]	203kg+ Ch, Pe		1,082lbs	1,231[d]	
Late 1970s			19 tons			

Sources: FBN, TODD, annual reports, including seizures, 1928–67; Interpol, usually UN, CND, E/CN.7/236–447, "Illicit Traffic" and "Clandestine Laboratories" reports, or as "International Criminal Police Organization," 1951–64. See notes below for specific sources.

Note: g=grams, oz=ounces, lbs=pounds, kg=kilograms; Bl=Bolivia, Ch=Chile, Cu=Cuba, Ec=Ecuador, Ja=Japan, Mx=Mexico, Pe=Peru, Pn=Panama.

[a] BNDD, "Domestic Seizures of Cocaine," 1972, tables 1–2, unpublished document from the DEA Library (VF, "Cocaine").

[b] "Cocaine Project," BNDD, 1968; NA, RG170, Box 54, Inter-American Conferences, Dec. 1968, unpublished document from the DEA Library (VF, "Cocaine").

[c] BNDD, Bulletin, Annual Report, 1973.

[d] Report of Federal Cocaine Policy Task Force, July 1974, pt. 3, Seizure and Arrest Statistics, unpublished document from the DEA Library (VF, "Cocaine").

NOTES

CD	*Chemist and Druggist*, London	
CM	*La Crónica Médica*, Lima	
DEA	Drug Enforcement Administration Library and Information Center, Arlington, Va.	
	VF	Vertical Files (subjects)
Dept.	Department	
EC	*El Comercio* (Lima)	
e-com.	electronic communication	
EH	*El Huallaga* (Huánuco)	
EP	*El Peruano* (Lima)	
exp.	*expediente*	
FBN	Federal Bureau of Narcotics (or BNDD, 1960s)	
	TODD	U.S. Treasury Department, *Traffic in Opium and Other Dangerous Drugs*, annual reports
GL	*Guía Lascano del Perú*	
GML	*Gaceta Médica de Lima*	
INPL	Interpol	
lg.	*legado*	
LN	League of Nations	
	OAC	Advisory Committee on Traffic in Opium and Other Dangerous Drugs (Opium Advisory Committee)
	PCOB	Permanent Central Opium Board
MEC	*Memoria del Estanco de la Coca* (ENACO), in Peru, Caja de Depósitos y Consignaciones	
MHP	*Memorias de Ministerio de Hacienda del Perú* (title varies)	
MM	*El Monitor Médico*, Lima	
MP	Memorias de Prefecturas (prefect reports)	
ms.	*manuscrito*	
NA	U.S. National Archives	
	RG43, IC	Records of International Conferences, Commissions, and Expositions
	RG59, DF	Department of State, Decimal Files
		B/N Bolivia/Narcotics (subject heading)
		P/N Peru/Narcotics (subject heading)
	RG59, LOT	Department of State, LOT Files (Office Subject Files)
	RG59, M155	Department of State, Despatches from U.S. Consuls in Callao
	RG59, SN	Department of State, Subject-Numeric Files

D/B   Drugs, Beverages

NMJ   *New York Medical Journal*

NYT   *New York Times*

ODR   *Oil, Paint, and Drug Reporter*, New York

oral-com.   oral communication

Pref.   Prefecturas

PRO, FO   Public Record Office, Records of the Foreign Office, London

Prot.   Protocoles

RA   *La Riqueza Agrícola*, Lima

RG   record group

RM   *La Reforma Médica*, Lima

TG   *Therapeutic Gazette*, Detroit

UN   United Nations

  CND   Commission on Narcotic Drugs

  ECSOC   Economic and Social Council

VA   *La Vida Agrícola*, Lima

INTRODUCTION

1. Gootenberg, "Case of Scientific Excellence."

2. On Balarezo, see Gootenberg, "Pre-Colombian Drug Trafficking."

3. Goodman, Lovejoy, and Sherratt, *Consuming Habits*; Schivelbusch, *Tastes of Paradise*; Courtwright, *Forces of Habit*; or Jankowiak and Bradburd, *Drugs and Colonial Expansion*. For trends, see Gootenberg, "Scholars on Drugs."

4. Anthropologist Sidney Mintz's term: *Sweetness and Power*, 99. Robbins, "Commodity Histories," for critical genre review.

5. LaBarre, "Old and New World Narcotics," or Schultes and Hoffman, *Plants of the Gods*. For a few of many such monographs on "drug" commodities, see Coe and Coe, *True History of Chocolate*; Goodman, *Tobacco in History*; Pendergrast, *History of Coffee*; and Valenzuela-Zapata and Nabhan, *Tequila!*

6. On the perils of estimating the global cocaine economy, see Reuter, "Political Economy of Drug Smuggling": some $38 billion (66 percent) of some $57.3 billion of U.S. (domestic) illegal drug expenditures are still for pricey cocaine (table 7.1). "Guestimates" of the value of the world drug trade run as high $400 billion, or 8 percent of all international trade (UNDCP, *World Drug Report*, ch. 4); Thoumi, *Illegal Drugs in Andes*. On coffee's culture, see Roseberry, "Rise of Yuppie Coffee."

7. For background, see Walker, *Drug Control in Americas*, or his compilation, *Drugs in Western Hemisphere*. Mexico attracts most new works on drugs: Astorga, *Mitología del narcotraficante* or *Siglo de las drogas*; Pérez Montfort, *Yerba, goma y polvo*, and a special drugs edition of *Revista de UNAM* (Dec. 2003) edited by Pérez Montfort.

8. Robertson, "Glocalization." For hemispheric transnationalism, see Joseph, LeGrande, and Salvatorre, *Close Encounters of Empire*, or Kaplan and Pease, *Cultures of United States Imperialism*. On drug globalism, see Stares, *Global Habit*; McAllister, *Drug Diplomacy*; Gootenberg, *Global Histories*; Courtwright, *Forces of Habit*; Davenport-Hines, *Pursuit of Oblivion*; or encyclopedic surveys such as Escohotado's *Historia de las drogas*.

9. For historical cocaine commodity chains, see Gootenberg, "Cocaine in Chains," and, in general, Topik, Marichal, and Frank, *From Silver to Cocaine*. Contemporary cocaine has gained much of this analysis: Vellinga, *Political Economy of Drug Industry*, or Bellone, "Cocaine Commodity Chain." Other relevant commodity studies include Bauer, *Goods, Power, History*; Douglas and Isherwood, *World of Goods*; Ortiz, *Cuban Counterpoint*; Mintz, *Tasting Food, Tasting Freedom*; and Topik and Pomeranz, *World that Trade Created*, ch. 3.

10. Appadurai, *Social Life of Things*, 27, and Kopytoff's "Cultural Biography of Things" in the same volume; on cultural commodities, see Appadurai, *Modernity at Large*, or Brewer and Trentmann, *Consuming Cultures, Global Perspectives*. A pioneer look at illicit goods is van Schendel and Abraham, *Illicit Flows and Criminal Things*.

11. Drug studies classics are Zinberg, *Drug, Set, and Setting*, and Weil, *Natural Mind*, influenced by sociologist Howard S. Becker's 1950s–60s research. Constructivism is now the mainstay of "drug studies," e.g., Edwards, *Matters of Substance*, or DeGrandpre's *Cult of Pharmacology*, on "pharmacologicalism" (biochemical reductionism) in shifting definitions of "demon" and "angel" drugs. Recent "poststructuralist" drug studies stretch these ideas, e.g., Lenson, *On Drugs*, or Ronell, *Crack Wars*. On excesses of constructivism, see Hacking, *Social Construction of What*; for skepticism around drugs, see Courtwright, "Mr. ATOD's Wild Ride."

12. On distinguishing coca and cocaine, see Mayer, "Uso social de la coca," or Weil, "Politics of Coca." On coca history and anthropology, see Gagliano, *Coca Prohibition*, or Boldó i Climent, *Coca andina*.

13. This bias is partly offset with other sources, including a few feasible cocaine oral histories. On such source challenges generally, see Cobb, *Police and People*, or Ginzburg, "Inquisitor as Anthropologist." On drug discourses, see Kohn, *Narcomania*, or Gootenberg, "Talking Like a State"; on drugs as inquisition, see Szasz, *Ceremonial Chemistry*.

CHAPTER ONE

1. Marx, "The Fetishism of Commodities and the Secret Thereof," in *Capital* (orig. 1887), 1:71–93; anthropologized by Kopytoff, "Cultural Biography of Things." For Andes, see Taussig's *Devil and Commodity Fetishism*.

2. In Bolivia, the term for "chewer" is *acullicador*. Coca overviews include Pacini and Franquemont, *Coca and Cocaine*; Carter, *Ensayos sobre la coca*; Instituto Indigenista Interamericano, *La coca*; and Boldó i Climent, *Coca andina*.

3. DeGrandpre, *Cult of Pharmacology*, ch. 1, for new pharmacological insight and the social implications of the cocaine-Ritalin equivalence.

4. On cocaine generally, consult Grinspoon and Bakalar, *Cocaine*; for its use, see

Waldorf, Reinarman, and Murphy, *Cocaine Changes*; on gauging the illicit economy, see Reuter, "Political Economy of Drug Smuggling."

5. Weil, "Politics of Coca"; Mayer, "Uso social de la coca," 124. There are epistemological (knowledge) differences as well: cocaine is the domain of chemists, medical professionals, criminologists, the police, or political economists, whereas the study of coca mainly belongs to anthropologists. Note the absence of historians from both fields. "Traditional" use can be a misleading term, as these uses are also historically created and include migrant worker streams of coca as well as some middle-class adoption. In Bolivia, such use today has generalized to, e.g., lowland truck drivers, and indeed ethnically specific terms like *coquero* are rarely deployed. See the case in Rivera's "Here Even Legislators Chew Them." In Ecuador, coca abated in the colonial era, and in Colombia (despite spiraling illicit coca cultivation from the 1990s) chewing is historically delimited to small indigenous groups such as the Paez.

6. Courtwright, *Forces of Habit*; Schivelbusch, *Tastes of Paradise*; or Goodman, "Excitantia." Coe and Coe, *True History of Chocolate*; Mintz, *Sweetness and Power*; and Goodman, *Tobacco in History* (medical filters), or Foster and Cordell, *Chiles to Chocolate*.

7. Goodman, *Tobacco in History*, 49–51, for analysis of coca vs. tobacco; Courtwright, *Forces of Habit*, ch. 3, for regional drugs. Both discussions are valuable (i.e., regarding the contaminating effects of coca's association with the Incas) but not fully convincing. To wit, tobacco smoking was also at first a repulsive use form to Europeans and rife with alien shamanism, as was cacao. See Gagliano, *Coca Prohibition*, chs. 3–4, for Peru debates.

8. Kennedy, *Coca Exotica*, ch. 6, for a genealogy.

9. Ibid., ch. 7, and Gagliano, *Coca Prohibition*, ch. 5, are surveys; a feel for this contentious era is found in Mortimer, *History of Coca*, ch. 10.

10. Kennedy, *Coca Exotica*, ch. 7, a suggestive narrative; Byck, *Cocaine Papers*, for Germanic texts and contexts; or Friman, "Germany and Cocaine." Scherzer, *Voyage on the Novara*, 3:402–9. Gaedke date is uncertain: it might be 1855, 1857, or 1858.

11. Kennedy, *Coca Exotica*, ch. 8. On Freud and cocaine, a rich bibliography holds three divergent views. Besides Bernfield's 1953 foray (in Byck, *Cocaine Papers*, ch. 22), Byck's *Cocaine Papers*, in the cocaine culture of the 1970s, revived Freud as the father of modern "psychopharmacology." Jones's official biography, *Life of Freud*, ch. 6, "The Cocaine Episode (1884–1887)," dismisses it as digressive minor episode in Freud's career. Cf. Thorton, *Freudian Fallacy*, which uses Fliess letters to show Freud's longer-term interest in cocaine (and personal drug issues). As a polemic, Thorton regards the theory of psychoanalysis as a product of Freud's drug-induced sexual delirium.

12. Kennedy, *Coca Exotica*, 69–72. Pernick, *Calculus of Suffering*, for genealogy of pain management; like Beard's age of neurasthenia, Charles Peirce (the great American philosopher) dubbed his age "the century of pain" (104).

13. Mariani, *Coca and Its Applications*; Kennedy, *Coca Exotica*, ch. 10 (quote, 63); Eyguesier, *Freud devint drogman*; Helfand, "Vin Mariani"; Madge, *White Mischief*, ch. 4.

14. My interpretation. Vin Mariani and its cultural and commodity circuits are in dire need of serious research.

15. Martindale, *Cocaine and Its Salts*. Tibbles, *Erythroxylon Coca*: a masterpiece of the "brain exhaustion" genre, Tibbles was Britain's unsung Mariani or Beard. M. Morris, "Coca," *BMI* 25 (1889); Kennedy, *Coca Exotica*, 55–56, 59–60.

16. Musto, *American Disease*; DeGrandpre, *Cult of Pharmacology*. Starr, *Transformation of American Medicine*, ch. 2; Griggs, *Green Pharmacy*; and Rorabaugh, *Alcoholic Republic*.

17. Lutz, *American Nervousness*; Giswijt-Hofstra and Porter, *Cultures of Neurasthenia*, for European variants. Beard's 1881 *American Nervousness* did not itself extol coca.

18. Searle, *New Form of Nervous Disease*; Dupré report, *AD* 9 (1887); H. H. Rusby, "Coca at Home and Abroad," *TG* 12 (Mar.–May 1888): 158–65, 303–7; Lloyd Brothers, *Treatise on Coca*. Gagliano, *Coca Prohibition*, 108–9.

19. Mariani, *Coca and Its Applications*, 10 (quote); Spillane, *Cocaine*, 8–12.

20. Pendergrast, *God and Coca-Cola*, ch. 2, sketches this coca culture.

21. Mortimer, *History of Coca*, a trove of coca data and opinion. I tried to research Mortimer and his audience but found only elegant New York addresses and evidence of his fame as an amateur magician.

22. Spillane, *Cocaine*, chs. 1–2, fine revisionism of muckrakers, then and now, who read cocaine's spread as a lapse of medical judgment.

23. "The Indiscriminate Use of Cocaine," New York Academy of Medicine symposium, in *NMJ*, 26 Nov. 1889.

24. See chapter 2 for colonization schemes. U.S. Navy, "Report on Coca or Cuca," *Sanitary and Medical Reports* (Washington, D.C., 1875), 675–76; Consul-Gen. Gibbs, "The Coca Plant," *Leonard's Illustrated Medical Journal*, Apr. 1886; for long view of the U.S.-Peru relation, see Gootenberg, "Between Coca and Cocaine."

25. My treatment of Bignon-Freud is Gootenberg, "Case of Scientific Excellence." Cueto, *Excelencia científica*. For a fanciful reading of Freud's tie to Peru, try Marez, *Drug Wars*, ch. 6.

26. On centrality of cultural nationalism, see Anderson, *Imagined Communities*, chs. 2, 5, 9–11, and Hobsbawm and Ranger, *Invention of Tradition*. Fischer, "Culturas de coca," compares coca histories. Traces of a coca nationalism appear ahead, in Fuentes, *Memoire sur le coca*, and in the Paz Soldán anticoca *indigenismo* of the 1920s (chapter 4). The depth of elite nationalism in Peru has long been at issue: for recent interpretations, see Thurner, *Two Republics to One Divided*, or Gootenberg, *Between Silver and Guano*.

27. Bauer, *Goods, Power, History*, ch. 5. For era's technology nationalism, see Gootenberg, *Imagining Development*, 103–11. Commodity writers like Lissón are related below.

28. For split nationalism, see Thurner, "Peruvian Genealogies of History." For transnational modernists, see Poole, *Vision, Race, and Modernity*; López-Ocon, "El nacionalismo y la Sociedad Geográfica"; or analysis of scientific nationalism in Lomnitz, "Nationalism's Dirty Linen."

29. Gagliano, *Coca Prohibition*, 82–83, 102; Kennedy, *Coca Exotica*, 53; Cueto, *Excelencia científica*, 39–42; Unánue, "Disertación sobre la coca," *Museo Erudito*

(Cuzco), 3/1–7 (15 Apr.–15 June 1837). During the 1940s, anticoca scientists (e.g., Marroquín) revisited the lime thesis.

30. "La coca peruana," *GML* 3/51 (31 Oct. 1858): 60; also see A. Raimondi, "Elementos de botánica aplicada a la medicina y a la industria," *GML* 13/264 (15 Jan. 1868): 125.

31. Kennedy, *Coca Exotica*, 61–62; Byck, *Cocaine Papers*, 55, 69, Freud (he also cites Unánue). "Revista médica de Paris — T. Moreno y Maíz," *GML* 6/129 (31 Jan. 1862); esp. "De la coca," 6/141 (31 July 1862); Juan Copello, "Clamor coca," 7/2 (31 Aug. 1862).

32. Dr. Tomás Moreno y Maíz, "Sobre el 'Erythroxylum Coca' del Perú, y sobre la 'Cocaína,'" Investigaciones químico-fisiológicas, *GML*, 2nd ser., 2/8 (18, 26 Feb. 1876): 58–142. Moreno y Maíz, *Recherches chimques et physiologiques* (1868). Moreno y Maíz is the most slighted by history: a top military surgeon, he barely makes Lastres's authoritative survey, *Historia de medicina*, vol. 3.

33. Fuentes, *Memoire sur le coca*, 7. Fuentes, a key figure in Lima society, knew and admired coca but was said to have had a run-in with Moreno y Maíz. The playful title of his 1877 *Hojas de coca* collection reveals his fascination: "Aqui entra una explicación: La coca merece todos los elogios que han predigado, desde el tiempo de los Incas (nuestros antesesores) y mucho más" (1:31). Von Tschudi, *Travels in Peru*, 450. On Raimondi, see Bonfiglio, *Antonio Raimondi*; on French influences, see Cueto, *Excelencia científica*, 45–46.

34. José A. de los Rios, "La coca peruana," *GML* 12/256 (15 Sept. 1867): 26–28 (2nd half lost?). Obit. in *CM* 17/278 (31 July 1900); Raimondi, "Elementos de botánica," 125. Farmacología, Eduardo Nuñez del Prado, "Estudio sobre la coca," *GML* 1/29–35 (30 Oct.–11 Dec. 1875). Nuñez was later credited with study of coca as antidote to mercury poisoning: "Informe sobre la coca," *CM* 6/6 (1889): 29.

35. "Comisión nombrada para estudiar el procedimiento del Sr. A. Bignon," *MM* 1/2 (15 June 1885); "Informe sobre la coca," *CM* 6/6 (1889). Monsalve, "Civilized Society and the Public Sphere," ch. 7, on racial and disciplinary roles of medical societies. "Free" academies arose against President Iglesia's war intervention of San Marcos University.

36. Cueto, *Excelencia científica*; or classic survey, Bambarén, "La medicina en la República." Bignon is unknown: he merits two brief cites in Gagliano, *Coca Prohibition* (114, 117), and none in Cueto's post-1890 analysis of Peruvian science, yet two hagiographic essays in a flash of World War II chemical nationalism: Tejeda B., "Talento olvidado," and Vallejos S., "Estudios sobre coca."

37. Biographical details, not all accurate, in Tejeda B., "Talento olvidado"; Lastres, *Historia de medicina*, 3:175–76 (quote). I located two uninformative Bignon wills in Lima. AGN, Testimonios (M. Iparraguirre), A. Bignon, 8 June 1889 (112.v), 25 June 1895 (126.v).

38. "Informe de la comisión nombrada para estudiar el procedimiento del Sr. Bignon para extraer la cocaína," *BAM*, 13 Mar. 1885 sess., 77–86 (rare copy in U.S. National Library of Medicine), and notes, 12 Jan. 1885; *CM* 2/18 (June 1885); preface, "La cocaína," by chemist Andrés Muñoz, whose thesis was on caffeine, *MM* 1/2 (15 June 1885); Bignon, "Nuevo método para la extracción de algunos de los alcaloídes," *MM* 1/4 (Oct. 1885): 191–93.

39. Sr. A. Bignon, Comunicación, "Acción fisiológica de la cocaína," *MM* 2/8 (15 Sept. 1886): 117–20; Trabajos Nacionales, "Acción fisiológica de la cocaína" and "Cocaína y sus sales," *MM* 11/8 (Dec. 1886): 231; Terapéutica, "Propiedades de la coca y la cocaína," *MM*, Feb. 1886, 245–46. Most had versions in *BAM* (with discrepant dates), i.e., "Acción fisiológica," 4 May 1886 sess., 319–39, at twenty pages, then "Comunicación: Sobre la acción fisológica," 15 June 1886. "Comunicaciones: Posología de la cocaína," *BAM*, 1 Apr. 1886, 306–11.

40. Unlike Freud, who reveled in cocaine's energizing effects, Bignon never broached such details.

41. Bignon, "Sobre el valor comparativo de las cocaínas," *BAM*, 4 Sept. 1886, 37–39.

42. Coca extracts, ads, patents of Velázquez (a leading pharmacy professor), *BAM*, 24 Feb. 1887; Bignon, Trabajos Nacionales, "Estudio experimental del antagonismo de la estricnina y de la cocaína," *MM* 11/14 (15 Dec. 1886; orig. Sept. 1886).

43. Bignon, Comunicación, "Sobre la utilidad de la cocaína en cólera," *BAM*, Jan. 1887, 128–32.

44. For other original works, see Espinosa, *Ensayo sobre koca*, a ninety-page 1875 Buenos Aires thesis found in the New York Academy of Medicine; for Mexico, Gómez y Couto, *La coca*, an 1876 thesis revealing of coca in the Latin American pharmacopoeia; or Gabriel Covarrubias, "Estudio sobre el muriato de cocaína," *Revista Médica de Chile* 15 (1886–87): 60–119, which discusses Bignon. Bignon's analogue of lost excellence on the periphery was Enrique Pizzi, the Italian pharmacist teaching in Bolivia rumored to have concocted cocaine in situ in 1857, before Gaedke's try and Niemann's isolation. For a recent Bolivian view of Pizzi, see Mendoza, "Verdadera historia de cocaína," and clues in "Cocaine in 1857," *CD*, 27 Mar. 1886, 226; Mortimer, *History of Coca*, 294.

45. A. Bignon, "Soluciones de cocaína," *BAM*, 6 Apr. 1887 sess., Feb. 1888, 198–99. S. Freud, "Craving for and Fear of Cocaine," July 1887, in Byck, *Cocaine Papers*, ch. 15; ch. 9, "Contribution to the Knowledge of the Effect of Cocaine," Jan. 1885, is Freud's scientific effort.

46. Bignon, "Pureza terapéutica de los medicamentos," *BAM*, 1 Apr. 1886, 311–13. For references to Bignon: Mortimer, *History of Coca*, 304, 311, 433; "Preparation of Cocaine," *AD*, Jan. 1886, 11; "Cocaine Factory in Lima," *AD*, 1888, 105; "Note on Cocaine," *AD*, Dec. 1886 (patents); Martindale, *Cocaine and Its Salts*, 53; Pozzi-Escot, "Recherches sur l'industrie de cocaïne." Overseas publications include: A. Bignon, "Note on the Properties of Coca and Cocaine," *Pharmaceutical Journal and Transactions* 16 (1885): 256–66; "Cocaine as a Dental Anaesthetic," *NMJ* 594 (1886); "Cocaine as an Antidote to Strychnine," *NMJ* 198 (Aug. 1887). Some of these originated in French, German, and Argentine publications.

47. San Marcos University, Escuela de Medicina, thesis catalogue (Showing now lost). For later example, see Lambruschini, *La cocaïne et ses dangers*, a 1936 Parisian medical thesis by a Huánuco native, ex-student of anticoca *huanuqueño* psychologist Hermilio Valdizán. For the 1920–50s scientific struggle between Gutiérrez-Noriega's pharmacology school, which saw coca as a degenerative poison addiction of natives, and the Andean biologists, see Gagliano, *Coca Prohibition*, ch. 7, or Cueto, *Excelencia científica*, ch. 5. There is recent research in Peru: e.g., Raúl Jeri, who

in fact began in the 1940s anticoca movement, produced 1970s work on cocaine addiction ("basuca") with global repercussions.

48. Sección Editorial, "La cocaína," *MM* 1/4: 99–100; see also *CM* 2/18: 61–66.

49. A. Butler, "La cocaína en las quemaduras," *CM* 2/16 (Apr. 9885): note the gender of cocaine (as in later *pichicata*, or "white lady"), though the noun is also feminine.

50. Bolivia in this interregnum exported some twenty-two thousand kilos annually; by 1897, Peru's coca exports averaged half a million kilos. Nystrom, *Informe sobre una expedición*; Maúrtua, *Porvenir del Perú*, table, 29; Martinet, *L'agriculture au Pérou*, 98–99; Peacock, *Resources of Peru*; Duffield, *Prospects of Peru*. Notations on coca were still mostly medical: "This product [coca] is perhaps one of the most useful to introduce among our armies, in our factories, and with our office workers (*gens de bureau*) and letters . . . for rest and stomachaches" (Carrey, *Le Pérou*, 96).

51. Esteves, *Apuntes para historia económica*, 78, 75; Gootenberg, *Imagining Development*, ch. 7 (Esteves and regional ideals); Thorp and Bertram, *Peru*, pt. 2, on Peru's new economy.

52. For a history of jungle fantasies, see Werlich, "Conquest of the Montaña," or García Jordán, *Cruz y arado*. Markham, *Travels in Peru*, 232–39, the figure who took "Peru bark" to Asian plantations; Herndon and Gibbon, *Exploration of Amazon*, 88, 130, 190.

53. Raimondi, *Apuntes sobre Loreto*, 59; Sobrevilla, "Creación de Pozuzo."

54. Albornoz, *Apuntes sobre regiones amazónicas*, 36–37.

55. Lissón, *Sociología del Perú*, 20 (quote), 63, 67; cf. Clavero, *Tesoro*, 46–47. For glorification of cocaine, see chapter 2.

56. Guillaume, *Amazon Provinces of Peru*, frontispiece, 35, 111–12. No Spanish version was published.

57. Ibid., 112.

58. "Informe sobre la coca," *CM* 6/6 (1889): 31 (report dated 31 Oct. 1888). The deeper mystery here is why Bignon himself was not a member of the commission and why his research was bypassed: personal conflicts? Bignon's anticoca stance? As a general retreat from national scientific initiatives, see chapter 2.

59. Asuntos Generales, "Informe sobre la coca," *Anales universitarios del Perú* 15–16 (24 July 1888): 256–57, in December forwarded to minister of education for dissemination.

60. "Informe sobre la coca," *CM* 6/6 (1889): 27.

61. Ibid., 28–29. This was a pat observation about dental health, but indigenous sugar use was low compared to that of coastal Peruvians. Espinoza was the Argentine researcher cited above; for Mantegazza, see Kennedy, *Coca Exotica*, 57.

62. Mortimer, *History of Coca*; Rusby, "Coca at Home and Abroad," *TG* 12 (1888); or Searle, *New Form of Nervous Disease*, for medicinal controversies.

63. Schivelbusch, *Tastes of Paradise*, or Mintz, *Sweetness and Power*, for capitalism's stimulants.

64. "Informe sobre la coca," *CM* 6/6 (1889): 31. Spillane, *Cocaine*, ch. 5, for what they missed, the heady growth of cocaine-laced popular products of the 1890s; Courtwright, *Forces of Habit*, on capitalism's "Psychoactive Revolution."

65. "Informe sobre la coca," *CM* 6/6 (1889): 30–31. Promotional coca literature

for crops and export came in the 1890s–1900s. Given early hopes, the cola industry might be judged as coca's historic success or, in longer readings, the illegal crack boom of the 1980s, which attracted mass consumers: e.g., Mintz, "Forefathers of Crack."

66. "Cocaine in Peru," *CD*, 29 May 1886.

CHAPTER TWO

1. Spillane, *Cocaine*, ch. 1, for cocaine as first "modern" drug, an idea traced globally in Gootenberg, *Global Histories*.

2. Motley sources indicate that in 1886 Bolivia sent 22,000 kilos of coca to Europe (one-fourth of coca imports), which halved to 10,800 in 1900 (one-tenth of European coca). In 1877, before the Pacific War, Peru exported only 7,955 kilos of coca (Walger, "Coca Distribution," 151), making the rest from Bolivia's *yungas*. For nascent coca culture, see Pendergrast, *God and Coca-Cola*, ch. 2; Kennedy, *Coca Exotica*, ch. 10; or Madge, *White Mischief*, ch. 4.

3. Friman, "Germany and Cocaine," 84–87, or his *Narco-Diplomacy*, ch. 2; context in Byck, *Cocaine Papers*, esp. Merck study; *Guide of German Industry*, 36–48. Spillane, *Cocaine*, table 3.3, 53, 86. German cocaine climaxed, with a hoarding of twenty tons, on the eve World War I; global consumption likely peaked earlier. Musto, "International Traffic in Coca," fig. 1, blurs timing with lumping of coca-cocaine circuits.

4. Spillane, *Cocaine*, ch. 3, "Making Cocaine," 68–73 (Parke, Davis), or his "Making a Modern Drug," and Spillane research in MacCoun and Reuter, *Drug War Heresies*, ch. 9.

5. Spillane, *Cocaine*, tables 3.6–3.7; peak is likely an overestimate including beverage coca.

6. Lloyd Brothers, *Treatise on Coca*. Like French coca culture, U.S. coca mania begs for cultural research. Spillane's *Cocaine* carefully distinguishes the two commodities; Pendergrast's *God and Coca-Cola*, ch. 2, sets context for the drink.

7. From study of New York *ODR*, 1880s. NA, RG170, Box 19, Coca Beverages, 1915–45, "Imitations of Coco-Cola," 18 May 1916, which lists 122 drug-tested competitors.

8. Musto, "International Traffic in Coca," for global standardization of 1880–1930s. See Appendix: Quantifying Cocaine for my evaluation. A critique of cocaine statistics, including unit confusions, is in the Soininen thesis "Geographies of Cocaine." On Peru's exports overall, see Hunt, "Price and Quantum Exports"; for economic history, Thorp and Bertram, *Peru*, chs. 3–4.

9. Calculated from *Memorias de Ministerio de Hacienda* (*MHP*, AGN H-4 versions), 1891, 1899, 1910, plus regional breakdowns for 1891, 1910, and 1897. Maúrtua, *Porvenir del Perú*, table "Valor de Exportaciones del Perú" (1877–1910); also in *BSG* 27 (1911). German statistics from Friman, "Germany and Cocaine," table 4.1; cf. Spillane, *Cocaine*, table 3.3.

10. Heroic attempts at such statistics in Thorp and Bertram, *Peru* (29, devaluation), and Boloña, *Políticas arancelarias*. New York's *ODR* (1884–) has monthly wholesale

11. *MM*, 1/1 (1885), 1/10–12 (Sept.–Dec. 1885). Some pharmacy ads boasted imported "Medicinas Extranjeras de las mejors fábricas" (e.g., including the ad for Chlorihidrato de Cocaína, Antigua Botica Inglesa-Italiano, Mar.–Sept. 1885), and others included ads for local elixirs of coca.

12. Correspondencia, *MM*, 1/10 (14 Oct. 1885): 193–94; cocaine ads in Lima journals, 1885–90.

13. "Informe: La cocaína y sus sales preparadas por Meyer y Hafemann," *BAM*, sess. 7, Dec. 1885, 265–68; also 30 July. "Cocaína y sus sales," *MM* 1/7 (15 Sept. 1885): 193–94. Clavero, *Tesoro*, 47 (German merchants).

14. E-com., Jyri Soininen (Helsinki, July 2006) on request queried leading cocaine chemists (i.e., John F. Casale, ex-DEA) to clarify confusions in police and other writings between crude cocaine, coca paste, and *pasta básica de cocaína*. They are, it turns out, chemically the same: sulfates exhibiting only differing degrees of moisture and oxidation. Gootenberg, "Case of Scientific Excellence," for Bignon as technical grandfather of global cocaine traffic.

15. "Cocaine in Peru," *CD*, 29 May 1886. Friman, "Germany and Cocaine," 84–87, table 4.1; Spillane, *Cocaine*, 53 (prices).

16. For syrup circuit, see Gootenberg, "Secret Ingredients"; on German agents, Friman, "Germany and Cocaine," 86–87, or Spillane, *Cocaine*, 50–54. Schaeffer papers (dated 1903) from Boehringer-Ingelheim Archives, supplied by T. Holzer.

17. "Crude Cocaine," *CD*, 31 Aug. 1889; cf. "Peru-Coca," *CD*, 27 Dec. 1890. Some reports refer to "Remy" method (to Pedro Remy of Lima's Cocaine Commission, not the Cuzco elixir) or to later conflations as the "Kitz"/"Bignon" method.

18. *CD*, 17 Mar. 1894, 389. Velázquez, "that clever Peruvian pharmacist" (Clavero, *Tesoro*, 47), was head of the Lima Pharmacists Society, penned authoritative pharmacy texts, and bragged about his fresh, superior "100% Peruvian" product; also, Cisneros, *Reseña económica*, 243.

19. Renoz, *Pérou*, 161; Garland, *Perú en 1906*, 143; Cisneros, *Reseña económica* (1906 ed.), directory, 129. Walger, "Coca Distribution," 140.

20. "La cocaína de Bignon," *MM* 1/5 (Aug. 1885): 100; Tejeda B., "Talento olvidado," 613 (dates off). For references to Bignon, see Mortimer, *History of Coca*, 304, 311, 433; "Preparation of Cocaine," *AD*, Jan. 1886, 11; "Cocaine Factory in Lima," *AD*, 1888, 105; "Note on Cocaine," *AD*, Dec. 1886 (patents); Martindale, *Cocaine and Its Salts*, 53; Pozzi-Escot, "Recherches sur l'industrie de cocaïne," 615–16; and Bignon's own translated publications abroad, cited in notes to chapter 1.

21. This section draws on close of Gootenberg, "Case of Scientific Excellence"; commodity chains examined in chapter 3 below. On French and German medical currents, see Parascandola, *American Pharmacology*, or, generally, Bynum, *Science and Medicine*.

22. Bignon, "Acción fisiológica de la cocaína," *MM* 2/8 (Sept. 1886): 120; E. R. Squibb, "Hydrochorate of Cocaine, or Muriate of Cocaine," *Pharmaceutical Journal and Transactions* 15 (Mar. 1885): 774–76; "The Preparation of Cocaine," *ODR*, 26 Nov. 1894.

23. Ads, *CM*, late 1880s–90s; *"Peru": Yearbook*, listing 53, ex-firm.

24. See Gootenberg, "Case of Scientific Excellence," for oblivion. Post-1930s scientists (e.g., Gutiérrez-Noriega) regarded Indian coca use as form of cocaine "toxicomanía," thus erasing the chemical, biological, or social distinctiveness of coca; they rarely cited Bignon. Earlier, Bignon still found local admirers, as in a 1918 San Marcos thesis of Vinelli, *Estudio de coca*, 26.

25. Mark Twain, "The Turning Point of My Life" (1910), in Strausbaugh and Blaise, *Drug User*, 148–50; Gibbs, "Coca Plant" (1886).

26. *BMI* 25 (Jan., Sept. 1889). Dissemination in Karch, *Mystery of Coca* (esp. Walger, "Coca Distribution"); Soininen, "Geographies of Cocaine," ch. 5, for colonization and Karch errors. For Colombia promotion, e.g., see "Sección científica: La coca," *El Empresario* (Tunja), 1 Oct. 1880 (document supplied by Malcolm Deas).

27. Rusby, *Jungle Memories*, chs. 1, 8. The title of his original field report, "Coca at Home and Abroad" (*TG*, 1888), refers to coca's medicinal powers: better in the Andes ("at home") then with stale leaves "abroad." Rusby also blamed U.S. tariffs (an "absurd system of taxation") for keeping imported coca extract out of needed use by the "poorer classes" (307). He later sought an extract business in Bolivian Larini liquor with his British explorer peer in London's drug firm Burroughs-Wellcome (ibid., 343). Rusby reappears in the FDA 1911 Coca-Cola trials, discussed below.

28. "Cultivation of the Coca Plant in the United States," *AD*, Jan. 1885, 15; "Cocaine Factory in Lima," *AD*, Nov. 1885, 109; "Coca Leaves and Cocaine" and "Cocaine," *AD*, June 1887, 107. Similar reports in *ODR*: "The Coca Plant in India," 14 Mar. 1888; "The Cultivation of Coca," 13 Feb. 1889; "The High Price of Coca Leaves," 14 Mar. 1892.

29. "Crude Cocaine," *CD*, 31 Aug. 1889.

30. Clements R. Markham, "Coca Cultivation," *CD*, 17 Mar. 1894, 389; includes "An Uncommercial Coca-Lecture," 387–88. See "Production and Use of Coca Leaves," *BII* 8 (1910): 388–92 for outcomes. For wider angle, see Brockway, *Science and Expansion*.

31. This analysis lacks two elements: first, the delayed post-1900 minor-power Dutch coca colonialism (dating to prior botanical interest), seen in chapter 4; second, the long U.S. preference for coca over crude cocaine (reinforced by tariffs), which led not to coca colonialism but to a typical U.S. informal sway in Andean coca zones. See "Coca Leaves," *AD*, 23 (Jan. 1891), or the series "Coca Culture," *AD*, 15 Jan. 1891.

32. For coca exporting of the south, see Bonilla, *Gran Bretaña y el Perú*, quote from Robilliard, Mollendo, 1887 (4:11); BNP, MR, D3993, *MP* (Huánuco, Freire, 19 July 1889), an. 1, "Cultivo de la coca."

33. Sobrevilla, "Creación de Pozuzo"; Chocano, *Desenvolvimiento comercial*, for geography, 98–103; P. D. G. Clark, "Informe sobre el territorio central del Perú a ...La Peruvian Corporation Ltd.," *EP*, May 1892, 52–54. I visited Pozuzo in 1998; a vestige of Kitz's factory remains (e-com., M. Lacuisse, June 2008).

34. Stiglich, *Informe de comisión explorador*.

35. Poeppig, *Pampanaco*; Scherzer, *Voyage on the Novara*, 3:409, italics in original; Sobrevilla, "Creación de Pozuzo," 117. Scherzer ran into "Germans" en route to Pozuzo and filed a report on the colony.

36. AGN, H-6, Tierras de Montaña, Resoluciones, 0254 (1895), partners E. Weck-

warlt, E. Dibos (?), 23 Jan. 1888; ARH, Prot., Ramírez, 21 May 1904, "Kitz & Co." Tulumayo passed over the years from Kitz to Durand to the Japanese firm Hoshi to become a U.S. agricultural station and colonization site, and by the 1970s it had passed to traffickers: see chapter 7. Morales, *Cocaine*, 75, on past "German" visitors.

37. Tamayo, *Informe sobre Pozuzo*, 111–12. Walger, "Coca Distribution," 134–35. BNP, MR, D4949, "Expediente sobre el reclamo formulado por A. Kitz y Co. para que se le devuleva cantidades de soles que se le cobró por impuesto de la cocaína," 19 Nov. 1895; also Ministerio de Gobierno, *EP*, 23 Oct. 1895.

38. Tamayo, *Informe sobre Pozuzo*, 112. By 1910, the same author did not even note cocaine in his "Colonias de Oxapampa y Pozuzo" (*BSG* 19/25 [1910]: 362–68), nor did Walger in his 1913 "Coca Distribution," 122–40, though detailing both "German settlement" and Pampa Hermosa.

39. NA, RG59, M155, Callao, vol. 13, no. 65, 4 Apr. 1891, Dougherty, "Reply . . . on Subject of Cocaine."

40. Vivian, *Peru and Development*, 173, for thirty figure; Garland, *Reseña industrial*, 78, 143–45 (quote); "Coca Leaves in Hamburg," *CD*, 8 Jan. 1887.

41. BNP, MR, E44, MP (Huanta, 25 May 1903), "Industrias"; BNP, MR, E47, MP (Ayacucho, Benavides, 1905), "Nueva Industria," 51; Bonilla, *Gran Bretaña y el Perú*, vol. 4, southern exports; Walger, "Coca Distribution," 129–35, coca valleys, plant closures.

42. "Coca and Cocaine in Peru," *AD*, 30 (10 Mar. 1897): 174 (orig. in *El Comercio*, La Paz), repr., *BAR*, 1897. Cisneros, *Atlas del Perú*, 14 (coca geography).

43. Paz-Soldán, *Diccionario biográfico*, 312–13. Risco was briefly in Huánuco as a Montero partner in 1897; Higuera y Paz Soldán, *Impresiones y datos de Trujillo* (Acharán, Goicochea, Pinillos). For later Maywood circuit, see Pilli, "Coca Industry," 16–20.

44. *Guía comercial* (1921), 30, 451–52, 458 (photo Vergel, also as Verjil and Vergil). This circuit still runs: Michael W. Miller, "Quality Stuff: Firm Is Peddling Cocaine, and Deals Are Legit," *Wall Street Journal*, 27 Oct. 1994.

45. Plowman, "Botanical Origins," 13.

46. Werlich, "Conquest of the Montaña"; García Jordán, *Cruz y arado*. "Monografía de la Provincia de Huánuco," *BSG* 7 (1897): 68; P. D. G. Clark, "Informe sobre la Peruvian Corporation," *EP*, May 1892, 52–54, cites coca as "esta valiosa planta" for "consumo local," noting Huánuco. The issue is what might have ensued with a strong British interest in coca as a modern "plantation" crop in these Perenne or Satipo colonies, analogous to Hoshi in Tulumayo.

47. Pavletich, *Autopsía de Huánuco*, 5.

48. Herndon and Gibbon, *Exploration of Amazon*, 132, chs. 6–7. Varallanos, *Historia de Huánuco*, 626–30. MP (Huánuco, Delfin, 1874) in *EP*, 23–24 Aug. 1874; "Huánuco y 'El Perú' de Antonio Raimondi, Montañas de Chinchao y Tingo María," in Cloud, *Antología huanuqueña*, 3:153–62; Walger, "Coca Distribution," 135–38.

49. "Monografía de Huánuco," *BSG*, 1897, 61–105; Durand, *Ferrocarril al Huallaga*, 6–17; Lafosse, *Algo sobre Huamalíes*, 74–75, Monzón. Later (1929), Diez-Canseco, *Red nacional*, 141–47, reports 80 percent of all cocaine originated in Chinchao, between Rios Chinchao and Monzón.

50. Thudichem, *Coca of Peru*, 11–12, 17–20; a former professor of "pathological

chemistry," he used sources well in the era of the Searle, Mariani, and Martindale science genre of coca trade pamphlets.

51. AGN, H-4, Ministerio de Hacienda, 0400, "Censo General del Perú—1876" (Lima, 1878), vol. 5, Huánuco, Chinchao.

52. "Coca," *BMI*, 25 Jan. 1889: one of dozens in the era's mystifying botanic-alkaloidal debates over Erythroxylum species, a Spruce-Rusby tradition continued in Karch, *Mystery of Coca*. For clarification, Plowman, "Botanical Origins," 11–12. Confusions remain, as one variety of coca's two commercial species is *named* "Coca Huánuco," the chief cultivar from Ecuador to Bolivia (now hybridized in Colombia).

53. Plowman, "Botanical Origins," Chinchao, 12. For commercial eye, see Pilli, "Coca Industry," 3–7. Bignon, "Sobre una coca del norte" (1887), 36–39; Mortimer, *History of Coca*, 342–45, notes high alkaloids of Huánuco but argues, in a classic prococa move, that Indians purposely seek the least cocaine-bearing leaf.

54. BNP, MR, D3993, MP (Huánuco, Freire, 1889), an. 1, "Cultivo de la coca" (and *Registro oficial*, 13 Sept. 1889); AGN, Tierras de Montaña, vol. 1; AGN, H-6, Prefecturas, 0245 (1895), Obras Públicas, "Leyes y Resoluciones referentes a terrenos de montaña." Claims also appeared in *EP*.

55. BNP, MR, D4689 (MP, Huánuco, Huapaya, 1899); BNP, MR, E832 (MP, Huánuco, 1900); BNP, MR, E925 (MP, Huánuco, Rodríguez, 1904); BNP, MR, E025 (MP, Huánuco, 1905). Lafosse, *Algo sobre Huamalíes*, 58, 74–75, for new Monzón factories like Marte. *BAR*, 1897, 545, reports ten factories, five in Huánuco, one in Monzón. Garland, *Reseña industrial*, 78.

56. For the group, see Spoja Cortijo, *Croatas en Huánuco*; "Monografía de Huánuco," *BSG*, 1897, 79–80, 99–100. A few Jews wandered in, too: Pedro Rubín and José Rosenthal (municipal president in 1905), and in the 1870s "Sr. Bar," a Portuguese trader (?) and governor of Monzón, lauded by authorities for his promotion of "Christianity"! MP, Huánuco, Delfin, 1874, in *EP*, 29 May 1874. Kawell stresses immigrants in "Essentially Peruvian."

57. NA, RG59, M155, Callao, vol. 13, no. 65, 4 Apr. 1891; "La Acción pro-indígena—Esclavitud en Huánuco," *EC*, 27 Dec. 1912. ARH, Sucesiones (wills), Juan Plejo, 1927: his "inventory of goods" illuminates a working *cocal*. Croat origins in ARH, Expedientes Civiles, Minutario, and Protocoles of 1890s. *Peru at Louisiana Exposition*, "List of the Peruvian Exhibitors," cites E. Gonzáles Orbegoso (coca, Trujillo), Mariano Vargas (coca, Cuzco), and Mariano Paucar (coca, Vitor), with two medals.

58. These bios emerge from a maze of ARH Protocoles (named notary books), e.g., Ramírez (1901–02, 1909–10), Robles (1902, 1907–08, 1910–14, 1915–16), and Roncillo (1917–18). Garinovich, Milosovich, Sarinivich, and Beraún, plus non-Croats Minoya and Ibérico, also ran factories.

59. ARH, Municipalidad, "Impuesto de la Coca," lg. 271, Libro de la Adminstración de la Coca, 1902. There are other fragments, e.g., lg. 99, "Relación de las guís de Coca y Café, por los vigilantes de Tingo y Ambo," 1903–4, or (missing) lg. 183, "Arbitrios de la Coca, 1896–1910."

60. See chapter 4 for cocaine reformers. Pedro Paulet, "Industrias—La Cocaína," *BMF* 1/9 (1903): 25–42; Alfredo Rabines, "The Production of Cocaine in Peru," *Peru To-Day* 3 (Sept. 1911): 31–33; Reens, *Coca de Java*, 75–76.

61. See *Cultivo de coca*, a nineteen-page 1896 rarity in the Biblioteca Felix Denegri Luna, or the above-cited "Cultivo de la coca" (BNP, MR, D3993, MP [Huánuco, Freire, 19 July 1889], an. 1). Bües, *La coca*, 18 (quote). Bolivia had more early extension works, with its active elite Sociedad de Propietarios de Yungas, e.g., Álvarez Daza's 1899 *Cultivo de coca*.

62. Mario A. Durand, "Coca: Dos palabras," *EH*, Oct. 1916; Bües, *La coca*; A. Martín Lynch, "Factores que determinan la riqueza de cocaína en las hojas de coca" (and Jacob studies), *RA* 7/10 (1912): 388–90.

63. "Augusto Durand: Su—Personalidad—Su Vida," *La República* (Lima), Apr. 1923, "El Hombre de Negocios."

64. Bios: Parker, *Peruvians To-day*, 341–42; Paz-Soldán, *Diccionario biográfico*; a few note his "industrialización de la coca." Durand, *Ferrocarril al Huallaga*, 57–58. Pavletich, *No se suicidan*, won Peru's 1959 Premio Nacional de Novela.

65. "Su fortuna, su tiempo, su genio, su hacienda, su vida misma, todo lo había puesto al servicio de la política," in obituary "El Hombre Político," *La República*, Apr. 1923. Eastern coca politics exemplified in Méndez, *Plebeian Republic*, esp. 70–74, 151–52.

66. Prefects saw Durand's 1890s revolts as the obstacle to area progress (BNP, MR, D4689, MP, Huánuco, 1899, 35–36), a document that still omits Durand from among cocaine makers Plejo, Más, Nesanovich, and bygone Kitz (27). My grasp of Durand was aided by interviews with family descendants (two are academics, Francisco and Jorge Durand) and by ARH, Protocoles (1890s–1920).

67. Bits of *El Huallaga* (Huánuco) were found in the BNP Sala de Investigaciones and Colección Manuel Nieves in Huánuco: "Memoria de Juan Durand, Alcalde," Jan. 1904; "El impuesto de la coca," "Reunión de los hacendados," Apr. 1904; "Remate de coca," 13 July 1904; "El nuevo Municipio," 4 Nov. 1916. Durand's own Lima paper, *La Prensa*, said little about cocaine.

68. Durand, *Ferrocarril al Huallaga*, 16–17, 29–30; Durand, *Noticias sobre gomales*. Durand writings pervade the *BSG*, 1900–1910 (e.g., "Ferrocarril al Oriente," 18 [1906]; "De Huánuco a las montañas de Monzón," 23 [1908]). See *BSG* 12 (1902): 14–73 for opposing plans.

69. "Grand Trust de Cocaína," *EH*, 17 Oct. 1911; oral-com., A. Quiroz, 1997, on Durand and banks; details in ARH, Prot., Roncillo and Cox, 1917–18. On *cocaleros*, see "Los caminos a las montañas de Derrepente," *EH*, 18 Apr. 1918, or "Protesta del pueblo huanuqueño," *EH*, 23 Apr. 1919, which lauds Durand for "popularizing Huánuco in foreign markets." For European syndicates, see Friman, "Germany and Cocaine," and de Kort, "Doctors, Diplomats, and Businessmen."

70. Thorp and Bertram, *Peru*, pt. 2, "The Rise and Fall of a Local Developmental Effort: 1890–1930"; on its politics, Burga and Flores Galindo, *Apogeo de República Aristocrática*.

71. See Bauer, *Goods, Power, History*, chs. 5–6, for "modernizing" and "developing" goods; Spillane, Kohn, and Roldán essays in Gootenberg, *Global Histories*, for "modern" cocaine, also noted by Kawell in "Essentially Peruvian." Gootenberg, *Imagining Development*.

72. Clavero, *Tesoro*, 46; Rodríguez, *Estudios económicos-financieros*, 470; Garland, *Las industrias*, 29; Garland, *Export from Peru*, 7–8, 15; Garland, *Reseña industrial*, 43, 78, 145; Garland, *Perú en 1906*, 181. Lissón, *Sociología de Perú*, 63.

73. Gibson, "Coca, alcohol y música incaíca," 9; Chocano, *Desenvolvimiento comercial*, 95, which cites "Mortimer en su interesante 'The History of Coca' que tenemos aqui a la vista."

CHAPTER THREE

1. Gereffi and Korzeniewicz, introduction to *Commodity Chains*, built from sociologist Immanuel Wallerstein's idea of a grand "modern world system"; see also Korzeniewicz and Smith, *Latin America and World Economy*. Contemporary cocaine has received wide treatment as a commodity chain: see Wilson and Zambrano, "Cocaine Commodity Chains"; Bellone, "Cocaine Commodity Chain"; and Vellinga, *Political Economy of Drug Industry*. Gootenberg, *Global Histories*, is also organized around commodity chains; for drugs as global goods, see Stares, *Global Habit*, or Pomeranz and Topik, *World that Trade Created*, esp. ch. 3, "The Economic Culture of Drugs." For commodity chains as Latin American history, see Topik, Marichal, and Frank, *From Silver to Cocaine*, esp. introduction, "Commodity Chains" (Gootenberg's ch. 12 deals with cocaine).

2. For more cultural or Polanyi-esque approaches, see Appadurai, *Social Life of Things*, with its concept of "commodity ecumene," or Mintz's *Sweetness and Power*, for the cultural history of a specific global commodity, sugar. My approach here is hardly the only feasible conception of transnational forces. For example, rather than commodity flows, one might foreground cocaine's culturally articulated "contact zones"— a concept mined from anthropologist Fernando Ortiz's classic commodity "transculturation" (Ortiz, *Cuban Counterpoint*) by Pratt in *Imperial Eyes*, an analysis drawing on Peru, applied by Lomnitz in "Nationalism's Dirty Linen." Recently, uneven crosscurrents of transnational culture drive postcolonial theory, e.g., Marez, *Drug Wars*.

3. See Appendix: Quantifying Cocaine for a detailed discussion of sources and quantitative problems. A recent aggregate study is Musto's "International Traffic in Coca," a team effort to piece together historical statistics on licit coca trades. This chapter makes limited use of Musto's figures, for reasons outlined in the appendix. Commodity chains help counter the biases of standardized quantification by stressing differences in providence and between coca and cocaine flows, for example by distinguishing the trade in cocaine from longstanding regional trades in coca leaf (e.g., Bolivia's) or in the production of coca for extracts (e.g., U.S. beverage syrups from northern Peru).

4. Scherzer, *Voyage on the Novara*, vol. 3; Byck, *Cocaine Papers*; Kennedy, *Coca Exotica*, 57–58.

5. See Spillane, *Cocaine*, ch. 1, for cocaine's scientific modernism; Bynum, *Science and Medicine*, ch. 4, on German currents. I rely here on industrial ideal types distinguished by Gerschenkron (whom I have written about elsewhere) in *Economic Backwardness in Perspective*. However, Germanic scientific practice should not be confused with cultural determinism: e.g., homeopathy, a foil of allopathic medicine, was eminently German (of Hahnemann, inspired by cinchona) and still enjoys its greatest legitimacy in Europe.

6. Friman, "Germany and Cocaine"; "Markham on Coca-Cultivation," *CD*, 17

Mar. 1894; Mortimer, *History of Coca*, 317. Projects surveyed in Walger, "Coca Distribution," 146–49.

7. This interaction is the theme of my "Case of Scientific Excellence"; Spillane, *Cocaine*, 51, and Friman, "Germany and Cocaine," 87.

8. Scherzer, *Voyage on the Novara*, 3:409; Tamayo, *Informe sobre Pozuzo*, 111–12.

9. Statistics amended from "Cocaine-Manufacture in Peru," *CD*, 9 Apr. 1904; coca guesses come from travelers like Markham, who likely repeat late colonial figures; Garland, *Perú en 1906*, 180–82, 213. Soininen, "Geographies of Cocaine," ch. 5, 28; ch. 6, 58.

10. Mariani, *Coca and Its Applications*; Hefland, "Vin Mariani." Not only is French coca interest understudied, but its contrast with Germany is problematic, as nineteenth-century French scientists pioneered both alkaloidal sciences and drug-related fields like neurology.

11. "Coca," *BMI*, 25 (Jan. 1889); Martindale, *Cocaine and Its Salts*; "Production and Use of Coca Leaves," *BII* 7 (1910): 388–92; "Armbrecht's Coca Wine," *CD*, 18 Apr. 1891; 17 Mar. 1894. Brockway, *Science and Expansion*; Stockwell, *Nature's Pharmacy*.

12. For this and other reasons, one resists simply labeling the Bolivian circuit as "traditional." Bolivian coca had its own historical dynamic, often articulated to highly monetized sectors of Andean society. See esp. Klein, "Coca in the Yungas."

13. Loza Balsa, *Monografía de coca*, esp. chs. 2–4; Soux, *Coca liberal*, historical. Historians will recognize this pattern from Assadourian's colonial model, *Sistema de economía colonial*; see Langer, *Economic Change in Bolivia*, on postcolonial patterns.

14. Lema, "Coca de las Americas," or edited English version, "Coca Debate and Landowners"; Fischer, "Culturas de coca," for coca politics. Rusby, *Jungle Memories*, ch. 5 (quote).

15. Rusby, *Jungle Memories*, chs. 5, 8, or his "Coca at Home and Abroad," *TG*, Mar.–May 1888; Mariani, "Coca and Its Applications," 13; "Erythroxylon Coca," *ODR*, 23 Sept. 1885 (Merriam report); Gibbs, "Coca Plant," *Leonard's Illustrated Journal*, Apr. 1886.

16. "Market for Coca," *CD*, 15 Apr. 1885 (costs). Canelas Orellana and Canelas Zanner, *Bolivia*, 104–8; by 1950, Cochabamba (i.e., the *yungas* and Chapare) produced a third of crops. For a detailed view of the *yungas*, see Walger, "Coca Distribution."

17. In political terms, coca was to La Paz and Bolivia as coca was regionally to Huánuco Province in Peru, as seen, also in 1902, in chapter 2. See Soux, *Coca liberal*, for 1902 survey and, on politics, Lema, "Coca de las Americas." Rivera, "Here Even Legislators Chew Them." Tastes for coca would spread in Argentina, and by the 1940s moved with internal migrants well into Buenos Aires. There is the unverified "Bolivian" claim of the very first "industrialization of coca" in La Paz by pharmacist Enrique Pizzi in 1857, three years before Niemann (Mortimer, *History of Coca*, 294); a few Bolivian coca elixirs also won fame.

18. Searle, *New Form of Nervous Disease*; U.S.-published Mariani, "Coca and Its Applications."

19. Mortimer, *History of Coca*; on British-U.S. herbal traditions, see Griggs, *Green Pharmacy*.

20. See Gootenberg, "Between Coca and Cocaine," on American chain overall or, for coca promotion, 122–23, 123n5. Rusby, *Jungle Memories*, chs. 1, 8.

21. Spillane, *Cocaine*, ch. 3, or his "Making a Modern Drug."

22. "Peru: Coca and Cocaine," *BAR*, 4 (1896/97): 111–12. For syrup circuit and its political economy, see Gootenberg, "Secret Ingredients," and for later circuits, Pilli, "Coca Industry," 33–34.

23. See Musto, *American Disease*, or Spillane's updated look at anticocainism (*Cocaine*, chs. 5–8). Some resistance arose to subsuming coca in the crusade from herbalists like Mortimer or the Lloyd brothers, but the conflation reflected the victory of allopathic medicine and pharmacological science.

24. PRO, FO 228/2202, Imperial Institute, "Memorandum on the Production, Distribution, Sale and Physiological Effects of Cocaine," Dec. 1909–June 1910; the institute published a version, "Production and Use of Coca Leaves," *BII* 8:388–92. For era's drug cultures, see Davenport-Hines, *Pursuit of Oblivion*, ch. 7; Dikötter, Laamann, and Xun, *Narcotic Culture*, ch. 10, in China.

25. Higginson's reports are in *BRE*, vols. 1–9 (1904, 1907, 1912).

26. For U.S. campaign, see Gootenberg, "Reluctance or Resistance"; see de Kort, "Doctors, Diplomats, and Businessmen," Karch, "Japan and Cocaine," and Friman, "Germany and Cocaine," for new twentieth-century chains.

27. On some origins, see Karch, *Brief History*, chs. 2, 6, and context in Rush, *Opium to Java*.

28. De Kort, "Doctors, Diplomats, and Businessmen," based on his 1995 Dutch doctoral thesis; Reens, *Coca de Java* (orig. 1917). There is discrepancy in these sources on the question whether any form of crude cocaine was made in Java.

29. See chain-crossing reports of Peruvian diplomat M. A. Derteano, "Informe que presenta el cónsul sobre la coca de la isla de Java," *BRE* 15 (1918): 347–48 (orig. 1914, Hong Kong). Merck Corporate Archives, RG 2.7.6, 3.8.6, 3.97, for Tjitembong, originally a Merck of Darmstadt lease.

30. These European "cartels" were more genuinely cartel-like than their illicit Colombian namesakes of the 1980s. De Kort, "Doctors, Diplomats, and Businessmen," 126–43: American forces made coca eradication a precondition for the brief Dutch reoccupation of Java after 1945.

31. Friman, *Narco-Diplomacy*, ch. 3; Karch, *Brief History*, chs. 6, 10, or his "Japan and Cocaine of Asia." Tulumayo sources in NA, RG59, DF823.114, P/N, "Alleged Traffic in cocaine and other alkaloids by Japanese Agriculturalists," 15 Jan. 1923. Takamine owned an elegant townhouse in Manhattan and was the force behind Japan's cherry tree gifts in America.

32. Friman, *Narco-Diplomacy*, offers a balanced analysis comparing Japan and Germany; Jennings, *Opium Empire*, if sparse on cocaine, is dispassionate on Japan's role. Karch's indictment in *Brief History*, ch. 10, uses no Japanese sources.

33. Karch, *Brief History*, ch. 10, estimates Japanese production, using acreage and alkaloid ratios, at seven metric tons (above world licit supply); this estimate is critiqued in Soininen, "Geographies of Cocaine," ch. 7, 76–81, esp. notes 31, 34, and 35. Dikötter, Laamann, and Xun, *Narcotic Culture*, 196–97.

34. "Mancha india" (Indian stain) is a racist term for Peru's southern Andean provinces of Cuzco, Ayacucho, and Puno. Pilli, "Coca Industry," 4–5, 8; Pilli offers

another estimate—by bulk?—with 70 percent for chewing, 15 percent for exports, and 15 percent for cocaine. Paz Soldán's 1937 *Coca peruana* (xvi) puts Cuzco at 50 percent, Huánuco at 21 percent, La Libertad at 7 percent, Ayacucho at 17 percent, and other areas at 5 percent. *Perú en marcha*, 183–87, table 18.

35. Paz Soldán, "Problema médico-social de coca"; Gootenberg, "Reluctance or Resistance," 56–63; Gagliano, *Coca Prohibition*, chs. 6–7.

36. Gootenberg, "Secret Ingredients," from NA, RG170, Boxes 19, 20, Beverages; for figures, see FBN, *TODD*, 1960, table 10, "Opium and coca leaves imported into the U.S. . . . 1929–59."

37. For pressures, see Gootenberg, "Reluctance or Resistance," based on FBN foreign country papers (NA, RG170, 0660); for global picture, consult McAllister, *Drug Diplomacy*.

38. Pilli, "Coca Industry"; NA, RG59, DF823.114, P/N, Burdett, "Manufacture of the derivative of the coca leaf in Peru," Apr. 1932; Reid, "Coca" (orig. 1918?).

39. NA, RG170, Box 18, File 0605, World Narcotics Factories: such detailed 1928–38 surveys as these, some of which list capital, capacity, and agents, are not found in official League documents.

40. For related territorial or field of power models, see Wacquant and Bourdieu, *Invitation to Reflexive Sociology*, or Mann, *Sources of Social Power*, vol. 1.

CHAPTER FOUR

1. Gagliano, *Coca Prohibition*, chs. 6–7; Fischer, "Culturas de coca"; Bauer, *Goods, Power, History*, for the idea of modernizing Latin American commodities.

2. This image dates to von Tschudi in the 1840s; Esteban Pavletich (the leftist *huanuqueño* journalist) left the classic account of an evil landowner (Durand) in *No se suicidan*.

3. Gutiérrez-Noriega and Zapata, *Estudios sobre coca y cocaína*, despite its title, does not cite Bignon; Hermilio Valdizán, "El cocainismo y la raza indígena," *CM*, 30 (1913): 263–65 was among the first anticoca manifestos. For context in neo-Lamarckian genetics, see Stepan, *Hour of Eugenics*, esp. ch. 3.

4. See Cueto, *Excelencia científica*, ch. 5, for Monge Medrano's movement. The now-dominant "ethnographic" or cultural defense of coca—as not only benign but essential to indigenous ethnic survival—did not begin until after the 1960s, e.g., Boldó i Clement, *Coca andina*.

5. Fascinating lags pervade these representations. For example, into the 1990s, illustration plates of national products (for study by millions of Peruvian children) portrayed a hyperscientific "Extracción de la cocaína" versus a backward "Chacchar coca: Vicio del Indio" (Colección Huascarán, no. 124, "La Coca"). Sociologically, Peru's anticoca movement was akin to the elite "tortilla discourse" in Porfirian Mexico, which tried to extinguish Indian use of maize as a modernizing hygienic measure: Pilcher, *Que vivan los tamales*, ch. 4.

6. Paz Soldán, *Coca peruana*, table 4, graphs a, b; Hohagen, *Sumario sobre exportaciones*, "Coca-Cocaine," 75–85.

7. E. Higginson, "Porvenir de los productos peruanos en Nueva York," *BRE* 1/5 (1905): 186–87; reports reprinted in *BMF*, 1903, *EH*, agricultural journals (e.g.

RA 2 [1912], "Hojas de Coca"); also *Peru To-Day* 1/2 (Apr. 1909): 5–7. Higginson, "Memoria que presenta el Cónsul General del Perú en Nueva York," *BRE*, 1905, 72–73; 1906, 186–87.

8. Higginson, "Memoria consular," "Revista de productos peruanos importados a los E.U.," *BRE*, 1907, 186–87.

9. Higginson, "Memoria del Cónsul-General del Perú en Nueva York para el año de 1912," *BRE* 10/69 (1913): 92, 110–11; excerpted in *RA* 1/11 (Nov. 1912): 509–14. M. A. Derteano, "Informe...sobre la coca de la Isla de Java," *BRE* 15 (1918): 347–58.

10. P. Paulet, "Industrias: La cocaína," *BMF* 1/9 (Sept. 1903): 25–42; Higginson, "Coca y cocaína," *BMF* 2 (1904): 97–98; A. Rabines, "The Production of Cocaine in Peru," *Peru To-Day* 3 (1911): 31–33.

11. Pozzi-Escot, "Recherches sur l'industrie de cocaïne" (repr., *L'agronomie tropicale*, Apr.–June 1913); here, he is identified as a chemistry professor at the Peruvian Institute of Agronomy. Cueto, *Excelencia científica*, 94–95, classes Pozzi-Escot among Peru's thirty-two "elite" scientists.

12. See *Cultivo de coca* and the same title on the *yungas* by Álvarez Daza (1899).

13. Bües, *La coca* (published in 1911, it dates to before the crash, with data only to 1904). Johannes Wille, "Los insectos dañinos a la coca en el Perú," *VA*, Dec. 1937, 1003–9, from 1930s fieldwork in Huánuco and Otuzco.

14. Bües, "La coca en el Perú."

15. A. Martín Lynch, "Factores que determinan la riqueza de cocaína en las hojas de coca," *RA* 7/10 (1912): 288–90; A. M. Linch (*sic*), "Breves notas sobre el cultivo de la coca," *Agronomía* 72 (Oct.–Dec. 1952): 77–80; H. Jacob and C. Deneumostier, "La coca en la montaña de Huánuco," *RA* 1/11 (Nov. 1912): 500–502; H. Jacob, "Apuntes sobre el cultivo de la coca," *RA* 4 (1913): 693–97.

16. Vinelli, *Estudio de coca*, quotes 1, 30; published in *BMF*, 1919.

17. Mario A. Durand, "Coca: Dos palabras," *EH* (496–502), 7–14 Oct.–18 Nov. 1916. This work is a rare find from the BNP, as it never appeared in separate pamphlet form.

18. Luzio, "Tecnología de cocaína," 51, 55; NA, RG59, DF823.114, P/N, Apr. 1940.

19. BNP, Dante Binda, "La cocaína: Problema industrial en el Perú," *Actas y trabajos del Segundo Congreso Peruano de Química* 1 (23 Oct. 1943): 375–79, quotes 375, 379. See also Dr. Alberto González Z., "Algunos privilegios naturales y especiales riquezas del Perú" (industrializing coca), *Boletín de la Sociedad Química del Perú*, Dec. 1943, or its editorial for III Congreso National de Química (15/2, 1949). Gootenberg, *Imagining Development*, ch. 5.

20. Varallanos, *Historia de Huánuco*, 588–90; Parker, *Peruvians To-day*, 57, 97; Paz-Soldán, *Diccionario biográfico* (3 entries); *La República* (Lima), Apr. 1923.

21. Juan Durand, *Noticias sobre gomales* and *Ferrocarril al Huallaga*.

22. "Gran trust de cocaína," *EH*, 14 Oct. 1911 (involving Pedro Wiese and El Banco del Perú y Londrés); ARH, Prot. (Roncillo), 1917–19, for Durand network and contracts.

23. "El hombre de negocios," *La República* (Lima), Apr. 1923; Chocano, *Desenvolvimiento comercial*, ads; oral-coms. with descendants Francisco and Jorge Durand, 1998–99.

24. Hohagen, *Sumario sobre exportaciones*, entries "Coca," "Cocaine"; costs, 84. These numbers (note his odd units) and my manipulations of them must be taken with many grains of salt.

25. NA, RG170, 0660, Box 18, World Narcotics Factories, "Producers of refined cocaine in Peru," Nov. 1928, memo 238, for (outdated) capacity, as follows: Huánuco at 1,400 kilos (Durand, 1,000; Soberón, 400); Trujillo at 1,500 kilos (Pinillos, 800, plus Vergel, Fan, Risco, Ayllon). "Informe relativo al control de sustancias narcóticos," *BSP*, 22 June 1928.

26. *Anuario de América Latina* (Paris, 1914), 1432; vol. 2, 1920–21 (Huánuco; Cocaína, Fábricas), 1653; ARH, Prot. (Roncillo), May 1917; Prot./Prefs. of 1920s–40s; Sucesiones, Viuda de Soberón, 1957; "Informe relativo al control de sustancias narcóticos," *BSP*, 22 June 1928; NA, RG170, 0660, Box 18, World Narcotics Factories, "Opium and Coca Industry in Peru," 1928.

27. Interview, Dr. Nilo Lambruschini, Huánuco, July 1998; ARH, Pref., lg. 33, exp. 463, "Inventario de la fábrica de cocaína de D. Andrés A. Soberón," 24 May 1949. Soberón's kin include a grandson, Ricardo Soberón, who is a drug and human rights expert in Lima.

28. NA, RG59, DF823.114, P/N, Burdett, "Manufacture of the Derivatives of the Coca Leaf in Peru," 22 Apr. 1932; for marketing, see DF823.114, McKesson and Robbins etc., 22 Oct. 1931.

29. NA, RG59, DF823.114, P/N, Burdett, "Visit to Huánuco," 22 Apr. 1932.

30. E.g., Dunn, *Peru Handbook*, 142–43; F. E. Class, "The Sacred Coca Plant," *Pan-American Magazine*, Dec. 1922; "Coca," in "Peruvian Handbook," *West Coast Leader*, Oct. 1921; "Coca—Whence Cocaine," in *Peru: The Cradle*, 10 Apr. 1925; cf. prococa article "Coca, the Cocaine of Commerce," *BAR*, 1910, 1076–77.

31. Diez-Canseco, *Red nacional*, 142, share. ARH, Pref., lgs. 23–26 (1930s *guías*) and lg. 34, no. 473; Pref., "Asociación de Productores de Coca," (new), Dec. 1949; Sucesiones (69–2154, 1971), F. Rada; AGN, H-6-406, Ministerio del Hacienda, Censo Nacional de Población y Ocupación, 1940, vol. 1, table 83 (16 men and 1 woman); *GL* (1946), "Huánuco—Agricultura y Ganadería"; NA, RG170, Box 18, World Narcotics Factories, 1936; Pilli, "Coca Industry," 31–32, 40.

32. NA, RG59, DF823.114, P/N, 15 Jan. 1923, "Alleged Traffic in Cocaine and other Alkaloids by Japanese Agriculturalists"; enclosure, "Japanese Quietly Exporting Cocaine from Interior of Peru," *Christian Science Monitor*, 12 Aug. 1922; export via northern Eten was U.S. concern.

33. *Tulumayo*, a 1942 compendium. NA, RG59, DF823.114, P/N, "Activities of Japanese Firm in Production of Narcotics in Peru," 23 Sept. 1936; ARH, Pref., lgs. 22–26, 1940s.

34. Pilli, "Coca Industry," 17–20; Gootenberg, "Secret Ingredients," 244–46. The spelling of Vergel's name varies.

35. NA, RG170, Box 18, World Narcotics Factories, "Opium and Coca Industry in Peru," 1928; *Guía comercial* (1921), 158–59 (Vergel); Paz-Soldán, *Diccionario biográfico*, 312–13 (Pinillos); *GL* (1920s–46), entry "La Libertad."

36. Paz Soldán, "Problema médico-social de coca"; "La coca peruana y su futuro régimen político," *RM*, Jan. 1934, 69–77, 98–99, and Feb. 1934. For context, see Cueto, *Excelencia científica*, bio, 205; Cueto, "Andean Biology"; or Stepan, *Hour*

of Eugenics, 180–81. Paz Soldán was often regarded as a dilettante by the rising medical establishment.

37. Paz Soldán, "Problema médico-social de coca," pts. 1–3.

38. Ibid., pt. 3, 597–603.

39. Ricketts, *Ensayos pro-indígena*. Gagliano, *Coca Prohibition*, chs. 6–7, a Ricketts optic. A man with a flawed 1930s memory, Ricketts the later anticommunist saw cocaine as a global plot.

40. For context, see Gootenberg, "Secret Ingredients." NA, RG59, DF823.114, P/N, "Subject: Dr. Antonio Pagador," 12 Dec. 1930 (and Shreve, 3 Nov. 1930); DF511.4, A7/12, Hobson, 6 Sept. 1930; RG170, 0660, Peru, Nov. 1930.

41. NA, RG170, 0660, Peru, "Visit of Mr. Schaefer," 10 Mar. 1933; Paz Soldán, "Problema médico-social de coca," epigraph; "La coca peruana," *RM*, Jan. 1934; Ricketts, *Ensayos pro-indígena*, 33–34; Fuchs, *Política fiscal*, "Coca y cocaína," 20–23. Guildhall Library, London, Gibbs Papers, ms. 16, 882, file 25, no. 631–35, Jan.–Mar. 1930. Schieffelin was former head of the National Retail Drug Association, the powerful U.S. drug lobby.

42. NA, RG59, DF823.114, P/N, 3, 19 May 1933 (clippings, *La Industria* [Trujillo]); Paz Soldán, "La coca peruana," *RM*, 1 Feb., 15 June 1934; Bües, "La coca en el Perú."

43. Paz Soldán, *Coca peruana* (SNA, *RM*, 1936), including historical, statistical appendices.

44. "La Coca en peligro," *VA*, 1 Mar. 1936; SNA, "La cuestión de la Coca"; "Publicaciones recibidas: La Coca Peruana," June 1936; Dir. Gen. de Salubridad, "Oficial: Producción cocalera"; "La situación de la industria cocalera," *VA*, all June, Aug. 1936.

45. *EC*, 15 Mar., 9 May 1936; *La Prensa* (Lima), 6 Apr. 1936. NA, RG59, DF823.114, P/N, 4, 13 Apr. 1936; NA, RG170, 0660, Peru, "Approaching Narcotics Conference Interests Peru," 13 Apr. 1936, "Peru's Attitude at Narcotics Conference," 1 June, 14 Aug. 1936.

46. "La industria cocalera," *EC*, 19 May 1936, 15 Mar. 1935. NA, DF823.114, P/N, "Commission Appointed to Study the Peruvian Coca Industry," 23 Mar. 1936. Ricketts, *Ensayos pro-indígena*, "La oposición al proyecto de restringir el abuso de la coca," 33–36.

47. NA, RG59, DF823.114, P/N, "Confidential Biographic Data (Enrique Trujillo Bravo)," Apr., 13 Oct. 1936. Bravo is described as an irrigation engineer, "Personality: Pleasing," "Influence: Not Important," desiring a diplomatic passport for European vacations. "Tráfico de Estupefacientes," *BRE*, 15 Apr., 31 Jan. 1936. McAllister, *Drug Diplomacy*, ch. 4.

48. LN, OC1760, "Latin American Mission," 24 Apr. 1939, 5–7; NA, RG59, DF823.114, P/N, Anslinger, 7 Mar. 1938.

49. LN, OC1760, "Latin American Mission," 24 Apr. 1939, includes Ekstrand, "Report of the Director," and app., "Peru," 5–7.

50. "Visita de una misión de la Liga de las Naciones," *BRE*, 6 Jan., 8 Mar. 1938, esp. "Memorandum del Director...sobre el libro 'La Coca Peruano,'" Apr. 1938, 248–59 (Ekstrand); "El control internacional de los estupefacientes y la coca peruana," *VA*, July 1938, 595–97. Paz Soldán, "Luchamos contra la esclavitud del cocaismo

indígena," *RM*, 1 Jan. 1939, 19–24, or parting shot, "La coca y el prestigio del Perú," Jan. 1949, for UN coca mission of 1948–50.

51. ARH, Municpalidad, "Administración de la Coca y la Cocaína," 1902, and Municipalidad, lg. 99, "Relación de Guías de la Coca y Café," 1903–4; Hohagan, *Sumario sobre exportaciones*, "Cocaína"; Fuchs, *Política fiscal*, 20–23.

52. Lorente and Caravedo, *Bases de defensa contra la toxicomanía*, 5; also in *BSP*, 1927. The report ignores alcohol, long an elite worry for Indians. *La Reforma Farmacéutica*, 1927; Rubio Correa, *Legislación sobre drogas*, annex, 37–38.

53. NA, RG59, DF823.114, P/N, Burdett, 13, 21 Apr. 1932. *BSP*, decrees 1923–26, esp. Aug. 1923, Sept. 1925, Feb. 1928, and "Informe relativo al control de sustancias narcóticas," *BSP*, 156–59, 30 June 1935. *Prontuario de legislación sanitaria*, 3 vols. (1928–35).

54. "Permiso para fabricar cocaína," *EC*, 19 Apr. 1932; "La producción de cocaína en el Perú," 4 Aug. 1932. ARH, Pref., esp. lgs. 44–46, 1930s–40s cocaine sales; B. Caravedo, "La asistencia de los toxicomanías en los E.U.A.," *Archivos Peruanos de Higiene Mental*, 1940, 47–69.

55. "Discubrieron las autoridades un laboratorio clandestina de drogas heróicas en Miraflores," *El Universal*, 31 Mar. 1939 (from NA, RG59, DF823.114, 1 Apr. 1939). DF823.114, P/N, "Peruvian Legislation Affecting the Trade in and Manufacture of Narcotic Drugs," 30 Apr. 1940; *EC*, 4 Dec. 1939, 5 Sept. 1940.

56. Rubio Correa, *Legislación sobre drogas*, 21–22; Pilli, "Coca Industry," 47–48; *EC*, 23 Mar. 1945; *Revista de Sanidad de la Policía*, 1948–54. Professional journals (e.g., *Farmacia y Química*, 1944–45) also trace state role. Interview, Dr. Virgilio López Calderón, Huánuco, 1998.

57. A full cite for this fieldwork-based study is Emile R. Pilli, "The Coca Industry in Peru," report for Merck, New Jersey (Rahway: 1943). DEA Library holds a rare copy, not found in Merck Archives.

58. Ibid., 4–7; unclear origin of usage figure. See Bües, "La coca en el Perú," for more precise estimate: 8 million kilos (17.6 million lbs.) of coca, with 3 percent in "export." If cocaine exports reached 1,000 kilos (a high number for the decade) and had a 150–180 (or high 200–1) coca-cocaine ratio, cocaine end use may have reached 200,000 kilos, or 2–2.5 percent of national coca. *Perú en marcha* (1942) has 3 percent as coca export (185). If recalculated from its 1940 export data in table 18, the result is 1.6 percent for cocaine and 5.5 percent for coca exports (7.1 percent total exportable), leaving 6.1 metric tons in internal consumption.

59. Pilli, "Coca Industry," 9–15 (unclear sources on past or 1943 plant numbers); Bües, *La coca*.

60. Pilli, "Coca Industry," 17–20.

61. Ibid., 20–27.

62. My sense is that Waiy, sizing up the market, quickly abandoned his (short-lived) cocaine foray. The 1940 *GL* lists factories of Soberón, Baroli, Funegra, the Durands, Pampayacu, and few Chinese merchants, save Weng, owner of Santo Toribio. Authorized shipments (ARH, Pref., 1936–40) show Sawada, Éxito, Cóndor, Rada, and Roncagliolo, yet Soberón dominates. Local *patentes* business taxes (ARH, Municipalidad, lg. 79, 1941) show similar trends, naming Soberón, Baroli, Orfanides, and Chinese in the "coffee-coca" trades. The city's three cocaine factories paid the

largest *industriales* tax: "Julio Chan Way" for *S*/567 (behind Soberón's *S*/771+) but crossed out, suggesting a bankruptcy. AGN, H-6, 1081 (Contribuciones, Huánuco, 1951) no longer has any Chinese presence. U.S. reports confirm this interpretation: NA, RG59, DF823.114, P/N, 4 Dec. 1941, "Cocaine Stocks in Peru," notes Waiy's Inca as one of eight factories (120 kilos of 1,200 total), with Soberón and Rada as leaders.

63. Pilli, "Coca Industry," 32–33.

64. Ibid., 39; Huánuco tax registers show a different order.

65. Ibid., 42; cost structure, 42–43, 45 (last quote): this has a very different cost structure from Hohagen's 1927 *Sumario sobre exportaciones*, analyzed above.

66. Pilli, "Coca Industry," 44–48; wrongly, he notes that if coca gets scarce, "it will not be at all surprising to see the U.S. government become financially interested in a cocaine manufacturing plant in Peru" (50).

CHAPTER FIVE

1. For labeling theory, see Becker, *Outsiders*; on regimes, Nadelmann, *Cops Across Borders*.

2. We lack a social or cultural theory to explain the turn to prohibitions in drug history similar to the understanding we have of the genesis of drug cultures in the early modern world. Leading histories stumble on the problem: Schivelbusch, *Tastes of Paradise*, ch. 8; McAllister, *Drug Diplomacy*, 16–20. Courtwright's *Forces of Habit*, chs. 9–10, uses a broad commodity lens: coca/cocaine, one of the historic "little three" regional goods (in contrast to rooted drugs like alcohol), came under medical indictments for hygienic social costs, its deviant users, or as a threat to national youth. See DeGrandpre, *Cult of Pharmacology*, chs. 4–5, on U.S. history, or Hickman, *Secret Leprosy*.

3. This cycle was replicated in the 1980s fall of glamorous powder cocaine to crack. Musto, *American Disease*, has no specific argument on cocaine, but his "America's First Cocaine" does. See Courtwright, "Rise and Fall of Cocaine," for who uses and cocaine and racism. For contexts, see Walker, *Drug Control Policy*, or Erien and Spillane, "Federal Drug Control."

4. See Hickman, "Mania Americana," for prohibition "othering," or his *Secret Leprosy*, 106–11, on criminality. Micro-view is Foster, "Road to Drug-Free Tennessee." Grinspoon and Bakalar, *Cocaine*, is thin on shift; cf. Bakalar's "Drugs and Medical Culture," professionalization thesis.

5. Spillane, *Cocaine*, chs. 6–7, or "Making a Modern Drug." Spillane also disputes prohibition's impact per se on cocaine's transformations, many of which were already underway.

6. On tariffs, *ODR*, 1891–92, 1894; "Coca," *BII*, 1910, 389; Kebler, *Habit-Forming Agents*.

7. Cocaine's postwar monopolization (misread in Coca-Cola histories as the end of Coke's coca flavoring and leaf imports) from FDA archives: a 2001 Freedom of Information Act request resulted in inspection papers of Maywood processes (FDA, EI, 9/21, 22, 23/77, 1948–78, esp. "History of Business"). Other revelations include

U.S. destruction of pre-1938 Maywood records and postwar physician complaints of overzealous prohibition, resulting in medicinal cocaine shortages.

8. Spillane, "Making a Modern Drug." U.S. Treasury Dept., "Report of Commissioner of Internal Revenue" and "Traffic in Narcotic Drugs" reports, 1915–20.

9. Spillane, *Cocaine*, chs. 4, 7; Hickman, *Secret Leprosy*, 117–18, on corporate discourse; Weinstein, *Corporate Ideal*; Block, "Snowman Cometh," illicit scare. Drug conference transcripts include NA, RG43, IC, Entry 48, Box 2, Opium Commission Correspondence (Wright, 1909).

10. U.S. House of Representatives, 63rd Congress, "Memorandum as to the Importation of Coca Leaves and Cocaine in the Continental U.S. since Jan. 1, 1910," 11, 19, 22 (Harrison Act).

11. National Library of Medicine, Ms. FB102, National Drug Trade Conference, "Minutes of a Special Meeting," May 1917; NA, RG170, Box 34, Early League Documents, "Export-Import Law of 1922," and Nutt, "Conference Held March 27, 1923, between the Advisory Committee of the Federal Narcotics Control Board and Narcotic Drug Manufacturers." On Anslinger, see McWilliams, *The Protectors*.

12. Detailed in Gootenberg, "Secret Ingredients."

13. Pendergrast, *God and Coca-Cola*, chs. 6–8, on coca culture, conflicts, accommodation. NA, RG170, Box 19, D/B, Coca, 1915–45, "Imitations of Coco-Cola," 18 May 1916, for 122 drug-tested brands, including health drink Dr. Pepper.

14. Boehringer-Ingelheim Archives, Schaeffer documents, 1903/58; FDA, *Notices of Judgment*, Case 1455, *U.S.A. vs. Forty Barrels and Twenty Kegs of Coca-Cola*, 1909, Schaeffer decocainization, 39–40; Miller, "Quality Stuff," for continuing processing of coca in Maywood "Building II."

15. Pendergrast, *God and Coca-Cola*, ch. 7, app. "The Sacred Formula" (from Russian archive); Allen, *Secret Formula*, 42–44, 48 (cult), 195: Candler wanted cocaine out by 1892 and tapped Schaeffer for process; Kahn, *Big Drink*. FDA, *Notices of Judgment*, Case 1455, *U.S.A. v. Forty Barrels*, Feb. 1912, 2–57; U.S. Court of Appeals, 6th Circuit, 1913, pt. 2, "Forty Barrels," esp. 786–807.

16. NA, RG170, Box 19, D/B, 1915–45, J. L. White (Joel Blanc), "The Coco-Cola 'joker' in the Harrison Narcotic Law," 29 Apr. 1916 (broadside). RG170, "Coca," 1915–45, Treasury, 26 Mar. 1915, 7 Mar., 13 Dec. 1916 (Schaeffer sample analysis). Treasury collected crank letters, often from rivals, on "cocaine" in Coca-Cola, e.g., Porter, 15 Dec. 1925.

17. NA, RG170, Box 19, "Coca," 1915–45, 21 June 1929, 31 Mar. 1928. RG59, LOT55D607, Drugs, Box 4, Coca-Cola Extract; FBN, *TODD*, 1930, "Conference at Bureau of Narcotics regarding...Manufacture of Flavoring Extract from Special Coca Leaves at Maywood Chemical Works," 3–5, 10; Bureau of Narcotics, *Regulations No. 2 Relating to Importation...of Opium or Coca Leaves or Any Compound, Manufacture, Salt, Derivative or Preparation thereof*, 1938, sec. 6.

18. FBN, *TODD*, 1965, table 11, "Opium and Coca Leaves Imported into the United States...1925–64." NA, RG170, Box 19, Coca, "Visit to Simbal," 8 Apr. 1940; and Cantrell, "Coca Leaves: Historical Development of the Coca Leaves Industry," 5 Nov. 1943; Pilli, "Coca Industry," 17–22.

19. Gootenberg, "Secret Ingredients," from NA, RG170, Boxes 19–20, De-cocainized Coca Leaves and Drugs — Coca, Beverages, quote, Box 19, Hirsch to Brokmeyer, 18

Jan. 1933. On United Fruit, see Bucheli and Read, "Banana Boats"; on Coca-Cola imperialism, see Kuisel, *Seducing the French*, 52–69 (note book's French Coke cover). Merck was far less active here.

20. "Classic" Coca-Cola still contains coca extract. Few Coke lovers realize that the mid-1980s consumer fiasco of a "New Coke" concerned an experimental cocaless formula, giving new meaning to the "classic" branding now used with the drink. Pendergrast, *God and Coca-Cola*, chs. 16–19.

21. Spillane, "Building Drug Control," 32–33; FBN, *TODD*, 1925–50s reports, including 1932, 12, and 1938, 14. Works on fading cocaine after 1920 include Musto, "America's First Cocaine"; Courtwright, "Rise and Fall of Cocaine"; and Phillips and Wynne, *Cocaine*, chs. 6–7: the latter speculate on substitution by amphetamine or heroin, a burnout of nonaddicted users, and the impact of alcohol prohibition on criminal networks.

22. Taylor, *American Diplomacy*; Bewley-Taylor, *U.S. and Drug Control*; McAllister, *Drug Diplomacy* or "Habitual Problems"; Walker, *Drug Control Policy*.

23. See McAllister, *Drug Diplomacy*, for developments, ch. 7 for 1961; he stresses that bureaucratic politics, compromised by conflicting global drug interests, undercut serious efforts.

24. For varied views, see Taylor, *American Diplomacy*, chs. 2–4; McAllister, *Drug Diplomacy*, 30–31; Musto, *American Disease*, ch. 3. NA, RG43, IC, entries 38/39, Opium Conference, 1909–11; entry 37, Wright letter book, 1909–15. Friman, "Germany and Cocaine," 91–97; Karch, "Japan and Cocaine." PRO, FO 228/2202, Embassy and Consular Archives, China, "Cocaine," 1909–10.

25. 63rd Congress, Senate doc. 157, "Second International Opium Conference," Wright, 9, 10 Aug. 1913. NA, RG43, IC, entry 41, June–Aug. 1912, 1 Oct. 1912, and to Wright, 3 July 1913; RG59, DF511.4A1–1390. PRO, FO, *Opium Trade*, 2:77 (1912, Peru).

26. NA, RG43, IC, entries 41–43, Wright to Pezet, Feb. 1912; for Bolivia, RG43, IC, entry 41, American Legation at La Paz, June–Aug. 1912.

27. NA, RG43, IC, Second International Opium Conference, minutes (1913), 2, 90; enclosures, Senate doc. 157 (the Netherlands), 4 Feb. 1913; H. Wright, "The International Opium Conference," *American Journal of International Law*, Oct. 1912, 870–71, 87.

28. McAllister, "Habitual Problems," 183, as the "extreme supply-control position"; Walker, *Drugs in Western Hemisphere*, xvii. U.S. Congress, House, Fourth International Conference, *International Control of Traffic in Habit-Forming Narcotic Drugs*, 1924, 13, 29, 31–3 (Porter), 289, 293–94 (Wright).

29. Taylor, *American Diplomacy*; McAllister, *Drug Diplomacy*; Bruun, Pan, and Rexed, *Gentlemen's Club*; Lowes, *Genesis of Control*. Renborg, *International Control* (1947), among other testimonies of 1920s and 30s (e.g., Willoughby, *Opium as International Problem*).

30. LN, Second Opium Conference, o.172.M.47.1924.XI; or C.641.M.303.1933. XI (OC 14729[1]), "Questionnaire Regarding the Coca Leaf" (Geneva), 31 May 1933. O.L.198.1934XI, "Situation of Certain Countries of Latin America." OC1472, "Preliminary Report on the Substitution of Other Crops for the Coca Plant and the Opium Poppy," 6 Aug. 1924. LN, C.760.M.260.1924 XI, Records of Second

Opium Conference, vol. 1, app. 1, "Draft Treaty Relating to the Coca Leaf," 381–88. PCOB, C.24.M241944.XI, "Pre-War Production and Distribution of Narcotic Drugs and their Raw Materials" (1944), 14–19, 25–27; OAC, OC445, "Coca Producers Association" (Amsterdam, Nov. 1925–May 1926); OC1133, "Syndicate of Cocaine and Morphine Manufacturers," 16 Jan. 1930; OC1760, "Latin American Mission," 24 Apr. 1939. Renborg, *International Control*, ch. xi, "Limits of Raw Material," does not note coca. Khat (or Qat), unrelated to coca, is a leafy stimulant from East Africa.

31. Anti-Opium Information Bureau, "Strange Omissions" (Geneva, 1928–34), 26 May 1931, 14. Willoughby, *Opium as International Problem*, ch. 20, "Production of Coca Leaf."

32. "Informe relativo al control de sustancias narcóticos," *BSP*, 22 June 1928; NA, RG170, 0660, Box 18, World Narcotics Factories, "Opium and Coca Industry in Peru," 1928; LN, OAC, OC153, 12 July 1923; C.L.182.1935, Annual Reports, "Situation of Certain Countries of Latin America," Nov. 1935; OC1143(2), "List of Firms Authorized to Manufacture Drugs," 17 Mar. 1936. ARE, Liga de Naciones, sections 7-0, 7-0-B, 1921–40s (and *BRE*, 1910–50s).

33. LN, OAC, OC1760, Ekstrand, "Latin American Mission," Peru, 5–7, app. "Visita de una misión de la Liga de las Naciones," 6 Jan., 8 Mar. 1938; *BRE*, esp. "Memorandum del Director," Apr. 1938, 248–59; *VA*, July 1938, 595–97.

34. Lema, "Coca de las Americas," 1–12, for local debate (lacking League records cited below); edited English version, Lema, "Coca Debate and Landowners," esp. 104–6.

35. LN, OAC, OC158, "Letter from the Bolivian Government on the Coca Industry and the Preparation of Cocaine," 28 Aug. 1923 (SPY); OAC, C.397.M146, 1924, minutes of 6th sess., 46, 50, an. 12, memorandum of M. Pinto-Escalier, "Observations of the Bolivian Government Regarding the Proposal to Restrict the Cultivation of Coca." C.760.M.260.1924 XI, Records of 2nd Opium Conference, vol. 1, Aug. 1925, 63–64; app. 1, "Draft Treaty Relating to the Coca Leaf."

36. Fernández, *Coca boliviana* (excerpt, Walker, *Drugs in Western Hemisphere*), ch. 17; ch. 18, Pérez retort, 1942. Lema, "Coca Debate and Landowners," 106. In 1948, the SPY reacted similarly to the UN Mission of Enquiry into Coca-Leaf: NA, RG170, 0660, Bolivia, J. M. Gamarra, "Bolivian Coca Is Not a Narcotic," from *Última Hora*, 3 Feb. 1948.

37. Friman, *Narco-Diplomacy*, ch. 2; Karch, "Japan and Cocaine"; de Kort, "Doctors, Diplomats, and Businessmen."

38. See Nadelmann, *Cops Across Borders*, for slow spread of policing. On the interwar era, see Meyer and Parssinen, *Webs of Smoke*, chs. 4–9. On FBN foreign policy politics, see Kinder and Walker, "Stable Force in a Storm."

39. NA, RG170, Box 18, World Narcotics Factories, 1927–39, "Producers of Refined Cocaine in Peru," 8 Nov. 1928. RG59, DF823.114, P/N, "Exportation of Coca Leaves from Peru," Jan. 1924. RG170, 0660, Peru, "Production of Coca Leaf in Peru," May 1933, or Nov. 1938.

40. NA, RG170, 0660, Bolivia, 1933–55, Fernand, "Coca Leaf in Bolivia," 12 Apr. 1933; Forsyth, "The Yungas Region of Bolivia," 12 Jan. 1937. Bolivia Decimal Files lag until about 1950.

41. NA, RG59, DF823.114, P/N, Burdett, "Manufacture of the Derivatives of the Coca Leaf in Peru," 22 Apr. 1922, "Visit to Huánuco" (quotes); marketing, DF823.114, Peru, Soberón to McKesson and Robbins (22 Oct. 1931), and to Merck, Markt, and Hammacher.

42. NA, RG59, DF823.114, P/N, Burdett, Apr. 1922.

43. NA, RG170, 0660, Peru, "Manufacture of the Derivatives of the Coca Leaf in Peru," 21 Apr. 1932, and all 1930s, e.g., "Cocaine Factories," Apr. 1938, and "Consumption of Coca Leaves," Nov. 1938. RG59, DF823.114, all 1930s, e.g., "Narcotics Questionnaire," May 1936; July 1936.

44. For details, see Gootenberg, "Secret Ingredients," from FBN documents (NA, RG170, Boxes 19–20, Beverages); cf. Reiss, "Policing for Profit," stressing cocaine's economic weight.

45. NA, RG59, LOT55D607, Box 4, Coca-Cola Extract, "Preliminary History," 1933. Pendergrast, *God and Coca-Cola*, 187–89, lacks FBN sources. Allen, *Secret Formula*, 180, 192–97.

46. NA, RG170, Box 19, D/B, De-cocainized Coca Leaves, Federal Narcotics Control Board, 21 June 1929, 15 Feb., 1 Mar. 1930, USDA (FDA) to Nutt.

47. NA, RG59, LOT55D607, Drugs, Box 4, Canada, Dept. of Pensions and National Health, 9 Mar. 1933; Sharman to Anslinger, 17 Nov. 1932. RG170, Box 63, D/B, 1932–33.

48. NA, RG170, Box 63, D/B, Fuller file (State Dept.), 3 Mar. 1933; Brokmeyer to Fuller, "Confidential: Bureau of Narcotics," 19 Jan. 1933. RG59, LOT55D607, Drugs, Box 4, Coca-Cola Extract, Hayes to Fuller, 28 Feb. 1938; RG170, Box 19, all 1937–38.

49. NA, RG170, Peru, "Visit of Mr. Eugene Schaeffer — Import of Coca into U.S. for Industrial Purposes," 10 Mar. 1933; and Anslinger to Hartung, 21 Feb. 1940.

50. See Gootenberg, "Reluctance or Resistance" or "Secret Ingredients," for details. Decades later, when Peru enacted ENACO in the 1950s, the U.S. reaction was still to demand low prices for Coca-Cola: NA, RG59, DF823.53, P/N, "Proposed Coca Leaf Monopoly," 7 Nov. 1955.

51. NA, RG170, Box 19, D/B, "Coca," 1915–45, 15, 20 July 1936, 28 Feb. 1940; an undated mid-1930s clipping, "The Coca-Cola Industry," tells of a mysterious "small plant in Peru." On war, see RG170, Box 20, Drugs/Coca Leaves, 1933–53, letters 1939–45, esp. Murlock, 18 Mar. 1942, Hayes to Anslinger, 2 July 1942. Pendergrast, *God and Coca-Cola*, chs. 11–13.

52. See, e.g., Andreas, "When Policies Collide." This is a contradiction seized upon by some anti–drug war libertarians.

53. Paz Soldán, "Problema médico-socio de coca"; Luzio, "Tecnología de cocaína"; "Ten Years of Coca Monopoly in Peru," *BN* 14/1 (1962): 9–17. UN Archive, TE 322/Per (9), 1957–60, Caron, "Cocaína — comercialización de la cocaína por el Perú," 15 Dec. 1961.

54. E.g., NA, DF823.114, P/N, 12 Dec. 1930, 19 May 1933, 24 Oct. 1940, and 17 June 1944. RG170, Box 19, De-cocainized Coca Leaves, Hartung to Brokmeyer, 15, 27 Apr. 1940; Box 20, Drugs/Coca Leaves, "Visit to Simbal," 8 Apr. 1940.

55. Friman, *Narco-Diplomacy*, chs. 4–5. This analysis follows dense war documentation in NA, RG170, 0660, Peru, all 1940–44, and RG59, DF823.114, P/N, 1944–45. RG170, 0660, Peru, "Japanese Inquiries," 6 Dec. 1941.

Caron, "Cocaína — Comercialización de la Cocaína por el Perú," 15 Dec. 1961. *MEC*,
1955–60s, "Laboratorios Fiscales de Industrialización de la Coca y sus Derivados."
NA, RG59, DF823.53, P/N, 1955.

57. NA, RG170, 0660, Peru, Maywood to Anslinger, Feb., May 1940, Apr.–May
1942; "Narcotics in Peru," Apr. 1942; "Exports of Coca, Cocaine," 1943; "Raw
Cocaine in Peru," Dec. 1941. RG59, DF823.114, P/N, orders, intelligence reports.
Walker, *Drug Control in Americas*, 157–58; Pendergrast, *God and Coca-Cola*, ch. 12.
Joseph Heller's satirical war novel *Catch-22* portrays Minderbinder's M and M
Enterprises running the war for world capitalism.

58. E.g., NA, RG170, 0660, Peru, Mar. 1942, "Confidential," July 1943, 17 June
1944; RG59, DF823.114, Apr. 1942. See Kohn, "Cocaine Girls," for war discourses; in
contrast, for war as space of drug running and official collaboration, see Marshall,
"Opium and National Security."

59. NA, RG170, 0660, Peru, "Control of Soda Ash in Peru," Mar. 1942. RG59,
DF823.114, P/N, Mar. 1939, Apr.–Aug. 1941, Jan.–June 1942, Jan. and Apr. 1943,
Apr.–May 1944, Jan. 1945. *Acción oficial en Tingo María*, 110–1l.

60. NA, RG170, 0660, Peru, Nov. 1942. Sáenz, *La coca*; Gutiérrez-Noriega and
Zapata, *Estudios sobre coca y cocaína*; Gagliano, *Coca Prohibition,* 146–54; Cueto,
"Andean Biology."

61. NA, RG170, 0660, Peru, Feb. 1940, Maywood, Apr. 1940, Mar. 1944; Ministerio
de Relaciones Exteriores, Sept. 1944; RG59, DF823.114, P/N, Apr. 1940, Mar. 1942,
1944.

62. McAllister, *Drug Diplomacy*, ch. 6. UN, CND, 1st–2nd sess., 1946–48, "Illicit
Traffic in Narcotic Drugs, World Trends, 1939–45," 1947. On U.S. anxieties, see
Jonnes's literal *Hep-Cats and Pipe Dreams*, ch. 6.

63. UN, CND, Annual Reports of Governments, E/NR 1950, *Peru: Annual Report
for 1950*, "Laws and Publications," 3–14 (translations); NA, RG59, DF823.114, P/N,
all 1947–50, degree laws. A compendium is Rubio Correa, *Legislación sobre drogas*,
82–93, from *EP*, 1947–50.

64. On APRA and drugs, see NA, RG59, LOT61D45, Subject Files Relating to
Peru, 1950–58, esp. Morlock, 24 Mar. 1950; NA, RG170, 0660, Peru, all Feb.–Mar.
1950. See analysis by Dorn, "American Reputation." For drug sweeps, see *EC*,
21–22, 27 Apr., and esp. 28–30 Apr. 1949; 1, 3–4, 7, 14, 19, 23 May; 27 July; 20, 23,
25, 31 Aug.; and 9 Sept. 1949.

65. NA, RG170, 0660, South America, Box 30, "Confidential," 6-1998 (Peña), 14
Dec. 1948; RG170, 0660, Box 63, Drugs-Cocaine, "Cocaine Renaissance," 27 Feb.
1950. "Peru: The White Goddess," *Time*, 11 Apr. 1949.

66. NA, RG170, 0660, Box 63, Drugs-Cocaine, all 1949–50, esp. "Program for
elimination of the movement of cocaine from the West Coast of South America to
the United States," 20 Oct. 1949; RG59, DF823.114, P/N, Williams, "Memorandum
for Anslinger," 17 May 1949; Hoover, "Peruvian Narcotics Traffic," 22 Apr. 1949;
Ryan, "Illicit Cocaine Traffic," 3 Dec. 1949; "Afirman que la producción de cocaína
peruana es una amenaza para el mundo," *La Prensa* (Lima), 19 Apr. 1949.

67. Anslinger and Tompkins, *Traffic in Narcotics*, 281, 16–18; FBN, *TODD*, 1949–50.
NA, RG170, 0660, Peru, "Illicit Traffic in Cocaine from Peru," 2 May 1949.

68. INPL, UN, ECSOC, E/CN.7/236–447, "Illicit Traffic," "Clandestine Laboratories,"

1951–63. FBN, *TODD*, 1953–66; NA, RG170, Box 54, "Inter-American Conferences," "Cocaine Conferences," 1961–64; UN, CND, E/CN7, 393, 28 Apr. 1960; *BN* 16/3 (July–Sept. 1964): 25–32. See Valentine, *Strength of the Wolf*, for FBN oral histories affirming pre-1970s drug wars.

69. Gagliano, *Coca Prohibition*, ch. 7, for UN mission; Bewley-Taylor, *U.S. and Drug Control*, 86–87, as imperial; Reiss, "Policing for Profit," ch. 3, as conspiratorial. See timely survey by Carlos Monge M., "El problema de la coca en el Perú," *Anales de la Facultad de Medicina* 29/4 (1946): 2207–11, esp. research of F. Cabieses. UN, CND, E/575, 12 Sept. 1947; E/CN.7/W.34, 1 May, 14 June 1948 (its "Study on Coca Leaves" cites an old "very interesting note" of Alfredo Bignon, 18). NA, RG170, Box 20, Drugs, Coca Leaves, 8 Nov., 20 Dec. 1950, 2 Jan. 1951, 25 Mar. 1952.

70. UN, CND, E/NR 1950/97, *Peru: Annual Report for 1950*, 17 Jan. 1952, 25–27, "Mission of Experts for Reorganization of Narcotics Administration" (Logan Mission). NA, RG170, Box 8, Drugs, Coca Chewing, 1937–63, 8 July 1952. Anslinger now knew the Coca-Cola exception was complicating his job abroad, though the firm helped his 1950s domestic rein. See Box 8, Sept.–Oct. 1950, for Anslinger campaign to quash even U.S. medical research on coca: a Massachusetts General–Navy coca project on high-altitude stress in pilots at the advent of cold war jet aviation.

71. UN, ECSOC, *Report of the Commission of Enquiry on the Coca Leaf*, 5th year, 12th sess., Special Supplement (July 1950); or related, e.g., E/1666, "Answer to Statements of the Representatives of Peru and Bolivia in Commission on Narcotic Drugs," 8 June 1951. "Llegada de la Comisión de las NU que estudiará el problema de la coca," *EC*, 12 Sept. 1949.

72. Monge M., "Réplica," *Perú Indígena* 3/7–8 (Sept.–Dec. 1952); also as *Counter-Reply of Peruvian Commission*; *EC*, 14 Sept. 1949.

73. UN, CND, E/NR 1950/97, *Peru: Annual Report for 1950*; E/CN.7/242/, 25 Mar. 1953, "Export of Coca Leaf from Peru"; CND, NR 1951–54, 13 Mar. 1956, "Annual Reports Communicated by the Gov. of Peru"; E/CN.7/370, 15 Apr. 1959, "The Question of the Coca Leaf." NA, RG170, 0660, Bolivia, 1933–55, "Problem of Bolivian Coca," 27 Feb. 1948, esp. *Última Hora*, 3 Feb. 1948.

74. UN Archive, TE 322/Per (9), June 1957–19 Sept. 1960; 26 Feb. 1962, Caron, "Cocaína," 15 Dec. 1961; *MEC*, 1955–60s, "Laboratorios Fiscales de Industrialización de la Coca y sus Derivados." NA, RG59, DF823.53, P/N, 1955.

75. Summary of Gootenberg, "Secret Ingredients," 254–65, esp. ALAKEA, 262–64; Pennsylvania State University Library, Harry J. Anslinger Papers, for 1950s.

CHAPTER SIX

1. On this secret war, see Valentine, *Strength of the Wolf*, or Astorga, *Drogas sin fronteras*.

2. Cobb, *Police and People*; Ginzburg, "Inquisitor as Anthropologist." On drug control discourse, see Astorga, *Mitología del narcotraficante*; Gootenberg, "Talking like a State"; or Kohn, *Narcomania*. On traffickers in historical research, besides Astorga or Sáenz Rovner, *Conexión cubana*, see Meyer and Parssinen's Asian-oriented *Webs of Smoke*; Recio, "Prohibition and Drug Trade"; and Block, "European Drug Traffic."

3. For transnational Americas, see Joseph, LeGrande, and Salvatorre, *Close Encounters of Empire*; Smith, "Political Culture of Drug Control," on cold war antidrug culture; and for the U.S.-Andean cold war, Pike, *United States and Andean Republics*, chs. 10–11.

4. For models of illicit economy, see Reuter, *Disorganized Crime*; Haller, "Illegal Enterprise"; or van Schendel and Abraham, *Illicit Flows and Criminal Things*.

5. ARH, Pref., exp. 463, oficio 82, Soberón bankruptcy, 1949; lg. 80, exp. 1212, 1948, last sale.

6. Spillane, *Cocaine*, chs. 6–7; Block, "Snowman Cometh"; Kohn, *Dope Girls*. On the "Dusters," see Asbury, *Gangs of New York* (orig. 1927), 237–39, 298–300.

7. Musto, "America's First Cocaine"; see Treasury Department's *Reports of Commissioner of Internal Revenue* (GPO, 1915–20s) on seizures, mainly from doctors and dentists.

8. Block, "Snowman Cometh"; Morgan, *Yesterday's Addicts*; Courtwright, Joseph, and Jarlais, *Addicts Who Survived*; Starks, *Cocaine Fiends and Reefer Madness*, ch. 4. Phillips and Wynne, *Cocaine*, chs. 6–7; Ashley, *Cocaine*, ch. 6.

9. Karch, "Japan and Cocaine"; Friman, *Narco-Diplomacy*; Davenport-Hines, *Pursuit of Oblivion*, 217, 265, 286–88; Guy, *Sex and Danger*, 148–50. I. C. Chopra and R. N. Chopra, "The Cocaine Problem in India," *BN* 10/2 (1958): 12–24, a case open for research.

10. FBN, *TODD*, all 1930–45.

11. Renborg, *International Control*, 147–48. NA, RG59, LOT55D607, Subject Files Relating to Control of Narcotics Traffic, despatch 487 (NN3 59 88–7), "Name File of Suspected Narcotics Traffickers, 1927–1942." "Descubrieron . . . un laboratorio clandestino de drogas heroícas en Miraflores," *El Universal*, 31 Mar. 1938. RG170, 0660, Bolivia, Box 6, 10 May 1960. Bácula, from a French cell, was rumored to send Slavic chemists to Lima (20 Apr. 1954), and his sister was married in the 1950s to the ex–cocaine maker Salvador Nesanovich. Interview, Dr. Virgilio López Calderón, Huánuco, July 1998. Nineteen forty-three was also the year of murky rumored "Aerolineas Q" drug flights between Cuba and the Andes.

12. NA, RG59, DF823.114, P/N, July 1940, 7 Oct. 1943; DF823.114, 1–1347, P/N, 23 Jan. 1947, 2 Jan. 1948. FBN, *TODD*, 1946–47.

13. NA, RG170, 0660, Box 30, South America, "Confidential," 6-1998 (Peña), 14 Dec. 1948, emphasis in original; Box 63, Drugs-Cocaine, "Program for elimination of the movement cocaine from . . . South America to U.S.," 20 Oct. 1949, and "Cocaine Renaissance," 27 Feb. 1950. On bop-era New York cocaine scene, see Davis, *Miles*, 86, 95; others downplay drugs, e.g., DeVeaux, *Birth of Bebop*, 446–47.

14. For Balarezo, see NA, RG59, DF823.114, P/N, esp. 24 Aug. 1949, clippings. On APRA, see RG59, DF825.53, Chile, Narcotics, 1950–59, "Apristas Protest Bureau of Narcotics," or anti-Aprista polemics, e.g., Enríquez, *Haya de la Torre*, 121–33, "Haya y el tráfico de narcóticos."

15. Dorn, "American Reputation"; Kinder, "Bureaucratic Cold Warrior" generally.

16. NA, RG59, DF825.53, Enclosure no. 3, Mar. 1950; DF823.114, P/N, 1948–49, esp. Williams, "Illicit Cocaine Traffic," 17 May 1949, 1 Nov. 1948, 7 June, 14 Dec. 1949. Peru's output of the 1940s was less than half a ton, but the FBN claimed a

twenty-seven-kilo daily capacity, or seven tons yearly worth $35 million in New York.

17. *EC*, all Apr.–May 1949; UN, CND, E/NR 1950/07, *Peru, Annual Report for 1950*, 35–40, add. "Cocaine and Crude Cocaine," 17 Jan. 1952.

18. NA, RG59, DF823.114, P/N, 7 June 1949 (Prados); DF823.114, 8–2548, "Fabricación de cocaína clandestina" (Ayllon); DF823.114, no. 302, 7 Dec. 1948.

19. ARH, Pref., lg. 80, no. 905, 3 July 1948. NA, RG59, DF823.114, P/N, 25 Aug. 1948, "Clandestine Traffic"; UN, CND, E/NR 1950/07 *Peru: Annual Report for 1950*, 35–36.

20. NA, RG170, 0660, Box 8, Ecuador, "Illicit Narcotic Traffic in Peru," 7 May 1953, López, 30 Apr. 1953, and "A Report on Observation in Peru regarding Illicit Drug Traffic," 24 Apr. 1953. Novelist Vargas Llosa, in *Fish in Water*, recounts Lima's bohemian scene in 1952, when as a young journalist he snorted coke at the "Negro-Negro" located in a "basement underneath the arcades of the Plaza San Martín" (147), i.e., near the Hotel Bolívar trafficker haunt.

21. Cases from NA, RG59, DF823.114, P/N, all 1949–55; RG170, Box 30, Trafficking, Mexico, Mar. 1961. Cubans included Martínez del Rey, Ara, Escalona, Flaifel, and Portella. Repeat offenders included Steel, Morales, Quiroz, Pandura, and Puttkammer.

22. NA, RG59, DF825.53, Narcotics, Chile, 1955–, no. 000254, "Control of Narcotic Drugs," Jan. 1959; RG170, Box 19, Drugs, Cocaine, 4-29-52; *Vistazo*, 20 Jan. 1959; also "Soy un traficante de drogas heróicas," *Véa*, 29 Jan. 1959. INPL, UN, ECSOC, E/CN.7/388, "Illicit Traffic," 1959, and 1962 report. FBN, *TODD*, 1959.

23. UN, ECSOC, E/CN.7/420, add. 1, "The Question of the Coca Leaf: Report by the National Health Services of Chile," 2 Mar. 1962, 3.

24. NA, RG170, Box 30, Subject Files—Trafficking, Mexico, 13 Mar. 1961.

25. NA, RG59, DF825.53, Chile, Narcotics, 29 Jan. 1963. RG170, Box 18, World Narcotics Factories, 17 Oct. 1966; UN, GEN/NAR/64Conf.2.6, Inter-American Consultative Group on the Coca Leaf, report "Illicit Traffic in Cocaine," 1 Sept. 1964, 6, 14; FBN, *TODD*, 1964, 18.

26. UN, TAO/LAT/72, "Report of the UN Study Tour of Points of Convergence of the Illicit Traffic in Coca Leaf and Cocaine in Latin America," 28 Feb. 1967, 14, 44; U.S. House Committee on Foreign Affairs, *World Narcotics Problem*, 1973; cf. U.S. Senate Committee on the Judiciary, *World Drug Traffic*, 1972, 157: Squella-Avendaño was "slated to receive an important post in the Allende government," making this an anticommunist drug scandal.

27. Schwartz, *Pleasure Island*, 24; Cirules, *Mafia in Havana*; Sáenz Rovner, *Conexión cubana*.

28. FBN, *TODD*, 1957, "Cuba," and 1960–62 reports; INPL, UN, ECSOC, E/CN.7/388, "Illicit Traffic" and "Clandestine Laboratories" reports, 1953–61.

29. Messick and Goldblatt, *Mobs and Mafia*, 5, 202–4. NA, RG170, Box 54, Inter-American Conferences, 1960–64, "Statement of the USA Delegation," Rio, Feb. 1960.

30. FBN, *TODD*, 1961–64 reports.

31. NA, RG170, Box 30, Traffickers, "Cocaine Traffic between South America, Central America and the U.S.," New York, 1961, enclosures (Mexico), and 19 July

32. NA, RG170, 0660, Box 8, Cuba, 1958–59; RG59, DF837.53, Cuba, 1955–59, no. 1037, 19 Mar. 1959. DF837.53, 23 Mar. 1962, "Rejection of Cuban Note on Narcotics"; also in Walker, *Drugs in Western Hemisphere*, 170–72.

33. Pennsylvania State University Library, Harry J. Anslinger Papers, Box 6, Scrapbooks, June 1962 clippings; NA, RG170, 0660, Bolivia, Box 6, 1955–62, "Confidential," Report of the U.S. Delegation, Rio Conference, 1961.

34. UN GEN/NAR/64Conf.2.6, "Illicit Traffic in Cocaine," 1 Sept. 1964, "Memo for Inter-American Consultative Group on Coca Leaf Problems," La Paz, Nov. 1964, 3–4; UN, E/CN.7 R.12/add. 31, 1962, 3.

35. UN, ECSOC, INPL, E/CN.7/388, 447, 1959, 1962, and PCOB, "Traffic in Narcotic Drugs," 1960; INPL, "Clandestine Laboratories," 1945–60 (Paris, 1961 — no UN class), 72–73. NA, RG170, Box 30, Trafficking, 12 Oct. 1960.

36. UN, CND, 14th sess., Gen. E/CN.7/R.12, "Restricted," add. 24, "Illicit Traffic, Brazil," 1959, add. 31, 1962, 2–5 (DEA Library). D. Parreiras, "Data on the Illicit Traffic in Cocaine and Coca Leaves in South America, with an Annex on Narcotics Control in Brazil," *BN* 13/4 (Oct.–Dec. 1961): 33–36.

37. UN, CND, 15th sess., Gen. E/CN.7/R.12, add. 31, "Illicit Traffic, Brazil," 1962, 4–5.

38. Agnew, *Undercover Agent — Narcotics*, ch. 10. UN, CND, E/CN.7/393, Illicit Traffic, "Inter-American Conference on the Illicit Traffic in Cocaine and Coca-Leaf," Rio de Janeiro, Apr. 1960 (varied designations and delegation reports).

39. UN, GEN/NAB/64/Conf.2/6, Inter-American Consultative Group on Coca-Leaf Problems, "Illicit Traffic in Cocaine," Nov. 1964, 5–6.

40. NA, RG170, 0660, Box 54, Ecuador, 1961; RG170, Box 161, Panama, "Subject: South America," 31 July 1964 (Blades); RG170, 0660, Box 8, Colombia (1960s), 12 Jan. 1959, Cuba file, Herrán Olazaga, otherwise sparse. UN, TAO/LAT/72, "UN Study Tour of Points of Convergence of the Illicit Traffic in Coca Leaf and Cocaine," 1967; PCOB, 89th sess., E/OB/W/A.1, "Mission to Honduras, Colombia, Ecuador," 5 Sept. 1966, 8; FBN, *TODD*, 1961. For Colombia, see Roldán, "Cocaine Miracle," or Kenney, "History of Colombian Trade," based on Sáenz Rovner, "Pre-historia del narcotraficante": these latter documents reveal little "prehistory."

41. Astorga, "Cocaine in Mexico," 185; Astorga, *Drogas sin fronteras*, 296–98, 300–304, for same incidents.

42. INPL, UN, ECSOC, E/CN.7/388, 26 Mar. 1956. NA, RG170, Box 30, Trafficking, "Cocaine Trafficking b/n S. America, Central America and the U.S.," 15 Nov. 1961; RG170, 0660, Box 2, Mexico, July–Aug. 1960; FBN, *TODD*, 1958–65 reports.

43. NA, RG170, Box 30, "Cocaine Trafficking," 1961; RG170, 0660, Box 54, Mexico, 1964–65; RG170, 0660, Mexico, Box 161, "Case: George Asaf de Bala," Nov. 1959; Astorga, *Drogas sin fronteras*, 300–303. Astorga (oral-com., Aug. 2004) links these pioneers and the 1980s Sonorans, apprenticed in cocaine by jailed Cubans in Mexico.

44. Dunkerley, *Rebellion in Veins*, 308–26, for later cocaine; on coming peasant migrations, see Sanabria, *Coca Boom*.

45. NA, RG170, 0660, Box 19, Bolivia, Williams, 8 Mar. 1950; 15 Feb. 1950; "Attention G. Morlock," Dept. of State, 11 Apr. 1950, for Peru origins; "Information from Confidential Source," 19 June 1950; "Alleged Smuggling of Cocaine to Brazil," 16 May 1950.

46. NA, RG170, Box 19, 23 July 1951, "Bolivian Police Uncover Narcotics Organization," 16 Oct. 1951; "Further Developments in . . . Narcotics Trade," 28 Nov. 1951; 5 Mar. 1953; RG170, Box 1, Ecuador, 30 Apr. 1953. DF824.53/4–450, B/N, 23 July 1951.

47. NA, RG59, DF824.53/8–1253, B/N, 12 Aug.–2 Sept. 1953, clippings; DF824,53/5–554, 5 May 1954. DF825.53/254, Embassy, Santiago, "Control of Narcotic Drugs," 22 Jan. 1959.

48. FBN, *TODD*, 1955, "Cocaine." NA, RG170, Box 19, Bolivia, 1957–64; INPL, UN, ECSOC, E/CN.7, 1953–60, Bolivia.

49. NA, RG59, DF824.53/2.2956, B/N, 27–29 Feb. 1956; DF411.24342, Jan.–Feb. 1961, July 1962. RG170, Box 6, 13 Apr. 1962. Spitzer, *Hotel Bolivia*; for Jewish traffickers generally, see Block, "European Drug Traffic," 324–25. For Nazis and later drug roles, see Cockburn and St. Clair, *Whiteout*: Klaus Barbie, the fugitive "Butcher of Lyon" in Bolivia and, by 1957, U.S. citizen, became one of Banzar's notorious drug and political allies in the 1970s. Cockburn implies he was running "coca paste" from the lowlands by 1967 after aiding the 1964 coup (176).

50. NA, RG59, DF824.53/22956, B/N, 23 Mar. 1956; DF824.53/5–2958, "Fábrica de Jabones y Champú se elaborada cocaína," *La Nación*, 29 May 1958.

51. NA, RG170, 0660, Bolivia, "Investigation of cocaine smuggler Blanca Ibáñez de Sánchez of La Paz, Bolivia," 12 Nov., 16 Apr. 1958; RG170, Box 54, Conferences, "Blanca Ibáñez de Sánchez Gang of International Illicit Cocaine Traffickers," 26 Nov. 1962; RG170, 0660, Cuba, 28 Apr. 1961, and "Cocaine Traffic," 15 Nov. 1961.

52. FBN, *TODD*, 1960, "Bolivia," 41–42; NA, RG59, DF824.53/5–260, B/N, 2 May 1960; INPL, UN, ECSOC, E/CN.7/388, "Illicit Traffic," 1960, Argentina; "Clandestine Laboratories," 1960, 73.

53. NA, RG59, DF411.24342/2–761, "Narcotics Trafficker Blanca Ibáñez de Sánchez," photos; DF824.53/5–2460, B/N, 24 May 1960.

54. NA, RG170, 0660, Box 6, Bolivia, 1955–62, 10 July, 18 Aug. 1957; Lechín, 15 Sept 1961.

55. NA, RG59, DF824.53/9–1561, B/N, 15 Sept. 1961, enclosures. RG170, Box 6, Bolivia, "Controversy Over Illegal Narcotics Activity in Argentina," 14 Sept. 1961.

56. NA, RG59, DF824.53/11–1161, B/N, no. 246, 15 Nov. 1961, Karp to embassy, clippings.

57. Dunkerley, *Rebellion in Veins*, 108. NA, RG59, DF 824.53/11–1161, B/N, clippings *Última Hora*, *El Diario*; RG170, 0660, Box 6, "Press Round-up on Luis Gayán," Dec. 1961 and all Jan.–Feb. 1962. UN, CND, E/CN.7/L257, Consultative Group on Coca-Leaf Problems, Lima, 1962, "Question of the Coca-Leaf," 24 Apr. 1963; "Report of Delegation to 2nd Meeting of Inter-American Consultative Group," Jan. 1962; and Rio report, 27 Nov.–7 Dec. 1961, 15.

58. NA, RG59, DF824.53/1246, B/N, "Arrest of Members of Narcotic Ring," 4 Dec.

1961; RG170, 0660, Box 6, Bolivia, 30 Mar. 1962 and all 1962–65, including "Bolivian
Cops Sniff Way to Coke Cookers," *Sunday News*, 11 July 1965.

59. NA, RG170, Box 8, "Drugs—Coca Chewing" (Coca Reports, 1937–63). Bascopé Aspiazu, *Veta blanca*, 60; Cockburn and St. Clair, *Whiteout*, 174, 180–81, which puts Barbie with fascist Croats.

60. UN, C/CN.7/L.257, Bolivian Health Ministry, "Question of the Coca Leaf," 24 Apr. 1963; NA, RG170, 0660, Box 6, Bolivia, "Classified Report of U.S. Delegation," Dec. 1961; Rio Conference, "Illicit Traffic in Cocaine," 1 Sept 1964; McVickers, Cochabamba, 18 Nov. 1965, 20 July, 22 Aug. 1966. UN, CND, E/CN.7/R.11, add. 40, "Illicit Traffic Brazil," 7 Apr. 1961.

61. NA, RG170, 0660, Box 6, Bolivia, Durkin to INPL, 2 June 1967; "Bi-Annual Summary...of Manufacture and Traffic of Narcotics in Bolivia," July–Dec. 1966.

62. See Kenney, *From Pablo to Osama*, ch. 1, for insights on such networks.

63. Block, "European Drug Traffic"; Meyer and Parssinen, *Webs of Smoke*. Valentine, *Strength of the Wolf*, 325–28, 370–72, notes attempted Corsican mafia cocaine trading by 1965 (Ricord's Group France, Mondoloni, Croce) in Mexico and Argentina—a "triangle of death" of South American coke for French heroin. Sáenz Rovner, *Conexión cubana*, ch. 9.

CHAPTER SEVEN

1. Laussent-Herrera, "Presencia japonesa en Huánuco-Pucallpa"; *Tulumayo* (1942).

2. E. Salgado, "The Peruvian Central Highway," *Bulletin of the Pan-American Union* 49 (1935): 825–30; Werlich, "Conquest of the Montaña"; Herndon and Gibbon, *Exploration of Amazon*; Durand, *Ferrocarril al Huallaga*. AGN, H-6, 1081, Contribuciones, Padrón de giro de impuestos, Huánuco, 1951.

3. *Acción oficial en Tingo María*, a 177-page 1943 report; Hanson, *The Amazon*, 27–28; *Viajes de estudio*; de las Casas, *Provincia de Huánuco*, 227; "Tingo María, ciudad adolecente," *EC*, July 1949. NA, RG166, Foreign Agricultural Service, Peru, Attaché reports, Boxes 349–51, 1942–.

4. UN, CN.7/474/add. 4, 1962. NA, RG166: Foreign Agricultural Service, Narrative Reports, Boxes 888–90 (1940s); Technical Collaboration Branch, Peru, Boxes 18–22, 1942–53, reports to 1960s, when project folded into US-AID. *MEC*, 1955. Pilli, "Coca Industry," 31.

5. We may never know the full story of the Huallaga, for Peru's Sendero Luminoso guerrillas, exploiting the valley's coca peasants and drug levies in the 1980s and 1990s, burned, French Revolution style, provincial records in Tingo María. On growth, see *Departamento de Huánuco*, 29–36.

6. Aramburú, "Expansión de la frontera en selva alta"; Aramburú, Bedoya, and Recharte, *Colonización en Amazonía*; Werlich, *Peru*, ch. 10.

7. For migration and coca, see Aramburú, "Economía parcelaria y cultivo de coca"; Rumrill, "Penélope en la Huallaga" (from 1975 fieldwork with coca peasants); Morales, *Cocaine*, esp. ch. 5; and for Bolivian lowlands, see Sanabria, *Coca Boom*.

8. NA, RG59, SN, 11.5, A-308, "Narcotic Situation in Peru," Lima, 16 Oct. 1971;

11.5, A-215, Confidential, Narcotics Control, "Action Plan—Peru, Description of Drug Situation in Peru" (n.d., ca. 1972); and 11.5, 4705, Lima, Peru, 12 Aug. 1970.

9. *La Trinchera* (Huánuco), 1974–75, esp. 10 June, 22 July 1974; 4 Feb., 25 Mar., 30 Sept., 11 Nov. 1975. Thanks to Maestro Manuel Nieves for opening his personal newspaper collection. ARH, Penales, 1972–76, confirm spiking local drug cases.

10. On PBC and crude cocaine, see Gootenberg, "Case of Scientific Excellence," n39, or BNDD papers, e.g., NA, RG170, Box 18, "Process for Manufacture of Cocaine Paste," Mar. 1966 (of "detained traffickers"). Morales, *Cocaine*, 75, for peasant claim that "Germans" (Kitz, *pozuzeños*, or Merck lineage?) left the technique. Léon and Castro de la Mata, *Pasta básica*.

11. "Capturan narcotraficantes—Cáen traficantes," *La Trinchera* (Huánuco), 11 Nov. 1975. For the Huallaga's 1980s boom, see Kawell, "Coca." That marginal Huallaga peasants had no supraorganization enabled coca's volatility after 1970 and its takeover by Sendero Luminoso in the 1980s. Bolivian coca peasants, on the other hand, managed to forge more political ties, organization, and identities rooted in coca, thus becoming long-term players in Bolivian politics.

12. Uncertainty surrounds the role of the 1950s Herrán Olazaga brothers, noted in chapter 6. Historians seeking a longer role for Colombians are Sáenz Rovner, "Pre-historia del narcotraficante," used in Kenney, "History of Colombian Trade" (his phases 1 and 2 are otherwise the best map); and Camacho-Guizado and López-Restrepo, "Smugglers to Drug Lords." Informed secondary accounts concur with my periodization: Orlando Melo, "Drug Trade and Economy"; Thoumi, *Illegal Drugs in Andes*; Roldán, "Cocaine Miracle"; and Henman, *Mama Coca*.

13. In Colombia, the logic goes, it was as if Bolivia's weak state faced Chilean-style economic elites: Thoumi, *Illegal Drugs in Andes*, ch. 3. Bentancourt and García, *Contrabandistas y mafiosos*; Camacho-Guizado and López-Restrepo, "Smugglers to Drug Lords," stress desensitizing 1950s violence.

14. See Roldán, "Cocaine Miracle"; for origins, Orlando Melo, "Drug Trade and Economy," 68–70; or for zone overall, Appelbaum, *Muddied Waters*.

15. NA, RG59, SN, Narcotics, Soc 11-5, 203727 (telegram, 14 Dec. 1970); Soc 11-5, 203727 (14 Dec. 1970); Soc 11-5, 165739 (7 Oct. 1970); also 4485, 4499. Castillo, *Jinetes de cocaína*, 6, 29–30.

16. "Production of Cocaine in Chile Described," *Última Hora*, 5 July 1972 (from DEA, VF, "Cocaine," "Illicit Traffic"); "Cocaine Gains Cited," *NYT*, 24 Apr. 1975 (Gage series) and 10 Sept. 1974. Phillips and Wynne, *Cocaine*, ch. 13, "Trafficking in Cocaine: Getting it Here," for Jerry Strickler, DEA, an error-marred source based on Plate interviews in "Coke: The New Big Easy Entry Business," *NYT Magazine*, Oct. 1973; Grinspoon and Bakalar, *Cocaine*, 53–54, also from *NYT* reportage. Authorities even tried to frame Chilean solidarity networks as cocaine related in a bizarre 1975 trial of University of Wisconsin journalism professor Marion Brown: *NYT*, 31 July 1975. E-com., Daniel Palma, Santiago, Feb. 2006. William Walker III (e-com., Oct. 2006) reports from an old interview of former agent Saucedo that the new DEA was not thrilled with Pinochet's move: it felt it could have nipped cocaine in the bud given its concentration in Chile, a plan foiled by this dispersal.

17. L. Rohter, "Former Aide Says Pinochet and a Son Dealt in Drugs," *NYT*, 11 July 2006. For an exposé, see Francisco Marín, "Narcodictador," *Proceso* (Mexico)

1551 (23 July 2006): 54–58. Accusations tie General Manuel Contreras, notorious head of the Dirección Nacional de Inteligencia, to Italian fascist Valerio Borhese and jailed dealer Frankel Baramdyka. Some charges of drug financing date as early as the 1976 Letelier assassination in Washington, D.C., when Chile's military used rightist Cuban exile groups dealing in cocaine. Dinges and Landau, *Assassination*, 264n, implies that in league with the Cubans, the DINA took over abandoned trafficker plants.

18. Castillo, *Jinetes de cocaína*, ch. 2; Antonil, *Mama Coca*, 76–96, 98–99, for initial conditions.

19. Kenney, "History of Colombian Trade," phase 3; Thoumi, *Illegal Drugs in Andes*, 84–5 (interview of early trafficker); Chaparro, *Cartel de Cali*, 161–63, 235–40; N. Gage, "Herreras among Biggest of Cocaine Organizations," *NYT*, 21 Apr. 1975.

20. Escobar left sources, including R. Escobar, *Mi hermano Pablo*; memoirs; and a family documentary, Beaufort, *Archivos privados de Escobar*. There is much journalism: Salazar, *Escobar*; Legara, *Verdadero Pablo*; or Mollison, *Memory of Escobar*, a photographic homage. See Kirk, *More Terrible than Death*, 78–87, for reliable narrative.

21. N. Gage, "Latins Now Leaders in Hard-Drug Trades," *NYT*, 21–24 Apr. 1975; *NYT Magazine*, 1 Sept. 1974.

22. Grinspoon and Bakalar, *Cocaine*, 50–51; Phillips and Wynne, *Cocaine*, 182–83; DEA, VF, "Cocaine" (1970s), "Report of the Federal Cocaine Policy Task Force," July 1974, and George Gaffney, "Narcotic Drugs—Their Origins and Routes of Traffic," June 1968. NA, RG59, SN, Soc 11–15, 12, 1972, untitled BNDD documentation. A pioneer was legendary 1960s folksinger Dave Van Ronk, whose cover of the 1920s ditty "Cocaine Blues" on *Dave Van Ronk and the Hudson Dusters* (Verve-Forecast Records, FTS-3041, 1968) was a staged act of cultural memory, as the Dusters (on the cover) imitated the city's notorious coke gang of the teens, which had operated around Van Ronk's Greenwich Village stomping grounds.

23. Epstein, *Agency of Fear*; Massing, *The Fix*. I contest here Massing's notion that Nixon, by making drug control a social policy, got the drug war right. Warring on other fronts worked far more eventual harm than methadone clinics alleviated. Davenport-Hines, *Pursuit of Oblivion*, ch. 13.

24. G. Volsky, "Illicit Traffic in Cocaine Growing by Leaps and Bounds in Miami," *NYT*, 1 Feb. 1970. Kamastra's 1974 *Weed*, 276–77, notes smugglers' shift; Corben's *Cocaine Cowboys*, a documentary on early Miami traffickers, shows move from Colombian angle.

25. Phillips and Wynne, *Cocaine*, ch. 11, "Current Use of Cocaine in the U.S."

26. UN, TAO/LAT/72, "Report of the United Nations Study Tour of Points of Convergence of the Illicit Traffic in Coca Leaf and Cocaine in Latin America," 28 Feb. 1967; NA, RG170, 0660, Box 54, Conferences and Commissions, UN Latin American Study Tour, 1969.

27. NA, RG170, 0660, Box 54, Inter-American Conferences, "Cocaine Project," Dec. 1968. House Committee on Foreign Affairs, *International Aspects of Narcotics Problem* and *World Narcotics Problem*; House Select Committee on Narcotics Abuse and Control, *Cocaine*.

28. Documents found in DEA, VF, "Cocaine" (1970s): "Report of the Federal

Cocaine Policy Task Force" (typescript, 19 July 1974); "White Paper on Drug Abuse" (Report to the President, Domestic Council Drug Abuse Task Force, Sept. 1975, 24–25, 33). Petersen and Stillman, *Cocaine: 1977*, introduction, 1; BNDD, "Annual Report of Office of Deputy Director"— "Operations," 1971, 17–19, Operation Condor. The latter was badly named, given Pinochet's later international terror ring against leftist opponents (also code-named Condor), now tied to cocaine financing.

29. Musto, "America's First Cocaine": Musto is not wrong about the forgetting, but there is also a hidden history between the two booms and a major cultural shift with cocaine's 1970s return.

30. Ann Crittenden and Michael Ruby, "Cocaine: The Champagne of Drugs," *NYT Magazine*, 1 Sept. 1974; Brecher, *Licit and Illicit*, pt. 5, a consumer report. See Torgoff, *Can't Find My Way*, ch. 10, a cultural analysis (cf. Jonnes, *Hep-Cats and Pipe Dreams*, chs. 15–18); Biskind, *Easy Riders*; and, on semiotics of cocaine consumerism, Lenson, *On Drugs*, ch. 9.

31. Phillips and Wynne, *Cocaine*, 182–83. Best-seller "fictionalized" 1970s accounts of cocaine include Woodley, *Dealer*, which inspired *Superfly*; Sabbag, *Snowblind*; and amateur guides like Ashley's 1975 *Cocaine* or the *Gourmet Cokebook*, which spoke directly to its culture.

32. On crack hysteria, "babies" and all, see Reinarman and Levin, *Crack in America*; Reeves and Campbell, *Cracked Coverage*; or Bourgois, *Search of Respect*.

33. Davenport-Hines, *Pursuit of Oblivion*, ch. 13. Clawson and Lee, *Andean Cocaine Industry*, ch. 1, table 1.1, figure 1.4; Painter, *Bolivia and Coca*, table 3.10, "Coca-Cocaine Economies." For update, see Vellinga, *Political Economy of Drug Industry*.

34. Weil, "Politics of Coca"; J. Tierney, "Reading the Coca Leaves," *NYT*, 23 Sept. 2006; M. Ryzik, "Cocaine: Hidden in Plain Sight," *NYT*, 10 June 2007. My estimate of current users uses Rospigliosi's Peru research in "Coca legal y illegal" (81, 94–95), plus a doubling (for population growth and wider usage) of 1980s figures in Carter and Mamami, *Coca en Bolivia*, table 1–19. Among Peru's 4 million users, Rospigliosi finds only a million "habitual" users, who account for four-fifths of all coca consumption.

35. *International Narcotics Control Strategy* (2000), 35–45; *NACLA* 2002–03 drug war issues (35/1, 36/2); Kenney, "From Pablo to Osama." J. Forero, "Hide and Seek Among the Coca Leaves," *NYT*, 9 June 2004; W. Hoge, "Global Drug Use and Production Slowing, U.N. Finds," *NYT*, 26 June 2007; *NYT*, 28 Apr. 2005, 19 Aug. 2006, 3 Oct. 2007.

36. Scott, *Seeing Like a State*, ch. 9: his subtitle seems tailor-made for American drug policy. See my "Talking Like a State" for a related analysis of antidrug discourse. If *metis* is indeed the concept, I wonder about another big "Scottian" implication: illicit actors in cocaine (traffickers, peasants) acting out of "resistance" against modernist states and legal regimes. See Kenney, *From Pablo to Osama*, 4–5, for discussion of *metis* (intuitive skills) versus *techne* (abstract, artifact knowledge) among adaptive traffickers.

37. Nadelmann, "U.S. Drug Policy."

38. See my "Between Coca and Cocaine" for a long view of the U.S.-Andean relationship.

39. Walker, *Drug Control in Americas*; Walker himself suggested this revision.

40. For an update, see J. Forero, "Colombia's Coca Survives U.S. Plan to Uproot It," *NYT*, 19 Aug. 2006. Many recent books expose the absurdities and damage of our drug war, e.g., Malamud-Goti, *Smoke and Mirrors*; Reinarman and Levin, *Crack in America*; Duke and Gross, *America's Longest War*; and Youngers and Rosen, *Drugs and Democracy*.

41. Merton, "Unanticipated Consequences" (1936), usually referred to as "unintended"; his concept of "self-fulfilling prophecy" is newer, dating to 1948.

APPENDIX

1. See Reuter, "Political Economy of Drug Smuggling," on price-inflated drug estimates; Karch, *Brief History*, ch. 10, on fishy official Japanese statistics. On illicitness problems, see van Schendel and Abraham, *Illicit Flows and Criminal Things*, or ch. 3, Gootenberg, "Talking Like a State."

2. Musto, "International Traffic in Coca." Even the sober historian Spillane occasionally resorts to this lumping in *Cocaine*, e.g., table 3-6. Karch compounds ratio errors (using poor arithmetic and ratios) while trying to redress Japan's cocaine statistics in *Brief History*, 137–38 (see Soininen, "Geographies of Cocaine," ch. 7, 79–88, for detailed critique of this medical cliometrics).

3. Soininen, "Geographies of Cocaine": we shared multiple e-coms. over 2005–7 about such source problems. Fogel and Elton, *Views of History*, for dilemmas of source thinness and robustness shared by narrative and quantitative historians alike.

BIBLIOGRAPHIC ESSAY

1. For more details and copious primary footnotes from these historiographical eras, consult Gootenberg, "Hidden Histories"; Mortimer, *History of Coca*; Karch, *Mystery of Coca*, for documents. Musto, *American Disease*, xi–xii.

2. Byck, *Cocaine Papers*; Andrews and Solomon, *Coca and Cocaine*; Ashley, *Cocaine*; two synthetic essays were Musto, "America's First Cocaine," and Courtwright, "Rise and Fall of Cocaine." More 1970s volumes are cited ahead.

3. For recent Asian advances, see Dikötter, Laamann, and Xun, *Narcotic Culture*; Brook and Wakabayashi, *Opium Regimes*; or, on India and marijuana, Mills, *Cannabis Britannica*.

4. Such new works are cited below.

5. Courtwright, *Forces of Habit*; Topik, Marichal, and Frank, *From Silver to Cocaine*; Bauer, *Goods, Power, History*; Schivelbusch, *Tastes of Paradise*; Goodman, Lovejoy, and Sherratt, *Consuming Habits*.

6. Byck, *Cocaine Papers*; Andrews and Solomon, *Coca and Cocaine*; Grinspoon and Bakalar, *Cocaine*; Phillips and Wynne, *Cocaine*; Kennedy, *Coca Exotica*.

7. Gootenberg, *Global Histories*, including chapters by Spillane, Kohn, Friman, and de Kort; Spillane, *Cocaine* (Spillane has other indispensable essays cited in the secondary bibliography and researched the cocaine history chapter, ch. 9, in MacCoun and Reuter's *Drug War Heresies*); Pendergrast, *God and Coca-Cola*; Friman,

Narco-Diplomacy; Kohn, *Dope Girls*; Karch, *Brief History* and *Mystery of Coca*; Musto, "International Traffic in Coca."

8. Thorp and Bertram, *Peru*; Werlich, *Peru*; Gagliano, *Coca Prohibition*; Morales, *Cocaine*; Soux, *Coca liberal*; Pacini and Franquemont, *Coca and Cocaine*; Weil, "Politics of Coca." Other contributing works to coca history include Klein, "Coca in the Yungas," in Pacini and Franquemont (1985); Romano, "Coca buena," in Boldó i Climent, *Coca andina* (1986); Fischer, "Culturas de coca," 16–26; and Lema, "Coca de las Americas."

9. Musto, *American Disease*; McAllister, *Drug Diplomacy*; Walker, *Drugs in Western Hemisphere*; McCoy, "Stimulus of Prohibition"; Nadelmann, "Drug Prohibition." New work is emerging here, too, about cocaine, e.g., Suzanna Reiss's dissertation, "Policing for Profit" (2005), and writer JoAnn Kawell's still unpublished history, "Going to the Source."

10. Meyer and Parssinen, *Webs of Smoke*; Astorga, *Mitología del narcotraficante*. Astorga has two other books on drugs in Mexico, *Siglo de las drogas* and *Drogas sin fronteras*. Block, "Snowman Cometh" and "European Drug Traffic"; Valentine, *Strength of the Wolf*; Torgoff, *Can't Find My Way*. Sáenz Rovner's *Conexión cubana* has a chapter on traffickers. A special issue of *Revista UNAM* (Dec. 2003), edited by Ricardo Pérez Montfort, is dedicated to drug history in Mexico, as is Campos-Costero's "Marijuana, Madness, and Modernity," a dissertation, and research in progress by historian Elaine Carey on female traffickers on the Mexico-U.S. border.

11. Kenney, *From Pablo to Osama* and "History of Colombian Trade"; Roldán, "Cocaine Miracle" (cf. Sáenz Rovner, "Pre-historia del narcotraficante"); Thoumi, "Why Illegal Drugs"; Henman, *Mama Coca*; Beaufort, *Archivos privados de Escobar*.

12. Waldorf, Reinarman, and Murphy, *Cocaine Changes*; Reinarman and Levin, *Crack in America*; Bourgois, *Search of Respect*; Clawson and Lee, *Andean Cocaine Industry*; Malamud-Goti, *Smoke and Mirrors*. There are many other books, of course, on contemporary cocaine.

13. Ashley, *Cocaine*; Streatfield, *Cocaine*; Madge, *White Mischief*; *Gourmet Cokebook*; Woodley, *Dealer*; Hyde and Zanetti, *White Lines*.

BIBLIOGRAPHIC ESSAY

A Guide to the Historiography of Cocaine

Readers eager to learn more about cocaine history will have to wade through a swamp of journalistic, fictionalized, and quasi-sociological writings on the drug. Most of it is speculation on today's illicit cocaine trade from South America, recycled with anecdotal sound bites from cocaine's past. Rigorous or comprehensive primary research on cocaine's hidden and global history is just beginning. The aim of this bibliographic essay is twofold: first, to introduce readers to the drug's "historiography" (the historical trends in research and writing about the cocaine), which may suggest why cocaine has suffered historical neglect, and second, to guide readers to a few of the serious (in my estimation) works on cocaine in the "new drug history."

In light of the scant research on cocaine, it may be premature to speak of a formal historiography of cocaine. There have been, however, four recognizable stages in global historical studies of cocaine and coca. The first was the frenzied curiosity stirred by the novel drug itself during cocaine's first medical boom at the end of the nineteenth century (1860–1905). Hundred of notes, essays, scholarly monographs, and pamphlets (medical, botanical, and historical) circulated among coca and cocaine enthusiasts and scientists in Europe, the United States, and even in unexpected sites like Peru. Some of these works, such as New York physician W. Golden Mortimer's encyclopedic 1901 *History of Coca: "The Divine Plant" of the Incas*, plumbed extant historical or ethnographic knowledge to make claims about the medicinal uses or social utility of coca and cocaine. Many of these notes serve today as indispensable primary documents on this active phase of cocaine's emergence. The second stage, from 1905 through 1970, in contrast, saw a long dearth in the study of cocaine. As the drug's legal and medicinal prestige fell and cocaine became a pariah drug and disappeared in the United States, few saw the need for, or found any support for, further research. As medical historian David Musto suggests, especially in the United States, this meant a kind of social amnesia or collective memory loss about cocaine, even about its societal and medical dangers.[1] Americans, for example, would not have recognized after 1920 why their national soft drink, Coca-Cola, prominently displayed the C-word, and by mid-century few remembered this relic drug's potential threats to body and mind. Furthermore, with its misleading legal classification as a narcotic after 1914, cocaine lost much of its separate historical identity.

The third wave, one of renewed fascination with cocaine (1970–90), broke when the drug suddenly resurfaced around 1970 as a glamorous "soft" drug. Again, as with the nineteenth-century boom, a flood of essays, articles, and now edited collections on cocaine ensued, many based on the rediscovery and recycling of the older cocaine research. Most notable were the timely 1974 republication of both Sigmund Freud's mid-1880s "cocaine papers" (and his resuscitation as a pioneer psycho-pharmacologist) and Mortimer's *History of Coca*.[2] Some of these surveys helped establish a better chronology, or periodization, for the drug. This output was heavily sociological and journalistic due to the longer gestation period required for new medical or historical research, and some of was it openly advocative (like cocaine coffee table books and user guides, often spiced up with tidbits of history). With the arrival of the violent mid-1980s crack epidemic in the United States and its ensuing drug panic, the celebratory spirit waned, replaced by sensationalist exposes of ne'er-do-wells like the Colombian cartels, and, with Ronald Reagan's cocaine-escalated drug war, renewed scholarly pleas for a more reasoned approach to drug policy reform. Whatever the tone, cocaine's genealogy remained at an anecdotal, moralistic, incidental level — a repeating kind of "great man" history, with obligatory reference to the Incas, Freud, Sherlock Holmes, Coca-Cola, and later Pablo Escobar, John Belushi, and Richard Pryor. Little new historical research occurred.

During the 1990s, for the reasons noted in the introduction, a new kind of drug history began to stir. It is more global, invested in primary research, and draws on interdisciplinary currents from drug studies and other fields. So far, Asian opiates have received more sophisticated and wider treatment than Latin American drugs, and many works stay within the bounds of diplomatic history, focusing on conventional subjects such as the genesis of American or global narcotics policy.[3] Solid social and cultural histories have also emerged on drug usage in Europe and the United States, as have transnational studies of drugs of empire, although these mostly focus on opiates. (Marijuana, like cocaine, is a historically orphaned drug, perhaps due to its "soft" image.) Nonetheless, a fourth wave of cocaine history, which at last distinguishes cocaine from narcotics, is starting to gather, probably because we are now more removed from its politically inflammatory booms and busts since the 1970s. For example, we now have a comprehensive social and business history of cocaine's first pharmaceutical boom in the United States (1880–1920), which sheds light on the politics of American cocaine prohibition. We know more about that era's nascent illicit drug markets peopled with cocaine "fiends" (users) and "combinations" (dealer gangs). Globally, we have new collations of coca leaf export statistics, innovative cultural studies of cocaine haunts in turn-of-the-century London, drug policy analysis that compares manufacturing nations such as 1920s Germany and Japan, European dissertations and document collections about the commercial dissemination of coca botany to colonial Java and Formosa, and research on a few pioneer Cuban cocaine traffickers of the 1950s. For the Andes, we have a social history monograph about Bolivian coca growers, an essay on Bolivian reactions to anticoca diplomacy in the 1920s, and a long-term narrative on Peruvian religious and medical controversies about coca leaf from the Spanish conquest through the 1950s. There are even clues emerging now to the origins of the Colombian traffickers of the 1970s.[4]

However, the majority of topics in cocaine history remain wide open to historical research. Tempting examples include the nineteenth-century coca mania in France, colonial coca and cocaine panics in India, the vanishing of illicit coke in the interwar United States, the rise of cocaine in revolutionary Bolivia and that country's historical coca politics, the mambo-flavored Cuban consumption culture of the 1950s, and the birth of Colombian traffickers and the new U.S. cocaine demand of the 1970s. I hope that this book's interpretation will help spur research interest in these crucial gaps.

For readers eager to sample a few of the existing serious works on cocaine and related drug history, I can make the following annotated recommendations. For a broad commodity perspective on global drug history, a fine start is David T. Courtwright's accessible and accurate *Forces of Habit: Drugs and the Making of the Modern World* (2001). A new set of historical essays on Latin American commodity chains (to which I contribute the titular cocaine) is coedited by Steven Topik, Carlos Marichal, and Zephyr Frank: *From Silver to Cocaine: Latin American Commodity Chains and the Building of the World Economy, 1500–2000* (2006). Arnold J. Bauer's *Goods, Power, History: Latin America's Material Culture* (2001) offers an evocative overview of the material and commodity history of Latin America. Two works that exemplify how well commodities, drugs, and cultural history intersect are Wolfgang Schivelbusch's *Tastes of Paradise: A Social History of Spices, Stimulants, and Intoxicants* (1992, orig. 1980) and Jordan Goodman, Paul E. Lovejoy, and Andrew Sherratt's edited volume, *Consuming Habits: Drugs in History and Anthropology* (1995), which contains Courtwright's periodizing essay "The Rise and Fall of Cocaine in the United States."[5]

During the return of illicit coke as a pleasure drug in the 1970s and 1980s, a number of surveys and document collections were cobbled together about cocaine. Three still-valuable volumes of primary documents from this wave are Robert Byck, ed., *Cocaine Papers by Sigmund Freud* (1974), on the drug's initial scientific culture; George Andrews and David Solomon, eds., *The Coca Leaf and Cocaine Papers* (1975); and Joel L. Phillips and Ronald D. Wynne's notably historical *Cocaine: The Mystique and the Reality* (1980), which also documents the 1970s cocaine revival. Noted already is Mortimer's *History of Coca*, a classic on nineteenth-century coca cultures, reissued in 1974 by the Fitz Hugh Ludlow Memorial Library. A serious overall survey of the drug remains Lester Grinspoon and James B. Bakalar's *Cocaine: A Drug and Its Social Evolution* (1976), although some of its concerns seem dated by the crack boom of the 1980s. Joseph Kennedy's *Coca Exotica: The Illustrated History of Cocaine* (1985), a decently researched coffee table book, also springs from this wave of mass fascination with drugs and attempts to trace the historical relationship of coca leaf and cocaine cultures.[6]

New scholarship is gathering in global cocaine history. This latest wave of work is represented in Paul Gootenberg, ed., *Cocaine: Global Histories* (1999), in which, following a historiographic introduction, the seven chapters (original contributions on the United States, Peru, Britain, Germany, the Netherlands, Japan, Mexico, and Colombia) are organized in terms of global commodity chains. On the United States and early cocaine, we now have Joseph F. Spillane's masterful social, political, and business history, *Cocaine: From Medical Marvel to Modern Menace in the United States, 1884–1920* (2000), plus his other published essays, including "Making a Modern Drug: The Manufacture, Sale, and Control of Cocaine in the United States, 1880–1920," in *Cocaine: Global Histories*. On American coca culture, see Mark Pendergrast's popular *For God, Country, and Coca-Cola: The Unauthorized History of the Great American Soft Drink and the Company that Makes It* (1993), especially chapters 1–2. For European circuits, see H. Richard Friman's comparative work, *Narco-Diplomacy: Exploring the U.S. War on Drugs* (1996), chapters 2 and 5, and his "Germany and the Transformations of Cocaine, 1880–1920," also in *Cocaine: Global Histories*. For early-twentieth-century Britain, we have Marek Kohn's creative cultural history of cocaine's original fall from grace, *The Dope Girls: The Birth of the British Drug Underground* (1992). As for the Netherlands, see Marcel de Kort, "Doctors, Diplomats and Businessmen: Conflicting Interests in the Netherlands and Dutch East Indies," in *Cocaine: Global Histories*, based on his published 1995 Dutch doctoral thesis. On Japan and the Asian colonial networks, try chapter 3 in Friman's *Narco-Diplomacy*, along with the de Kort essay. Steven B. Karch's *A Brief History of Cocaine* (1998), less reliably, also has a good deal to say about the Asian drug connection. Karch recently put out an English edition of European documents on historical cocaine titled *A History of Cocaine: The Mystery of Coca Java and the Kew Plant* (2003), including translated excerpts of rare doctoral theses by French, German, and Dutch colonial agronomists. David Musto's team effort, "International Traffic in Coca through the Early Twentieth Century" (*Drug and Alcohol Dependence*, 1998) is a heroic attempt to trace the leaf's licit global commerce between the 1890s and 1930s, flawed by its lumping of coca and cocaine statistics.[7] Four sites that beg for research on their coca and cocaine histories are France, Bolivia, India, and Colombia.

For Peruvian cocaine, consult the list of Gootenberg essays cited in the this volume's bibliography of secondary sources. On the country's larger commodity history, we are lucky to have Rosemary Thorp and Geoffrey Bertram's *Peru, 1890–1977: Growth and Policy in an Open Economy* (1978). My best pick for a general history of Peru, with its strong coverage of Amazonia, is David P. Werlich's *Peru: A Short History* (1978). For long-term discourse about coca, at times blending into cocaine, there is Joseph Gagliano's *Coca Prohibition in Peru: The Historical Debates* (1994). Edmundo Morales's *Cocaine: White Gold Rush in Peru* (1989) is an ethnography of the peasant rush into Huallaga Valley cocaine in the 1970s and 1980s. Bolivia has a smattering of solid social history works on coca, mainly in Spanish, for example, María Luisa Soux, *La coca liberal: Producción y circulación a principios del s. xx* (1993). On Andean coca leaf generally, one of the most informative, if scarce, volumes in English is Deborah Pacini and Christine Franquemont's edited *Coca and Cocaine: Effects on People and Policy in Latin*

America (1985). Andrew Weil, M.D., America's popular new age health guru (who is actually a Harvard-trained ethnobotanist), provides an eye-opening update on Andean coca in "The New Politics of Coca" (*New Yorker*, 1995), which likely needs a renewed look given the leaf's progressive revaluation in places like Bolivia.[8]

On the history of drug prohibition (if mainly on opiate politics), see David Musto's still authoritative *The American Disease: Origins of Narcotic Control* (1973 and subsequent editions) or, from a global archival perspective, William B. McAllister's *Drug Diplomacy in the Twentieth Century: An International History* (2000). William O. Walker III has published a number of books on hemispheric "drug control: a fine set of historical documents, including quite a few on coca and cocaine politics, is found in his *Drugs in the Western Hemisphere: An Odyssey of Cultures in Conflict* (1996). A striking global survey of modern drug prohibitions, if thin on cocaine, is Alfred W. McCoy's "The Stimulus of Prohibition: A Critical History of the Global Narcotics Trade," in *Dangerous Harvest: Drug Plants and the Transformation of Indigenous Landscapes*, edited by Michael K. Steinberg, Joseph J. Hobbs, and Kent Mathewson (2004). A corrective to official and often popularly held views on drug policy is Ethan Nadelmann's "Drug Prohibition in the United States: Costs, Consequences and Alternatives" (*Science*, 1989).[9]

Drug traffickers have attracted scant genuine research. I can only recommend a few works: Kathryn Meyer and Terry Parssinen's *Webs of Smoke: Smuggling, Warlords, Spies, and the History of the International Drug Trade* (1998), largely about Asian opiates; and sociologist Luis Astorga's Spanish-language books on northern Mexican drug smuggler culture, especially *Mitología del "narcotraficante" en México* (1995), a sample of which is had in his essay "Cocaine in Mexico: A Prelude to 'los Narcos,'" in *Cocaine: Global Histories*. Criminologist Alan A. Block has written two outstanding articles on illicit trades: "The Snowman Cometh: Coke in Progressive New York" (*Criminology*, 1979), a rare peek at the first phase of illicit cocaine based on the Kehillah of New York archives in Jerusalem (as cocaine dealing was then a Jewish problem), and, on opiates, "European Drug Traffic and Traffickers between the Wars: The Policy of Suppression and Its Consequences" (*Journal of Social History*, 1989). Douglas Valentine's *The Strength of the Wolf: The Secret History of America's War on Drugs* (2004), an oral history of FBN drug agents, is remarkable for its information about the origins of modern postwar drug trades (though scant on cocaine) if readers can get past the book's conspiracy theories. An incisive history of

Martin Torgoff's *Can't Find My Way Home: America in the Great Stoned Age, 1945–2000* (2004).[10]

Surprisingly or not, the vast literature on Colombian drug trafficking (in both English and Spanish) is overwhelmingly ahistorical and usually poor. A recent exception, political scientist Michael Kenney's *From Pablo to Osama: Trafficking and Terrorist Networks, Government Bureaucracies, and Competitive Adaption* (2007), in chapters 1–4 provides great insight into the structure and strategy of Colombian drug traders, but the book omits Kenney's earlier historical research. Historian Mary Roldán uses a fine regional lens in "Colombia: Cocaine and the 'Miracle' of Modernity in Medellín," in *Cocaine: Global Histories*. Economist Francisco E. Thoumi assesses his country well in answering the question implied in the title of his essay "Why the Illegal Psychoactive Drugs Industry Grew in Colombia" (*Journal of Interamerican Studies and World Affairs*, 1992). An ethnographic feel for this chaotic era in Colombia comes from *Mama Coca* (1987) by Anthony Henman, a.k.a. Antonil. For a strikingly different view of South American traffickers, the 2002 documentary film *Los archivos privados de Pablo Escobar*, directed by Marc de Beaufort, exploits the family's home movies and recollections.[11]

On contemporary cocaine, I would turn to Dan Waldorf, Craig Reinarman, and Sheigla Murphy's realistic 1991 volume *Cocaine Changes: The Experience of Using and Quitting*; Reinarman and Harry G. Levin's later edited volume, *Crack in America: Demon Drugs and Social Justice* (1997); Phillipe Bourgois's innovative ethnographic study *In Search of Respect: Selling Crack in El Barrio* (1995); Patrick L. Clawson and Rensselaer W. Lee III's hard-nosed *The Andean Cocaine Industry* (1996); or Jaime Malamud-Goti's grassroots view of the drug war in Bolivia, *Smoke and Mirrors: The Paradox of the Drug Wars* (1992).[12] Two recent special issues of *NACLA: Report on the Americas* ("Widening Destruction: Drug Wars in the Americas" 35/1 [July 2003] and "Drug Economies of the Americas" 36/2 [Sept.–Oct. 2002]) provide reliable updates on the persistent conflict between Latin American economies and North American drug demands.

For the guilty pleasures of the countless popular or confessional guides to cocaine, one might indulge in Richard Ashley's *Cocaine: Its History, Uses, and Effects* (1975), the newer *Cocaine: An Unauthorized Biography*, by Dominic Streatfield (2001), which includes on pages 180–86 a good-humored encounter with this author, or Tim Madge's *White Mischief: A Cultural His-*

tory of Cocaine (2001), which is not too bad. For a 1970s period piece, try the anonymous *The Gourmet Cokebook: A Complete Guide to Cocaine* (1972) or Richard Woodley's *Dealer: Portrait of a Cocaine Merchant* (1971), the inspiration for Hollywood's "Superfly" character. Literary readers may want to snort some of *White Lines: Writers on Cocaine*, edited by Stephen Hyde and Geno Zanetti (2002).[13] I cannot honestly recommend any of the scores of badly fictionalized books and memoirs that purport to expose the behavior of international cocaine cartels.

BIBLIOGRAPHY

ARCHIVES

Germany
Boehringer-Ingelheim Archives, Mannheim
    Late-nineteenth-century papers, courtesy of Tilmann Holzer

Peru
Archivo del Ministerio de Relaciones Exteriores del Perú, Lima
    Conferencias Internacionales
    Liga de Naciones, Comité Central del Opio (Section 7-0-D)
    Liga de Naciones, Naciones Unidas (Section 7-0 to 7-0-B, 7-1-B), 1917–50s
Archivo General de la Nación, Archivo Histórico, Lima
    Anuario/Extracto Estadísticas, H-6
    Archivo de Fuero Agrario
    Boletines (ministerial bulletins)
    Dirección de Fomento, H-6
    Imigrantes, books 75–76
    Libros Manuscritos Republicanos, H-4 (1877, 1940 census, tax matrículas,
        Dir. de Estadística, Aduanas, Fomento, Hacienda y Comercio,
        Exportación)
    Ministerio de Relaciones Exteriores
    Oficios, O.L. (Prefecturas)
    Prefecturas, H-6, 1889–1921
    Testimonios (wills)
    Tierras de Montaña, 1887–1964
Archivo Sub-Regional del Huánuco, Archivo Departamental, Huánuco
    Expedientes Civiles, Minutario, 1880s–1910
    Municipalidad (Legados 38–146, 1900–1950s Libros de Actas, Internación y
        Guías de Coca, Provincia de Huánuco, Patentes, Presupuestos)
    Penales (police), 1965–79

Prefecturas, Legados 23–149, 1910s–60s

Protocoles (Notaries), 1880s–1950

Sucesiones (wills), 1920s–70s

Biblioteca Felix Denegri Luna (now housed at La Pontificia Universidad Católica del Perú), Lima

    Anales universitarios del Perú, 1880s–90s

    Rare pamphlets, books, clippings, journals

Biblioteca Nacional del Perú, Sala de Investigaciones, Lima

    Boletín de Ministerio de Fomento del Perú, 1890s–1920s

    Commercial and industrial guides (e.g., *Guía Lascano*, 1921–66)

    Manuscritos Republicanos (Republican manuscript collection, e.g., Memorias de Prefecturas, 1889–1913)

    Memorias de Ministerio de Gobierno, 1890s–1920s

    Old monographs, pamphlets, journals, and periodicals

    El Peruano, Registro oficial (official gazettes), 1890s–1950s

Universidad Mayor de San Marcos, Lima

    Facultad de Medicina, thesis collection

    General thesis archive (nineteenth century—La Casona)

United Kingdom

Burroughs-Wellcome Company Records Centre, London

Guildhall Library, London

    Gibbs Papers, commercial affairs

Public Record Office, London

    FO 177, British legations in Lima, commercial reports, opium

Royal Botanic Gardens at Kew Archive, London

    Bulletin of Miscellaneous Information

    Correspondence on coca, miscellaneous reports, Imperial Institute

Wellcome Institute for the History of Medicine, London

United States

Drug Enforcement Administration Library and Information Center, Arlington, Va.

    Historical addiction essays, laws, and monographs; League of Nations narcotics conferences

    Publications: *Drug Enforcement, DEA Intelligence Division*, 1976–93

    UN Inter-American Conferences on Coca Leaf Problems, Documents, U.S. Reports, 1960–64

    Vertical files (topical clippings, memos): "Addiction in History," "Andean Region," "Anslinger," "Coca to 1970," "Cocaine," "Cocaine History," "Harrison Act," "Illicit Traffic," "Internal Control," "Laws and Legislation," "Latin America," "Narcotic History," "New York," "Peru," "Routes," 1920s–80s

Food and Drug Administration Archive, Rockville, Md.

    FDA *Notices of Judgment*

    Maywood, Merck papers

Mallinckrodt Chemical Company Archives, Saint Louis
  Early-twentieth-century papers, courtesy of Joseph Spillane
Merck Corporate Archives, White House, N.J.
  Rows 3–6 (1920s–40s): Cocaine, Coca leaves, Java coca plantation–
    Tjitembong, Rahway manufacturing, narcotics/opium, old Merck,
    annual reports
National Library of Medicine, Bethesda, Md.
  Manuscripts
  Peruvian and Latin American medical and pharmacy journals
  Surgeon general's list of medical publications (nineteenth century)
Parke, Davis and Company Archives, Detroit
  Early-twentieth-century papers, courtesy of Joseph Spillane
Pennsylvania State University Library, Historical Collections and Labor Archives
  Harry J. Anslinger Papers, Boxes 2–11
    Correspondence, 1922–64
    Scrapbooks, 1930s–40s
United Nations Archive, New York
  Central Files, ECSOC, Narcotics, Internal Drug Control, 1960–74
  Commission of Enquiry into the Effects of Chewing Coca Leaf, 1948–52
  Narcotics, 1948–50s
  Register Archive Group, RAG 2–3, Advisory Groups, Technical Assistance
  Yearbooks, 1946–60
United Nations Library, New York
  Commission on Narcotic Drugs (Economic and Social Council), documents
U.S. National Archives, College Park, Md.
  RG43, Records of International Conferences, Commissions, and Expositions
    Opium Conferences, Commissions, General Correspondence, 1909–15
  RG59, Department of State, Consular Trade Reports, 326 (Microfilm) Peru,
    1925–50
  RG59, Department of State, Decimal Files (Central Office Files)
    Bolivia, Narcotics (series 824.114, 824.53), 1945–63
    Chile, Narcotics (825.53), 1950–63
    Cuba, Narcotics (837.53), 1950–59
    Mexico, Narcotics (812.53), 1950s
    Panama, Narcotics (819.120/53), 1950–64
    Peru, Narcotics (series 823.114, 823.53, 823.711), Boxes 5709, 5299, 1920s–50s
  RG59, Department of State, LOT Files (Office Subject Files)
    55D607 Far Eastern Affairs, Control of Narcotics Traffic, 1903–55
    Name File of Suspected Narcotics Traffickers (15 boxes)
    63D434, 66D13 (also Box 209), Records Relating to Peru, 1956–64
    Boxes 1, 4, 9, 10, 16, 26, Factories, Coca, Cocaine, Individual
      Commodities, Drugs and Chemicals, *Coca-Cola* Extract
  RG59, Department of State, National Archives — Northeast Region
    (New York), Microfilm
    M155, Despatches from U.S. Consuls in Callao, 1854–1906, Microfilm
      Rolls 7–17

T52, Despatches from U.S. Ministers to Peru, 1826–1906, Rolls 41–66

T802, Notes from Peruvian Legation in the United States, 1827–1906, Rolls 5–6

RG59, Department of State, Subject-Numeric Files, SOC 11.5, 1963–73 (Peru, Latin America, Narcotics)

RG97, U.S. Department of Agriculture, Records of the Bureau of Agricultural and Industrial Chemistry, Hearings, Pharmaceutical Manufacturers, Imports, 1907–18

RG166, U.S. Department of Agriculture, Foreign Agricultural Service

  Boxes 18–22, Records of the Technical Collaboration Branch, Peru, 1942–53

  Box 22, Reports from Agricultural Attachés, Peru, 1930s–50s

  Box 51, Narrative Reports, 1966–67

  Box 66, Narrative Reports, 1969–70

  Boxes 260–67, Narrative Reports, 1962–65

  Boxes 349–60, Narrative Reports, Peru, 1942–45

  Box 430, Narrative Reports, 1904–39

RG170, Bureau of Narcotics and Dangerous Drugs (FBN, BNDD, DEA), all 0060 — Subject Files of the Bureau of Narcotics

  Box 1–2, Foreign Countries (Mexico) through 1966

  Box 4 (old Box 8), Foreign Countries (Brazil to Ecuador), 1950s–60s

  Box 6, Foreign Countries (Bolivia), 1955–64

  Box 7, Conference on Production, 1930s

  Box 8, League of Nations, 1935–36

  Box 9, Foreign Countries (Hong Kong to Thailand), 1932–67

  Box 18, World Narcotics Factories, 1927–66

  Box 19, Foreign Countries (Bolivia); De-cocainized Coca Leaves, 1915–47

  Box 20, Drugs — Coca Leaves, Beverages, 1930s–60s

  Box 23, Foreign Countries (Peru), 1926–44

  Box 29 (new Box 161), Foreign Countries (Mexico to Peru), 1932–67

  Box 30, South America, 1940s–60s

  Box 34, Narcotics, Prohibition Unit, 1920–24

  Boxes 37–38, Single Convention, 1957–61

  Box 54 (old Box 10), Inter-American Conferences, 1960–64

  Box 63, Drugs — Cocaine, Beverages, 1933–62

  Box 161, Mexico to Peru, 1955–67

PAMPHLET AND NEWSPAPER COLLECTIONS

Peru

Biblioteca Felix Denegri Luna, Lima

Biblioteca Municipal de Huánuco, Huánuco

Biblioteca Nacional del Perú, Sala de Investigaciones, Lima

Colección Manuel Nieves (rare local periodicals, 1920s–70s), Huánuco

United Kingdom

Bodleian Library, Oxford

Wellcome Institute for the History of Medicine, London

Babst Library, New York University (League of Nations depository collection), New York, N.Y.

Columbia University Libraries (Butler, Law, Rare Book and Manuscript, Annex, Long Health Sciences, Archives and Special Collections, and Columbiana Archive), New York, N.Y.

Firestone Library, Princeton University, Princeton, N.J.

Library of Congress, Washington, D.C.

New York Academy of Medicine, New York, N.Y.

New York Historical Society, New York, N.Y.

New York Public Library (Humanities and Social Sciences Library and Science, Industry, and Business Library), New York, N.Y.

Pan-American Union Library, Washington, D.C.

Sterling Memorial Library (Manuscripts and Archives), Yale University, New Haven, Conn.

Widener Library, Harvard University, Cambridge, Mass.

OFFICIAL DOCUMENTS

International

Interpol

  UN, ECSOC, E/CN.7, "Illicit Traffic," "Clandestine Laboratories," 1951–64

League of Nations (depository collections: Babst Library, New York University, and United Nations Library)

  Advisory Committee on Traffic in Opium and Other Dangerous Drugs, 1921–40s

  Annual Reports of Governments, 1938–40s

  Annual Reports of the Traffic in Opium and Other Dangerous Drugs, Traffic in Opium (United States, Latin America, Peru, Japan, Netherlands, etc.)

  Minutes of Annual Sessions

  Opium Commissions, Advisory Committees, Conferences, 1923–46 (Mainly O.C. denomination, Geneva, or C, Conferences)

  Permanent Central Opium Board, Series XI, Estimated World Requirements of Dangerous Drugs, 1930s–40s

  Records of the Conference for the Suppression of the Illicit Traffic in Narcotic Drugs, Series XI, Geneva, 1936 and 1939

  Records of the Conference on the Limitation of the Manufacture of Narcotic Drugs, C 587–, Geneva, 1930–31

  Records of the Second Opium Conference, C 684–760, Geneva, 1924–25

  World Narcotic Defense Association, 1930s

United Nations (UN Library and New York University depository collection)

  Annual Reports of Governments, E/NR Bolivia, Peru, Chile, Colombia, etc., 1944–60

  Bulletin on Narcotics, vols. 1–15, 1949–62

  Commission on Narcotic Drugs (ECSOC), Lake Success, N.Y. E.CN.7

    Memorandum on the Illicit Drug Traffic in Narcotic Drugs, 1949–

Preparatory Work for International Conference . . . Limiting . . . Coca Leaf, 1947

Sessions and documents, 1–16, 1946–60s

Supplemental reports, Coca Leaf, 1946, 1947, 1948, 1950, 1951, 1952, 1960 (includes "Report of the Commission of Enquiry on the Coca Leaf," May 1950)

Illicit Traffic in Narcotic Drugs, Summary of Illicit Transactions and Seizures E/NS, 1945–50

Permanent Central Opium Board, Geneva, EOB, 1–8, 1946–54

Permanent General Narcotics Board, Geneva, E/OB/W, 1960s

Peru

Boletín de Dirección de Salubridad, Salud Pública y Asistencia Social (title varies), 1920s–40s

Caja de Depósitos y Consignaciones, *Memorias del Estanco de la Coca* (ENACO), 1952–68

Dirección de Colonización y Asuntos Orientales, 1890s–1910s

Ministerio de Fomento y Obras Públicas, 1890s–1920s

Memorias de Ministerio de Hacienda del Perú, 1870s–1930s

Prontuario de legislación sanitaria del Perú, Dirección de Salubridad Pública, 1928–35

United Kingdom

Public Record Office, Foreign Office, *The Opium Trade, 1910–1941* (collection of Foreign Office documents published by Scholarly Resources, Wilmington, 1974, 6 vols.)

United States

Commissioner of Internal Revenue, 1915, 1920

New York State, Department of Narcotics, and Narcotics Control, 1919–20s

President of the United States. *The Opium Evil.* 62nd Cong., 2nd sess., 1912. Washington, D.C.: Government Printing Office, 1912.

U.S. Congress. House. Committee on Foreign Affairs. *Limiting Production of Habit-Forming Drugs and Raw Materials from Which They are Made.* 67th Cong., 4th sess., 1924. Washington, D.C.: Government Printing Office, 1924.

———. Committee on Foreign Affairs. *International Aspects of the Narcotics Problem.* 92nd Cong., 1st sess., 1971. Washington, D.C.: Government Printing Office, 1971.

———. Committee on Foreign Affairs. *The World Narcotics Problem: The Latin American Perspective.* 93rd Cong., 1st sess., 1973. Washington, D.C.: Government Printing Office, 1973.

———. Committee on Ways and Means. *Bureau of Narcotics, Hearings. . . .* 71st Cong., 2nd sess., 1930. Washington, D.C.: Government Printing Office, 1930.

———. Select Committee on Narcotics Abuse and Control. *Cocaine: A Major Drug Issue of the Seventies.* 96th Cong., 1st sess., 1980. Washington, D.C.: Government Printing Office, 1980.

U.S. Congress. Senate. Committee on the Judiciary. *World Drug Traffic and its Impact on U.S. Security*. 92nd Cong., 2nd sess., 1972. Washington, D.C.: Government Printing Office, 1972.

———. Sub-Committee on Improvements in Federal Criminal Code. *Illicit Narcotics Traffic, Hearings. . . .* 84th Cong., 1st sess., 1955. Washington, D.C.: Government Printing Office, 1955.

U.S. Department of Agriculture, 1910–11

U.S. Public Health Service, 1915

U.S. Treasury Department, "Traffic in Narcotic Drugs," 1919; "Traffic in Habit-Forming Narcotic Drugs," 1923–25; Federal Bureau of Narcotics, *Traffic in Opium and Other Dangerous Drugs*, 1926–67

PERIODICALS

Chile
Revista Médica de Chile, 1886

Cuzco
Museo Erudito, 1837

Huánuco
El Espéctador, 1926–29
El Huallaga, 1904–45
El Pueblo, 1917
La Trinchera, 1970–76

Lima
Agronomía, 1938–40
Anales de la Facultad de Medicina de Lima, 1918–51
Archivos Peruanos de Higiene Mental, 1939–41
Boletín de la Academia Libre de Medicina, 1885–87
Boletín de la Dirección de Agricultura y Ganadería, 1934–36
Boletín de la Sociedad Geográfica de Lima, 1891–1910
Boletín de la Sociedad Química del Perú, 1935–48
Boletín del Círculo Médico Peruano, 1926
Boletín del Ministerio de Relaciones Exteriores del Perú, 1904–41
El Comercio, 1929–51
La Crónica Médica, 1884–1900
La Farmacia Peruana, 1893–94
Farmacia y Química, 1944–45
Gaceta Médica de Lima, 1856–75
La Industria, 1897–1928
El Mercurio Peruano, 1929–30
El Monitor Médico, 1885–96
El Mundo, 1928–30
Perú Indígena, 1952–55

Bibliography

Peru To-Day, 1909–14
La Prensa, 1915–17
La Reforma Farmacéutica, 1927–29
La Reforma Médica, 1920–50
La República, 1923
Revista de Sanidad de la Policía, 1948–54
La Riqueza Agrícola, 1912–14
La Vida Agrícola, 1934–38
West Coast Leader, 1921–28

London
British Medical Journal, 1900–1905
Bulletin of the Imperial Institute, 1900–12
Chemist and Druggist, 1885–1910

Paris
Bulletin des Sciences Pharmacologiques, 1913–14

United States
American Druggist (New York), 1884–93; *American Druggist and Pharmaceutical Record*, 1894–1910
American Journal of Pharmacy (Philadelphia), 1883–1905
Boletín de la Unión Sanitaria Panamericana (Washington, D.C.), 1937–49
Bulletin of the Bureau of American Republics
Journal of the American Medical Association (Chicago), 1901–40s
National Druggist (St. Louis), 1882–86
New York Medical Journal (New York), 1883–1923
New York State Journal of Medicine (New York), 1901–20
New York Times, 1890–1915, 1948–52, 1970–79
Oil, Paint, and Drug Reporter (New York), 1882–1923
Therapeutic Gazette (Detroit), 1884–89

INTERVIEWS

All interviews were conducted by the author in 1997–99.

Dr. Fernando Cabieses (Lima)
Baldomero Cáceres (Lima)
Guillermo Casteñeda (Huánuco)
Adolfo Cavalié (Huánuco)
Augusto, Carmen Rosa, Francisco, and Jorge Durand (Lima, New York)
Dr. Nilo Lambruschini (Huánuco)
Dr. Virgilio López Calderón (Huánuco)
Ricardo Soberón (Lima)
José Spoya Costijo (Lima)

La acción oficial en la colonización de Tingo María (años 1944–46). Lima: Ministerio de Agricultura, Dirección de Colonización y Asuntos Orientales, 1947.

Agnew, Derek. *Undercover Agent—Narcotics: The Dramatic Story of the World's Secret War against Drug Racketeers.* London: Souvenir, 1959.

Albornoz, Mariano Martín. *Breves apuntes sobre las regiones amazónicas.* Lima: Imp. del Progreso, 1885.

Álvarez Daza, Lizandro. *Cultivo de la coca.* La Paz: Talleres Gráficas La Prensa, 1899.

Anslinger, Harry J., and William F. Tompkins. *The Traffic in Narcotics.* New York: Funk and Wagnalls, 1953.

Bambarén, Carlos A. "La medicina en el primer centenario de la República." *La Crónica Médica* 1921: 189–221.

Beard, George M. *American Nervousness: Its Causes and Consequences.* New York: G. P. Putnam's Sons, 1881.

Bües, Carlos. *La coca: Apuntes sobre la planta, beneficio, enfermedades y aplicación.* Lima: Ministerio de Fomento, 1911.

———. "La coca en el Perú." *Boletín de la Dirección de Agricultura y Ganadería* 18 (1935): 29–62.

Carrey, Émile. *Le Pérou: Tableau descriptif, historique, et anaytique.* Paris: Garnier Frs., 1875.

Chocano, Abelardo. *El desenvolvimiento comercial e industrial del Perú.* Lima: Sociedad Nacional de Industrias, 1925.

Cisneros, Carlos B. *Atlas del Perú: Político, minero, agrícola, industrial y comercial. . . .* Lima: Imprenta Gil, 1900.

———. *Reseña económica del Perú.* Lima: Imprenta del Estado, 1902–8.

———. *Frutos de la paz.* Lima: La Opinión Nacional, 1908.

Clavero, José G. *El tesoro del Perú.* Lima: Imprenta de Torre Aguirre, 1896.

Counter-Reply of the Peruvian Commission for the Study of the Coca Problem to the Commission of Enquiry of the United Nations on the Coca Leaf. Lima: Ministerio de Salud Pública, 1951.

Cultivo de la coca. Lima: Biblioteca del Agricultor Práctica, Ed. J. Gallard, 1896.

De las Casas, Enrique. *Provincia de Huánuco: Apuntes monograficos.* Lima: Imprenta Gil, 1935.

Diez-Canseco, Ernesto. *Peru: Red nacional de carreteras.* Lima: Ministerio de Fomento, 1929.

Duffield, A. J. *The Prospects of Peru.* London: Newman, 1881.

Dunn, William E. *Peru: A Commercial and Industrial Handbook.* Washington, D.C.: U.S. Department of Commerce, Bureau of Foreign and Domestic Commerce, 1925.

Durand, Juan E. *Ferrocarril de Lima a Yurimaguas a orillas del Huallaga.* Lima: Imprenta de la Cámera de Diputados, 1903.

———. *Noticias sobre los gomales de la región de Monzón.* Lima: La Voce d'Italia, 1909.

Enríquez, Luis. *Haya de la Torre: La estafa política más grande de América*. Lima: Ed. Pacífica, 1951.

Espinosa, Manuel M. *Ensayo esperimental sobre el el Erythroxylum Koca*. Buenos Aires: Pablo Conti, 1875.

Esteves, Luis. *Apuntes para la historia económica del Perú*. 1882. Reprint, Lima: Centro de Estudios de Población y Desarrollo, 1971.

Fernández, Dr. Nicanor T. *La coca boliviana: Maravillosas propiedades y cualidades de la coca*. La Paz: Sociedad de Propietarios de Yungas, 1932.

Fuchs, Fernando. *Política fiscal y desarrollo industrial*. Lima: Imprenta Americana, 1935.

Fuentes, Manuel A. *Memoire sur le coca du Pérou.* . . . Paris: Ad. Laine et Havard, 1866.

———. *Hojas de coca: Colección de artículos publicados.* . . . Lima: Imprenta de Estado, 1877.

Garland, Alejandro. *Las industrias en el Perú*. Lima: Imprenta de Estado, 1896.

———. *Export from Peru, 1896–1900*. Lima: Imprenta la Industria, 1901.

———. *Reseña industrial del Perú*. Lima: Imprenta la Industria, 1905.

———. *El Perú en 1906*. Lima: Imprenta la Industria, 1907.

Geographical and Statistical Synopsis of Peru, 1895 to 1898. Lima: Leonidas H. Jiménez, 1899.

Gibson, Percy. *Coca, alcohol, música incaíca y periódismo: Discurso pronunciado por su autor en el Teatro Olímplica.* . . . Arequipa: Tip. Sanguinetti, 1920.

Gómez y Couto, Vicente. *La Coca: Estudio fisiológico y terapéutico*. Mexico: Imprenta de Comercio, 1876.

Guía comercial e industrial del Perú. Lima: Cámara del Comercio, 1921.

Guía Lascano: Gran guía general y de la industria, profesionales. . . . 18 editions. Lima: J. Oscar Lascano, 1923–66.

Guide through the Exhibition of the German Chemical Industry. Chicago: Columbian Exhibition, 1893.

Guillaume, H. *The Amazon Provinces of Peru as a Field for European Emigration*. London: Wyman and Sons, 1888.

Gutiérrez-Noriega, Carlos, and Vicente Zapata Ortiz. *Estudios sobre la coca y la cocaína en el Perú*. Lima: Dirección de Educación Artística y Extensión Cultural, 1947.

Hanson, Earl Parker. *The Amazon: A New Frontier?* New York: Foreign Policy Association, 1944.

Herndon, Lt. William L., and Lardner Gibbon. *Exploration of the Valley of the Amazon Made under Direction of the Navy Department*. 2 vols. Edited by Gary Kinder. 1854. Reprint, New York: Grove Press, 2000.

Higuera y Paz Soldán, Marcel. *Impresiones y datos de Trujillo y de los valles de Santa Catalina y de Chicama*. Lima: n.d., ca. 1915.

Hohagen, Jorge. *Sumario de informaciones sobre exportaciones del Perú*. Lima: Casa Nacional de Moneda, 1927.

Kebler, L. F. *Habit-Forming Agents: Their Indiscriminate Sale and Use a Menace to the Public Welfare*. Washington, D.C.: Government Printing Office, 1910.

Lafosse, Alfredo P. *Algo referente a la Provincia de Huamalíes*. Lima: Imp. La Revista, 1907.

Lambruschini, Dr. Nilo S. *La cocaïne et ses dangers*. Paris: Libraire Picart, 1936.

Lissón, Carlos. *Breves apuntes sobre la sociología del Perú en 1886*. Lima: Imprenta Gil, 1887.

Lloyd Brothers. *A Treatise on Coca (Erythroxylum Coca): The Divine Plant of the Incas*. Cincinnati: Lloyd Brothers, 1913.

Lorente, Sebastian, and Baltazar Caravedo. *Bases fundamentales de la organización de la defensa social contra la toxicomanía*. VIII Conferencia Sanitaria Pan-Americana. Lima: Imp. de Castro, 1927.

Luzio A., Federico. "Tecnología: La fabricación de cocaína en Huánuco." *Agronomía: Organo del Centro de Estudiantes de la Molina* 3/15 (Nov. 1938): 44–55.

Mariani, Angelo. *La coca et la cocaine*. Paris: Libraire Delahaye et Lecrosnier, 1885.

———. *Coca Erythroxylon (Vin Mariani): Its Uses in the Treatment of Disease*. New York: Mariani, 1886.

———. *Coca and Its Therapeutic Applications*. 2nd ed. New York: J. N. Jaros, 1890.

Markham, Clements R. *Travels in Peru and India while Supervising the Collection of Chinchona Seeds and Plants in South America. . . .* London: John Murray, 1862.

Martindale, William. *Coca, Cocaine and Its Salts*. London: H. K. Lewis, 1886.

Martinet, J. B. H. *L'agriculture au Pérou*. Paris: Société des Agriculteurs de France, 1878.

Maúrtua, Aníbal. *El porvenir del Perú*. Lima: Tip. Carlos Fabri, 1911.

Merck. *E. Merck Darmstadt: A History of Chemical Achievement, 1827–1937*. Darmstadt: Merck, n.d., ca. 1938.

Moreno y Maíz, Tomás. *Recherches chimques et physiologiques sur L'erythroxylum Coca du Pérou et la cocaine*. Paris: L. Leclerc Ed., 1868.

Mortimer, W. Golden, M.D. *History of Coca: "The Divine Plant" of the Incas*. 1901. Reprint, San Francisco: Fitz Hugh Ludlow Memorial Library, 1974.

Nystrom, Juan G. *Informe al Supremo Gobierno del Perú sobre una expedición al interior de la República*. Lima: Imp. Prugue, 1868.

Parker, William B. *Peruvians of To-day*. Lima: Hispanic Society of Americas, 1919.

Pavletich, Esteban. *Autopsía de Huánuco*. Lima: Talleres Gráficos de la Ed. Numen, 1937.

———. *No se suicidan los muertos*. 1957. Reprint, Huánuco: Empresa Periodística PERU, 1994.

Paz Soldán, Carlos Enrique. "El problema médico-social de la coca en el Perú." *El Mercurio Peruano* 19 (1929): 135–36, 584–603.

———. *La coca peruana: Memorandum sobre su situación actual*. Lima: Sociedad Nacional Agraria, 1936.

Paz-Soldán, Juan Pedro. *Diccionario biográfico de peruanos contemporáneos*. Lima: Imprenta Gil, 1917.

Peacock, George. *The Resources of Peru*. Exeter: W. Pollard, 1874.

Peru at the Louisiana Purchase Exposition. St. Louis: n.p., ca. 1904.

El Perú en marcha: Ensayo de geografía económica. Lima: Banco de Crédito del Perú, 1942.

Peru: The Cradle of South America. London: Consulate of Peru, 1925.

"Peru": Yearbook of Foreign Trade. Lima: Sanmorlí y Cia., 1941.

Pilli, Emile R. "The Coca Industry in Peru." Unpublished monograph for Merck, New Jersey. Rahway: 1943.

Poeppig, Eduard. *Pampanaco: Deutches Forfeberleben in Urwald Sudamerilas*. Postdam: n.p., n.d.; reprint, 1934.

Pozzi-Escot, Emmanuel. "Recherches sur l'industrie de la cocaïne au Pérou: La coca et se culture; Extraction de la cocaïne." *Bull. des sciences pharmacologiques* (Paris) 20 (1913): 608–17.

Prontuario de legislación sanitaria del Perú. 3 vols. Dirección de Salubridad. Lima: Imp. Americana, 1937.

Raimondi, Antonio. *Apuntes sobre la provincia litoral de Loreto*. Lima: Tip. Nacional, 1862.

Reens, Emma. "La coca de Java: Monographie historique botanique, chimique et pharmacologique." Thesis in pharmacy, Université de Paris, 1919. Edited version in *A History of Cocaine: The Mystery of Coca Java and the Kew Plant*, by Steven B. Karch, ch. 5. London: Royal Society of Medicine Press, 2003.

Reid, William A. "Coca: A Plant of the Andes." Commodities of Commerce Series no. 20. Washington, D.C.: Pan-American Union, 1928.

Renborg, Bertil. *International Drug Control: A Study of International Administration by and through the League of Nations*. Washington, D.C.: Carnegie Endowment for International Peace, 1947.

Renoz, Charles. *Le Pérou: Histoire, description physique et politique, productions, commerce, immigration et colonization*. Brussels: Weissenbruch Imp., 1897.

Ricketts, Carlos. *Ensayos de legislación pro-indígena*. Arequipa: Tip. Cuadros, 1936.

Rodríguez, José M. *Estudios económicos-financieros y ojeada sobre las hacienda pública del Perú y la necesidad de su reforma*. Lima: Librería y Imprenta Gil, 1895.

Rusby, Henry Hurd. *Jungle Memories*. New York: McGraw-Hill, 1933.

Sáenz, Luis N. *La coca: Estudio médico-social de la gran toxicomanía peruana*. Lima: La Guardia Civil y Policía, 1938.

Scherzer, Karl D. C. *Voyage on the Novara: Narrative of the Circumnavigation of the Globe by the Austrian Frigate Novara*. 3 vols. London: Saunders, Otley, 1861–63.

Searle, William S. *A New Form of Nervous Disease (together with an Essay on Erythroxylon Coca)*. New York: Fords, Howard and Hulbert, 1881.

Stiglich, Germán. *Informe del jefe de la comisión explorador de las regiones de Ucayali, Fiscarraldo i Madre de Dios*. Lima: La Opinión Nacional, 1907.

Tamayo, Augusto E. *Informe sobre las colonias de Oxapampa y Pozuzo y los Rios Palcazu y Pichis*. Lima: Imprenta Liberal Unión, 1904.

Tejeda B., Aurea. "Un talento olvidado: Alfredo Bignon." In *Actas y trabajos*, 609–15. Lima: Primero Congreso Farmacéutico Peruano, 1943.

Thudichem, J. L. W., M.D. *The Coca of Peru and Its Immediate Principles*. London: Bailièrre, Tindall and Cox, 1885.

Tibbles, W., M.D. *Erythroxylon Coca: A Treatise on Brain Exhaustion as the Cause of Disease.* Helmsley, U.K.: Ryedale Printing Office, 1877.

El Tulumayo: Documentos justificativos del dominio y posesión que mantiene en aquella florestia nacional el Dr. Hajime Hoshi. Lima: Cía de Impresiones y Publicidad, 1942.

Vallejos S., Luis. "Estudios científicos sobre la coca peruana desde H. Unánue hasta A. Bignon." In *Actas y trabajos*, 578–83. Lima: Primero Congreso Farmacéutico Peruano, 1943.

Viajes de estudio: Crónica del viaje Lima-Pucallpa. Lima: San Marcos University, Instituto de Geografía, 1949.

Vinelli, Manuel. *Contribución al estudio de la coca.* Lima: Imprenta San Pedro, 1918.

Vivian, E. C. *Peru: Physical Features, Natural Resources, Means of Communications, Manufactures and Industrial Development.* New York: Appleton, 1914.

Von Tschudi, Johan J. *Travels in Peru, during the Years 1838–42. . . .* London: D. Bogue, 1846.

Walger, Theodor. "Coca: Its History, Geographic Distribution and Economic Significance." Thesis, Universität zu Giessen, Berlin, 1914/17. Edited version in *A History of Cocaine: The Mystery of Coca Java and the Kew Plant*, by Steven B. Karch, ch. 7. London: Royal Society of Medicine Press, 2003.

Willoughby, W. W. *Opium as an International Problem: The Geneva Conferences.* Baltimore: Johns Hopkins University Press, 1925.

Wright, Marie Robinson. *The Old and the New Peru.* Philadelphia: George Barrie and Sons, 1908.

SECONDARY SOURCES

General and Comparative

Allen, Frederick. *Secret Formula: How Brilliant Marketing and Relentless Salesmanship Made Coca-Cola the Best-Known Product in the World.* New York: HarperCollins, 1994.

Anderson, Benedict. *Imagined Communities: Reflections on the Origins and Spread of Nationalism.* London: Verso, 1983.

Appadurai, Arjun, ed. *The Social Life of Things: Commodities in Cultural Perspective.* Cambridge: Cambridge University Press, 1986.

———. *Modernity at Large: Cultural Dimensions of Globalization.* Minneapolis: University of Minnesota Press, 1996.

Asbury, Herbert. *The Gangs of New York: An Informal History of the Underworld.* Foreword by Jorge Luis Borges. 1927. Reprint, New York: Thunder's Mouth, 1998.

Bauer, Arnold J. *Goods, Power, History: Latin America's Material Culture.* Cambridge: Cambridge University Press, 2001.

Becker, Howard B. *Outsiders: Studies in the Sociology of Deviance.* New York: Free Press, 1963.

Brewer, John, and Frank Trentmann, eds. *Consuming Cultures, Global Perspectives: Historical Trajectories, Transnational Exchanges.* Oxford: Berg, 2006.

398

Brockway, Lucille H. *Science and Colonial Expansion: The Role of the British Royal Botanical Gardens*. New York: Academic Press, 1979.

Bucheli, Marcelo, and Ian Read. "Banana Boats and Baby Food: The Banana in U.S. History." In *From Silver to Cocaine: Latin American Commodity Chains and the Building of the World Economy, 1500–2000*, edited by Steven Topik, Carlos Marichal, and Zephyr Frank, ch. 8. Durham: Duke University Press, 2006.

Bynum, W. F. *Science and the Practice of Medicine in the Nineteenth Century*. Cambridge: Cambridge University Press, 1994.

Cirules, Enrique. *The Mafia in Havana: A Caribbean Mob Story*. Translated by D. E. LaPrade. Melbourne: Ocean Press, 2004.

Cobb, Richard. *The Police and the People: French Popular Protest, 1789–1920*. New York: Oxford University Press, 1970.

Coe, Sophie, and Michael D. Coe. *The True History of Chocolate*. London: Thames and Hudson, 1996.

Davis, Miles, with Quincy Troupe. *Miles: The Autobiography*. New York: Simon and Schuster, 1989.

DeVeaux, Scott. *The Birth of Bebop: A Social and Musical History*. Berkeley: University of California Press, 1999.

Dinges, John, and Saul Landau. *Assassination on Embassy Row*. New York: McGraw-Hill, 1980.

Douglas, Mary, and Baron Isherwood. *The World of Goods*. New York: Basic Books, 1979.

Fogel, Robert W., and G. R. Elton. *Two Views of History*. New Haven: Yale University Press, 1983.

Foster, Nelson, and Linda S. Cordell, eds. *Chiles to Chocolate: Food the Americas Gave the World*. Tucson: University of Arizona Press, 1992.

Gereffi, Gary, and Miguel Korzeniewicz, eds. *Commodity Chains and Global Capitalism*. Westport: Greenwood Press, 1994.

Gerschenkron, Alexander. *Economic Backwardness in Historical Perspective: A Book of Essays*. Cambridge: Harvard University Press, Belknap Press, 1962.

Ginzburg, Carlo. "The Inquisitor as Anthropologist." In *Clues, Myths, and the Historical Method*, by Carlo Ginzburg, 156–64. Baltimore: Johns Hopkins University Press, 1992.

Giswijt-Hofstra, Marijke, and Roy Porter, eds. *Cultures of Neurasthenia: From Beard to the First World War*. Amsterdam: Rodopi, 2001.

Goodman, Jordan. *Tobacco in History: The Cultures of Dependence*. London: Routledge, 1993.

Griggs, Barbara. *Green Pharmacy: The History and Evolution of Western Herbal Medicine*. Rochester, Vt.: Healing Arts Press, 1981.

Guy, Donna J. *Sex and Danger in Buenos Aires: Prostitution, Family, and Nation in Argentina*. Omaha: University of Nebraska Press, 1991.

Hacking, Ian. *The Social Construction of What?* Cambridge, Mass.: Harvard University Press, 1999.

Haller, Mark H. "Illegal Enterprise: A Theoretical and Historical Interpretation." *Criminology* 28/2 (1990): 207–36.

Hobsbawm, Eric, and Terrence C. Ranger, eds. *The Invention of Tradition*. Cambridge: Cambridge University Press, 1983.

Jones, Ernest. *The Life and Work of Sigmund Freud*. New York: Anchor Books, 1963.

Joseph, Gilbert, Catherine LeGrande, and Ricardo Salvatorre, eds. *Close Encounters of Empire: Writing the Cultural History of Latin American–U.S. Relations*. Durham: Duke University Press, 1998.

Kahn, E. J., Jr. *The Big Drink: The Story of Coca-Cola*. New York: Random House, 1959.

Kaplan, Ann, and Donald Pease, eds. *Cultures of United States Imperialism*. Durham: Duke University Press, 1993.

Kopytoff, Igor. "The Cultural Biography of Things: Commoditization as Process." In *The Social Life of Things: Commodities in Cultural Perspective*, edited by Arjun Appadurai, 64–94. Cambridge: Cambridge University Press, 1986.

Korzeniewicz, Roberto P., and William C. Smith, eds. *Latin America and the World Economy*. Westport: Greenwood, 1990.

Kuisel, Richard F. *Seducing the French: The Dilemma of Americanization*. Berkeley: University of California Press, 1993.

Lomnitz, Claudio. "Nationalism's Dirty Linen: 'Contact Zones' and the Topography of National Identity." In *Deep Mexico, Silent Mexico: An Anthropology of Nationalism*, 125–44. Minneapolis: University of Minnesota Press, 2001.

Lutz, Tom. *American Nervousness, 1903: An Anecdotal History*. Ithaca: Cornell University Press, 1991.

Mann, Michael. *The Sources of Social Power: A History of Power from the Beginnings to A.D. 1760*. 2 vols. Cambridge: Cambridge University Press, 1986.

Marx, Karl. *Capital: A Critique of Political Economy*. 3 vols. 1887. Reprint, New York: International Publishers, 1967.

Merton, Robert K. "The Unanticipated Consequences of Purposeful Social Action." *American Sociological Review* 1/6 (Dec. 1936): 894–904.

Messick, Hank, and Burt Goldblatt. *The Mobs and the Mafia: The Illustrated History of Organized Crime*. New York: Thomas Crowell, 1972.

Mintz, Sidney W. *Sweetness and Power: The Place of Sugar in Modern History*. New York: Viking, 1985.

———. *Tasting Food, Tasting Freedom: Excursions into Eating, Culture, and the Past*. Boston: Beacon, 1996.

Nadelmann, Ethan. *Cops Across Borders: The Internationalization of U.S. Criminal Law Enforcement*. University Park: Pennsylvania State University Press, 1993.

Ortiz, Fernando. *Cuban Counterpoint: Tobacco and Sugar*. Translated by Harriet de Onís. 1947. Reprint, Durham: Duke University Press, 1995.

Parascandola, John. *The Development of American Pharmacology*. Baltimore: Johns Hopkins University Press, 1992.

Pendergrast, Mark. *The History of Coffee and How It Transformed Our World*. New York: Basic Books, 1999.

Pernick, Martin S. *A Calculus of Suffering: Pain, Professionalization, and Anesthesia in Nineteenth-Century America*. New York: Columbia University Press, 1985.

Pilcher, Jeffrey M. *¡Que Vivan los Tamales! Food and the Making of Mexican Identity*. Albuquerque: University of New Mexico Press, 1998.

Pomeranz, Kenneth, and Steven Topik. *The World that Trade Created: Society, Culture, and the World Economy, 1400 to the Present*. Armonk, N.Y.: M. E. Sharp, 1999.

Pratt, Mary Louise. *Imperial Eyes: Travel Writing and Transculturation*. London: Routledge, 1992.

Reuter, Peter. *Disorganized Crime: The Economics of the Visible Hand*. Cambridge, Mass.: MIT Press, 1983.

Robertson, Roland. "Glocalization: Time-Space, Homogeneity-Heterogeneity." In *Global Modernities*, edited by M. Featherstone, Scott Lash, and Roland Robertson, 25–44. London: Sage, 1995.

Roseberry, William. "The Rise of Yuppie Coffee and the Reimagination of Class in the United States." *American Anthropologist* 98/4 (Dec. 1996): 762–75.

Schwartz, Rosalie. *Pleasure Island: Tourism and Temptation in Cuba*. Lincoln: University of Nebraska Press, 1997.

Scott, James C. *Seeing Like a State: How Certain Schemes to Improve the Human Race Have Failed*. New Haven: Yale University Press, 1998.

Starr, Paul. *The Social Transformation of American Medicine*. New York: Basic Books, 1982.

Stepan, Nancy Leys. *"The Hour of Eugenics": Race, Gender, and Nation in Latin America*. Ithaca: Cornell University Press, 1991.

Stockwell, Christine. *Nature's Pharmacy: A History of Plants and Healing*. London: Royal Botanical Gardens / Arrow Books, 1988.

Topik, Steven, Carlos Marichal, and Zephyr Frank, eds. *From Silver to Cocaine: Latin American Commodity Chains and the Building of the World Economy, 1500–2000*. Durham: Duke University Press, 2006.

Valenzuela-Zapata, Ana G., and Gary Paul Nabhan. *¡Tequila! A Natural and Cultural History*. Tucson: University of Arizona Press, 2003.

Van Schendel, Willem, and Itty Abraham, eds. *Illicit Flows and Criminal Things: States, Borders, and the Other Side of Globalization*. Bloomington: Indiana University Press, 2005.

Wacquant, Loic, and Pierre Bourdieu. *An Invitation to Reflexive Sociology*. Chicago: University of Chicago Press, 1992.

Weinstein, James C. *The Corporate Ideal in the Liberal State, 1900–1918*. Boston: Beacon, 1968.

Drugs and Cocaine

Andreas, Peter. "When Policies Collide: Market Reform, Market Prohibition, and Narcotization of the Mexican Economy." In *The Illicit Global Economy and State Power*, edited by H. Richard Friman and P. Andreas, ch. 5. Lanham, Md.: Rowan and Littlefield, 1999.

Andrews, George, and David Solomon, comps. *The Coca Leaf and Cocaine Papers*. New York: Harcourt, Brace and Jovanovich, 1975.

Ashley, Richard. *Cocaine: Its History, Uses, and Effects*. New York: St. Martin's, 1975.

Astorga, Luis. *Mitología del "narcotraficante" en México*. Mexico: Plaza y Valdés, 1995.

——. *El siglo de las drogas: Usos, percepciones, y personajes*. Mexico: Espasa-Hoy, 1996.

——. "Cocaine in Mexico: A Prelude to 'los Narcos.'" In *Cocaine: Global Histories*, edited by Paul Gootenberg, ch. 9. London: Routledge, 1999.

——. *Drogas sin fronteras: Los expedientes de una guerra permanente*. Mexico: Editorial Grijalbo, 2003.

Bakalar, James B. "Drugs and Medical Culture: Cocaine as a Historical Example." Paper presented at the American Association for the Advancement of Science Symposium on Cocaine, Boston, Mass., 1978.

Bellone, Amy. "The Cocaine Commodity Chain and Developmental Paths in Peru and Bolivia." In *Latin America and the World Economy*, edited by Roberto P. Korzeniewicz and William C. Smith, ch. 2. Westport: Greenwood, 1990.

Bewley-Taylor, David R. *The United States and International Drug Control*. London: Pinter, 1999.

Biskind, Peter. *Easy Riders, Raging Bulls: How the Sex-Drugs-and-Rock'n'Roll Generation Saved Hollywood*. New York: Simon and Schuster, 1998.

Block, Alan A. "The Snowman Cometh: Coke in Progressive New York." *Criminology* 17/1 (May 1979): 75–99.

——. "European Drug Traffic and Traffickers between the Wars: The Policy of Suppression and Its Consequences." *Journal of Social History* 23 (Winter 1989): 314–37.

Bourgois, Philippe. *In Search of Respect: Selling Crack in El Barrio*. Cambridge: Cambridge University Press, 1995.

Brecher, Edward M., and the editors of *Consumer Reports*. *Licit and Illicit Drugs: The Consumers Union Report on Narcotics, Stimulants, Depressants, Inhalants, Hallucinogens, and Marijuana—Including Caffeine, Nicotine, and Alcohol*. Boston: Little, Brown, 1972.

Brook, Timothy, and Bob Tadashi Wakabayashi, eds. *Opium Regimes: China, Britain and Japan, 1839–1952*. Berkeley: University of California Press, 2000.

Bruun, Kettil, Lynn Pan, and Ingemar Rexed. *The Gentlemen's Club: International Control of Drugs and Alcohol*. Chicago: University of Chicago Press, 1975.

Byck, Robert, ed. *Cocaine Papers by Sigmund Freud*. New York: Stonehill Books, 1974.

Cajas, Juan. *El truquito y la maroma, cocaína, traquetos y pistoleros en Nueva York: Una antropología de la incertidumbre y lo prohibido*. Mexico: CONACULTA-INAH, 2004.

Cockburn, Alexander, and Jeffrey St. Clair. *Whiteout: The CIA, Drugs, and the Press*. London: Verso, 1998.

Courtwright, David T. "The Rise and Fall of Cocaine in the United States." In *Consuming Habits: Drugs in History and Anthropology*, edited by Jordan Goodman, Paul Lovejoy, and Andrew Sherratt, ch. 10. London: Routledge, 1995.

——. *Forces of Habit: Drugs and the Making of the Modern World*. Cambridge, Mass.: Harvard University Press, 2001.

———. "Mr. ATOD's Wild Ride: What Do Alcohol, Tobacco, and Other Drugs Have in Common?" *Social History of Alcohol and Drugs* 20 (2005): 105–40.

Courtwright, David T., Herman Joseph, and Don des Jarlais, eds. *Addicts Who Survived: An Oral History of Narcotic Use in America, 1923–1965.* Knoxville: University of Tennessee Press, 1989.

Davenport-Hines, Richard. *The Pursuit of Oblivion: A Global History of Narcotics.* New York: W. W. Norton, 2001.

DeGrandpre, Richard. *The Cult of Pharmacology: How America Became the World's Most Troubled Drug Culture.* Durham: Duke University Press, 2006.

De Kort, Marcel. "Doctors, Diplomats, and Businessmen: Conflicting Interests in the Netherlands and Dutch East Indies, 1860–1950." In *Cocaine: Global Histories,* edited by Paul Gootenberg, ch. 6. London: Routledge, 1999.

Dikötter, Frank, Lars Laamann, and Zhou Xun. *Narcotic Culture: A History of Drugs in China.* Chicago: University of Chicago Press, 2004.

Duke, Steven B., and Albert C. Gross. *America's Longest War: Rethinking our Tragic Crusade against Drugs.* New York: G. P. Putnam's Sons, 1993.

Edwards, Griffith. *Matters of Substance: Drugs—and Why Everyone's a User.* London: Allen Lane, 2004.

Epstein, Edward Jay. *Agency of Fear: Opiates and Political Power in America.* 2nd ed. London: Verso, 1990.

Erien, Jonathan, and Joseph Spillane, eds. *Federal Drug Control: The Evolution of Policy and Practice.* New York: Pharmaceutical Products Press, 2004.

Escohotado, Antonio. *Historia de las drogas.* 3 vols. Madrid: Alianza Editorial, 1989.

Eyguesier, Pierre. *Comment Freud devint drogman: Études sur la coca et la cocaïne à la Belle Époque.* Paris: Navarin Edituer, 1983.

Foster, Jeffrey Clayton. "The Rocky Road to a 'Drug-Free Tennessee': A History of the Early Regulation of Cocaine and the Opiates, 1897–1913." *Journal of Social History* 29/3 (1995): 547–64.

Friman, H. Richard. *Narco-Diplomacy: Exporting the U.S. War on Drugs.* Ithaca: Cornell University Press, 1996.

———. "Germany and the Transformations of Cocaine, 1880–1920." In *Cocaine: Global Histories,* edited by Paul Gootenberg, ch. 4. London: Routledge, 1999.

Goodman, Jordan. "Excitantia; or, How Enlightenment Europe Took to Soft Drugs." In *Consuming Habits: Drugs in History and Anthropology,* edited by Jordan Goodman, Paul Lovejoy, and Andrew Sherratt, 126–47. London: Routledge, 1995.

Goodman, Jordan, Paul Lovejoy, and Andrew Sherratt, eds. *Consuming Habits: Drugs in History and Anthropology.* London: Routledge, 1995.

Gootenberg, Paul, ed. *Cocaine: Global Histories.* London: Routledge, 1999.

———. "Cocaine: Hidden Histories." In *Cocaine: Global Histories,* edited by Paul Gootenberg, ch. 1. London: Routledge, 1999.

———. "Secret Ingredients: The Politics of Coca in US-Peruvian Relations, 1915–65." *Journal of Latin American Studies* 36/2 (May 2004): 233–66.

———. "Talking Like a State: Drugs, Borders, and the Language of Control."

In *Illicit Flows and Criminal Things*, edited by Willem van Schendel and Itty Abraham, ch. 3. Bloomington: Indiana University Press, 2005.

———. "Scholars on Drugs: Some Qualitative Trends." *Qualitative Sociology* 28/4 (Winter 2005): 479–91.

———. "Cocaine in Chains: The Rise and Demise of a Global Commodity." In *From Silver to Cocaine: Latin American Commodity Chains and the Building of the World Economy, 1500–2000,* edited by Steven Topik, Carlos Marichal, and Zephyr Frank, ch. 12. Durham: Duke University Press, 2006.

———. "The 'Pre-Colombian' Era of Drug Trafficking in the Americas: Cocaine, 1945–1965." *The Americas* 64/2 (Oct. 2007): 133–76.

The Gourmet Cokebook: A Complete Guide to Cocaine. New York: White Mountain, 1972.

Grinspoon, Lester, and James B. Bakalar. *Cocaine: A Drug and Its Social Evolution.* New York: Basic Books, 1976.

Hefland, William. "Vin Mariani." *Pharmacy in History* 22/1 (1980): 11–19.

Henman, Anthony (Antonil). *Mama Coca.* London: Hassle Free Press, 1987.

Hickman, Timothy A. "'Mania Americana': Narcotic Addiction and Modernity in the United States, 1870–1920." *Journal of American History* 90/4 (May 2004): 1269–94.

———. *The Secret Leprosy of Modern Days: Narcotic Addiction and Cultural Crisis in the United States, 1870–1920.* Amherst: University of Massachusetts Press, 2007.

Hyde, Stephen, and Geno Zanetti, eds. *White Lines: Writers on Cocaine.* New York: Thunder's Mouth, 2002.

International Narcotics Control Strategy Report. Washington, D.C.: Bureau of International Narcotics and Law Enforcement Affairs, 2000.

Jankowiak, William, and Daniel Bradburd, eds. *Drugs, Labor and Colonial Expansion.* Tucson: University of Arizona Press, 2003.

Jennings, John M. *The Opium Empire: Japanese Imperialism and Drug Trafficking in Asia, 1895–1945.* New York: Praeger, 1995.

Jonnes, Jill. *Hep-Cats, Narcs, and Pipe Dreams: A History of America's Romance with Illegal Drugs.* New York: Scribner, 1996.

Kamastra, Jerry. *Weed: Adventures of a Dope Smuggler.* Santa Barbara: Ross-Erikson, 1974.

Karch, Steven B., M.D. *A Brief History of Cocaine.* Baton Rouge: CRC, 1998.

———. "Japan and the Cocaine Industry of Southeast Asia, 1864–1944." In *Cocaine: Global Histories,* edited by Paul Gootenberg, ch. 7. London: Routledge, 1999.

———. *A History of Cocaine: The Mystery of Coca Java and the Kew Plant.* London: Royal Society of Medicine Press, 2003.

Kawell, JoAnn. "Drug Economies of the Americas." *NACLA Report on the Americas* 36/2 (Sept.–Oct. 2002): 8–13.

Kennedy, Joseph. *Coca Exotica: The Illustrated History of Cocaine.* New York: Cornwall Press, 1985.

Kenney, Michael. "From Pablo to Osama: Counter-Terrorism Lessons from the War on Drugs." *Survival* 45/3 (Autumn 2003): 187–206.

——. "A History of the Colombian Drug Trade." Ms., 2005.

——. *From Pablo to Osama: Trafficking and Terrorist Networks, Government Bureaucracies, and Competitive Adaptations*. University Park: Pennsylvania State University Press, 2007.

Kinder, Douglas C. "Bureaucratic Cold Warrior: Harry J. Anslinger and Illicit Drugs Traffic." *Pacific Historical Review* 50/2 (1981): 169–91.

Kinder, Douglas C., and William O. Walker III. "Stable Force in a Storm: Harry J. Anslinger and United States Narcotic Foreign Policy, 1930–1962." *Journal of American History* 72/4 (1986): 908–27.

Kohn, Marek. *Narcomania: On Heroin*. London: Faber and Faber, 1987.

——. *The Dope Girls: The Birth of the British Drug Underground*. London: Lawrence and Wishart, 1992.

——. "Cocaine Girls: Sex, Drugs, and Modernity in London during and after the First World War." In *Cocaine: Global Histories*, edited by Paul Gootenberg, ch. 5. London: Routledge, 1999.

LaBarre, Winston. "Old and New World Narcotics: A Statistical Question and Ethnological Reply." *Economic Botany* 24 (1970): 73–80.

Lenson, David. *On Drugs*. Minneapolis: University of Minnesota Press, 1995.

Léon, Federico, and Ramiro Castro de la Mata, eds. *Pasta básica de cocaína: Un estudio multidisciplinario*. Lima: CEDRO, 1989.

Lowes, Peter D. *The Genesis of International Narcotics Control*. Geneva: Librairie Droz, 1966.

MacCoun, Robert J., and Peter Reuter. *Drug War Heresies: Learning from Other Vices, Times, and Places*. Cambridge: Cambridge University Press, 2001.

Madge, Tim. *White Mischief: A Cultural History of Cocaine*. New York: Thunder's Mouth, 2001.

Malamud-Goti, Jaime. *Smoke and Mirrors: The Paradox of the Drug Wars*. Boulder: Westview, 1992.

Marez, Curtis. *Drug Wars: The Political Economy of Narcotics*. Minneapolis: University of Minnesota Press, 2004.

Marshall, Jonathan. "Opium, Tungsten, and the Search for National Security, 1940–1952." In *Drug Control Policy: Essays in Historical and Comparative Perspective*, edited by William Walker III, 89–116. University Park: Pennsylvania State University Press, 1992.

Massing, Michael. *The Fix*. New York: Simon and Schuster, 1998.

McAllister, William B. *Drug Diplomacy in the Twentieth Century: An International History*. London: Routledge, 2000.

——. "Habitual Problems: The United States and International Drug Control." In *Federal Drug Control: The Evolution of Policy and Practice*, edited by Jonathan Erien and Joseph Spillane, 175–207. New York: Pharmaceutical Products Press, 2004.

McCoy, Alfred W. "The Stimulus of Prohibition: A Critical History of the Global Narcotics Trade." In *Dangerous Harvest: Drug Plants and the Transformation of Indigenous Landscapes*, edited by Michael K. Steinberg, Joseph J. Hobbs, and Kent Mathewson, 24–111. New York: Oxford University Press, 2004.

McWilliams, John C. *The Protectors: Harry J. Anslinger and the Federal Bureau of Narcotics, 1930–1962*. Newark: University of Delaware Press, 1990.

Meyer, Kathryn, and Terry Parssinen. *Webs of Smoke: Smuggling, Warlords, Spies, and the History of the International Drug Trade*. London: Rowman and Littlefield, 1998.

Mills, James H. *Cannabis Britannica: Empire, Trade, and Prohibition*. Oxford: Oxford University Press, 2003.

Mintz, Sidney W. "The Forefathers of Crack." *NACLA Report on the Americas* 22/6 (March 1989): 31–32.

Morgan, H. Wayne. *Yesterday's Addicts: American Society and Drug Abuse, 1865–1920*. Norman: University of Oklahoma Press, 1974.

Musto, David F., M.D. *The American Disease: Origins of Narcotic Control*. New Haven: Yale University Press, 1973. Rev. ed., New York: Oxford University Press, 1987.

———. "America's First Cocaine Epidemic." *Wilson Quarterly* (Summer 1989): 59–64.

———. "International Traffic in Coca through the Early Twentieth Century." *Drug and Alcohol Dependence* 19 (1998): 145–56.

Nadelmann, Ethan. "U.S. Drug Policy: A Bad Export?" *Foreign Policy* 70 (1988): 97–108.

———. "Drug Prohibition in the United States: Costs, Consequences and Alternatives." *Science* 245 (1989): 939–47.

North American Congress on Latin America. "Widening Destruction: Drug War in the Americas." *NACLA Report on the Americas* 35/1 (July 2003): 12–51.

Pacini, Deborah, and Christine Franquemont, eds. *Coca and Cocaine: Effects on People and Policy in Latin America*. Ithaca: LASP–Cornell University; Cambridge, Mass.: Cultural Survival, 1985.

Pendergrast, Mark. *For God, Country, and Coca-Cola: The Unauthorized History of the Great American Soft Drink and the Company that Makes It*. New York: Scribner, 1993.

Pérez Montfort, Ricardo. *Yerba, goma y polvo: Drogas, ambientes y policías en México, 1900–1940*. Mexico: INAH–Ediciones ERA, 1999.

Petersen, Robert C., and Richard C. Stillman, eds. *Cocaine: 1977*. NIDA Research Monograph 13. Rockville, Md.: Department of Health, Education, and Welfare, 1977.

Phillips, Joel L., and Ronald D. Wynne. *Cocaine: The Mystique and the Reality*. New York: Avon Books, 1980.

Recio, Gabriela. "Drugs and Alcohol: US Prohibition and the Origins of the Drug Trade in Mexico, 1910–1930." *Journal of Latin American Studies* 34/1 (2002): 21–41.

Reeves, Jimmie L., and Richard Campbell. *Cracked Coverage: Television News, the Anti-Cocaine Crusade, and the Reagan Legacy*. Durham: Duke University Press, 1994.

Reinarman, Craig, and Harry G. Levin, eds. *Crack in America: Demon Drugs and Social Justice*. Berkeley: University of California Press, 1997.

Reuter, Peter. "The Political Economy of Drug Smuggling." In *The Political*

Economy of the Drug Industry: Latin America and the International System, edited by Mario Vellinga, ch. 7. Gainesville: University Press of Florida, 2004.

Rivera Cusicanqui, Silvia. "'Here Even Legislators Chew Them': Coca Leaves and Identity Politics in Northern Argentina." In *Illicit Flows and Criminal Things: States, Borders and the other Side of Globalization*, edited by Willem Van Schendel and Itty Abraham, 128–52. Bloomington: Indiana University Press, 2005.

Robbins, Bruce. "Commodity Histories." *Publications of the Modern Language Association of America* 120/2 (2005): 454–63.

Ronell, Avital. *Crack Wars: Literature, Addiction, Mania*. Lincoln: University of Nebraska Press, 1992.

Rorabaugh, William J. *The Alcoholic Republic: An American Tradition*. New York: Oxford University Press, 1979.

Rush, James R. *Opium to Java: Revenue Farming and Chinese Enterprise in Colonial Indonesia, 1860–1910*. Ithaca: Cornell University Press, 1990.

Sabbag, Robert. *Snowblind: A Brief Career in the Cocaine Trade*. New York: Grove, 1976.

Sáenz Rovner, Eduardo. *La conexión cubana: Narcotráfico, contrabando y juego en Cuba entre los años 20 y comienzos de la Revolución*. Bogotá: Universidad Nacional de Colombia, 2005.

Schivelbusch, Wolfgang. *Tastes of Paradise: A Social History of Spices, Stimulants, and Intoxicants*. New York: Vintage Books, 1992.

Schultes, Richard Evans, and Albert Hoffman. *Plants of the Gods: Their Sacred, Healing, and Hallucinogenic Powers*. Rochester, Vt.: Healing Arts, 1992.

Spillane, Joseph F. "Making a Modern Drug: The Manufacture, Sale, and Control of Cocaine in the United States, 1880–1920." In *Cocaine: Global Histories*, edited by Paul Gootenberg, ch. 2. London: Routledge, 1999.

———. *Cocaine: From Medical Marvel to Modern Menace in the United States, 1884–1920*. Baltimore: Johns Hopkins University Press, 2000.

———. "Building a Drug Control Regime, 1919–1930." In *Federal Drug Control: The Evolution of Policy and Practice*, edited by Jonathan Erien and J. Spillane, 25–60. New York: Pharmaceutical Products Press, 2004.

Stares, Paul B. *Global Habit*. Washington, D.C.: Brookings Institution, 1996.

Starks, Michael. *Cocaine Fiends and Reefer Madness: An Illustrated History of Drugs in the Movies*. London: Cornwall Books, 1982.

Strausbaugh, John, and Donald Blaise, eds. *The Drug User: Documents, 1840–1960*. New York: Blast Books, 1991.

Streatfield, Dominic. *Cocaine: An Unauthorized Biography*. London: Virgin, 2001.

Szasz, Thomas. *Ceremonial Chemistry: The Ritual Persecution of Drugs, Addicts, and Pushers*. Garden City, N.Y.: Doubleday-Anchor, 1974.

Taylor, Arnold H. *American Diplomacy and the Narcotics Traffic, 1900–1939*. Durham: Duke University Press, 1969.

Thorton, E. M. *The Freudian Fallacy: Freud and Cocaine*. 1983. Reprint, London: Palladin Grafton Books, 1986.

Thoumi, Francisco E. "Why the Illegal Psychoactive Drugs Industry Grew in Colombia." *Journal of Interamerican Studies and World Affairs* 34/3 (1992): 37–63.

Torgoff, Martin. *Can't Find My Way Home: America in the Great Stoned Age, 1945–2000*. New York: Simon and Schuster, 2004.

UNDCP (United Nations International Drug Control Program). *World Drug Report*. New York: Oxford University Press, 1997.

Valentine, Douglas. *The Strength of the Wolf: The Secret History of America's War on Drugs*. London: Verso Books, 2004.

Vellinga, Menno, ed. *The Political Economy of the Drug Industry: Latin America and the International System*. Gainesville: University Press of Florida, 2004.

Waldorf, Dan, Craig Reinarman, and Sheigla Murphy. *Cocaine Changes: The Experience of Using and Quitting*. Philadelphia: Temple University Press, 1991.

Walker, William O., III. *Drug Control in the Americas*. Albuquerque: University of New Mexico Press, 1981; rev. ed., 1989.

———, ed. *Drug Control Policy: Essays in Historical and Comparative Perspective*. University Park: Pennsylvania University Press, 1992.

———, ed. *Drugs in the Western Hemisphere: An Odyssey of Cultures in Conflict*. Wilmington, Del.: Scholarly Resources, 1996.

Weil, Andrew, M.D. *The Natural Mind: An Investigation of Drugs and the Higher Consciousness*. Boston: Houghton Mifflin, 1972.

———. "The New Politics of Coca." *New Yorker*, 15 May 1995, 70–80.

Wilson, Suzanne, and Marta Zambrano. "Cocaine, Commodity Chains and Drug Politics: A Transnational Approach." In *Commodity Chains and Global Capitalism*, edited by Gary Gereffi and Miguel Korzeniewicz, 297–316. Westport: Greenwood, 1994.

Woodley, Richard. *Dealer: Portrait of a Cocaine Merchant*. New York: Holt, Rinehart and Winston, 1971.

Youngers, Coletta A., and Eileen Rosen, eds. *Drugs and Democracy in Latin America: The Impact of U.S. Policy*. Boulder: Lynne Rienner, 2005.

Zinberg, Norman E. *Drug, Set, and Setting: The Basis for Controlled Intoxicant Use*. New Haven: Yale University Press, 1984.

Andean History

Appelbaum, Nancy. *Muddied Waters: Race, Region, and Local History in Colombia, 1846–1948*. Durham: Duke University Press, 2003.

Aramburú, Carlos E. "La expansión de la frontera demográfica y económica en la selva alta peruana." In *Colonización en la Amazonía*, edited by Carlos E. Aramburú, Enrique Bedoya, and Jorge Recharte, 1–40. Lima: Ed. CIPA, 1982.

———. "La economía parcelaria y el cultivo de la coca: El caso del Alto Huallaga." In *Pasta básica de cocaína: Un estudio multidisciplinario*, edited by Federico Léon and Ramiro Castro de la Mata, 231–59. Lima: CEDRO, 1989.

Aramburú, Carlos E., Enrique Bedoya, and Jorge Recharte, eds. *Colonización en la Amazonía*. Lima: Ed. CIPA, 1982.

Assadourian, Carlos Sempat. *El sistema de la economía colonial: Mercado interno, regiones y espacio económico*. Lima: Instituto de Estudios Peruanos, 1982.

Bascopé Aspiazu, René. *La veta blanca: Coca y cocaína en Bolivia*. La Paz: Ediciones Aquí, 1982.

Bentancourt, Darío, and Martha Luz García. *Contrabandistas, marimberos y mafiosos: Historia social de la mafia colombiana (1965–1992)*. Bogotá: Tercer Mundo Eds., 1994.

Boldó i Climent, Joan, ed. *La coca andina: Visión indígena de una planta satanizada*. Mexico: Instituto Indigenista InterAmericano, 1986.

Boloña, Carlos. *Políticas arancelarias en el Perú, 1880–1980*. Lima: Instituto de Economía de Libre Mercado, 1994.

Bonfiglio, Giovanni. *Antonio Raimondi: El mensaje vigente*. Lima: Banco de Crédito del Perú, 2004.

Bonilla, Heraclio, comp. *Gran Bretaña y el Perú, 1826–1919: Informes de los cónsules británicos*. 5 vols. Lima: Instituto de Estudios Peruanos, Banco Industrial del Perú, 1976.

Burga, Manuel, and Alberto Flores Galindo. *Apogeo y crisis de la República Aristocrática*. Lima: Ediciones Rikchay Perú, 1979.

Camacho-Guizado, Álvaro, and Andrés López-Restrepo. "From Smugglers to Drug-Lords to *Traquetos*: Changes in the Colombian Illicit Drug Organizations." In *Peace, Democracy, and Human Rights in Colombia*, edited by Christopher Welna and Gustavo Gallón, 60–89. South Bend: University of Notre Dame Press, 2007.

Canelas Orellana, Amado, and Juan Carlos Canelas Zanner. *Bolivia—Coca cocaína: Subdesarrollo y poder político*. La Paz: Los Amigos de Libro, 1982.

Carter, William E., and Mauricio Mamami. *Coca en Bolivia*. La Paz: U.S. National Institute of Drug Abuse, 1980.

———, ed. *Ensayos científicos sobre la coca*. La Paz: Editorial Juventud, 1983.

Castillo, Fabio. *Los jinetes de la cocaína*. 1987. Reprint, Bogotá: Nizkor web version, n.d., ca. 2001.

Chaparro, Camilo. *Historia del cartel de Cali*. Bogotá: Intermedio Eds., 2005.

Clawson, Patrick L., and Rensselaer Lee III. *The Andean Cocaine Industry*. New York: St. Martin's, 1996.

Cloud, Andrés, ed. *Antología huanuqueña*. Huánuco: Universidad Hermilio Valdizán, 1989.

Cueto, Marcos. *Excelencia científica en la periferia: Actividades científicas e investigación biomédica en el Perú, 1890–1950*. Lima: CONCYTEC, 1989.

———. "Andean Biology in Peru: Scientific Styles in the Periphery." *ISIS* 80 (1989): 640–58.

Departamento de Huánuco. 3rd ed. Lima: Colección Documental del Perú, 1971.

Dorn, Glenn J. "'The American Reputation for Fair Play': Víctor Raúl Haya de la Torre and the Federal Bureau of Narcotics." *Historian* 48 (2003): 59–81.

Dunkerley, James. *Rebellion in the Veins: Political Struggles in Bolivia, 1952–1982*. London: Verso, 1982.

Escobar Gaviria, Roberto. *Mi hermano Pablo*. Bogotá: Quintero Eds., 2000.

Fischer, Thomas. "¿Culturas de coca? El debate acerca de los grupos que produjeron y consumieron la coca en los países andinos, años veinte a cuarenta." *Revista de UNAM* (Dec. 2003): 16–26.

Gagliano, Joseph. *Coca Prohibition in Peru: The Historical Debates*. Tucson: University of Arizona Press, 1994.

García Jordán, Pilar. *Cruz y arado, fúsiles y discursos: La construcción de los orientes el el Perú y Bolivia, 1820–1940*. Lima: Instituto de Estudios Peruanos, 2001.

Gootenberg, Paul. *Between Silver and Guano: Commercial Policy and the State in Postindependence Peru*. Princeton: Princeton University Press, 1989.

———. *Imagining Development: Economic Ideas in Peru's 'Fictitious Prosperity' of Guano, 1840–1880*. Berkeley: University of California Press, 1993.

———. "Reluctance or Resistance? Constructing Cocaine (Prohibitions) in Peru, 1910–50." In *Cocaine: Global Histories*, edited by Paul Gootenberg, ch. 3. London: Routledge, 1999.

———. "Between Coca and Cocaine: A Century or More of U.S.-Peruvian Drug Paradoxes, 1860–1980." *Hispanic American Historical Review* 83/1 (Feb. 2003): 119–50.

———. "A Forgotten Case of 'Scientific Excellence' on the Periphery: The Nationalist Cocaine Science of Alfredo Bignon in Lima, 1884–1887." *Comparative Studies in Society and History* 49/1 (Jan. 2007): 1–32.

Hunt, Shane J. *Price and Quantum Estimates of Peruvian Exports, 1830–1962*. Discussion paper, Research Program in Economic Development, no. 33. Princeton: Woodrow Wilson School of Public and International Affairs, 1973.

Instituto Indigenista Interamericano, comp. *La coca . . . tradición, rito, identidad*. Mexico: Instituto Indigenista Interamericano, 1989.

Kawell, JoAnn. "Coca: The Real Green Revolution." *NACLA Report on the Americas* 22/6 (March 1989): 13–21, 25–30, 33–38.

———. "The 'Essentially Peruvian Industry': Legal Cocaine Production in the Nineteenth Century." Paper presented at the Russell Sage Foundation symposium "Cocaine: From Miracle to Menace," New York, N.Y., May 1997.

———. "Going to the Source." Manuscript, Berkeley, 1997/2005.

Kirk, Robin. *More Terrible than Death: Massacres, Drugs, and America's War on Drugs*. New York: Public Affairs Books, 2003.

Klein, Herbert S. "Coca Production in the Bolivian Yungas in the Colonial and Early National Periods." In *Coca and Cocaine: Effects on People and Policy in Latin America*, edited by Deborah Pacini and Christine Franquemont, 53–64. Ithaca: LASP–Cornell University; Cambridge, Mass.: Cultural Survival, 1985.

Langer, Erik D. *Economic Change and Rural Resistance in Southern Bolivia, 1880–1930*. Stanford: Stanford University Press, 1989.

Lastres, Juan. *Historia de la medicina peruana*. 3 vols. Lima: Universidad Nacional Mayor San Marcos, 1951.

Laussent-Herrera, Isabele. "La presencia japonesa en el eje Huánuco-Pucallpa entre 1918 y 1982." *Revista Geográfica* (Mexico) 107 (Jan.–June 1988): 93–118.

Legara, Astrid. *El verdadero Pablo*. Bogotá: Gato Azul, 2005.

Lema, Ana María. "La coca de las Americas: Partido renido entre la Sociedad Propietarios de Yungas y la Sociedad de Naciones." *I Coloquio Cocayapu* (La Paz) 1992, 1–12.

———. "The Coca Debate and Yungas Landowners in the First Half of the Twentieth Century." In *Coca, Cocaine, and the Bolivian Reality*, edited by Madeline Barbara Léons and Harry Sanabria, 99–117. Albany: State University of New York Press, 1997.

López-Ocon Cabrera, Leoncio. "El nacionalismo y los orígenes de la Sociedad Geográfica de Lima." In *Saberes andinos: Ciencia y tecnología en Bolivia, Ecuador y Perú*, edited by Marcos Cueto, 109–25. Lima: Instituto de Estudios Peruanos, 1995.

Loza Balsa, Gregorio. *Monografía de la coca*. La Paz: Sociedad Geográfica de La Paz, 1992.

Mayer, Enrique. "El uso social de la coca en el mundo andino: Contribución a un debate y un tomo de posición." *América Indígena* 38/4 (1978): 849–65.

Méndez, Cecilia. *The Plebeian Republic: The Huanta Rebellion and the Making of the Peruvian State, 1829–1850*. Durham: Duke University Press, 2005.

Mendoza, Javier. "La verdadera historia del descubrimiento de la cocaína." *Revista Unitas* 11 (1993): 21–33.

Mollison, James. *The Memory of Pablo Escobar*. London: Chris Boot, 2007.

Morales, Edmundo. *Cocaine: White Gold Rush in Peru*. Tucson: University of Arizona Press, 1989.

Orlando Melo, Jorge. "The Drug Trade, Politics and the Economy: The Colombian Experience." In *Latin America and the Multinational Drug Trade*, edited by Elizabeth Joyce and Carlos Malamud, ch. 3. London: Institute of Latin American Studies, 1998.

Painter, James. *Bolivia and Coca: A Study in Dependency*. Boulder: Lynne Rienner, 1994.

Pike, Frederick B. *The United States and the Andean Republics*. Cambridge, Mass.: Harvard University Press, 1977.

Plowman, Timothy. "Coca Chewing and the Botanical Origins of Coca (*Erythroxlylum SPP.*) in South America." In *Coca and Cocaine: Effects on People and Policy in Latin America*, edited by Deborah Pacini and Christine Francamante, 5–34. Ithaca: LASP–Cornell University; Cambridge, Mass.: Cultural Survival, 1985.

Poole, Deborah. *Vision, Race, and Modernity: A Visual Economy of the Andean Image World*. Princeton: Princeton University Press, 1997.

Roldán, Mary. "Colombia: Cocaine and the 'Miracle' of Modernity in Medellín." In *Cocaine: Global Histories*, edited by Paul Gootenberg, ch. 8. London: Routledge, 1999.

Romano, Ruggiero. "¿Coca buena, coca mala? Su razón histórica en el caso peruano." In *La coca andina: Visión indígena de una planta satanizada*, edited by Joan Boldó i Climent, 297–352. Mexico: Instituto Indigenista InterAmericano, 1986.

Rospigliosi, Fernando. "Coca legal y illegal en el Perú." *Debate Agrario* 39 (2005): 81–107.

Rubio Correa, Marcial. *Legislación peruana sobre drogas a partir de 1920*. Monograph 2. Lima: CEDRO, 1988. Rev. as monograph 10, 1994.

Rumrill, Roger. "El narcotráfico en el Perú: Penélope en el Valle de la Huallaga." In *La coca y las economías de exportación en América Latina*, edited by Hermes Tovar Pinzón, 71–86. Sevilla: Universidad Hispanoamericana Santa María de la Rábida, 1993.

Sáenz Rovner, Eduardo. "La pre-historia del narcotraficante en Colombia." *Innovar: Revista de Ciencias Administrativas y Sociales* 8 (July–Dec. 1996): 65–92.

Salazar, J. Alonso. *Pablo Escobar: Auge y caída de un narcotraficante*. Bogotá: Planeta Singular, 2001.

Sanabria, Harry. *The Coca Boom and Rural Social Change in Bolivia*. Ann Arbor: University of Michigan Press, 1993.

Sobrevilla, Natalia. "La creación de la colonia de Pozuzo." In *La presencia europea en el Perú*, edited by Giovanni Bonfiglio, 166–230. Lima: Fondo Editorial del Congreso, 2001.

Soux, María Luisa. *La coca liberal: Producción y circulación a principios del s. xx*. La Paz: CID, 1993.

Spitzer, Leo. *Hotel Bolivia: The Culture of Memory in a Refuge from Nazism*. New York: Hill and Wang, 1998.

Spoja Cortijo, José. *Croatas en Huánuco*. Lima: privately printed, 1996.

Taussig, Michael. *The Devil and Commodity Fetishism in South America*. Chapel Hill: University of North Carolina Press, 1980.

Thorp, Rosemary, and Geoffrey Bertram. *Peru, 1890–1977: Growth and Policy in an Open Economy*. London: Macmillan, 1978.

Thoumi, Francisco E. *Illegal Drugs, Economy and Society in the Andes*. Washington, D.C.: Woodrow Wilson Center; Baltimore, Md.: Johns Hopkins University Press, 2003.

Thurner, Mark. *From Two Republics to One Divided: Contradictions of Postcolonial Nation-Making in Andean Peru*. Durham: Duke University Press, 1997.

———. "Peruvian Genealogies of History and Nation." In *After Spanish Rule: Postcolonial Predicaments in the Americas*, edited by Mark Thurner and Andrés Guerrero, ch. 6. Durham: Duke University Press, 2003.

Varallanos, José. *Historia de Huánuco: Introducción para el estudio de la vida social de una región del Perú*. Buenos Aires: Imprenta López, 1959.

Vargas Llosa, Mario. *A Fish in the Water: A Memoir*. Translated by Helen Lane. New York: Farrar, Straus, Giroux, 1994.

Werlich, David P. *Peru: A Short History*. Carbondale: Southern Illinois University Press, 1978.

Unpublished Theses

Campos-Costero, Isaac. "Marijuana, Madness, and Modernity in Global Mexico, 1545–1920." Ph.D. diss., Harvard University, 2006.

Kenney, Michael. "Outsmarting the State: A Comparative Case Study of the Learning Capacity of Colombian Drug Trafficking Organizations and Government Counter-Narcotics Agencies." Ph.D. diss., University of Florida–Gainesville, 2002.

Monsalve, Martín. "Civilized Society and the Public Sphere in Multiethnic Societies: Struggles over Citizenship in Lima, Peru, 1850–1880." Ph.D. diss., Stony Brook University, 2005.

Reiss, Suzanna J. "Policing for Profit: United States Imperialism and the International Drug Economy." Ph.D. diss., New York University, 2005.

Smith, Nathaniel L. "The Political Culture of Drug Control: The Rise of a Punitive Regime, 1951–1956." M.A. thesis, Department of History, University of North Carolina at Chapel Hill, 2002.

Soininen, Jyri. "Industrial Geographies of Cocaine." M.A. thesis, Department of Geography, University of Helinski, 2008.

Werlich, David P. "The Conquest and Settlement of the Peruvian Montaña." Ph.D. diss., University of Minnesota, 1968.

Films and Documentaries

Beaufort, Marc de, dir. *Los archivos privados de Pablo Escobar*. Colombia, 2002.

Corben, Billy, dir. *Cocaine Cowboys*. Miami Beach: Rakontur, 2005.

Robles Godoy, Armando, dir. *La muralla verde* (The Green Wall). Peru, 1970; Chicago: Facets Multimedia, 1990.

INDEX

Abdallah, Mario, 283
Academia Libre de Medicina de
 Lima, 1, 36, 38, 43, 45
Academia Nacional de Medicina, 36
"Acción fisiológica de la cocaína"
 (Bignon), 39
Acharán clan, 83
Acosta, José de, 19
Addiction: to Coca-Cola, 138, 200;
 criminalization of, 206; to
 opiates, 28, 30
Addiction to cocaine: hospitalization
 for, 179; likelihood of, 10, 17, 25;
 in Peru, 179; in U.S., 30, 204–5,
 249–50
Advertising: for cocaine, 59, 60, 66;
 for coca leaf, 25
African Americans: Coca-Cola
 consumption by, 198–99; crack
 cocaine use by, 312; heroin use
 by, 308; in prison, 313; and U.S.
 anticocainism, 193
Agency: in rise of cocaine, 9, 56, 70,
 318–20
Agnew, Derek, 272
A. Goicochea and Company, 82, 83
Agriculture, U.S. Department of, 294
Agriculture au Pérou, L' (Martinet), 45
Agronomy: in Peru, 151–54, 293–94

Aguillera, Lucho, 269
Aid, U.S.: to Bolivia, 284; to Peru, 297
ALAKEA project, 241
Álamos, Guillermo, 303
Álamos, Olmedo, 303
Alarcón, Rafael, 303
Alba Medina, Junto, 269
Albornoz, Mariano Martín, 47–49
Alcohol: coca as substitute for, 28,
 60; coca combined with, 25–26,
 28, 57, 61; U.S. consumption of,
 27, 28
Aldaña Conde, María, 302
Alianza Popular Revolucionaria
 Americana (APRA) Party, 162, 168,
 233, 248, 256–57
Alipaz, Alfredo, 281
Alkaline ash, 16
Alkaloids: isolation of, 22
Allende, Salvador, 303, 309
Alliance for Progress, 284
Alvarado Velasco, Juan, 296
Álvarez, Carlos, 305
Amazonia: cocaine production in, 65,
 76–83. See also Huallaga Valley
Amazon Provinces of Peru as a Field
 for European Emigration, The
 (Guillaume), 49
Amazon River, 77

American Druggist (journal), 74

American Medical Association
(AMA), 27, 193

Amphetamine, 308

Amsterdam, 126

Andean region: agency in, 9, 56,
70, 318–20; centrality in history
of cocaine, 6, 318; cocaine as
construction of, 55–56; coca use in
culture of, 10, 16–18, 20; colonial
era in, 3, 4, 18–21; establishment
of national states of, 21

Anesthetic, cocaine as: discovery
of, 1, 23, 108; German role in
developing, 24, 108–9; new drugs
replacing, 124, 127; in Peru, 34, 39;
physiological effects of, 17; prices
affected by, 109; in U.S., 29, 30

Animal experiments, 34, 38, 39, 41

Anslinger, Harry J.: on Balarezo
gang, 2, 256, 257; Coca-Cola and,
201, 202–4, 223–25, 240–41; in
coça import regulation, 196–97;
on Cuban trafficking, 267, 268;
illicit cocaine as focus of, 240–41;
on illicit cocaine use, 251, 252;
intelligence gathering under, 218;
and international anticocainism,
206; and Peruvian prohibition of
cocaine, 233, 235; pharmaceutical
industry collaboration with,
198; retirement of, 241, 268;
stockpiling by, 131; and UN
Commission of Enquiry on
the Coca Leaf, 237, 238; in UN
Commission on Narcotic Drugs,
231; and U.S.-Andean commodity
chain, 124; during World War II,
227, 228

Anthropology: on coca leaf use, 9–10;
in drug studies, 3

Anticocainism, international, 189–
241; Bolivian responses to, 207,
211–12, 214–16, 239, 240; current
status of, 315; development of,
207–9; and Japanese cocaine,
130–31; League of Nations in,
124, 127, 138, 211–17; versus
narcotics problem, 205; Peru as
target of, 207, 210; and Peruvian
nationalization, 137, 167, 168–69,
173; Peruvian responses to, 136,
209–14; rise of, in illicit cocaine,
190, 287; social consequences of,
190; start of, 124; U.S. push for,
124, 137, 190, 191, 205–11, 217–26;
between world wars, 138; after
World War II, 230–39

Anticocainism, U.S.: Coca-Cola in,
198–205, 221–25; and commodity
chain with Peru, 137–41; current
status of, 323–24; cycles of drug
use and prohibition in, 27, 122,
192; development of, 137–41;
export of, 190, 191, 205–11; federal
legislation in, 102, 124, 191, 195,
200–201; global prohibition
as goal of, 124, 137, 138;
nonmedicinal coca in, 201; origins
of, 119, 122, 191–98; paradoxes
in, 322–24; Peruvian cooperation
with, 220–21, 229–30; Peruvian
responses to, 123–24, 139, 148,
220–21; pharmaceutical industry
in, 137–38, 193–98; political
economy of, 191, 194–98; racism
in, 192–93; reasons for turn to,
191–94; rise of, in illicit cocaine,
190; structure of, 191–98; between
world wars, 138; during World
War II, 139–40. *See also* War on
drugs, U.S.

Anticocainism League (Peru), 230

Antidrug campaigns, international: cocaine in agenda of, 207–9; opiates in, 206, 207–8; origins of, 205–7. *See also* Anticocainism, international

Antinarcotics diplomacy, U.S., 138–39

Anti-Opium Information Bureau, 212

Antioquía Department (Colombia), 302

Aphrodisiac: coca as, 26

Ara, José, 265

Argentina: bureaucratic authoritarianism in, 289; illicit cocaine in, 268–70, 282, 283–84

Arica (Chile): illicit cocaine in, 261–63

Aristocratic Republic (1895–1919), 36, 96

Asaf y Bala, Jorge, 275

Asian cocaine: in competition with Peruvian cocaine, 124; in Japanese Pan-Asian commodity chain, 107, 124, 128–32

Association of Coca Producers (Dutch), 128

Asthma, 30

Aucuyacu (Peru), 296

Aulet Curbelo, Carlos, 265

Austriácos, 90

Austrian peasants: in Pozuzo, 47, 77, 78, 111

Ávalos, Carlos, 180, 235, 259

Avendaño, Leonidas, 37

Ayacucho (Peru), 81

Ayllon, Ricardo Martín, 83, 259

Ayllon, Santiago Martín, 259

Aymara Indians, 16, 116

Bácula, Carlos Fernández, 252

Bain, Joseph, 26

Bakalar, James, 193

Balarezo, Carmen, 255

Balarezo, César, 258

Balarezo, Eduardo: bust of, 1–2, 254–55; Peruvian politics in case of, 256–58; sources of cocaine, 257–58; trial and conviction of, 255–56

Balarezo gang, 234, 237–38, 254–56

Baramdyka, Frankel, 373 (n. 17)

Baroli, Carlos, 164

Barranchea, Julio, 164

Barrientos, René, 285

Bauer, Arnold, 32

Beard, George, 27

Belaúnde Terry, Fernando, 295, 296

Bello, Alfredo, 271

Benavides, Oscar, 172, 173, 292

Bentley, W. H., 28

Berckemeyer, Ambassador, 235

Bermúdez Pérez, Humberto, 267

Berry, Eduardo, 267

Bicarbonate of soda, 39, 93

Bignon, Alfredo: attitudes toward coca influenced by, 31, 45; career of, 37–38; Coca Commission of 1888 and, 71, 345 (n. 58); cocaine papers of, 36–44; cocaine production technique of, 1, 38–39, 44, 66, 68, 111; commercial efforts of, 68, 70–72; end of studies by, 67, 70–72; German competitors of, 71, 111; on inferiority of coca, 40–41, 51; life of, 37; on medical use of cocaine, 39–42, 50; modern cocaine influenced by, 299; Moreno y Maíz and, 33, 38, 40, 71; in nationalist coca movement, 33, 45, 51; productivity of, 38, 41, 42; reputation of, 38, 43, 72; in rise of cocaine, 16, 53, 65–66

Bignon, Luis, 37

Binda, Dante, 156–57

Binker, Louis, 267

Blades, Rubén, 273

Blow (film), 311

Boehringer and Sohn, 58, 59, 69, 111, 122, 199

Boerhaave, Herman, 21, 22

Boeschel, Carlos, 70

Boletín de Agricultura y Ganadería, 172–73

Bolivia: coup of 1964 in, 285; Croats in, 91, 285; in Pacific War, 45; cocaine scandal of 1961 in, 282–85; responses to international anticocainism, 211–12, 214–16, 239, 240; revolution of 1952 in, 276, 277, 282, 284; U.S. intervention in, 282–84

Bolivian coca: attitudes toward, 18, 32, 114–15, 137, 144, 341 (n. 5); colonial scientific missions for, 21; in commodity chains, 106–7, 113–18; cultivation of, 113–15; current status of, 314–15; geography of, 116; Indian use of, 214–16; international anticocainism targeting, 207; lack of cocaine production from, 80, 81, 113, 275; versus Peruvian coca, 113–14; U.S. intelligence gathering on, 219

Bolivian coca exports: to France, 57, 115–16; lack of development of, 73, 113, 116–18; to U.S., 30, 120–21; volume of, 346 (n. 2)

Bolivian cocaine, illicit, 275–86; Argentine connection to, 268–69, 283–84; Chilean connection to, 262–63, 277; Cuban connection to, 265, 278, 280; German connection to, 284–85; origins of, 240, 275–76; peasants in, 285, 286; Peruvian connection to, 260–61; phases of development, 276; prohibition of, 240, 283–84, 320; volume of, 285–86

Boloña, Carlos, 328

Bonpland, Aimé, 21

Borhese, Valerio, 373 (n. 17)

Bosch, Carlos, 281

Bosch, Raúl, 279, 285

Botanical imperialism, 30

Botanico Medical College of Georgia, 29

Bourbons (Spanish Crown), 21

Boyanovich, Juan, 89, 90

Bradbie, Juanita, 263

Bravo, Alberto, 304

Bravo, Enrique Trujillo, 174, 214

Bravo clan, 306

Brazil: bureaucratic authoritarianism in, 289; illicit cocaine in, 270–72

Brent, Bishop, 206

Breves apuntes sobre la sociología del Perú en 1886 (Lissón), 48

Britain: anticocainism in, 192; cocaine production in, 58, 74–75; in commodity chains, 112–13; on dangers of cocaine, 123; in international antidrug conventions, 208; rediscovery of coca in, 26, 112–13; scientific research on coca in, 113; in World War II, 229

British Foreign Office, 123

British Medical Association (BMA), 26

British Medical Journal, 113

Brokmeyer, Eugene, 200, 223

Brun, Luis, 277

Bües, Carlos, 151–52, 172–73

Bulletin of Foreign Affairs, 147

Bulletin of the Ministry of Promotion, 149

Bulnes, Francisco, 48

Burck, Willem, 125

Burdett, William C.: 1932 report on Peruvian coca, 163–64, 178, 219–20

Bureaucratic authoritarianism, 289

Bureau of Narcotics and Dangerous Drugs (BNDD): on Bolivian trafficking, 284, 285; Coca-Cola and, 241; on Colombian trafficking, 302; on Panamanian trafficking, 273; on 1970s revival of cocaine, 309; as source on illicit cocaine, 10–11, 335; on U.S. cocaine use, 307

Burn patients, 43, 44

Burt, Donald, 285

Bush, George W., 312

Bustamante, José Luis, 232–33

Butler, Almenara, 43, 44

Cacahuatl (chocolate), 19

Cacao, 20

Caffeine: coca combined with, 28; versus cocaine, 36

Caicido, Jaime, 304

Cajabamba (Peru), 82

Cajamarca (Peru), 81–82

Calcite, 21

Cali (Colombia), 304–5

Callao (Peru): cocaine production in, 69, 70; cocaine sales through, 63; Merchandise No. 5 in, 222

Camacho, Carlos, 278

Canada, 223

Candler, Asa G., 62, 199

Cañete, Marqués de, 19

Capitalism: coca's role in, 52

Caravedo, Baltazar, 177–79

Cárdenas Xiquez, Markos, 267

Cardiovascular system, 17

Cartels: Colombian, 300, 301, 315; European, 109, 354 (n. 30); Peruvian, 159; problems with concept, 17, 301

Carter, Jimmy, 310

Carter Silva, Guillermo, 257–58

Castillo, Elmer, 302

Castillo, Juan C., 41

Castillo, Lucindo del, 42

Castro, Fidel, 267–68

Caudillo: Augusto Durand as, 95–100

Central Intelligence Agency (CIA), 235, 284

Cerro de Pasco (Peru), 33, 37, 85

Ceylon, 123

Chacchador, 16

Chachapoyas (Peru): coca cultivation in, 47, 81–82

Chemist and Druggist (journal), 53–54, 74–75, 113

Chile: coup of 1973 in, 303–4; illicit cocaine in, 261–64, 277, 289, 303–4, 309; in Pacific War, 36, 45–46

China: dangers of cocaine in, 123, 208; German cocaine in, 129; Japanese cocaine in, 131

Chinchao (Peru): coca cultivation in, 85–87, 184; cocaine production in, 89; Pilli's 1943 report on, 184

Chinese immigrants: in Huánuco, 91–92, 164, 183–84; opium smoking by, 177–78

Chocano, Eduardo, 102

Chocano, Geraldo Tapías, 255

Cholera, 42

Chon Fan, 166

Christison, Sir Robert, 24, 26, 29

Chuncho Indians, 84

Cigarettes, coca-tobacco, 27

418

Index

Cinchona bark, 48–49, 66, 75
"Clamor coca" (Copello), 34
Clavero, José, 101
Cobb, Richard, 11
Cobo, Bernabé, 19
Coca. *See* Coca leaf
Coca-Beef Tonic, 28
Coca beer, 70
Coca-Bola, 28, 60
Coca chocolates, 70
Coca-Cola: addiction to, 138, 200;
    in anticocainism efforts of U.S.,
    198–205, 221–25; Bignon and,
    41; coca content of, 198, 199;
    cocaine removed from, 62, 121–22,
    199; coca sales to, 83, 119, 121,
    166; competitors of, 198, 202–4,
    225; critics of, 198, 199–200;
    development of, 28–29, 62; FBN's
    compact with, 198, 201–5, 222,
    224–25, 240–41; federal legislation
    protecting, 200–201; inspections
    of facilities, 200, 201; launch of,
    119; Merchandise No. 5 in, 121,
    138, 196, 199, 200–201, 222–24;
    on nationalization in Peru, 226;
    Peruvian factory of, 222–24;
    success of, 28, 50, 62, 119, 198; and
    U.S.-Andean commodity chain,
    124; Vin Mariani as precursor to,
    26, 62; during World War II, 204,
    225, 227–28
"Coca-Cola imperialism," 200
Coca Commission of 1888, 35, 37, 39,
    50–53, 61, 71, 345 (n. 58)
Coca cultivation, 16; in Bolivia,
    113–15; European attempts at, 30,
    72, 73, 113; in Formosa, 129, 131,
    132; improvements in methods
    of, 94–95, 151–52, 155; in India,
    72, 73, 75, 113, 152; in Java, 95,

125, 126; labor systems in, 94–95;
    profitability of, 86; in U.S., 72–74.
    See also Peruvian coca cultivation;
    specific locations
Coca diplomacy, 30
"Coca en el Perú, La" (Bües), 152,
    172–73
Coca exports: from Java, 125; versus
    local use in Andes, 4, 10. *See also*
    Bolivian coca exports; Peruvian
    coca exports
Cocaína bruta, 39
"Cocaína en las quemadas, La"
    (Butler), 43
"Cocaína y sus sales, La" (Bignon), 39
"Coca Industry in Peru, The" (Pilli),
    139, 181–88
Cocaine: as Andean construction,
    55–56; differences between
    cocaine and coca leaf, 9–10,
    16–18; discovery of, 1, 22–23; gaps
    in history of, 5; as good versus
    bad drug, 3; historic uses of, 17;
    ingestion of, 17; pharmacological
    action of, 17; physiological effects
    of, 17, 29; stages of emergence
    of, 2–3, 5; toxicity of, 25, 30, 40.
    See also Illicit cocaine; Prices of
    cocaine; Production of cocaine
Cocaine Commission of 1885, 37, 50,
    66, 67
Cocaine hydrochloride (HCl):
    Bignon's research on, 38, 39;
    identification of formula for, 23;
    use in scientific research, 108
Cocaine sulfate: Bignon's research
    on, 38, 39, 41
Coca leaf: differences between coca
    leaf and cocaine, 9–10, 16–18;
    cocaine production from, 1, 58,
    59, 68; in colonial era, 19–21;

cultural role of, 10, 16–18, 20; current status of, 314–15; dangers of, 144–45; definition of, 16; hierarchy of coca leaf and cocaine, 40–41, 51; historical research on, 9–10; ingestion methods for, 16, 19, 25–26; local use versus export of, 4, 10; physiological effects of, 9–10, 16, 51; reasons for use of, 9–10, 16; transport of, 20, 22, 58, 82, 116; varieties of, 41, 62, 88, 350 (n. 52); wine combined with, 25–26, 28, 57, 61. *See also* Bolivian coca; Coca cultivation; Europe, coca in; Indian coca use; Javan coca; Medical use of coca; Peruvian coca; United States, coca in

Cocaleros, 17

Coca paste, 17

"Coca peruana, La" (Ríos), 35

Coca taxes. *See* Taxes, coca

Codeine, 180

Coffee: coca as replacement for, 50, 52; colonial export of, 4; economic role of, versus cocaine, 4

Cold war: and Bolivian illicit cocaine, 276, 282; in rise of illicit cocaine, 246–47, 289

Colombian coca cultivation, 315

Colombian cocaine, illicit, 301–6; cartels in, 300, 301, 315; Chilean connection to, 303–4; current status of, 17, 315; lack of, before 1970s, 273; origins of, 245, 301–4; rise of, 289, 291, 297, 301, 304–6; sociopolitical conditions encouraging, 301–4

Colonial era, 18–21; coca leaf in, 19–21; psychoactive stimulants in, 3, 4, 18

Colonization in Peru: of Huallaga Valley, 292–96; of Huánuco, 90; of *montaña* region, 46–49, 292–93; of Pozuzo, 47, 77, 90

Colson, Jesse, 262

Columbian exchange, 4, 18

Colunga, Miguel, 35, 37, 50

Comercio, El (newspaper), 174, 221, 257

Comisión de Coca. *See* Coca Commission

Commission of Enquiry on the Coca Leaf, UN, 236–39

Commission on Narcotic Drugs (CND), UN, 207, 231

Commodities: coca as national commodity, 32; cocaine as national commodity, 5, 15, 31, 55, 56–65; colonial, 3, 4; drugs as, 3, 4, 8; in drug studies, 3, 8

Commodity chains, 105–41; anticocainism and, 122–24; applications of concept, 105–6, 352 (n. 3); Bolivian coca in, 113–18; competing forms of, 8; current status of, 313–14; definition of, 8, 105; Dutch colonial, 107, 124–28; German/European-Andean, 106–18; global reach of, 122–23; illicit, 287; Japanese Pan-Asian, 107, 124, 128–32; noneconomic flows in, 8; for *pasta básica de cocaína*, 297; political constraints on, 122–24; shifts in, 316–17, 320–21; U.S.-Andean, 106, 107, 118–22, 124, 132, 137–41; during World War II, 139–40

Commodity ecumene, 8

Commodity studies, 3, 8

Communism: and Bolivian trafficking, 282; and Cuban trafficking, 267–68

Cóndor factory (Lima), 164, 179

Congress, Peruvian, 96

Congress, U.S., 309

Constructionism: of Andean cocaine, 55–56; and commodity chains, 106; influence on drug studies, 3–4, 8–9; rise of, 3–4

Consumer fraud: Coca-Cola charged with, 199

Consumption of cocaine: culture of, 311, 312; current status of, 312–16; diversification of, 18; 1910–50 decline in, 124; in nineteenth-century U.S., 58–60, 121; prevalence of, 18; in twentieth-century U.S., 137, 291, 306–13

Consumption of drugs: colonial expansion of, 18; U.S. versus international, 26–27

Contact zones, 352 (n. 2)

Contreras, Manuel, 373 (n. 17)

Copello, Juan, 34

Coquero, 16

Corning, J. Leonard, 28, 29

Courtwright, David T., 18

Crack cocaine, 17, 312, 314

"Craving for and Fear of Cocaine" (Freud), 42

Crespo, Pedro, 33

Criminalization: of addiction, 206; of Peruvian cocaine, 232; and U.S. anticocainism, 193

Croatian immigrants: in Bolivia, 91, 285; in Huánuco, 83, 90–93, 162, 164

Crónica Médica, La (journal), 36–37, 43

Crude cocaine: cocaine production from, 39, 58, 68, 74, 317; as competition for coca, 53; decline of, 126; in evolution of industry, 65, 317; German influence on

exports of, 109; "on the spot" processing of, 74–75, 111; from Pozuzo, 78; rise of, 53, 109

Cuba: in Bolivian trafficking, 265, 278, 280; illicit cocaine in, 240, 264–68, 304; in Mexican trafficking, 274–75

Cuban Revolution of 1959–61, 240, 247, 264, 266–68

Cuero-Giron, Efraín, 302

Cueto, Marcos, 37

Cultural biography of goods, 8

Cultural studies, 3–4

Culture: coca leaf use in Andean, 10, 16–18, 20; of consumption, 311, 312. *See also* Drug culture

Curbelo, Aulet, 267

Currencies, 63, 328

Cuzco (Peru), 49, 81

Dammert, Adolf, 180

Dammert and Sons, 69, 163

Dasso, Davíd, 227

Dávila, Eduardo, 305

Davis, George, 73

Defence of the Realm Act (Britain), 208–9

De Jong, A. W. K. (Anna), 125, 126

De Jussieu, Joseph, 21

"De la coca" (Moreno y Maíz), 34

Delfin, José Antonio, 82

DeLorean, John, 311

Demand for coca, European, 48, 50–51, 126–27

Demand for cocaine, U.S.: post-1960s, 291, 306–13

Deneumostier, C., 153

Dental health, 51, 345 (n. 61)

Departamento Administrativo de Seguridad (DAS), Colombian, 306

Dependency theory, 106

Depp, Johnny, 311
Depression: economic, 172;
    psychological, 30
Derteano, M. D., 148
Development, Peruvian Ministry
    of, 48
Developmental imagination,
    Peruvian, 46, 100
Díaz, Isías, 279
Dibós family, 80
Didero, José, 159
Diez Canseco, Víctor, 43
Diplomacy: antinarcotics, 138–39;
    coca, 30
Dirección de Salubridad Pública,
    Sección de Narcóticos of, 177
Disco, 311
Dopamine uptake, 17
Dorn, Glenn, 256
Dougherty, A. J., 80
Drug control. *See* Anticocainism,
    international; Anticocainism,
    U.S.; Antidrug campaigns,
    international; War on drugs, U.S.
Drug culture: cocaine use in, 18; and
    drug studies, 3; in 1960s in U.S.,
    308, 310; in 1970s in U.S., 310–12
Drug Enforcement Agency (DEA),
    U.S.: on Chilean trafficking, 303;
    on Colombian trafficking, 306;
    establishment of, 307; and price
    of cocaine, 313, 315; priorities
    of, 309–10; as source on illicit
    cocaine, 326
Drug history, new, 3–5
Drug regimes: historical study of, 3
Drugs. *See specific drugs*
Drug studies, 3–5; emergence of field,
    3; methodologies used in, 6–9;
    social constructionism in, 3–4,
    8–9

Drug war, U.S. *See* War on drugs,
    U.S.
Duboe Osmara, Lara, 269
Dunkerley, James, 284
Durand, Augusto: as caudillo of
    cocaine, 95–100; coca cultivation
    by, 96–97; cocaine production
    by, 97–99; cocaine production
    method used by, 93, 95; death
    of, 100, 159; in exile, 96, 98;
    Éxito factory under, 86, 97, 99;
    German connections of, 111–12;
    in Huánuco, 84, 89, 90, 95–100,
    157–59; industry controlled by,
    56, 65, 84, 89, 95–96, 157; life of,
    95–96; Marinovich family and,
    91; modern cocaine influenced
    by, 299; political career of,
    95–96, 98, 99, 157–59; reputation
    of, 95; response to cocaine
    crisis, 159; response to U.S.
    anticocainism, 123–24; Soberón
    family and, 162
Durand, Emilia, 98, 159
Durand, Gregorio, 90, 96, 98
Durand, Juan: career of, 96, 98–99;
    in Huánuco, 89, 90, 98–99; on
    regional development, 98–99,
    159
Durand, Mario A., 154
Durand, Rosa, 160
Durand family: coca cultivation
    by, 97; after death of Augusto
    Durand, 159–60; decline of, 157,
    159–60; diversification by, 159,
    160; and Japanese investors,
    165; Nesanovich and, 91, 97; in
    politics, 96, 98
Du Reis, Adolfo Costa, 216
Dutch colonial commodity chain,
    107, 124–28

Easy Rider (film), 310
Economic Commission for Latin
    America (CEPAL), 155
Economic history, 10
Economy: of cocaine, 4–5, 17,
    339 (n. 6); of drug trade, 4–5;
    Peruvian, 45–46; political
    economy of U.S. anticocainism,
    191, 194–98
Ecuador: colonial scientific missions
    to, 21; illicit cocaine in, 273
Egg, Luis, 77
Ekstrand, Eric, 175–76, 212, 214, 216
Elite, Bolivian: attitudes toward coca,
    32, 114–15, 144; Croats as, 91, 285
Elite, Peruvian: attitudes toward
    coca, 31–33, 36, 144, 319–20; Croats
    as, 90; Japanese as, 166
Elmore, Enrique, 34
Elsburg, Louis, 28
Empresa Nacional de Coca (ENACO)
    (Peru), 225, 226, 240
Energy enhancement, 17, 51
Enganchados, 86
England. *See* Britain
Enlightenment, 19–20
Entrepreneurs: Chilean, 261;
    Colombian, 302; Peruvian, 55–56,
    62–63, 157–67, 318–19; U.S., 311
Epilepsy, 42
Erosion, 184
E. R. Squibb and Company, 58
Erythroxylon coca, 9, 16, 21, 41, 84, 88
Erythroxylon novogranatense, 41, 82, 125
Escalona, Régulo, 265, 274, 278
Escobar, Gustavo, 305
Escobar, Pablo, 304, 305–6, 315
Escobar, Roberto, 305, 306
Espinoza, Manuel M., 51
Espionage, industrial, 181. *See also*
    Intelligence gathering, U.S.

Estación Experimental Agrícola de
    Tingo María, 229, 293–94
Estanco de la Cocaína y la Coca, 167
Esteves, Luis, 46
"Estudio experimental del
    antagonismo de la estricnina y de
    la cocaína" (Bignon), 41–42
Ethnicity: in coca cultivation, 87
Ethnobotany, 3, 16
Eugenics, 145, 168
Europe: cocaine production in,
    57–58; colonial era of, 3, 4, 18–21;
    in commodity chains, 109–13;
    illicit cocaine use in, 249, 250; in
    Peruvian colonization plans, 49;
    psychoactive revolution in, 18–19
Europe, coca in, 19–26; attitudes
    toward, 19–22; colonial
    cultivation of, 30, 72, 73, 113;
    demand for, 48, 50–51; end of
    demand for, 126–27; rediscovery
    of, 24–26, 107–8, 112–13; scientific
    research on, 20–22, 26, 33–35, 72
European Convention of Cocaine
    Producers, 128
European immigrants: in Huánuco,
    90–91; in Pozuzo, 47, 77–78, 80
Europeans: in Huánuco, 87, 90
Exchange rates, 64, 328
Éxito factory, 86, 95, 97, 99, 159–60
Exportation. *See* Bolivian coca
    exports; Coca exports; Peruvian
    coca exports; Peruvian cocaine
    exports

Factories and workshops, Peruvian:
    in Chinchao, 86; in Huánuco,
    164–65; licensing of, 179; location
    of first, 81–83; in northern Peru,
    166–67; number of, 80; in Pozuzo,
    78–80; production technique

used by, 93; purity of products from, 93; statistics on, 330, 333; in twentieth century, 164–67. *See also* Production of cocaine

Farbwerke, 109, 126

Fauvell, Charles, 26

Federal Bureau of Investigation (FBI), 257

Federal Bureau of Narcotics (FBN): annual drug reports of, 251; on Bolivian trafficking, 276–81; on Brazilian trafficking, 272; Burdett's report on Peruvian coca to, 219–20; in bust of Balarezo gang, 2, 255–56; on Chilean trafficking, 261; Coca-Cola's compact with, 198, 201–5, 222, 224–25, 240–41; coca imports regulated by, 195; cocaine production regulated by, 138, 200; on Cuban trafficking, 264, 266–67; illicit cocaine seized by, 251–53, 335; inspectors in Peru from, 240; intelligence gathering in Peru by, 139, 218, 219; and international antidrug campaigns, 206; on Mexican trafficking, 273, 274; and nationalization of Peruvian cocaine, 172; and Peruvian regulation, 179; pharmaceutical industry collaboration with, 198; after prohibition of cocaine, 235–36; shift to focus on illicit cocaine, 240–41; as source on illicit cocaine, 10–11, 326; stockpiling by, 131; after World War II, 231

Fernández, Davíd, 278

Fernández, Nicanor T., 216

Ferreyra, Leandro, 258

Fertilizer trade (guano), 46, 101

Feuchtuger, Berthold, 180

Figueroa, Humberto, 262

Figueroa, María, 297

Fiscal Laboratories for the Industrialization of Coca, 240

Flaifel Yapur, Nicolás, 265

Florentino, Jaime, 277

Flórez, R. L., 37, 41

Florida: illicit cocaine in, 264, 266, 308, 311

Fonda, Howard B., 237, 238

Fontaine, Luis, 303

Food and Drug Administration (FDA), 124, 191, 223

Foreign Affairs, Bolivian Ministry of, 214

Foreign Affairs, Peruvian Ministry of, 213, 214

Formosa (Taiwan): coca cultivation in, 129, 131, 132, 165

Formulas, cocaine, 1, 23, 38–39. *See also* Production of cocaine

Frampton, John, 20

France: Bolivian coca exportation to, 115–16; cocaine production in, 58; coca nationalism in, 32; in commodity chains, 112, 115–16; influence on Peruvian cocaine, 111; Peruvian cocaine exportation to, 71; rediscovery of coca in, 25–26, 112; scientific research on coca in, 33–35

Franco, Ebar, 280

Frank of Lima, 235

Fraud, consumer: Coca-Cola charged with, 199

Freebasing, 17

Freifeld, Hersh and Zelda, 279

Freire, Ramón, 88

Freud, Sigmund: Bignon compared to, 42–43; on cocaine as

anesthetic, 34; cocaine papers of, 1, 23–24, 31, 42–43; Moreno y Maíz cited by, 34; role in research on cocaine, 108
Fruscher, León, 279
Fuchs, Fernando, 172
Fuentes, Manuel A., 35, 343 (n. 33)
Fuller, Stuart, 201, 206, 223
Funegra, Víctor, 164, 180
Funtowitcz, Salomo, 279

Gaceta Médica de Lima (journal), 33–36
Galdames, Ruth, 303
Gallardo, Fernando, 164
Galvano, Josefina, 271
Gamarra family, 114–15
Gamonales, 96
García, Angélica, 267
Garcia, Jerry, 311
García Céspedes, Pedro, 258
García de Freites, Fabio, 271
Garcilaso de la Vega, 33
Garland, Alejandro, 80–81, 101, 123, 150
Garrido Cruz, María, 274
Gayán Contador, Luis, 262, 278, 282–83
Gehe and Company, 58
Gender: and coca chewing, 135
Geneva Conference for the Suppression of the Illicit Trade in Dangerous Drugs (1936), 207
Geneva Conference on the Limitation of Manufacture of Narcotic Drugs (1931), 128, 206–7
Geneva Convention (1931), 170, 173, 174
Geneva Convention on Opium and Other Drugs (1925), 128, 175, 206
German immigrants: in Pozuzo, 77–78, 80, 90; trafficking by, 279

Germany: anticocainism in, 192; in Bolivian trafficking, 284–85; cocaine exports from, through Japan, 129; cocaine production in, 29, 56–59, 64, 68–69, 108–9, 126, 140; in commodity chain with Andes, 106–18; as competition of Bignon, 71, 111; in competition with U.S., 121; discovery of cocaine in, 22; in European Convention of Cocaine Producers, 128; in international antidrug conventions, 208; Peruvian coca exports to, 63; Peruvian cocaine exports to, 67–70, 109–12, 126, 132; and Peruvian cocaine reform, 155; and Peruvian cocaine regulation, 179–80; scientific research in, 23–25, 57, 107–8; in World War II, 228
Gibbs, Consul-General, 30
Gibson, Percy, 102
Ginzburg, Carlo, 11
Giralt, Gabriella, 266
Global studies, 7
Glucose absorption, 16
Goicochea clan, 83
Goldberg, Isaac, 283
Gómez, Anatolio, 252
Gómez, Nilda, 274
Goncalves, Nelson, 271
González, Bravo, 302
González, Juan, 298
González, Luis, 283
González, Miguel, 265, 274, 282
González, Ramón, 274
González clan: in Chilean trafficking, 265; in Mexican trafficking, 274
Göttingen University, 22, 23
Grace Line, 253, 255, 261
Grant, Ulysses S., 29

Gran Trust de Cocaína, 159
Great Britain. *See* Britain
Greek traffickers, 278–79
Green Wall, The (film), 296
Greshoff, Maurits, 125
Grinspoon, Lester, 193
Gruenbaum, Corina, 283
Guano, 5, 32, 45, 101
Guarana, 4
Guevara, Ernesto "Che," 279, 285, 286
Guevara, Walter, 283
Guillaume, H., 49
Gutiérrez-Noriega, Carlos, 43, 72,
    230, 238

Habich, Eduardo, 31
Hacienda Victoria, 78
Hackman, Gene, 308
Hague International Opium
    Conventions: 1912, 124, 148, 206,
    209–10, 214; 1913–14, 206
Halsted, William S., 24, 29
Hamburg (Germany): cocaine
    production in, 58, 63, 68, 108–9
Hammond, William, 24, 30
Harb, Antonio N., 277
Harb, César, 261
Harb, Emilio, 284
Harb, José Luis, 278
Harb, Luisa Huasaff, 261
Harb, Ramis, 262–63, 278, 282
Harb, Said, 277
Harrison Narcotics Tax Act of 1914,
    124, 191, 197, 200, 206
Hartung, H. J., 224, 230
Hasskarl, J. K., 125
Havana (Cuba): illicit cocaine in,
    264–66
Haya de la Torre, Víctor Raúl, 168,
    169, 233, 235, 256
Hay fever, 30

Health, Peruvian Bureau of, 180, 213,
    219
Herbalist medicine, 27
Hercovici, Itzchak, 279
Heredia, Cayetano, 35
Herndon, William L., 47, 85, 293
Heroin: in Mexico, 274; trafficking
    of, versus cocaine, 287; U.S.
    consumption of, 250, 308
Herrera, Benjamín, 304–5
Herrera, "Tacho," 252
Herzog, Enrique, 283
Higginson, Eduardo: reports on coca
    by, 123–24, 147–49
Hippies, 310–11
Hirsch, Harold, 202
Hiss, Alger, 2, 256
*Historia medicinal de los cosas que traen
    de las Indias* (Monardes), 20
Historical constructionism, 8–9
Historiography of cocaine, 377–84
History, field of: in drug studies, 3–5
History of Coca (Mortimer), 29, 32, 61,
    80, 119, 215
Hoffman, Abbie, 311
Hohagen, Jorge, 160–61
Holistic medicine, 27
Hollywood, 250, 310
Holquín, Carlos, 236
Hooker, Sir William, 113
Hoover, J. Edgar, 235
Horowitz, Sybil, 263
Hoshi, Hajime, 129, 165
Hoshi Pharmaceuticals, 129, 165–66,
    292
Hotel de Turistas (Tingo María), 294
Huallaga, El (newspaper), 98, 154
Huallaga Valley (Peru): coca
    cultivation in, 47, 84, 86–87, 296;
    cocaine production in, 56, 65, 84;
    colonization of, 292–96; current

status of, 313; European travelers in, 86; illicit cocaine in, 84, 291–300; Japanese plantations in, 129, 165; regional development in, 159, 292, 295–96; as river system, 84; U.S. intelligence gathering in, 166, 219; U.S. research station in, 229, 293–94. *See also* Huánuco

Huamachuco (Peru), 82

Huanta (Peru), 47, 81

Huánuco (Peru), 83–100; Burdett's 1932 report on, 163–64, 178, 219–20; centrality in history of cocaine, 6–7, 76, 83, 111, 165, 318; Chinese immigrants in, 91–92, 164, 183–84; coca cultivation in, 47, 49, 76, 85–90; cocaine production in, 56, 65, 76, 79, 83–84, 89–95, 111–12, 164–65; cocaine production technique used in, 93–94; coca leaf variety from, 62, 88, 350 (n. 52); coca taxes in, 88, 89, 91–93, 98; colonization of, 90; competition and rivalries in, 89; Croats in, 83, 90–93, 162, 164; diversification in, 159, 161–62; Augusto Durand in, 84, 89, 90, 95–100, 157–59; end of cocaine production in, 247–48; entrepreneurial response to decline in, 157–67; illicit cocaine in, 252, 258–60, 287, 297–99; Japanese investors in, 165–66; Kitz in, 78–79, 90, 111; location and accessibility of, 84–85; Pilli's 1943 report on, 183–85; population of, 88, 89; reform attempts in, 154–55; regional development in, 98–99, 159; stages of cocaine industry in, 83–84; U.S. intelligence gathering on, 219–20; during World War II, 139, 165

Huánuco Department (Peru): coca cultivation in, 89; population of, 87–88

Huánuco Province (Peru): cocaine industry in, 77, 111–12; geography of, 84; origins of cocaine in, 77

Huasaff, Amanda, 261–62, 278

Huasaff, Luisa, 263

Huasaff, René Harb, 262, 263

Huasaff, Rubén Sacre, 261, 278

Huasaff-Harb clan: in Bolivia, 277–78, 284; in Chile, 261–63; in Mexico, 274, 275

Humoral system, 20, 22

Hunger suppression, 34

Hurtado, Alberto, 229

Hygienic qualities of coca, 52

Hysteria, 27, 42

Ibáñez de Sánchez, Blanca, 265, 269, 279–81

Ichantequi, Juan, 81

Identity, Peruvian: coca in, 31–32; cocaine in, 101

Ilipta, 16

Illicit cocaine, 245–89, 291–324; anticocainism in rise of, 190, 287; in Argentina, 268–70, 282, 283–84; in Bolivia, 260–61, 275–86; in Brazil, 270–72; in Chile, 261–64, 289, 303–4, 309; cold war in, 246–47, 289; in Colombia, 301–6; commodity chains of, 287; in Cuba, 240, 264–68, 304; in Europe, 250; FBN's focus on, 240–41; in Mexico, 263, 273–75; origins of, 84, 190, 234, 245; prohibition of cocaine coinciding with, 233–34, 248–49; social roles of, 17; sources on, 10–11, 326; stages of development of, 2–3, 246–47; in U.S., 204–5, 249–52, 306–12;

World War II in rise of, 179–81, 252–53. *See also* Peruvian cocaine, illicit; Trafficking, cocaine

Illicit drugs: boundaries between legal and, 3; cocaine's status as, 2–3; in commodity studies, 8; and links between U.S. and Latin America, 4

Illicit Drug Trafficking Conference (1936), 174–75

Imperial Institute, 75, 123

Imperialism: botanical, 30; Coca-Cola, 200

Incas: coca leaf use by, 19, 26, 27

India: coca cultivation in, 72, 73, 75, 113, 152; cocaine problem in, 123; illicit cocaine in, 250; Japanese cocaine in, 131, 250

Indian coca use, 9–10; by Aymara, 16, 116; benefits of, 9–10, 102, 145; in Bolivia, 214–16; dangers of, 144–45, 170, 230; by Incas, 19, 26, 27; Pilli's 1943 report on, 185; racism and, 136, 145; scientific research on, 145, 229–30; *toxicomanía* and, 177; UN report on, 238

Indians: in Huánuco coca cultivation, 87, 90; psychoactive substances used by, 4

Indigenistas, 46, 144, 171

Indigenous communities. *See* Indians; *specific groups*

Indonesia, 125

Industria, La (newspaper), 172

Industrial good: Peruvian cocaine as, 65–76

Industrialization of coca: in Huánuco, 83; in Peruvian nationalism, 44; success of, in Peru, 80–81; twentieth-century hopes for, 155–57. *See also* Production of cocaine

Infanzón, Ramiro, 267

Ingestion methods: for cocaine, 17; for coca leaf, 16, 19, 25–26; for crack cocaine, 17

Innovation: from periphery, 31, 37

Instituto de Medicina Social (Lima), 168

Intelligence gathering, U.S.: on Japanese drug activities, 166; Maywood Chemical Works and, 202, 218; on Peruvian coca, 139, 166, 171, 217–21; after prohibition of cocaine, 235–36; in World War II, 166, 179–80, 181, 228

Inter-American Coca Leaf Consultative Seminars, UN, 284, 286

Inter-American Conference on the Illicit Traffic in Coca-Leaf and Cocaine (1960), 271–72

Inter-American Development Bank, 296

Interpol: on Argentine trafficking, 269, 270; Bolivian membership in, 283; on Bolivian trafficking, 278, 286; on Cuban trafficking, 265; as source on illicit cocaine, 335

Intoxicants: ethnobotany and, 3

Ipadu, 21

Irizarry, William, 267

Jacob, H., 153

Japan: coca cultivation in Formosa by, 129, 131, 132, 165; coca cultivation in Peru by, 165–66, 292; cocaine production in, 128–32, 140; and Javan coca, 128, 129; League of Nations and, 217; Pan-Asian commodity chain of, 107, 124, 128–32; trafficking by, between world wars, 250; in World War II, 128, 131–32, 227, 228

Jaramillo-Gutiérrez, Enrique, 302
Jaros, Julius, 28, 61
Javan coca: in competition with
    Peruvian coca, 95, 125, 126–27,
    148, 152–53; cultivation of, 95, 125,
    126; in Dutch colonial commodity
    chain, 124–28; Japan in, 128, 129;
    rise and fall of, 125–28
Jefferson Airplane, 311
Jesuits, 19
Jewish immigrants, 279, 350 (n. 56)
Jiménez García, Carlos, 262, 263
Johnson and Johnson, 129
Jones-Miller Act of 1922, 191, 195,
    196, 218
Joyfull News Out of the Newe World
    (Frampton), 20
Juan, Jorge, 21
Jung, George, 311
Junín (Peru), 49
Junta Departamental de
    Desocupados, 162

Karambelas (trafficker), 278–79
Karch, Steven B., 131
Karp, Samuel, 284
Kerosene: in cocaine production, 1,
    17, 38, 39, 66, 93
Kew, Royal Botanic Gardens at, 26,
    72, 113
Kissinger, Henry, 307
Kitz, Arnaldo: cocaine exportation
    by, 69, 78; commodity chains
    influenced by, 111; death of, 80; in
    Huánuco, 78–79, 90, 111; in Lima,
    65, 69, 75, 78–80, 111; modern
    cocaine influenced by, 299; in
    Pozuzo, 77–80, 111
Kitz and Company: cocaine
    exportation by, 69; cocaine
    production by, 70, 78, 92–93; after
    death of Kitz, 80; in Lima, 78–79

K.K.K.K. (consortium), 165
Knoll, Carlos, 80
Knoll and Company, 58
Kola nut, African, 28
Kolb, Lawrence, 250
Köller, Karl, 24, 29, 30, 34, 48, 108

Labeling, sociological, 190
Labor systems: in coca cultivation,
    94–95
Labs. *See* Factories and workshops,
    Peruvian
La Convención (Peru), 47, 81
La Libertad (Peru): coca cultivation
    in, 81–82; coca exports to U.S.
    from, 121, 202
Lamarck, Jean-Baptiste, 21
Languasco, Juan, 90
Lansky, Meyer, 265–66
La Paz (Bolivia): coca cultivation
    and, 114, 353 (n. 17); illicit cocaine
    in, 279, 280–81
Latin America: in global history of
    drugs, 4–5; U.S. relations with,
    during World War II, 226–29, 293.
    See also Andean region; *specific
    countries*
Laurencio, José, 91
Lavalle, Hernando de, 173
Law 4428 (Peru), 177
Law of Internal Security (Peru), 257
League of Nations: anticocainism
    in, 124, 127, 138, 211–17; antidrug
    conventions of, 206–7; Bolivian
    responses to, 214–16; on global
    cocaine production, 139–40;
    and Japanese cocaine, 130–31;
    and nationalization of Peruvian
    cocaine, 169, 171–76; Opium
    Advisory Committee of, 174–75,
    206, 213, 214, 230; Permanent
    Central Opium Board of, 206; on

Peruvian cocaine production, 164; Peruvian responses to, 211–14; problems with statistics sent to, 326; quotas from, 174, 175–76, 196, 216; U.S. influence on agenda of, 205, 206, 209, 211

Leary, Timothy, 311

Lechín, Juan, 282–85

Legislation, U.S. anticocaine, 102, 124, 191, 195, 200–201

Leguía, Augusto B.: cocaine regulation under, 177; Augusto Durand and, 96, 98, 99, 159; and nationalization of cocaine, 172; opium regulation under, 178; U.S. intelligence gathering under, 218

Lehder, Carlos, 304, 305

Leoncio Prado (Peru), 294

Leticia (Colombia), 297, 304

Levine, Sam, 278

Liberal Party (Bolivia), 115

Liberal Party (Peru), 95, 96, 99, 159

Licensing: Peruvian cocaine regulation through, 179, 180

Lietzenmayer, Otto, 180

Lima (Peru): cocaine production in, 65–76, 164; illicit cocaine in, 259–60; Kitz in, 65, 69, 75, 78–80, 111; Merck's mission to, 69, 75, 109, 111; scientific research on coca in, 34–36

Lime: coca combined with, 21, 33, 39; in cocaine production, 39

Lissón, Carlos, 48–49, 53, 101–2

Lloyd Brothers, 28, 60

Llujt'a, 16

Loayza, Gerónimo de, 19

Logan Mission, 237

Long y Cia, Tasy, 183

López, Nelson Alfred, 259–60

López, Vicente, 270

Lorente, Sebastian, 177–78

Lossen, Wilhelm, 23, 39

Loureiro, José, 271

Luciano, "Lucky," 2, 255, 265

Luna, Roberto, 271

Luzio, Federico, 155–56

Lynch, Alberto Martín, 151, 152–53

Mafia: in Argentina, 268; in Balarezo case, 2; in Cuba, 265, 266

Mallinckrodt Chemical, 59

Mancha india, 135, 354 (n. 34)

Mantegazza, Paolo, 21, 22, 51

Marañón Amazonian region, 82

Mariani, Angelo, 25–26, 28, 45, 57, 61, 112. *See also* Vin Mariani

Marijuana: in Colombia, 273, 302, 305; FBN focus on, 252; in Nixon's war on drugs, 308; in U.S. drug culture of 1960s, 308

Marimberos, 302

Marinovich, Estevan: Augusto Durand and, 99; in Huánuco, 90, 91

Marinovich, Manuel, 90, 91

Market, coca: commodity chains in, 106; decline of, 124–25; Dutch, 126; European demand in, 48, 50–51, 126–27; German, 63–64; nineteenth-century U.S., 60–62, 64–65, 118–19; for Trujillo variety, 81–82. *See also* Commodity chains

Market, cocaine: decline of, 124–25; differentiation of, 60; German, 63–64; nineteenth-century U.S., 58–60, 63–64, 118–19; in post-1960s U.S., 291, 306–13. *See also* Commodity chains

Markets: in commodity chains, 106; mental life of things and, 15

Markham, Clements R., 47, 75, 113

Martín, Enrique, 164

Martin, Frank, 280

Martin, Joseph, 2, 256

Martindale, William, 24, 26, 71

Martinet, J. B., 45

Martínez, Alicia, 257

Martínez, Felix, 266

Martínez del Rey, Abelardo, 264, 265

Martínez Rodríguez, Antonio, 267

Martínez Rodríguez, Jorge, 267

Martín family: and Japanese investors, 165; Tulumayo property under, 85–86, 165

Marx, Karl, 15

Más, José, 90

Mastrókola, Alfredo, 98, 159

Masulo, Genaro, 271

Matienzo, Juan, 19

Maximilian of Austria, 23

Mayer, Enrique, 18

Maywood Chemical Works: in anticocainism efforts, 137–38, 195–98, 202, 221–24; Coca-Cola working with, 69, 83, 122, 199; in coca import regulation, 197; cocaine production by, 195–96; and commodity chains, 137–38; establishment of, 69, 199; government inspections of, 201; intelligence gathering by, 202, 218; as intermediary between Coca-Cola and FBN, 198, 201–4, 222, 224–25; and illicit cocaine, 249; nationalization in Peru, 226; Peruvian coca exports to, 135, 166, 183, 201–2; after prohibition on cocaine, 241; under Schaeffer family, 199; during World War II, 230

McKesson and Robbins, 58

McVickers, Consul, 286

Medellín (Colombia), 300, 302

Medical societies, Peruvian, 36–37

Medical use of coca: Coca Commission of 1888 on, 51; in colonial era, 18–19; in Europe, 21–22, 25–26, 113; Peruvian research on, 35–36, 40–41; in U.S., 27–28, 119. *See also* Patent medicines

Medical use of cocaine, 2; categories of, 29–30; dangers of, 30, 40, 60, 72; decline in, 60, 72, 124, 138; European research on, 18–19, 23–24; German research on, 108; Peruvian research on, 39–44; prices affected by, 109; in U.S., 29–30, 121, 138, 193, 196; U.S. research on, 29–30. *See also* Anesthetic, cocaine as

Memorias de Ministerio de Hacienda del Perú, 44–45

Méndez Marfa, Manuel, 265, 274, 282

Méndez Pérez, Oscar, 265

Mental life of things, 15

Mercado, Rodolfo, 43

Mercado Terrazas, Ciro, 283

Merck, E. (Darmstadt), 1; cocaine exportation to, 67, 69, 75; cocaine production by, 57–59, 68, 108–9; and commodity chains, 137–38; diversification of products at, 109; mission to Lima by, 69, 75, 109, 111; Parke, Davis and, 28

Merck, Emmanuel: cocaine exportation to, 78, 80; cocaine production by, 23, 56–57, 108

Merck, New Jersey: in anticocainism of U.S., 137–39, 195–98; in coca import regulation, 196–97; intelligence gathering by, 218; and Javan coca, 126; and lack of illicit cocaine, 249; Pilli's report on Peruvian coca for, 181–87; U.S.

branch of, 122, 195; during World
   War II, 139
Mercurio Peruano, El (newspaper), 33,
   168
Mercury poisoning, 52
Mermelstein, Max, 311
Merton, Robert K., 323, 324
Methadone clinics, 308
Methodologies, 6–9
Metis, 318
Mexico: illicit cocaine in, 263, 273–75;
   marijuana in, 308
Meyer, J., 69, 75
Meyer and Hafemann, 66–67, 69
Miami: illicit cocaine in, 264, 266,
   308, 311
Miami Vice (TV show), 311
Mier y Terán, Alfonso, 2, 235, 255, 256
Military: coca use in Peru, 45;
   Coca-Cola consumption in U.S.,
   199, 228
Millias, Dunaldo, 302
Milosovich, Juan, 162
Mining: coca leaf in, 19, 52, 82, 85, 114
Mita workers, 19
Mitchell, Charles L., 60
Mob. *See* Mafia
Mollendo (Peru), 63, 81
Monardes, Nicolás, 20
Monge Medrano, Carlos: Bignon
   and, 43; and coca control, 171; on
   Indian coca use, 145, 229–30; UN
   Commission of Enquiry on the
   Coca Leaf and, 237, 238–39
Monitor Médico, El (journal), 36, 40,
   43–44, 66
Monopoly on coca and cocaine:
   in Peru, 75, 81, 93, 224, 240;
   in U.S., 122, 138, 195. *See also*
   Nationalization of Peruvian
   cocaine

Montaña region (Peru): coca
   cultivation in, 16, 45, 46–47, 76–77;
   colonization plans for, 46–49,
   292–93; European travelers in, 21
Montero brothers, 90, 164
Monzón (Peru): accessibility of, 86;
   coca cultivation in, 86; cocaine
   production in, 89–91; Croats in,
   90; Pilli's 1943 report on, 184
Monzón coca leaf, 88
Morales, "El Chino," 257, 274
Morales, Evo, 118, 215, 315, 320
Moreno y Maíz, Tomás: Bignon
   influenced by, 33, 38, 40, 71;
   national pride in, 48, 51; scientific
   research by, 33–35
Morphine: coca as treatment for
   addiction to, 28; isolation of,
   22; threat of, versus cocaine,
   205; trafficking of, 287; U.S.
   consumption of, 28, 29, 250
Mortimer, W. Golden, 29, 32, 41, 61,
   80, 119, 215, 342 (n. 21)
Moubarack, José Flaifel, 258, 265
Music: cocaine in, 307, 310, 311
Musto, David, 27, 122, 192, 310, 327,
   352 (n. 3)

Nación, La (newspaper), 42
Nacional, El (newspaper), 34
Nadelmann, Ethan, 321
Narcos: first pre-Colombian, 245–46,
   288–89, 297. *See also* Trafficking,
   cocaine
Narcotraficantes, Colombian, 291,
   301–6. *See also* Trafficking, cocaine
National Association of Retail
   Druggists, 200
National Coca Commission, 237
National Coca Company. *See*
   Empresa Nacional de Coca

National good: coca as, 32, 44–54,
319–20
National identity, Peruvian: coca in,
31–32; cocaine in, 101
National Institute on Drug Abuse
(NIDA), 310
Nationalism, Peruvian: coca and
cocaine in, 31–33, 43–44, 153–54,
319–20
Nationalization of Peruvian cocaine,
167–76; Japanese investors
affected by, 165–66, 292; Paz
Soldán in, 137, 155, 167–76; as
response to global anticocainism,
137, 167–69, 173; Tulumayo
property in, 131, 165–66, 292, 293;
U.S. position on, 224–26; U.S. role
in, 165–66, 171–72, 174
Navy, U.S., 30, 120–21
Negociación A. Durand, 98, 159–60
Nesanovich, Salvador, 90–93, 97
Netherlands: anticocainism in, 192;
cocaine production in, 125–26;
colonial commodity chain of,
107, 124–28; illicit cocaine in, 250;
scientific research on coca in,
125–26
Netherlandsch Cocainefabriek
(NCF), 125–28
Neurasthenia, 22, 27, 42, 52, 60, 119
Neurological effects: of cocaine, 30,
34, 39–42; of coca leaf, 21–22, 27,
52, 119
New drug history, 3–5
New Jersey, 58, 69, 122
Newsweek magazine, 310
New York Academy of Medicine, 30
New York City: cocaine trafficking
into, 1–2, 234–35, 238, 253; cocaine
use in, 197, 205, 249, 307, 311; first
cocaine busts in, 1–2, 253, 254–56;

in history of cocaine, 6; 1949 drug
scare in, 234–35; Vin Mariani in,
28, 61, 119
New York Daily Mirror, 2, 254
New York Herald, 171
New York Quinine and Chemical
Works, 59
New York Times, 309
Niemann, Albert, 22, 23, 25, 38, 39,
47, 108
Nisei community, Peru, 165, 166, 292
Nitrates, 45
Nixon, Richard M.: rise of cocaine
use under, 307–10
No se suicidan los muertos (Pavletich),
96
Novara mission, 22–23, 77, 108
Novocaine, 127
Nuñez del Prado, Eduardo, 36, 51
Nutt, Levi, 201, 223
Nystrom, Juan, 45

Ochoa clan, 306
Odría, Manuel, 233, 255–58
Ojen, Alfonso, 253
Oncenio dictatorship, 96
Operation Condor (1971), 309
Operation Intercept (1969), 308
Opiates: versus cocaine, 207–8;
cocaine as treatment for addiction
to, 30; history of, 5; international
campaigns against, 206, 207–8
Opium: coca as treatment for
addiction to, 28; cocaine as
replacement for, 123; in Dutch
colonies, 125; international
restrictions on, 206; isolation
of morphine from, 22; in Peru,
177–78; scientific research on, 35
Opium Advisory Committee (OAC),
174–75, 206, 213, 214, 230

Orfanides, Ascencio, 164
Ortiz, Fernando, 352 (n. 2)
Otuzco Province (Peru), 82
Overexcitation disorders, 42

Pacific War (1879–81), 32, 36, 45–46
Pagador, Antonio, 171, 172
Palmer, E. L., 28
Pampa Hermosa, 77
Pampayacu plantation, 129, 165, 292
Panama, 273
Pan-American Sanitary Conference,
    Eighth, 177
Pan-American Sanitary Union, 168
Panao (Peru), 85
Paris: Bignon in, 70, 71
Parke, Davis and Company: Andean
    mission of, 73–74, 120; cocaine
    production by, 29, 58–59, 68; coca
    medicines of, 119; and Japanese
    cocaine, 129; and Merck, 28
Party of the Institutional Revolution
    (PRI), 315
Pasqüero, Angela, 258
Pasta básica de cocaína (PBC):
    commodity chain of, 297; in illicit
    cocaine, 68, 93; in Peru, 297–99; in
    production of cocaine, 17
Patent medicines: coca in, 28, 60;
    cocaine in, 30, 60; critics of, 29,
    199; U.S. consumption of, 27, 28
Paulet, Pedro, 94, 149–50
Pavletich, Esteban, 84, 96
Paz Estenssoro, Víctor, 283–85
Paz Soldán, Carlos Enrique: Bignon
    and, 72; career of, 167–68, 176; on
    fall of cocaine exports, 146; on
    nationalization of cocaine, 137,
    155, 167–76; in reform attempts,
    149; views on coca and cocaine,
    168–69, 171

Peasants: in Bolivian illicit cocaine,
    285, 286; in Peruvian coca
    cultivation, 47, 77, 78, 111; in
    Peruvian illicit cocaine, 292, 293;
    in rise of illicit cocaine, 289
Pehovaz Frs., 69, 70
Pemberton, John: development of
    Coca-Cola by, 28–29, 50, 119,
    198; wine cola of, 28, 62. See also
    Coca-Cola
Peña, Rosa, 279
Peña, Salvadore, 234, 253–55
Penick, Saul, 204
Pepsi Cola, 204
Pérez, Cristóbal, 267
Pérez Fernández, José Gabriel, 265
Periphery: innovation from, 31, 37;
    power differentials between core
    and, 106
Permanent Central Opium Board
    (PCOB), 206, 223
Peru: Aristocratic Republic of, 36, 96;
    centrality in history of cocaine, 6,
    318; economy of, after Pacific War,
    45–46; in Hague Conventions,
    209; independence of, 33; medical
    societies in, 36–37; mining in,
    19; after Pacific War, 32, 36,
    45–46; responses to international
    anticocainism, 136, 209–14;
    responses to U.S. anticocainism,
    123–24, 139, 148, 220–21, 229–30;
    U.S. intervention in, 292, 293–94,
    297
Peru-bark (cinchona), 22, 48, 73
Peruvian coca: versus Bolivian coca,
    113–14; Coca Commission on
    commercialization of, 50–53;
    colonial attitudes toward, 19–21;
    in commodity chain with U.S.,
    118–22, 132–41; current status

of, 315; disdain for, 144–45, 170–71; elite attitudes toward, 31–33, 36, 144, 319–20; European scientific research on, 21, 33–35; Higginson's reports on, 123–24, 147–49; internal market for, 47, 135; Japanese coca in competition with, 165–66; Javan coca in competition with, 95, 125, 126–27, 148, 152–53; as national commodity, 32; as national good, 32, 44–54, 319–20; nationalist vindication of, 31–33; Peruvian colonization plans for, 46–49, 292–93; Peruvian scientific research on, 31–44, 144–45, 151–54; Pilli's 1943 report on, 181–88; after prohibition of cocaine, 240, 294–95; proposals for eradication of, 170–71, 236; reform attempts for, 151–56; transnational hopes for, 49; twentieth-century attitudes toward, 136, 144; U.S. intelligence gathering on, 166, 171, 217–21; varieties of, 62

Peruvian coca cultivation: expansion of, 76, 81–82, 116; in Huánuco, 47, 49, 76, 85–90; by Japan, 165–66, 292; in *montaña* region, 45, 46–47, 76–77; peasants in, 47, 77, 78, 111; Pilli's 1943 report on, 182–83; profitability of, 86; reform attempts in, 151–52, 155; regions of, in early twentieth century, 135

Peruvian coca exports: decline of, 126–27, 132, 135, 147, 160; 1890s expansion of, 53, 63–64, 75, 76; European demand for, 48, 50–51, 126–27; revenue from, 64, 75, 148; statistics on, 329; to U.S., 30, 64–65, 120–24, 135, 166, 183, 201–2;

volume of, 44–45, 62, 63–64, 112, 346 (n. 2)

Peruvian cocaine, 55–102; agency in, 9, 56, 70, 318–20; in Amazon, 65, 76–83; Bignon's papers on, 36–44; in commodity chain with U.S., 132–41, 321; crises of 1910–45 in, 143–49; effects of U.S. pressure on, 217–26; end of licit, 102, 160, 226–30; entrepreneurs in decline of, 157–67; entrepreneurs in rise of, 55–56, 62–63, 318–19; first commercial supply of, 53–54; global market for, 56–65; in Huánuco, 83–100; as industrial good, 65–76; international anticocainism targeting, 207, 210; in Lima, 65–76; methods of production, 149–50, 156–57, 317; as national commodity, 5, 15, 31, 55, 56–65; national pride in, 100–102; northern circuit of, 166–67; "on the spot" processing of, case for, 74–75, 78, 111; origins of, 1, 6; Peruvian scientific research on, 31–44, 70, 149–50; Pilli's 1943 report on, 181–88; reform attempts for, 149–57; technological lag in, 93, 149–50; twentieth-century attitudes toward, 136–37; U.S. intelligence gathering on, 217–21. *See also* Nationalization of Peruvian cocaine; Peruvian cocaine, illicit; Peruvian cocaine regulation

Peruvian cocaine, illicit, 247–61; Balarezo gang in, 254–56; in Huallaga Valley, 84, 291–300; in Huánuco, 252, 258–60, 297–99; legal cocaine's ties to, 258; nationalization and, 166; peasants

in, 292–96; during World War II,
179–81
Peruvian cocaine exports: decline
of, 132, 146–47; expansion of, 63,
75; German influence on, 109;
to Germany, 67–70, 109–12, 126,
132; international quotas on,
174–76; from Lima, 67–70; after
prohibition, 240; revenue from,
64, 75; statistics on, 63, 329; to
U.S., 74, 155; volume of, 63–64;
during World War II, 179–80, 227
Peruvian cocaine regulation:
Coca-Cola/Maywood's influence
on, 222; criminalization in, 232;
through licensing, 179, 180;
local control of, 178; policing
in, 180–81; prohibition in, 140,
231–33, 248, 320; rise of, 137,
176–81; through taxes, 176–77;
U.S. influence on, 225–26; U.S.
tracking of, 178–80; after World
War II, 231–33; during World War
II, 179–80, 227, 229–30
Peruvian Corporation, 84
Peruvian Investigative Police (PIP),
180, 297
Petriconi, Luis, 34
Petroleum jelly, 42, 43
Pezet, Francisco, 209
Pharmaceutical industry: Japanese,
129–31; U.S., 137–38, 193–98. See
also specific companies
Pharmacological action of cocaine, 17
Pharmacology of the Newer Materia
Medica, 59
Philippines, 206
Physiological effects: of cocaine, 17,
29; of coca leaf, 9–10, 16, 51
Piedras, Mack, 267
Piedras, Modina, 267

Pilli, Emile: "The Coca Industry in
Peru," 139, 181–88
Pinillos, Alfredo, 82–83, 166, 202,
224, 226
Pinillos, Goicochea y Cia, 83
Pinillos family, 138, 183
Pinochet, Augusto, 297, 303, 304
Pinto-Escalier, Arturo, 215
Pizarro, Héctor, 257
Pizzi, Enrique, 22, 344 (n. 44), 353
(n. 17)
Placebo: coca leaf medicine as, 27
Plan Cóndor, 304
Plejo, Juan, 80, 89–91, 93
Poeppig, Eduard, 21, 47, 78, 86, 107–8
Point Four technical assistance
programs, 293
Poisons Acts (Britain), 123
Police reports: as historical sources,
11
Policing, Peruvian: start of, 180–81
Polini, Judith, 277
Politics: cocaine commodity
chains constrained by, 122–24;
drug trade's influence on, 4; in
Huánuco, 95–96, 98, 157–59, 162;
1961 Bolivia scandal in, 282–85;
U.S. politics in rise of cocaine use,
307–9
Portella, Gustavo, 265
Porter, Stephen G., 201, 215
Porter Act of 1930, 195, 201, 222, 223
Porter Resolution of 1924, 210
"Posología de la cocaína" (Bignon),
41
Posology, 41
Potosí (Bolivia), 19, 20
Power differentials: between core
and periphery, 106
Powers-Weightman-Rosengarten, 59
Pozo, Ovidio, 283

Pozos (processing pits), 298–99

Pozuzo (Peru): cocaine production in, 76, 77–80; colonizing of, 47, 77, 90; factory in, 78–80; Kitz in, 77–80, 111; location and accessibility of, 77, 86

Pozzi-Escot, Emmanuel, 150

Prados, Gustavo, 83, 166, 257, 258

Prato, José, 184, 295

Precipitation methods, 1, 38

Prensa, La (newspaper), 95, 159, 174

Prensa Libra, La (newspaper), 268

Prescott, William H., 27

Prices of cocaine: DEA on, 313, 315; Durand family and, 99; in 1880s, 57, 58; German influence on, 57, 58, 64; Javan coca and, 127; Kitz on, 80; medical use and, 109; production from crude cocaine and, 68; and revival of U.S. use, 312; twentieth-century decline of, 132, 161, 312, 313; volatility of, 64

Prieto, Alberto, 305

Prío, Francisco, 280

Production of cocaine: Bignon's method for, 1, 38–39, 66, 111; from coca leaf, 1, 58, 59, 68, 88; from crude cocaine, 39, 58, 68, 74, 317; discovery of methods of, 1, 22–23; dispersal of, 76, 81, 109; diversification of, 18; early research on, 23; formulas for, 1, 23, 38–39; Huánuco method for, 93–94; mobility of, in *pozos*, 298–99; modern methods of, 298–99; Pilli's 1943 report on, 185–86; sites of, 17; stages of, 17, 93; volume of, 112; between world wars, 139–40. *See also specific locations*

Progressive movement, U.S., 194

Prohibition of cocaine: in Bolivia, 240, 283–84, 320; establishment of, after World War II, 230–39; events of 1950s after, 239–41; as goal of U.S. anticocainism, 124, 137, 138; in Peru, 140, 231–33, 248, 320; rise of illicit cocaine coinciding with, 233–34, 248–49; U.S. war on drugs and, 233–36

Promotion, Peruvian Ministry of, 76

"Propiedades de la coca y de la cocaína" (Bignon), 40–41

Protectionism, drug: in Peru, 174

Prüss, Bernard, 69, 70, 80

Prüss and Company, 80

Psychoactive revolution, 18–19

Psychoanalysis, 23

Public Health, Peruvian Bureau of, 178, 179

Pure Food and Drug Act of 1906, 62, 148, 191

Quebradas, 85

Quechua Indians, 16

Quinine, 22, 48, 293

Quotas, cocaine export: FBN on, 201; League of Nations on, 174, 175–76, 196, 216; UN on, 181

Rabines, Alfredo, 94, 150

Racial hierarchy: in Peru, 32

Racism: and Coca-Cola, 198–99; and crack cocaine, 312; and Indian coca use, 136, 145; and international anticocainism, 208; and U.S. anticocainism, 192–93

Rada, Fortunato, 164

Rahway (New Jersey), 58

Railway, trans-Andean, 98

Raimondi, Antonio, 31, 35–36, 47, 85

Ramírez clan, 164

Razón, La (newspaper), 282
Reagan, Ronald, 313
Recavarren, Uvalde, 260
Recreational use of cocaine: early,
    248, 249; in Europe, 249; in U.S.,
    249, 307–12. See also Illicit cocaine
Reens, Emma, 125
Reforma Médica, La (journal), 168, 172
Regalado, José, 267
Regional development: in Huallaga
    Valley, 159, 292, 295–96; in
    Huánuco, 98–99, 159
Remy, Pedro, 37, 81
Requeña, José, 283
Respiratory ailments, 30
Revista Agrícola, La (journal), 176
Revista de Sanidad de la Policía
    (journal), 180–81
Revolutionary Nationalist Movement
    (MNR), 282–85
Ricketts, Carlos, 171, 230, 358 (n. 39)
Riedel, I. D., 58
Rio (Brazil): illicit cocaine in, 270–71
Ríos, José Antonio de, 35, 37, 41, 50
Ríos Benze, José, 265
Risco, Genaro, 82, 166
Ritalin, 17
Ritual coca leaf use, 16
Rivera, Camilo, 303
Rivera, Wilson, 303
Rivera de Vargas, Verónica, 303
Road building: in Peru, 159, 292, 295
Robinson, Alberto, 277
Robles Godoy, Armando, 296
Rockefeller Foundation, 229
Rodríguez, José H., 267
Rodríguez, José M., 101
Rodríguez, Orestes, 257, 258
Rodríguez, Pedro, 302
Rodríguez, Roberto, 274
Rodríguez Gacha, González, 305

Rodríguez-Orjuela, Gilberto, 304
Rohawa Company, 222
Roland, Ralph, 253
Rolling Stone magazine, 310
Roncagliolo, José, 164, 258
Roosevelt, Franklin D., 199
Rothstein, Arnold, 249
Rubber trade, 78, 148, 293
Rubeiro Moreno, Julio, 275
Rubín, Enrique R., 179
Rusby, Henry Hurd, 28, 73–75, 120,
    199, 348 (n. 27)
Ryan, James C., 234–35

Sacamanca (Peru): coca cultivation
    in, 82, 166; illicit cocaine in, 258–59
Sadtler and Sons, 204
Sáenz, Luis, 230
Saipai farming colony, 294
Salaverry (Peru), 82, 83
Salgado, José, 279
Salvatierra, Álvaro, 260
Samayoa, Francisco, 274
San Carlos hacienda, 97, 98
Sanguinetti, Luis, 303
Sanitary projects, 176, 177
Sankyo Pharmaceuticals, 129
San Marcos University, 37, 50, 96, 145,
    168; Institute of Andean Biology,
    229–30; Medical School, 43
Santa Cecilia (ship), 253
Santa Cruz City (Bolivia), 284–86
Santa Cruz Province (Bolivia), 285,
    286
Santa Margarita (ship), 253
Santa María de Valle (Peru), 85
Santa Rosa de Quie hacienda, 91
Santiago Fernández, Paulo, 271
Sawada, Masao, 165, 166
Scandals, political: in Bolivia (1961),
    282–85

Schaeffer, Eugene, 172, 199, 222–24
Schaeffer, Louis, 69, 122, 199, 200
Schaeffer Alkaloid Works, 199–200
Schemel, Louis, 280
Scherzer, Karl, 22–23, 74, 77, 78, 108,
    111
Schieffelin Drug Company, 171
Schröder, C. M., 69
Scientific excellence, 31, 37
Scientific nationalism, Peruvian,
    31–33, 43–44, 153–54
Scientific research on coca: British,
    113; Dutch, 125–26; European,
    20–22, 26, 72; French, 33–35;
    German, 107–8; Peruvian, 31–44,
    144–45, 151–54; UN, 236–39
Scientific research on cocaine:
    European, 18–19; German, 23–25,
    57, 107–8; Japanese, 129; Peruvian,
    31–44, 70, 149–50; U.S., 29–30
Searle, William, 27, 119
Self-experimentation, 23, 24, 38, 39
Sertürner, Wilhelm, 22
Sexual effects, 26, 62
Shamanistic communities, 4
Shanghai Opium Commission
    (1909), 206
Sharman, H. L., 223
Ships: trafficking on, 253–54
Showing, Eduardo, 43
Shreve, R. Norris, 171
Sicarios, 305
Silver mining, 19
Sindicato de Cocaína, 159
Single Convention on Narcotic
    Drugs (1961), 204, 207, 283
Siragusa, Charles, 268
Smuggling. *See* Trafficking, cocaine
Snuff, coca leaf, 16, 21
Soberón, Andrés A.: in Bolivian
    trafficking, 276; Chinese

immigrants and, 183–84; cocaine
    defended by, 167; Croats and,
    91, 162; and decline of cocaine,
    84, 98, 161–64; diversification by
    Soberón family, 161–62; illicit
    cocaine production by, 258,
    259–60, 319; Japanese immigrants
    and, 166; licit cocaine production
    by, 162–64, 247–48; life of, 162;
    modern cocaine influenced
    by, 299; and nationalization
    of cocaine, 174; retirement of,
    247–48, 258; rise of, 135, 157,
    161–63; U.S. intelligence gathering
    on, 219–20
Soberón, Augusto, 163
Soberón, Manuel, 162
Soberón, Walter, 162, 233, 248,
    259–60
Sobosky, Adolfo, 303
"Sobre el Erythroxylon Coca del Perú
    y sobre la 'cocaína'" (Moreno y
    Maíz), 34–35
"Sobre el valor comparativo de las
    cocaínas" (Bignon), 41
"Sobre la utilidad de la cocaína en el
    cólera" (Bignon), 42
"Sobre una nueva coca del norte del
    Perú" (Bignon), 41
Social constructionism: and
    commodity chains, 106; influence
    on drug studies, 3–4, 8–9
Social life of things, 106
Social medicine: in Peru, 44, 168, 171
Sociedad Agrícola (Huánuco), 98
Sociedad de Amantes del País, 33
Sociedad de Medicina (Lima), 36
Sociedad de Patriotas de la
    Amazonas, 47
Sociedad de Propietarios de Yungas
    (SPY), 114–15, 214–16, 239, 275

Sociedad Médica Unión Fernandini, 36–37
Sociedad Nacional Agraria (SNA), 173, 176
Sociedad Obreros del Porvenir de la Amazonia, 47, 49
Soda ash, 1, 39
Soft drug: cocaine viewed as, 308, 309–10
Soil erosion, 184
Soininen, Jyri, 327
"Soluciones de cocaína" (Bignon), 42
Souze, Jorge, 173–74
Spain: colonies of, 4, 19–20; illicit cocaine in, 250
Spillane, Joseph, 23, 29, 60, 193
Spirituality: of coca leaf use, 16
Spruce, Richard, 21–23
Squella-Avendaño affair, 264
Squibb, Edward, 24, 28
Star Hotel, 280, 281
State Department, U.S.: in anticocainism, 197; in Balarezo case, 256–57; on coca, 30; Coca-Cola and, 225; intelligence web in Peru, 139; and nationalization of Peruvian cocaine, 172; on Peruvian illicit cocaine, 297
Statistics, 10, 63, 325–36
Steel, José, 258
Stepan Chemical Corporation, 199
Stewart, Francis E., 27
Stimson, Henry, 223
Stimulants: coca as, 16; cocaine as, 17, 30; in colonial era, 3, 18
Stockpiling of cocaine: by Japan, 131; by U.S., 131; in World War I, 109
Strychnine, 41
Studio 54, 311
Suárez, Juan, 280

Suárez, Manuel, 278
Suárez, Roberto, 285
Superfly, 312
Surgery: cocaine as anesthetic in, 24, 29, 30, 108–9
Surveillance. *See* Intelligence gathering, U.S.
Swan, Zachary, 311

Taiwan. *See* Formosa
Takamine, Jokichi, 129
Tanjun, Alfonso, 183
Tariffs, U.S., 194
Taxes, coca: in Huánuco, 78–79, 88–89, 91–93, 98; regulation through, 176–77
Tea: coca as replacement for, 50, 52; coca compared to, 10, 16, 26
Technological advances in cocaine production, 93, 149–50, 156–57
Tetanus, 41–42
Texas: illicit cocaine in, 311–12
Therapeutic Gazette (Parke, Davis), 59
Thorp, Rosemary, 100
Thoumi, Francisco, 301
Thudichum, J. L. W., 86–87
Time magazine, 2, 254–55, 310
Tingo María (Peru): coca cultivation in, 47, 85; colonization of, 292–94; illicit cocaine in, 296, 298; Japanese investment in, 165, 292; Kitz in, 78; Pilli's 1943 report on, 184, 186; U.S. research station in, 229, 293–94
Tittelman, Harold, 256
Tjitembong plantation (Java), 126
Toledo, Francisco, 19
Tonic: cocaine as, 30
Tónica Kola, 250
Torres, Victoria, 280
Toxicity: of cocaine, 25, 30, 40

Toxicomanía: definition of, 177; reports on, 177–78

Trade, drug: economic role of, 4–5; emergence of, 4; estimates of value of cocaine, 4, 17, 339 (n. 6); volume of coca, 44–45. *See also* Bolivian coca exports; Coca exports; Peruvian coca exports; Peruvian cocaine exports

Traffic in Opium and Other Dangerous Drugs reports, 195, 201, 251

Trafficking, cocaine, 245–89; in Argentina, 268–70, 282, 283–84; in Bolivia, 275–86; in Brazil, 270–72; in Chile, 261–64, 289, 303–4, 309; in Colombia, 301–6; in Cuba, 264–68, 304; development of rings in, 254, 256; first documented case of, 253; first major busts of, 1–2, 254–56; in Japan, 250; Latin American role in, 5; in Mexico, 273–75; start of, 234–35, 245, 248, 253; into U.S., 253–54; volume of, 17. *See also* Illicit cocaine

Tranquilandia, 306

Transnational discourses, 15

Transnational studies, 7

Transport of coca: from Bolivia versus Peru, 116; cost of, 82, 116; problems with, 20, 22, 58

Travelers, European, 21, 86

Treasury Department, U.S., 197, 200

Tremontona, Michael, 277

Trigo Paz, Milton, 270

Trinchera, La (newspaper), 297–99

Trujillo (Peru): coca cultivation in, 65; cocaine production in, 82–83; licensing in, 179; U.S. intelligence gathering on, 219

Trujillo variety of coca leaf, 41, 62, 64, 65, 81–82

Truman, Harry, 293

Trusts: attempts at formation of, 148, 159, 184

Tulumayo property: centrality in history of cocaine, 165; history of ownership of, 165, 349 (n. 36); Japanese ownership of, 129, 165; Kitz's purchase of, 78; under Martín family, 85–86; nationalization of, 131, 165–66, 292, 293; size of, 165; U.S. research station on, 294

Twain, Mark, 73, 119

"Über Coca" (Freud), 24, 34

Ulloa, Antonio de, 21

Ulloa, José Casimiro, 37; on Bignon's formula, 39; in Coca Commission, 37, 50, 51–52; on need for scientific research, 33, 43–44; Paz Soldán compared to, 167; scientific research by, 35

Unánue, José Hipólito, 33, 36, 51

Undercover Agent (Agnew), 272

United Fruit Company, 202

United Nations (UN): antidrug bodies of, 181, 207, 231; on Argentine trafficking, 269; on Bolivian trafficking, 286; on Brazilian trafficking, 270–71; on Chilean trafficking, 264; on medical use of cocaine, 124; Peruvian reports to, 257–58; on revival of cocaine in 1960s, 309; U.S. influence in, 207; U.S. vision for anticocainism in, 206, 207

United Nations Commission of Enquiry on the Coca Leaf, 236–39

United Nations Commission on Narcotic Drugs, 207, 231

United Nations Inter-American Coca Leaf Consultative Seminars, 284

United States: change of attitudes toward drugs in, 119, 122, 191–94;

in commodity chain with Andes, 106, 107, 118–22, 124, 132, 137–41; cycles of drug use and prohibition in, 27, 122, 192; foreign aid by, 284, 297; interventions in Bolivia, 282–84; interventions in Peru, 292, 293–94, 297; Latin American relations with, during World War II, 226–29, 293; in nationalization of Peruvian coca, 165–66, 171–72, 174; and Peruvian cocaine regulation, 178–80; stockpiling by, 131

United States, coca in: allure of, 26–29, 60–62, 118–19; cultivation of, 72–74; market for, from 1890 to 1910, 58–65, 118–19; medical use of, 27–28, 119; popularity of, in nineteenth century, 26–29, 60–62, 118–19

United States, cocaine in: abuse of, 30, 204–5, 249–50; current status of, 312–14; first bust of, 1–2, 254–56; illicit, 249–52, 306–12; market for, from 1890 to 1910, 58–65, 118–19; market for, after 1960s, 291, 306–13; medical use of, 29–30, 121, 138, 193, 196; paradoxes of history of, 321–24; production of, 29, 58–60, 68, 121, 195–96; recreational use of, 249, 307–12

United States coca imports: Bolivian, 30, 120–21; 1882–1931, 119–21; 1925–59, 201–2; Peruvian, 30, 64–65, 120–24, 135, 166; in political economy of anticocainism, 194–96; regulation of, 124, 195, 201; special permits for, 201

United States cocaine imports: versus coca imports, 194–95; federal ban on, 195; Peruvian, 74, 155; in political economy of anticocainism, 194–95

United States drug policy. *See* Anticocainism, U.S.; War on drugs, U.S.

Universidad Nacional Agraria de la Selva, 294

Urbina, Ramón, 253

Urea, 22, 40

Uriquen Bravo, Miguel, 268

Uzquiano, Miguel, 266

Valdizán, Hermilio, 72, 144–45

Van Ronk, Dave, 373 (n. 22)

Van Wettun, W. G., 212

Vázquez, Julio, 257, 258

Velázquez, Juan Trujillo, 297

Velázquez, Manuel, 41, 69–70, 347 (n. 18)

Vergel, Teofilo S., 82–83, 166–67, 172, 174

Versailles, Treaty of, 206, 210, 213

Viceroyalty of Peru, 19–20

Vida Agrícola, La (journal), 173

Villar, D. L., 37

Vinelli, Manuel, 153–54

Vin Mariani: Bolivian coca in, 57, 115; cocaine removed from, 62; in commodity chains, 112, 115; development of, 25–26; in U.S., 28, 61, 119

Violence: in trafficking, 17, 306; urban violence in U.S., 313

Vistazo (newspaper), 262

Vitamins: in coca leaf, 10, 16

Von Humboldt, Baron, 21, 33, 107–8

Von Tschudi, Johan Jacub, 21, 22, 35, 86, 107–8

Waiy, Julio Chan, 164, 183–84, 359 (n. 62)

Wallerstein, Immanuel, 8

Wanderley, Luiz, 271

War Commodities Board, 227

Warhol, Andy, 311

War on drugs, U.S.: coca leaf in, 9; current status of, 323–24; goal of, 323–24; incarceration in, 313; under Nixon, 307–9; Peruvian cooperation with, 234–36; under Reagan, 313; start of, 5, 233–34, 306. *See also* Anticocainism, U.S.

Weng, Augusto Kuan, 183

White, J. Leyden, 200

Wiese, Emiliano, 91

Wiley, Harvey W., 199

Wille, Johannes, 152

Williams, Garland, 234, 238, 256, 257, 276

Wilson, Woodrow, 209

Wine: coca leaf combined with, 25–26, 28, 57, 61

Wissmar, Raúl, 260

Witz, Leib, 279

Wöhler, Friedrich, 22–23, 108

Women: coca chewing by, 135; in trafficking, 279–80

Women's Christian Temperance Union, 199–200

Workers Society for the Amazon's Future. *See* Sociedad Obreros del Porvenir de la Amazonia

Working classes: coca's benefits for, 52

Workshops. *See* Factories and workshops, Peruvian

World systems theory, 105

World War I: cocaine stockpiling during, 109; international antidrug movement after, 206; and Javan coca, 126

World War II: antidrug campaigns in, 139–40; Coca-Cola in, 204, 225, 227–28; commodity chains during, 139–40; and end of licit Peruvian cocaine, 226–30; Huánuco cocaine production during, 139, 165; illicit categories in, 179–81, 252–53; international anticocainism after, 230–39; Japan in, 128, 131–32, 227, 228; and Javan coca, 128; nationalization of Peruvian coca and, 165–66; Peruvian cocaine regulation in, 179–80, 227; U.S.–Latin American relations during, 226–29, 293

Wright, Elizabeth Washburn, 206

Wright, Hamilton, 200, 206, 208, 209–10

Yerba maté, 4

YPFB, 282

Yungas region: coca cultivation in, 16, 32, 45, 47, 113–16

Yuppies, 311

Zeijo, Botano, 266

Zembrano, Carlos, 278, 282

Zulen, Pedro S., 90–91

Zuñiga, Antonio, 19